ENGLAND!
ENGLAND!

The Complete WHO'S WHO
of Players since 1946

ENGLAND! ENGLAND!

The Complete WHO'S WHO of Players since 1946

DEAN P. HAYES

FOREWORD BY **JOHN MOTSON**

SUTTON PUBLISHING

796.334

HAY

First published in the United Kingdom in 2004 by
Sutton Publishing Limited · Phoenix Mill
Thrupp · Stroud · Gloucestershire · GL5 2BU

British Library Cataloguing in Publication Data
A catalogue record for this book is available from the British Library.

ISBN 0-7509-3234-1

Author's note

Although every effort has been made and every care taken to ensure that this
book is statistically accurate, inevitably errors will creep in, for which I offer my
apologies in advance.

Typeset in 9.5/11.5 pt Joanna MT.
Typesetting and origination by
Sutton Publishing Limited.
Printed and bound in England by
J.H. Haynes & Co. Ltd, Sparkford.

Contents

Foreword

by John Motson

*H*aving been privileged to commentate on well over one hundred full internationals played by the England team over the last 30 years, I must confess the memory often stumbles over the precise career details of many of those who have worn the white shirt with the Three Lions proudly displayed. Anybody who has taken part in those popular football quiz sessions, which fascinate those in the game as well as supporters, knows that post-war England line-ups offer ample scope for debating who played how many times, against whom and how their international career began and ended. Now we need rack our brains no longer. Dean Hayes' exhaustive research has produced a precious volume that will not only settle those queries at a stroke but also serve as a reliable and ready point of reference for journalists and commentators whose shelves have been short of such a comprehensive work for all of a decade.

International football today is unrecognizable from the muddled scenario that Walter Winterbottom inherited when he became England's first full-time coach immediately after the war. Then, team selection was in the hands of a committee, England had yet to enter a World Cup and the European Championships had not been envisaged. The likes of Stanley Matthews, Tom Finney and Raich Carter were parading their skills in the Home International Championship and proudly taking on the rest of the world in prestige friendlies. How forties and fifties idols like these would have relished the millionaire status and celebrity lifestyles of David Beckham, Michael Owen and today's luminaries. Tommy Lawton was earning £12 a week, and Wilf Mannion's hat-trick in England's first official peacetime fixture would have attracted a fraction of the column inches that a Wayne Rooney fitness test commands today. And yet . . . an England cap, in some cases dozens of them, remains the benchmark of a career – a sign that promise was fulfilled. Centurions like Billy Wright, Bobby Moore and

Peter Shilton are listed alongside Danny Clapton, John Fantham and Paul Goddard – just three of those who were capped once and then internationally forgotten. In these pages, they have parity.

Dean Hayes has penned a mini-biography of nearly 500 players. All have their place in this compendium of talent. Tainted though it has sometimes been by horror and hooliganism, the reputation of the England team remains rooted in the birth of international football two centuries ago. Whatever the club game offers in the form of a week-to-week focus, however glamorous the pull of the Champions League, each and every England match carries an agenda and an attention span of its own.

After Winterbottom, Alf Ramsey insisted on sole selection and won the World Cup. He was followed by Don Revie, Ron Greenwood, Bobby Robson, Graham Taylor, Terry Venables, Glenn Hoddle, Kevin Keegan and Sven-Goran Eriksson. Joe Mercer and Howard Wilkinson had short spells as caretaker. At one time or another, I interviewed each and every one, often questioning why they had selected certain players above others. The answer, by and large, is that they picked the best Englishmen available at the time. Every single one of those chosen, from George Hardwick in 1946 to Scott Parker in 2004, has earned his place in this dedicated contribution to a football-lover's bookshelf.

John Motson
London 2004

Introduction

This who's who of England footballers revisits the many contrasting post-war experiences of the national side through its lifeblood – the players. Some are great, some good, some less than good, but all have one thing in common: all have pulled on the Three Lions and taken to the field to represent their country.

A total of 477 players have appeared for England in the post-war period. They appear here in chronological order – that is, in the order they made their international debut. There are, of course, matches where a number of players made their debut at the same time, and in such cases they are listed alphabetically. Should you be unsure of the decade in which a particular favourite played, there is an index at the back of the book for easy reference.

In a number of entries, reference is made to wartime caps. Though international games continued during hostilities, the Victory matches of 1946 and the wartime fixtures of 1939–45 were not recognized as full internationals and therefore these appearances are not included in the total number of caps won. In the statistics section at the head of each player's entry, match dates are listed according to the year that marked the end of the season in which the game was played. Every post-war game is included in the book up to the end of the qualifying rounds for the 2004 European Championships.

For each player I have aimed to provide the following information: full name, recognized position, period as an England player, height and weight, date and place of birth, date and place of death, career details, breakdown of appearances and goals scored for England, and biography. Weights should only be regarded as approximate figures since they obviously varied throughout the player's career.

This book is a collection of statistics and biographies. But I hope it is more than that: it is a celebration of the great game. Since international football resumed in 1946, a number of England records have been broken, anniversaries marked and personal bests established. These include the nation's first substitute, Jimmy Mullen, coming on and scoring in England's 4–1 defeat of Belgium in May 1950; Billy Wright becoming the first England player to register 100 caps (though Peter Shilton now holds the record with 125); Alan Mullery gaining the unwanted distinction of becoming the first England player to be sent off in a full international in June 1968; and of course Geoff Hurst netting the first hat-trick ever scored in a World Cup Final. Recently, Wayne Rooney of Everton, at 17 years 160 days, became the youngest ever player to make his full international start when in April 2003 he played against Turkey.

Every game and every championship brings a new chapter. The story will continue.

Dean P. Hayes
Pembrokeshire, April 2004

1946–49

Rebuilding

Walter Winterbottom was appointed England's first-team manager and coach in 1946. It was his job to prepare the players for matches, although he had no control over selection, except in an advisory capacity.

Buoyed by a huge upsurge of interest in the game at home, the post-war era saw England carry all before them. New arrivals like Tom Finney and Wilf Mannion joined a number of seasoned players anxious to make up for lost time. The selection panel put their trust in youth for the first post-war international against Northern Ireland at Windsor Park. This saw no fewer than nine players make their debut, but the lack of experience didn't matter much – England won 7–2. Then Tommy Lawton was soon among the goals, netting four in an 8–2 win over Holland, while the first post-war international at Wembley saw England draw 1–1 with Scotland.

After 1947 victories against Portugal (10–0) and Belgium (5–2) England were keen to test themselves against the best, and the defeat of Italy in Turin in 1948 by a 4–0 margin appeared as significant as the Battle of Highbury in throwing down a gauntlet to the world. But unfortunately the optimists were sadly mistaken, as the Republic of Ireland showed the following year when, at Goodison Park, they ended England's proud record of never having lost against 'continental' (i.e. non-Home Country) opposition.

The Home Internationals and the World Cup came together to make a qualifying group for the final stages of the competition to be played in Brazil. England beat Northern Ireland 9–2 with Jack Rowley netting four of the goals. They then took Wales 4–1, with Jackie Milburn scoring a hat-trick, while the clinching victory against Scotland, albeit by a single goal, was hard won at a Hampden Park packed to capacity with 133,250 partisan fans.

Raich CARTER

Position	Inside-forward
Born	Horatio Stratton Carter, Sunderland, 21 December 1913
Died	9 October 1994
Height	5ft 8in
Weight	10st 6lb
Clubs	Sunderland, Derby County, Hull City, Cork Athletic
England Caps	13 Goals 7

1934 v Scotland (won 3–0), v Hungary (lost 1–2)
1935 v Germany (won 3–0)
1936 v Ireland (won 3–1) 1 goal, v Hungary (won 6–2) 1 goal
1937 v Scotland (lost 1–3)
1946 v N. Ireland (won 7–2) 1 goal, v Eire (won 1–0), v Wales (won 3–0), v Holland (won 8–2) 2 goals
1947 v Scotland (1–1) 1 goal, v France (won 3–0) 1 goal, v Switzerland (lost 0–1)

CAPPED SIX TIMES before the Second World War and seven times after, Raich Carter had a 13-year international career, longer than any other England inside-forward. He was at his best though during the war years when he played between Stanley Matthews and Tommy Lawton in the unofficial internationals, playing in 17 and scoring 18 goals.

Raich was an excellent all-round athlete and could have been almost as successful as a cricketer, but since Durham did not have first-class status at that time he would have had to move and wait. After leaving school he became an errand boy and then an apprentice electrician, but his heart was not in electrical engineering and he jumped at the chance of a trial with Leicester City. Told he was too small for professional football, he joined his home-town club as an amateur before later being offered professional terms. The brilliance of Carter's performances for Sunderland, where he became a very young captain, helped the club win the League Championship in 1935/36. That season he scored 31 goals in 39 League games, including four goals in a 6–1 defeat of West Bromwich Albion. The following season he netted another hat-trick in a 4–1 win over Middlesbrough and led Sunderland to their first-ever FA Cup Final triumph.

The Second World War robbed Raich Carter of his best years. Bomb damage to the family home meant a move to Derby, and after the hostilities Carter joined the Rams on a permanent basis. With County he went on to win another FA Cup winners' medal, the only player to gain such a medal before and after the war.

He later stepped down to the Third Division with Hull City and was soon appointed player-manager. After leading the Tigers to the Third Division (North) Championship he had a spell with Cork Athletic. He later managed Leeds United, Mansfield Town and Middlesbrough before being dismissed following the Ayresome Park club's relegation to the Third Division.

Stanley Matthews in Blackpool kit. (Lancashire Evening Post)

Stanley MATTHEWS

Position	Outside-right
Born	Stanley Matthews, Hanley, 1 February 1915
Died	5 May 1999
Height	5ft 10in
Weight	11st 8lb
Clubs	Stoke City, Blackpool
England Caps	54 Goals 11

1934 v Wales (won 4–0) 1 goal, v Italy (won 3–2)

1935 v Denmark (won 3–0)

1937 v Scotland (lost 1–3), v Wales (won 2–1) 1 goal, v Czechoslovakia (won 5–4) 3 goals

1938 v Scotland (lost 0–1), v Germany (won 6–3) 1 goal, v Switzerland (lost 1–2), v France (won 4–2), v Wales (lost 2–4) 1 goal, v FIFA (won 3–0), v Norway (won 4–0), v Ireland (won 7–0) 1 goal

1939 v Scotland (won 2–1), v Italy (2–2), v Yugoslavia (lost 1–2)

1947 v Scotland (1–1), v Switzerland (lost 0–1), v Portugal (won 10–0) 1 goal, v Belgium (won 5–2), v Wales (won 3–0), v N. Ireland (2–2)

1948 v Scotland (won 2–0), v Italy (won 4–0), v Denmark (0–0), v N. Ireland (won 6–2) 1 goal, v Wales (won 1–0), v Switzerland (won 6–0)

1949 v Scotland (lost 1–3)

1950 v Spain (lost 0–1), v N. Ireland (won 4–1)

1951 v Scotland (lost 2–3)

1953 v Rest of Europe (4–4), v N. Ireland (won 3–1), v Hungary (lost 3–6)

1954 v Belgium (4–4), v Uruguay (lost 2–4), v N. Ireland (won 2–0), v Wales (won 3–1), v W. Germany (won 3–1)

1955 v Scotland (won 7–2), v France (lost 0–1), v Spain (1–1), v Portugal (lost 1–3), v Wales (lost 1–2)

1956 v Brazil (won 4–2), v N. Ireland (1–1) 1 goal, v Wales (won 3–1), v Yugoslavia (won 3–0), v Denmark (won 5–2)

1957 v Scotland (won 2–1), v Eire (won 5–1), v Denmark (won 4–1)

Honours	Footballer of the Year 1948 and 1963
	European Footballer of the Year 1956

ALTHOUGH HIS APPEARANCES in the England side were spasmodic during the latter part of his career, Stanley Matthews won 54 caps after making his international debut as a 19-year-old in 1934, playing his last game for England in 1957, aged 41. He also played in 29 wartime internationals.

Known as the 'Wizard of Dribble' because of his close ball control, Matthews was the biggest crowd-puller of the 1950s. The son of a boxing barber, he began his League career with Stoke City, helping the Potters win promotion to the First Division in his second season at the Victoria Ground. His fame grew quickly, fans trooping to matches in their thousands just to watch him.

Matthews liked the ball played to his feet. Stopping it dead with perfect control, he shuffled towards a full-back, teasing him with the ball. The full-back very rarely committed himself, fearing Matthews' reputation. Stan would approach slowly, swaying his body from side to side. The defender would retreat until he thought he knew the direction in which Matthews was going and then lunge for the ball. But Matthews had gone, switching the ball to the opposite side and sprinting down the wing.

When Matthews first asked Stoke for a transfer in 1938, there was a public outcry. Over 3,000 fans attended a protest meeting and another 1,000 paraded outside the ground with placards – he stayed. However, in 1947 he did move to Blackpool and was a member of the Seasiders team that lost to Manchester United in the 1948 FA Cup Final, though there was consolation for him in being elected Britain's first Footballer of the Year. It was the same story against Newcastle United in 1951, and in 1953 it looked like being a third losers' medal, for, with 20 minutes to play, Blackpool trailed Bolton Wanderers 3–1. But Matthews turned on a brilliant display and tore apart the Bolton defence. Blackpool won 4–3 and the match, one of the greatest seen at Wembley, is still hailed as the 'Matthews Cup Final'.

In 1956 he was voted European Footballer of the Year and was awarded the OBE the following year. In 1961 he rejoined Stoke City and helped the Potters return to the top flight, playing his 701st and last game against Fulham in February 1965 at the age of 50 years and five days. He was also knighted that year, the first footballer to be so honoured. Many consider him the greatest player to have ever lived.

Tommy LAWTON

Position	Centre-forward
Born	Thomas Lawton, Bolton, 6 October 1909
Died	Nottingham, 6 November 1996
Height	5ft 11in
Weight	12st 0lb
Clubs	Burnley, Chelsea, Everton, Notts County, Brentford, Arsenal
England Caps	23 Goals 22

1938 v Wales (lost 2–4) 1 goal, v FIFA (won 3–0) 1 goal, v Norway (won 4–0) 1 goal, v Ireland (won 7–0) 1 goal

1939 v Scotland (won 2–1) 1 goal, v Italy (2–2) 1 goal, v Yugoslavia (lost 1–2), v Romania (won 2–0)

1946 v N. Ireland (won 7–2) 1 goal, v Eire (won 1–0), v Wales (won 3–0) 1 goal, v Holland (won 8–2) 4 goals

1947 v Scotland (1–1), v France (won 3–0), v Switzerland (lost 0–1), v Portugal (won 10–0) 4 goals, v Belgium (won 5–2) 2 goals, v Wales (won 3–0) 1 goal, v N. Ireland (2–2) 1 goal, v Sweden (won 4–1) 1 goal

1948 v Scotland (won 2–0), v Italy (won 4–0) 1 goal, v Denmark (0–0)

TOMMY LAWTON is the only English player to have scored in five consecutive internationals twice. His first goal run was in 1939 and he went on another scoring spree in 1946, becoming in the process the first player since 1929 to score four goals in a match for England. Lawton is the England striker with the best post-war strike rate, scoring 16 goals in 15 games after 1945. He also scored the quickest-ever England goal, knocking one past Portugal in 1947 after just 17 seconds.

Lawton, who scored a staggering 570 goals in three seasons of schoolboy football, began his League career with Burnley. One of the greatest centre-forwards of all time, he made his debut four days after his 17th birthday, scoring a hat-trick against Tottenham Hotspur. In 1936 he joined Everton and after playing at inside-forward to accommodate Dixie Dean, he settled down at centre-forward. He topped the club's goalscoring charts in each of the three seasons leading up to the Second World War and in the 1938/39 season netted 34 goals in 38 games as the Blues won the League Championship.

After the war he became involved in a dispute with Everton and transferred to Chelsea. He spent two years at Stamford Bridge before a British record transfer fee of £20,000 took him to Notts County. After helping the Meadow Lane club win the Third Division Championship, he joined Brentford before ending his League career with Arsenal. He later managed Notts County.

Frank SWIFT

Position	Goalkeeper
Born	Frank Victor Swift, Blackpool, 24 December 1914
Died	Munich, 6 February 1958
Height	6ft 2in
Weight	14st 0lb
Clubs	Manchester City
England Caps	19
	1946 v N. Ireland (won 7–2), v Eire (won 1–0), v Wales (won 3–0), v Holland (won 8–2)
	1947 v Scotland (1–1), v France (won 3–0), v Switzerland (lost 0–1), v Portugal (won 10–0), v Belgium (won 5–2), v Wales (won 3–0), v N. Ireland (2–2), v Sweden (won 4–1)
	1948 v Scotland (won 2–0), v Italy (won 4–0), v Denmark (0–0), v N. Ireland (won 6–2), v Wales (won 1–0)
	1949 v Scotland (lost 1–3), v Norway (won 4–1)

IN 1935 FRANK SWIFT made an appearance for The Rest in a trial match against England, but it was not until after the war that he played a full international.

He appeared in many wartime internationals as well as gaining First and Second Division Championship medals and a 1934 FA Cup winners' medal. He had been captain of Manchester City for a couple of seasons when, in Italy 1948, he became the first goalkeeper to captain England.

Frank Swift set the standards for goalkeeping before and after the Second World War. Joining Manchester City from Fleetwood, he was ever-present in four consecutive seasons from 1934/35 onwards and missed just one game in 1938/39. In 1934 he was a member of the successful City side that lifted the FA Cup after beating Portsmouth 2–1. At half-time Pompey led 1–0, with Swift conceding that he might have saved the goal had he been wearing gloves. Fred Tilson hit two second-half goals and on the final whistle the 19-year-old Swift turned to collect his cap and gloves and fainted!

Swift had enormous hands, with a finger span of almost a foot – he would catch the ball in one hand and then hold it over the centre-forward's head, just out of reach. A spectacular goalkeeper, he was daring, sometimes even heading shots away.

He was also one of the first goalkeepers to elect to throw the ball to a colleague rather than opt for the long kick downfield typically used in those days.

Frank was killed in the Munich Air Disaster of 1958 when accompanying Manchester United as a newspaper reporter.

Laurie SCOTT

Position	Full-back
Born	Lawrence Scott, Sheffield, 24 April 1917
Died	7 July 1999
Height	5ft 10in
Weight	11st 8lb
Clubs	Bradford City, Arsenal, Crystal Palace
England Caps	17
	1946 v N. Ireland (won 7–2), v Eire (won 1–0), v Wales (won 3–0), v Holland (won 8–2)
	1947 v Scotland (1–1), v France (won 3–0), v Switzerland (lost 0–1), v Portugal (won 10–0), v Belgium (won 5–2), v Wales (won 3–0), v N. Ireland (2–2), v Sweden (won 4–1)
	1948 v Scotland (won 2–0), v Italy (won 4–0), v Denmark (0–0), v N. Ireland (won 6–2), v Wales (won 1–0)

LAURIE SCOTT began his Football League career with Bradford City before joining his ex-team-mate George Swindin at Arsenal in February 1937 in exchange for Ernest Tuckett. Unfortunately the war came at the time when Laurie Scott was making a name for himself. He served as a PT instructor in the RAF and during those years he developed into one of the country's finest full-backs, winning 16 England wartime international caps.

He missed only three League games during Arsenal's Championship season of 1947/48, but from then on was unfortunately dogged by injury for the rest of his career. He had an appendicitis operation during the summer of 1948, followed by a serious knee injury sustained in an international match against Wales. On his return to the League side, a recurrence of the injury resulted in him having to share the right-back position with Walley Barnes, while Lionel Smith was the regular left-back. With his first-class career coming to a close, he was transferred to Crystal Palace as player-manager in 1951.

Had it not been for the war years, Laurie Scott would surely have had a longer and more distinguished career. Even so, he was one of the most accomplished defenders the Highbury club has had, his speed, fine distribution and positional sense making him the complete full-back.

George HARDWICK

Position	Full-back
Born	George Francis Moutry Hardwick, Saltburn, 2 February 1920
Height	5ft 10in
Weight	12st 0lb
Clubs	Middlesbrough, Oldham Athletic
England Caps	13
	1946 v N. Ireland (won 7–2), v Eire (won 1–0), v Wales (won 3–0), v Holland (won 8–2)
	1947 v Scotland (1–1), v France (won 3–0), v Switzerland (lost 0–1), v Portugal (won 10–0),
	v Belgium (won 5–2), v Wales (won 3–0), v N. Ireland (2–2), v Sweden (won 4–1)
	1948 v Scotland (won 2–0)

ONE OF MIDDLESBROUGH'S best-known players, George Hardwick made his League debut in December 1937, scoring an own goal inside the first minute in a 2–1 home defeat at the hands of Bolton Wanderers!

During the Second World War, Hardwick served in the RAF Bomber Command. He also 'guested' for Chelsea and appeared in two wartime Wembley Cup Finals for the Stamford Bridge club. He was selected for 17 wartime internationals, all as captain.

After the resumption of League football in 1946/47, Hardwick was a virtual ever-present for the next five seasons, during which time his consistency in the Boro defence earned him 13 full caps for England. In fact, Hardwick captained his country in each of his international appearances and captained the Great Britain side that played against Europe.

Hardwick left Ayresome Park in November 1950 to become player-manager of Oldham Athletic. He exerted a great influence on the Boundary Park club and in 1952/53 the Latics won the Third Division (North) Championship. However, a lack of finance precluded any significant strengthening of the side and the following season the club were relegated. Hardwick resigned his post and, after spells coaching the US Army, PSV Eindhoven and the Dutch FA, he returned to Ayresome Park in 1961 as the club's youth-team coach. He later managed Sunderland and Gateshead, and in 1983 he and Wilf Mannion were given a joint testimonial by Middlesbrough. George Hardwick is a regular visitor to the club's Riverside Stadium, where he has a suite named after him.

Billy WRIGHT

Position	Centre-half
Born	William Ambrose Wright, Ironbridge, 6 February 1924
Died	Barnet, 3 September 1994
Height	5ft 8in
Weight	11st 6lb
Clubs	Wolverhampton Wanderers
England Caps	105 Goals 3
	1946 v N. Ireland (won 7–2), v Eire (won 1–0), v Wales (won 3–0), v Holland (won 8–2)

1947 v Scotland (1–1), v France (won 3–0), v Switzerland (lost 0–1), v Portugal (won 10–0), v Belgium (won 5–2), v Wales (won 3–0), v N. Ireland (2–2), v Sweden (won 4–1)

1948 v Scotland (won 2–0), v Italy (won 4–0), v Denmark (0–0), v N. Ireland (won 6–2), v Wales (won 1–0), v Switzerland (won 6–0)

1949 v Scotland (lost 1–3), v Sweden (lost 1–3), v Norway (won 4–1), v France (won 3–1) 1 goal, v Eire (lost 0–2), v Wales (won 4–1), v N. Ireland (lost 0–2), v Italy (won 2–0) 1 goal

1950 v Scotland (won 1–0), v Portugal (won 5–3), v Belgium (won 4–1), v Chile (won 2–0), v United States (lost 0–1), v Spain (lost 0–1), v N. Ireland (won 4–1) 1 goal

1951 v Scotland (lost 2–3), v Argentina (won 2–1), v France (2–2), v Wales (1–1), v N. Ireland (won 2–0), v Austria (2–2)

1952 v Scotland (won 2–1), v Italy (1–1), v Austria (won 3–2), v Switzerland (won 3–0), v N. Ireland (2–2), v Wales (won 5–2), v Belgium (won 5–0)

1953 v Scotland (2–2), v Argentina (0–0), v Chile (won 2–1), v Uruguay (lost 1–2), v United States (won 6–3), v Wales (won 4–1), v Rest of Europe (4–4), v N. Ireland (won 3–1), v Hungary (lost 3–6)

1954 v Scotland (won 4–2), v Yugoslavia (lost 0–1), v Hungary (lost 1–7), v Belgium (4–4), v Switzerland (won 2–0), v Uruguay (lost 2–4), v N. Ireland (won 2–0), v Wales (won 3–1), v W. Germany (won 3–1)

1955 v Scotland (won 7–2), v France (lost 0–1), v Spain (1–1), v Portugal (lost 1–3), v Denmark (won 5–1), v Wales (lost 1–2), v N. Ireland (won 3–0), v Spain (won 4–1)

1956 v Scotland (1–1), v Brazil (won 4–2), v Sweden (0–0), v Finland (won 5–1), v W. Germany (won 3–1), v N. Ireland (1–1), v Wales (won 3–1), v Yugoslavia (won 3–0), v Denmark (won 5–2)

1957 v Scotland (won 2–1), v Eire (won 5–1), v Denmark (won 4–1), v Eire (1–1), v Wales (won 4–0), v N. Ireland (lost 2–3), v France (won 4–0)

1958 v Scotland (won 4–0), v Portugal (won 2–1), v Yugoslavia (lost 0–5), v Soviet Union (1–1), v Soviet Union (2–2), v Brazil (0–0), v Austria (2–2), v Soviet Union (lost 0–1), v N. Ireland (3–3), v Soviet Union (won 5–0), v Wales (2–2)

1959 v Scotland (won 1–0), v Italy (2–2), v Brazil (lost 0–2), v Peru (lost 1–4), v Mexico (lost 1–2), v United States (won 8–1)

Honours   Footballer of the Year 1952

....

BILLY WRIGHT regarded playing for his country as the highest honour his chosen profession could give him. He captained England on 90 occasions. If one match more than any other can be described as the climax of his career, then it has to be England against Scotland at Wembley on 11 April 1959 – the match gave him his 100th cap and made him the first man in the history of football to pass this milestone. The previous year, just after the World Cup in Sweden, Wright had married Joy Beverley of the internationally known Beverley Sisters.

Billy Wright was the model professional. In 117 wartime outings, 654 League and Cup games and 105 internationals, he was never sent off or cautioned. A mark of the esteem in which he was held was his election as an honorary life member of the Football Association.

Billy Wright of Wolves.
(Wolverhampton Express & Star)

A centre-forward as a schoolboy, once scoring ten goals in a match, he was initially rejected by Major Frank Buckley as being too small. However, the Wolves manager changed his mind and signed him on amateur forms in 1939. During the war years, Wright broke his ankle and it was thought at that time that he would never play football again. He made his League debut in the first season of peacetime football and in 1947/48 he replaced Stan Cullis as captain of Wolverhampton Wanderers. He led Wolves to FA Cup success in 1949 and to the League Championship in 1953/54, 1957/58 and 1958/59.

At the end of the 1958/59 season, he decided to retire as a player while he was still at the top. He was 35 and though he could have held his place for another season or two, he knew in his heart that the pace was beginning to tell. Wright was awarded the CBE for his services to football and became manager of England's Under-23 and youth sides, an FA staff coach, a TV personality and disc jockey, a regular contributor to newspapers and magazines, and a players' agent. He became a Wolves director in 1990 and a new £5 million stand at Molineux has been named after him.

Neil FRANKLIN

Position	Centre-half
Born	Cornelius Franklin, Stoke-on-Trent, 24 January 1922
Died	Stoke-on-Trent, 17 February 1996
Height	5ft 11in
Weight	11st 4lb
Clubs	Stoke City, Sante Fe (Bogota), Hull City, Crewe Alexandra, Stockport County
England Caps	27
	1946 v N. Ireland (won 7–2), v Eire (won 1–0), v Wales (won 3–0), v Holland (won 8–2)
	1947 v Scotland (1–1), v France (won 3–0), v Switzerland (lost 0–1), v Portugal (won 10–0), v Belgium (won 5–2), v Wales (won 3–0), v N. Ireland (2–2), v Sweden (won 4–1)
	1948 v Scotland (won 2–0), v Italy (won 4–0), v Denmark (0–0), v N. Ireland (won 6–2), v Wales (won 1–0), v Switzerland (won 6–0)
	1949 v Scotland (lost 1–3), v Sweden (lost 1–3), v Norway (won 4–1), v France (won 3–1), v Eire (lost 0–2), v Wales (won 4–1), v N. Ireland (won 9–2), v Italy (won 2–0)
	1950 v Scotland (won 1–0)

IN THE HISTORY OF the game there has probably never been a more accomplished footballer in an English defence than Neil Franklin. After the Second World War, he was the unchallenged England centre-half for 27 consecutive matches. He had gained ten wartime caps as the successor to the legendary Stan Cullis, but his career was disrupted by a secret and ill-advised departure from Stoke City for the Sante Fe club of Bogotá, Colombia. Together with George Mountford, Franklin and his family left for South America in the spring of 1950, having signed contracts immediately after the end of the domestic season. He told the Football Association that he would not be available for the World Cup Finals in Brazil because his wife was expecting their

Neil Franklin of Stoke City.
(Lancashire Evening Post)

second child and she planned to have the baby in Bogotá. This was the era of the maximum wage of £20 a week in English football and there was no freedom of contract once a player had signed for a club. In spite of McGrory's dislike of Franklin's stylish, intelligent game, Stoke had refused Franklin's request for a move. In the event, his wife decided to fly home for the birth. The Stoke defender accompanied her as far as New York, as had been agreed, but then on finding no flight booked for his wife, flew back with her to England. For breach of contract at the Victoria Ground, Franklin was suspended without any pay until the following year. An illustrious career had been destroyed. He subsequently joined Hull City but was never again selected for England.

A cartilage operation curtailed his success at Boothferry Park and there followed spells with Crewe, Stockport County and Macclesfield before he entered management, first with Wellington Town and then Colchester United.

Henry COCKBURN

Position	Wing-half
Born	Henry Cockburn, Ashton-under-Lyne, 14 September 1923
Height	5ft 4in
Weight	10st 4lb
Clubs	Manchester United, Bury
England Caps	13
	1946 v N. Ireland (won 7–2), v Eire (won 1–0), v Wales (won 3–0)
	1948 v Scotland (won 2–0), v Italy (won 4–0), v Denmark (0–0), v N. Ireland (won 6–2), v Switzerland (won 6–0)
	1949 v Scotland (lost 1–3), v Sweden (lost 1–3)
	1951 v Argentina (won 2–1), v Portugal (won 5–2), v France (2–2)

HENRY COCKBURN, who won 13 caps for England, completed a quite formidable international half-back line with Stoke City's Neil Franklin and Wolves' Billy Wright. Despite standing only 5ft 4in, he became one of the finest wing-halves in English football in the immediate post-war years. He had joined Manchester United from local junior club, Goslings, then a Reds nursery club, and he made his first-team debut in wartime football. Cockburn's first England cap came after he had played in only a handful of League matches, although it should be said that the Football League proper had only just restarted after the war.

Cockburn's timing was perfect and he could outjump men much taller than himself. He was a great club player because he worked so hard for the team and his enthusiasm rubbed off on other people. His positional play was equally good, and he always wanted to win.

He won an FA Cup winners' medal in 1948 and a League Championship medal in 1951/52. On leaving Old Trafford, Cockburn joined neighbours Bury before entering non-League football with Peterborough United, who were then members of the Midland League. Spells with other non-League clubs Corby Town and Sankeys followed before he returned to the League scene as Oldham's assistant-trainer. His final move took him to Huddersfield Town, where he was involved in coaching.

Tom FINNEY

Position	Forward
Born	Thomas Finney, Preston, 5 April 1922
Height	5ft 8in
Weight	10st 6lb
Clubs	Preston North End, Distillery
England Caps	76 Goals 30

1946 v N. Ireland (won 7–2) 1 goal, v Eire (won 1–0) 1 goal, v Wales (won 3–0), v Holland (won 8–2) 1 goal

1947 v France (won 3–0) 1 goal, v Portugal (won 10–0) 1 goal, v Belgium (won 5–2) 2 goals, v Wales (won 3–0) 1 goal, v N. Ireland (2–2), v Sweden (won 4–1)

1948 v Scotland (won 2–0) 1 goal, v Italy (won 4–0) 2 goals, v N. Ireland (won 6–2), v Wales (won 1–0) 1 goal

1949 v Scotland (lost 1–3), v Sweden (lost 1–3) 1 goal, v Norway (won 4–1) 1 goal, v France (won 3–1), v Eire (lost 0–2), v Wales (won 4–1), v N. Ireland (won 9–2), v Italy (won 2–0)

1950 v Scotland (won 1–0), v Portugal (won 5–3) 4 goals; v Belgium (won 4–1), v Chile (won 2–0), v United States (lost 0–1), v Spain (lost 0–1), v Wales (won 4–24–)

1951 v Scotland (lost 2–3) 1 goal, v Argentina (won 2–1), v Portugal (won 5–2) 1 goal, v France (2–2), v Wales (1–1), v N. Ireland (won 2–0)

1952 v Scotland (won 2–1), v Italy (1–1), v Austria (won 3–2), v Switzerland (won 3–0), v N. Ireland (2–2), v Wales (won 5–2) 1 goal, v Belgium (won 5–0)

1953 v Scotland (2–2), v Argentina (0–0), v Chile (won 2–1), v Uruguay (lost 1–2), v United States (won 6–3) 2 goals, v Wales (won 4–1)

1954 v Scotland (won 4–2), v Yugoslavia (lost 0–1), v Hungary (lost 1–7), v Belgium (4–4), v Switzerland (won 2–0), v Uruguay (lost 2–4) 1 goal, v W. Germany (won 3–1)

1955 v Denmark (won 5–1), v Wales (lost 1–2), v N. Ireland (won 3–0) 1 goal, v Spain (won 4–1) 1 goal

1956 v Scotland (1–1), v Wales (won 3–1) 1 goal, v Yugoslavia (won 3–0), v Denmark (won 5–2)

1957 v Scotland (won 2–1), v Eire (won 5–1), v Denmaek (won 4–1), v Eire (1–1), v Wales (won 4–0) 1 goal, v France (won 4–0)

1958 v Scotland (won 4–0), v Portugal (won 2–1), v Yugoslavia (lost 0–5), v Soviet Union (1–1), v Soviet Union (2–2) 1 goal, v N. Ireland (3–3) 1 goal, v Soviet Union (won 5–0)

Honours	Footballer of the Year 1954 and 1957

A VERSATILE PLAYER, Tom Finney was able to play with equal ease on the right or left flank and even at centre-forward. He made his international debut for England against Northern Ireland in Belfast, scoring the first of 30 goals. He made 76 international appearances, 40 at outside-right, 33 at outside-left and three at centre-forward, his 30 goals for his country equalling the record that was held by Nat Lofthouse at the time. He began his England career at outside-right, the berth in which Stanley Matthews won worldwide renown. Soon, however, Matthews returned and Finney did more than settle contentedly for the role of outside-left. For years he figured in one of the greatest wing combinations the world has ever seen. The fans and critics compared his merits with those of Matthews. However, when people were unwise enough to ask a man of such modesty if he was better than his close friend, Finney would reply with sincerity, 'To me Stanley Matthews is phenomenal.'

Tom Finney of Preston North End.
(Lancashire Evening Post)

Finney spent his entire League career with his home-town club, Preston North End. He resisted all temptations to move on to more fashionable clubs, and because of this loyalty he failed to win any major domestic honours. He won wartime honours in the shape of a 1941 Cup Winners' medal and in July 1945 gained his first representative honours, for an FA XI in Zurich. In 1954 he appeared in the FA Cup Final but West Bromwich Albion deprived him of a major honour. However, he was elected Footballer of the Year that season and again in 1957, becoming the first man to win it twice. In 1957/58, playing at centre-forward, Finney scored 26 goals to help Preston finish runners-up in the First Division. He retired in 1960 at the age of 38, having devoted his entire career to North End and England. In 1963 he 'guested' in his only European club game for the Northern Irish team Distillery in their cup-tie against Benfica.

Known as the 'Preston Plumber', because he continued to run his plumbing business during his playing days, he was knighted in 1998 for his services to the game.

Wilf MANNION

Position	Inside-forward
Born	Wilfred Mannion, South Bank, 16 May 1918
Died	4 April 2000
Height	5ft 5in
Weight	11st 0lb
Clubs	Middlesbrough, Hull City
England Caps	26 Goals 10

1946 v N. Ireland (won 7–2) 3 goals, v Eire (won 1–0), v Wales (won 3–0) 2 goals, v Holland (won 8–2) 1 goal

1947 v Scotland (1–1), v France (won 3–0) 1 goal, v Switzerland (lost 0–1), v Portugal (won 10–0), v Belgium (won 5–2), v Wales (won 3–0), v N. Ireland (2–2) 1 goal, v Sweden (won 4–1)

1948 v Italy (won 4–0) •

1949 v Norway (won 4–1), v France (won 3–1), v Eire (lost 0–2)

1950 v Scotland (won 1–0), v Portugal (won 5–3), v Belgium (won 4–1) 1 goal, v Chile (won 2–0), v United States (lost 0–1), v N. Ireland (won 4–1), v Wales (won 4–2) 1 goal, v Yugoslavia (2–2)

1951 v Scotland (lost 2–3), v France (2–2)

KNOWN AS the 'Golden Boy' because of his blond hair, supreme dribbling skills and wonderful pace, Wilf Mannion began his League career with Middlesbrough and by the age of 17 was a regular in the club's First Division side. During the hostilities, he made four international appearances for England and also played for the Army side. He served with the Green Howards regiment and was evacuated from Dunkirk. He later served in the Middle East and Italy, but was invalided out of the army with shell-shock.

Mannion scored a hat-trick in his first full international against Northern Ireland, and had an outstanding game in May 1947, playing against the Rest of Europe at Glasgow. Playing at inside-right he scored the first goal and would have had a hat-trick had Lawton not touched one of his shots as it was crossing the line. He darted irrepressibly all over the field, pulling the hapless European defence to pieces – it was a marvellous exhibition.

At the beginning of the 1948/49 season, Mannion refused to re-sign for Middlesbrough, but in those days the clubs held all the aces and after losing a good deal of money in wages he was forced to return to the game with Boro. He spent five more seasons at Ayresome Park, taking his tally of goals to 110 in 368 games before deciding to retire. Hull City persuaded him to come out of retirement, but after just one season at Boothferry Park the Football League suspended him for refusing to give chapter and verse about alleged illegal payments to players. Mannion then went to play non-League football for Poole Town, King's Lynn, Haverfield Rovers and Earlstown before hanging up his boots.

Bobby LANGTON

Position	Outside-left
Born	Robert Langton, Burscough, 8 September 1918
Died	15 November 1996
Height	5ft 6in
Weight	10st 10lb
Clubs	Blackburn Rovers, Preston North End, Bolton Wanderers, Ards
England Caps	11 Goals 1
	1946 v N. Ireland (won 7–2) 1 goal, v Eire (won 1–0), v Wales (won 3–0), v Holland (won 8–2)
	1947 v France (won 3–0), v Switzerland (lost 0–1), v Sweden (won 4–1)
	1948 v Denmark (0–0)
	1949 v Sweden (lost 1–3)
	1950 v Scotland (won 1–0), v N. Ireland (won 4–1)

BOBBY LANGTON scored one of England's goals in a 7–2 defeat of Northern Ireland on what was his full international debut. His other ten appearances for his country were spread over four years.

He joined Blackburn Rovers from Southport League side Burscough Victoria in 1937 and within 12 months of his arrival at Ewood Park he had established himself as a first-team regular, helping the club win promotion to the First Division. During the war he was an infantryman in India and represented the Army in practically every game they played during his service. He appeared in the 1940 War Cup Final when Rovers lost 1–0 to West Ham United.

After the hostilities, Blackburn's fortunes began to wane and he was transferred to Preston North End. After just a handful of matches for the Lilywhites, Langton netted a goal just seven seconds from the kick-off in a game against Manchester City. In November 1949 Langton joined his third Lancashire club when he signed for Bolton Wanderers for £20,000. He remained at Burnden Park long enough to play in the famous 1953 FA Cup Final against Blackpool, before returning to play for Blackburn Rovers in September of that year. Although his speed had diminished somewhat in his second spell, he had added a great deal of guile and cunning to his play. He then had a spell playing for Ards in Northern Ireland before entering non-League football with Kidderminster Harriers, later playing for Wisbech Town and Colwyn Bay. After returning to his roots to become manager of Burscough Rangers, Langton ended his involvement with the game.

Harry JOHNSTON

Position	Wing-half
Born	Harry Johnston, Droylsden, 26 September 1919
Died	Blackpool, 12 October 1973
Height	5ft 11in
Weight	12st 4lb
Clubs	Blackpool
England Caps	10
	1946 v Holland (won 8–2)
	1947 v Scotland (1–1)
	1951 v Scotland (lost 2–3)
	1953 v Argentina (0–0), v Chile (won 2–1), v Uruguay (lost 1–2), v United States (won 6–3), v Wales (won 4–1), v N. Ireland (won 3–1), v Hungary (lost 3–6)
Honours	Footballer of the Year 1951

HARRY JOHNSTON'S international career was all too brief, at least as far as caps were concerned. He gained only ten in a seven-year period, although had it not been for the consistent Billy Wright he would surely have appeared many more times for his country.

Johnston played his early football for Droylsden Athletic before joining Blackpool in 1937. One of the youngest players to have represented the club, he was appointed the Seasiders' captain on the resumption of League football in 1946/47. He led Blackpool to the 1948 FA Cup Final, where they were beaten 4–2 by Manchester United. In 1951, Johnston led the Seasiders to another FA Cup Final, where they lost 2–0 to Newcastle United, and was voted Footballer of the Year. He later became the first Blackpool captain to hold aloft the FA Cup after the Seasiders had beaten Bolton Wanderers 4–3 in the famous 1953 Final. Though he was the subject of several big bids from the leading clubs of his day, Johnston remained a loyal one-club man. An essential member of the great Blackpool side of the 1950s, he was one of the greatest players ever to have turned out for the Seasiders. When he, Matthews and Mortensen were in the side, the away crowd, so it was said, would be twice as large as normal! On leaving Bloomfield Road, Johnston managed Reading, but later returned to the Fylde coast as Blackpool's chief scout. He subsequently ran a newsagent's in the town, but sadly died aged just 54.

Jimmy MULLEN

Position	Outside-left
Born	James Mullen, Newcastle upon Tyne, 6 January 1923
Died	Wolverhampton, 2 October 1987
Height	5ft 10in
Weight	11st 4lb
Clubs	Wolverhampton Wanderers
England Caps	12 Goals 6
	1947 v Scotland (1–1)
	1949 v Norway (won 4–1) 1 goal, v France (won 3–1)
	1950 v Belgium (won 4–1) 1 goal
	1950 v Chile (won 2–0), v United States (lost 0–1)
	1953 v Wales (won 4–1), v Rest of Europe (4–4) 2 goals, v N. Ireland (won 3–1)
	1954 v Scotland (won 4–2) 1 goal, v Yugoslavia (lost 0–1), v Switzerland (won 2–0) 1 goal

JIMMY MULLEN had the distinction of being England's first-ever substitute when he replaced the injured Stan Mortensen against Belgium in 1950, but he had made his England debut three years earlier. He appeared in two World Cups for England and scored against Switzerland on his last international appearance in 1954.

Jimmy Mullen is the youngest player ever to have appeared for Wolves in a first-class match. He was just 16 years and 43 days old when he made his League debut in

a 4–1 win over Leeds United in February 1939. During the Second World War he helped Wolves win the Wartime League Cup (North) when he was serving in the Army as a corporal. After the hostilities he gained three First Division Championship-winning medals in 1953/54, 1957/58 and 1958/59, as well as an FA Cup winners' medal in 1949. He was a virtual fixture in the Wolves side at No. 11 for eight seasons and he and his opposite number, Johnny Hancocks, were generally regarded as by far the best pair of wingers in the Football League during the early 1950s. He went on to score 112 goals in 486 games before leaving Molineux in the summer of 1959.

Jimmy Mullen of Wolves.
(Lancashire Evening Post)

Eddie LOWE

Position	Left-half/Full-back
Born	Edward Lowe, Halesowen, 11 July 1925
Height	5ft 11in
Weight	11st 3lb
Clubs	Aston Villa, Fulham, Notts County
England Caps	3
	1947 v France (won 3–0), v Switzerland (lost 0–1), v Portugal (won 10–0)

EDDIE LOWE began his League career with Aston Villa, joining the Midlands club in the summer of 1945. His performances in the Villa side in the first four seasons following the resumption of League football after the Second World War led to him winning full international honours in 1947, when he became Villa's first post-war international. He played in three internationals that year, his last in the 10–0 rout of Portugal.

In May 1950, he and his brother Reg joined Fulham. Able to play at full-back or wing-half, Lowe missed very few games over the next 13 seasons. He helped the Cottagers win promotion to the First Division in 1958/59, after which he pitted his wits against the best inside-forwards in the game and often came out on top. Unlucky not to add to his total of international caps while at Craven Cottage, he went on to appear in 511 games for Fulham before deciding to hang up his boots at the end of the 1962/63 season.

Lowe went into management with Notts County but had a disastrous first season as the Magpies were relegated to the Fourth Division. In an effort to rectify matters he made a comeback as a player just before his 40th birthday but things didn't work out and he was sacked. He later worked as a purchasing manager for a central-heating company in Nottingham while scouting for Plymouth Argyle.

Stan MORTENSEN

Position	Forward
Born	Stanley Harding Mortensen, South Shields, 26 May 1921
Died	Blackpool, 22 May 1991
Height	5ft 10in
Weight	11st 7lb
Clubs	Blackpool, Hull City, Southport
England Caps	25 Goals 24
	1947 v Portugal (won 10–0) 4 goals, v Belgium (won 5–2) 1 goal, v Wales (won 3–0) 1 goal, v N. Ireland (2–2), v Sweden (won 4–1) 3 goals
	1948 v Scotland (won 2–0) 1 goal, v Italy (won 4–0) 1 goal, v N. Ireland (won 6–2) 3 goals, v Wales (won 1–0)
	1949 v Scotland (lost 1–3), v Sweden (lost 1–3), v Norway (won 4–1), v Wales (won 4–1) 1 goal, v N. Ireland (won 9–2) 2 goals, v Italy (won 2–0)
	1950 v Scotland (won 1–0), v Portugal (won 5–3) 1 goal, v Belgium (won 4–1) 1 goal, v Chile (won 2–0) 1 goal, v United States (lost 0–1), v Spain (lost 0–1)

1951 v Scotland (lost 2–3), v Argentina (won 2–1) 2 goals
1953 v Rest of Europe (4–4) 1 goal, v Hungary (lost 3–6) 1 goal

STAN MORTENSEN made his international debut for Wales in wartime against his own country at Wembley on 25 September 1943. Mortensen, then 21, travelled to Wembley as an England reserve but finished up playing for an injury-hit Welsh side when left-half Ivor Powell had to leave the field. His first full game for England was against Portugal in Lisbon in 1947. It was a remarkable game – England won 10–0 and Mortensen scored four, the first of 24 goals for his country in 25 internationals. In fact, he was one of only four players in the twentieth century who achieved hat-tricks when making their England debut.

'The other Stanley', as he was proud to be known, joined the Blackpool groundstaff but was almost rejected as a player for being too slow. His career was cut short in its infancy when he received severe head and back injuries when the Wellington bomber he was piloting crashed. For years afterwards he suffered headaches and sleepless nights, but the fans never knew. Miraculously he overcame this serious injury to become one of the game's finest inside-forwards.

Stanley Matthews and Stan Mortensen (right) during a training session at Stamford Bridge, London, before a game against a Rest of the World team, 20 October 1953. (Reg Burkett/Getty Images).

Mortensen headed Blackpool's scoring charts for the first six seasons following the Second World War and found the net in every round of the 1947/48 FA Cup competition. He played in three FA Cup Finals, the best remembered of which is the 1953 Final when he notched a hat-trick in his side's 4–3 win over Bolton Wanderers. It was a sad day for him when in 1955, after scoring 222 goals in 354 games, the time came for him to leave Bloomfield Road.

Stan joined Hull City and later played for Southport before going out of the League with Bath City and Worcester. He then opened his sports shop close to Bloomfield Road and that was the last football saw of him until Blackpool called him back to manage them in February 1967 – he was thrilled at the challenge but unfortunately things didn't work out.

Tim WARD

Position	Wing-half
Born	Timothy Victor Ward, Cheltenham, 17 October 1917
Died	Barton-under-Needwood, 28 January 1993
Height	5ft 9in
Weight	11st 9lb
Clubs	Derby County, Barnsley
England Caps	2
	1947 v Belgium (won 5–2)
	1948 v Wales (won 1–0)

TIM WARD was outstanding in his first full international, helping England to a 5–2 win over Belgium in Brussels, but he was left out of the next five games before being recalled for the game against Wales at Villa Park, which England won 1–0.

Ward was signed by Derby County manager George Jobey after a successful trial in which he scored with his first kick! He missed very few games in the seasons leading up to the war. Slightly wounded in the D-Day landings, he nonetheless played in the Rams' first game of the 1945/46 FA Cup campaign at Luton. Army duties then took him back to Germany, where he played for the BAOR side, and he had no chance of winning back his place for the 1948 FA Cup Final when Derby lifted the trophy for the only time in their history. In 1951, in a move which disappointed Derby fans, Ward transferred to Barnsley when the Oakwell club sought a replacement for Danny Blanchflower. In March 1953 he accepted the job as manager of Exeter City but after only eight days he returned to Oakwell to take charge of Barnsley following the death of Angus Seed. At 34 he was the youngest manager in the League at the time. After relegation, Ward led the Tykes to the Third Division (North) Championship, but in 1960 he took over the reins at Grimsby Town. He took the Mariners to the runners-up spot in Division Three in 1961/62 before receiving a very good offer to take over at Derby County. Sadly, his time in charge at the Baseball Ground was unhappy and when his contract was not renewed he ended his involvement with the game as manager of Carlisle United.

Phil TAYLOR

Position	Right-half
Born	Philip Henry Taylor, Bristol, 18 September 1917
Height	5ft 10in
Weight	11st 2lb
Clubs	Bristol Rovers, Liverpool
England Caps	3
	1947 v Wales (won 3–0), v N. Ireland (2–2), v Sweden (won 4–1)

PHIL TAYLOR captained the Liverpool side that swept to the League title in 1947, a year in which he was also capped three times by England and was never on the losing side.

He began his playing career with Bristol Rovers in 1932 before, four years later, Liverpool paid £5,000 for his services and he began an illustrious career with the Anfield club that would stretch over 20 years. As for so many footballers of his generation, the arrival of war was to interrupt a blossoming career. He duly returned to League action when the hostilities ceased, but by then he was almost 30.

Composed, polished and a great reader of the game, he continued playing until 1954, then 37 years old, but when Liverpool were relegated he decided to call it a day and took up a post on the coaching staff. He rose through the ranks to become chief coach and when Don Welsh was taken ill he took over briefly as caretaker-manager. When Welsh decided in 1956 that he could no longer carry on, Taylor was appointed manager. Over the next three seasons, Taylor experienced the frustration of near misses as the Reds repeatedly failed to gain promotion to the top flight by a whisker. In November 1959, after his health suffered under the strain of the job, he resigned.

Stan PEARSON

Position	Inside-forward		
Born	Stanley Clare Pearson, Salford, 15 January 1919		
Died	20 February 1997		
Height	5ft 9in		
Weight	11st 0lb		
Clubs	Manchester United, Bury, Chester		
England Caps	8	Goals	5
	1948 v Scotland (won 2–0), v N. Ireland (won 6–2) 1 goal		
	1949 v Scotland (lost 1–3), v N. Ireland (won 9–2) 2 goals, v Italy (won 2–0)		
	1951 v Portugal (won 5–2)		
	1952 v Scotland (won 2–1) 2 goals, v Italy (1–1)		

WITHOUT DOUBT, the highlight of Stan Pearson's international career was scoring both goals in England's 2–1 victory over Scotland at Hampden Park in April 1952.

Stan was a player of immense power who had the ability to score goals as well as create them for others, and none can have been more important than the one he netted in the 1948 FA Cup Final against Blackpool, which gave United a lead they were not to relinquish. Pearson's hat-trick in the semi-final against Derby County had assured United of a Wembley place. He enjoyed a highly successful partnership with Jack Rowley and between them they scored 52 of United's 95 goals on their way to winning the League Championship of 1951/52. He could spray out some marvellous sweeping passes and was equally proficient at getting on the end of the resultant crosses. His lethal shot helped him to 149 goals in 345 games for United, but with Busby's youth policy bearing fruit he ended his 17-year career with the club and signed for Bury in 1954, later playing for Chester, where he eventually became manager. He found the managerial side of football much harder than playing and exchanged the pressure of League club management for the less demanding task of running a newsagent's shop.

Jack HOWE

Position	Left-back
Born	John Robert Howe, West Hartlepool, 7 October 1913
Died	Derby, 5 April 1987
Height	5ft 11in
Weight	12st 10lb
Clubs	Hartlepool United, Derby County, Huddersfield Town
England Caps	3
	1948 v Italy (won 4–0), v N. Ireland (won 6–2)
	1949 v Scotland (lost 1–3)

ONE OF DERBY COUNTY'S greatest defenders, Jack Howe won the first of his three England caps in 1948 – and it was considered long overdue.

One of the first professional sportsmen to wear contact lenses, Howe began his career with Hartlepool United, where his impressive performances led to Derby County manager George Jobey bringing him to the Baseball Ground. Able to kick a ball equally hard and accurately with either foot, and widely considered one of the best two-footed full-backs in the Football League, he was a regular in the Derby side until the outbreak of the Second World War, helping the Rams finish runners-up to Sunderland in Division One in 1935/36.

During the hostilities he joined the Cameron Highlanders, and while north of the border he 'guested' for Hearts, Falkirk, Aberdeen and St Mirren. He also played for the Scottish League against the British Army. After service in India, he was demobbed in time to earn an FA Cup winners' medal, playing centre-half in the semi-final and left-back in the 4–1 win over Charlton Athletic at Wembley.

Jack Howe never shirked a tackle and when Raich Carter left to play for Hull City, he took over the captaincy. After ending his League career with Huddersfield Town, he had spells as player-manager with King's Lynn and Long Sutton before managing Wisbech Town.

John ASTON

Position	Full-back
Born	John Aston, Manchester, 3 September 1921
Height	5ft 11in
Weight	12st 7lb
Clubs	Manchester United
England Caps	17

1948 v Denmark (0–0), v Wales (won 1–0), v Switzerland (won 6–0)

1949 v Scotland (lost 1–3), v Sweden (lost 1–3), v Norway (won 4–1), v France (won 3–1), v Eire (lost 0–2), v Wales (won 4–1), v N. Ireland (won 9–2), v Italy (won 2–0)

1950 v Scotland (won 1–0), v Portugal (won 5–3), v Belgium (won 4–1), v Chile (won 2–0), v United States (lost 0–1), v N. Ireland (won 4–1)

JOHN ASTON won 17 full caps for England at left-back, partnering several different right-backs, including Alf Ramsey.

He joined Manchester United as an amateur in 1937 but didn't turn professional until the end of the Second World War. Converted from inside-forward, Aston joined Johnny Carey as one of the most famous full-back pairings of the immediate post-war years, the two of them developing a great understanding. He was a member of United's first 1948 FA Cup-winning team and of the 1952 League Championship-winning side. Well-built, he used his weight to good advantage, but he was also a skilful player. During the 1950/51 campaign, he was often called upon to help out in the forward line when injuries took their toll, scoring 16 goals in 45 games, including 2 in a 3–1 win over Arsenal. Illness cut short his career and in April 1954 he played the last of his 253 games for United, scoring the opening goal in the club's 3–1 win over Sheffield United.

Aston took up scouting duties with the club and in 1970 became chief scout. The father of John Aston junior, a member of United's 1968 European Cup-winning team, he did not survive the upheaval of Frank O'Farrell's sacking in 1972 and left Old Trafford.

Jimmy HAGAN

Position	Inside-forward
Born	James Hagan, Washington, 21 January 1917
Died	Portugal, 27 February 1998
Height	5ft 8in
Weight	10st 10lb
Clubs	Liverpool, Derby County, Sheffield United
England Caps	1

1948 v Denmark (0–0)

JIMMY HAGAN was very unlucky to reach his footballing peak during the war years, when he rose to the rank of major and 'guested' for Aldershot. Winning 16 wartime caps, he once scored after only 50 seconds against Scotland at Wembley in 1942. Yet he won only one official England cap, in an undistinguished performance against Denmark in Copenhagen in September 1948.

Unable to make much headway with Liverpool, Jimmy Hagan began his professional career with Derby County, but there too he was unable to win a regular place – apparently he and manager George Jobey never got on – and so he moved to Sheffield United. That season his inspirational play led to promotion to the First Division and Hagan went on to become a legend at Bramall Lane.

A man with almost magical ball control, he was an inside-forward who could baffle opponents as well as his own team-mates. His artistry led some to suggest that the Yorkshire club were a one-man team and, to make the point, a photographer published a team photo featuring 11 Jimmy Hagan heads!

When he hung up his boots, Hagan joined Peterborough United as their manager. After their election to the Football League in 1960, he led them to the Fourth Division Championship in their first season. Following a dispute with the players he was sacked. He later joined West Bromwich Albion as manager, leading them to success in the League Cup Final of 1965. A controversial and sometimes volatile boss, Jimmy Hagan then took charge of Benfica, and in each of his three seasons they won the Portuguese Championship. He later managed Sporting Lisbon and Oporto, living in Portugal until his death.

Len SHACKLETON

Position	Inside-forward
Born	Leonard Francis Shackleton, Bradford, 3 May 1922
Died	Cumbria, 28 November 2000
Height	5ft 8in
Weight	11st 5lb
Clubs	Arsenal, Bradford Park Avenue, Newcastle United, Sunderland
England Caps	5 Goals 2
	1948 v Denmark (0–0), v Wales (won 1–0)
	1949 v Wales (won 4–1)
	1954 v Wales (won 3–1) 1 goal, v W. Germany (won 3–1) 1 goal

ONE OF THE GAME'S most entertaining players, Len Shackleton, who was nicknamed 'The Clown Prince of Soccer', won six caps for England over a period of five years. There were many who thought that he should be an England regular, but his international appearances were restricted because of his unwillingness to conform.

When Arsenal rejected him as a youngster, Len joined his local club, Bradford Park Avenue, just as the Second World War was beginning. In October 1946 he left the Yorkshire club to join Newcastle United, who paid £13,000 for him. He made a most spectacular debut for the Magpies, scoring six goals in United's 13–0 thrashing of Newport County, including three in the space of two-and-a-half minutes, which is believed to be the fastest first-class hat-trick of all time. He went on to score 29 goals in 64 games for the Magpies, taking part in the first half of the club's 1947/48 promotion campaign before a shake-up at Newcastle saw him join Sunderland in February 1948 for a fee of £20,000. By the time an ankle injury forced his retirement in September 1957, he had scored 101 goals in 348 games for the Black Cats.

He was a great humorist: a chapter in his autobiography was entitled 'What the average director knows about football' – Shackleton left the page blank!

Jackie MILBURN

Position	Centre-forward
Born	John Edward Thompson Milburn, Ashington, 11 May 1924
Died	Ashington, 9 October 1988
Height	6ft 0in
Weight	12st 9lb
Clubs	Newcastle United, Linfield
England Caps	13 Goals 7

1948 v N. Ireland (won 6–2) 1 goal, v Wales (won 1–0), v Switzerland (won 6–0) 1 goal
1949 v Scotland (lost 1–3) 1 goal, v Wales (won 4–1) 3 goals
1950 v Portugal (won 5–3), v Belgium (won 4–1), v Spain (lost 0–1), v Wales (won 4–2) 1 goal
1951 v Argentina (won 2–1), v Portugal (won 5–2), v France (2–2)
1955 v Denmark (won 5–1)

ALWAYS IN THE RECKONING for an England place, Jackie Milburn won only half the caps he should have done. Appearing in the ill-fated 1950 World Cup Finals, he netted a hat-trick for his country against Wales and hit two other trebles for the Football League XI.

Internationally known as 'Wor Jackie', he was a Geordie idol long after he ceased to wear the black and white stripes of Newcastle United. Having worked as a pit apprentice, he joined Newcastle as a right-winger, though he was to play in all other forward roles during his career with United. A former professional sprinter, he had devastating pace and a lethal shot in both feet. He is particularly remembered for his ability to swivel in tight situations and power a drive towards the net. Noted for his many spectacular goals, he relished the big-match atmosphere – his first-minute header in the 1955 FA Cup Final was one of the quickest-ever in a final (he also netted in every round of the 1951 FA Cup run to Wembley). No other Newcastle player has scored more goals in all competitions for the Magpies.

On leaving United he became popular in Northern Ireland, appearing for Linfield in European Cup football and scoring over 100 goals in only two seasons.

After a spell as manager of Ipswich Town, he returned to Tyneside to become a much-respected journalist for the News of the World, covering Newcastle's fortunes for over 20 years. He was given a belated testimonial at St James' Park in 1967 and a crowd of over 45,000 welcomed him home. Following his death from cancer, the whole of Newcastle came to a standstill for his funeral.

He was made a Freeman of the City and a statue on Newcastle's main thoroughfare recognizes the achievements of Jackie Milburn, the working man's hero.

Arsenal goalkeeper George Swindin reaches to collect the ball as it leaves Newcastle United striker Jackie Milburn's head during the 1952 FA Cup final at Wembley. The Magpies won 1–0. (Getty Images)

Ted DITCHBURN

Position	Goalkeeper
Born	Edwin George Ditchburn, Gillingham, 24 October 1921
Height	6ft 1in
Weight	12st 12lb
Clubs	Tottenham Hotspur
England Caps	6
	1948 v Switzerland (won 6–0)
	1949 v Sweden (lost 1–3)
	1953 v United States (won 6–3)
	1956 v Wales (won 3–1), v Yugoslavia (won 3–0), v Denmark (won 5–2)

UNFORTUNATE TO PLAY in an era when England were well served by Frank Swift and Bert Williams, both top-class keepers, Ted Ditchburn, who was a member of England's 1950 World Cup squad, deserved more than his six England caps spread over eight years.

The son of a professional boxer, he arrived at Tottenham via the Northfleet nursery in 1939. His debut was in the Football League South in May 1940 but National Service meant he was only able to play occasionally for Spurs. However, the war did allow him to get an early taste of representative football with the Royal Air Force and FA XIs, as well as two England wartime internationals. He missed just two League games in seven post-war seasons, which included an unbroken sequence of 247 outings between April 1948 and March 1954. He was ever-present in the Second Division Championship team of 1949/50 and in the First Division-winning team the following season.

Ted was a magnificent catcher of crosses, breathtakingly agile on his line, and with Alf Ramsey he pioneered the short throw-out, which was so important to Spurs' 'push-and-run' style of the early 1950s. In the mid-1950s, he lost his place for short spells to Ron Reynolds but fought his way back. His top-flight days ended, however, with a broken finger at Chelsea in August 1958 and eight months later he became player-manager at Romford.

He is one of the most beloved figures in the history of Tottenham Hotspur — only Pat Jennings and Steve Perryman have played more than Ditchburn's 453 games for Spurs, a remarkable statistic given that seven years of his career were lost to the Second World War.

Alf RAMSEY

Position	Right-back
Born	Alfred Ernest Ramsey, Dagenham, 22 January 1920
Died	Suffolk, 28 April 1999
Height	5ft 9in
Weight	12st 8lb
Clubs	Portsmouth, Southampton, Tottenham Hotspur
England Caps	32 Goals 3

1948 v Switzerland (won 6–0)
1949 v Italy (won 2–0)
1950 v Scotland (won 1–0), v Portugal (won 5–3), v Belgium (won 4–1), v Chile (won 2–0), v United States (lost 0–1), v Spain (lost 0–1), v N. Ireland (won 4–1), v Wales (won 4–2), v Yugoslavia (2–2)
1951 v Scotland (lost 2–3), v Argentina (won 2–1), v Portugal (won 5–2), v France (2–2), v Wales (1–1), v N. Ireland (won 2–0), v Austria (2–2) 1 goal
1952 v Scotland (won 2–1), v Italy (1–1), v Austria (won 3–2), v Switzerland (won 3–0), v N. Ireland (2–2), v Wales (won 5–2), v Belgium (won 5–0)
1953 v Scotland (2–2), v Argentina (0–0), v Chile (won 2–1), v Uruguay (lost 1–2), v United States (won 6–3), v Rest of Europe (4–4) 1 goal, v Hungary (lost 3–6) 1 goal

AS A PLAYER, Alf Ramsey was a strong, polished and distinguished defender who joined Portsmouth as an amateur in 1942. A year later he moved to the Dell to play for Southampton. He made his England debut in a 6–0 victory over Switzerland at Highbury in December 1948, before going on to make 28 consecutive appearances for his country, captaining the side in the absence of Billy Wright. In all he won 32 caps for England and represented the Football League on five occasions.

In May 1949 Ramsey moved to Tottenham Hotspur for £21,000, a record fee for a full-back. He was virtually an ever-present in the teams that won the Second Division and Football League titles in 1950 and 1951 respectively, but in May 1955, after appearing in 250 League and Cup games for the White Hart Lane club, he decided to retire.

He was appointed manager of Ipswich Town in August 1955 and immediately began to refashion the Portman Road side in a manner that was to herald the dawn of a new era. He led the club to the Third Division (South) title in 1956/57, the Second Division Championship in 1960/61 and the First Division Championship of 1961/62.

In January 1963 he was appointed full-time manager of England. His greatest triumph came in 1966 when England, playing on home territory, won the World Cup for the first and only time. In May 1974, after England had failed to qualify for the finals of that year's World Cup competition, he was sacked. Under Ramsey, England had lost only 17 out of 113 games and won 69 of these.

Shortly after the start of the 1977/78 season, Sir Alf Ramsey, who was by then a Birmingham City director, became the first knight to manage a League club, following the dismissal of Willie Bell. He held office for seven months before being forced to relinquish the position due to ill-health. His final appointment in 1980 saw him take the post of technical director with Panathinaikos, but his stay with the Athenian club also lasted only a few months.

Jack ROWLEY

Position	Forward
Born	John Frederick Rowley, Wolverhampton, 7 October 1918
Died	Shaw, 28 June 1998
Height	5ft 9in
Weight	12st 0lb
Clubs	Wolverhampton Wanderers, Bournemouth, Manchester United, Plymouth Argyle
England Caps	6 Goals 6
	1948 v Switzerland (won 6–0) 1 goal
	1949 v Sweden (lost 1–3), v Norway (won 4–1), v France (won 3–1), v N. Ireland (won 9–2)
	4 goals, v Italy (won 2–0) 1 goal

JACK ROWLEY'S GOALSCORING EXPLOITS – eight in one game for Wolves and seven in another for Spurs – won him a wartime cap against Wales in 1944, but he had to wait four years to win the first of his six full caps. He scored a goal per game at international level and his total included four in a World Cup qualifier against Northern Ireland in November 1949.

Born into a footballing family – his father was a goalkeeper with Walsall – Jack Rowley began his career as an outside-left with Major Buckley's famous nursery at Wolverhampton Wanderers. However, the Molineux club didn't rate him too highly and he was allowed to join Bournemouth. After scoring almost a goal a game for the Cherries, his form attracted a number of top clubs and in October 1937 he moved to Manchester United. After making his debut he needed time to settle into his new surroundings, but after a spell of reserve-team football he returned to score four goals in a 5–1 defeat of Swansea. After the war, he dominated United's scoring – especially on the big occasions – netting two in the 1948 FA Cup Final victory over Blackpool. He started the 1951/52 season in fine style, hitting hat-tricks in each of the club's first two games, and went on to score 30 goals – a club record only broken by Dennis Viollet in 1960. He appeared in 422 games for United, scoring 208 goals – his First Division tally alone was 182 in 380 games.

After 18 years with United he joined Plymouth Argyle as player-manager, leading them to promotion to Division Two. He later managed Oldham Athletic before succeeding Vic Buckingham as manager of Ajax. On returning to these shores, he had spells with Wrexham, Bradford, and Oldham again, before leaving the game to run a sub-post office.

He was the brother of the equally prolific Arthur – amazingly they both scored their 200th League goal on the same day, 22 October 1955, Jack reaching the milestone first by just 12 minutes!

Jack HAINES

Position	Inside-forward
Born	John Thomas Haines, Wickhamford, 24 April 1920
Died	Evesham, 19 March 1987
Height	5ft 9in
Weight	10st 11lb
Clubs	Liverpool, Swansea Town, Leicester City, West Bromwich Albion, Bradford Park Avenue, Rochdale, Chester City
England Caps	1 Goals 2
	1948 v Switzerland (won 6–0) 2 goals

THOUGH HIS EARLY MANAGERS were unsure how to make best use of Jack Haines, when he joined West Bromwich Albion he was positioned exclusively in the forward line and soon won an England cap, scoring twice against Switzerland.

Jack was a utility player whose early career was stymied by the outbreak of the Second World War. He had to wait until peacetime football resumed in 1946/47 to make his Football League debut for Swansea Town. During the hostilities he had 'guested' for a number of clubs, including Worcester City, Bradford Park Avenue, Doncaster Rovers, Lincoln City, Notts County and Wrexham.

At the end of that first season of League football, Haines left the Vetch Field to join Leicester City. At Filbert Street, the Leicester manager Johnny Duncan seemed uncertain as to his best position and in his brief stay with the club he wore five different-numbered outfield shirts. In March 1948 he joined West Bromwich Albion in a straight swap for Peter McKennan. After helping Albion win promotion to the top flight, he left to join Bradford Park Avenue, but his first season with the Yorkshire club ended in relegation as they dropped from the Second to the Third Division (North). He later played for Rochdale and Chester before ending his career in non-League circles with Wellington Town, Kidderminster Harriers and Evesham Town.

Johnny HANCOCKS

Position	Outside-right
Born	John Hancocks, Oakengates, 30 April 1919
Died	14 February 1994
Height	5ft 4in
Weight	9st 5lb
Clubs	Walsall, Wolverhampton Wanderers
England Caps	3　　Goals　　2
	1948 v Switzerland (won 6–0) 2 goals
	1949 v Wales (won 4–1)
	1950 v Yugoslavia (2–2)

GOALSCORING WINGER JOHNNY HANCOCKS began his Football League career with Walsall, but in May 1946 Wolves paid £4,000 to bring him to Molineux and he made his debut in a 6–1 win over Arsenal on the opening day of the 1946/47 season. His form during the club's FA Cup-winning season of 1948/49 led to the first of three full England caps – he scored twice in a 6–0 win over Switzerland.

He netted his first hat-trick for Wolves in December 1950 in a 3–1 home win over West Bromwich Albion and his second during the club's League Championship-winning season of 1953/54, when Wolves beat Chelsea 8–1. The following season, Hancocks was the club's leading scorer with 26 goals in 32 games, including hat-tricks against Huddersfield Town and Arsenal. Hancocks topped the goalscoring charts again in 1955/56, when he also netted his fifth and last treble for the club in a 9–1 demolition of Cardiff City. Sadly it was his last season in the first team. After scoring 168 goals in 378 League and Cup games, he spent a season in the club's Central League side before becoming player-manager of Wellington Town. He later ended his career with Cambridge United (who were then members of the Southern League), Oswestry and GKN Sankey.

Eddie SHIMWELL

Position	Right-back
Born	Edmund Shimwell, Wirksworth, 27 February 1920
Died	Matlock, 2 October 1988
Height	5ft 11in
Weight	12st 6lb
Clubs	Sheffield United, Blackpool, Oldham Athletic
England Caps	1
	1949 v Sweden (lost 1–3)

TOUGH-TACKLING FULL-BACK Eddie Shimwell won his only England cap as a replacement for the injured Alf Ramsey in a 3–1 defeat by Sweden in Stockholm. He had a disappointing game and was replaced by Southampton's Bill Ellerington for the next game of England's Scandinavian tour, against Norway five days later.

Shimwell began his career with Sheffield United, for whom he played throughout the Second World War. He asked permission from the United board to run a pub in the town, and when they refused he asked for a transfer, joining Blackpool in December 1946. He should have made his debut for the Seasiders in the match at Charlton Athletic but the train from his Chesterfield home was snowbound so he didn't arrive at the Valley until half-time! He eventually made his Blackpool debut on Christmas Day and he became a regular for the next nine seasons, forming a formidable full-back pairing with Tommy Garrett. Though he only scored a handful of goals, one, against Chester City in the fourth round of the FA Cup in January 1948, saw him lob the ball over the head of the opposing keeper from fully 60 yards, while in that season's FA Cup Final he became the first full-back to score in a Wembley final when he netted from the penalty spot. A dislocated shoulder ended his playing days at Bloomfield Road, and after a brief spell with Oldham Athletic he ended his career playing non-League football for Burton Albion.

Roy BENTLEY

Position	Centre-forward
Born	Roy Thomas Frank Bentley, Bristol, 17 May 1923
Height	5ft 10in
Weight	11st 7lb
Clubs	Bristol Rovers, Bristol City, Newcastle United, Chelsea, Fulham, Queen's Park Rangers
England Caps	12 Goals 9
	1949 v Sweden (lost 1–3)
	1950 v Scotland (won 1–0) 1 goal, v Portugal (won 5–3), v Belgium (won 4–1) 1 goal, v Chile (won 2–0), v United States (lost 0–1)
	1952 v Wales (won 5–2) 1 goal, v Belgium (won 5–0)
	1954 v Wales (won 3–1) 3 goals, v W. Germany (won 3–1) 1 goal
	1955 v Spain (1–1) 1 goal, v Portugal (lost 1–3) 1 goal

ROY BENTLEY appeared in the 1950 World Cup Finals in Brazil and in 12 games for England spread over six years, scoring nine goals, including a hat-trick in a 3–1 defeat of Wales.

He began his Football League career as an inside-forward with Newcastle United after playing for both Bristol clubs during the Second World War. But when he joined Chelsea in January 1948 he was tried at centre-forward, with great success. He captained the Stamford Bridge club to the League Championship in 1954/55 and gained many honours while with The Pensioners. After leaving Chelsea, he joined Fulham, where he was converted into an outstanding half-back, and during his second season at Craven Cottage he was instrumental in the club winning promotion to the First Division. After ending his playing career with Queen's Park Rangers, he was appointed manager of Reading. After three seasons at Elm Park, where he experimented with new methods of play, he left to take over at Swansea, leading the club to promotion to the Third Division at the end of his first season. After two seasons of mid-table placings, the Swans had a poor 1972/73 season, and Bentley lost his job. After managing non-League Thatcham Town, he later held the post of club secretary at both Reading and Aldershot.

Bill ELLERINGTON

Position	Right-back
Born	William Ellerington, Southampton, 30 June 1923
Height	6ft 0in
Weight	12st 3lb
Clubs	Southampton
England Caps	2
	1949 v Norway (won 4–1), v France (won 3–1)

ONE OF THE MOST CONSISTENT defenders in the Football League in the immediate post-war years, Bill Ellerington deservedly won two England caps, playing in victories over Norway and France.

Bill came from a football family, his father having played for The Saints during the First World War before later playing for Middlesbrough and then Sunderland. Bill also started his career with Southampton during a war, first playing in the 1940/41 Southern Regional League. He was one of the best full-backs ever to represent the club and went on to appear in 61 wartime games before making his Football League debut against Swansea Town on the opening day of the 1946/47 season. Initially he was competing with Alf Ramsey for the right-back position but more often than not he was the club's first choice, only losing his place when he caught pneumonia during the Saints' visit to Newcastle United later that season. Ramsey replaced him and went on to win almost immediate international recognition. When Ellerington finally recovered, after almost a year out of the game, the Southampton management found themselves with a superfluity of talent and experience in the full-back department, so they let Ramsey join Tottenham Hotspur. Ellerington went on to appear in 237 League and Cup games for the Saints during his ten years with the club, before joining Ted Bates' coaching staff.

Jimmy DICKINSON

Position	Left-half
Born	James William Dickinson, Alton, 24 April 1925
Died	Portsmouth, 8 November 1982
Height	5ft 10in
Weight	11st 0lb
Clubs	Portsmouth
England Caps	48
	1949 v Norway (won 4–1), v France (won 3–1), v Eire (lost 0–2), v Wales (won 4–1)
	1950 v Scotland (won 1–0), v Portugal (won 5–3), v Belgium (won 4–1), v Chile (won 2–0), v United States (lost 0–1), v Spain (lost 0–1), v N. Ireland (won 4–1), v Wales (won 4–2), v Yugoslavia (2–2)
	1951 v Wales (1–1), v N. Ireland (won 2–0), v Austria (2–2)
	1952 v Scotland (won 2–1), v Italy (1–1), v Austria (won 3–2), v Switzerland (won 3–0), v N. Ireland (2–2), v Wales (won 5–2), v Belgium (won 5–0)
	1953 v Scotland (2–2), v Argentina (0–0), v Chile (won 2–1), v Uruguay (lost 1–2),

v United States (won 6–3), v Wales (won 4–1), v Rest of Europe (4–4), v N. Ireland (won 3–1), v Hungary (lost 3–6)

1954 v Scotland (won 4–2), v Yugoslavia (lost 0–1), v Hungary (lost 1–7), v Belgium (4–4), v Switzerland (won 2–0), v Uruguay (lost 2–4)

1955 v Spain (1–1), v Portugal (lost 1–3), v Denmark (won 5–1), v Wales (lost 1–2), v N. Ireland (won 3–0), v Spain (won 4–1)

1956 v Scotland (1–1), v Wales (won 3–1), v Yugoslavia (won 3–0), v Denmark (won 5–2)

AN AUTOMATIC CHOICE for England for many years, Jimmy Dickinson played in the 1950 World Cup Finals in Brazil and was a member of the England team humiliated 1–0 by United States. The summer of 1954 saw him play in his second World Cup Finals in Switzerland, but unfortunately in the match against Belgium, which ended 4–4, he scored the first own goal of his career.

One of the greatest names in British football, Jimmy Dickinson holds the Portsmouth appearance record with 834 first-team matches and another 31 wartime games. He is second to Swindon's John Trollope (770) in terms of the most post-war Football League appearances for one club, having made 764.

Almost faultless in defence, he was instrumental in the club winning its first League Championship in 1948/49, winning the first of his 48 caps at the end of that season, following which he helped Pompey retain the title in 1949/50, when he was again in commanding form. At club level, he was an ever-present in seven of his 19 seasons of League football, twice playing in runs of more than 100 consecutive League matches.

Dickinson was awarded the MBE in the Queen's Birthday Honours List of 1964, and on hanging up his boots he took up a full-time post as Portsmouth's public relations officer. Three years later he became the club secretary and in May 1977 he took over from Ian St John as Portsmouth manager. In March 1979, following a 1–1 draw against Barnsley, Dickinson collapsed in the dressing-room with a massive heart attack. Despite making a recovery, he resigned his post as manager and took up the position of chief executive. Sadly, the legendary Pompey player suffered another heart attack and died at the age of 57. A private cremation was followed by a Memorial Service to 'Gentleman Jim'.

Johnny MORRIS

Position	Inside-left
Born	John Morris, Radcliffe, 27 September 1924
Height	5ft 8in
Weight	10st 8lb
Clubs	Manchester United, Derby County, Leicester City
England Caps	3 Goals 3

1949 v Norway (won 4–1) 1 goal, v France (won 3–1) 2 goals, v Eire (lost 0–2)

Jimmy Dickinson of Portsmouth heads a ball during training. (Getty Images)

AFTER DISAGREEING with Matt Busby on tactics, Johnny Morris left Manchester United to join Derby County for a British record fee of £24,500. His form led to three full caps for England, which he matched with three international goals.

Spotted by Louis Rocca, Johnny Morris was on the books at Old Trafford from the age of 15 and made his senior debut in wartime football while still a month short of his 17th birthday. By the time peace returned, he had also 'guested' for Bolton Wanderers, Wrexham and Charlton while on leave from his Royal Armoured Corps tank crew. Blessed with great dribbling skills and difficult to dispossess, he starred in United's early post-war forward line and helped engineer the club's 1948 FA Cup Final victory. Though he won international recognition while with the Rams, he left to join Second Division Leicester City. A regular at Filbert Street for four seasons, he helped the Foxes win the Second Division Championship in 1953/54 before switching from inside-forward to wing-half and winning a second Championship medal in 1956/57.

His off-field relations with the club management were not what they should have been and he even managed to get himself sent off for insulting the referee during City's public practice match in August 1957. At the end of that season he left the club to become player-manager of Southern League Corby Town, and later of Kettering, before ending his career with spells at Great Harwood and Oswestry Town.

Bert WILLIAMS

Position	Goalkeeper
Born	Bertram Frederick Williams, Bilston, 31 January 1922
Height	5ft 10in
Weight	12st 2lb
Clubs	Walsall, Wolverhampton Wanderers
England Caps	24

1949 v France (won 3–1), v Eire (lost 0–2), v Wales (won 4–1), v Italy (won 2–0)

1950 v Scotland (won 1–0), v Portugal (won 5–3), v Belgium (won 4–1), v Chile (won 2–0), v United States (lost 0–1), v Spain (lost 0–1), v N. Ireland (won 4–1), v Wales (won 4–2), v Yugoslavia (2–2)

1951 v Scotland (lost 2–3), v Argentina (won 2–1), v Portugal (won 5–2), v France (2–2), v Wales (1–1)

1954 v W. Germany (won 3–1)

1955 v Scotland (won 7–2), v France (lost 0–1), v Spain (1–1), v Portugal (lost 1–3), v Wales (lost 1–2)

QUITE BRILLIANT AT TIMES, agile, alert and reliable, Bert Williams, affectionately known as 'The Cat', was England's No. 1 goalkeeper in the early 1950s. He was England's World Cup keeper in 1950 and finished up on the losing side in only seven of the 24 internationals in which he played.

Williams was Wolves' first-choice goalkeeper from September 1945 until April 1957, a total of 12 seasons. During that time he appeared in 448 matches, the most by any keeper ever registered with the Molineux club. Before the outbreak of the

Bert Williams, goalkeeper for Wolves and England, 1952. (Charles Hewitt/Getty Images)

Second World War, he had turned professional with Walsall, but when the hostilities ended he joined Wolves. One of the greatest names in the history of Wolverhampton Wanderers, he won an FA Cup winners' medal in 1949, when Leicester City were beaten 3–1, and followed that up by earning a First Division Championship medal in 1953/54. Williams also played in the 1954 FA Charity Shield game against West Bromwich Albion at Molineux, a match which ended all square at 4–4. He finally retired at the end of the 1956/57 season, to run a highly successful sports outfitters in his home town of Bilston for a number of years as well as a goalkeeping school.

Bert MOZLEY

Position	Right-back
Born	Bertram Mozley, Derby, 21 September 1926
Height	5ft 9in
Weight	12st 2lb
Clubs	Nottingham Forest, Derby County
England Caps	3
	1949 v Eire (lost 0–2), v Wales (won 4–1), v N. Ireland (won 9–2)

BERT MOZLEY won three full caps for England, making his debut in what was the country's first defeat on home soil against non-home-team opposition when they went down 2–0 to Eire at Goodison Park in September 1949.

He began his Football League career with his home-town club Derby County, joining them in March 1945. Prior to that, he had played non-League football for Shelton United, and during the war he had a spell on Nottingham Forest's books as an amateur. Mozley was one of the quickest defenders in the Football League and was reckoned to be almost on a par with Arsenal's Laurie Scott. He was also cool and steady under pressure, had good distribution skills and was tough in the tackle. As well as his games for England, he also represented the Football League XI and, in 1950, toured Canada with the FA party. His performances on that tour proved what a high-class defender he was and, on his return, he continued to be an important member of the Derby County side, making 297 League appearances, before emigrating in January 1955 to the land of the maple leaf, where he still lives.

Peter HARRIS

Position	Outside-right
Born	Peter Philip Harris, Portsmouth, 19 December 1925
Died	17 December 2002
Height	5ft 7in
Weight	10st 2lb
Clubs	Portsmouth
England Caps	2
	1949 v Eire (lost 0–2)
	1954 v Hungary (lost 1–7)

A FLYING WINGER with an astonishing turn of speed and superb ball control, Peter Harris appeared twice for England, and both matches were memorable for the wrong reasons. The match against Eire was England's first defeat on home soil, while his second appearance against Hungary in Budapest five years later saw England lose 7–1.

Harris made his debut for Portsmouth as an 18-year-old against Watford in October 1944 and a week later scored two goals on his home debut in a 3–0 win over Aldershot. After establishing himself as a first-team regular in 1947/48, he ended the following season – the club won the League Championship – as joint-top scorer with 17 League goals. In the 7–0 FA Cup win over Stockport County, Harris hit the first of his eight senior hat-tricks. He scored 16 goals the following season as Portsmouth retained the League Championship, though his best seasons for Pompey in terms of goals scored were 1952/53, 1954/55 and 1955/56, in each of which he netted 23. On 3 September 1958 he scored all five Portsmouth goals in a 5–2 win over Aston Villa, but unfortunately his prolific goalscoring did not prevent Pompey from finishing bottom of the First Division and being relegated.

In November 1959, after a serious chest ailment had forced him to spend a long time in a sanatorium, Peter Harris played the last of his 520 games for Portsmouth, having scored a total of 208 goals for the club.

Jesse PYE

Position	Centre-forward
Born	Jesse Pye, Treeton, 22 December 1921
Died	20 February 1984
Height	5ft 10in
Weight	11st 7lb
Clubs	Sheffield United, Notts County, Wolverhampton Wanderers, Luton Town, Derby County
England Caps	1
	1949 v Eire (lost 0–2)

JESSE PYE averaged a goal every other game, a scoring record that earned him one full cap against Eire at Goodison Park in 1949. He had had an earlier outing in the Victory international against Belgium in 1946 and later played for the England 'B' team on three occasions and for the Football League XI.

Jesse was an amateur with Sheffield United when the Second World War broke out, and after serving with the Royal Engineers in a number of countries, where he also gained experience in Forces' football, he signed professional forms for Notts County. His goalscoring feats attracted the attention of Wolves, who beat off a number of leading clubs to secure his services for a fee of £12,000. He scored a hat-trick on his debut as Wolves beat Arsenal 6–1 on the opening day of the 1946/47 season, and he ended the campaign with 21 goals, including another treble in a 7–2 home win over Derby County. He continued to find the net on a regular basis and was top scorer in 1948/49 with another tally of 21 goals, including a hat-trick in a

7–1 defeat of Huddersfield Town. Pye also netted twice in the 1949 FA Cup Final as Wolves beat Leicester City 3–1. The following season he netted another hat-trick against Huddersfield Town, in a match which again finished 7–1 in favour of Wolves.

Pye went on to score 95 goals in 209 games for Wolves before signing for Luton Town in the summer of 1952. After scoring a goal every other game for the Hatters, he ended his League career with Derby County before becoming player-manager of Wisbech Town.

Bernard STRETEN

Position	Goalkeeper
Born	Bernard Reginald Streten, Gimingham, Norfolk, 14 January 1921
Died	North Walsham, Norfolk, 6 May 1984
Height	5ft 10in
Weight	11st 10lb
Clubs	Notts County, Shrewsbury Town, Luton Town
England Caps	1
	1949 v N. Ireland (won 9–2)

BERNARD STRETEN played his sole game for England against Northern Ireland in November 1949 in a 9–2 victory. A fortnight later he was replaced in goal by Bert Williams but was the reserve when England beat Italy 2–0.

After playing Norfolk junior football, Streten had a brief spell as an amateur with Notts County before joining Shrewsbury Town midway through the Second World War. Before he played for the Gay Meadow club, however, he 'guested' for Wolverhampton Wanderers, making four appearances in the Football League (North). His performances for Shrewsbury in the Midland League led to Luton manager George Martin securing his services for the Hatters in 1947.

A skilful, daring and often inspired goalkeeper, he was a virtual ever-present for Luton in his first couple of seasons with the club. Yet two months after making his England debut, he was out of the Luton first team and playing Combination football! He asked for a transfer, but his request was turned down, and he went on to prove himself a fine clubman for the Hatters, making 301 appearances in his ten years with the club.

After calling it a day, he was tempted out of retirement to play for King's Lynn in the Midland League and later played for Wisbech Town and Cambridge City before ending his career as a permit player for North Walsham in Norfolk, where he lived until his death.

Willie WATSON

Position	Right-half
Born	William Watson, Bolton-on-Dearne, 7 March 1920
Height	5ft 9in
Weight	11st 4lb
Clubs	Huddersfield Town, Sunderland, Halifax Town
England Caps	4
	1949 v N. Ireland (won 9–2), v Italy (won 2–0)
	1950 v Wales (won 4–2), v Yugoslavia (2–2)

ONE OF THE FEW people to be capped by England at football and cricket, Willie Watson made his debut for his country at soccer against Northern Ireland in a 9–2 win at Maine Road in November 1949. He also played in 22 Tests for England, having joined Yorkshire in 1939 and been awarded his county cap in 1947.

Willie began his career with Huddersfield Town, making 11 appearances before the outbreak of the Second World War. He signed for Sunderland in April 1946 and missed very few games over the next seven seasons, appearing in 223 League and Cup games before leaving to become player-manager of Halifax Town.

Watson had two spells in charge of Halifax but did not achieve much success. He helped produce a number of good players but the Yorkshire club were always in financial difficulties and were forced to sell them. He also managed Bradford City, where he laid the foundations for a future promotion side. His cricketing career was of a much higher profile. After leaving Yorkshire, he captained Leicestershire, before going on to become an England cricket selector and player-manager of the MCC tour party to East Africa in 1963.

Jack FROGGATT

Position	Centre-half/Outside-left
Born	Jack Froggatt, Sheffield, 17 November 1922
Died	Worthing, 17 February 1993
Height	5ft 8in
Weight	12st 4lb
Clubs	Portsmouth, Leicester City
England Caps	13 Goals 2
	1949 v N. Ireland (won 9–2) 1 goal, v Italy (won 2–0)
	1951 v Scotland (lost 2–3), v Austria (2–2)
	1952 v Scotland (won 2–1), v Italy (1–1), v Austria (won 3–2), v Switzerland (won 3–0),
	v N. Ireland (2–2), v Wales (won 5–2) 1 goal, v Belgium (won 5–0)
	1953 v Scotland (2–2), v United States (won 6–3)

CAPPED BY ENGLAND at both outside-left and centre-half, Jack Froggatt made 13 full appearances for England, his second cousin Redfern Froggatt playing alongside him in four of those games. Jack's father Frank had been a Sheffield Wednesday,

Notts County and Chesterfield player in the 1920s, and Redfern also played for the Owls.

Froggatt was still in the Royal Air Force when he was offered a trial with Portsmouth. He signed for the Fratton Park club as a centre-half and scored on his debut in the War League South game against Southampton, but he later managed to persuade Pompey manager Jack Tinn to play him at outside-left. This switch was vindicated shortly afterwards when Froggatt netted a hat-trick in a 6–0 win over Sheffield United. He was an important member of the Pompey side that won the League Championship in 1948/49 and 1949/50, and scored a goal on his international debut as England beat Northern Ireland 9–2 at Maine Road. In March 1954 he moved to Leicester City, becoming the final link in their promotion-winning side. He subsequently switched positions and shirts with unruffled ease until settling as ever-present centre-half and captain for the club's 1956/57 Second Division Championship season. He later moved to Kettering Town and was player-manager for successive relegation and promotion teams before reverting to the playing ranks only.

Froggatt retired in 1962 and thereafter ran a number of pubs in Portsmouth.

The Froggatt cousins, Jack and Redfern, during an England training session at Chelsea on the eve of an England match against Wales, 11 November 1952. (Getty Images)

1950–59

Frustration and Disappointment

England approached the 1950 World Cup tournament with a
ridiculous air of complacency. Drawn in Pool 2, they were placed
against Chile (considered part-time also-rans), the United States
(no-hopers in everyone's eyes) and Spain (the only side considered to be
of a decent standard by the English). In their first game England beat
Chile 2–0, but their single-goal defeat in their first-ever international
against the United States five days later has gone down as one of the low
points in the team's international record. Eleven strikes of the woodwork
counted for nothing as Haiti-born striker Larry Gaetjaens dented
England's hopes. Four changes were made for the game against Spain but
another 1–0 defeat sent them out of the tournament.

Three years later Hungary came to Wembley and won 6–3. It was an
earth-shattering blow, especially in an historic year that brought the
coronation, the ascent of Everest and the Matthews Cup Final. Stanley
Matthews, Billy Wright, Stan Mortensen and Alf Ramsey were all members
of the England side soundly beaten by the mercurial talents of Puskas,
Hidegkuti and Kocsis. In their last game before the 1954 World Cup,
England travelled to Budapest for a rematch but the 'Magnificent Magyars'
gave another devastating performance to secure a 7–1 win. In 1954

England topped their qualifying group to earn a quarter-final tie against holders Uruguay but they lost 4–2, Gil Merrick, one of those who had faced the Hungarians, being at fault for at least two of the goals.

England subsequently steadied the ship with a 16-game unbeaten run. Then three Manchester United players – Roger Byrne, Duncan Edwards and Tommy Taylor – were lost in the Munich air crash. The 1958 World Cup saw the first and only finals in which all four home countries would participate. England held eventual winners Brazil to a goalless draw – the only time Brazil failed to score in the tournament – but lost in the play-off against the Soviet Union. A far-sighted Winterbottom proposed a 'policy of developing a young team that would play together, mature together and be ready within a four-year cycle'. Unfortunately the idea was abandoned at his colleagues' insistence after a 3–2 defeat to Sweden, and it was 'back to the old regime'.

Bill JONES

Position	Full-back/Centre-half
Born	William Henry Jones, Whaley Bridge, 13 May 1921
Height	5ft 11in
Weight	13st 1lb
Clubs	Liverpool
England Caps	2
	1950 v Portugal (won 5–3), v Belgium (won 4–1)

THOUGH HE PLAYED most of his games for Liverpool at full-back, Bill Jones could play anywhere and enjoyed himself as much at centre-half as at centre-forward. In fact, he played at centre-half for his two England appearances against Portugal and Belgium.

Grandfather of the former Liverpool and England full-back Rob Jones, Bill Jones arrived at Anfield a year before the Second World War broke out. During the hostilities he won the Military Medal and did not make his Football League debut until the first season of peacetime football in 1946/47. Jones made 26 appearances in six different outfield positions for the Reds in that campaign, as they went on to win the League Championship. He also played for the Football League XI against the Irish League and was unlucky not to add to his tally of international appearances. He appeared at left-half for Liverpool in the 1950 FA Cup Final and in eight seasons of first-team football scored 17 goals in 278 games for the Reds.

Jones left Liverpool in May 1954 to become player-manager at Ellesmere Port, but returned to his beloved Anfield as a scout during the 1960s and 1970s.

Laurie HUGHES

Position	Centre-half
Born	Lawrence Hughes, Waterloo, 2 March 1924
Height	6ft 0in
Weight	12st 4lb
Clubs	Tranmere Rovers, Liverpool
England Caps	3
	1950 v Chile (won 2–0), v United States (lost 0–1), v Spain (lost 0–1)

LAURIE HUGHES was selected for England's trip to the 1950 World Cup Finals where he made three appearances, including the ill-fated game against the United States. They were to be his only games for his country.

Hughes began his career as an amateur with Tranmere Rovers in 1942, but within a year he had left Prenton Park and crossed the Mersey to play for Liverpool. After signing professional forms, he appeared in a number of different positions during the club's wartime games before settling at centre-half for the start of the 1946/47 season. In that first season after the hostilities, Hughes helped Liverpool win the League Championship, giving a series of dominant displays at the heart of the Reds' defence. A tall, strong centre-half, who occasionally turned out at left-half, for sheer consistency he took some beating. His other assets included good positional sense and outstanding heading ability. A member of Liverpool's 1950 FA Cup Final side that lost 2–0 to Arsenal, he returned to Anfield after the World Cup and, despite missing virtually two seasons through injury, he grossed over 300 League and Cup appearances for the Reds before retiring at the end of the 1959/60 season.

Bill ECKERSLEY

Position	Left-back
Born	William Eckersley, Southport, 16 July 1926
Died	Blackburn, 25 October 1982
Height	5ft 6in
Weight	10st 1lb
Clubs	Blackburn Rovers
England Caps	17
	1950 v Spain (lost 0–1), v Yugoslavia (2–2)
	1951 v Scotland (lost 2–3), v Argentina (won 2–1), v Portugal (won 5–2), v Austria (2–2)
	1952 v Austria (won 3–2), v Switzerland (won 3–0), v N. Ireland (2–2)
	1953 v Argentina (0–0), v Chile (won 2–1), v Uruguay (lost 1–2), v United States (won 6–3), v Wales (won 4–1), v Rest of Europe (4–4), v N. Ireland (won 3–1), v Hungary (lost 3–6)

BILL ECKERSLEY gained selection for England regularly as Alf Ramsey's partner, winning 17 caps between 1950 and 1953. Perhaps he should have had a lot more, for he was extremely tenacious, very fit and quick.

A former lorry driver, Eckersley might never have played for Blackburn Rovers had they not been short for an 'A' team fixture. He got to play that match in borrowed boots with only a couple of studs on each and string for shoelaces! He joined Rovers in November 1947 at a time when the club was struggling to recover from the repercussions of war, and over the next few seasons he matured into Blackburn's most outstanding player. Though lacking in height and weight, his tackling was keen and he had tremendous composure and style. He also had the clever knack of making attacking wingers go the way he wanted them to, and though he was often aggressive he could be very subtle too, when required. Despite his success on the international scene, club honours eluded him. A number of promotion near-misses and two FA Cup semi-finals were the most he achieved in his prime, and by the time Blackburn finally won promotion, in 1958, his career was coming to an end, plagued by injuries that saw him miss out on the club's FA Cup run of 1960.

Life outside the game wasn't kind to Eckersley, and after a failed confectionery business he returned to lorry driving before his early death at the age of 54. The ashes of this player of limitless talent were scattered on the Ewood Park turf by his sons in an emotional ceremony prior to a first-team game.

The Duke of Gloucester (left) shakes hands with Bill Eckersley before the kick-off of the 68th international match between England and Scotland at Wembley, 14 April 1951. England lost the match 2–3. (Getty Images)

Eddie BAILY

Position	Inside-forward
Born	Edward Francis Baily, Clapton, 6 August 1925
Height	5ft 7in
Weight	10st 13lb
Clubs	Tottenham Hotspur, Port Vale, Nottingham Forest, Leyton Orient
England Caps	9 Goals 5
	1950 v Spain (lost 0–1), v N. Ireland (won 4–1) 2 goals, v Wales (won 4–2) 2 goals, v Yugoslavia (2–2)
	1951 v Wales (1–1) 1 goal, v Austria (2–2)
	1952 v Austria (won 3–2), v Switzerland (won 3–0), v N. Ireland (2–2)

EDDIE BAILY FOLLOWED three caps for England 'B' with a full England debut in June 1950 against Spain in Rio de Janeiro during the World Cup Finals. As well as earning nine full caps, Baily also appeared for the Rest of the UK against Wales and was still considered good enough to play for an England team against Young England in May 1957.

One of the most important names in Spurs' post-war history, first as a player, later as assistant manager to Bill Nicholson, Eddie Baily might never have appeared in a Spurs shirt at all had it not been for the good grace of Chelsea! He signed as an amateur on leaving school but during the war he served with the Royal Scots Fusiliers. Spurs heard he had been reported missing in action and allowed his registration to lapse. When he returned to these shores he joined Chelsea, but when the Army's error became known, the Stamford Bridge club agreed to cancel his registration so that he could re-sign for Spurs. Known affectionately as 'The Cheeky Chappie', he was a key link in the 'push and run' team. A chirpy cockney character, he was also an off-the-field personality – even Alf Ramsey was forced to comment on Baily's humour in his autobiography. After ten years at White Hart Lane, he was allowed to join Port Vale, but nine months later he left to join Nottingham Forest, whom he helped gain promotion to the First Division. He ended his playing career with Leyton Orient before returning to White Hart Lane in October 1963, where he remained for 11 years as Bill Nicholson's assistant before leaving Tottenham again following Nicholson's resignation.

Allenby CHILTON

Position	Centre-half
Born	Allenby Chilton, South Hylton, 16 September 1918
Died	16 June 1996
Height	6ft 1in
Weight	12st 0lb
Clubs	Manchester United, Grimsby Town
England Caps	2
	1950 v N. Ireland (won 4–1)
	1951 v France (2–2)

REGARDED BY MATT BUSBY as his best-ever centre-half, Allenby Chilton won two England caps, his first against Northern Ireland in 1950.

Chilton joined Manchester United from Seaham Colliery and though he made his League debut against Charlton Athletic on 2 September 1939, war was declared the next day and he had to wait another seven years for his next League outing. Despite being wounded while on service in Normandy, he 'guested' for Charlton Athletic in wartime football and won a Wartime South Cup winners' medal when a crowd of 85,000 saw Charlton beat Chelsea at Wembley. In his early days at Old Trafford, Chilton received plenty of abuse from the crowd and there was a time when he gave up football to try boxing, but after six months in the ring he returned to soccer with no regrets whatsoever. A tall and powerful centre-half, he was United's only ever-present when they won the League Championship in 1952. He was the backbone of the Reds' defence and succeeded Johnny Carey as club captain. When he lost his place in the United line-up to Mark Jones in February 1955, he ended a run of 166 consecutive League appearances, a United record until Steve Coppell broke it during the 1980/81 season.

Chilton, who also won an FA Cup winners' medal in 1948, left Old Trafford in 1955 to become player-manager of Grimsby Town, inspiring them to the Third Division (North) title in 1955/56.

Jack LEE

Position	Centre-forward
Born	John Lee, Sileby, 4 November 1920
Died	Loughborough, 15 January 1995
Height	6ft 0in
Weight	12st 2lb
Clubs	Leicester City, Derby County, Coventry City
England Caps	1 Goals 1
	1950 v N. Ireland (won 4–1) 1 goal

JACK LEE began his career with Leicester City but it wasn't until he joined Derby County that he won his England cap, scoring in a 4–1 win over Northern Ireland in Belfast in 1950.

Lee joined the Foxes in 1940. During the war years he served with the RAF in India, which limited the number of games he could play. Though he had to overcome a couple of serious injury setbacks, he still registered a goal every other appearance before peacetime football returned in 1946/47.

He scored twice on his Football League debut for Leicester in a 2–1 win at Luton Town's Kenilworth Road, a ground which must surely have been his favourite away venue – in the FA Cup run of 1949 he netted four of City's goals in a 5–5 draw there! Lethal with both head and feet, he scored a number of spectacular goals during his stay at Filbert Street, perhaps none more dramatic than the equalizing goal at Ninian Park in the post-Cup Final game – the point gained helping Leicester keep their Second Division status. There were those who thought that if Jack Lee hadn't been switched to inside-right for the final against Wolves, the Foxes might have sprung a surprise.

When Leicester accepted Derby County's bid of £16,000 for Lee there was uproar among Leicester fans, and their disappointment deepened when he ended the season as the second-top-scorer in the First Division in his first season at the Baseball Ground.

Lee later ended his career with Coventry City, having scored 136 goals in 231 games for his three clubs.

Lionel SMITH

Position	Left-back
Born	Lionel Smith, Mexborough, 23 August 1920
Died	15 November 1980
Height	6ft 1in
Weight	11st 12lb
Clubs	Arsenal, Watford
England Caps	6
	1950 v Wales (won 4–2)
	1951 v Wales (1–1), v N. Ireland (won 2–0)
	1952 v Wales (won 5–2), v Belgium (won 5–0)
	1953 v Scotland (2–2)

IF IT HAD NOT BEEN for the war, Lionel Smith, who won six full international caps for England, might have challenged Eddie Hapgood for recognition as Arsenal's finest left-back.

Smith played junior football for home-town club Mexborough Albion and Denaby United before joining the Gunners as an amateur in April 1939. Unfortunately, war was declared only weeks after he turned professional, and during the conflict he was injured in a crane accident when serving as a sapper.

On returning to Highbury, he was made captain of the club's Combination side but eventually made his Football League debut as a replacement for Leslie Compton, who was playing cricket for Middlesex. Following an injury to Laurie Scott, Wally Barnes switched to right-back, allowing Smith to have an extended run in the left-back spot. He soon became recognized as one of the best left-backs in the country. His passing ability was exceptional, and he was good in the air and quick on the recovery. A member of Arsenal's FA Cup Final team against Newcastle United, he appeared in 31 of the Gunners' games when they won the League Championship in 1952/53.

In the summer of 1954 he was granted a free transfer and joined Watford. After one season at Vicarage Road, he left to manage Gravesend and Northfleet.

Leslie COMPTON

Position	Centre-half
Born	Leslie Harry Compton, Woodford, 12 September 1912
Died	Essex, 27 December 1984
Height	6ft 2in

Weight	13st 6lb
Clubs	Arsenal
England Caps	2
	1950 v Wales (won 4–2), v Yugoslavia (2–2)

LESLIE COMPTON won two full caps for England and, in doing so, became at 38 years and 64 days the oldest-ever debutant for England in a full international.

The longest-serving of all Arsenal's players, Compton joined the Gunners in August 1930 from Hampstead Town. Over the next 23 years, he served Arsenal in literally every position. At the beginning of Arsenal's 1932/33 League Championship-winning season, he played in four League games before losing his place first to Tom Parker and then to George Male. In the 1930s, he spent much of his time in the club's reserve side, yet he still appeared in the first of two England trials. By the time war was declared in September 1939, Compton was 27 years old and, because of the brilliance of Male and Hapgood, had played in fewer than 70 League games. However, he had the consolation of winning five Football Combination Championship medals. During the war years he played in 130 games for the club and, following his conversion to centre-forward, scored 93 goals. Later converted to centre-half, he helped Arsenal win the League Championship in 1947/48 and the following season was made captain. Though he didn't score too many goals, one of his most important came in the 1950 FA Cup semi-final against Chelsea, when he headed the equalizing goal from his brother Denis' corner.

Leslie, who was also Middlesex's wicket-keeper, became Arsenal's coach and scout. Suffering from arthritis, he later had a foot amputated before his death in December 1984.

Les MEDLEY

Position	Outside-left
Born	Leslie Dennis Medley, Edmonton, 3 September 1920
Height	5ft 7in
Weight	11st 3lb
Clubs	Tottenham Hotspur
England Caps	6 Goals 1
	1950 v Wales (won 4–2), v Yugoslavia (2–2)
	1951 v France (2–2) 1 goal, v Wales (1–1), v N. Ireland (won 2–0), v Austria (2–2)

ONCE HE MADE IT into the first division, Les Medley's displays won him international recognition. He was never on the losing side in his six appearances for England, four of which saw his Spurs team-mate Eddie Baily as his inside-forward partner.

A local schoolboy star, Les joined the professional staff at White Hart Lane, the outbreak of the Second World War gave him an earlier opportunity in the first team than might otherwise have been the case. Service in the Royal Air Force then took him to Canada, where he spent much of the war and met his wife. Returning to Spurs for the later war years, he soon established himself in the club's first team, but his wife became homesick, so in November 1946 he emigrated to Canada. There he played for Toronto Greenbacks and Ulster United, but in the early part of 1948 he returned to White Hart Lane.

It took him some time to adjust to English football, but when he did he became an important member of Spurs' 'push-and-run' team that won the Second and First Division titles in successive seasons in 1949/50 and 1950/51. A fast and direct winger, he was always liable to appear in the most unexpected of positions and this unpredictability helped him score many goals, especially from Alf Ramsey's flighted free kicks. He represented the Football League against the Scottish League and collected his last major representative honour when he played for the Rest of the United Kingdom against Wales in December 1951.

Nat LOFTHOUSE

Position	Centre-forward
Born	Nathaniel Lofthouse, Bolton, 27 August 1925
Height	5ft 10in
Weight	12st 2lb
Clubs	Bolton Wanderers
England Caps	33 Goals 30

1950 v Yugoslavia (2–2) 2 goals
1951 v Wales (1–1), v N. Ireland (won 2–0) 2 goals, v Austria (2–2) 1 goal
1952 v Scotland (won 2–1), v Italy (1–1), v Austria (won 3–2) 2 goals, v Switzerland (won 3–0) 2 goals, v N. Ireland (2–2) 1 goal, v Wales (won 5–2) 2 goals, v Belgium (won 5–0) 2 goals
1953 v Scotland (2–2), v Argentina (0–0), v Chile (won 2–1) 1 goal, v Uruguay (lost 1–2), v United States (won 6–3) 2 goals, v Wales (won 4–1) 2 goals, v Rest of Europe (4–4), v N. Ireland (won 3–1) 1 goal
1954 v Belgium (4–4) 2 goals, v Uruguay (lost 2–4) 1 goal, v N. Ireland (won 2–0)
1955 v Scotland (won 7–2) 2 goals, v France (lost 0–1), v Spain (1–1), v Portugal (lost 1–3), v Denmark (won 5–1) 2 goals, v Wales (lost 1–2), v Spain (won 4–1)
1956 v Scotland (1–1), v Finland (won 5–1) 2 goals
1958 v Soviet Union (won 5–0) 1 goal, v Wales (2–2)

Honours	Footballer of the Year 1953

....

NAT LOFTHOUSE was recognized at international level in November 1950 when he was chosen to lead England's forward line at Highbury in the match against Yugoslavia. He fulfilled his promise by scoring both goals in a 2–2 draw that was to be the start of a glittering career for England. In May 1952 he earned the tag 'Lion of Vienna' after his heroic performance against Austria, scoring twice in a 3–2 win. He won a total of 33 caps for England and to score what was then a record 30 goals for his country.

Attending the same school as the legendary Tommy Lawton, Lofthouse joined his home-town club Bolton Wanderers, playing his first game for the club at the age of

Nat Lofthouse, 16 November 1951.
(Getty Images)

15 years 207 days and scoring twice in a 5–1 win over Bury. The son of a coalman, he worked on the coalface during the war years, often going straight from the pit to assist the Wanderers in wartime games. In September 1952 he scored six goals for the Football League against the Irish League at Molineux and in the 1952/53 FA Cup he scored in every round of the competition, only for injury-hit Bolton to lose 4–3 to Blackpool in the final. He was voted Footballer of the Year at the end of that season and in 1955/56 he finished as the leading goalscorer in the First Division with 33 goals. In 1958 he captained Bolton to their FA Cup victory over Manchester United, scoring both goals in Wanderers' 2–0 win.

After a severely damaged ankle forced him into retirement, Bolton immediately appointed him assistant manager and in 1968 he took over as manager. He had two separate spells in charge before deciding to take a back seat. After becoming executive club manager, he later became Bolton's president, thus continuing his devotion to Lancashire's oldest club.

Harold HASSALL

Position	Inside-left
Born	Harold William Hassall, Tyldesley, 4 March 1929
Height	5ft 11in
Weight	11st 8lb
Clubs	Huddersfield Town, Bolton Wanderers
England Caps	5 Goals 4
	1951 v Scotland (lost 2–3) 1 goal, v Argentina (won 2–1), v Portugal (won 5–2) 1 goal, v France (2–2)
	1953 v N. Ireland (won 3–1) 2 goals

HAROLD HASSALL won the first four of his five international caps while with Huddersfield Town, scoring on his debut against Scotland at Wembley.

Though he played his early football for Astley and Tyldesley collieries just outside Bolton, Harold began his professional career with Huddersfield, where he had the distinction of saving a penalty from the great Tom Finney. This came about after he had to stand in for the Huddersfield keeper, who was injured. He left Leeds Road in January 1952, joining Bolton Wanderers for a fee of £27,000. At Burnden Park he joined the Wanderers' all-international forward line and won another international cap in 1953, along with an FA Cup runners-up medal.

On New Year's Day 1955 he sustained a serious knee injury, which ended his career as a professional footballer. He then fell back on his qualification as a teacher. He added a physical education diploma and a postgraduate diploma in management studies, and in 1958 he was appointed manager-coach of the England Youth team. During 1966, Hassall received further recognition when FIFA invited him to report on World Cup games and, with another three coaches, to submit findings on aspects of all games played during the competition. In later years he was appointed general secretary of the Amateur Swimming Association.

Jim TAYLOR

Position	Centre-half
Born	James Guy Taylor, Hillingdon, 5 November 1917
Height	5ft 11in
Weight	11st 10lb
Clubs	Fulham, Queen's Park Rangers
England Caps	2
	1951 v Argentina (won 2–1), v Portugal (won 5–2)

JIM TAYLOR, who joined Fulham from non-League Hillingdon, was the club's first England international, winning caps against Argentina and Portugal in the Festival of Britain matches in 1951. As with many other players of his generation, the Second World War delayed his introduction to League football, though he did appear in 88 wartime games for the Cottagers. As well as playing for England, he also represented the Football League in March 1948 and toured Canada with the FA in 1950.

Taylor was 28 years old when he made his League debut in a 7–2 defeat at Bury on the opening day of the 1946/47 season, a campaign in which he went on to be an ever-present. A no-nonsense centre-half, he in fact missed very few games over the next seven seasons, helping the Cottagers win the Second Division Championship in 1948/49.

Taylor left Craven Cottage in the summer of 1952 to play for Queen's Park Rangers, but after just one season at Loftus Road he opted to become player-manager of Tunbridge Wells. He later ended his involvement with the game following a spell as manager of Yiewsley Town.

Vic METCALFE

Position	Outside-left
Born	Victor Metcalfe, Barrow, 3 February 1922
Died	6 April 2003
Height	5ft 8in
Weight	11st 0lb
Clubs	Huddersfield Town, Hull City
England Caps	2
	1951 v Argentina (won 2–1), v Portugal (won 5–2)

VIC METCALFE won two England caps and played for the Football League in 1951, but that could not temper his disappointment at Huddersfield's relegation to the Second Division that season.

Metcalfe, whose father played Rugby League for Barrow, began his career with Huddersfield Town, turning professional in December 1945 after wartime service as an RAF radio operator. On the resumption of League football in 1946/47, Metcalfe became a valued member of the Huddersfield side and his place on the left wing was virtually unchallenged over the next 12 seasons. Along with Jimmy Glazzard, he proved a key figure in Town's fight to regain their top-flight status in the early 1950s.

Huddersfield won promotion to the First Division in 1952/53, when Metcalfe was one of seven ever-presents. He had scored 90 goals in 459 games for Huddersfield when, with the club trying to reduce the average age of the first-team squad, he was allowed to join Hull City. He was with the Tigers when they clinched promotion to the Second Division in 1958/59, but midway through the following season he decided to hang up his boots.

Metcalfe later returned to Leeds Road as a member of the club's coaching staff before joining Halifax Town as assistant-coach and scout. In April 1966, when Willie Watson left to take charge at Bradford City, he became Halifax's manager. After being succeeded by Alan Ball senior, he scouted for Bradford City.

Bill NICHOLSON

Position	Right-half
Born	William Edward Nicholson, Scarborough, 26 January 1919
Height	5ft 9in
Weight	11st 8lb
Clubs	Tottenham Hotspur
England Caps	1 Goals 1
	1951 v Portugal (won 5–2) 1 goal

BILL NICHOLSON'S one and only appearance for England against Portugal at Goodison Park saw him score from long distance with his first kick of the game after just a matter of seconds.

Bill's career as a player was interrupted by the war, but after the hostilities he played in Arthur Rowe's side that won the Second Division Championship in 1949/50 and the League title the season after.

One of the greatest managers of British soccer, Bill was the architect of one of the finest club sides the world has ever seen. In the early 1960s, his Spurs team played exhilarating, flowing football. They won the League and FA Cup double in 1960/61, the first club to do so in the twentieth century. This remarkable triumph was followed by a steady stream of Cup successes as Spurs went marching on.

Nicholson surprised most people by resigning after 16 years in charge. The players and the directors tried to persuade him to change his mind, but to no avail. He took a deserved rest from the game before returning to work as consultant to West Ham United, but within months he was back at White Hart Lane as chief adviser and scout. He was awarded the OBE in 1975, a testimonial game at Spurs in 1983 and the PFA Merit Award in 1984. In May 1991 he was appointed Spurs' president, an office he still holds.

Arthur WILLIS

Position	Left-back
Born	Arthur Willis, Denaby Main, 2 February 1920
Died	Haverfordwest, 7 November 1987
Height	5ft 7in
Weight	11st 2lb
Clubs	Tottenham Hotspur, Swansea Town
England Caps	1
	1951 v France (2–2)

SHORTLY AFTER WINNING a regular place with Spurs and helping the White Hart Lane club win the League Championship, Arthur Willis won his one and only international cap against France in October 1951.

Willis was working as a miner when he received offers to embark on a football career from Barnsley, Sunderland and Spurs. He chose to join the North London club's amateur staff, but because of the advent of the Second World War he played for Finchley. He worked in a local engineering factory, and made his debut for Spurs during the war. After signing as a professional, he played regularly in one of the full-back positions until losing his place to Sid Tickridge in September 1947. He did not get back into the team until the last couple of matches of the 1949/50 season, but he held his place the following season when the famous 'push and run' side won the League title.

Quick, neat and studious, Willis left White Hart Lane in September 1954, following Ron Burgess to Swansea Town, after sharing the left-back duties with Charlie Withers. He played for the Vetch Field club for four seasons, helping them to the Welsh Cup Final in 1956, and later joined the coaching staff before taking over as player-manager of Haverfordwest in the Welsh League.

Malcolm BARRASS

Position	Centre-half
Born	Malcolm Williamson Barrass, Blackpool, 13 December 1924
Height	5ft 11in
Weight	12st 7lb
Clubs	Bolton Wanderers, Sheffield United
England Caps	3
	1951 v Wales (1–1), v N. Ireland (won 2–0)
	1953 v Scotland (2–2)

MALCOLM BARRASS followed in the footsteps of his father, Matt, who played League football for Blackpool, Sheffield Wednesday and Manchester City. After playing three trial games for Wolverhampton Wanderers and being offered terms, Malcolm opted instead to join Bolton Wanderers. In 1944/45, his first season with the club, he scored 22 goals in 40 games from the inside-forward position. He showed no signs of being overawed by the big step into wartime League football, and honours soon came his way when he was chosen to play for England in the Victory international against Wales at the Hawthorns.

Barrass became a versatile player, once scoring four goals from the centre-forward position against Manchester City, but it was at centre-half that he won his three full caps for England. Two weeks after appearing in the last of these matches, he returned to Wembley as Bolton's centre-half in the FA Cup Final against his home-town club, Blackpool. After 12 years with the Wanderers he joined Sheffield United and later became player-manager of then non-League Wigan Athletic. He ended his career with a two-and-a-half year spell at Southern League Nuneaton Borough before settling in the Bury area as a sales representative.

Tommy THOMPSON

Position	Inside-right
Born	Thomas Thompson, Fencehouses, 10 November 1929
Height	5ft 6in
Weight	10st 4lb
Clubs	Newcastle United, Aston Villa, Preston North End, Stoke City, Barrow
England Caps	2
	1951 v Wales (1–1)
	1957 v Scotland (won 2–1)

SMALL BUT STRONGLY BUILT, Tommy Thompson developed into one of the fifties' top inside-forwards, but in his early days at Newcastle United he was given only a few chances to impress after being blooded in the club's promotion-winning season of 1947/48. After leaving to join Aston Villa, he blossomed as a free-scoring inside-forward, good enough to earn England recognition. However, he had to wait six years before winning his second cap.

Nicknamed 'Topper', Thompson grabbed 76 goals in 165 games for Villa before moving to Deepdale, where he became the perfect foil for Tom Finney. He scored after just two minutes of his North End debut in a 4–0 win at Everton and over the next six seasons he enjoyed his most productive spell in the game as he and Finney scored 203 First Division goals between them. In 1957/58 he peaked with 34 goals as North End finished runners-up to Wolves in the First Division. Thompson had the rare gift of being both a prolific scorer and the perfect team man, always aware of what was going on around him. One of his hat-tricks for Preston came against Chelsea, but the Pensioners won 5–4 with all their goals scored by a certain Jimmy Greaves!

Following the club's relegation in 1960/61, Thompson was allowed to move to Stoke City, where he played his part in the Potters' promotion to the First Division, before ending his playing career with Barrow.

Birmingham City's Gil Merrick shows the hands with which he hoped to keep Manchester City at bay in the FA Cup Final, May 1956. In fact, Man City won 3–1. (Getty Images)

Gil MERRICK

Position	Goalkeeper
Born	Gilbert Harold Merrick, Birmingham, 26 January 1922
Height	6ft 1in
Weight	13st 0lb
Clubs	Birmingham City
England Caps	23

1951 v N. Ireland (won 2–0), v Austria (2–2)
1952 v Scotland (won 2–1), v Italy (1–1), v Austria (won 3–2), v Switzerland (won 3–0),
  v N. Ireland (2–2), v Wales (won 5–2), v Belgium (won 5–0)
1953 v Scotland (2–2), v Argentina (0–0), v Chile (won 2–1), v Uruguay (lost 1–2), v Wales
  (won 4–1), v Rest of Europe (4–4), v N. Ireland (won 3–1), v Hungary (lost 3–6)
1954 v Scotland (won 4–2), v Yugoslavia (lost 0–1), v Hungary (lost 1–7), v Belgium (4–4),
  v Switzerland (won 2–0), v Uruguay (lost 2–4)

ON THE LOSING SIDE in only five of his 23 internationals – though these included two heavy defeats by Hungary – goalkeeper Gil Merrick always modelled himself on his childhood favourite, Harry Hibbs.

Merrick joined Birmingham City and in the summer of 1939 appeared in 172 games for the Blues during the hostilities. Following the resumption of League football in 1946/47, he missed just one game in a campaign that saw the St Andrew's club finish third in the Second Division. The following season he helped the club win the Second Division Championship and in 1951 he won his first international cap,

keeping a clean sheet in a 2–0 win over Northern Ireland. He was Birmingham's first-choice keeper for 13 seasons and was ever-present in 1949/50 and 1950/51, when he appeared in 126 consecutive League games. He helped the Blues win the Second Division Championship again in 1954/55 and played in the 1956 FA Cup Final when Birmingham lost 3–1 to Manchester City. Merrick, who holds the club record for the number of first-team appearances, with 551 games to his name, retired at the end of the 1959/60 season and was appointed the club's new manager. Almost immediately he saw Birmingham lose to Barcelona in the second leg of the Inter Cities Fairs Cup Final in Spain, and he remained in that country to study Spanish football methods and organizations. Though they were constantly fighting against relegation during Merrick's term of office, Birmingham did beat Aston Villa over two legs to win the 1963 League Cup Final.

After parting company with the club, he had spells in charge of Bromsgrove Rovers and Atherstone Town before ending his involvement with the game.

Jackie SEWELL

Position	Inside-forward
Born	John Sewell, Kells, 24 January 1927
Height	5ft 8in
Weight	11st 4lb
Clubs	Notts County, Sheffield Wednesday, Aston Villa, Hull City
England Caps	6 Goals 3
	1951 v N. Ireland (won 2–0)
	1952 v Austria (won 3–2) 1 goal, v Switzerland (won 3–0) 1 goal, v N. Ireland (2–2)
	1953 v Hungary (lost 3–6) 1 goal
	1954 v Hungary (lost 1–7)

AS WELL AS WINNING six full England caps, in which he scored a goal every other game, Jackie Sewell scored a hat-trick for the Football League against the League of Ireland at Maine Road.

Beginning his career with Notts County, Sewell played alongside the legendary Tommy Lawton, and in 179 League games scored 97 goals as well as helping the Meadow Lane club win the Third Division (South) Championship in 1949/50. In March 1951, Sheffield Wednesday paid £34,500 – a British record at the time – for his services. Though he scored six goals in ten appearances, he was unable to save the Owls from relegation to the Second Division. However, in 1951/52 he scored 23 goals as Wednesday won the Second Division title, including all four goals in a 4–2 win over Cardiff City. He also netted a hat-trick against Plymouth Argyle on the opening day of the 1955/56 season, but midway through the campaign, having scored 92 goals in 175 games, he left to join Aston Villa. Though not quite matching the strike rate he'd achieved with his previous two clubs, he went on to score 40 goals in 144 outings and won an FA Cup winners' medal in 1957 as Villa beat Manchester United in the Wembley final. He later played for Hull City before coaching in Zimbabwe, Zambia and Zaire.

Len PHILLIPS

Position	Inside-left
Born	Leonard Horace Phillips, Hackney, 11 September 1922
Height	5ft 8in
Weight	11st 0lb
Clubs	Portsmouth
England Caps	3
	1951 v N. Ireland (won 2–0)
	1954 v Wales (won 3–1), v W. Germany (won 3–1)

LEN PHILLIPS formed a terrific partnership with winger Peter Harris and, after helping Portsmouth win a second successive League Championship, he earned the first of three England caps playing against Northern Ireland at Villa Park in 1951. He was never on the losing side when he represented his country and was unfortunate not to win more honours.

After playing his early football with Hackney Boys, Phillips was called up into the Royal Marines, serving on assault landing craft and taking part in the Normandy D-Day landings. Discovered while playing for the Royal Marines, he signed for Portsmouth in February 1946, making his first appearance for Pompey later that month against Wolverhampton Wanderers. He made his League debut for the Fratton Park club in a 1–0 win at Blackburn Rovers in December of that year but did not establish himself in the first team until midway through the 1948/49 season, a campaign in which the club won its first-ever League Championship. As a forward, Phillips was fast and incisive, showing great poise and control. Later in his career he moved from inside-forward to wing-half, but these qualities were still much in evidence. However, after tearing a ligament in an FA Cup tie at Grimsby in January 1956, Phillips was forced to leave the League scene after scoring 50 goals in 270 games, though he later played non-League football for Poole Town, Chelmsford and Bath City.

Arthur MILTON

Position	Outside-right
Born	Clement Arthur Milton, Bristol, 10 March 1928
Height	5ft 9in
Weight	10st 0lb
Clubs	Arsenal, Bristol City
England Caps	1
	1951 v Austria (2–2)

ARTHUR MILTON will be remembered for having played both football and cricket for England, winning his solitary cap against Austria in November 1951, after just 12 first-team appearances for Arsenal.

Milton joined the Gunners as an amateur in April 1945, and just over a year later turned professional. He had still to make his Football League debut for Arsenal when he was called up for National Service. He returned to Highbury two years later but had to wait until March 1951 before making his League debut against Aston Villa. He became the club's first-choice outside-right at the beginning of the 1951/52 campaign and the following season helped the Gunners win the League Championship. In the two seasons that followed he found himself in and out of the side, and in February 1955 he left Highbury to join his home-town club, Bristol City. However, after just one season with the Ashton Gate club he retired to concentrate on his cricket career.

During his 23-year association with Gloucestershire County Cricket Club, he totalled over 30,000 runs and played in six Test matches for England.

Ivor BROADIS

Position	Inside-forward
Born	Ivan Arthur Broadis, Isle of Dogs, 18 December 1922
Height	5ft 9in
Weight	11st 0lb
Clubs	Carlisle United, Sunderland, Manchester City, Newcastle United, Queen of the South
England Caps	14 Goals 8
	1951 v Austria (2–2)
	1952 v Scotland (won 2–1), v Italy (1–1) 1 goal
	1953 v Scotland (2–2) 2 goals, v Argentina (0–0), v Chile (won 2–1), v Uruguay (lost 1–2),
	v United States (won 6–3) 1 goal
	1954 v Scotland (won 4–2) 1 goal, v Yugoslavia (lost 0–1), v Hungary (lost 1–7) 1 goal,
	v Belgium (4–4) 2 goals, v Switzerland (won 2–0), v Uruguay (lost 2–4)

IVOR BROADIS had a fine record in an England shirt, grabbing eight goals in 14 appearances. Four of the goals came in the 1954 World Cup Finals.

Broadis was one of the most skilful inside-forwards of his generation, a player with excellent ball control, the ability to make space and create chances for others and a keen eye that brought him his fair share of goals. Though he played a number of wartime games for Spurs as an amateur and 'guested' for Bradford Park Avenue, Manchester United and Millwall, he not only turned professional with Carlisle United but was also their player-manager. He was highly successful with the Third Division (North) club and in February 1949 transferred himself to Sunderland! In his second season at Roker Park, he helped the Wearsiders finish third in the First Division. His form led to him being a member of England's 1950 World Cup squad. On Boxing Day of that year he scored his only hat-trick for Sunderland in a 5–3 victory over Manchester United, but within a year he had left the north-east to play for Manchester City. He spent two years at Maine Road before returning to the north-east with Newcastle United. Here he continued to find the net on a regular basis and appeared for England in the 1954 World Cup Finals. After displaying some good form in United's FA Cup run in 1955, he was surprisingly left out of the Wembley line-up and he moved on within weeks of the Magpies' victory. He returned to Carlisle as player-coach, and three years later ended his career as a player with Queen of the South.

Newcastle United winger Ivor Broadis crosses the ball during a match against Arsenal at Highbury on 27 November 1953. (Getty Images)

Tommy GARRETT

Position	Full-back
Born	Thomas Garrett, Whiteless, 28 February 1927
Height	5ft 10in
Weight	12st 0lb
Clubs	Blackpool, Millwall
England Caps	3
	1952 v Scotland (won 2–1), v Italy (1–1)
	1953 v Wales (won 4–1)

ONE OF BLACKPOOL'S longest-serving players, Tommy Garrett made a handful of international appearances, partnering Alf Ramsey in the England defence.

When Blackpool signed him in the summer of 1942, Garrett was a miner playing for Horden Colliery. He joined the Seasiders as an inside-forward but he was converted to full-back with great success. Though he made his League debut at Derby County in March 1948, Garrett only made a few appearances over the next couple of seasons due to the fine form of Ron Suart. When Suart left to play for Blackburn Rovers, Garrett won a regular place in the side and was a mainstay of the Blackpool defence for 12 seasons. Equally at home on either flank, he appeared in the 1951 and 1953 FA Cup Finals, although he played in the 4–3 victory over Bolton Wanderers with a broken nose sustained a week earlier at Manchester City. During that Cup run, Garrett scored a remarkable goal in the fourth-round game against Huddersfield Town. The game was goalless and seemingly heading for a replay when Garrett, in his own half of the pitch, lobbed the ball over the Yorkshire club's keeper to put the Seasiders into the fifth round.

After 19 years with the Bloomfield Road club, he left to join Millwall. After just one season with the Lions, he returned to the north-west to play non-League football for Fleetwood before having a spell in Australian football with Newcastle.

Billy ELLIOTT

Position	Outside-left/Defender
Born	William Henry Elliott, Bradford, 20 March 1925
Height	5ft 7in
Weight	10st 7lb
Clubs	Bradford Park Avenue, Burnley, Sunderland
England Caps	5 Goals 3
	1952 v Italy (1–1), v Austria (won 3–2), v N. Ireland (2–2) 1 goal, v Wales (won 5–2), v Belgium (won 5–0) 2 goals

SUCH WAS Billy Elliott's impact during his first season in the top flight that he was chosen to go on England's European Tour in the summer of 1952. However, he was probably at his peak the following season, appearing in three further internationals, scoring three goals and playing three times in Football League representative matches.

Elliott was spotted playing schoolboy football in his home town by Bradford Park Avenue during the war and after joining them as an amateur he turned professional in March 1942. He was a regular in Bradford's Second Division side of the late 1940s, but in the summer of 1951 Burnley paid a club-record fee of £25,000 to bring Elliott to Turf Moor. He was soon a big favourite with the Clarets' fans. His speed and power down the left touchline became a feature of Burnley's style of play and his ferocious low crosses led to countless goals for his colleagues. Known as one of the game's hard men, Elliott was the only Burnley player to be sent off in the twenty years following the resumption of League football in 1946. In June 1953 he left Burnley to play for Sunderland for a record £26,000 and to become part of the then most expensive side ever assembled in England, the so-called Millionaires team.

Elliott played in just one more representative match while with the Wearsiders, scoring a goal in a 4–2 victory for the Football League against the Irish League at Anfield. Following Sunderland's relegation in 1958, Elliott spent one more season at Roker Park before joining Wisbech Town of the newly established Premier Division of the Southern League.

On hanging up his boots, he became national coach to Libya – the first of many coaching and managerial appointments that he held. He had a spell as caretaker-manager of Sunderland, steering the Wearsiders to within a point of promotion from the Second Division in 1979, following which he spent four years managing Darlington before retiring from the game.

Ronnie ALLEN

Position	Forward
Born	Ronald Allen, Fenton, 15 January 1929
Died	9 June 2001
Height	5ft 8in
Weight	10st 9lb
Clubs	Port Vale, West Bromwich Albion, Crystal Palace
England Caps	5 Goals 2
	1952 v Switzerland (won 3–0)
	1954 v Scotland (won 4–2) 1 goal, v Yugoslavia (lost 0–1), v Wales (won 3–1) 1 goal,
	v W. Germany (won 3–1)

THOUGH HE ONLY WON five full international caps for England, Ronnie Allen proved to be a prolific goalscorer for West Bromwich Albion, scoring 234 times in 458 games. His record of 208 League goals for the club stood until Tony Brown went better in 1979. One record that he will never lose is the unique distinction of being the only player to score in each of the first 20 post-war seasons.

Allen began his Football League career with Port Vale, making his debut in an FA Cup first-round tie against Wellington Town in November 1945 and turning professional the following April. He started out as a right-winger but later moved to centre-forward. He was a two-footed striker blessed with a powerful shot in both feet. He left Vale Park to join West Bromwich Albion in March 1950, scoring in his first match against Wolves and continuing to find the net with great regularity throughout 11 seasons with the Albion. New manager Vic Buckingham built the team round Allen's skill and vision and they went on to win the FA Cup in 1954 – with Allen scoring twice in a 3–2 win over Preston North End – and finish runners-up in the League.

Allen left the Hawthorns in May 1961 to play for Crystal Palace, later turning to coaching with Wolverhampton Wanderers. He became manager at Molineux in 1966 and led the club back into the top flight two years later. He later managed Atletico Bilbao, Sporting Lisbon, Walsall, West Bromwich Albion (twice), the Saudi Arabian national team and Panathinaikos.

Redfern FROGGATT

Position	Inside-forward
Born	Redfern Froggatt, Sheffield, 23 August 1923
Height	5ft 11in
Weight	11st 1lb
Clubs	Sheffield Wednesday
England Caps	4 Goals 2
	1952 v Wales (won 5–2), v Belgium (won 5–0) 1 goal
	1953 v Scotland (2–2), v United States (won 6–3) 1 goal

REDFERN FROGGATT was a clever inside-forward who scored more than his fair share of goals. He was chosen to play for England 'B' against Switzerland in 1950 before winning his first full cap against Wales at Wembley two years later. In all, he won four full caps, forming a left-wing partnership with his cousin, Portsmouth's Jack Froggatt, in the 4–2 win over Scotland.

The son of Frank Froggatt, a determined hard-tackling defender who captained Sheffield Wednesday to the Second Division Championship in 1925/26, he too joined the Owls, making his debut in a League Cup (North) game against Grimsby Town during the Second World War. He went on to make 86 wartime appearances for the Hillsborough club before making his Football League debut on the opening day of the 1946/47 season. During his time with Wednesday he established a post-war scoring record of 149 goals, helping the Owls win promotion four times and collecting three Second Division Championship medals in the process. His best season in terms of goals scored was 1958/59, when he netted 26 times in 37 League games, including a hat-trick in a 6–0 defeat of Sunderland. That season he followed in his father Frank's footsteps by captaining the side to the Second Division title. He played the last of his 458 games for Wednesday against West Ham United on the final day of the 1959/60 season.

Tommy TAYLOR

Position	Centre-forward
Born	Thomas Taylor, Smithies, 29 January 1932
Died	Munich, 6 February 1958
Height	6ft 0in
Weight	12st 11lb
Clubs	Barnsley, Manchester United
England Caps	19 Goals 16
	1953 v Argentina (0–0), v Chile (won 2–1) 1 goal, v Uruguay (lost 1–2) 1 goal
	1954 v Belgium (4–4), v Switzerland (won 2–0)
	1956 v Scotland (1–1), v Brazil (won 4–2) 2 goals, v Sweden (0–0), v Finland (won 5–1),
	v W. Germany (won 3–1), v N. Ireland (1–1), v Yugoslavia (won 3–0) 2 goals, v Denmark
	(won 5–2) 3 goals
	1957 v Eire (won 5–1) 3 goals, v Denmark (won 4–1) 2 goals, v Eire (1–1), v Wales
	(won 4–0), v N. Ireland (lost 2–3), v France (won 4–0) 2 goals

TOMMY TAYLOR won the first of his 19 England caps in the abandoned game against Argentina in May 1953 – a week later he scored the first of his 16 England goals in a 2–1 defeat of Chile. Although he played twice in the 1954 World Cup Finals, he did not establish himself as an England regular until he replaced Bolton's Nat Lofthouse in 1956. Scoring consecutive hat-tricks against Denmark and Eire, he helped his country qualify for the 1958 World Cup Finals but by the time England took their place in Sweden he had tragically lost his life at Munich.

Taylor was a superb leader of Manchester United's attack in the years leading up to the Munich Air Disaster. A powerful header of the ball, he began his Football League career with Barnsley, where he was an inside-forward, but after joining Manchester United in March 1953 he was converted into a centre-forward. United paid £29,999 for his services, Matt Busby not wanting to burden him with a £30,000 tag! In five years at Old Trafford, he won two League Championship medals and scored United's only goal in the 1957 FA Cup Final defeat against Aston Villa. Europe provided Taylor's greatest stage: he scored 11 goals in 14 European Cup matches, his performance in the 3–0 defeat of Atletico Bilbao in the 1956/57 quarter-finals being his greatest.

Tommy Taylor.
(Getty Images)

Johnny BERRY

Position	Winger
Born	John Reginald Berry, Aldershot, 1 May 1926
Died	15 September 1994
Height	5ft 5in
Weight	9st 9lb
Clubs	Birmingham City, Manchester United
England Caps	4
	1953 v Argentina (0–0), v Chile (won 2–1), v Uruguay (lost 1–2)
	1956 v Sweden (0–0)

JOHNNY BERRY, who gained four England caps and represented England 'B' and the Football League XI, was a brilliant winger who was discovered for Birmingham City by former Blues half-back Fred Harris when they played together in the Army.

Though he signed professional forms for the St Andrew's club in December 1944, he did not get a chance to play in the club's League side until September 1947, when he played in a 1–0 defeat at Newcastle United. He established himself in the Birmingham side midway through the following campaign and was a virtual ever-present until September 1951, when Manchester United manager Matt Busby, needing a replacement for Irish international Jimmy Delaney, paid £25,000 for his services. He made his United debut in a 1–0 defeat at Bolton but, despite this disappointing start, he ended his first season with a League Championship winners' medal. When United won the title again in 1955/56, Berry and Roger Byrne were the only survivors of the previous Championship success and they won a third Championship medal the following year.

Sadly, the injuries he received in the Munich Air Crash meant that he never played again.

Albert QUIXALL

Position	Inside-forward
Born	Albert Quixall, Sheffield, 9 August 1933
Height	5ft 8in
Weight	11st 5lb
Clubs	Sheffield Wednesday, Manchester United, Oldham Athletic, Stockport County
England Caps	5
	1953 v Wales (won 4–1), v Rest of Europe (4–4), v N. Ireland (won 3–1)
	1955 v Spain (1–1), v Portugal (lost 1–3)

CAPPED FIVE TIMES by the full England side, 'Golden Boy' Albert Quixall also played for his country at Schoolboy, 'B' and Under-23 levels and represented the Football League XI.

He began his career with his home-town club Sheffield Wednesday, making his debut with his long-term wing partner Alan Finney against Chelsea at Hillsborough in

1950, when he scored in a 2–2 draw. He was an important member of Wednesday's Second Division Championship-winning sides of 1951/52 and 1955/56, and was in outstanding form during the club's run to the FA Cup semi-finals in 1954. In 1956/57 he was the Owls' leading scorer with 24 goals, though it was often said that he didn't reach his full potential while at Hillsborough. In September 1958, the youthful-looking Quixall, who ironically had captained Wednesday against United in the Reds' first game after Munich, moved to Manchester United for a fee of £45,000 – almost £10,000 more than the then British record. He had scored 65 goals in 260 games for Sheffield Wednesday, yet in his first season at Old Trafford his goalscoring touch deserted him. He rediscovered his goalscoring form the following season, going on to net 56 goals in 183 games and to win an FA Cup winners' medal as Manchester United beat Leicester City 3–1 in the 1963 final. A year later he joined Oldham Athletic but soon moved on to Stockport County, where he ended his League career.

Quixall had a brief spell playing non-League football for Altrincham before concentrating on his scrap-metal business.

Dennis WILSHAW

Position	Forward
Born	Dennis James Wilshaw, Stoke, 11 March 1926
Height	5ft 11in
Weight	11st 8lb
Clubs	Walsall, Wolverhampton Wanderers, Stoke City
England Caps	12 Goals 9
	1953 v Wales (won 4–1) 2 goals
	1954 v Switzerland (won 2–0), v Uruguay (lost 2–4)
	1955 v Scotland (won 7–2) 4 goals, v France (lost 0–1), v Spain (1–1), v Portugal (lost 1–3),
	v Wales (lost 1–2), v N. Ireland (won 3–0) 2 goals
	1956 v Finland (won 5–1) 1 goal, v W. Germany (won 3–1), v N. Ireland (1–1)

DENNIS WILSHAW was capped 12 times by England, his first international appearance coming in October 1953 when he scored twice in a 4–1 win over Wales. He played in the World Cup Finals in Switzerland the following year, and in his first Wembley game he scored four goals as England hammered the Scots 7–2 in April 1955.

After some prolific goalscoring feats in the North Staffordshire League, Wilshaw signed professional forms for Wolverhampton Wanderers in 1944 but was allowed to join Walsall on loan. He did so well with the Saddlers, scoring 21 goals in 87 games, that he was recalled to Molineux midway through the 1948/49 season. On his League debut for Wolves he blasted a quickfire hat-trick in a 3–0 win over Newcastle United and ended the season with 10 goals in 11 games. He was nevertheless still classed a reserve to players like Jesse Pye and Roy Swinbourne, and over the next three seasons he struggled to make much of an impact. He finally established himself as a first-team regular in 1952/53 and the following season, when the club won the League Championship for the first time in their history, Wilshaw was the top scorer with 25 goals, including a hat-trick in an 8–1 win over Chelsea. He stayed at

Molineux, where he scored 117 goals in 232 games, until December 1957, when he was transferred to his home-town club, Stoke City.

Wilshaw spent four years at the Victoria Ground before a broken leg in a match at Newcastle United forced him into retirement.

Derek UFTON

Position	Centre-half
Born	Derek Gilbert Ufton, Crayford, 31 May 1928
Height	6ft 0in
Weight	12st 4lb
Clubs	Charlton Athletic
England Caps	1
	1953 v Rest of Europe (4–4)

A ONE-CLUB MAN, Derek Ufton gave impressive performances at the heart of the Charlton Athletic defence and this resulted in him winning international recognition in 1953 when he played for England against the Rest of Europe. The game ended all square at 4–4 as Ufton and his fellow defenders were given a rough time by the FIFA team's forwards.

Ufton had been an amateur on Cardiff City's books and played non-League football for Dulwich Hamlet, Bexleyheath and Welling United before joining Charlton Athletic in September 1948. A cultured centre-half, Ufton was also a strong tackler and was a regular for most of his 12 seasons at the Valley, despite him dislocating his shoulder 20 times during his career! Ufton went on to play in 277 games for Charlton before injury eventually forced his retirement.

On leaving the Valley, he joined Plymouth Argyle as coach to Malcolm Allison, and when Allison left to join Manchester City Ufton became manager. Although he made a profit on the transfer market, he sold some of the club's best players and in the 1967/68 season, after only three wins in 25 games, he was sacked. Currently President of Kent County Cricket Club, Ufton was also an accomplished cricketer, playing in 148 matches for his county between 1949 and 1962, scoring 3,919 runs and recording 314 dismissals as a wicket-keeper. His other roles include that of a photographic model, being chairman of the Lord's Taverners, and playing an important part in Charlton Athletic's return to the Valley in December 1992.

Stan RICKABY

Position	Right-back
Born	Stanley Rickaby, Stockton, 12 March 1924
Height	6ft 0in
Weight	13st 0lb
Clubs	Middlesbrough, West Bromwich Albion
England Caps	1
	1953 v N. Ireland (won 3–1)

STAN RICKABY'S consistent displays for West Bromwich Albion saw him rewarded at full international level in November 1953 when he played in the 3–1 win over Northern Ireland in a World Cup qualifying match.

Rickaby was languishing in Middlesbrough's reserve team when, in February 1950, West Bromwich Albion manager Jack Smith brought him to the Hawthorns. He soon developed into a fine defender, strong in the tackle and showing good positional sense. Over the next few seasons, Rickaby missed very few matches as Albion challenged for League Championship honours. He was injured in the club's 2–1 FA Cup semi-final win over Port Vale, an injury that cost him a winners' medal after Albion went on to defeat Preston North End 3–2 in the 1954 Final. In fact, the injury was so severe that it shortened his first-class career, and at the end of the following season he left the Hawthorns to become player-manager of Poole Town. He later reverted simply to playing and had spells with Weymouth and Newton Abbot Spurs before hanging up his boots.

After working in a life insurance firm in Birmingham, the former Albion defender emigrated to Australia in 1969.

Ernie TAYLOR

Position	Inside-right
Born	Ernest Taylor, Sunderland, 2 September 1925
Died	Birkenhead, 9 April 1985
Height	5ft 4in
Weight	10st 4lb
Clubs	Newcastle United, Blackpool, Manchester United, Sunderland, Derry City
England Caps	1
	1953 v Hungary (lost 3–6)

ERNIE TAYLOR'S one and only England cap came in the 6–3 1953 home defeat by Hungary, after which, along with several others, he was discarded from the international scene.

Ernie began his footballing career with Newcastle United, joining the St James' Park playing staff from Hylton Colliery Juniors in 1942. During the war he served in the Royal Navy before going on to play in 143 games for the Magpies. In October 1951 he signed for Blackpool just six months after helping Newcastle beat the Seasiders in the FA Cup Final at Wembley. Once Stanley Matthews had recovered from injury, he and Taylor created one of the best right-wing partnerships in the Football League. He was perhaps the unsung hero of Blackpool's win at Wembley in 1953, for it wasn't until Taylor started to hit some slide-rule passes to the feet of Matthews that the great man began to make his mark on the match. Though he only stood 5ft 4in, Taylor was surprisingly lethal in front of goal and had the ability to split defences wide open with a single devastating pass.

Following the Munich Air Disaster, Taylor left Bloomfield Road to join Manchester United, making his debut for the Reds in the emotional FA Cup match against

Sheffield Wednesday. He played in that season's FA Cup Final but Bolton ended his dream of picking up an FA Cup winners' medal with three different clubs.

Taylor later returned to his home-town team of Sunderland before going into non-League football with Altrincham. He then played for Irish club Derry City before emigrating for New Zealand to coach the Christchurch club, New Brighton. On his return to these shores, he worked in the Vauxhall car plant at Hooton, Cheshire.

George ROBB

Position	Outside-left
Born	George Robb, Finsbury Park, 1 June 1926
Height	5ft 8in
Weight	11st 12lb
Clubs	Tottenham Hotspur
England Caps	1
	1953 v Hungary (lost 3–6)

ENGLAND AMATEUR INTERNATIONAL George Robb joined Spurs in the summer of 1944, but when the White Hart Lane club failed to offer him professional terms he became a schoolmaster. He continued to play as an amateur for Finchley, whom he had first joined in 1942, and won 18 amateur caps in his nine years with them. He again signed amateur forms for Spurs in December 1951 and scored on his League debut in a 3–0 win over Charlton Athletic. Signing professional forms in the summer of 1953, he played under three managers in a period of under-achievement by the club.

In 1953/54, his first full season, he scored 16 goals in 37 outings and was rewarded with a full cap for the match against Hungary at Wembley, which the Magyars won 6–3. Continuing to perform reliably at club level, Robb enjoyed an active FA Cup campaign in 1956. After scoring three times in the early rounds, he was about to push the ball into an empty net for the equalizer in the semi-final against Manchester City when Bert Trautmann appeared to grab his legs. Amazingly no penalty was given.

Robb suffered a serious knee injury during the 1957/58 season, which forced him into retirement in May 1960 and a full-time return to the classroom.

Ron STANIFORTH

Position	Right-back
Born	Ronald Staniforth, Manchester, 13 April 1924
Height	5ft 11in
Weight	11st 0lb
Clubs	Stockport County, Huddersfield Town, Sheffield Wednesday, Barrow
England Caps	8
	1954 v Scotland (won 4–2), v Yugoslavia (lost 0–1), v Hungary (lost 1–7), v Belgium (4–4), v Switzerland (won 2–0), v Uruguay (lost 2–4), v Wales (won 3–1), v W. Germany (won 3–1)

RON STANIFORTH, who won eight full caps for England in the space of nine months in 1954, served with the Navy during the Second World War before becoming a milkman. He wrote to Stockport County asking for a trial, which resulted in him signing amateur forms in August 1946. His ability was so obvious that he had signed professional forms within six weeks and made his League debut against Tranmere Rovers shortly afterwards. When County manager Andy Beattie left to take over at Huddersfield Town, Staniforth, who had made 245 appearances for the Hatters, followed him.

Although he only spent a short time at Leeds Road, he helped Town reclaim the First Division place they had lost 12 months earlier. He subsequently helped them attain third place at the end of the following campaign but was later dropped after being given the runaround by Newcastle's Bobby Mitchell. He never regained his first-team place and left to play for Sheffield Wednesday.

He remained at Hillsborough for four years, winning Second Division Championship medals in his first and last seasons before leaving to become player-manager of Fourth Division Barrow.

After hanging up his boots, Staniforth remained as Barrow's manager until 1964, his new role proving disappointingly unsuccessful. He later had two spells on the coaching staff at Hillsborough.

Roger BYRNE

Position	Left-back
Born	Roger William Byrne, Manchester, 8 February 1929
Died	Munich, 6 February 1958
Height	5ft 9in
Weight	11st 7lb
Clubs	Manchester United
England Caps	33

1954 v Scotland (won 4–2), v Yugoslavia (lost 0–1), v Hungary (lost 1–7), v Belgium (4–4), v Switzerland (won 2–0), v Uruguay (lost 2–4), v N. Ireland (won 2–0), v Wales (won 3–1), v W. Germany (won 3–1)

1955 v Scotland (won 7–2), v France (lost 0–1), v Spain (1–1), v Portugal (lost 1–3), v Denmark (won 5–1), v Wales (lost 1–2), v N. Ireland (won 3–0), v Spain (won 4–1)

1956 v Scotland (1–1), v Brazil (won 4–2), v Sweden (0–0), v Finland (won 5–1), v W. Germany (won 3–1), v N. Ireland (1–1), v Wales (won 3–1), v Yugoslavia (won 3–0), v Denmark (won 5–2)

1957 v Scotland (won 2–1), v Eire (won 5–1), v Denmark (won 4–1), v Eire (1–1), v Wales (won 4–0), v N. Ireland (lost 2–3), v France (won 4–0)

CAPPED 33 TIMES by England in consecutive internationals, Roger Byrne was a player with a great tactical foresight that enabled him to dictate the course of play. A confident ball-playing full-back, he was one of the fastest in that position. On the rare occasions he was beaten he could recover instantly.

Byrne joined Manchester United as an amateur in March 1949 but had to wait until November 1951 before making his League debut in a goalless draw at Anfield as a

replacement at left-back for Bill Redman. Converted to outside-left for the last six
games of the season, he scored seven goals as United won the League Championship.

Byrne succeeded Johnny Carey as captain and was no exception to the great
tradition of United skippers established by Matt Busby. He led the Reds to successive
League Championship wins in the mid-1950s and to the FA Cup Final of 1957.
When he led the side to Wembley that year, Manchester United were attempting to
become the first team that century to achieve the League and Cup double.

Byrne perished at Munich with, among others, seven of his team-mates. His
remark after the 1957 FA Cup Final defeat by Aston Villa had been, 'Never mind,
we'll be back next year.' Poignantly, though Manchester United were back, Roger
Byrne was not. Eight months after his death, his wife Joy gave birth to a son, whom
she named Roger. Had Roger senior survived Munich, he would have gone on to
become one of England's greatest captains.

Harry CLARKE

Position	Centre-half
Born	Harold Alfred Clarke, Woodford, 23 February 1923
Died	16 April 2000
Height	6ft 3in
Weight	12st 8lb
Clubs	Tottenham Hotspur
England Caps	1
	1954 v Scotland (won 4–2)

HARRY CLARKE'S consistent performances for his only club, Tottenham Hotspur, were
rewarded with an appearance for England 'B' against West Germany in March 1954
and a full cap the following month as England beat Scotland 4–2 at Hampden Park.

A stalwart centre-half in Arthur Rowe's 'push and run' Tottenham team of the
early 1950s, Clarke joined the White Hart Lane club from Southern League Lovells
Athletic in March 1949, having previously gained experience with the RAF
Command XI. Spurs pitched him straight into the first team and, despite such a late
entry into the League arena, he was ever-present for the next two seasons as the
club won the Second Division and League Championship in successive years. At 6ft
3in, Clarke was once described as a 'shy giant' – he was a cool, commanding figure
both in the air and on the ground, attributes that were vital to Spurs' dashing style.

Clarke went on to appear in 322 League and Cup games for Spurs before retiring
midway through the 1956/57 season. He remained at White Hart Lane as coach to
the juniors until taking the manager's job at Llanelli. He later had a spell in the
same capacity with Romford before working as an officer for a security transit
company in Ilford.

Johnny NICHOLLS

Position	Inside-right
Born	John Nicholls, Wolverhampton, 3 April 1931
Died	West Bromwich, 1 April 1995
Height	5ft 9in
Weight	11st 0lb
Clubs	Wolverhampton Wanderers, West Bromwich Albion, Cardiff City, Exeter City
England Caps	2 Goals 1
	1954 v Scotland (won 4–2) 1 goal, v Yugoslavia (lost 0–1)

ON HIS INTERNATIONAL DEBUT, which was also his 23rd birthday, Johnny Nicholls lined up alongside his Albion team-mate Ronnie Allen and scored one of England's goals in a 4–2 defeat of Scotland at Hampden Park.

After an early association with his home-town club, Wolverhampton Wanderers, Nicholls moved to West Bromwich Albion, spending his first season at the Hawthorns flitting in and out of the side. However, his form at the start of the 1953/54 season was outstanding – forming a deadly partnership with Ronnie Allen, he went on to score 28 goals. That season, Albion won the FA Cup and finished third in the First Division, but during the early part of the following campaign Nicholls developed an ankle problem and was transferred to Cardiff City. His stay at Ninian Park was both brief and unhappy, and it was only when he moved to Exeter City that he rediscovered his scoring form. Subsequently, after drifting through the non-League scene with Worcester and Wellington Town, he decided to retire.

Nicholls died of a heart attack while returning home from an Albion game against Middlesbrough in April 1995.

Sid OWEN

Position	Centre-half
Born	Sidney William Owen, Birmingham, 29 September 1922
Died	16 January 1999
Height	6ft 0in
Weight	11st 10lb
Clubs	Birmingham City, Luton Town
England Caps	3
	1954 v Yugoslavia (lost 0–1), v Hungary (lost 1–7), v Belgium (4–4)
Honours	Footballer of the Year 1959

A MEMBER OF the 1954 England World Cup party, Sid Owen was also chosen for the Football League XI and captained FA touring parties to South Africa, the West Indies and Australia.

One of Luton Town's greatest-ever players, Owen began his career with Birmingham City. However, his chances of success with the Blues were baulked by the consistency of Ted Duckhouse, so in June 1947 he joined the Hatters. He made his debut for the Kenilworth Road club in a 3–0 win at Brentford, a match in which Hugh Billington netted a hat-trick. A dominant centre-half, Owen also captained the club, manager Dally Duncan building the team round him. In 1954/55 he led the Hatters to promotion to the First Division, and at the end of the season, following Tim Kelly's departure, he was made club coach. In 1959 he captained Luton in the FA Cup Final against Nottingham Forest and was voted Footballer of the Year.

At the end of the 1958/59 season, Owen, having played in 413 games for the Hatters, hung up his boots and took over as the club's manager. Sadly, he did not have a happy time, frequently being at loggerheads with the club's directors over the signing of new players. After Luton were relegated to the Second Division, he left to work alongside Don Revie at Leeds United during the Yorkshire club's great days of the 1960s and early 1970s. In 1978 he was appointed Manchester United's youth-team coach before eventually becoming a scout at Old Trafford, a position he held until his retirement in 1982

Bedford JEZZARD

Position	Centre-forward
Born	Bedford Alfred George Jezzard, Clerkenwell, 19 October 1926
Height	5ft 11in
Weight	13st 4lb
Clubs	Fulham
England Caps	2
	1954 v Hungary (lost 1–7)
	1955 v N. Ireland (won 3–0)

BEDFORD JEZZARD, one of Fulham's best-ever centre-forwards and later to become one of the club's most successful managers, had the misfortune to make his full international debut for England in the 7–1 defeat by Hungary in Budapest in 1954.

Jezzard was working on the staff of the Old Merchant Taylor's sports ground when Fulham asked him to join them in the summer of 1948. During his first season with the Cottagers, he helped them win the Second Division Championship, and over the next three seasons he was a regular in the club's First Division side. But it was following Fulham's relegation to the Second Division that he developed into a prolific goalscorer. In 1952/53 he was the club's top scorer with 35 goals, establishing a club record when he found the net in nine consecutive League games. He scored a number of hat-tricks for the Cottagers, and during the course of the 1956/57 season he scored all five goals in a 5–0 rout of Hull City.

Jezzard was on tour with an FA XI in South Africa when he sustained an ankle injury that was prematurely to end his career at the age of 28, after he had scored 154 goals in 306 games. He became Fulham's youth-team coach before being appointed manager in 1958. In his first season in charge he led the club to promotion to the First Division and remained at the helm until the sale of Alan Mullery to Spurs in 1964. That transfer, arranged without his knowledge, prompted him to leave the club.

Bill McGARRY

Position	Right-half
Born	William Harry McGarry, Stoke, 10 June 1927
Height	5ft 8in
Weight	11st 0lb
Clubs	Port Vale, Huddersfield Town, Bournemouth
England Caps	4
	1954 v Switzerland (won 2–0), v Uruguay (lost 2–4)
	1955 v Denmark (won 5–1), v Wales (lost 1–2)

BILL McGARRY is as well known for his managerial wanderings as for his dependable displays as a powerful wing-half. Discovered by Port Vale, he was a virtual ever-present in their side for a number of seasons before he joined Huddersfield Town in March 1951. He soon established himself in the First Division, his performances earning him international recognition when he played for England in the World Cup Finals in Switzerland. He also played for the Football League and went on the FA's 1956 South African tour.

Remembered for his competitiveness during his ten years at Leeds Road, he carried that approach into his management career when he became Bournemouth's first-ever player-manager. He was later appointed manager of Watford before enjoying some success with Ipswich Town, but his best years as a manager were spent in charge of Wolverhampton Wanderers.

He took them back into Europe and to success in the 1974 League Cup Final before being sacked in 1976 after Wolves were relegated. He later coached in Saudi Arabia and managed Newcastle United. There followed spells as Brighton scout, Zambian national team manager and a period coaching in South Africa, before he spent 61 days in a second spell managing Wolves. Disillusioned, McGarry then quit the game altogether.

Ray WOOD

Position	Goalkeeper
Born	Raymond Ernest Wood, Hebburn-on-Tyne, 11 June 1931
Died	Bexhill, 7 July 2002
Height	5ft 11in
Weight	11st 12lb
Clubs	Newcastle United, Darlington, Manchester United, Huddersfield Town, Bradford City, Barnsley
England Caps	3
	1954 v N. Ireland (won 2–0), v Wales (won 3–1)
	1956 v Finland (won 5–1)

TO MANY FOOTBALL FOLLOWERS, the name Ray Wood conjures up memories of the incident during the 1957 FA Cup Final when, as Manchester United's goalkeeper, he left the field with a fractured cheekbone after only six minutes, following a controversial collision with Peter McParland. His injury certainly dashed the Reds' hopes of clinching the century's first League and Cup double.

After being on amateur forms with Newcastle United, Wood signed for Darlington, but after just 12 appearances for the Quakers he was on his way to Old Trafford. He was signed as cover for Jack Crompton, but when United then signed Reg Allen he had to be content with a further spell in the Central League. When Allen was forced to retire through illness, Wood started the 1954/55 season as the club's first-choice keeper. He helped United win two successive League Championships before being replaced by Harry Gregg. He survived the Munich Air Disaster but made only one more appearance following his return from serious injury. United transferred him to Huddersfield Town, where he steadied the club's hard-pressed defence. After a spell in Canadian football, Wood returned to play for both Bradford City and Barnsley before coaching in a number of countries, including Zambia, Cyprus, Greece, Kuwait, the United Arab Emirates and Kenya.

Bill FOULKES

Position	Centre-half
Born	William Anthony Foulkes, St Helens, 5 January 1932
Height	5ft 11in
Weight	12st 4lb
Clubs	Manchester United
England Caps	1
	1954 v N. Ireland (won 2–0)

BILL FOULKES made his Manchester United debut at right-back in a 2–1 win at Liverpool in 1952. In those days he was a rather raw and ungainly defender, and it was in the No. 2 shirt that he won his one and only full international cap against Northern Ireland two years later. In 1955 he played in two England Under-23 matches and for the Football League, but that was the extent of his representative football.

Foulkes was a strong and reliable defender, giving United sterling service during his 18 years in the first team. He survived Munich to become the backbone of United's defence after being converted to centre-half. Captain of the new-look Reds side in the 1958 FA Cup Final when they lost 2–0 to Bolton Wanderers, he gained compensation for two losers' medals (having also been in the 1957 side that lost to Aston Villa) when, in 1963, United beat Leicester City 3–1. Though not a great goalscorer, he was on the scoresheet in United's 3–3 draw with Real Madrid that put the club into the 1968 European Cup Final, where they beat Benfica. Foulkes played the last of his 682 first-team games against Southampton at the start of the 1969/70 season. He had won four League Championship medals, played in three FA Cup Finals and been a member of United's European Cup-winning team.

On retirement he was appointed the club's youth-team coach and a year later promoted to reserve-team coach. He then went to America to manage Chicago Stings and later Tulsa Roughnecks before taking charge of Norwegian side Lillestrom and finally Japanese side Mazda.

Johnny WHEELER

Position	Right-half
Born	John Edward Wheeler, Crosby, 26 July 1928
Height	5ft 9in
Weight	12st 2lb
Clubs	Tranmere Rovers, Bolton Wanderers, Liverpool
England Caps	1
	1954 v N. Ireland (won 2–0)

JOHNNY WHEELER began his career with Tranmere Rovers, where the club's trainer was Bill Ridding. When Ridding left to manage Bolton Wanderers, Wheeler followed him to Burnden Park. He made rapid progress with the Wanderers, establishing himself at right-half and playing in the 1953 FA Cup Final against Blackpool. In January of that year he had turned out as an emergency centre-forward against Blackpool and hit a hat-trick in a 4–0 win. International honours came his way, with five appearances for England 'B' along with Football League representative games, and in October 1954 he won his only England cap, against Northern Ireland in Belfast.

In September 1956, Wheeler moved to Liverpool, where he played his last two seasons under Bill Shankly, and, though his best days were behind him, he was a useful servant to the club. By the time the Reds finally escaped from their lower-division days, his career was almost over and he made just one appearance during Liverpool's Second Division Championship-winning season of 1961/62.

The following season, Wheeler was appointed player-manager of New Brighton but he never took up the post, becoming assistant-trainer at Bury instead.

Ray BARLOW

Position	Left-half
Born	Raymond John Barlow, Swindon, 8 August 1926
Height	6ft 0in
Weight	13st 6lb
Clubs	West Bromwich Albion, Birmingham City
England Caps	1
	1954 v N. Ireland (won 2–0)

QUITE TALL for a creative midfield player, Ray Barlow was the mainstay of the West Bromwich Albion side for almost the whole of the 1950s and should have won more than the single cap he earned against Northern Ireland in 1954.

Barlow was spotted playing for Wiltshire-based works side Garrards by former West Bromwich Albion centre-forward Jimmy Cookson and made his debut for the Baggies in wartime football. His debut in League football was an auspicious one, scoring one of the goals in Albion's 7–2 win at Newport County. During the club's promotion-winning season of 1948/49, he played a number of games at inside-forward and scored one of the goals in the win at Leicester City that clinched the club's place back in the top flight. Though he was later converted to left-half, Barlow also played at centre-half and centre-forward in emergencies.

Towards the end of his days at the Hawthorns, Barlow, who in total played almost 500 games, was made captain, but in the summer of 1960 he left to end his playing career with Birmingham City.

Don REVIE

Position	Inside-forward
Born	Donald George Revie, Middlesbrough, 10 July 1927
Died	Edinburgh, 26 May 1989
Height	5ft 11in
Weight	12st 9lb
Clubs	Leicester City, Hull City, Manchester City, Sunderland, Leeds United
England Caps	6 Goals 4
	1954 v N. Ireland (won 2–0) 1 goal
	1955 v Scotland (won 7–2) 1 goal, v France (lost 0–1), v Denmark (won 5–1) 2 goals, v Wales (lost 1–2)
	1956 v N. Ireland (1–1)
Honours	Footballer of the Year 1955

DON REVIE won recognition at both Football League and full international level during the latter stages of his time with Manchester City.

Revie began his Football League career with Leicester City but took some time to be appreciated by the Filbert Street crowd. However, his performances in the club's run to the 1949 FA Cup Final, during which he scored two goals in the semi-final victory over Portsmouth, won them over. Sadly he missed the Wembley game due to broken blood vessels in his nose. He was sold to Hull City in November 1949 but lost his form and was switched to wing-half to recover some of his confidence. Following Raich Carter's decision to leave Boothferry Park, Revie asked for a transfer and in October 1951 joined Manchester City for £25,000. Over the next six seasons he became an integral member of the City side. He was the tactical architect of what became known at Maine Road as the 'Revie Plan'. Revie played as a deep-lying centre-forward, prompting his inside-forwards rather than playing in the traditional style of an out-and-out striker. He masterminded the club's 1956 FA Cup Final victory over Birmingham before leaving for Sunderland. After the Wearsiders had been relegated he joined Leeds United as player-manager, before eventually hanging up his boots to concentrate solely on management.

In 1963/64 the Yorkshire club powered their way to the Second Division title. They made an immediate impact in the top flight and in ten years won two League titles, the FA Cup, the League Cup and two Fairs Cups, as well as appearing in numerous other finals. During his reign at Elland Road, Revie was named Manager of the Year in 1969, 1970 and 1972, and was awarded the OBE in January 1970.

In July 1974 he became manager of England but later left to coach the United Arab Emirates. Struck down by motor neurone disease, he spent his last years confined to a wheelchair.

Johnny HAYNES

Position	Inside-forward
Born	John Norman Haynes, Kentish Town, 17 October 1934
Height	5ft 10in
Weight	11st 10lb
Clubs	Fulham
England Caps	56 Goals 19

1954 v N. Ireland (won 2–0) 1 goal

1955 v N. Ireland (won 3–0), v Spain (won 4–1)

1956 v Scotland (1–1) 1 goal, v Brazil (won 4–2) 2 goals, v Sweden (0–0), v Finland (won 5–1) 1 goal, v W. Germany (won 3–1) 1 goal, v Wales (won 3–1) 1 goal, v Yugoslavia (won 3–0)

1957 v Eire (won 5–1), v Denmark (won 4–1) 1 goal, v Eire (1–1), v Wales (won 4–0) 2 goals, v N. Ireland (lost 2–3), v France (won 4–0)

1958 v Scotland (won 4–0), v Portugal (won 2–1), v Yugoslavia (lost 0–5), v Soviet Union (1–1), v Soviet Union (2–2), v Brazil (0–0), v Austria (2–2) 1 goal, v Soviet Union (lost 0–1), v N. Ireland (3–3), v Soviet Union (won 5–0) 3 goals, v Wales (2–2)

1959 v Scotland (won 1–0), v Italy (2–2), v Brazil (lost 0–2), v Peru (lost 1–4), v Mexico (lost 1–2), v United States (won 8–1) 1 goal, v N. Ireland (won 2–1)

1960 v Yugoslavia (3–3) 1 goal, v Spain (lost 0–3), v Hungary (lost 0–2), v N. Ireland (won 5–2), v Spain (won 4–2), v Wales (won 5–1) 1 goal

1961 v Scotland (won 9–3) 2 goals, v Mexico (won 8–0), v Portugal (1–1), v Italy (won 3–2), v Austria (lost 1–3), v Wales (1–1), v Portugal (won 2–0), v N. Ireland (1–1)

1962 v Austria (won 3–1), v Scotland (lost 0–2), v Switzerland (won 3–1), v Peru (won 4–0), v Hungary (lost 1–2), v Argentina (won 3–1), v Bulgaria (0–0), v Brazil (lost 1–3)

....

THE CAREER OF JOHNNY HAYNES was one of the most contradictory in the history of British football. He was the country's first £100-a-week player, one of the first to use his fame for advertising and to have an agent, and captain of England on 22 occasions, gaining the most satisfaction of his career from his games for England, for whom he won 56 caps. He scored a hat-trick in a 5–0 Wembley win over the Soviet Union but his best game in England colours was the 9–3 defeat of Scotland in 1961.

Though he could have joined Spurs, Haynes opted for Fulham and was a regular for the Cottagers for 18 seasons after making his debut against Southampton on Boxing Day 1952. When Fulham won promotion to the First Division in 1958/59, Haynes was the club's leading scorer with 26 goals in 34 games, including all four in a 4–2 victory over Lincoln City. In August 1962, soon after the disappointing World Cup in Chile, Haynes was involved in a car crash in Blackpool. It was to end his international career and put his whole playing future in jeopardy. Aged 29, he did not play for a year and was even told by doctors that he would never play again.

Considering his role as a leader of men with Fulham and England, it is strange that Haynes didn't go into management when his playing career ended. He did in fact take charge of Fulham for 17 days when Bobby Robson was sacked, but stepped down in favour of Bill Dodgin.

Johnny Haynes of Fulham. (Lancashire Evening Post)

Haynes scored 157 goals in 657 games for the Cottagers, and when he left the club in 1970 many expected him to join former Fulham player Jimmy Hill as a television personality, but instead he moved to South African football, where he won his first honour – as a member of the Durban City side that clinched the League title.

Brian PILKINGTON

Position	Outside-left
Born	Brian Pilkington, Leyland, 12 February 1933
Height	5ft 5in
Weight	10st 11b
Clubs	Burnley, Bolton Wanderers, Bury, Barrow
England Caps	1
	1954 v N. Ireland (won 2–0)

BRIAN PILKINGTON was serving his apprenticeship with Leyland Motors as a coach painter when he joined Burnley in April 1951. His early displays for the Clarets were so good that manager Frank Hill let regular left-winger Billy Elliott join Sunderland. Pilkington's fast direct wing play soon caught the eye of the international selectors and in March 1954 he won his first representative honours, collecting an England 'B' cap against Scotland at Roker Park. In October of that year he played in his only full international, replacing Tom Finney in a 2–0 victory over Northern Ireland in Belfast.

Pilkington missed very few matches during his First Division career at Turf Moor, his sheer consistency eventually leading to the Clarets winning the League Championship in 1959/60. Fittingly, it was Pilkington who scored the first of Burnley's goals in the 2–1 win against Manchester City at Maine Road that saw the title come to Turf Moor. Rather surprisingly, he was subsequently allowed to join Bolton Wanderers. He spent three years at Burnden Park, but never quite hit the form he was capable of. After the Wanderers lost their top-flight status he moved to Bury, but after a year at Gigg Lane he joined Fourth Division Barrow, where, after helping them win promotion, he ended his League career.

Now a magistrate, he had spells as manager of both Leyland Motors and Chorley.

Bill SLATER

Position	Left-half
Born	William John Slater, Clitheroe, 29 April 1927
Height	6ft 0in
Weight	12st 7lb
Clubs	Blackpool, Brentford, Wolverhampton Wanderers
England Caps	12
	1954 v Wales (won 3–1), v W. Germany (won 3–1)
	1958 v Scotland (won 4–0), v Portugal (won 2–1), v Yugoslavia (lost 0–5), v Soviet Union (1–1), v Soviet Union (2–2), v Brazil (0–0), v Austria (2–2), v Soviet Union (lost 0–1), v Soviet Union (won 5–0)
	1960 v Scotland (1–1)
Honours	Footballer of the Year 1960

CAPPED 21 TIMES by England as an amateur, Bill Slater won the first of 12 full international caps when he played in a 3–1 win over Wales at Wembley in 1954.

Slater joined Blackpool as an inside-left soon after the war and made his debut against Aston Villa in September 1949, but he found himself competing with Allan Brown for the No. 10 shirt. Unable to be guaranteed a first-team place, he joined Brentford in December 1951, but not before setting two interesting records: he is the last amateur to have appeared in an FA Cup Final at Wembley, for Blackpool in 1951, and he scored Blackpool's quickest-ever goal, which came after only 11 seconds of their game against Stoke City in December 1949. Unable to settle at Griffin Park, he joined Wolves in August 1952 and signed semi-professional forms in February 1954.

When Wolves won the League Championship for the first time in 1953/54, Slater played at wing-half. He won further League Championship medals in 1957/58 and 1958/59, and in 1960, when Wolves won the FA Cup, he was voted Footballer of the Year. He left Molineux in the summer of 1963 to rejoin Brentford, but after just one season he joined non-League Northern Nomads, where he saw out the rest of his playing career.

Slater subsequently became deputy director of the Crystal Palace sports centre and later worked as director of Physical Education at Liverpool and Birmingham universities. In 1982 he was awarded the OBE for his services to sport, and after five years as director of National Services he was elected president of the British Gymnastic Association.

Frank BLUNSTONE

Position	Outside-left
Born	Frank Blunstone, Crewe, 17 October 1934
Height	5ft 9in
Weight	10st 7lb
Clubs	Crewe Alexandra, Chelsea
England Caps	5
	1954 v Wales (won 3–1)
	1955 v Scotland (won 7–2), v France (lost 0–1), v Portugal (lost 1–3)
	1956 v Yugoslavia (won 3–0)

FRANK BLUNSTONE'S sparkling form during Chelsea's League Championship-winning season of 1954/55 earned him international honours against Wales, Scotland, France and Portugal, followed by a further cap in 1956 against Yugoslavia.

Frank arrived at Stamford Bridge as an 18-year-old in February 1953, having learned his trade in the Third Division (North) with his home-town club, Crewe Alexandra. He quickly became an automatic choice at outside-left, helped on his way by a goal scored on his debut in the London derby against Spurs. His return to the Chelsea side following a lengthy lay-off was an important factor in the surge that brought the Blues the League title. After numerous games for the Army during his National Service, he returned to the Chelsea side for the fourth-round FA Cup tie at White Hart Lane, only to sustain a fractured leg. He tried making his comeback too soon and, after suffering a recurrence of the injury, was out of action for more than a year. A fast, direct attacking winger, Blunstone showed his supreme professionalism by adapting to Tommy Docherty's new methods as Chelsea won promotion to the top flight in 1962/63. However, just as he was about to share in the club's exciting pursuit of honours, he damaged an Achilles tendon during the club's Caribbean tour – an injury that ended his playing career.

Blunstone subsequently managed Brentford and worked with Tommy Docherty at Manchester United and Derby County, but later declined the manager's chair at Stamford Bridge following Dave Sexton's departure.

Jimmy MEADOWS

Position	Right-back
Born	James Meadows, Bolton, 21 July 1931
Died	16 January 1994
Height	6ft 0in
Weight	12st 1lb
Clubs	Southport, Manchester City
England Caps	1
	1955 v Scotland (won 7–2)

A WINGER WHO CONVERTED to full-back, Jimmy Meadows began his Football League career with Southport. In March 1951 he moved to Manchester City and while with the Maine Road club he won his one and only cap when he played in England's 7–2 victory over Scotland at Wembley.

An injury he received in the 1955 FA Cup Final defeat by Newcastle United brought a premature end to his playing career.

Meadows joined the club's training staff and remained at Maine Road until the mid-1960s, when he was appointed manager of Stockport County. He led the Edgeley Park club to the Fourth Division Championship in 1966/67 before leaving to become assistant manager of Bury. He later held a similar post with Blackpool before becoming manager of Bolton Wanderers. His stay at Burnden Park was brief and he left to take over the reins at Southport. After taking the Sandgrounders to the Fourth Division title in 1972/73, he had spells coaching in both Kuwait and Sweden.

Ken ARMSTRONG

Position	Right-half
Born	Kenneth Armstrong, Bradford, 3 June 1924
Died	New Zealand, 13 June 1984
Height	5ft 8in
Weight	11st 0lb
Clubs	Chelsea
England Caps	1
	1955 v Scotland (won 7–2)

A MEMBER OF Chelsea's League Championship-winning side of 1954/55, Ken Armstrong's outstanding displays earned him full international honours, playing with Chelsea colleague Frank Blunstone in England's 7–2 win over Scotland at Wembley.

Armstrong played his early football for Bradford Rovers and in the Army before joining Chelsea in December 1946. Constructive, enthusiastic and tenacious to a degree, he could also play in a number of other positions and often turned out at centre- or inside-forward. When he did so he rarely failed to get on the scoresheet. Armstrong went on to play 362 League games for Chelsea – a club record until surpassed by Peter Bonetti in 1969/70 – before emigrating for New Zealand in the summer of 1957.

In New Zealand, Armstrong played for Eastern Union, Gisborne City and North Shore United, his performances leading to him making 13 appearances for the New Zealand national side. Later made chief coach to the New Zealand FA, he retired from playing at the age of 47. His son Ron also appeared for New Zealand on 27 occasions.

Duncan EDWARDS

Position	Left-half
Born	Duncan Edwards, Dudley, 1 October 1936
Died	Munich, 21 February 1958
Height	5ft 11in
Weight	13st 0lb
Clubs	Manchester United
England Caps	18 Goals 5

1955 v Scotand (won 7–2), v France (lost 0–1), v Spain (1–1), v Portugal (lost 1–3)
1956 v Scotland (1–1), v Brazil (won 4–2), v Sweden (0–0), v Finland (won 5–1),
   v W. Germany (won 3–1) 1 goal, v N. Ireland (1–1), v Denmark (won 5–2) 2 goals
1957 v Scotland (won 2–1) 1 goal, v Eire (won 5–1), v Denmark (won 4–1), v Eire (1–1),
   v Wales (won 4–0), v N. Ireland (lost 2–3) 1 goal, v France (won 4–0)

DUNCAN EDWARDS was the youngest-ever England player when he was given his first cap against Scotland in April 1955 at the age of 18 years 183 days. After England beat West Germany 3–1 in the Olympic Stadium in Berlin in 1956, he became known as 'Boom Boom' on account of the power he packed into his shots. Receiving the ball on the left of his own penalty area from keeper Reg Matthews, he beat one man and advanced to the halfway line. He beat another, then three more inside the German half and then, from fully 30 yards out, he hit a left-footer into the roof of the net like a rocket.

Snatched from under the noses of several Midlands clubs, Duncan Edwards began his career with Manchester United. Once at Old Trafford he soon impressed, making an immediate impact in the newly launched FA Youth Cup in 1952/53. He played a big part in helping United establish themselves as the masters of the Youth Cup, as they won the competition for five successive seasons following its inception – Edwards playing in the first three.

Duncan Edwards in action in January 1958. (Getty Images)

He made his League debut at the age of 16 years 185 days, and by the time he had reached 20 he was controlling games to such an extent that people were hailing him as the most complete footballer of any era.

'Big Dunc' was the golden youth who could well have become the greatest soccer immortal of them all had his career not been cut short scarcely after it had begun. The Munich Air Crash in February 1958 not only crushed the might of a fine Manchester United side but denied supporters the world over the opportunity of watching this Black Country boy so dedicated to the game he loved. After 15 days fighting as valiantly for his life as he had fought on a football field, he died aged only 21.

Peter SILLETT

Position	Right-back
Born	Richard Peter Sillett, Southampton, 1 February 1933
Died	14 March 1998
Height	6ft 2in
Weight	12st 7lb
Clubs	Southampton, Chelsea
England Caps	3
	1955 v France (lost 0–1), v Spain (1–1), v Portugal (lost 1–3)

PETER SILLETT WAS able to play on either flank, and his versatility meant that he was a regular member of the party selected for international matches – he travelled to the 1958 World Cup without getting a game. However, the lack of a regular partner at club level hampered his efforts to add to the three caps he won on the summer tour in 1955.

Sillett followed in his father's footsteps by joining his home-town club, Southampton. He played for the Saints for two seasons before being sold to Chelsea in May 1953 for 'financial reasons'. In his first season at Stamford Bridge he made only a dozen appearances, but midway through the next campaign he broke into the team and made a significant contribution to the Blues' League Championship triumph. A hard, uncompromising defender, his fiercely struck free kicks yielded a number of spectacular goals, perhaps none more so than the 40-yard effort against Manchester United in September 1959 that whistled past Harry Gregg into the net. However, the majority of his goals were from the penalty spot. An automatic choice for six seasons, he missed very few games except for the period following a knee operation. He succeeded Derek Saunders as Chelsea captain in 1959 but a broken leg in the third game of the 1961/62 season effectively ended his Chelsea career. Despite offers to join a number of League clubs, he opted to play non-League football for Guildford City, concerned that his leg would not be strong enough to cope with the demands of League football.

Ron FLOWERS

Position	Wing-half		
Born	Ronald Flowers, Edlington, 28 July 1934		
Height	5ft 11in		
Weight	12st 11lb		
Clubs	Wolverhampton Wanderers, Northampton Town		
England Caps	49	Goals	10
	1955 v France (lost 0–1)		
	1958 v Wales (2–2)		
	1959 v Scotland (won 1–0), v Italy (2–2), v Brazil (lost 0–2), v Peru (lost 1–4), v Mexico		
	(lost 1–2), v United States (won 8–1) 2 goals, v Wales (1–1), v Sweden (lost 2–3),		
	v N. Ireland (won 2–1)		

Ron Flowers of Wolves in action for
England. (Getty Images)

1960 v Scotland (1–1), v Yugoslavia (3–3), v Spain (lost 0–3), v Hungary (lost 0–2),
 v N. Ireland (won 5–2), v Luxembourg (won 9–0), v Spain (won 4–2), v Wales (won 5–1)
1961 v Scotland (won 9–3), v Mexico (won 8–0) 1 goal, v Portugal (1–1) 1 goal, v Italy
 (won 3–2), v Austria (lost 1–3), v Luxembourg (won 4–1), v Wales (1–1), v Portugal
 (won 2–0), v N. Ireland (1–1)
1962 v Austria (won 3–1) 1 goal, v Scotland (lost 0–2), v Switzerland (won 3–1) 1 goal,
 v Peru (won 4–0) 1 goal, v Hungary (lost 1–2) 1 goal, Argentina (won 3–1) 1 goal,
 v Bulgaria (0–0), v Brazil (lost 1–3), v France (1–1) 1 goal, v N. Ireland (won 3–1),
 v Wales (won 4–0)
1963 v France (lost 2–5), v Scotland (lost 1–2), v Switzerland (won 8–1)
1964 v Eire (won 3–1), v United States (won 10–0), v Portugal (1–1), v Wales (won 2–1),
 v Holland (1–1)
1965 v W. Germany (won 1–0)
1966 v Norway (won 6–1)

RON FLOWERS joined the Wolves nursery side Wath Wanderers in the summer of
1950, before turning professional two years later. He scored on his debut in a 3–2
defeat at Blackpool and thereafter was a virtual ever-present in the Molineux club's
side. After helping Wolves win the League Championship in 1953/54, he began to
produce performances that led to his winning the first of 49 caps for England when
he played against France in May 1955. His last game for England came 11 years later
in a 6–1 win over Norway in 1966, the year in which he was a member of England's
World Cup forty.

Flowers won further League Championship medals in 1957/58 and 1958/59, and
in 1960 won an FA Cup winners' medal when Wolves beat Blackburn Rovers 3–0. He
spent 15 years as a professional at Molineux, scoring 37 goals in 512 games before
joining Northampton Town in September 1967.

Flowers later became player-coach of the Cobblers before becoming player-
manager of non-League Wellington Town, whom he guided to the FA Trophy Final,
by which time they had been renamed Telford United. In 1971 he left the club to run
his own sports shop in Wolverhampton.

Ron BAYNHAM

Position	Goalkeeper
Born	Ronald Leslie Baynham, Birmingham, 10 June 1929
Height	6ft 0in
Weight	12st 2lb
Clubs	Luton Town
England Caps	3
	1955 v Denmark (won 5–1), v N. Ireland (won 3–0), v Spain (won 4–1)

RON BAYNHAM made his breakthrough at the highest level during the 1955/56 season, making three full international appearances for England. It came as a great shock when he was left out of the party to tour Europe at the end of the season, but he had played for the Football League in an unexpected defeat by the Irish League and this was put forward as the explanation for his omission from the England line up.

Baynham did not play any competitive football until serving in the Army, where he impressed Wolves' manager Stan Cullis, who arranged a trial for the young keeper. Baynham, however, failed to turn up at Molineux, thinking he wasn't good enough. After spells with Erdington Rovers and Bromford Amateurs, he joined Worcester City. Within two years he was on his way to Luton Town, where, after a series of impressive displays, he displaced England keeper Bernard Streten. He quickly developed into one of the club's best-ever keepers, his judgement and all-round efficiency aided by his height and litheness. Baynham missed very few games for the Hatters and was in goal when they lost 2–1 to Nottingham Forest in the 1959 FA Cup Final. Despite relegation the following season, he kept his place in the Luton side for a further five seasons, clocking up 432 appearances.

Forced to retire through injury, it was later discovered that Baynham had played with part of his pelvic structure pulled away following torn muscles and tendons, a condition that only by great good fortune had not left him crippled.

Jeff HALL

Position	Right-back
Born	Jeffrey James Hall, Scunthorpe, 7 September 1929
Died	Birmingham, 4 April 1959
Height	5ft 8in
Weight	11st 4lb
Clubs	Birmingham City
England Caps	17
	1955 v Denmark (won 5–1), v Wales (lost 1–2), v N. Ireland (won 3–0), v Spain (won 4–1)
	1956 v Scotland (1–1), v Brazil (won 4–2), v Sweden (0–0), v Finland (won 5–1), v W. Germany (won 3–1), v N. Ireland (1–1), v Wales (won 3–1), v Yugoslavia (won 3–0),
	v Denmark (won 5–2)
	1957 v Scotland (won 2–1), v Eire (won 5–1), v Denmark (won 4–1), v Eire (1–1)

DURING THE COURSE OF the 1955/56 season, in which Birmingham City reached the FA Cup Final, Jeff Hall won the first of 17 full caps for England in the 5–1 win over Denmark in Copenhagen. Hall in fact was only on the losing side once during his lengthy international career.

Though he didn't consider himself good enough for League football, Jeff Hall signed professional forms for Birmingham City in May 1950. After being converted from right-half to full-back and turning in a number of solid performances for the club's reserve side, he made his League debut against Bury in January 1951. After a handful of appearances the following season, he established himself as a first-team regular in 1952/53 and during the following campaign he scored his only goal for the club in a 3–2 defeat of Stoke City, when he was asked to play outside-right in an emergency. He helped the Blues win the Second Division Championship in 1954/55 and the following season he was part of the team that reached the FA Cup Final, where they lost 3–1 to Manchester City.

Hall had appeared in 265 games for Birmingham when he contracted polio and died at the tragically young age of 29. A Jeff Hall memorial scoreboard and clock were erected at the City End of St Andrew's to commemorate a player whose death was a sad loss to both Birmingham City and England.

Geoff BRADFORD

Position	Inside-forward
Born	Geoffrey Reginald William Bradford, Bristol, 18 July 1928
Died	Bristol, 31 December 1994
Height	6ft 1in
Weight	12st 7lb
Clubs	Bristol Rovers
England Caps	1 Goals 1
	1955 v Denmark (won 5–1) 1 goal

GEOFF BRADFORD is the only Bristol Rovers player ever to turn out for England. He scored in a 5–1 win over Denmark, but was never given another chance to represent his country.

Without doubt Bradford was Rovers' greatest-ever player. Not only was he the club's most prolific scorer, with 260 goals in 511 League and Cup games, but he also possessed a technical talent that enabled him to do his job with ruthless efficiency. He was as clean, accurate and powerful a striker of the ball as could be found anywhere outside the top flight. He could hit the target with either foot, had splendid ball control and an intuitive aerial ability. He also possessed a natural resilience that saw him bounce back from serious leg injuries sustained at Plymouth in 1953 and Doncaster in 1956.

When Rovers won the Third Division (South) Championship in 1952/53, he netted a hat-trick against Newport County, which clinched promotion to the second Division, and then on the opening day of the new season in the higher grade he scored another treble against Fulham. One of his best performances was reserved for his comeback game following his horrific injury against Plymouth when, after a six-month lay-off, he returned with his knee swathed in bandages to score yet another hat-trick, against Stoke City at Eastville.

Ronnie CLAYTON

Position	Right-half
Born	Ronald Clayton, Preston, 5 August 1934
Height	5ft 10in
Weight	11st 4lb
Clubs	Blackburn Rovers
England Caps	35

1955 v N. Ireland (won 3–0), v Spain (won 4–1)

1956 v Brazil (won 4–2), v Sweden (0–0), v Finland (won 5–1), v W. Germany (won 3–1), v N. Ireland (1–1), v Wales (won 3–1), v Yugoslavia (won 3–0), v Denmark (won 5–2)

1957 v Scotland (won 2–1), v Eire (won 5–1), v Denmark (won 4–1), v Eire (1–1), v Wales (won 4–0), v N. Ireland (lost 2–3), v France (won 4–0)

1958 v Scotland (won 4–0), v Portugal (won 2–1), v Yugoslavia (lost 0–5), v Soviet Union (lost 0–1), v N. Ireland (3–3), v Soviet Union (won 5–0), v Wales (2–2)

1959 v Scotland (won 1–0), v Italy (2–2), v Brazil (lost 0–2), v Peru (lost 1–4), v Mexico (lost 1–2), v United States (won 8–1), v Wales (1–1), v Sweden (lost 2–3), v N. Ireland (won 2–1)

1960 v Scotland (1–1), v Yugoslavia (3–3)

RONNIE CLAYTON made his League debut for Blackburn Rovers at the age of 16 in the final game of the 1950/51 season. He had natural leadership qualities which showed early in his career. In September 1955 he won his first Under-23 cap and a month later he appeared for the England 'B' team. In November of that year he completed the international sequence when he made his debut for the full England team.

Clayton was a tremendous driving force in Blackburn's promotion back to the First Division in 1957/58. An energetic wing-half, strong in the tackle and a brilliant timer of the ball in the air, he also liked to power forward and instigate attacking moves. He appeared in the final stages of the 1958 World Cup in Sweden and succeeded Billy Wright as captain for the last five of his 35 England appearances. He then lost favour with the England selectors and surprisingly didn't play again for his country after 1960. He continued to give good service to Blackburn, leading them to Wembley in 1960, only for them to lose 3–0 to Wolverhampton Wanderers. Remaining loyal to what many would class an unfashionable club, Ronnie Clayton experienced the highs and lows but always maintained the same level of enthusiasm and endeavour. As age began to slow him down he moved to play at the heart of the defence, where his reading of the game provided the solid defensive platform for the team. He had appeared in 665 games for Blackburn when he left Ewood Park to become player-manager of Morecambe. He later returned to north-east Lancashire to end his career with Great Harwood.

Ronnie Clayton of Blackburn Rovers.
(Lancashire Evening Post)

England! England! - *Ronnie Clayton* **97**

Bill PERRY

Position	Outside-left
Born	William Perry, Johannesburg, 10 September 1930
Height	5ft 8in
Weight	10st 7lb
Clubs	Blackpool, Southport
England Caps	3 Goals 2
	1955 v N. Ireland (won 2–0), v Spain (won 4–1) 2 goals
	1956 v Scotland (1–1)

WHEN BLACKPOOL FINISHED runners-up to Manchester United in 1955/56, their highest-ever position in the Football League, Bill Perry's goalscoring exploits led to him winning the first of three full caps for England, against Northern Ireland, qualifying due to his father's birthplace.

Bill Perry was recommended to Blackpool by former Bolton Wanderers star Billy Butler, who managed Johannesburg Rangers for whom Perry was playing at the time. He had earlier turned down a move to Charlton Athletic but the lure of First Division football with the Seasiders won him over. Though not a prolific scorer, he did hit a number of vital goals, including the winner against Birmingham City in the FA Cup semi-final replay of 1951. The Seasiders lost 2–0 to Newcastle United in the final. When Blackpool returned to Wembley two years later, Bill Perry scored the injury-time winner in the 4–3 defeat of Bolton Wanderers. Perry netted his first hat-trick for the club in April 1955 in a 6–1 win at Manchester City, a prelude to his best season in terms of goals scored, 20 in 1955/56.

A cartilage operation virtually ended his Bloomfield Road career and when he left the club in 1962 he had scored 129 goals in 436 League and Cup games. He had a season with Southport before trying his luck in Australia. On his return to England he set up in business as a promotional match-book manufacturer.

John ATYEO

Position	Centre-forward
Born	Peter John Walter Atyeo, Westbury, 7 February 1932
Died	Bristol, 16 June 1993
Height	6ft 0in
Weight	12st 4lb
Clubs	Portsmouth, Bristol City
England Caps	6 Goals 5
	1955 v Spain (won 4–1) 1 goal
	1956 v Brazil (won 4–2), v Sweden (0–0)
	1957 v Eire (won 5–1) 2 goals, v Denmark (won 4–1) 1 goal, v Eire (1–1) 1 goal

THE GREATEST GOALSCORER in the history of Bristol City and the holder of the Robins' appearance record, John Atyeo won selection for an FA XI, and this was quickly followed by England Under-23 and 'B' caps. He made his full international debut in November 1955 when he scored in a 4–1 win over Spain. He went on to score five goals in six games for England, his last coming in a World Cup qualifier against Eire.

Atyeo was playing in the Wiltshire League for Westbury when he signed amateur forms for Portsmouth. However, when the Portsmouth management asked him to live locally, Atyeo, who had played in two First Division games for Pompey, left to join Bristol City. He was City's leading scorer in 11 of his 15 seasons at Ashton Gate, with a best of 29 goals in 1955/56. The following season he scored the club's fastest-ever goal after just nine seconds of the match against Bury. When the Robins beat Chichester City 11–0 in the first round of the 1960–61 FA Cup competition, John Atyeo, who netted 16 hat-tricks for the club, scored five of the goals. Despite the interest of a number of bigger clubs, including Chelsea and Liverpool, he remained loyal to Bristol City.

Throughout his career, in which he scored 351 goals in 645 games, Atyeo remained a part-time professional, finally qualifying as a quantity surveyor and later as a teacher.

Reg MATTHEWS

Position	Goalkeeper
Born	Reginald Derrick Matthews, Coventry, 20 December 1932
Died	7 October 2001
Height	5ft 11in
Weight	11st 7lb
Clubs	Coventry City, Chelsea, Derby County
England Caps	5
	1956 v Scotland (1–1), v Brazil (won 4–2), v Sweden (0–0), v W. Germany (won 3–1), v N. Ireland (1–1)

REG MATTHEWS joined his home-town club Coventry City, where he soon became the undisputed star of an ailing Highfield Road side.

He progressed through the England ranks at Under-23 and 'B' team level, but because England had an embarrassing supply of international-class goalkeepers, including Bert Williams and Gil Merrick, many thought it would be impossible for a Third Division player to break into the England team. However, with some stirring performances for Coventry keeping him in the headlines, he eventually made his international debut against Scotland at Hampden Park in April 1956 and gave a creditable performance in a 1–1 draw.

Coventry directors constantly denied that he would move on, but the club had struggled to maintain an average side since being relegated in the early 1950s and any player of potential was soon sold. Practically overnight, Reg Matthews left Coventry for Chelsea for a then record fee for a goalkeeper of £22,500 in November 1956.

His move to Stamford Bridge was probably the biggest mistake Matthews ever made. Unable to settle in London, he continued to live in Coventry and so was unable to train with his new team-mates on a regular basis. Soon he was facing fierce competition from Peter Bonetti, and in October 1961 he moved to Derby County. His acrobatic saves and courage in hurling himself at forwards' feet were adored by County fans and he set a club record, later beaten by Colin Boulton, for goalkeeping appearances.

Colin GRAINGER

Position	Outside-left
Born	Colin Grainger, Havercroft, 10 June 1933
Height	5ft 9in
Weight	10st 12lb
Clubs	Wrexham, Sheffield United, Sunderland, Leeds United, Port Vale, Doncaster Rovers
England Caps	7 Goals 3
	1956 v Brazil (won 4–2) 2 goals, v Sweden (0–0), v Finland (won 5–1), v W. Germany
	(won 3–1) 1 goal, v N. Ireland (1–1), v Wales (won 3–1)
	1957 v Scotland (won 2–1)

COLIN GRAINGER, the 'singing winger', a well-known crooner on the Northern pub and club circuit, began his career with Wrexham, turning professional in 1950. In July 1953 he joined Sheffield United and it was while at Bramall Lane that he won the first of his seven England caps, netting twice in a 4–2 win over Brazil at Wembley. He had scored 26 goals in 88 games for the Blades when Sunderland signed him for a fee of £7,000 in February 1957. Grainger missed very few games over the next three seasons. In the 1957/58 season, despite the club being relegated to the Second Division for the first time in their history, Grainger was one of Sunderland's better players, his performances earning him his final cap against Scotland at Wembley.

In August 1960 he was on the move again, this time to Leeds United. The fast, direct winger failed to find his form at Elland Road and within a little over a year had signed for Port Vale. Injuries restricted his appearances for the Valiants and he moved to Doncaster Rovers before ending his career with then non-League Macclesfield Town.

Gordon ASTALL

Position	Outside-right
Born	Gordon Astall, Horwich, 22 September 1927
Height	5ft 9in
Weight	11st 13lb
Clubs	Plymouth Argyle, Birmingham City, Torquay United
England Caps	2 Goals 2
	1956 v Finland (won 5–1) 1 goal, v W. Germany (won 3–1) 1 goal

GORDON ASTALL won international recognition during Birmingham City's run to the 1956 FA Cup Final, scoring in each of his international appearances as England beat Finland and West Germany.

Astall began his career as an amateur with Southampton before joining Plymouth Argyle while serving with the Royal Marines. During his six seasons at Home Park, he scored 42 goals in 188 games and helped Argyle win the Third Division (South) Championship in 1951/52. In October 1953 he was transferred to Birmingham City and soon settled into the St Andrew's side, teaming up with Noel Kinsey in the Blues' attack. He was an important member of the Blues' Second Division Championship-winning side of 1954/55, scoring 11 goals in 33 games. In 1955/56 he had his best season in terms of goals scored, netting 12 in the League and another three in the club's run to Wembley, including one in the semi-final victory over Sunderland. A member of the City side that lost to Barcelona in the final of the Inter Cities Fairs Cup, he went on to score 67 goals in 271 games before leaving St Andrew's to join Torquay United, where he took his tally of goals to 112, a good return for a winger.

Johnny BROOKS

Position	Inside-forward
Born	John Brooks, Reading, 23 December 1931
Height	5ft 10in
Weight	11st 9lb
Clubs	Reading, Tottenham Hotspur, Chelsea, Brentford, Crystal Palace
England Caps	3 Goals 2
	1956 v Wales (won 3–1) 1 goal, v Yugoslavia (won 3–0) 1 goal, v Denmark (won 5–2)

A NATURALLY GIFTED PLAYER, Johnny Brooks had brilliant dribbling skills and an amazing body swerve. He also possessed a superb touch with either foot and his shooting ability soon caught the eye of the England selectors. He won his first cap against Wales in November 1956 and scored, as he did in his second match against Yugoslavia. However, his third, against Denmark, was his last as he did not fit in with Johnny Haynes, England's senior schemer.

After beginning his career with his home-town club Reading, Brooks joined First Division Tottenham Hotspur, where he at first found it difficult stepping up to the higher grade of football as Arthur Rowe set about major surgery to his beloved 'push and run' title winners. However, by the end of the 1954/55 season he had established a regular place and when Eddie Baily left in January 1956 he assumed the main creative role. In December 1959 he moved to Chelsea in a £20,000 part-exchange deal for Les Allen. Having helped stave off relegation, he didn't stay long at Stamford Bridge, seeing out the rest of his career in the lower divisions with Brentford and Crystal Palace, helping the Bees win the Fourth Division Championship.

Alan HODGKINSON

Position	Goalkeeper
Born	Alan Hodgkinson, Rotherham, 18 August 1936
Height	5ft 9in
Weight	11st 5lb
Clubs	Sheffield United
England Caps	5
	1957 v Scotland (won 2–1), v Eire (won 5–1), v Denmark (won 4–1), v Eire (1–1)
	1960 v Wales (won 5–1)

ALAN HODGKINSON, who won the first of his five international caps against Scotland in 1957, was in contention for an England place for several years, and in 1962 he travelled to Chile with England's World Cup squad as reserve goalkeeper.

Hodgkinson was playing non-League football for Worksop Town when Sheffield United manager Ray Freeman persuaded him to join the Bramall Lane club. The Blades' first-choice keeper was Ted Burgin, known to supporters as 'The Cat'. Though he was never awarded a full cap, Burgin was chosen for the England 'B' team, was an England reserve and went on the FA tour of Australia, and he was to teach Hodgkinson many of the arts and crafts of goalkeeping, often during the many afternoons they returned for extra training. Over the next couple of years, Hodgkinson learned a great deal playing for the Army while completing his National Service. He played in what might be termed 'a fairly useful side' with players of the calibre of Bobby Charlton, Duncan Edwards, Cliff Jones and Dave Mackay in the team! On his return to Bramall Lane, he became the Blades' first-choice keeper and in 1956/57 he represented the Football League against the Scottish League.

Only Joe Shaw, who played in 631 League games, made more appearances for Sheffield than Alan Hodgkinson, who appeared in 576. One of Britain's most respected goalkeeping coaches, he now coaches custodians all over the British Isles, including the Scottish national team.

Derek KEVAN

Position	Inside-forward
Born	Derek Tennyson Kevan, Ripon, 6 March 1935
Height	5ft 11in
Weight	12st 13lb
Clubs	Bradford Park Avenue, West Bromwich Albion, Chelsea, Manchester City, Crystal Palace, Peterborough United, Luton Town, Stockport County
England Caps	14 Goals 8
	1957 v Scotland (won 2–1) 1 goal, v Wales (won 4–0), v N. Ireland (lost 2–3)
	1958 v Scotland (won 4–0) 2 goals, v Portugal (won 2–1), v Yugoslavia (lost 0–5), v Soviet Union (1–1) 1 goal, v Soviet Union (2–2) 1 goal, v Brazil (0–0), v Austria (2–2) 1 goal, v Soviet Union (lost 0–1)
	1959 v Mexico (lost 1–2) 1 goal, v United States (won 8–1) 1 goal
	1961 v Mexico (won 8–0)

ALTHOUGH HE LACKED finesse, Derek Kevan made up for it with pure strength, often bulldozing his way through both First Division and international defences – he scored eight goals in 14 England appearances, including one on his debut as England beat Scotland 2–1 at Wembley in 1957.

Derek 'The Tank' Kevan became Vic Buckingham's first signing for West Bromwich Albion when the latter bought him from his own former club Bradford Park Avenue. He remained at the Hawthorns for the next ten years, usually as top scorer. In 300 games for the Albion he scored almost 200 goals, including five in one First Division game against Everton in 1960. In 1961/62 he topped the First Division scoring charts with an Albion post-war best of 33 goals, and the following year, when he was surprisingly sold to Chelsea after falling out with manager Archie Macaulay, he scored a hat-trick on his final Albion appearance. Another disagreement, this time with Chelsea manager Tommy Docherty, resulted in his stay at Stamford Bridge being a brief one and after just seven games he was on his way to Manchester City, where his 30 goals helped the Maine Road side return to the top flight. Unsuccessful spells at Crystal Palace, Peterborough and Luton Town followed before he won the first medal of his career with Fourth Division Stockport County in 1967.

David PEGG

Position	Outside-left
Born	David Pegg, Doncaster, 20 September 1935
Died	Munich, 6 February 1958
Height	5ft 10in
Weight	11st 11lb
Clubs	Manchester United
England Caps	1
	1957 v Eire (1–1)

WINGER DAVID PEGG played for England at Schoolboy, 'B' and Under-23 levels before he was capped at full level in May 1957 in a 1–1 draw against Eire in a World Cup qualifying match.

Pegg joined Manchester United straight from school and was a member of the club's splendid left-wing trio – Duncan Edwards and Albert Scanlon were the others – who destroyed Wolverhampton Wanderers in the first leg of the first-ever FA Youth Cup Final in 1953. That evening Pegg played at inside-left as United built up a 7–1 lead over the Molineux club, but it was at outside-left that he played all his first-team games for the Reds. He made his League debut for United just three months after his 17th birthday as they beat Middlesbrough 3–2, and went on to win two League Championship medals, in 1955/56 and 1956/57, and to play in the 1957 FA Cup Final, which United lost 2–1 to Aston Villa. He later came under pressure from Albert Scanlon and, just prior to the European Cup match against Red Star Belgrade, lost his place. However, he still made that fateful trip which was to cost him his life.

Eddie HOPKINSON

Position	Goalkeeper
Born	Edward Hopkinson, Wheatley Hill, 19 October 1935
Height	5ft 9in
Weight	11st 7lb
Clubs	Oldham Athletic, Bolton Wanderers
England Caps	14

1957 v Wales (won 4–0), v N. Ireland (lost 2–3), v France (won 4–0)
1958 v Scotland (won 4–0), v Portugal (won 2–1), v Yugoslavia (lost 0–5)
1959 v Scotland (won 1–0), v Italy (2–2), v Brazil (lost 0–2), v Peru (lost 1–4), v Mexico (lost 1–2), v United States (won 8–1), v Wales (1–1), v Sweden (lost 2–3)

DESPITE BEING ONE OF the smallest goalkeepers in the First Division, Eddie Hopkinson made his first full international appearance against Wales in October 1957, going on to play against all three countries in the Home Internationals and eventually collecting 14 caps.

Eddie Hopkinson of Bolton Wanderers. (Lancashire Evening Post)

The holder of Bolton Wanderers' appearance record, with 578 first-team outings between 1956 and 1969, Eddie Hopkinson began his career with Oldham Athletic and was only 16 years old when he played in three Third Division (North) games for the Latics. He joined the Wanderers in 1952 but only won a regular place when the club's first-choice keeper Ken Grieves couldn't be released from his cricketing duties with Lancashire, who were chasing Championship honours. Hopkinson kept a clean sheet in the 1958 FA Cup Final as Bolton beat Manchester United 2–0 at Wembley and was a virtual ever-present for Bolton over the next ten years. At Norwich, in January 1969, he broke the club's long-standing appearance record set by Alex Finney, and but for an injury that kept him out of the side for most of the 1958/59 season, and another that put him out of action for a 10-match spell in 1963/64, he would have passed Finney's record much earlier.

After injury finally forced his retirement, he became assistant-trainer at Burnden Park before joining Stockport County as assistant manager. He later rejoined the Wanderers as a goalkeeping coach but eventually left the game to work for a chemical company.

Don HOWE

Position	Right-back
Born	Donald Howe, Wolverhampton, 12 October 1935
Height	5ft 11in
Weight	10st 13lb
Clubs	West Bromwich Albion, Arsenal
England Caps	23

1957 v Wales (won 4–0), v N. Ireland (lost 2–3), v France (won 4–0)

1958 v Scotland (won 4–0), v Portugal (won 2–1), v Yugoslavia (lost 0–5), v Soviet Union (1–1), v Soviet Union (2–2), v Brazil (0–0), v Austria (2–2), v Soviet Union (lost 0–1), v N. Ireland (3–3), v Soviet Union (won 5–0), v Wales (2–2)

1959 v Scotland (won 1–0), v Italy (2–2), v Brazil (lost 0–2), v Peru (lost 1–4), v Mexico (lost 1–2), v United States (won 8–1), v Wales (1–1), v Sweden (lost 2–3), v N. Ireland (won 2–1)

THOUGH HE JOINED West Bromwich Albion soon after his 17th birthday in October 1952, Don Howe had to wait almost three years before making his League debut, gaining a regular place afterwards. While with the Albion, he played in 23 consecutive international matches for England and appeared in the 1958 World Cup Finals in Sweden.

Howe spent nearly 12 years at the Hawthorns, playing in almost 400 games and scoring 19 goals, mostly from the penalty spot, although he did have short spells in midfield and up front. Very outspoken as a player, he led the players' 'strike' at the Hawthorns in 1962/63 before leaving the club the following year to sign for Arsenal at what was then a record fee for a full-back of £40,000. During the course of the 1964/65 campaign, Howe was made club captain but the following season he broke a leg in a match against Blackpool at Highbury. Over the next two years he tried un-successfully to regain full fitness and eventually became the club's reserve-team coach.

Following Dave Sexton's departure he was appointed Arsenal's first-team coach and was the mastermind behind the Gunners' double-winning side of 1970/71. He left Arsenal amid great controversy to join West Bromwich Albion as manager in July 1971. After spells at Galatasaray and Leeds as coach, he rejoined Arsenal as chief coach. Around this time he took on the role of coach to the England national team. Later he spent two years as manager of Arsenal, before coaching spells with Wimbledon and Queen's Park Rangers and another spell in management with Coventry City. Appointed technical coaching director in the England set-up, he later became a media commentator, covering Italian football for Channel Four.

Bryan DOUGLAS

Position	Forward
Born	Bryan Douglas, Blackburn, 27 May 1934
Height	5ft 5in
Weight	9st 10lb
Clubs	Blackburn Rovers
England Caps	36 Goals 10

1957 v Wales (won 4–0), v N. Ireland (lost 2–3), v France (won 4–0)
1958 v Scotland (won 4–0) 1 goal, v Portugal (won 2–1), v Yugoslavia (lost 0–5), v Soviet Union (1–1), v Soviet Union (2–2), v Brazil (0–0), v Austria (2–2), v Wales (2–2)
1959 v Scotland (won 1–0)
1960 v Yugoslavia (3–3), v Hungary (lost 0–2), v N. Ireland (won 5–2) 1 goal, v Luxembourg (won 9–0), v Spain (won 4–2) 1 goal, v Wales (won 5–1)
1961 v Scotland (won 9–3) 1 goal, v Mexico (won 8–0) 2 goals, v Portugal (1–1), v Italy (won 3–2), v Austria (lost 1–3), v Luxembourg (won 4–1), v Wales (1–1) 1 goal, v Portugal (won 2–0), v N. Ireland (1–1)
1962 v Scotland (lost 0–2), v Peru (won 4–0), v Hungary (lost 1–2), v Argentina (won 3–1), v Bulgaria (0–0), v Brazil (lost 1–3)
1963 v Scotland (lost 1–2) 1 goal, v Brazil (1–1) 1 goal, v Switzerland (won 8–1) 1 goal

BRYAN DOUGLAS joined his home-town club Blackburn Rovers, but National Service disrupted his early career and he did not make his debut until September 1954. During his early days in the team he was often criticized for being over-elaborate and too selfish. Deceptively frail-looking, he was later to confound the critics and become one of England's greatest post-war footballers. He made his England debut during Rovers' promotion-winning season of 1957/58, wearing Stanley Matthews' No. 7 shirt. Considering Douglas played in the era of Finney, Matthews, Charlton, Haynes and Greaves, he did well to appear for his country so often.

Blackburn preferred to use Douglas as a scheming inside-forward. He had the most perfect close control you could hope to see. His shuffling feet carved up opposing defences for more than a decade, during which he helped a succession of forwards – notably Fred Pickering and Andy McEvoy – to become frequent goalscorers. A member of the Blackburn side that reached the 1960 FA Cup Final, he played in all four of England's games in the 1962 World Cup Finals in Chile. A cartilage operation coupled with other injuries meant that he missed most of Blackburn's struggle against relegation in 1965/66.

Douglas' final years at Ewood Park were dogged by injury and at the end of the 1968/69 season, after which he had scored 111 goals in 503 games, he left the club and spent a couple of seasons playing non-League football for Great Harwood with Ronnie Clayton and Roy Vernon.

Alan A'COURT

Position	Outside-left
Born	Alan A'Court, Rainhill, 30 September 1934
Height	5ft 8in
Weight	10st 7lb
Clubs	Liverpool, Tranmere Rovers
England Caps	5 Goals 1
	1957 v N. Ireland (lost 2–3) 1 goal
	1958 v Brazil (0–0), v Austria (2–2), v Soviet Union (lost 0–1), v Wales (2–2)

AFTER JOINING LIVERPOOL on his 18th birthday, winger Alan A'Court made his debut in a 3–2 win at Middlesbrough, but over the next two seasons he drifted in and out of the side, only getting a chance when Scottish international Billy Liddell was selected at centre-forward. He eventually established himself in the side during the Reds' first season following relegation to the Second Division and was an important member of the team that achieved promotion in 1961/62. After representing the Football League and making seven appearances for England Under-23s, he made his full international debut against Northern Ireland in 1957, scoring in a 3–2 defeat. The following year he appeared in the World Cup Finals in Sweden.

With the emergence of Peter Thompson, A'Court found himself squeezed out of the Liverpool side, so, after scoring 63 goals in 362 games, he left to join Tranmere Rovers. He spent two seasons at Prenton Park, helping Rovers finish fifth in the Fourth Division in each campaign, and netted his only Football League hat-trick in a 4–2 win at Bradford City.

On leaving Tranmere, he held various coaching jobs at Norwich, Chester, Crewe and Stoke, as well as in Zambia.

Bobby ROBSON

Position	Wing-half/Inside-forward
Born	Robert William Robson, Sacriston, 18 February 1933
Height	5ft 10in
Weight	11st 10lb
Clubs	Fulham, West Bromwich Albion
England Caps	20 Goals 4
	1957 v France (won 4–0) 2 goals
	1958 v Soviet Union (1–1), v Soviet Union (2–2), v Brazil (0–0), v Austria (2–2)

1960 v Spain (lost 0–3), v Hungary (lost 0–2), v N. Ireland (won 5–2), v Luxembourg
(won 9–0), v Spain (won 4–2), v Wales (won 5–1)
1961 v Scotland (won 9–3) 1 goal, v Mexico (won 8–0) 1 goal, v Portugal (1–1), v Italy (won
3–2), v Luxembourg (won 4–1), v Wales (1–1), v Portugal (won 2–0), v N. Ireland (1–1)
1962 v Switzerland (won 3–1)

ONE OF THE GAME'S most successful managers, Bobby Robson began his career as an
amateur with Middlesbrough but was playing for another local side, Langley Park
Juniors, when Fulham manager Bill Dodgin secured his services in May 1950. He
soon established himself in the Cottagers' side and formed a good understanding with
Bedford Jezzard and, in particular, Johnny Haynes. Robson's performances attracted a
number of top-flight clubs and in March 1956 West Bromwich Albion manager Vic
Buckingham paid £25,000 to take him to the Hawthorns. In 1958 he renewed his

Bobby Robson, 17 August 1965. (Getty Images)

partnership with Johnny Haynes, scoring twice on his international debut as England beat France 4–0. Robson, like Haynes, lost his place in the international side after the 1962 World Cup finals.

During his seven seasons with Albion, Robson was converted from inside-forward to wing-half, but that didn't stop him scoring 61 goals in 240 League games for the Baggies. In the summer of 1962 he linked up with Haynes again, when he rejoined the Cottagers for a second spell. He took his tally of goals for Fulham to 80 in 370 games before leaving to manage Vancouver Royals. Within six months he was back at Craven Cottage as manager, but he was sacked a year later after failing to arrest the club's decline. After a short spell scouting for Chelsea, he was appointed manager of Ipswich Town. Gradually he put together a useful side and they finished fourth in the First Division in 1972/73 and 1973/74, third in 1974/75, 1976/77 and 1979/80, and runners-up in 1980/81 and 1981/82. The club won the UEFA Cup in 1980, but Robson's greatest triumph came in the 1978 FA Cup Final when Town beat Arsenal 1–0. In July 1982, Robson replaced Ron Greenwood as manager of England and in 1986 they reached the World Cup quarter-finals before losing to Argentina. In 1990 he took England to the World Cup semi-finals, where they were unfortunate to lose to West Germany on penalties. In August 1990 he took over at PSV Eindhoven, who won the Dutch title in 1990/91 and 1991/92. Robson later managed Sporting Lisbon and Benfica before replacing Ruud Gullit as manager of Newcastle United and leading the Magpies into Europe.

Jim LANGLEY

Position	Left-back
Born	Edward James Langley, Kilburn, 7 February 1929
Height	5ft 9in
Weight	11st 5lb
Clubs	Leeds United, Brighton and Hove Albion, Fulham, Queen's Park Rangers
England Caps	3
	1958 v Scotland (won 4–0), v Portugal (won 2–1), v Yugoslavia (lost 0–5)

AFTER PLAYING AS AN AMATEUR for Yiewsley, Hayes and Brentford, Jim Langley had nine League games as an outside-left for Leeds United. He then moved to Brighton and Hove Albion and was converted into a full-back, his performances for the Seagulls leading to three England 'B' caps and a place in the Football League side. In February 1957 he was transferred to Fulham and soon became a great favourite with the Craven Cottage crowd. He won three England caps and was a Fulham first-team regular for eight seasons, helping the club win promotion to the First Division in 1958/59. He had scored 33 goals in 356 games for Fulham when he was surprisingly allowed to join Queen's Park Rangers in the summer of 1965. He was a key member of the Rangers side that won the League Cup and Third Division Championship in 1966/67, but shortly afterwards Langley, who was only the second full-back in the League to score over 50 League goals, left to manage non-League Hillingdon Borough, whom he took to Wembley in 1971.

Bobby and Jackie Charlton, 1965.
(Getty Images)

Bobby CHARLTON

Position	Forward
Born	Robert Charlton, Ashington, 11 October 1937
Height	5ft 9in
Weight	11st 2lb
Clubs	Manchester United, Preston North End
England Caps	106 Goals 49

1958 v Scotland (won 4–0) 1 goal, v Portugal (won 2–1) 2 goals, v Yugoslavia (lost 0–5), v N. Ireland (3–3) 2 goals, v Soviet Union (won 5–0) 1 goal, v Wales (2–2)

1959 v Scotland (won 1–0), v Italy (2–2) 1 goal, v Brazil (lost 0–2), v Peru (lost 1–4), v Mexico (lost 1–2), v United States (won 8–1) 3 goals

1959 v Wales (1–1), v Sweden (lost 2–3) 1 goal

1960 v Scotland (1–1) 1 goal, v Yugoslavia (3–3), v Spain (lost 0–3), v Hungary (lost 0–2), v N. Ireland (won 5–2) 1 goal, v Luxembourg (won 9–0) 3 goals, v Spain (won 4–2), v Wales (won 5–1) 1 goal

1961 v Scotland (won 9–3), v Mexico (won 8–0) 3 goals, v Portugal (1–1), v Italy (won 3–2), v Austria (lost 1–3), v Luxembourg (won 4–1) 2 goals, v Wales (1–1), v Portugal (won 2–0), v N. Ireland (1–1) 1 goal

1962 v Austria (won 3–1) 1 goal, v Scotland (lost 0–2), v Switzerland (won 3–1), v Peru (won 4–0), v Hungary (lost 1–2), v Argentina (won 3–1) 1 goal, v Bulgaria (0–0), v Brazil (lost 1–3)

1963 v France (lost 2–5), v Scotland (lost 1–2), v Brazil (1–1), v Czechoslovakia (won 4–2) 1 goal, v E. Germany (won 2–1) 1 goal, v Switzerland (won 8–1) 3 goals, v Wales (won 4–0) 1 goal, v Rest of the World (won 2–1), v N. Ireland (won 8–3)

1964 v Scotland (lost 0–1), v Uruguay (won 2–1), v Portugal (won 4–3) 1 goal, v Eire (won 3–1), v United States (won 10–0) 1 goal, v Brazil (lost 1–5), v Argentina (lost 0–1), v N. Ireland (won 4–3), v Holland (1–1)

1965 v Scotland (2–2) 1 goal, v Wales (0–0), v Austria (lost 2–3) 1 goal, v N. Ireland (won 2–1), v Spain (won 2–0)

1966 v W. Germany (won 1–0), v Scotland (won 4–3) 1 goal, v Yugoslavia (won 2–0) 1 goal, v Finland (won 3–0), v Norway (won 6–1), v Poland (won 1–0), v Uruguay (0–0), v Mexico (won 2–0) 1 goal, v France (won 2–0), v Argentina (won 1–0), v Portugal (won 2–1) 2 goals, v W. Germany (won 4–2 aet), v N. Ireland (won 2–0), v Czechoslovakia (0–0), v Wales (won 5–1) 1 goal

1967 v Scotland (lost 2–3), v Wales (won 3–0) 1 goal, v N. Ireland (won 2–0) 1 goal, v Soviet Union (2–2)

1968 v Scotland (1–1), v Spain (won 1–0) 1 goal, v Spain (won 2–1), v Sweden (won 3–1) 1 goal, v Yugoslavia (lost 0–1), v Soviet Union (won 2–0) 1 goal, v Romania (0–0), v Bulgaria (1–1)

1969 v Romania (1–1), v N. Ireland (won 3–1), v Wales (won 2–1) 1 goal, v Scotland (won 4–1), v Mexico (0–0), v Brazil (lost 1–2), v Holland (won 1–0), v Portugal (won 1–0)

1970 v Holland (0–0), v Wales (1–1), v N. Ireland (won 3–1) 1 goal, v Colombia (won 4–0) 1 goal, v Ecuador (won 2–0), v Romania (won 1–0), v Brazil (lost 0–1), v Czechoslovakia (won 1–0), v W. Germany (lost 2–3 aet)

Honours	Footballer of the Year 1966, World Cup winners England 1966
	European Footballer of the Year 1966

IN FEBRUARY 1958 after a European Cup tie in Belgrade, Manchester United's plane crashed in thick snow at Munich Airport. Bobby Charlton was thrown 50 yards and escaped with just a deep cut to his head.

After his return to Old Trafford it didn't take long for Bobby to reach the footballing heights, for within a little over two months he made his international debut against Scotland, marking the occasion with a spectacular goal. By 1966 and the World Cup Finals in England, Charlton's skills had reached their full maturity. He opened England's scoring with a typical long-distance blast and went on to score some thrilling goals in the tournament, including both goals in England's 2–1 semi-final win over Portugal. At the end of that season, he won both the Footballer of the Year and the European players' awards.

The nephew of the legendary centre-forward Jackie Milburn, Bobby Charlton joined Manchester United straight from school and was a member of the sides that won the FA Youth Cup in 1953/54, 1954/55 and 1955/56. He made his United debut in October 1956 and though he scored twice in a 4–2 win over Charlton Athletic, manager Matt Busby felt that the young striker needed time to mature. In May 1968 he scored two goals in the emotionally charged European Cup Final against Benfica at Wembley as United won 4–1. After 106 caps and 49 goals, his international career ended in Mexico in dramatic fashion. He was substituted in order to keep him fresh for the semi-finals as England led West Germany 2–0, but it wasn't to be, the Germans running out winners 3–2. He pulled on a Manchester United shirt for the last time at Stamford Bridge in 1973, setting appearance records for both club and country.

Charlton joined Preston North End as player-manager but didn't have the same success off the field as he'd enjoyed on it, and he duly retired. He was an active director of Wigan Athletic, whom he managed for a brief spell at the end of the 1982/83 season, before establishing the famous Bobby Charlton soccer schools for children. Knighted for his services to football, he has helped make Manchester United the most famous club in the world and was without doubt one of the most talented and popular footballers of all time.

Colin McDONALD

Position	Goalkeeper
Born	Colin Agnew McDonald, Tottington, 15 October 1930
Height	6ft 0in
Weight	12st 0lb
Clubs	Burnley
England Caps	8
	1958 v Soviet Union (1–1), v Soviet Union (2–2), v Brazil (0–0), v Austria (2–2), v Soviet Union (lost 0–1), v N. Ireland (3–3), v Soviet Union (won 5–0), v Wales (2–2)

IT WAS INEVITABLE that Colin McDonald's goalkeeping displays would attract the attention of the international selectors and in March 1958 he played for the Football League in a 4–1 win over the Scottish League. He soon progressed to the full England side and played in all four of their 1958 World Cup games, giving an outstanding display of goalkeeping in the goalless draw against the eventual World Champions, Brazil, in Gothenburg.

McDonald had made his Central League debut for Burnley in May 1950 but then, while on National Service, he had a spell on loan with Headington United (later to become Oxford United) of the Southern League. After beating Wycombe Wanderers in the FA Cup, the Manor Ground club were thrown out of the competition because of McDonald's apparent ineligibility to play for the club in the FA Cup. On his return to Turf Moor he had to wait until April 1954 before making his League debut, but from then on he hardly missed a game, turning in numerous near-faultless performances.

Sadly, in March 1959 tragedy struck. While playing for the Football League against the League of Ireland in Dublin, he broke his leg, and as a result he never played first-class football again. On leaving Turf Moor he coached Wycombe Wanderers before later scouting for both Bury and Bolton. He rejoined the Shakers as General Manager before acting as team manager for a three-month spell. He later coached Oldham Athletic and Tranmere Rovers before ending his involvement with the game.

Tommy BANKS

Position	Left-back
Born	Thomas Banks, Farnworth, 10 November 1929
Height	5ft 8in
Weight	12st 0lb
Clubs	Bolton Wanderers
England Caps	6
	1958 v Soviet Union (1–1), v Soviet Union (2–2), v Brazil (0–0), v Austria (2–2), v Soviet Union (lost 0–1), v N. Ireland (3–3)

TOMMY BANKS reached his peak towards the end of his Bolton career. After earning an FA Cup winners' medal against Manchester United in May 1959, he won the first of six England caps when he played against the Soviet Union in Moscow. He later played in the World Cup Finals in Sweden.

Left-back Banks was one of the 'hard men' of the Bolton Wanderers side during the 1950s, reputedly depositing opposition wingers on to the cinder track around the pitch on more than one occasion. On his arrival at Burnden Park, however, he had found his first-team opportunities limited by his older brother Ralph, who occupied one of the full-back berths. Despite making his League debut in a 1–0 defeat at Wolverhampton Wanderers in April 1948, it was to be 1953/54 before he won a regular place in the side. In fact, the tough-tackling left-back made only 12 first-team appearances in his first five seasons with the club.

The subject of transfer interest from Manchester United during their rebuilding after the Munich Air Disaster, Banks later ended his career by playing non-League football for Altrincham before concentrating on the building trade.

Eddie CLAMP

Position	Wing-half
Born	Harold Edwin Clamp, Coalville, 14 September 1934
Died	Wednesfield, 11 December 1995
Height	5ft 11in
Weight	11st 10lb
Clubs	Wolverhampton Wanderers, Arsenal, Stoke City, Peterborough United
England Caps	4
	1958 v Soviet Union (1–1), v Soviet Union (2–2), v Brazil (0–0), v Austria (2–2)

ONE OF THE GAME'S great characters in the 1950s and 1960s, Eddie Clamp was signed by Wolverhampton Wanderers midway through his newspaper round! After playing for the club's nursery side, Wath Wanderers, he turned professional and made his League debut against Manchester United at Old Trafford in March 1954. Affectionately nicknamed 'Chopper', he represented the Football League before winning four full caps for England – all the matches were drawn. The half-back line-up in the games he played read Clamp–Wright–Slater.

Clamp won two League Championship medals in 1957/58 and 1958/59 and an FA Cup winners' medal in 1960 as Blackburn Rovers were beaten 3–0. He had scored 25 goals in 241 games for Wolves when, in November 1961, he was transferred to Arsenal for £30,000. The Gunners had hoped his experience would guide the younger players within their squad. However, after less than a year at Highbury he was sold to Stoke City. In his first season at the Victoria Ground he helped the Potters win the Second Division Championship, despite being sent off in a home game against Burnley after a fracas with fellow England international John Connelly. He later ended his first-class career with Peterborough United before playing non-League football for Worcester City.

Peter BRABROOK

Position	Outside-right
Born	Peter Brabrook, East Ham, 8 November 1937
Height	5ft 11in
Weight	12st 0lb
Clubs	Chelsea, West Ham United, Leyton Orient
England Caps	3
	1958 v Soviet Union (lost 0–1), v N. Ireland (3–3)
	1960 v Spain (lost 0–3)

WHILE AT STAMFORD BRIDGE, Peter Brabrook became the first product of the Chelsea Juniors to play for England, making his full international debut in the play-off game against the Soviet Union in the 1958 World Cup in Sweden. Despite Brabrook hitting the post twice, England lost 1–0.

Brabrook made three appearances for Chelsea during the club's League Championship-winning season of 1954/55. He established himself in the side the following season and over the next five years was unchallenged as the Blues' first-choice outside-right. Pace and good ball control with both feet made Brabrook a formidable opponent. He was a direct, attacking winger who ran at defences and frequently left them trailing in his wake. He had scored 47 goals in 251 League games when in October 1962, following the appointment of Tommy Docherty as manager, he was transferred to West Ham United. With the Hammers, he went on to win an FA Cup winners' medal in 1964 and helped them lift the European Cup Winners' Cup the following season. He was also a member of the Hammers side that lost to West Bromwich Albion in the two-legged League Cup Final of 1966. He later ended his career with Leyton Orient after having helped them win the Third Division Championship in 1969/70.

Peter BROADBENT

Position	Inside-forward
Born	Peter Frank Broadbent, Dover, 15 May 1933
Height	5ft 10in
Weight	11st 6lb
Clubs	Brentford, Wolverhampton Wanderers, Shrewsbury Town, Aston Villa, Stockport County
England Caps	7 Goals 2
	1958 v Soviet Union (lost 0–1), v N. Ireland (3–3), v Wales (2–2) 2 goals
	1959 v Scotland (won 1–0), v Italy (2–2), v Brazil (lost 0–2)
	1960 v Scotland (1–1)

INSIDE-FORWARD PETER BROADBENT was capped seven times by England, his only goals for his country coming against Wales at Villa Park in November 1958 when he scored twice in a 2–2 draw.

Broadbent joined Brentford as a professional from Dover FC in the summer of 1950, but after just 16 League outings for the Bees he left Griffin Park to join Wolverhampton Wanderers in February 1951. Over the next 14 seasons Broadbent went on to give Wolves great service both as a goal-maker and goalscorer. He won three League Championship medals in the seasons 1953/54, 1957/58 and 1958/59 and an FA Cup winners' medal in 1960 as Wolves defeated ten-man Blackburn Rovers 3–0. His best season for Wolves in terms of goals scored was the League Championship-winning season of 1958/59 when he top-scored with 22 goals, including a hat-trick in a 5–3 win at Portsmouth. He went on to score 145 goals in 497 games before leaving Molineux for Shrewsbury Town in January 1965. He later played for Aston Villa and Stockport County before ending his career playing non-League football for Bromsgrove Rovers.

Wilf McGUINNESS

Position	Wing-half
Born	Wilfred McGuinness, Manchester, 25 October 1937
Height	5ft 8in
Weight	10st 10lb
Clubs	Manchester United
England Caps	2
	1958 v N. Ireland (3–3)
	1959 v Mexico (lost 1–2)

A FORMER ENGLAND Schoolboy and Youth captain and Under-23 international, Wilf McGuinness was capped at full level against Northern Ireland in 1958 and everything looked rosy for this talented wing-half. But in December 1959 he broke his leg playing against Stoke City in a Central League game at Old Trafford. The injury ended his playing career at the age of just 22.

One of a number of players to emerge from Manchester United's youth policy of the early 1950s, Wilf McGuinness won three FA Youth Cup medals with the Reds. After impressing in the club's Central League side, he made his Football League debut for United against Wolverhampton Wanderers in October 1955, but did not make the left-half position his own until after the Munich Air Disaster when the great Duncan Edwards lost his life. Even then he could not retain the position for the 1958 FA Cup Final against Bolton Wanderers, being replaced by the more experienced Stan Crowther.

Following his enforced retirement, McGuinness joined United's backroom staff and was involved in the preparation of several England teams, including the 1966 World Cup squad, before succeeding Sir Matt Busby at the helm in the summer of 1969. He had only been in charge for six months when he lost the position, reverting to trainer-coach of the reserve team. He probably found it difficult to manage players who were established internationals and who had achieved so much more than him as a player. He later managed Greek club Aris Salonika and then York City before joining the coaching staff at Bury. He is now much sought after for his wit as an after-dinner speaker.

Graham SHAW

Position	Left-back
Born	Graham Laurence Shaw, Sheffield, 9 July 1934
Height	5ft 8in
Weight	11st 0lb
Clubs	Sheffield United, Doncaster Rovers
England Caps	5
	1958 v Soviet Union (won 5–0), v Wales (2–2)
	1959 v Scotland (won 1–0), v Italy (2–2)
	1962 v Wales (won 4–0)

STRONG IN THE TACKLE and an intelligent user of the ball, Graham Shaw helped Sheffield United win the Second Division Championship in 1952/53. His performances in the top flight led to five full caps for England, his last in November 1962 as Wales were beaten 4–0.

Shaw, who was an ABA Schools' Boxing Champion, began his career with his home-town club, Sheffield United. He made his Football League debut in the Sheffield derby at Hillsborough on 5 January 1952, when a post-war record attendance of 65,384 packed into the ground to see the Blades win 3–1. Just 17 years old, it was a tribute to his character and his manager's judgement that he didn't let the side down. He rapidly developed into a most stylish and cool defender, though the following season, after being injured in the match against Southampton, he moved into the forward line and scored two late goals in a 4–4 draw. Though he didn't score too many other goals – just 12 in 442 League games for United – one in particular is worth recalling. It came in a 3–1 home win over Portsmouth in September 1960, Shaw scoring from a 50-yard free kick.

On leaving Bramall Lane, Shaw ended his League career with Doncaster Rovers before taking over as player-manager of non-League Scarborough.

Danny CLAPTON

Position	Outside-right
Born	Daniel Robert Clapton, Stepney, 22 July 1934
Died	16 June 1986
Height	5ft 9in
Weight	10st 2lb
Clubs	Arsenal, Luton Town
England Caps	1
	1958 v Wales (2–2)

DANNY CLAPTON'S searing pace, devastating body swerve and cheeky back-heels soon made him a huge favourite with Arsenal fans, and in 1958/59 he not only helped the Gunners to their highest League position for 12 seasons (third), but also won an England cap, playing in a 2–2 draw against Wales at Villa Park.

Clapton was working as a Billingsgate market porter and playing for his local amateur side Leytonstone when he wrote to Arsenal manager Tom Whittaker asking for a trial. The Highbury boss was instantly impressed and the enterprising winger became a regular in the club's Football Combination side before making his League debut against Chelsea on Christmas Day 1954.

One aspect of Clapton's play that was often criticized was his poor scoring record. His finishing tended to be wayward, despite occasionally scoring a spectacular goal.

Sadly, a career that had looked so promising petered out shortly after his 28th birthday, when he lost his place in the side following the signing of Johnny MacLeod. He was transferred to Luton Town but after only a handful of games he went to Australia to play for Corinthians of Sydney. He headed home in 1970 and, though troubled by ill-health, took a pub in Hackney before dying in tragic circumstances in June 1986.

Doug HOLDEN

Position	Winger
Born	Albert Douglas Holden, Manchester, 28 September 1930
Height	5ft 9in
Weight	10st 9lb
Clubs	Bolton Wanderers, Preston North End
England Caps	5
	1958 v Wales (2–2)
	1959 v Scotland (won 1–0), v Italy (2–2), v Brazil (lost 0–2), v Peru (lost 1–4)

THOUGH HE SCORED his fair share of goals, winger Doug Holden's chief asset was his crossing ability. When he made his international debut his crosses provided Peter Broadbent with two clear-cut chances, both gratefully accepted, in England's 2–2 draw with Wales.

Holden signed as an amateur for Bolton Wanderers in 1948 and appeared for the England Youth side before completing his National Service. He made his League debut for the Wanderers in a 1–1 draw against Liverpool at Anfield in November 1951 and, despite being only 17, he quickly proved that he possessed the temperament for the big occasion. Though he played primarily on the left flank, it was on the opposite wing that he made a name for himself in the 1953 FA Cup Final.

Five years later he reverted to the left wing for the 1958 FA Cup Final against Manchester United – he and Nat Lofthouse being the only Bolton players to appear in both finals. In November 1962, after scoring 44 goals in 463 games for the Wanderers, he left to play for Preston North End, for whom he appeared in the 1964 FA Cup Final against West Ham United. Holden later emigrated for Australia, where he played for the national side.

Jimmy ARMFIELD

Position	Right-back
Born	James Christopher Armfield, Denton, 21 September 1935
Height	5ft 11in
Weight	12st 12lb
Clubs	Blackpool
England Caps	43
	1959 v Brazil (lost 0–2), v Peru (lost 1–4), v Mexico (lost 1–2), v United States (won 8–1)
	1960 v Scotland (1–1), v Yugoslavia (3–3), v Spain (lost 0–3), v Hungary (lost 0–2),
	v N. Ireland (won 5–2), v Luxembourg (won 9–0), v Spain (won 4–2), v Wales (won 5–1)
	1961 v Scotland (won 9–3), v Mexico (won 8–0), v Portugal (1–1), v Italy (won 3–2),
	v Austria (lost 1–3), v Luxembourg (won 4–1), v Wales (1–1), v Portugal (won 2–0),
	v N. Ireland (1–1)
	1962 v Austria (won 3–1), v Scotland (lost 0–2), v Switzerland (won 3–1), v Peru (won 4–0),
	v Hungary (lost 1–2), v Argentina (won 3–1), v Bulgaria (0–0), v Brazil (lost 1–3), v France
	(1–1), v N. Ireland (won 3–1), v Wales (won 4–0)
	1963 v France (lost 2–5), v Scotland (lost 1–2), v Brazil (1–1), v E. Germany (won 2–1),

v Switzerland (won 8–1), v Wales (won 4–0), v Rest of the World (won 2–1), v N. Ireland (won 8–3)

1964 v Scotland (lost 0–1)

1966 v Yugoslavia (won 2–0), v Finland (won 3–0)

AFTER PLAYING FOR the Football League XI and England Under-23s, Jimmy Armfield and Jimmy Greaves were flown out to Rio de Janeiro, where Armfield made his full England debut in front of 175,000 volatile South Americans. Armfield was at

Jimmy Armfield of Blackpool. (Lancashire Evening Post)

left-back and up against the flying Julinho as England lost 2–0 to the World Cup holders. Perhaps his best international came against Spain at Wembley in 1960. England won 4–2 and Armfield's complete dominance over Real Madrid's Gento earned him a standing ovation.

While at school, Jimmy Armfield played more rugby than soccer and actually appeared for Lancashire Schoolboys in the former. However, following his National Service he turned professional with Blackpool, where he was converted from winger to full-back, with immediate effect. Though he made his League debut for the Seasiders against Portsmouth in December 1954, it was an injury to Eddie Shimwell midway through the 1955/56 season that gave Armfield a chance to re-establish himself. Acknowledged as one of the game's first overlapping full-backs, there is no doubt that his early days as a winger gave Armfield a taste for the attacking aspects of the game. Sharp in the tackle and quick to recover if a winger went past him, he also timed his runs perfectly and invariably crossed to good effect. Following his display in the 1962 World Cup in Chile, this stylish player was voted the best right-back in the world. He captained England on 15 occasions after taking over from the injured Johnny Haynes and at one stage played in 37 consecutive international matches. He helped Blackpool win promotion to the top flight in 1969/70 but at the end of the following season, after 19 years with the club, he left Bloomfield Road after appearing in 627 League and Cup games.

Armfield then became manager of Bolton Wanderers, leading the then Burnden Park club to the Third Division Championship. He then took over at Leeds United, but after taking the Yorkshire club to the 1975 European Cup Final he left to become a full-time journalist. Always playing with great enthusiasm, he was a model player both on and off the field.

Norman DEELEY

Position	Outside-right
Born	Norman Victor Deeley, Wednesbury, 30 November 1933
Height	5ft 4in
Weight	10st 3lb
Clubs	Wolverhampton Wanderers, Leyton Orient
England Caps	2
	1959 v Brazil (lost 0–2), v Peru (lost 1–4)

THE SMALLEST PLAYER to represent England at Schoolboy level – being just 4ft 4in tall when he played in 1947/48 – Norman Deeley later played in two full internationals for England, against Brazil and Peru in 1959.

His size did not deter Wolverhampton Wanderers, who signed him as an amateur. He turned professional in December 1950. He played his first game for the club at right-half as Wolves beat Arsenal 2–1 at Molineux. After two years' National Service, Deeley was switched to the right wing and scored his first goal for the club in the FA Charity Shield match against West Bromwich Albion in September 1954. However, it wasn't until the 1957/58 season that Deeley established himself as a first-team member, after which he missed very few games. He won League Championship medals in 1957/58 and 1958/59, scoring 23 and 17 League goals respectively. In September 1959 he scored four of Wolves' goals in a 9–0 demolition of Fulham and also netted twice in the 1960 FA Cup Final as Wolves beat Blackburn Rovers 3–0.

In February 1962, Deeley, who had scored 75 goals in 237 games – an excellent return for a winger – joined Leyton Orient. On leaving Brisbane Road, he had spells with a number of non-League clubs, including Worcester City, Bromsgrove Rovers and Darlaston Town.

Jimmy GREAVES

Position	Inside-forward
Born	James Peter Greaves, East Ham, 20 February 1940
Height	5ft 8in
Weight	10st 8lb
Clubs	Chelsea, AC Milan, Tottenham Hotspur, West Ham United
England Caps	57 Goals 44

1959 v Peru (lost 1–4) 1 goal, v Mexico (lost 1–2), v United States (won 8–1), v Wales (1–1) 1 goal, v Sweden (lost 2–3)

1960 v Yugoslavia (3–3) 1 goal, v Spain (lost 0–3), v N. Ireland (won 5–2) 2 goals, v Luxembourg (won 9–0) 3 goals, v Spain (won 4–2) 1 goal, v Wales (won 5–1) 2 goals

1961 v Scotland (won 9–3) 3 goals, v Portugal (1–1), v Italy (won 3–2) 1 goal, v Austria (lost 1–3) 1 goal

1962 v Scotland (lost 0–2), v Switzerland (won 3–1), v Peru (won 4–0) 3 goals, v Hungary (lost 1–2), v Argentina (won 3–1) 1 goal, v Bulgaria (0–0), v Brazil (lost 1–3), v France (1–1), v N. Ireland (won 3–1) 1 goal, v Wales (won 4–0) 1 goal

1963 v France (lost 2–5), v Scotland (lost 1–2), v Brazil (1–1), v Czechoslovakia (won 4–2) 2 goals, v Switzerland (won 8–1), v Wales (won 4–0) 1 goal, v Rest of the World (won 2–1) 1 goal, v N. Ireland (won 8–3) 4 goals

1964 v Uruguay (won 2–1), v Portugal (won 4–3), v Eire (won 3–1) 1 goal, v Brazil (lost 1–5) 1 goal, v Portugal (1–1), v Argentina (lost 0–1), v N. Ireland (won 4–3) 3 goals, v Belgium (2–2), v Holland (1–1) 1 goal

1965 v Scotland (2–2) 1 goal, v Hungary (won 1–0) 1 goal, v Yugoslavia (1–1), v Wales (0–0), v Austria (lost 2–3)

1966 v Yugoslavia (won 2–0) 1 goal, v Norway (won 6–1) 4 goals, v Denmark (won 2–0), v Poland (won 1–0), v Uruguay (0–0), v Mexico (won 2–0), v France (won 2–0)

1967 v Scotland (lost 2–3), v Spain (won 2–0) 1 goal, v Austria (won 1–0)

ARGUABLY THE GREATEST GOALSCORER in the history of British football, Jimmy Greaves made his League debut for Chelsea against Spurs on the opening day of the 1957/58 season. He scored then, in a 1–1 draw, as he was to score on all of his debut days. It was the first of 357 goals in the Football League, all of them in the First Division. After only six games for Chelsea, he made his debut for the England Under-23 side and scored twice against Bulgaria. His full England debut came in May 1959, when he scored his country's only goal in a 4–1 defeat by Peru.

Jimmy Greaves of Spurs. (Lancashire Evening Post)

Greaves stayed at Chelsea until June 1961, when he joined AC Milan. His goal-scoring debut came in a friendly against Botafoga and, despite the tough defensive tactics of the Italian League, he scored nine goals in 14 games. However, he was not able to stomach the petty disciplines the Italians imposed on their players and in December 1961 he returned to the Football League with Tottenham Hotspur, Spurs' manager Bill Nicholson paying £99,999 – refusing to pay a six-figure fee. Greaves responded with a hat-trick at home to Blackpool. He won an FA Cup winners' medal in his first season, scoring the opening goal at Wembley. He scored twice in the European Cup Winners' Cup Final the following year and ended the 1962/63 season with Spurs' highest-scorer-in-a-season record with 37 League goals. When he topped the First Division scoring charts in 1964/65 he became the first player to do so for three consecutive seasons. A serious illness in 1965/66 meant that he was unable to reach full fitness for the World Cup finals that summer.

In March 1970 Greaves left Spurs to join West Ham United. He scored twice on his Hammers debut but retired at the end of the 1970/71 season. In October 1972 a crowd of 45,799 turned out to pay tribute in his testimonial match against Feyenoord. He responded in the only way he knew by scoring after only three minutes. He later fell victim to alcoholism, a problem that threatened to kill him. Rehabilitation was followed by new stardom as a TV pundit, a role in which he revelled.

Warren BRADLEY

Position	Outside-right
Born	Warren Bradley, Hyde, 20 June 1933
Height	5ft 4in
Weight	9st 10lb
Clubs	Manchester United, Bury
England Caps	3 Goals 2
	1959 v Mexico (lost 1–2), v United States (won 8–1) 1 goal, v Italy (2–2) 1 goal

A SMALL, QUICK-THINKING and speedy winger, Warren Bradley played his early football for Durham City and, after being rejected by Bolton Wanderers, joined one of the leading amateur sides of the day, Bishop Auckland. While with Bishop Auckland, he won two FA Amateur Cup winners' medals and 11 England amateur caps. A schoolteacher by profession, he joined Manchester United after the Munich Air Disaster, signing professional forms in November 1958. Five months later, Bradley won the first of three full caps for England. Though his stay at Old Trafford was relatively brief, he had a good striking record for a winger and was an important part of the post-Munich rebuilding process at the club.

In March 1962 he joined Bury for a fee of £40,000 and later played non-League football for Northwich Victoria, Macclesfield and Bangor City while continuing to work as a teacher. After a year out of the game, he rejoined Macclesfield, but left again to take over as head teacher of a Manchester comprehensive school.

Tony ALLEN

Position	Left-back
Born	Anthony Allen, Stoke-on-Trent, 27 November 1939
Height	5ft 9in
Weight	11st 12lb
Clubs	Stoke City, Bury
England Caps	3
	1959 v Wales (1–1), v Sweden (lost 2–3), v N. Ireland (won 2–1)

AN ENGLAND YOUTH INTERNATIONAL, left-back Tony Allen won a full England cap before he had turned 20 years of age, playing against Wales at Ninian Park in October 1959, just two years after making his League debut for Stoke City. Capped three times by England, he also won seven Under-23 caps and made two appearances for the Football League XI.

A very stylish full-back, Allen, who appeared in 473 first-team games for Stoke, played an important role during the Matthews revival period at the Victoria Ground and the club's consolidation in the top flight. He won a Second Division Championship medal in 1962/63 and a League Cup runners-up medal in 1963/64, when the Potters lost 4–3 to Leicester City over two legs. Towards the end of his career at the Victoria Ground he began to lose a little of his pace and was moved to centre-half, but in the early part of 1970 he left the Potters to play for Bury. At Gigg Lane he was the experienced defender the club had been looking for, but after just one season with the Shakers he left to play in South African football for Hellenic. He later returned to these shores and saw out his career in non-League football with Stafford Rangers.

Trevor SMITH

Position	Centre-half
Born	Trevor Smith, Quarry Bank, 13 April 1936
Height	6ft 1in
Weight	13st 7lb
Clubs	Birmingham City, Walsall
England Caps	2
	1959 v Wales (1–1), v Sweden (lost 2–3)

AFTER PLAYING IN the same schools side as Duncan Edwards, centre-half Trevor Smith joined Birmingham City as an amateur in the summer of 1951 and the following year was a member of the Blues side that won the European Youth Cup in Switzerland. He made his League debut in a 4–2 win at Derby County in October 1953, and though Army service was to disrupt his progress later in the decade, he was the club's first-choice centre-half for 11 seasons. His outstanding performances at the heart of the Blues defence were eventually rewarded when he replaced Billy Wright of Wolves to win two full England caps. In 1954/55 he helped the Blues win the Second

Division Championship and he was a member of the Birmingham side that lost 3–1 to Manchester City in the 1956 FA Cup Final. In 1960 he played in the Inter Cities Fairs Cup Final and three years later he helped the Blues beat Aston Villa in the League Cup Final.

Smith went on to appear in 430 first-team games for the St Andrew's club before leaving in October 1964 to join Walsall, but after just 11 appearances for the Saddlers he decided to hang up his boots.

John CONNELLY

Position	Outside-right
Born	John Michael Connelly, St Helens, 18 July 1938
Height	5ft 8in
Weight	11st 2lb
Clubs	Burnley, Manchester United, Blackburn Rovers, Bury
England Caps	20 Goals 7

1959 v Wales (1–1), v Sweden (lost 2–3) 1 goal, v N. Ireland (won 2–1)
1960 v Scotland (1–1)
1961 v Wales (1–1), v Portugal (won 2–0) 1 goal
1962 v Austria (won 3–1), v Switzerland (won 3–1) 1 goal, v Wales (won 4–0) 1 goal
1963 v France (lost 2–5)
1965 v Hungary (won 1–0), v Yugoslavia (1–1), v Sweden (won 2–1) 1 goal, v Wales (0–0),
   v Austria (lost 2–3) 1 goal, v N. Ireland (won 2–1)
1966 v Scotland (won 4–3), v Norway (won 6–1) 1 goal, v Denmark (won 2–0),
   v Uruguay (0–0)

JOHN CONNELLY was a member of Burnley's League Championship-winning side of 1959/60, scoring 20 goals in 34 games. It was his form that season that led to the first of his 20 full caps for England, when he played in the match against Wales at Ninian Park.

Connelly joined the Clarets from his home-town team St Helens in 1956 but remained an amateur until he had completed his apprenticeship as a joiner at the age of 21. In his early days with Burnley it was immaterial as to which flank the notably two-footed Connelly occupied. He was direct and always seeking to have a shot on goal, and was one of the top-scoring wingmen in the game throughout the late fifties and early sixties. He scored two hat-tricks for Burnley, at Fulham in 1961/62 and at Manchester United in 1962/63. This led to a number of clubs vying for his services and in April 1964, after scoring 105 goals in 265 games, he joined Manchester United for £60,000. In his first campaign at Old Trafford, he helped United win the League Championship and thus collected his second Championship medal, but after two years at Old Trafford he left to play for Blackburn Rovers. He continued to find the net on a regular basis before ending his League career with Bury and retiring to take over a fish-and-chip shop.

John Connelly in England strip, 1959.
(Getty Images)

Brian CLOUGH

Position	Centre-forward
Born	Brian Howard Clough, Middlesbrough, 21 March 1935
Height	5ft 11in
Weight	11st 11lb
Clubs	Middlesbrough, Sunderland
England Caps	2
	1959 v Wales (1–1), v Sweden (lost 2–3)

ONE OF NINE CHILDREN, Brian Clough worked as a clerk with ICI while playing for Billingham Synthonia and Great Broughton before joining Middlesbrough. He soon established himself in the Boro side, top-scoring in 1956/57 with 40 goals in 44 games, including four in a 7–2 win over Huddersfield Town. Clough continued to find the back of the net the following season, when his total of 42 goals included four in both the 5–0 defeat of Doncaster Rovers and the 5–2 win over Ipswich Town. He headed the Second Division goalscoring charts for three consecutive seasons, netting 43 goals in 1958/59, including five in the 9–0 rout of Brighton and Hove Albion on the opening day of the season. This led to his selection for England but the prolific Clough failed to find the net on either of his two appearances.

Over three seasons at Ayresome Park, Clough had put in numerous transfer requests, all of which were turned down. He topped the 40-goal mark again the following season but in 1960/61 he failed for the first time to pass 40, though his total of 36 included his 17th hat-trick for the club. Clough, who had scored 204 goals in 222 games, was eventually allowed to join Sunderland for a fee of £45,000 in the summer of 1961. He scored 63 goals in 74 games for the Wearsiders before an injury received against Bury on Boxing Day 1962 virtually ended his playing career.

After a spell on Sunderland's coaching staff, Clough took his first steps in management with Hartlepool United. After turning the club's fortunes around, he and his partner Peter Taylor moved to Derby County. He helped the Rams win the Second Division title in 1970/71 and then led the club to the League Championship the following season, after which, in 1972/73, he steered them to the semi-finals of the European Cup. On leaving the Baseball Ground, he had brief spells in charge of Brighton and Leeds before being appointed manager of Nottingham Forest in January 1975. Over the next 18 years he was to produce some golden moments for Forest, including a League Championship, four League Cup wins and two European Cup successes. Beyond question, he was one of the greatest managers of all time. Amid adverse publicity, Clough decided to retire in May 1993, having won just about everything there is to win in the game.

Edwin HOLLIDAY

Position	Outside-left
Born	Edwin Holliday, Barnsley, 7 June 1939
Height	5ft 9in
Weight	10st 12lb
Clubs	Middlesbrough, Sheffield Wednesday, Workington, Peterborough United
England Caps	3
	1959 v Wales (1–1), v Sweden (lost 2–3), v N. Ireland (won 2–1)

OUTSIDE-LEFT EDWIN HOLLIDAY was an important member of the Middlesbrough attack, his pinpoint crosses providing Brian Clough and Alan Peacock with numerous chances, most of which they tucked away. After two seasons in the Ayresome Park club's first team, he won international recognition when he was selected for England at Under-23 level. A month later, in October 1959, Holliday made his full international debut alongside Brian Clough in a 1–1 draw against Wales at Ninian Park. He won two further caps with Boro before leaving Ayresome Park in March 1962 to join Sheffield Wednesday.

Holliday never really settled at Hillsborough and after just 55 League appearances for the Owls he rejoined Middlesbrough. He took his tally of goals in his two spells with the club to 25 in 169 games, but following the north-east club's relegation to the Third Division at the end of his first season, back he left to play Southern League football for Hereford United. In February 1968 he returned to League football with Workington, but after making 56 appearances he left to play for Peterborough United. After making just 16 appearances for 'Posh' he broke his leg and had to retire.

Ron SPRINGETT

Position	Goalkeeper
Born	Ronald Derrick Springett, Fulham, 22 July 1935
Height	5ft 10in
Weight	12st 1lb
Clubs	Queen's Park Rangers, Sheffield Wednesday
England Caps	33
	1959 v N. Ireland (won 2–1)
	1960 v Scotland (1–1), v Yugoslavia (3–3), v Spain (lost 0–3), v Hungary (lost 0–2),
	v N. Ireland (won 5–2), v Luxembourg (won 9–0), v Spain (won 4–2)
	1961 v Scotland (won 9–3), v Mexico (won 8–0), v Portugal (1–1), v Italy (won 3–2),
	v Austria (lost 1–3), v Luxembourg (won 4–1), v Wales (1–1), v Portugal (won 2–0),
	v N. Ireland (1–1)
	1962 v Austria (won 3–1), v Scotland (lost 0–2), v Switzerland (won 3–1), v Peru (won 4–0),
	v Hungary (lost 1–2), v Argentina (won 3–1), v Bulgaria (0–0), v Brazil (lost 1–3), v France
	(1–1), v N. Ireland (won 3–1), v Wales (won 4–0)
	1963 v France (lost 2–5), v Switzerland (won 8–1)
	1965 v Wales (0–0), v Austria (lost 2–3), v Norway (won 6–1)

From left to right, goalkeepers Peter Bonetti (Chelsea), Gordon Banks (Leicester) and Ron Springett (Sheffield Wednesday) wear their new World Cup uniforms to the Anglo-American Sporting Club dinner at the Hilton Hotel, 21 June 1966. (Getty Images)

RON SPRINGETT began his career with Queen's Park Rangers but his spectacular performances between the posts were soon recognized by the bigger clubs, and in March 1958 he was transferred to Sheffield Wednesday, where he still holds the record for being the club's most-capped international. Despite some heroic performances for the Owls in his first season at Hillsborough, he couldn't save the Yorkshire club from relegation to the Second Division. However, he was a key member of the Wednesday side that won the Second Division Championship the following season, keeping 13 clean sheets in the 32 matches in which he played. In 1959/60 he made the first of nine appearances for the Football League against the Irish League, and won the first of 33 caps for England when he played against Northern Ireland.

It was Springett's fine goalkeeping that kept Sheffield Wednesday in the upper reaches of the First Division for six seasons in the early 1960s and yet, though he appeared in 384 games in his nine full seasons, he was never an ever-present. The 1966 FA Cup Final, when the Owls lost 3–2 to Everton, was the closest he got to glory at club level. In 1967 he returned to Queen's Park Rangers in a unique deal that saw his brother Peter go to Hillsborough. Later involved in a gardening business, he twice played in the same game as Peter, once while a Wednesday player and once while with Queen's Park Rangers – the Owls won on both occasions.

Ken BROWN

Position	Centre-half
Born	Kenneth Brown, London, 16 February 1934
Height	6ft 0in
Weight	13st 1lb
Clubs	West Ham United, Torquay United
England Caps	1
	1959 v N. Ireland (won 2–1)

ONE OF A LONG LINE of outstanding West Ham centre-halves, Ken Brown was still serving in the Army when he made his debut for the club at Rotherham United in February 1953. However, most of his early days at Upton Park were spent in the reserves, where he played an important role in Football Combination League and Cup successes of the mid-1950s. Eventually replacing Malcolm Allison, he was a great success in the club's promotion-winning season of 1957/58 and in 1959 he won his only full international cap when he played for England in their 2–1 win over Northern Ireland at Wembley.

Brown continued to play for the Hammers until 1967, winning an FA Cup winners' medal in 1964 and a European Cup Winners' Cup medal in 1965. After appearing in 455 first-team games, he left Upton Park and played for Torquay United for a couple of seasons before joining Hereford United and then Bournemouth as trainer-coach. He joined John Bond as his assistant at Norwich City, taking over the reins when Bond left to manage Manchester City. He led the Canaries to their League Cup success over Sunderland and twice into the First Division, but after a disappointing 1987/88 season he was sacked. He later managed Plymouth Argyle but relinquished the post in 1991 to become director of Lakenham Leisure Centre near Norwich.

Joe BAKER

Position	Centre-forward		
Born	Joseph Henry Baker, Liverpool, 17 July 1940		
Height	5ft 8in		
Weight	11st 7lb		
Clubs	Hibernian, Torino, Arsenal, Nottingham Forest, Sunderland, Raith Rovers		
England Caps	8	Goals	3
	1959 v N. Ireland (won 2–1) 1 goal		
	1960 v Scotland (1–1), v Yugoslavia (3–3), v Spain (lost 0–3), v Hungary (lost 0–2)		
	1965 v N. Ireland (won 2–1) 1 goal, v Spain (won 2–0) 1 goal		
	1966 v Poland (1–1)		

JOE BAKER began his career in 1957 with Hibernian and in four seasons at Easter Road he scored 102 League goals in 117 games. This form won him the first of his eight England caps when he played against Northern Ireland in November 1959. In doing so, he became the first Englishman to play for his country while with a Scottish club. His new England team-mates found his broad Scottish accent rather amusing!

In the summer of 1961 he decided to join Jimmy Greaves and his good friend Denis Law in Italy. Unfortunately his spell at Torino was short-lived and in July 1962 he became Billy Wright's first signing for a new record Arsenal transfer fee of £72,500. In 1963/64 he was joint-top scorer with Geoff Strong. He headed the scoring charts again the following season and after a five-year break won back his England place. With Arsenal having a poor season in 1965/66, he opted to join Nottingham Forest. While at the City ground he was picked but not selected in the original 40 for the England 1966 World Cup squad. He later had a spell with Sunderland before returning north of the border to play for both Hibernian and Raith Rovers.

Ray PARRY

Position	Inside-left
Born	Raymond Alan Parry, Derby, 16 January 1936
Died	23 May 2003
Height	5ft 9in
Weight	10st 8lb
Clubs	Bolton Wanderers, Blackpool, Bury
England Caps	2 Goals 1
	1959 v N. Ireland (won 2–1) 1 goal
	1960 v Scotland (1–1)

WHEN RAY PARRY made his debut for Bolton Wanderers against Wolverhampton Wanderers at Molineux on 13 October 1951, he became the youngest player in First Division history, at 15 years 267 days. He was given two outings that season before gradually settling into the side at inside-forward. One of a famous footballing family, Ray Parry developed into a player who could pass the ball with great accuracy yet strike it with equal power. He was the scorer of some vital goals, perhaps none more so than the one against Wolves in the FA Cup sixth-round tie of 1958. A member of that season's FA Cup-winning side, he also won two caps for England, scoring in a 2–1 win over Northern Ireland on his international debut.

Parry had scored 79 goals in 299 games for the Wanderers when, in October 1960, he was transferred to Blackpool. After four years at Bloomfield Road he moved to Bury, where he made his debut in the local derby against his former club Bolton. He remained with the Shakers until 1972, before ending his playing days with non-League New Brighton.

1960-69

Champions of the World

Walter Winterbottom approached his fourth – and last – World Cup in the hope that circumstances would no longer conspire to blight the national side's bid for glory. But despite the presence of such talents as Greaves, Haynes, Moore, Wilson and Bobby Charlton, England lost in the 1960 quarter-finals to Brazil, who were on their way to a second successive win. Winterbottom gave way to Alf Ramsey in 1963, Ramsey having been chosen because of his success with Ipswich Town. Early omens were poor – two straight losses, away to France and at home to Scotland – but everything then came good. England lost just four of the next 42 matches.

The team's crowning achievement was, of course, the 1966 World Cup, for which England automatically qualified as hosts. The tournament opened with a dull, goalless draw between England and Uruguay before the home nation defeated Mexico and France to reach the quarter-finals. Opponents Argentina resorted to vicious tactics. Captain Antonio Rattin led the way in the assaults and verbal abuse, and inevitably was sent off. England won 1–0 with a Geoff Hurst goal and Alf Ramsey dubbed the Argentinians 'animals'. The semi-finals paired England with Portugal, featuring the talented Eusebio, and in a superb game – a match that was a credit to both English and Portuguese football – England won 2–1 thanks to two Bobby Charlton goals.

The 1966 World Cup Final – England v West Germany – is a piece of history. The Germans led through Haller after 13 minutes. Hurst equalized and the teams were level until 13 minutes from time, when Martin Peters secured what seemed to be the winning goal. Then, in the last minute, an equalizer from Weber sent the match into extra time. There then followed Hurst's and England's legendary but controversial third goal, before victory was sealed late on by Hurst's third of the match.

With their tails still up, England went on to register their best-ever placing – third – in the 1968 European Championship. The semi-final against Yugoslavia – lost to a single goal late in the game – is remembered for the historic dismissal of Spurs' midfielder Alan Mullery, the first England player to be sent off in an international.

Ray WILSON

Position	Left-back
Born	Ramon Wilson, Shirebrook, 17 December 1934
Height	5ft 8in
Weight	11st 6lb
Clubs	Huddersfield Town, Everton, Oldham Athletic, Bradford City
England Caps	63

1960 v Scotland (1–1), v Yugoslavia (3–3), v Spain (lost 0–3), v Hungary (lost 0–2)

1961 v Wales (1–1), v Portugal (won 2–0), v N. Ireland (1–1)

1962 v Austria (won 3–1), v Scotland (lost 0–2), v Switzerland (won 3–1), v Peru (won 4–0), v Hungary (lost 1–2), v Argentina (won 3–1), v Bulgaria (0–0), v Brazil (lost 1–3), v France (1–1), v N. Ireland (won 3–1)

1963 v Brazil (1–1), v Czechoslovakia (won 4–2), v E. Germany (won 2–1), v Switzerland (won 8–1), v Wales (won 4–0), v Rest of the World (won 2–1)

1964 v Scotland (lost 0–1), v Uruguay (won 2–1), v Portugal (won 4–3), v Eire (won 3–1), v Brazil (lost 1–5), v Portugal (1–1), v Argentina (lost 0–1)

1965 v Scotland (2–2), v Hungary (won 1–0), v Yugoslavia (1–1), v W. Germany (won 1–0), v Sweden (won 2–1), v Wales (0–0), v Austria (lost 2–3), v N. Ireland (won 2–1), v Spain (won 2–0)

1966 v Poland (1–1), v W. Germany (won 1–0), v Yugoslavia (won 2–0), v Finland (won 3–0), v Denmark (won 2–0), v Poland (won 1–0), v Uruguay (0–0), v Mexico (won 2–0), v France (won 2–0), v Argentina (won 1–0), v Portugal (won 2–1), v W. Germany (won 4–2 aet), v N. Ireland (won 2–0), v Czechoslovakia (0–0), v Wales (won 5–1)

Ray Wilson playing for England, May 1964. (Getty Images)

1967 v Scotland (lost 2–3), v Austria (won 1–0), v N. Ireland (won 2–0), v Soviet Union (2–2)

1968 v Scotland (1–1), v Spain (won 1–0), v Spain (won 2–1), v Yugoslavia (lost 0–1), v Soviet Union (won 2–0)

Honours   World Cup winners England 1966

SAID TO HAVE BEEN NAMED after the prewar film star Ramon Navarro, Ray Wilson – a tough-tackling defender with a superb tactical knowledge – ranks as one of the game's all-time great full-backs, winning a World Cup winners' medal in 1966.

Wilson was recommended to Huddersfield Town while working as a railwayman. He turned professional three months after his arrival at Leeds Road and was switched from wing-half to full-back by Bill Shankly. Despite Huddersfield being an average Second Division club, Wilson soon established himself as one of the best defenders in the game. He stayed with the Yorkshire club for 12 seasons before signing for Everton in July 1964. He helped Everton beat Sheffield Wednesday in the FA Cup Final of 1966 but his career in the top flight ended in the summer of 1968 when, following Everton's defeat in the FA Cup Final against West Bromwich Albion, a knee injury sustained in training required surgery. He fought back but, although the fitness that had been the hallmark of his play was still in evidence, some of his old speed and confidence were missing. Given a free transfer, he joined Oldham Athletic, but 12 months later he was appointed Bradford City's youth-team player-coach and later worked as assistant manager and caretaker-boss. In December 1971, a month after playing his final match, he joined his brother-in-law in the family joinery and undertaking business at Outlane near Huddersfield.

Peter SWAN

Position	Centre-half
Born	Peter Swan, South Elmsall, 8 October 1936
Height	6ft 1in
Weight	12st 0lb
Clubs	Sheffield Wednesday, Bury
England Caps	19

1960 v Yugoslavia (3–3), v Spain (lost 0–3), v Hungary (lost 0–2), v N. Ireland (won 5–2), v Luxembourg (won 9–0), v Spain (won 4–2), v Wales (won 5–1)

1961 v Scotland (won 9–3), v Mexico (won 8–0), v Portugal (1–1), v Italy (won 3–2), v Austria (lost 1–3), v Luxembourg (won 4–1), v Wales (1–1), v Portugal (won 2–0), v N. Ireland (1–1)

1962 v Austria (won 3–1), v Austria (lost 0–2), v Switzerland (won 3–1)

PETER SWAN made his Football League debut for Sheffield Wednesday in the local derby against Barnsley in November 1955, eventually displacing Don McEvoy at the heart of the Owls' defence. He was a regular in the Wednesday side for eight seasons until his suspension in 1964. In 1958/59 he helped Wednesday win the Second Division Championship and won three caps for England at Under-23 level. In 1959/60 he was ever-present as the Owls finished fifth in the First Division and won the first of 19 full caps for his country when he played in the 3–3 draw against Yugoslavia at Wembley. A key figure in the Wednesday team that did so well in the early part of the 1960s, he was ever-present again in 1962/63, but at the end of the following season he was one of the Sheffield Wednesday players banned from the game for match-fixing. In 1972 his life ban was lifted and he returned to Hillsborough, hoping to make up for the eight years he had lost. In the event he played in a further 15 games bringing his total number of first-team appearances for the club to 301 before moving to end his first-class career with Bury.

Dennis VIOLLET

Position	Inside-forward
Born	Dennis Sydney Viollet, Manchester, 20 September 1933
Died	United States, 6 March 1999
Height	5ft 8in
Weight	11st 0lb
Clubs	Manchester United, Stoke City, Linfield
England Caps	2 Goals 1
	1960 v Hungary (lost 0–2)
	1961 v Luxembourg (won 4–1) 1 goal

CAPPED TWICE for the full England team, Dennis Viollet won League Championship medals with Manchester United in 1955/56 and 1956/57, and an FA Cup runners-up medal in 1958 when the Reds were beaten by Bolton Wanderers.

Though he began his career with Manchester United, he lived near Maine Road and his parents were avid supporters of Manchester City! Yet after Matt Busby and Jimmy Murphy had chatted with the family, both parents seemed happy for him to wear the red of United. He was frail in appearance, but his frame belied his skills and stamina. Viollet snapped up half-chances at a terrific rate. In his 13 years with United he scored seven hat-tricks, the first coming in October 1954 as the Reds won a remarkable match at Stamford Bridge, beating Chelsea 6–5. In 1959/60 he scored 32 League goals – still a United record. In all matches for United he scored 178 goals, 160 of them coming in his 259 League games. Viollet was a compelling performer at inside- or centre-forward, possessing superb ball control, a delicate body swerve and a powerful shot. He played in 12 European ties for the Reds and scored 13 goals.

Viollet moved to Stoke City in January 1962 and in his five seasons at the Victoria Ground scored a further 59 goals in 182 appearances, as well as helping the Potters win the Second Division Championship in 1962/63. He then spent 18 months in the United States, playing in the NASL with Baltimore Boys. He returned to these shores to play non-League football for Witton Albion but later joined Linfield as their player-manager and won an Irish Cup winners' medal. He later coached Preston and Crewe before managing the Gresty Road outfit. On returning to the States he set up the Dennis Viollet Dolphin Soccer Camps in addition to fulfilling his duties as head coach of Jacksonville University.

Mick McNEIL

Position	Left-back
Born	Michael McNeil, Middlesbrough, 7 February 1940
Height	5ft 11in
Weight	12st 2lb
Clubs	Middlesbrough, Ipswich Town
England Caps	9
	1960 v N. Ireland (won 5–2), v Luxembourg (won 9–0), v Spain (won 4–2), v Wales (won 5–1)
	1961 v Scotland (won 9–3), v Mexico (won 8–0), v Portugal (1–1), v Italy (won 3–2), v Luxembourg (won 4–1)

MICK McNEIL began his Football League career with his home-town club, making his debut in a remarkable 6–4 win for Middlesbrough at Brighton and Hove Albion in December 1958. His early appearances for the club were at left-half, but after losing his place to Ray Yeoman he switched to full-back and never regretted the move. In 1959/60 McNeil was ever-present as Boro finished fifth in the Second Division. He was selected for an FA XI against the Army at St James' Park and followed this up with a number of appearances for the England Under-21 side. His performances in the Middlesbrough defence led to him winning nine full caps for England, never once appearing on the losing side.

In the summer of 1964, after appearing in 193 games for Boro, McNeil was allowed to join Ipswich Town. Although he did not add to his international caps while at Portman Road, he did captain an FA XI to a 10–0 win over Jersey in a match played to commemorate the centenary of the Jersey FA. He played the last of his 173 first-team games for Ipswich in February 1972 before entering non-League football with Cambridge City.

Bobby SMITH

Position	Centre-forward		
Born	Robert Alfred Smith, Langdale, 22 February 1933		
Height	5ft 9in		
Weight	12st 11lb		
Clubs	Chelsea, Tottenham Hotspur, Brighton and Hove Albion		
England Caps	15	Goals	11
	1960 v N. Ireland (won 5–2) 1 goal, v Luxembourg (won 9–0) 2 goals, v Spain (won 4–2) 2 goals, v Wales (won 5–1) 1 goal		
	1961 v Scotland (won 9–3) 2 goals, v Portugal (1–1)		
	1962 v Scotland (lost 0–2)		
	1963 v France (lost 2–5), v Scotland (lost 1–2), v Brazil (1–1), v Czechoslovakia (won 4–2), v E. Germany (won 2–1), v Wales (won 4–0) 2 goals, v Rest of the World (won 2–1), v N. Ireland (won 8–3) 1 goal		

Bobby Smith playing for Spurs in 1962.
(Lancashire Evening Post)

THE SON OF a Yorkshire miner, Bobby Smith was not the prettiest of footballers to watch, but his job was to score goals and this he did with relish, scoring 11 in 15 games for England before unexpectedly being discarded.

Smith joined the Chelsea groundstaff and made his first-team debut for the Stamford Bridge club at the age of 17, helping them to avoid relegation. After six years, in which he scored 30 goals in 86 senior games, he joined Spurs in December 1955. In his first five years at White Hart Lane he became the highest scorer in Tottenham history – he exceeded 30 League and Cup goals in each of the four seasons between 1957/58, in which he notched 38 in 40 outings, and 1960/61, the year of the 'double'. However, there were times when Spurs manager Bill Nicholson preferred the subtlety of Les Allen, meaning that Smith was left out of the team. At the end of the 1963/64 season, Nicholson decided that Frank Saul should partner Jimmy Greaves up front and Smith was allowed to move on to Brighton and Hove Albion. His 18 goals in 31 appearances helped the Seagulls win the Fourth Division Championship in his only season at the Goldstone Ground. He fell out with Brighton over comments in some newspaper articles and was sacked.

Smith later entered non-League football with Hastings United, where he played until March 1967, later ending his career with Banbury United.

Gerry HITCHENS

Position	Centre-forward
Born	Gerald Archibald Hitchens, Cannock, 8 October 1934
Died	13 April 1983
Height	5ft 11in
Weight	12st 2lb
Clubs	Cardiff City, Aston Villa, Inter Milan, Torino, Atalanta, Cagliari
England Caps	7 Goals 5

1961 v Mexico (won 8–0) 1 goal, v Italy (won 3–2) 2 goals, v Austria (lost 1–3)
1962 v Switzerland (won 3–1) 1 goal, v Peru (won 4–0), v Hungary (lost 1–2), v Brazil (lost 1–3) 1 goal

GERRY HITCHENS, who won the last four of his international caps while with Inter Milan, began his Football League career with Cardiff City when he joined the Bluebirds from Kidderminster Harriers in 1953. At Ninian Park he scored 40 goals in 95 League games before signing for Aston Villa in December 1957.

Hitchens made his debut for Villa in a disastrous derby defeat at the hands of Birmingham City, but scored three goals in his next two games to give notice of his goalscoring ability. His first hat-trick for the club came the following season, a ten-goal spree over three successive games, including five in the 11–1 thrashing of Charlton Athletic, which equalled the club record for the most goals scored by one player in a League game. That season he topped the club's scoring charts with 23 goals as they won the Second Division Championship. In 1960/61 he achieved the feat again with 29 goals. He also helped Villa to the League Cup Final, scoring in every round of the competition. Despite those 11 goals, he missed the Final against

Rotherham United because it had been put back to the start of the following season and by that time he had joined Italian giants Inter Milan.

A most popular player, Hitchens stayed in Italy for eight years, playing for Torino, Atalanta and Cagliari after his days at Inter were over. He returned to England in 1969 to play for Worcester City and then retired after a short spell with Merthyr Tydfil.

John ANGUS

Position	Right-back
Born	John Angus, Amble, 2 September 1938
Height	6ft 0in
Weight	12st 0lb
Clubs	Burnley
England Caps	1
	1961 v Austria (lost 1–3)

UNFORTUNATE TO BE around at the same time as Blackpool's Jimmy Armfield, John Angus won only one full cap for England, when he was asked to play left-back against Austria in 1961, though he had won seven Under-23 caps and represented England Youth.

It was following injuries to a number of key defenders that John Angus made his Football League debut for Burnley in a 2–1 home victory over Everton in September 1956. He went on to be the club's first-choice right-back for the next 15 seasons. During his time with Burnley, Angus won a League Championship medal in 1959/60 and an FA Cup runners-up medal in 1962. He was ever-present in 1962/63, when the Clarets finished third in the First Division.

One of the best right-backs in the top flight, Angus, whose career spanned three decades, represented the Football League and went on to appear in 521 League and Cup games for Burnley, scoring four goals. Two of his strikes came in the same match in October 1964 as the Clarets lost 3–2 to Arsenal.

When his playing days were over, Angus severed all connections with the game and went to live and work in his native Northumberland.

Brian MILLER

Position	Wing-half
Born	Brian George Miller, Hapton, 19 January 1937
Height	6ft 1in
Weight	12st 10lb
Clubs	Burnley
England Caps	1
	1961 v Austria (lost 1–3)

BRIAN MILLER made his Burnley debut in the club's marathon FA Cup tie against Chelsea at Stamford Bridge in February 1956. However, it was to be the following campaign before he became a regular in the Burnley side. He kept his place for the next 11 seasons. When the club won the League Championship in 1959/60, Miller was ever-present, his form that season earning him selection for the England Under-23 side. After another successful season in 1960/61, he won his only full cap for England against Austria in Vienna in May 1961. Unfortunately, he was asked to play at right-half in a match that England lost 3–1.

Miller went on to play in 455 games for the Clarets, scoring 37 goals, two of which came in the two-legged European Fairs Cup match against Eintracht Frankfurt in 1966/67. Only four days after the second leg of that tie, Miller twisted a knee in a 1–0 win at Aston Villa – an injury that ended his playing career.

At the end of the 1966/67 season Miller joined the Turf Moor club's coaching staff before replacing Harry Potts as manager in October 1979. He led the Clarets to the Third Division Championship in 1981/82, but with the club struggling in the lower reaches of the Second Division he was sacked in January 1983. In the summer of 1986 he was asked to manage the club for a second time but the following season, after being knocked out of the FA Cup by Telford, the club only just managed to stave off relegation to the Vauxhall Conference. After losing his position to Frank Casper, he was appointed the Clarets' chief scout.

John FANTHAM

Position	Inside-forward
Born	John Fantham, Sheffield, 6 February 1939
Height	5ft 7in
Weight	11st 3lb
Clubs	Sheffield Wednesday, Rotherham United
England Caps	1
	1961 v Luxembourg (won 4–1)

JOHN FANTHAM IS THE holder of Sheffield Wednesday's post-war aggregate scoring record. His achievements were recognized in the early 1960s, when he won FA, Under-23 and Football League honours, and there is no doubt that he deserved more than the one England cap he was awarded against Luxembourg in 1961.

Fantham only came into his own at the start of the 1958/59 season, following the departure of Albert Quixall to Manchester United. In his first full season he won a Second Division Championship medal and in 1959/60 he topped the Wednesday scoring charts for the first of what was to be five occasions. His best season in terms of goals scored was 1961/62, when he netted 24 times, including scoring his first hat-trick in the Football League as Wednesday beat Birmingham City 5–1.

Fantham scored 167 goals in 435 League and Cup games for the Owls before manager Danny Williams opted to sell the ace marksman to neighbours Rotherham United for just £5,000 in October 1969. On leaving Millmoor, Fantham went on to become a successful businessman.

Ray POINTER

Position	Centre-forward
Born	Raymond Pointer, Cramlington, 10 October 1936
Height	5ft 9in
Weight	10st 10lb
Clubs	Burnley, Bury, Coventry City, Portsmouth
England Caps	3 Goals 2
	1961 v Luxembourg (won 4–1) 1 goal, v Wales (1–1), v Portugal (won 2–0) 1 goal

IN 1958/59 RAY POINTER ended his first full season with Burnley as the club's leading scorer, with 27 goals in 37 League games. The following season, when the Clarets won the League Championship, Pointer played in every League and Cup game, scoring 23 goals, including a hat-trick in a 5–2 win at Arsenal. On 16 September 1961, he netted his second hat-trick for the club in a 6–2 win at Birmingham City, his prolific marksmanship earning him his first full England cap some 12 days later. Leading his country's attack, he found the net in a 4–1 win over Luxembourg at Highbury. In 1961/62 Pointer scored 26 goals, as he had done the previous season, and played for Burnley in the FA Cup Final defeat against Tottenham Hotspur.

In April 1963 Pointer chipped a bone in his foot in the match at Nottingham Forest and though he returned to take his tally of goals to 133 in 270 games, he was never the same player again. In December 1965 he joined Bury, but after scoring 17 goals in just 19 appearances he was on the move again, this time to Coventry City. Shortly afterwards, with the Sky Blues heading towards the top flight, he joined Portsmouth, where he combined his playing duties with coaching the club's youngsters. In 1973 he teamed up with former Burnley manager Harry Potts again as Blackpool's youth coach, before ending his involvement with the game with a spell as Burnley's youth team manager.

Johnny BYRNE

Position	Inside-forward
Born	John Joseph Byrne, West Horsley, 13 May 1939
Died	Cape Town, 27 October 1999
Height	5ft 9in
Weight	11st 7lb
Clubs	Crystal Palace, West Ham United, Fulham
England Caps	11 Goals 7
	1961 v N. Ireland (1–1), v Switzerland (won 8–1) 2 goals
	1964 v Scotland (lost 0–1), v Uruguay (won 2–1) 1 goal, v Portugal (won 4–3) 3 goals,
	v Eire (won 3–1) 1 goal, v Brazil (lost 1–5), v Portugal (1–1), v Argentina (lost 0–1), v Wales
	(won 2–1)
	1965 v Scotland (2–2)

NICKNAMED 'BUDGIE' because of his constant chattering on and off the field, Johnny Byrne joined Crystal Palace in 1956 and became the first Fourth Division player to be capped by England at Under-23 level. In 1960/61 he scored 30 goals, which helped Palace win promotion to the Third Division, and the following season he won full international recognition when he played for England against Northern Ireland at Wembley. He went on to make 11 appearances for his country, netting a hat-trick in a 4–3 win over Portugal in Lisbon in 1964, the winning goal coming three minutes from time.

In March 1962 Byrne joined West Ham United for £65,000, a record transfer between English clubs, and during his time at Upton Park he won an FA Cup winners' medal in 1964 as the Hammers beat Preston North End 3–2. Unfortunately he was forced to miss the following season's European Cup Winners' Cup Final due to injury, but he played in the 1966 League Cup Final defeat by West Bromwich Albion.

In February 1967, after scoring 107 goals in 205 games, Byrne returned for a brief spell with Crystal Palace before spending a season at Fulham. He then emigrated for South Africa, where he became manager of Durban City and later coached Hellenic.

Ray CRAWFORD

Position	Centre-forward
Born	Raymond Crawford, Portsmouth, 13 July 1936
Height	5ft 10in
Weight	11st 10lb
Clubs	Portsmouth, Ipswich Town, Wolverhampton Wanderers, West Bromwich Albion, Charlton Athletic, Colchester United
England Caps	2 Goals 1
	1961 v N. Ireland (1–1)
	1962 v Austria (won 3–1) 1 goal

RAY CRAWFORD began his League career with his home-town club Portsmouth, but after just 22 games, in which he scored 12 goals, he joined Ipswich Town. He ended his first season at Portman Road as Town's leading scorer with 25 goals, including hat-tricks in the wins over Swansea Town and Brighton and Hove Albion. When Ipswich won the Second Division Championship in 1960/61, Crawford had a remarkable season, netting three hat-tricks and scoring 40 out of the club's 100 goals. The following season he continued to find the net with great regularity and became the first Ipswich player to gain an England cap when he played against Northern Ireland at Wembley. It was Crawford who provided the cross for Bobby Charlton to score in a 1–1 draw.

Ipswich's first experience of European football came in 1962/63, and when they beat Maltese champions Floriana 10–0 at Portman Road, Crawford scored five of the goals to establish a scoring record for any British player in any European competition – since equalled by Chelsea's Peter Osgood. Crawford also netted a hat-trick for the Football League in the game against the Irish League at Carrow Road.

In September 1963 he was surprisingly allowed to leave and had spells with both Wolverhampton Wanderers and West Bromwich Albion before Bill McGarry brought him back to Portman Road in March 1966. He took his tally of goals for Ipswich to

228 in 354 games before leaving to play for Charlton Athletic. There then followed a spell of non-League football with Kettering before signing for Colchester United. Not only did he score both of Colchester's goals in a 3–2 Cup defeat by First Division leaders Leeds United, but after netting a hat-trick in an earlier round of that season's FA Cup competition, he became the first player to score trebles in the Football League, FA Cup, League Cup and European Cup.

Stan ANDERSON

Position	Wing-half
Born	Stanley Anderson, Hordern, 27 February 1934
Height	5ft 9in
Weight	11st 12lb
Clubs	Sunderland, Newcastle United, Middlesbrough
England Caps	2
	1962 v Austria (won 3–1), v Scotland (lost 0–2)

STAN ANDERSON had the distinction of captaining all three major north-east clubs: Sunderland, Newcastle United and Middlesbrough. The tough-tackling wing-half won two full caps for England in 1962 but never added to his collection, probably because he had been sent off in an Under-23 international against Bulgaria five years earlier.

After playing his first game for the Wearsiders against Portsmouth in October 1952, Anderson was a virtual ever-present in the Sunderland side for the next 11 seasons. Though he failed to win any domestic honours with Sunderland, he did take the club to two FA Cup semi-finals, but in November 1963, after scoring 35 goals in 447 League and Cup games, he moved to arch-rivals Newcastle United. The move shocked the Sunderland faithful, who nevertheless were soon to see their club promoted to the First Division. Anderson made a dramatic impact on the Newcastle side and was instrumental in their promotion from the Second Division in 1964/65.

After joining Middlesbrough as player-coach, Anderson was appointed manager in April 1966 and brought about a revival at Ayresome Park as he led them back into the Second Division. After two seasons of going close to promotion to the top flight, he left to manage AEK Athens. He later replaced Ian Greaves as manager of Bolton Wanderers, but after they were relegated he was sacked, with almost two years of his contract still to run.

Roger HUNT

Position	Inside-forward		
Born	Roger Hunt, Golborne, 20 July 1938		
Height	5ft 9in		
Weight	11st 10lb		
Clubs	Liverpool, Bolton Wanderers		
England Caps	34	Goals	17

1962 v Austria (won 3–1) 1 goal

1963 v E. Germany (won 2–1) 1 goal

1964 v Scotland (lost 0–1), v United States (won 10–0) 4 goals, v Portugal (1–1) 1 goal, v Wales (won 2–1)

1965 v Spain (won 2–0) 1 goal

1966 v Poland (1–1), v W. Germany (won 1–0), v Scotland (won 4–3) 2 goals, v Finland (won 3–0) 1 goal, v Norway (won 6–1), v Poland (won 1–0) 1 goal, v Uruguay (0–0), v Mexico (won 2–0) 1 goal, v France (won 2–0) 2 goals, v Argentina (won 1–0), v Portugal (won 2–1), v W. Germany (won 4–2 aet), v N. Ireland (won 2–0) 1 goal, v Czechoslovakia (0–0), v Wales (won 5–1)

1967 v Spain (won 2–1) 1 goal, v Austria (won 1–0), v Wales (won 3–0), v N. Ireland (won 2–0), v Soviet Union (2–2)

1968 v Spain (won 1–0), v Spain (won 2–1), v Sweden (won 3–1), v Yugoslavia (lost 0–1), v Soviet Union (won 2–0), v Romania (0–0)

1969 v Romania (1–1)

Honours	World Cup winners England 1966

ROGER HUNT was one of the most prolific goalscorers of the 1960s, but he had his critics, even among England supporters. With Jimmy Greaves around, some thought he wasn't worth his England place. But Alf Ramsey remained an admirer of his poaching instincts, and his inclusion in the 1966 World Cup squad instead of Greaves was to prove crucial to England's fortunes.

For many years Hunt held the Liverpool record for the number of goals scored for the club as well as the highest goal tally for a season. He came to Anfield from Stockton Heath in 1958 and remained with the club for 11 seasons, during which time he struck 285 League goals. He made his first appearance in a red shirt in September 1959 and went on to make 489 appearances, hitting more than 20 League goals in a season on seven occasions, his best tally being during the 1961/62 season when he netted 41 League goals to create a new club record and help the Reds lift the Second Division Championship. There were some who thought he would find life in the First Division more difficult but, on the contrary, Hunt warmed to his task. Dubbed 'Sir Roger' by the Kop, he formed an effective goalscoring partnership with Ian St John, always seeming to be in the right place at the right time.

In December 1969 Hunt joined Bolton Wanderers, the club he had supported as a boy. Unable to revive their struggling fortunes, however, he retired to work in the family haulage business.

Bobby MOORE

Position	Left-half
Born	Robert Frederick Chelsea Moore, Barking, 12 April 1941
Died	24 February 1993
Height	6ft 0in
Weight	12st 13lb
Clubs	West Ham United, Fulham
England Caps	108 Goals 2

The most famous image in English football. Bobby Moore, 1966. (Lancashire Evening Post)

1962 v Peru (won 4–0), v Hungary (lost 1–2), v Argentina (won 3–1), v Bulgaria (0–0),
v Brazil (lost 1–3), v France (1–1), v N. Ireland (won 3–1), v Wales (won 4–0)

1963 v France (lost 2–5), v Scotland (lost 1–2), v Brazil (1–1), v Czechoslovakia (won 4–2),
v E. Germany (won 2–1), v Switzerland (won 8–1), v Wales (won 4–0), v Rest of the
World (won 2–1), v N. Ireland (won 8–3)

1964 v Scotland (lost 0–1), v Uruguay (won 2–1), v Portugal (won 4–3), v Eire (won 3–1),
v Brazil (lost 1–5), v Portugal (1–1), v Argentina (lost 0–1), v N. Ireland (won 4–3),
v Belgium (2–2)

1965 v Scotland (2–2), v Hungary (won 1–0), v Yugoslavia (1–1), v W. Germany (won 1–0),
v Sweden (won 2–1), v Wales (0–0), v Austria (lost 2–3), v N. Ireland (won 2–1), v Spain
(won 2–0)

1966 v Poland (1–1) 1 goal, v W. Germany (won 1–0), v Scotland (won 4–3), v Norway
(won 6–1) 1 goal, v Denmark (won 2–0), v Poland (won 1–0), v Uruguay (0–0), v Mexico
(won 2–0), v France (won 2–0), v Argentina (won 1–0), v Portugal (won 2–1),
v W. Germany (won 4–2 aet), v N. Ireland (won 2–0), v Czechoslovakia (0–0),
v Wales (won 5–1)

1967 v Scotland (lost 2–3), v Spain (won 2–0), v Austria (won 1–0), v Wales (won 3–0),
v N. Ireland (won 2–0), v Soviet Union (2–2)

1968 v Scotland (1–1), v Spain (won 1–0), v Spain (won 2–1), v Sweden (won 3–1),
v W. Germany (lost 0–1), v Yugoslavia (lost 0–1), v Soviet Union (won 2–0), v Romania
(0–0), v Bulgaria (1–1)

1969 v France (won 5–0), v N. Ireland (won 3–1), v Wales (won 2–1), v Scotland (won 4–1),
v Mexico (0–0), v Uruguay (won 2–1), v Brazil (lost 1–2), v Holland (won 1–0), v Portugal
(won 1–0)

1970 v Belgium (won 3–1), v Wales (1–1), v N. Ireland (won 3–1), v Scotland (0–0),
v Colombia (won 4–0), v Ecuador (won 2–0), v Romania (won 1–0), v Brazil (lost 0–1),
v Czechoslovakia (won 1–0), v W. Germany (lost 2–3 aet), v E. Germany (won 3–1)

1971 v Greece (won 3–0), v Malta (won 5–0), v N. Ireland (won 1–0), v Scotland (won 3–1),
v Switzerland (won 3–2), v Switzerland (1–1), v Greece (won 2–0)

1972 v W. Germany (lost 1–3), v W. Germany (0–0), v Wales (won 3–0), v Scotland
(won 1–0), v Yugoslavia (1–1), v Wales (won 1–0)

1973 v Wales (1–1), v Scotland (won 5–0), v N. Ireland (won 2–1), v Wales (won 3–0),
v Scotland (won 1–0), v Czechoslovakia (1–1), v Poland (lost 0–2), v Soviet Union
(won 2–1), v Italy (lost 0–2), v Italy (lost 0–1)

Honours   Footballer of the Year 1964, World Cup winners England 1966

....

THE GREATEST West Ham United player of all time, Bobby Moore was the first
captain to lift three trophies at Wembley in three consecutive years. He lifted the FA
Cup in 1964, the European Cup Winners' Cup in 1965 and of course the World Cup
in 1966. Moore's development was steady – he played a record 18 times for England's
Youth before following the conventional route towards the international team with
eight Under-23 caps, after which he made his full international debut in Peru in May
1962. He had played 17 times for his country when, in May 1963, he was made
England's youngest captain for the match against Czechoslovakia.

At West Ham, Moore and his team-mates suddenly became successful. They won
the 1964 FA Cup Final, beating Preston North End 3–2, and Moore was elected
Footballer of the Year. Cup victory sent the Hammers into Europe and they produced

what many people still regard as the finest performance by a British side in Europe, beating TSV Munich 2–0 in the European Cup Winners' Cup Final. Moore was now in the front line of international defenders, his natural ability refined by his managers, Ron Greenwood at West Ham and Alf Ramsey for England. At the end of the 1966 World Cup tournament, he won the Player of Players award, such was the calibre of his performance. Despite West Ham's decline at this time, his game was completely unaffected, his distribution of the ball from deep remaining impeccable.

In 1973, after appearing in 642 games for West Ham, he joined Fulham, and two years later appeared for the Second Division Cottagers against the Hammers in the FA Cup Final.

After breaking Bobby Charlton's England appearance record, he played just one more game for his country before leaving the international scene. Still England's second-most-capped player in history, the whole country mourned when Bobby Moore died of cancer in 1993.

Maurice NORMAN

Position	Centre-half
Born	Maurice Norman, Mulbarton, 8 May 1934
Height	6ft 1in
Weight	12st 2lb
Clubs	Norwich City, Tottenham Hotspur
England Caps	23
	1962 v Peru (won 4–0), v Hungary (lost 1–2), v Argentina (won 3–1), v Bulgaria (0–0), v Brazil (lost 1–3), v France (1–1)
	1963 v Scotland (lost 1–2), v Brazil (1–1), v Czechoslovakia (won 4–2), v E. Germany (won 2–1), v Wales (won 4–0), v Rest of the World (won 2–1), v N. Ireland (won 8–3)
	1964 v Scotland (lost 0–1), v Uruguay (won 2–1), v Portugal (won 4–3), v United States (won 10–0), v Brazil (lost 1–5), v Portugal (1–1), v Argentina (lost 0–1), v N. Ireland (won 4–3), v Belgium (2–2), v Holland (1–1)

THOUGH HE WAS a member of England's 1958 World Cup squad, Maurice Norman had to wait until 1962 for his first full cap.

Making his name as an uncompromising centre-half in the Spurs 'double' team, he had arrived at White Hart Lane in November 1955 from Norwich City. A giant of a player whose shock of wavy black hair made him appear even taller than his 6ft 1in, he was a commanding figure in the air and an awesome tackler. He had played only 35 games for the Canaries when he joined Spurs in a deal engineered by Jimmy Anderson which saw Johnny Gavin go from Tottenham to Carrow Road. Norman won his first England Under-23 cap against Scotland in February 1956 and two more the following season, but it wasn't until the autumn of 1957 that he could call the centre-half position at Spurs his own. Apart from his 1960/61 club honours, he won an FA Cup winners' medal the next season and was a member of the 1963 European Cup Winners' Cup team.

Norman's career suffered an abrupt end in 1965 when his left leg was broken in five places in a home friendly against a Hungarian XI. Despite a two-year fight for fitness, during which his shinbone had to be reset, he was forced to retire.

Alan PEACOCK

Position	Centre-forward
Born	Alan Peacock, Middlesbrough, 29 October 1937
Height	6ft 0in
Weight	11st 4lb
Clubs	Middlesbrough, Leeds United, Plymouth Argyle
England Caps	6　　Goals　3
	1962 v Argentina (won 3–1), v Bulgaria (0–0), v N. Ireland (won 3–1), v Wales (won 4–0) 2 goals
	1965 v Wales (0–0), v N. Ireland (won 2–1) 1 goal

ALAN PEACOCK began his League career with his home-town team of Middlesbrough, establishing himself in the club's first team midway through the 1957/58 season. During that campaign he netted 15 goals in 22 games, including his first hat-trick for the club in a 4–1 defeat of Cardiff City. Forming a lethal striking partnership with Brian Clough, he scored 19 goals in 1958/59 and the following season netted four of Boro's goals in a 7–1 win at the Baseball Ground as Derby County were completely overrun. Once Clough left Ayresome Park, Peacock came into his own and in 1961/62 he top-scored with 24 goals, including another four in a 5–1 win over Rotherham United. His form that season earned him a place in the England squad for the 1962 World Cup Finals in Chile and he went on to win six caps.

Peacock's best season for Boro in terms of goals scored was 1962/63, when he netted 31 in 40 games, including his sixth hat-trick for the club. He had scored 141 goals in 238 games for Middlesbrough when, in February 1964, he left to play for Leeds United. At Elland Road he won a Second Division Championship medal and appeared in the 1965 FA Cup Final against Liverpool, before ending his career with Plymouth Argyle, where a knee injury forced his retirement.

Mike HELLAWELL

Position	Winger
Born	Michael Stephen Hellawell, Keighley, 30 June 1938
Height	5ft 11in
Weight	11st 6lb
Clubs	Queen's Park Rangers, Birmingham City, Sunderland, Huddersfield Town, Peterborough United
England Caps	2
	1962 v France (1–1), v N. Ireland (won 3–1)

SPEEDY WINGER MIKE HELLAWELL had a trial with Huddersfield Town before joining Queen's Park Rangers in the summer of 1955. While at Loftus Road he played for the Third Division (South) XI against the Third Division (North), but he was far too good a player for that standard of football and in May 1957 he joined

Birmingham City. He took a while to settle at St Andrew's, and it wasn't until 1959/60, following the departure of Harry Hooper, that he began to establish himself in the Blues' side. He played in the 1961 Fairs Cup Final and the following season, in which he was ever-present, won two full caps for England against France and Northern Ireland in October 1962.

In January 1965 Hellawell, who had scored 33 goals in 213 games for Birmingham, moved to Sunderland. A little over a year later he joined Huddersfield Town, later ending his League career with Peterborough United before a brief spell playing non-League football for Bromsgrove Rovers.

Chris CROWE

Position	Inside-forward
Born	Christopher Crowe, Newcastle-upon-Tyne, 11 June 1939
Died	2003
Height	5ft 7in
Weight	11st 0lb
Clubs	Leeds United, Blackburn Rovers, Wolverhampton Wanderers, Nottingham Forest, Bristol City, Walsall
	England Caps 1
	1962 v France (1–1)

CHRIS CROWE had the distinction of playing for both Scotland Schoolboys and the full England team! He had moved to Edinburgh with his family and had a trial with Hearts before joining Leeds United as an amateur in October 1954. He won eight England Youth caps before turning professional in the summer of 1956. Playing alongside the great John Charles, Crowe showed himself to be good on the ball and able to shoot with both feet. In March 1960 he was allowed to join Blackburn Rovers, but it was not until he moved to Wolverhampton Wanderers in February 1962 that he reached his peak, winning a full cap against France in October of that year to add to four Under-23 appearances.

In August 1964 Crowe followed Alan Hinton to Nottingham Forest before, in January 1967, Fred Ford signed him to boost Bristol City's relegation fight. He then had a brief spell playing for Auburn FC in Australia before returning to end his Football League career with Walsall. The much-travelled Crowe went into management with Greenaway Sports and Fram in Norway, before briefly coming out of retirement to play for Bath City. He then had a succession of jobs – among others, working as a newsagent, shoe-shop owner, estate agent and taxi driver – until ill-health forced his retirement.

Ray CHARNLEY

Position	Centre-forward
Born	Raymond Ogden Charnley, Lancaster, 29 May 1935
Height	6ft 0in
Weight	11st 12lb
Clubs	Blackpool, Preston North End, Wrexham, Bradford Park Avenue
England Caps	1
	1962 v France (1–1)

RAY CHARNLEY was playing non-League football for Morecambe when Blackpool manager Joe Smith persuaded him to join the Seasiders in the summer of 1957. In his first season with the club he scored twice in Blackpool's biggest-ever home victory, 7–0 over Sunderland, before going off with a gashed forehead. Charnley topped the Blackpool scoring charts for the first of five consecutive seasons in 1958/59, with a best of 36 goals in 1961/62. During the course of that season he netted four of Blackpool's goals in a 7–2 home win over Wolverhampton Wanderers and scored hat-tricks in the defeats of Chelsea and Leyton Orient. This form led to his only full international cap for England in the match against France at Hillsborough.

Charnley scored ten hat-tricks for the Bloomfield Road club in a total of 222 goals in 407 games, before Stan Mortensen made the unpopular decision to transfer him to rivals Preston North End. He returned to Bloomfield Road just nine days after putting pen to paper and scored against his former club! He later had a brief spell with Wrexham before ending his League career with Bradford Park Avenue.

Alan HINTON

Position	Outside-left		
Born	Alan Thomas Hinton, Wednesbury, 6 October 1942		
Height	5ft 10in		
Weight	11st 5lb		
Clubs	Wolverhampton Wanderers, Nottingham Forest, Derby County		
England Caps	3	Goals	1
	1962 v France (1–1)		
	1964 v Belgium (2–2) 1 goal, v Wales (won 2–1)		

WINGER ALAN HINTON began his Football League career with his local club Wolverhampton Wanderers, establishing himself as a first-team regular midway through the 1961/62 season. He ended the following campaign as the club's leading scorer with 19 goals in 38 League games, which included a hat-trick in a 5–0 win at Fulham. Having earned England Youth and Under-23 honours, Hinton won the first of three full caps for England in October 1962 when he played in a 1–1 draw with France.

Hinton had scored 29 goals in 78 games for Wolves when, in January 1964, he was transferred to Nottingham Forest. It was at the City ground that Hinton won his other two caps, missing very few games in a three-and-a-half year stay at the City Ground before Brian Clough paid £30,000 to take the speedy winger to Derby County. At the Baseball Ground, Hinton helped the Rams win the Second Division title and two League Championships, scoring 64 goals in 253 League appearances.

After leaving the Football League scene, Hinton went to play in the NASL for a variety of teams – Dallas Tornado, Vancouver Whitecaps, Tulsa Roughnecks, Seattle Sounders and Tacoma Stars, whom he continued to play for in the Major Indoor League after the NASL folded.

Brian LABONE

Position	Centre-half
Born	Brian Leslie Labone, Liverpool, 23 January 1940
Height	6ft 1in
Weight	12st 11lb
Clubs	Everton
England Caps	26
	1962 v N. Ireland (won 3–1), v Wales (won 4–0)
	1963 v France (lost 2–5)
	1967 v Spain (won 2–0), v Austria (won 1–0)
	1968 v Scotland (1–1), v Spain (won 2–1), v Sweden (won 3–1), v W. Germany (lost 0–1),
	v Yugoslavia (lost 0–1), v Soviet Union (won 2–0), v Romania (0–0), v Bulgaria (1–1)
	1969 v N. Ireland (won 3–1), v Scotland (won 4–1), v Mexico (0–0), v Uruguay (won 2–1),
	v Brazil (lost 1–2)
	1970 v Belgium (won 3–0), v Wales (1–1), v Scotland (0–0), v Colombia (won 4–0),
	v Ecuador (won 2–0), v Romania (won 1–0), v Brazil (lost 0–1), v W. Germany
	(lost 2–3 aet)

BRIAN LABONE was one of the greatest players ever to wear the royal blue of Everton. When he won the first of his 26 caps against Northern Ireland in 1962, he became the first Everton player since the Second World War to secure an England place.

A player who won almost every honour in the game, Labone was given the runaround by Bobby Smith in a 4–3 win for Spurs in only his second appearance and was dropped. It was almost a year later before he regained his first-team place when he replaced the injured Tommy E. Jones.

He was a great influence on the club's League Championship-winning campaign in 1962/63, but after holding aloft the FA Cup in 1966 he asked to be excused from England's World Cup party to concentrate on his wedding plans! He then astounded the football world in 1967 by announcing his retirement. Having lost both form and confidence, he told the Everton board that he would part company with them in 18 months' time or as soon as a suitable replacement could be found. Thankfully he changed his mind, and after returning to peak form he resurrected his international career and in 1969/70 won another League Championship medal. He stayed in the side until 1971, when an Achilles injury ended his career.

Appearing in a total of 530 games for the Blues, he was described by Harry Catterick as 'the last of the great Corinthians'.

Brian Labone of Everton in England strip. (Lancashire Evening Post)

Freddie HILL

Position	Inside-forward
Born	Frederick Hill, Sheffield, 17 January 1940
Height	5ft 11in
Weight	11st 11lb
Clubs	Bolton Wanderers, Halifax Town, Manchester City, Peterborough United
England Caps	2
	1962 v N. Ireland (won 3–1), v Wales (won 4–0)

FREDDIE HILL turned down an offer from his home-town team Sheffield Wednesday in the hope of getting regular first-team football with Bolton Wanderers. Hill also almost joined Liverpool early in his career but the transfer fell through when it was discovered that he had high blood pressure. He finally made his Wanderers debut in a 1–1 home draw with Newcastle United in April 1958 as a replacement for the injured Dennis Stevens. When Nat Lofthouse retired, Stevens moved to centre-forward to accommodate Freddie Hill on a permanent basis as the club's inside-left. The young Yorkshireman responded by netting his first hat-trick for the club in a 6–0 defeat of Chelsea. After only three seasons of first-team football, Hill was selected for the England Under-23 side and in October 1962 won the first of two caps for England when he played in a 3–1 victory over Northern Ireland in Belfast. In March 1963 he netted his second hat-trick for Bolton as they beat Sheffield United 3–2 – it was Bolton's first home game for three months following one of the worst winters on record.

Hill went on to score 79 goals in 412 games for the Trotters before leaving Burnden Park in 1969 to play for Halifax Town. His stay at the Shay was brief and he returned to top-flight action with Manchester City before joining Peterborough United, whom he helped win the Fourth Division Championship in 1973/74.

Mike O'GRADY

Position	Outside-left		
Born	Michael O'Grady, Leeds, 11 October 1942		
Height	5ft 9in		
Weight	11st 0lb		
Clubs	Huddersfield Town, Leeds United, Wolverhampton Wanderers, Birmingham City, Rotherham United		
England Caps	2	Goals	3
	1962 v N. Ireland (won 3–1) 2 goals		
	1969 v France (won 5–0) 1 goal		

MIKE O'GRADY had a meteoric rise to the top after making his League debut for Huddersfield Town in 1959/60 when only 17 years of age. Only in his second season of first-team football when he won the first of three England Under-23 caps, he went on to gain his first full England cap in October 1962, scoring twice in a 3–1 win over

Northern Ireland in Belfast. He then faded from the international scene for the next seven years, returning when a Leeds United player to again find the net in a 5–0 rout of France.

O'Grady realized his ambition of playing a higher grade of football in 1965 when he moved to Elland Road, and although injuries restricted his opportunities, he still won Fairs Cup and League Championship winners' medals.

In September 1969 he moved to Wolverhampton Wanderers but a tendon injury kept him out of action for over a year. Unable to hold down a regular spot in the Molineux side, he moved to Birmingham City on loan. Again injuries hampered his progress, and he returned to Yorkshire to play for Rotherham United. One of the game's bravest fighters, he was forced into premature retirement, having played in all four divisions of the Football League.

Bobby TAMBLING

Position	Forward
Born	Robert Victor Tambling, Storrington, 18 September 1941
Height	5ft 8in
Weight	11st 8lb
Clubs	Chelsea, Crystal Palace
England Caps	3 Goals 1
	1962 v Wales (won 4–0)
	1963 v France (lost 2–5) 1 goal
	1966 v Yugoslavia (won 2–0)

BOBBY TAMBLING scored on his League debut for Chelsea as they beat West Ham United 3–2 in February 1959, but it was another couple of seasons before he won a regular place in the Blues' starting line-up. Following Jimmy Greaves' departure to Italy, Tambling ended the 1961/62 campaign as the club's leading scorer with 20 goals in 34 games. The following season, aged just 21, he became the youngest player to have captained a promotion-winning side. It certainly didn't affect his goalscoring, for he found the net 35 times – 25 of the goals coming in the 22 games before the big freeze. Included in this total were four goals in the crucial promotion battle against Portsmouth. This form led to him winning the first of his three caps against Wales, when he had a hand in all of England's goals in a 4–0 win.

Tambling – who held the club's record with 202 goals – scored four goals for Chelsea on four occasions, and in the match against Aston Villa in 1966 he netted five times. Sadly, the latter stages of his career at Stamford Bridge were blighted by injury, and after a cartilage operation he joined Crystal Palace, spending four seasons at Selhurst Park before spells in Irish football with Cork City, Waterford and Shamrock Rovers.

Ron HENRY

Position	Left-back
Born	Ronald Patrick Henry, Shoreditch, 17 August 1934
Height	5ft 10in
Weight	11st 13lb
Clubs	Tottenham Hotspur
England Caps	1
	1963 v France (lost 2–5)

RON HENRY won a League Championship medal in 1961, FA Cup winners' medals in 1961 and 1962, and a European Cup Winners' Cup medal in 1963. His consistency for Spurs was rewarded with an England cap against France in February 1963, but, in what was manager Alf Ramsey's first match, England were beaten 5–2 and Henry never got another chance at the top level.

Spotted as a teenage outside-left when stationed at Woolwich during his National Service, Henry was converted into a left-half, made his senior debut for Tottenham Hotspur at centre-half against Huddersfield Town in 1955, then finally became a left-back. It was an injury to Mel Hopkins, who broke his nose in an international for Wales against Scotland, that brought him permanently into the Spurs team. He missed only one of the next 188 games, during which time he formed an excellent full-back partnership with Peter Baker. The only goal of his 14-year career was a speculative 35-yarder against eventual champions Manchester United – a goal that both amazed and delighted the Spurs crowd.

Troubled by a cartilage injury in the later stages of his career, Henry moved into coaching the Spurs juniors following his retirement from playing.

Gordon BANKS

Position	Goalkeeper
Born	Gordon Banks, Sheffield, 30 December 1937
Height	6ft 1in
Weight	13st 6lb
Clubs	Chesterfield, Leicester City, Stoke City
England Caps	73
	1963 v Scotland (lost 1–2), v Brazil (1–1), v Czechoslovakia (won 4–2), v E. Germany (won 2–1), v Wales (won 4–0), v Rest of the World (won 2–1), v N. Ireland (won 8–3)
	1964 v Scotland (lost 0–1), v Uruguay (won 2–1), v Portugal (won 4–3), v United States (won 10–0), v Portugal (1–1), v Argentina (lost 0–1), v N. Ireland (won 4–3)
	1965 v Scotland (2–2), v Hungary (won 1–0), v Yugoslavia (1–1), v W. Germany (won 1–0), v Sweden (won 2–1), v N. Ireland (won 2–1), v Spain (won 2–0)
	1966 v Poland (1–1), v W. Germany (won 1–0), v Scotland (won 4–3), v Yugoslavia (won 2–0), v Finland (won 3–0), v Poland (won 1–0), v Uruguay (0–0), v Mexico (won 2–0), v France (won 2–0), v Argentina (won 1–0), v Portugal (won 2–1), v W. Germany (won 4–2 aet), v N. Ireland (won 2–0), v Czechoslovakia (0–0), v Wales (won 5–1)

Gordon Banks. (Lancashire Evening Post)

1967 v Scotland (lost 2–3), v Wales (won 3–0), v N. Ireland (won 2–0), v Soviet Union
   (2–2)
1968 v Scotland (1–1), v Spain (won 1–0), v W. Germany (lost 0–1), v Yugoslavia (lost 0–1),
   v Soviet Union (won 2–0), v Romania (0–0)
1969 v Romania (1–1), v France (won 5–0), v N. Ireland (won 3–1), v Scotland (won 4–1),
   v Uruguay (won 2–1), v Brazil (lost 1–2)
1970 v Holland (0–0), v Belgium (won 3–1), v Wales (1–1), v N. Ireland (won 3–1),
   v Scotland (0–0), v Colombia (won 4–0), v Ecuador (won 2–0), v Romania (won 1–0),
   v Brazil (lost 0–1), v Czechoslovakia (won 1–0)
1971 v Malta (won 1–0), v Greece (won 3–0), v Malta (won 5–0), v N. Ireland (won 1–0),
   v Scotland (won 3–1), v Switzerland (won 3–2), v Greece (won 2–0)
1972 v W. Germany (lost 1–3), v W. Germany (0–0), v Wales (won 3–0), v Scotland
   (won 1–0)

Honours   World Cup winners England 1966, Footballer of the Year 1972

ARGUABLY THE GREATEST goalkeeper of all time, Gordon Banks was outstanding at his job and accepted any praise with dignity. Even after England's 1966 World Cup win he remained quite unmoved by the fame. The Banks legend took root at Wembley in 1966, and his success and amiable personality gave a new aura and stature to goalkeeping. In the World Cup Finals of 1970 he made a save that is still frequently shown on TV, and is claimed by many to be the best save ever: following a header by the legendary Pele, who, it is reported, shouted 'Goal' as he made contact, Banks threw himself to his right and turned the ball over the bar.

Banks was first noticed in Chesterfield's unexpected progress to the FA Youth Cup Final in 1956. He had played in just 23 games for the Spireites when Leicester City manager Matt Gillies took him to Filbert Street. Here he quickly developed into one of the best keepers in the country, basing his game on an uncanny sense of positioning, superb reflexes and agility. He won the first of his 73 caps for England when he played in the 2–1 defeat by Scotland at Wembley in April 1963. The rise of Peter Shilton spelt a controversially premature end to Banks' Leicester City career and in April 1967 he joined Stoke City for a fee of £52,000. In 1972 he inspired the Potters to their first-ever trophy, the League Cup, and in that same year he was named Footballer of the Year.

Tragically, Banks' world was shattered in October 1972 when, returning home after treatment, he was involved in a road accident that cost him the sight of his right eye. He fought hard to regain his position after a long lay-off, but it wasn't to be. There followed stints coaching Stoke and Port Vale before managing Telford United. An immensely likeable man, his consistency was legendary, and for many he was simply the best.

Gerry BYRNE

Position	Left-back
Born	Gerald Byrne, Liverpool, 29 August 1938
Height	5ft 10in
Weight	12st 6lb
Clubs	Liverpool
England Caps	2
	1963 v Scotland (lost 1–2)
	1966 v Norway (won 6–1)

GERRY BYRNE, who won two full caps for England, albeit three years apart, was the famed Liverpool full-back of the 1960s, whose finest moment came at Wembley in 1965 as the Reds lifted the FA Cup for the first time in their history, beating Leeds United 2–1. Injured after just three minutes, Byrne bravely played on into extra time as if nothing had happened. It was only revealed after the game that the attacking full-back had in fact broken his collarbone!

Byrne joined the Anfield staff straight from school in 1955, but his early career with the Reds looked unpromising. After putting through his own goal on his Liverpool debut, he was largely ignored until the arrival of new manager Bill Shankly, turned him into one of the surest defenders in the First Division. Byrne went on to play in 273 games for Liverpool, winning League Championship honours as well as that FA Cup winners' medal. A stylish full-back who could play on either the left or the right, Byrne formed an effective partnership with Chris Lawler that was the backbone of an outstanding Liverpool side. Injury forced him to retire in 1969, upon which he joined the Anfield club's coaching staff for a short while.

Jimmy MELIA

Position	Inside-forward
Born	James Melia, Liverpool, 1 November 1937
Height	5ft 9in
Weight	10st 12lb
Clubs	Liverpool, Wolverhampton Wanderers, Southampton, Aldershot, Crewe Alexandra
England Caps	2 Goals 1
	1963 v Scotland (lost 1–2), v Switzerland (won 8–1) 1 goal

JIMMY MELIA joined the Anfield staff in 1953 and made his Football League debut for Liverpool two years later. Capped at schoolboy and youth level, he eventually won a full England cap in 1963 and gained a second later that year as England beat Switzerland 8–1 in Basle, with Melia scoring one of the goals. It was to be the final cap for a useful inside-forward always prepared to carry the ball into the area.

Unfortunately, most of Melia's football was played in the lower divisions, with his best season being 1961/62, when the Reds won the Second Division Championship. Life in the top flight was much harder, and after a couple of seasons he lost his place and was transferred to Wolverhampton Wanderers. Eight months later he moved to Southampton, where he played a significant part in the Saints' promotion to the First Division in 1965/66. His vast experience helped the south coast club avoid relegation during their first season in the top flight, but in November 1968 he left to play for Aldershot, later ending his career with Crewe Alexandra.

Melia tried his hand in management with the Railwaymen, and then Stockport County, before moving first to the Middle East and subsequently to the United States. He later returned to these shores and in a brief spell as manager of Brighton and Hove Albion took them to a Wembley Cup Final before going to work in Portugal.

Gordon MILNE

Position	Wing-half
Born	Gordon Milne, Preston, 29 March 1937
Height	5ft 8in
Weight	11st 3lb
Clubs	Preston North End, Liverpool, Blackpool
England Caps	14
	1963 v Brazil (1–1), v Czechoslovakia (won 4–2), v E. Germany (won 2–1), v Wales (won 4–0), v Rest of the World (won 2–1), v N. Ireland (won 8–3)
	1964 v Scotland (lost 0–1), v Uruguay (won 2–1), v Portugal (won 4–3), v Eire (won 3–1), v Brazil (lost 1–5), v Argentina (lost 0–1), v N. Ireland (won 4–3), v Belgium (2–2)

GORDON MILNE was capped 14 times by England and was included in the 1966 World Cup squad. The son of former Preston North End manager Jimmy Milne, he began his career with non-League Morecambe before joining his home-town team. A strong, constructive wing-half, he replaced Tommy Docherty in the North End side, but after a couple of seasons as a Deepdale regular he was made a scapegoat after a poor start to what proved to be the club's relegation season of 1960/61. Three days after being dropped, he was transferred to Liverpool, where he enjoyed his greatest success. Although he missed the 1965 FA Cup Final through injury, he played in two League Championship-winning sides and a Second Division title side as well as a European Cup Winners' Cup Final.

Milne left Anfield in May 1967 and joined Blackpool, making his Seasiders debut on his old hunting ground of Deepdale. Blackpool just missed out on promotion to the First Division in Milne's first season at Bloomfield Road, and thereafter injuries and a loss of form severely curtailed his appearances.

In January 1970 Milne was allowed to join Wigan Athletic as player-manager. He then held managerial posts with Coventry City and Leicester City, whom he helped into the First Division. Though he was later sacked by the Foxes, Milne managed the England Youth side before moving to Turkey, where he had great success managing Besiktas.

George EASTHAM

Position	Inside-forward
Born	George Edward Eastham, Blackpool, 23 September 1936
Height	5ft 8in
Weight	9st 13lb
Clubs	Ards, Newcastle United, Arsenal, Stoke City
England Caps	19 Goals 2

1963 v Brazil (1–1), v Czechoslovakia (won 4–2), v E. Germany (won 2–1), v Wales (won 4–0), v Rest of the World (won 2–1), v N. Ireland (won 8–3)

1964 v Scotland (lost 0–1), v Uruguay (won 2–1), v Portugal (won 4–3), v Eire (won 3–1) 1 goal, v United States (won 10–0), v Brazil (lost 1–5), v Argentina (lost 0–1)

1965 v Hungary (won 1–0), v W. Germany (won 1–0), v Sweden (won 2–1), v Spain (won 2–0)

1966 v Poland (1–1), v Denmark (won 2–0) 1 goal

GEORGE EASTHAM came from a footballing family, his father George having appeared for Bolton and England and his elder brother Harry for Liverpool and Newcastle United during the Second World War. A member of England's World Cup squads in both 1962 and 1966, he and his father were for many years the only father and son pair to have appeared for their country.

Eastham played alongside his father in Northern Ireland for Ards before joining the Magpies, where he developed rapidly alongside the 'Welsh Wizard' Ivor Allchurch. After becoming a regular for the Young England side, Eastham became embroiled in a major dispute with Newcastle – an unsavoury affair, firstly over money and a club-house and then eventually over the basic right of a footballer to ply his trade wherever he chooses. Backed by the Players' Union, he took the authorities and Newcastle United to the High Court and won a historic litigation battle. By the time the long legal process was resolved, Eastham had joined Arsenal, for whom he scored twice on his debut in a 5–1 win over Bolton Wanderers. During his stay with Arsenal, he was a great inspiration to the club, captaining them for three seasons. However, after the 1965/66 season, the Gunners' worst campaign for many a year, he could not agree terms and was transferred to Stoke City. He spent eight seasons at the Victoria Ground, helping Stoke win their first major honour, the League Cup, in 1971/72.

After retiring, Eastham coached and managed Stoke City before later emigrating to South Africa. Awarded the OBE in 1975, he settled in Johannesburg, where he operated a sportswear company.

Ken SHELLITO

Position	Right-back
Born	Kenneth John Shellito, East Ham, 18 April 1940
Height	5ft 10in
Weight	12st 12lb
Clubs	Chelsea
England Caps	1
	1963 v Czechoslovakia (won 4–2)

KEN SHELLITO won what promised to be the first of many England caps on the 1963 tour of Eastern Europe, but in October of that year he damaged his left knee in the match against Sheffield Wednesday. He had to undergo four cartilage operations in the next three years as he battled with great courage to save his career.

Though he made his Football League debut for Chelsea in 1959, Shellito spent the next couple of seasons in the club's reserve side, honing his technique. When the chance he had been waiting for finally arrived, the young defender secured his place with a series of polished displays. His reputation began to blossom during the club's Second Division promotion-winning season of 1962/63 when playing alongside Eddie McCreadie. Shellito rarely wasted possession and was keen to support the attack at every opportunity. Helping to pioneer the overlap, he often surged down the right flank, linking with his forwards and delivering a telling centre.

Shellito took over the Chelsea captaincy, only for the knee injury to put an end to his career. The home leg of the Fairs Cup tie against Wiener of Austria in December 1965 proved to be his last first-class game. Forced to abandon his fight for fitness, he joined the Stamford Bridge coaching staff, succeeding his old full-back partner Eddie McCreadie as manager in 1977.

Terry PAINE

Position	Outside-right
Born	Terence Lionel Paine, Winchester, 23 March 1939
Height	5ft 8in
Weight	10st 6lb
Clubs	Southampton, Hereford United
England Caps	19 Goals 7
	1963 v Czechoslovakia (won 4–2), v E. Germany (won 2–1), v Wales (won 4–0), v Rest of the World (won 2–1) 1 goal, v N. Ireland (won 8–3) 3 goals
	1964 v Scotland (lost 0–1), v Uruguay (won 2–1), v United States (won 10–0) 2 goals, v Portugal (1–1), v N. Ireland (won 4–3)
	1965 v Hungary (won 1–0), v Yugoslavia (1–1), v W. Germany (won 1–0) 1 goal, v Sweden (won 2–1), v Wales (0–0), v Austria (lost 2–3)
	1966 v Yugoslavia (won 2–0), v Norway (won 6–1), v Mexico (won 2–0)

WHEN ENGLAND BEAT Northern Ireland 8–3 in November 1963, Terry Paine became the first outside-right since Stanley Matthews to score a hat-trick in an international

Terry Paine of Southampton. (Lancashire Evening Post)

match. He was part of Alf Ramsey's plans for the 1966 World Cup, but in that tournament he only played in the 2–0 win over Mexico, a match in which he was injured. It was his last appearance for England, with all of his caps being won while he was a Second Division player.

Paine began his career with his home-town club Winchester, then managed by former Southampton forward Harry Osman. He recommended the young Paine to Southampton manager Ted Bates, and in August 1956 he was added to the club's playing staff. After working his way up through the ranks, Paine was ever-present from 1958 to 1961, helping the club to win the Third Division Championship in 1959/60 and then scoring 25 goals during the club's first season back in the Second Division. On 18 November 1961 he missed the match against Sunderland after appearing in 160 consecutive League games, but in 1962/63 he was again ever-present. An important member of the Southampton side that won promotion to the First Division in 1965/66, he was yet again ever-present the following season when his endless stream of pinpoint crosses brought Ron Davies 37 goals in 41 games. Staying free from injury, Paine broke both the club appearance and goalscoring records, playing in 801 League and Cup games and scoring 183 goals.

In 1974 Paine left the Dell to join Hereford United, helping them to a Third Division title two seasons later. Awarded the MBE for his services to football, he now works as a football coach in South Africa.

Tony KAY

Position	Wing-half
Born	Anthony Herbert Kay, Sheffield, 13 May 1937
Height	5ft 8in
Weight	12st 0lb
Clubs	Sheffield Wednesday, Everton
England Caps	1 Goals 1
	1963 v Switzerland (won 8–1) 1 goal

THOUGH HE MADE his Sheffield Wednesday debut in 1954, red-haired Tony Kay didn't become a first-team regular until the arrival of manager Harry Catterick four years later. He played in seven England Under-23 matches and represented the Football League on three occasions. An ever-present in seasons 1960/61 and 1961/62, Kay went on to play in 203 League and Cup games before being transferred to Everton in December 1962 for £55,000 – then a record fee for a half-back. In 1963 he won his one and only full England cap, scoring a goal in the 8–1 win over Switzerland in Zurich.

Appointed captain during Harry Catterick's reign as Everton manager, he played a leading role in the club's League Championship success of 1962/63. However, he was at the centre of one of football's greatest-ever scandals when in 1965 he was sent to prison and banned for life after the infamous soccer bribes trial. It was a very sad end to the career of a man who was without doubt one of the most talented wing-halves of his day.

George Cohen (see p. 168) and Martin Peters in action for England during the World Cup Final against West Germany at Wembley, 30 July 1966. (Getty Images)

Bobby THOMSON

Position	Left-back
Born	Robert Anthony Thomson, Smethwick, 5 December 1943
Height	6ft 0in
Weight	11st 6lb
Clubs	Wolverhampton Wanderers, Birmingham City, Walsall, Luton Town, Port Vale
England Caps	8
	1963 v N. Ireland (won 8–3)
	1964 v United States (won 10–0), v Portugal (1–1), v Argentina (lost 0–1), v N. Ireland (won 4–3), v Belgium (2–2), v Wales (won 2–1), v Holland (1–1)

LEFT-BACK BOBBY THOMSON was a polished defender whose performances in schoolboy football led to a number of Midlands clubs trying to sign him. Wolves won the chase and it wasn't long before he established himself as a first-team regular. He developed into an international player, gaining eight full caps for England before he was 22, having also appeared for the England Under-23s and the Football League.

Having helped Wolves win promotion to the First Division in 1966/67, and after playing in 300 games for the Molineux club, he joined Birmingham City in March 1969. He was an ever-present in his first season at St Andrew's, but after losing his place to Ray Martin he went on loan to Walsall before joining Luton Town. His stay at Kenilworth Road was brief and he moved on to Port Vale, where he ended his League career.

Thomson subsequently dropped into non-League football as player-manager of Stafford Rangers before leaving to run a sports shop in Sedgley.

George COHEN

Position	Right-back
Born	George Reginald Cohen, Kensington, 22 October 1939
Height	5ft 10in
Weight	12st 7lb
Clubs	Fulham
England Caps	37
	1964 v Uruguay (won 2–1), v Portugal (won 4–3), v Eire (won 3–1), v United States (won 10–0), v Brazil (lost 1–5), v N. Ireland (won 4–3), v Belgium (2–2), v Wales (won 2–1), v Holland (1–1)
	1965 v Scotland (2–2), v Hungary (won 1–0), v Yugoslavia (1–1), v W. Germany (won 1–0), v Sweden (won 2–1), v Wales (0–0), v Austria (lost 2–3), v N. Ireland (won 2–1), v Spain (won 2–0)
	1966 v Poland (1–1), v W. Germany (won 1–0), v Scotland (won 4–3), v Norway (won 6–1), v Denmark (won 2–0), v Poland (won 1–0), v Uruguay (0–0), v Mexico (won 2–0), v France (won 2–0), v Argentina (won 1–0), v Portugal (won 2–1), v W. Germany (won 4–2 aet), v N. Ireland (won 2–0), v Czechoslovakia (0–0), v Wales (won 5–1)
	1967 v Scotland (lost 2–3), v Spain (won 2–0), v Wales (won 3–0), v N. Ireland (won 2–0)
Honours	World Cup winners England 1966

GEORGE COHEN played his first game for Fulham in a 2–1 home defeat at the hands of Liverpool in March 1957. It was his only appearance that season, but midway through the 1957/58 campaign he won a regular spot in the Cottagers' side, helping them to that season's FA Cup semi-final. In 1958/59 he missed just one game as Fulham won promotion to the First Division and over the next nine seasons the speedy full-back missed just a handful of games due to injury. In 1961/62 he helped the club to another FA Cup semi-final, before winning the first of 37 caps for England in May 1964, against Uruguay at Wembley. He was in the England side that won the World Cup in 1966, forming a formidable full-back pairing with Ray Wilson, and was the last Fulham player to win an England cap.

Sadly for Fulham and England, Cohen received a nasty knee injury in the First Division game against Liverpool in December 1967, and, though he tried to make a comeback, it virtually ended his career. Having appeared in 459 games for the Cottagers, he had a brief spell coaching the club's juniors before leaving to develop his business interests. After a five-year battle with cancer he combined his interests in building and property development with raising money for cancer charities.

Peter THOMPSON

Position	Winger
Born	Peter Thompson, Carlisle, 27 November 1942
Height	5ft 8in
Weight	11st 6lb
Clubs	Preston North End, Liverpool, Bolton Wanderers
England Caps	16
	1964 v Portugal (won 4–3), v Eire (won 3–1), v United States (won 10–0), v Brazil (lost 1–5), v Portugal (1–1), v Argentina (lost 0–1), v N. Ireland (won 4–3), v Belgium (2–2), v Wales (won 2–1), v Holland (1–1)
	1965 v Scotland (2–2), v N. Ireland (won 2–1)
	1967 v N. Ireland (won 2–0)
	1968 v W. Germany (lost 0–1)
	1969 v Holland (won 1–0)
	1970 v Scotland (0–0)

DURING THE 1960s there were few more exciting sights in the Football League than to see Peter Thompson running at defenders, the ball at his feet, as the red shirts of Liverpool swarmed towards the Kop. Thompson arrived at Anfield from Preston North End in the summer of 1963, manager Bill Shankly paying £35,000 for his services. He was then 21 and already receiving rave notices. In nine seasons at Anfield he played in just over 400 games, scoring 54 goals. In his first season with the Reds he won four England Under-23 caps and also played in his first full international as England beat Portugal 4–3. He was eventually capped 16 times for England while at Anfield, collecting League and FA Cup honours as well.

After losing his place to Steve Heighway, Thompson joined Bolton Wanderers on loan in December 1973. A month later he signed on a permanent basis, giving the Wanderers an exciting new attacking dimension. A great crowd favourite, he helped the club enjoy one of its most exciting periods, but at the end of the 1977/78 season he left the game to run a hotel in the Lake District.

Peter Thompson. (Lancashire Evening Post)

Tony WAITERS

Position	Goalkeeper
Born	Anthony Keith Waiters, Southport, 1 February 1937
Height	6ft 2in
Weight	13st 12lb
Clubs	Blackpool, Burnley
England Caps	5
	1964 v Eire (won 3–1), v Brazil (lost 1–5), v Belgium (2–2), v Wales (won 2–1), v Holland (1–1)

TONY WAITERS won England Amateur honours while at Loughborough College and then played for Bishop Auckland and Macclesfield before joining Blackpool in October 1959. He set about replacing Blackpool's Scottish international keeper George Farm, who had been at Bloomfield Road for well over a decade, making his debut in a 1–0 win over Blackburn Rovers on Boxing Day 1959. After that the first-team jersey was his, though he did have to fight off another future England goalkeeper in Gordon West. Waiters was a fitness fanatic and worked consistently at developing and improving his skills. He won his first representative honour in October 1963, when representing the Football League against the League of Ireland in Dublin. He went on to win five full caps for England, including an appearance against Brazil in the Maracana Stadium in Rio de Janeiro when the Pele-inspired opposition won 5–1.

All his Blackpool career was spent in the top flight, and he decided to retire when the Seasiders were relegated in 1966/67. He became the FA's north-west regional coach, later joining Liverpool as the Anfield club's youth coach. In July 1970 he joined Burnley as coach, but following an injury to Peter Mellor, was persuaded to resurrect his playing career. He had a season as the Turf Moor club's keeper before joining Coventry City as director of coaching. After a spell as England Youth-team manager he took charge of Plymouth Argyle and led them to promotion to the Second Division. Later, after a number of years as coach of Vancouver Whitecaps, he coached the Canadian national team to the 1986 World Cup Finals in Mexico.

Mike BAILEY

Position	Midfielder
Born	Michael Alfred Bailey, Wisbech, 27 February 1942
Height	5ft 8in
Weight	11st 4lb
Clubs	Charlton Athletic, Wolverhampton Wanderers, Hereford United
England Caps	2
	1964 v United States (won 10–0)
	1965 v Wales (won 2–1)

MIKE BAILEY played his early football with non-League Gorleston before being signed by Charlton Athletic in the summer of 1958. His performances for the Addicks led to him winning five England Under-23 caps and two at full level, Bailey developing into one of the best wing-halves in the country. Having become Charlton's captain, he broke a leg in the match against Middlesbrough in October 1964 but recovered well to play in a total of 169 games, before joining Wolverhampton Wanderers for £40,000 in March 1966. The following season he helped Wolves win promotion to the First Division and was voted Midland Footballer of the Year. When Wolves reached the final of the 1972 UEFA Cup against Spurs, he was on the bench, but he skippered the side to victory against Manchester City in the League Cup Final of 1974. When he left Molineux in the summer of 1977, he had scored 25 goals in 436 games for the club.

Bailey joined Minnesota Kicks in the NASL before later becoming player-coach of Hereford United and then manager of Charlton Athletic. He was appointed too late to prevent Athletic's relegation but the following season he helped them bounce straight back to be Second Division, the club securing promotion in third place. After later managing Brighton and Hove Albion, he went to coach abroad.

Fred PICKERING

Position	Centre-forward
Born	Frederick Pickering, Blackburn, 19 January 1941
Height	5ft 11in
Weight	12st 8lb
Clubs	Blackburn Rovers, Everton, Birmingham City, Blackpool
England Caps	3 Goals 4
	1964 v United States (won 10–0) 3 goals, v N. Ireland (won 4–3) 1 goal, v Belgium (2–2)

FRED PICKERING scored a hat-trick on his international debut as the United States were routed 10–0, beginning his career as a full-back with Blackburn Rovers. He enjoyed success in the Ewood Park club's junior teams, helping to win the FA Youth Cup in 1959, but when he was given a chance in the first team he failed to impress. Rovers' manager Jack Marshall decided to gamble with him at centre-forward, after some powerful displays in that position with the reserves. Blessed with the happy knack of putting the ball in the net, Pickering soon began to create a name for himself. In fact, he became so prolific, scoring 59 goals in 123 League games for Rovers, that when Everton's bid of £85,000 for his services was accepted, there was outrage in Blackburn.

Pickering signalled his arrival on Merseyside with a hat-trick on his debut as Everton thrashed Nottingham Forest 6–1. Pickering's best season was 1964/65, when he scored 37 goals in 51 League and Cup games, including another treble in a 4–1 defeat of Tottenham Hotspur. The following season he suffered a cartilage problem and had to miss the club's semi-final victory over Manchester United. Though Pickering passed himself fit for the final, Catterick didn't select him and it became clear his days at Goodison were numbered. Having scored 68 goals in 107 games for the Toffees, he was allowed to join Birmingham City. He later went back to the north-west to play for Blackpool, but after helping the Seasiders win promotion he returned to Ewood Park, where he ended his career.

Terry VENABLES

Position	Inside-forward
Born	Terence Frederick Venables, Bethnal Green, 6 January 1943
Height	5ft 8in
Weight	11st 8lb
Clubs	Chelsea, Tottenham Hotspur, Queen's Park Rangers, Crystal Palace
England Caps	2
	1964 v Belgium (2–2), v Holland (1–1)

TERRY VENABLES was a stylish player with four London clubs and won an FA Cup and League Cup winners' medal during his career. Starting out with Chelsea, he won FA Youth Cup winners' medals in 1960 and 1961, and became the first player to represent England at five different levels – schoolboy, amateur, youth, Under-23 and full. After 237 games for the Stamford Bridge club, he moved to Tottenham Hotspur for £80,000 in May 1966. In his first season with Spurs he won an FA Cup winners' medal against his former club, but overall failed to win over the critical White Hart Lane fans. In the summer of 1969 he joined Queen's Park Rangers, spending five years at Loftus Road before moving on to Crystal Palace.

His playing career was near its end and Venables soon retired to become coach at Selhurst Park. When Malcolm Allison left, Venables became Palace manager and in his first season led the Eagles to promotion from the Third Division. In 1978/79 they won the Second Division championship, but Venables parted company with the club in October 1980 after a boardroom row. Immediately joining Queen's Park Rangers as manager, he led them to an FA Cup Final in 1982 and the Second Division title in 1983. In May 1984 he received an offer to manage Barcelona, and in his first season with the Spanish giants he led them to the League title. They reached the European Cup Final the following year but lost on penalties to Steaua Bucharest. He later returned to England to manage Spurs, taking them to the 1991 FA Cup Final, where they beat Nottingham Forest 2–1. His contribution at Tottenham was always full of incident, culminating in public conflict with Alan Sugar in 1993. His eventual dismissal provoked fierce protest among his many devoted fans, but in 1994 he was appointed England coach, leading them to the semi-finals of Euro '96. He subsequently focused on his role as a TV pundit before being persuaded to return to management, helping Middlesbrough retain their Premiership status. Venables subsequently became manager of Leeds United, following the dismissal of David O'Leary, but his time there, in what was a turbulent time for the club, proved an unhappy one, and in 2003 he was replaced by Peter Reid.

Gerry YOUNG

Position	Wing-half
Born	Gerald Morton Young, South Shields, 1 October 1936
Height	5ft 11in
Weight	11st 10lb
Clubs	Sheffield Wednesday
England Caps	1
	1964 v Wales (won 2–1)

UNFORTUNATELY, Gerry Young's name will always be associated with Sheffield Wednesday's 1966 FA Cup Final appearance against Everton, when he failed to cut out a long clearance, allowing Derek Temple to run on and score the winning goal. However, the popular wing-half was a model professional and gave the Owls great service, winning international honours for England against Wales at Wembley in November 1964. He was due to make his second appearance against Holland a few weeks later, but a ruptured thigh muscle cost him his place.

Young arrived at Hillsborough in May 1955 and made his first-team debut at Blackpool in March 1957, but it wasn't until Tony Kay left to join Everton that he won a regular first-team place. In 1963/64 he was the club's only ever-present as they finished sixth in the First Division. Young went on to make 345 League and Cup appearances for Wednesday before hanging up his boots in 1971. He then joined the club's coaching staff. However, after taking temporary charge of team affairs, he was sacked when Steve Burtenshaw departed.

Frank WIGNALL

Position	Centre-forward		
Born	Frank Wignall, Blackrod, 21 August 1939		
Height	5ft 11in		
Weight	12st 0lb		
Clubs	Everton, Nottingham Forest, Wolverhampton Wanderers, Derby County, Mansfield Town		
England Caps	2	Goals	2
	1964 v Wales (won 2–1) 2 goals, v Holland (1–1)		

FRANK WIGNALL was capped twice by England in 1964, scoring both goals on his debut as England beat Wales 2–1. Later that year he broke his leg in a county cup-tie and didn't return to first-team action until midway through the 1965/66 season.

Playing his early football with Horwich RMI in the Lancashire Combination, Frank Wignall's powerful displays and prolific scoring attracted the attention of a number of top clubs, and in May 1958 he joined Everton. He had made just 33 appearances for the Toffees when he left to play for Nottingham Forest in April 1963. In his first campaign with the club, Wignall was Forest's leading scorer with 16 goals, including a hat-trick in a 3–2 win over Bolton Wanderers, the club he had supported as a boy. After his lengthy lay-off following his leg-break, Wignall was back to his best, acting as the perfect foil to Joe Baker. The goals dried up, however, in 1967/68, and in March of that season he was allowed to join Wolves. His stay at Molineux was brief and he moved on to Derby County, whom he helped win the Second Division Championship. He ended his first-class career with Mansfield Town before playing non-League football for King's Lynn and Burton Albion. He later coached the Qatar national side and managed Shepshed Charterhouse.

Alan MULLERY

Position	Wing-half
Born	Alan Patrick Mullery, Notting Hill, 23 November 1941
Height	5ft 9in
Weight	12st 4lb
Clubs	Fulham, Tottenham Hotspur
England Caps	35 Goals 1

1964 v Holland (1–1)

1967 v Spain (won 2–0), v Austria (won 1–0), v Wales (won 3–0), v N. Ireland (won 2–0), v Soviet Union (2–2)

1968 v Scotland (1–1), v Spain (won 1–0), v Spain (won 2–1), v Sweden (won 3–1), v Yugoslavia (lost 0–1), v Romania (0–0), v Bulgaria (1–1)

1969 v France (won 5–0), v N. Ireland (won 3–1), v Scotland (won 4–1), v Mexico (0–0), v Uruguay (won 2–1), v Brazil (lost 1–2), v Holland (won 1–0), v Portugal (won 1–0)

1970 v Holland (0–0), v Wales (1–1), v N. Ireland (won 3–1), v Scotland (0–0), v Colombia (won 4–0), v Ecuador (won 2–0), v Romania (won 1–0), v Brazil (lost 0–1), v Czechoslovakia (won 1–0), v W. Germany (lost 2–3 aet) 1 goal, v E. Germany (won 3–1)

1971 v Malta (won 1–0), v Greece (won 3–0), v Switzerland (won 3–2)

Honours	Footballer of the Year 1975

ONLY 17 WHEN he made his League debut for Fulham, Alan Mullery soon established himself as a permanent member of the Cottagers' side, his impressive performances in the top flight leading to him winning the first of three England Under-23 caps when he played against Italy in November 1960. He had appeared in 218 games for Fulham when, in March 1964, Spurs paid £72,500 for his services. Two months later he played for the Football League against the Italian League, and after one more outing with the Football League he won his first full cap against Holland in December of that year. Restricted at international level by the performances of Nobby Stiles, he did not win his second cap until May 1967, four days after winning an FA Cup winners' medal against Chelsea. After that he became an England regular, winning 33 more caps.

In 1968 Mullery became club captain and led Spurs to victory in the 1971 League Cup Final. However, in October of that year he suffered a deep-seated pelvic strain, which put him out of action for six months. Having recovered, he went on loan to Fulham, but after a few weeks he was recalled owing to a lengthy injury list at White Hart Lane. Leading the club into their UEFA Cup semi-final with AC Milan, he clinched the tie with a brilliant 20-yard volley at the San Siro Stadium before going on to secure

Alan Mullery. (Lancashire Evening Post)

the trophy with a header – knocking himself out in the process – in the second leg of the final against Wolves. He returned to Craven Cottage on a permanent basis in the summer of 1972, after appearing in 429 games for Spurs. In 1975 he won an FA Cup runners-up medal after the Cottagers had been beaten 2–0 by West Ham United.

Mullery was elected Footballer of the Year and awarded the MBE. Having scored 42 goals in 412 games during his time with Fulham, he went into management with Brighton. He led the Seagulls from the Third to the First Division before later managing Charlton Athletic, Crystal Palace and Queen's Park Rangers, finally finishing his career with another spell at Brighton.

Nobby STILES

Position	Wing-half
Born	Norbert Peter Stiles, Manchester, 18 May 1942
Height	5ft 6in
Weight	10st 10lb
Clubs	Manchester United, Middlesbrough, Preston North End
England Caps	28 Goals 1

1965 v Scotland (2–2), v Hungary (won 1–0), v Yugoslavia (1–1), v Sweden (won 2–1), v Wales (0–0), v Austria (lost 2–3), v N. Ireland (won 2–1), v Spain (won 2–0)

1966 v Poland (1–1), v W. Germany (won 1–0) 1 goal, v Scotland (won 4–3), v Norway (won 6–1), v Denmark (won 2–0), v Poland (won 1–0), v Uruguay (0–0), v Mexico (won 2–0), v France (won 2–0), v Argentina (won 1–0), v Portugal (won 2–1), v W. Germany (won 4–2 aet), v N. Ireland (won 2–0), v Czechoslovakia (0–0), v Wales (won 5–1)

1967 v Scotland (lost 2–3)

1968 v Soviet Union (won 2–0)

1969 v Romania (1–1)

1970 v N. Ireland (won 3–1), v Scotland (0–0)

Honours	World Cup winners England 1966

....

NOBBY STILES wore the No. 4 shirt throughout England's triumphant World Cup in 1966, making his mark as a world-class player with his brilliant covering, especially against Portugal's Eusebio in the semi-final. No one will forget Nobby's antics after England had won the World Cup, putting the trophy on his head and dancing with delight.

One of the hardmen of British football, Stiles was just 18 when he made his League debut for Manchester United against Bolton Wanderers in October 1960. Staying in the side for the rest of the season, he shared in United's successful 1963 FA Cup run, though he didn't win a place in the final. Having helped the Reds win the League Championship in 1964/65, he hardly missed a match as the club repeated the feat in 1966/67 and then won the European Cup in 1968.

It has been said that many of Nobby's awkward-looking tackles in the early days were the result of him not wearing his spectacles, his tackling improving after he was fitted with contact lenses! Whatever the case, the fans abroad certainly didn't like him: he was called an assassin in South America, spat at in Italy and hit on the head by a bottle in Madrid. Playing without his false teeth made him look like Dracula, and according to the French, who met him in the 1966 World Cup tournament, he was twice as dangerous!

In May 1971, after two cartilage operations, Stiles was transferred to Middlesbrough, but after two seasons in the north-east he joined Preston North End. He had just one season playing for the Deepdale club, but spent the next seven years there as coach and manager. On leaving North End he teamed up with his brother-in-law Johnny Giles as coach of Vancouver Whitecaps, before following him in a similar capacity to West Bromwich Albion. He later coached the juniors at Old Trafford.

Nobby Stiles, September 1965. (Getty Images)

Jack CHARLTON

Position	Centre-half
Born	Jack Charlton, Ashington, 8 May 1935
Height	6ft 2in
Weight	12st 8lb
Clubs	Leeds United
England Caps	35 Goals 6

1965 v Scotland (2–2), v Hungary (won 1–0), v Yugoslavia (1–1), v W. Germany (won 1–0), v Sweden (won 2–1), v Wales (0–0), v Austria (lost 2–3), v N. Ireland (won 2–1), v Spain (won 2–0)

1966 v Poland (1–1), v W. Germany (won 1–0), v Scotland (won 4–3), v Yugoslavia (won 2–0), v Finland (won 3–0) 1 goal, v Denmark (won 2–0) 1 goal, v Uruguay (0–0), v Mexico (won 2–0), v France (won 2–0), v Argentina (won 1–0), v Portugal (won 2–1), v W. Germany (won 4–2 aet), v N. Ireland (won 2–0), v Czechoslovakia (0–0), v Wales (won 5–1) 1 goal

1967 v Scotland (lost 2–3) 1 goal, v Wales (won 3–0)

1968 v Spain (won 1–0)

1969 v Romania (1–1) 1 goal, v France (won 5–0), v Wales (won 2–1), v Holland (won 1–0), v Portugal (won 1–0) 1 goal

1970 v Holland (0–0), v Czechoslovakia (won 1–0)

Honours	World Cup winners England 1966, Footballer of the Year 1967

'BIG JACK' was part of the Elland Road scene for 21 years. His uncles, George, Jim and Jack Milburn, all started with Leeds United, and it was Jim who recommended the gangling centre-half to the Yorkshire club. After National Service with the Royal Horse Guards, Charlton occupied the centre-half spot vacated by John Charles, who had switched to the attack. In October 1957 he played for the Football League against the League of Ireland. International honours looked likely but his career reached a temporary plateau when he found himself in a struggling Leeds team. He won a belated first cap against Scotland in 1965, joining his brother Bobby, already a household name with Manchester United, in the side. The brothers played vital roles in England's 1966 World Cup success and Jack, who won 35 caps, was voted Footballer of the Year in 1967.

Jack had a brief spell as captain of Leeds United but gave it up because of a superstition that it was best to come on to the pitch last. Playing alongside Norman Hunter, Charlton, a supreme header of the ball, developed into probably the best centre-half in the First Division. He figured in Leeds' early successes under Don Revie and won an FA Cup winners' medal in 1972, two days before his 37th birthday.

In 1973 Charlton left Leeds to become manager of Middlesbrough, and by the end of his first season at Ayresome Park the club had won the Second Division title. They later won the Anglo-Scottish Cup, but in April 1977 Charlton resigned to take charge of Sheffield Wednesday. He swiftly created a team that won promotion to the Second Division, but then left to manage Newcastle United. His time with the Magpies proved an unhappy one for the big Geordie, and after being barracked by the crowd he resigned in August 1985. Six months later he was approached by the Irish FA to take over the running of the national side on a part-time basis. In 1988, the Republic reached the European Championship Finals for the first time, and in 1990 they went a step further, making the World Cup Finals, where they lost 1–0 to Italy in the quarter-finals. They reached the World Cup Finals again in 1994, but midway through the 1995/96 season Charlton stepped down to be replaced by Mick McCarthy.

Barry BRIDGES

Position	Forward
Born	Barry John Bridges, Horsford, 29 April 1941
Height	5ft 9in
Weight	11st 11lb
Clubs	Chelsea, Birmingham City, Queen's Park Rangers, Millwall, Brighton and Hove Albion
England Caps	4 Goals 1
	1965 v Scotland (2–2), v Hungary (won 1–0), v Yugoslavia (1–1) 1 goal, v Austria (lost 2–3)

A FORMER ENGLAND schoolboy international, Barry Bridges joined Chelsea's groundstaff in the summer of 1956, signing professional forms two years later. Following the departure of Jimmy Greaves to AC Milan, Bridges began to establish himself in the Chelsea side, and in April 1965 won the first of four full caps for England when he played in the 2–2 draw against Scotland at Wembley.

Bridges went on to score 93 goals in 205 games for the Stamford Bridge club, before a fee of £55,000 took him to Birmingham City. He made his debut in the local derby against Wolves on the opening day of the 1966/67 season, two goals from his former Chelsea team-mate Bert Murray giving the Blues a 2–1 win. Ending his first season at St Andrew's with 18 goals, he finished the next as the club's leading scorer with 29 goals, including a hat-trick in a 4–1 home win over Rotherham United. He left Birmingham in the close season to join Queen's Park Rangers, later ending his career with spells at Millwall and Brighton and Hove Albion.

Alan BALL

Position	Midfielder
Born	Alan James Ball, Farnworth, 5 May 1945
Height	5ft 7in
Weight	10st 0lb
Clubs	Blackpool, Everton, Arsenal, Southampton, Bristol Rovers
England Caps	72 Goals 8
	1965 v Yugoslavia (1–1), v W. Germany (won 1–0), v Sweden (won 2–1) 1 goal, v Spain (won 2–0)
	1966 v Poland (1–1), v W. Germany (won 1–0), v Scotland (won 4–3), v Finland (won 3–0), v Denmark (won 2–0), v Poland (won 1–0), v Uruguay (0–0), v Mexico (won 2–0), v France (won 2–0), v Argentina (won 1–0), v Portugal (won 2–1), v W. Germany (won 4–2 aet), v N. Ireland (won 2–0), v Czechoslovakia (0–0), v Wales (won 5–1)
	1967 v Scotland (lost 2–3), v Spain (won 2–0), v Austria (won 1–0) 1 goal, v Wales (won 3–0) 1 goal, v Soviet Union (2–2) 1 goal

1968 v Scotland (1–1), v Spain (won 1–0), v Spain (won 2–1), v Sweden (won 3–1),
v W. Germany (lost 0–1), v Yugoslavia (lost 0–1), v Romania (0–0)
1969 v Romania (1–1), v N. Ireland (won 3–1), v Wales (won 2–1), v Scotland (won 4–1),
v Mexico (0–0), v Uruguay (won 2–1), v Brazil (lost 1–2), v Portugal (won 1–0)
1970 v Belgium (won 3–1) 2 goals, v Wales (1–1), v Scotland (0–0), v Colombia (won 4–0)
1 goal, v Ecuador (won 2–0), v Romania (won 1–0), v Brazil (lost 0–1), v Czechoslovakia
(won 1–0), v W. Germany (lost 2–3 aet), v E. Germany (won 3–1)
1971 v Malta (won 1–0), v Greece (won 3–0), v Malta (won 5–0), v Scotland (won 3–1),
v Switzerland (1–1), v Greece (won 2–0)
1972 v W. Germany (lost 1–3), v W. Germany (0–0), v Scotland (won 1–0) 1 goal,
v Yugoslavia (1–1), v Wales (won 1–0)
1973 v Wales (1–1), v Scotland (won 5–0), v N. Ireland (won 2–1), v Czechoslovakia (1–1),
v Poland (lost 0–2), v Portugal (0–0)
1975 v W. Germany (won 2–0), v Cyprus (won 5–0), v Cyprus (won 1–0), v N. Ireland (0–0),
v Wales (2–2), v Scotland (won 5–1)

Honours   World Cup winners England 1966

GIVEN HIS ENGLAND DEBUT against Yugoslavia in 1965, Alan Ball went on to star
the following year in the World Cup Finals. Without doubt his best match was the
final itself. His tirelessness, especially during extra time, has become legendary, and he
set up the third and decisive goal for Geoff Hurst. The sight of him running with
socks down round his ankles during the World Cup Final endeared him to the public.

After unsuccessful trials with Wolves and Bolton, it was only the persistence of his
footballing father Alan Ball senior that persuaded Blackpool to sign him. He made his

Alan Ball takes on Kenny Dalglish in a match against Scotland at Wembley on 19 May
1973. (Getty Images)

first-team debut for the Seasiders against Liverpool at Anfield in 1962 at 17 years of age. Within 12 months he had become a regular in the Bloomfield Road club's side, and he went on to play in 126 games for them before joining Everton in August 1966, immediately after the World Cup. The £110,000 fee was then the highest to pass between British clubs. Ball made his Everton debut on the opening day of the 1966/67 season, scoring the game's only goal. He was the club's leading scorer in his first two seasons with the Toffees, and in 1967/68, when he scored 20 League goals, he netted four in the 6–2 win at West Bromwich Albion. Playing alongside Colin Harvey and Howard Kendall in the Everton midfield, he was instrumental in the Blues winning the League Championship in 1969/70. For no apparent reason, the side broke up, and in 1971, after scoring 78 goals in 249 games, Ball was sold to Arsenal for another record fee of £220,000.

After a successful career at Highbury, Ball moved to Southampton in March 1976, then to Blackpool as manager in 1980. He resigned a year later and returned to Southampton, playing his last game in the top flight in October 1982. After a short spell in Hong Kong, he resumed his playing career with Bristol Rovers before managing Portsmouth. After taking Pompey into the First Division, he had spells managing Stoke City, Exeter City, Southampton and Manchester City, before returning to Fratton Park for a second spell as Portsmouth boss.

Mick JONES

Position	Centre-forward
Born	Michael David Jones, Worksop, 24 April 1945
Height	5ft 11in
Weight	11st 11lb
Clubs	Sheffield United, Leeds United
England Caps	3
	1965 v W. Germany (won 1–0), v Sweden (won 2–1)
	1970 v Holland (0–0)

AN AGGRESSIVE non-stop centre-forward, Mick Jones began work in a cycle factory while playing for Dinnington Miners' Welfare. His impressive displays attracted a number of local League clubs, and in the summer of 1962 he signed for Sheffield United. His early performances for the Blades led to him winning England Under-23 honours and then, following a successful partnership with Alan Birchenall, he won full international honours when called up for the game against West Germany, which England won 1–0.

Jones, who was Sheffield United's leading scorer for three seasons in succession, left Bramall Lane in September 1967, when Leeds United paid £100,000 to take him to Elland Road. With Leeds he won two League Championship medals, an FA Cup winners medal and two Inter Cities Fairs Cup medals. His partnership with Allan Clarke proved highly successful, yet it was never tried at international level. Many will remember how, when Leeds beat Arsenal to lift the 1972 FA Cup, Jones broke his arm while setting up the winning goal and went up to the royal box with his arm in a sling.

Sadly, a serious knee injury ended Jones' career in 1975. He left Leeds to become a representative for a sports goods company, before running a sports shop in Maltby.

Derek TEMPLE

Position	Outside-left
Born	Derek William Temple, Liverpool, 13 November 1938
Height	5ft 8in
Weight	11st 4lb
Clubs	Everton, Preston North End
England Caps	1
	1965 v W. Germany (won 1–0)

WINGER DEREK TEMPLE joined Everton straight from school. A former England schoolboy, his form with the Everton Colts was amazing – in one season alone he scored 70 goals, including six in one match and five on a number of occasions. His form was such that he soon made his first-team debut for the Toffees in a 2–1 win over Newcastle United in March 1957. An important member of the Everton side, he missed the majority of the club's League Championship winning season of 1962/63 through injury, but bounced back to win full international honours in 1965 in England's 1–0 win over West Germany in Nuremberg. The following season he won a place in Everton's 'Hall of Fame' when he scored the winning goal in the Blues' marvellous 3–2 win over Sheffield Wednesday in the FA Cup Final at Wembley.

Temple went on to score 82 goals in 273 League and Cup games, including a hat-trick in a 5–2 defeat of Ipswich Town in September 1961, before leaving to play for Preston North End. In three seasons at Deepdale he played in a variety of roles, subsequently seeing out his career with then non-League Wigan Athletic.

Norman HUNTER

Position	Central defender
Born	Norman Hunter, Middlesbrough, 29 October 1943
Height	6ft 0in
Weight	12st 8lb
Clubs	Leeds United, Bristol City, Barnsley
England Caps	28 Goals 2
	1965 v Spain (won 2–0)
	1966 v W. Germany (won 1–0), v Yugoslavia (won 2–0), v Finland (won 3–0)
	1967 v Austria (won 1–0)
	1968 v Spain (won 2–1) 1 goal, v Sweden (won 3–1), v W. Germany (lost 0–1), v Yugoslavia (lost 0–1), v Soviet Union (won 2–0)
	1969 v Romania (1–1), v Wales (won 2–1)
	1970 v Holland (0–0), v W. Germany (lost 2–3 aet)
	1971 v Malta (won 1–0)
	1972 v W. Germany (lost 1–3), v W. Germany (0–0), v Wales (won 3–0), v N. Ireland (lost 0–1), v Scotland (won 1–0), v Wales (won 1–0)
	1973 v Wales (1–1) 1 goal, v Soviet Union (won 2–1), v Austria (won 7–0), v Poland (1–1)
	1974 v N. Ireland (won 1–0), v Scotland (lost 0–2), v Czechoslovakia (won 3–0)
Honours	Footballer of the Year 1974

Norman Hunter of Leeds United. (Lancashire Evening Post)

NORMAN 'BITE YER LEGS' HUNTER was one of the game's fiercest competitors. The Elland Road defender began his career with Leeds United, and became renowned for his tackling – his reputation often disguising the fact that he was a very good footballer. He was the first England player to be capped as a substitute, when he played against Spain just a few weeks after his full debut against West Germany. Only the presence of England captain Bobby Moore stopped him from earning more international honours than his 28 caps.

Hunter was remarkably consistent, being ever-present in five seasons and featuring in all Leeds' Cup Final teams from 1965 to 1975. During that time he won two League Championship medals, an FA Cup winners' medal, a League Cup winners' medal and two Inter Cities Fairs Cup winners' medals. He also had the honour of being voted the PFA's first-ever Player of the Year in 1974.

In October 1976 he joined Bristol City, where he was a great favourite with the Ashton Gate crowd. Then, after three seasons with the Robins, he was appointed player-coach with Barnsley, taking over the reins at Oakwell after manager Allan Clarke left, but after steering the club into the Second Division, he was surprisingly sacked. He subsequently had a spell as assistant manager at West Bromwich Albion before going to Rotherham as manager. Dismissed in December 1987, he returned to Elland Road on the coaching staff but lost his job when Howard Wilkinson was sacked. He had a brief spell as Terry Yorath's assistant at Bradford City, but now works as a summarizer for BBC Radio Leeds.

Gordon HARRIS

Position	Inside-forward
Born	Gordon Harris, Worksop, 2 June 1940
Height	5ft 10in
Weight	13st 1lb
Clubs	Burnley, Sunderland
England Caps	1
	1966 v Poland (1–1)

GORDON 'BOMBER' HARRIS was working down the pit and representing his colliery at Firbeck when Burnley signed him in January 1958. However, despite some impressive displays in the club's Central League side, it was 1960/61 before he established himself as a first-team regular, scoring 14 goals in 31 games, including a hat-trick in a 4–0 League Cup win at Cardiff City. The following season was Harris' best in terms of goals scored, as he netted 17 times. He also appeared in the Burnley side that lost 3–1 to Spurs in the FA Cup Final. His form led to him winning his first representative honours when, in November 1961, he played for the Football League against the Irish League. A week later he represented the England Under-23s against Israel and in January 1966 he won his only full cap when he played in the 1–1 draw against Poland at Goodison Park.

Appointed Burnley captain for the 1967/68 season, he was dropped, surprisingly, just before Christmas and disciplined following differences of opinion with other players during training. Shortly afterwards, having scored 81 goals in 313 games, he left to join Sunderland. Though not as prolific on Wearside, he had three impressive seasons before seeing out his career in non-League football with South Shields.

Keith NEWTON

Position	Full-back
Born	Keith Robert Newton, Manchester, 23 June 1941
Died	16 June 1998
Height	5ft 11in
Weight	11st 2lb
Clubs	Blackburn Rovers, Everton, Burnley
England Caps	27

1966 v W. Germany (won 1–0), v Scotland (won 4–3)
1967 v Spain (won 2–0), v Austria (won 1–0), v Wales (won 3–0)
1968 v Scotland (1–1), v Spain (won 1–0), v Spain (won 2–1), v Sweden (won 3–1),
   v W. Germany (lost 0–1), v Yugoslavia (lost 0–1), v Romania (0–0), v Bulgaria (1–1)
1969 v France (won 5–0), v N. Ireland (won 3–1), v Wales (won 2–1), v Scotland (won 4–1),
   v Mexico (0–0), v Uruguay (won 2–1), v Brazil (lost 1–2)
1970 v Holland (0–0), v Belgium (won 3–1), v N. Ireland (won 3–1), v Scotland (0–0),
   v Colombia (won 4–0), v Ecuador (won 2–0), v Romania (won 1–0), v Czechoslovakia
   (won 1–0), v W. Germany (lost 2–3 aet)

KEITH NEWTON suffered several major injuries that dogged his career and cost him many representative honours. He injured a knee in training with England and had to have a cartilage operation. Once fully recovered he won the first of his 27 caps for England in a 1–0 win over West Germany, but just before the interval he was carried off with a suspected broken leg.

A member of the successful Blackburn Rovers FA Youth Cup-winning side of 1959, Newton made his first-team debut at left-half but was soon switched to left-back. Sharp in the tackle and sound in the air, he was noted for his attacking runs down the flank. He finally settled into the right-back spot, and won his first major honours in 1964, gaining the first of several England Under-23 caps against Scotland at St James' Park. Newton began to develop into a world-rated player, so it was no surprise when, with Blackburn struggling in the lower reaches of the Second Division, he joined Everton.

He helped the Blues win the League Championship in 1969/70, but injuries prevented him playing in enough games to warrant a medal. He later became unsettled at the way he was being asked to play, and after losing his place he joined Burnley. An ever-present when the Clarets won the 1972/73 Second Division Championship, he missed very few games in six seasons at Turf Moor. Newton later had brief spells in non-League football with Morecambe and Clitheroe before his untimely death in the summer of 1998.

Geoff HURST

Position	Forward
Born	Geoffrey Charles Hurst, Ashton-under-Lyne, 8 December 1941
Height	6ft 0in
Weight	12st 9lb
Clubs	West Ham United, Stoke City, West Bromwich Albion
England Caps	49 Goals 24

1966 v W. Germany (won 1–0), v Scotland (won 4–3) 1 goal, v Yugoslavia (won 2–0), v Finland (won 3–0), v Denmark (won 2–0), v Argentina (won 1–0) 1 goal, v Portugal (won 2–1), v W. Germany (won 4–2 aet) 3 goals, v N. Ireland (won 2–0), v Czechoslovakia (0–0), v Wales (won 5–1) 2 goals

1967 v Scotland (lost 2–3) 1 goal, v Spain (won 2–0), v Austria (won 1–0), v Wales (won 3–0), v N. Ireland (won 2–0) 1 goal, v Soviet Union (2–2)

1968 v Scotland (1–1), v Sweden (won 3–1), v W. Germany (lost 0–1), v Soviet Union (won 2–0) 1 goal, v Romania (0–0), v Bulgaria (1–1) 1 goal

1969 v Romania (1–1), v France (won 5–0) 3 goals, v N. Ireland (won 3–1) 1 goal, v Scotland (won 4–1) 2 goals, v Mexico (0–0), v Uruguay (won 2–1) 1 goal, v Brazil (lost 1–2), v Holland (won 1–0)

1970 v Holland (0–0), v Belgium (won 3–1) 1 goal, v Wales (1–1), v N. Ireland (won 3–1) 1 goal, v Scotland (0–0), v Colombia (won 4–0), v Ecuador (won 2–0), v Romania (won 1–0) 1 goal, v Brazil (lost 0–1), v W. Germany (lost 2–3 aet), v E. Germany (won 3–1)

1971 v Greece (won 3–0) 1 goal, v Wales (0–0), v Scotland (won 3–1), v Switzerland (won 3–2) 1 goal, v Switzerland (1–1), v Greece (won 2–0) 1 goal

1972 v W. Germany (lost 2–3)

Honours	World Cup winners England 1966

THOUGH GEOFF HURST had to suffer the torment of sitting on the sidelines to watch England struggle through the first three matches of the 1966 World Cup, he came into the team for the quarter-final and scored the only goal of the game against Argentina. In the final he demonstrated his all-round talent with three goals in the 4–2 extra-time win over West Germany – one with his head, one with his right foot and the last with his left.

During his early days in the game, Hurst was a dogged wing-half and little more. Indeed, he had become so disillusioned with his lack of progress that he was ready to change clubs. West Ham manager Ron Greenwood, however, saw in Hurst the strength of character and eagerness to learn that he needed for the tactical revolution he was about to undertake. Hurst was exactly the forward of brains and vision that Greenwood was looking for: he provided a mobile target for passes from defence, was an elusive, unpredictable 'wall' off whom attacks could be built in the opponents' half, and then would arrive late, unmarked, to sweep in on goal and deliver the killer shot. In 1963/64, his first full season in his new position, he netted 26 goals, including the Hammers' second in the 3–2 FA Cup Final win over Preston North End. Despite this, however, he was still barracked by a section of the Upton Park crowd.

A man who shared Greenwood's perception of Hurst's abilities was England manager Alf Ramsey, and in the 1965/66 season, after scoring 40 goals in 59 games,

Hurst won selection for the England team. In 1968/69 he scored six goals in one game as Sunderland were beaten 8–0, ending the campaign with 41 goals in 49 games. He played a total of 499 first-team games for the Hammers, scoring 248 goals, before joining Stoke City prior to the start of the 1972/73 season, with whom he spent three seasons before ending his Football League career with West Bromwich Albion.

After a season in the United States with Seattle Sounders, Hurst became player-manager of Telford United, before moving into full-time management with Chelsea. He left Stamford Bridge in 1981 to work in the insurance business.

Martin PETERS

Position	Midfielder
Born	Martin Stanford Peters, Plaistow, 8 November 1943
Height	6ft 1in
Weight	11st 11lb
Clubs	West Ham United, Tottenham Hotspur, Norwich City, Sheffield United
England Caps	67 Goals 20

1966 v Yugoslavia (won 2–0), v Finland (won 3–0) 1 goal, v Poland (won 1–0), v Mexico (won 2–0), v France (won 2–0), v Argentina (won 1–0), v Portugal (won 2–1), v W. Germany (won 4–2 aet) 1 goal, v N. Ireland (won 2–0) 1 goal, v Czechoslovakia (0–0), v Wales (won 5–1)

1967 v Scotland (lost 2–3), v Wales (won 3–0) 1 goal, v N. Ireland (won 2–0), v Soviet Union (2–2) 1 goal

1968 v Scotland (1–1) 1 goal, v Spain (won 1–0), v Spain (won 2–1) 1 goal, v Sweden (won 3–1) 1 goal, v Yugoslavia (lost 0–1), v Soviet Union (won 2–0), v Romania (0–0), v Bulgaria (1–1)

1969 v France (won 5–0), v N. Ireland (won 3–1) 1 goal, v Scotland (won 4–1) 2 goals, v Mexico (0–0), v Uruguay (won 2–1), v Brazil (lost 1–2), v Holland (won 1–0), v Portugal (won 1–0)

1970 v Holland (0–0), v Belgium (won 3–1), v Wales (1–1), v N. Ireland (won 3–1) 1 goal, v Scotland (0–0), v Colombia (won 4–0) 2 goals, v Ecuador (won 2–0), v Romania (won 1–0), v Brazil (lost 1–2), v Czechoslovakia (won 1–0), v W. Germany (lost 2–3 aet) 1 goal, v E. Germany (won 3–1) 1 goal

1971 v Malta (won 1–0) 1 goal, v Greece (won 3–0), v Malta (won 5–0), v N. Ireland (won 1–0), v Wales (0–0), v Scotland (won 3–1) 1 goal, v Switzerland (won 3–2), v Greece (won 2–0)

1972 v W. Germany (lost 1–3), v W. Germany (0–0), v N. Ireland (lost 0–1)

1973 v Scotland (won 5–0), v N. Ireland (won 2–1), v Wales (won 3–0) 1 goal, v Scotland (won 1–0) 1 goal, v Czechoslovakia (1–1), v Poland (lost 0–2), v Soviet Union (won 2–1), v Italy (lost 0–2), v Austria (won 7–0), v Poland (1–1), v Italy (lost 0–1)

1974 v Portugal (0–0), v Scotland (lost 0–2)

Honours	World Cup winners England 1966

Martin Peters. (Lancashire Evening Post)

TAGGED 'ten years ahead of his time' by England manager Sir Alf Ramsey in 1966, Martin Peters was probably the least famous of the three West Ham players who did so much to help the country win the World Cup, scoring one of the goals in the 4–2 defeat of West Germany.

Peters made his West Ham United debut in a 4–1 win over Cardiff City on Good Friday 1962 and went on to appear in every position for the club, including goalkeeper. A member of West Ham's European Cup Winners' Cup team of 1965 and League Cup Final team of 1966, he played in 364 games for the Hammers, scoring exactly 100 goals, including a hat-trick in a 4–0 win over West Bromwich Albion in August 1968. An elegant goalscoring midfield player with first-class technical skills and a high work rate, he left Upton Park for Spurs in March 1970 for a then British record fee of £200,000, with Jimmy Greaves going to West Ham in part-exchange. A member of the Spurs team that won the League Cup in 1971 and 1973, and the UEFA Cup in 1972, he also appeared in the UEFA Cup Final of 1974. He had scored 87 goals in 287 appearances for the White Hart Lane club, when in March 1975 he moved to Norwich City, going on to play in 207 games for the Canaries before being appointed player-manager of Sheffield United, where he took his total Football League appearances for his four League clubs past the 700 mark.

Peters was awarded the MBE in the 1978 New Year's Honours List. After leaving Bramall Lane, he teamed up with Geoff Hurst to work for a motor insurance company.

Ian CALLAGHAN

Position	Midfielder
Born	Ian Robert Callaghan, Liverpool, 10 April 1942
Height	5ft 7in
Weight	11st 1lb
Clubs	Liverpool, Swansea City, Crewe Alexandra
England Caps	4
	1966 v Finland (won 3–0), v France (won 2–0)
	1977 v Switzerland (0–0), v Luxembourg (won 2–0)
Honours	Footballer of the Year 1974

LIVERPOOL'S MOST LOYAL SERVANT, Ian Callaghan joined the Anfield club's groundstaff in 1957 and began his career as an outside-right, but as the role of the out-and-out winger disappeared, he was converted into a midfielder. In 21 years at Anfield, he played in a record 636 League games and a total of 843 games in all competitions, winning European, League Championship and FA Cup winners' medals; he was also awarded the MBE and was voted the Football Writers' Player of the Year in 1974. Another, and more unusual, record he holds is that of the longest gap between caps. Having played twice for England in 1966, he was not chosen again until October 1977, an interval of 11 years and 49 days!

Callaghan left Liverpool in 1978 to join Swansea, and in his first season at the Vetch Field he helped the club win promotion to the Second Division. As the club consolidated their position, he went on to equal Stanley Matthews' record by appearing in his 85th FA Cup tie at the age of 37, and a few weeks later he established a new record when he appeared for the Swans against West Ham United at Upton Park. After leaving South Wales, he had a spell playing for Cork Hibs in Ireland, before ending his first-class career with Crewe Alexandra.

Peter BONETTI

Position	Goalkeeper
Born	Peter Phillip Bonetti, Putney, 27 September 1941
Height	5ft 10in
Weight	11st 3lb
Clubs	Chelsea
England Caps	7
	1966 v Denmark (won 2–0)
	1967 v Spain (won 2–0), v Austria (won 1–0)
	1968 v Spain (won 2–1)
	1969 v Holland (won 1–0), v Portugal (won 1–0)
	1970 v W. Germany (lost 2–3 aet)

HAVING CONCEDED just one goal in his first six international appearances, Peter Bonetti's last game for England was a nightmare, in which he bore the brunt of criticism for England's 3–2 defeat by West Germany in the 1970 World Cup quarter-finals.

Bonetti's future in professional football was shaped before he left school, when in 1957 his mother wrote to Ted Drake, then Chelsea's manager, to ask if he would give a trial to her son, who 'might make you a useful goalkeeper'. He soon established himself as the club's first-choice keeper and in 1962/63 helped Chelsea win promotion to the First Division. He was in goal two seasons later when the club won the League Cup, and in 1967 – the season he was voted Chelsea's first Player of the Year – he made his first appearance at Wembley when Spurs beat them in the FA Cup Final. Bonetti's daring and spectacular play thrilled the crowds and was a decisive factor in Chelsea's cup triumphs of the early 1970s. In the 1970 FA Cup Final at Wembley, he touched world class in extra time to deny Leeds United the victory their superiority deserved. In the replay at Old Trafford, with his left knee badly swollen following a collision with Mick Jones, he showed great courage when, twice in the space of a minute, he dived to save fierce shots from Terry Cooper. He took his place in the Chelsea side to face Real Madrid in the European Cup Winners' Cup Final after a bout of pneumonia and produced three superb extra-time saves to take the game to a replay. During the rematch he produced one of his greatest saves when, with Chelsea leading 2–1, he sprang to his left to clutch Zoco's last-minute point-blank header.

Nicknamed 'The Cat', he played in 728 games for Chelsea before moving to the Isle of Mull. There he combined life as a guest-house owner with occasional appearances for Dundee United. Since then he has acted as goalkeeping coach for Chelsea and been involved with the England set-up.

Peter Bonetti. (Lancashire Evening Post)

John HOLLINS

Position	Midfielder
Born	John William Hollins, Guildford, 16 July 1946
Height	5ft 8in
Weight	11st 5lb
Clubs	Chelsea, Queen's Park Rangers, Arsenal
England Caps	1
	1967 v Spain (won 2–0)

JOHN HOLLINS comes from a footballing family, with three of his brothers, his father and his grandfather having played League football. He joined Chelsea and soon won a regular place in the club's starting line-up. An outstanding attacking wing-half, he served the Blues with distinction for 12 seasons, taking part in all the club's successes in that period. He won just one cap for England, against Spain in 1967, shortly after playing in a losing FA Cup Final side against Spurs.

Hollins made up for that Spurs defeat when he won an FA Cup winners' medal in 1970 against Leeds United, and the following year Chelsea won the European Cup Winners' Cup Final against Real Madrid in Athens. When Chelsea lost their top-flight status, however, he left to play for Queen's Park Rangers, helping them to runners-up spot in the First Division in 1975/76, his first season with the club. After four seasons at Loftus Road he moved to Arsenal, before returning to Stamford Bridge as the club's player-coach. In his first season back at Chelsea he helped them win promotion to the First Division. He eventually retired a couple of seasons later, having scored 48 goals in 465 games for Chelsea, and shortly afterwards he was appointed the club's manager.

The teams Hollins put together during his spell as manager were considered efficient but dull, and so he was not popular with Chelsea fans. He enjoyed a brief spell as reserve-team coach for Queen's Park Rangers before taking over the reins at Swansea City and, more recently, Rochdale.

David SADLER

Position	Central defender
Born	David Sadler, Yalding, 5 February 1946
Height	6ft 0in
Weight	12st 3lb
Clubs	Manchester United, Preston North End
England Caps	4
	1967 v N. Ireland (won 2–0), v Soviet Union (2–2)
	1970 v Ecuador (won 2–0), v E. Germany (won 3–1)

DAVID SADLER, who had been capped at Youth and Under-23 levels, won the first of four full international caps, in each of which he was never on the losing side, against Northern Ireland in November 1967.

Manchester United won the race to sign Maidstone United's England Amateur international inside-forward in November 1962. Sadler made his United debut as a replacement for the injured David Herd in a 3–3 draw at Sheffield Wednesday on the opening day of the 1963/64 season, but is best remembered for netting a hat-trick that season in the second leg of the FA Youth Cup Final win over Swindon Town. Yet, shortly after this, he was converted into a centre-half. Tall and well-built, Sadler's style was unspectacular but effective. He helped United win the League Championship in 1966/67 and a year later was a member of the side that beat Benfica 4–1 at Wembley in the final of the European Cup. After playing in 333 League and Cup games for United, he turned out for Miami Toros in the United States during the summer of 1973 before returning to these shores to join Preston North End. He stayed with the Lilywhites until May 1977, when injury forced his retirement, but returned to Deepdale as the club's manager in 1981.

Cyril KNOWLES

Position	Left-back
Born	Cyril Barry Knowles, Fitzwilliam, 13 July 1944
Died	31 August 1991
Height	6ft 0in
Weight	11st 13lb
Clubs	Middlesbrough, Tottenham Hotspur
England Caps	4
	1967 v Soviet Union (2–2)
	1968 v Spain (won 1–0), v Sweden (won 3–1), v W. Germany (lost 0–1)

A GREAT ATTACKING FULL-BACK, Cyril Knowles began his career with Middlesbrough, where almost immediately he caught the eye of Spurs' manager Bill Nicholson. He had made just 39 appearances for Boro when in May 1964 he joined the White Hart Lane club. The brother of Peter Knowles, who gave up his professional career with Wolves to become a Jehovah's Witness, he spent his initial North London season at right-back, moving to the left at the start of the 1965/66 season to replace Ron Henry. He was a member of the Spurs FA Cup-winning team in 1967, after which he won the first of four full caps for England. He also played in the 1971 and 1973 League Cup Final wins and the 1972 UEFA Cup success, becoming a cult figure when the pop song 'Nice One Cyril' became a national catchphrase.

From December 1973, Knowles was troubled by a serious knee injury, and although he recovered enough to help save the club from relegation in 1974/75 – with two goals in the final match at Leeds – the injury flared up again the following season and he was forced into premature retirement.

Knowles went on to become a successful coach at Middlesbrough and manager of Darlington, Torquay United and Hartlepool. A brain illness forced him to quit Hartlepool in June 1991, and two months later he died, at the early age of 47.

Mike SUMMERBEE

Position	Winger
Born	Michael George Summerbee, Cheltenham, 15 December 1942
Height	5ft 11in
Weight	12st 4lb
Clubs	Swindon Town, Manchester City, Burnley, Blackpool, Stockport County
England Caps	8 Goals 1
	1968 v Scotland (2–2), v Spain (won 1–0), v W. Germany (lost 0–1)
	1971 v Switzerland (1–1) 1 goal
	1972 v W. Germany (0–0), v Wales (won 3–0), v N. Ireland (lost 0–1), v Soviet Union
	(won 2–1)

CAPPED EIGHT TIMES by England, Mike Summerbee was a West Country boy from a footballing family, his uncle George having been a professional with Chester, Preston and Barrow. When he left school he played for his home-town team of Cheltenham until Swindon Town spotted his potential. He played in more than 200 games for the Wiltshire club, helping them clinch promotion from the Third Division in 1962/63. Inevitably his dashing excursions along the wings caught the eyes of some of the bigger clubs, and in August 1965 he became the first of Manchester City manager Joe Mercer's signings.

Summerbee's first season at Maine Road saw City win the Second Division Championship and then, in a three-year spell between 1968 and 1970 – the most successful in the club's history – he played a significant role in City's triumphs. Primarily right-footed, he made an immediate impression at Maine Road with his diligence and industry, always ready to tackle back and shoulder his share of defensive duties. A confident player on the field, deputizing as a central striker when the club had injuries, he was a fashionable dresser, and part-owner, with Manchester United's George Best, of a boutique.

Summerbee spent ten seasons with Manchester City before joining Burnley in the summer of 1965. His career later took him to Blackpool and then to the player-manager's job at Edgeley Park, where he ended his playing days.

Alex STEPNEY

Position	Goalkeeper
Born	Alexander Cyril Stepney, Mitcham, 18 September 1942
Height	6ft 0in
Weight	11st 9lb
Clubs	Millwall, Chelsea, Manchester United
England Caps	1
	1968 v Sweden (won 3–1)

A SOLID if unspectacular keeper, Alex Stepney was capped just once by England – although he was also chosen for the 1970 World Cup squad, he did not actually play then.

Stepney began his career with non-League Tooting and Mitcham before turning professional with Millwall in 1963. He had made almost 150 appearances for the Lions when, in May 1966, Tommy Docherty signed him for Chelsea, but four months later, having made just one League appearance for the Stamford Bridge club, he was transferred to Manchester United for £55,000. At least Chelsea made a profit out of the deal, but given the magnificent service that Stepney had given to United, the Blues might later have regretted letting him go.

Stepney made his United debut in the Manchester derby, a Denis Law goal giving the Reds a 1–0 win. In his first season at Old Trafford, United lifted the League Championship and then, in 1968, the European Cup. It was the heroics of Alex Stepney, with two instinctive saves from Eusebio in the closing minutes of normal time, which kept United alive in the final against Benfica. The extra-time goals will always be the highlight of the famous victory, but Stepney's part should never be forgotten. He went on to play in 535 League and Cup games for United and even scored a couple of goals from the penalty spot in the Reds' relegation season of 1973/74. After that, he won a Second Division Championship medal to add to his League Championship medal, and later an FA Cup winners' medal when United beat Liverpool 2–1.

After 12 seasons with United Stepney left to play in the States with Dallas Tornadoes, before returning to play for Altrincham. After retiring, he was Rochdale's commercial manager for a short spell before acting as goalkeeping coach of Manchester City.

Colin BELL

Position	Midfielder
Born	Colin Bell, Heselden, 26 February 1946
Height	6ft 0in
Weight	11st 12lb
Clubs	Bury, Manchester City
England Caps	48 Goals 9

1968 v W. Germany (lost 0–1), v Bulgaria (1–1)
1969 v France (won 5–0), v Wales (won 2–1), v Uruguay (won 2–1), v Brazil (lost 1–2)
   1 goal, v Holland (won 1–0) 1 goal, v Portugal (won 1–0)
1970 v Holland (0–0), v N. Ireland (won 3–1), v Brazil (lost 0–1), v Czechoslovakia
   (won 1–0), v W. Germany (lost 2–3 aet)
1971 v N. Ireland (won 1–0), v Greece (won 2–0)
1972 v W. Germany (lost 1–3), v W. Germany (0–0), v Wales (won 3–0) 1 goal,
   v N. Ireland (lost 0–1), v Scotland (won 1–0), v Yugoslavia (1–1), v Wales (won 1–0) 1 goal
1973 v Wales (1–1), v Scotland (won 5–0), v N. Ireland (won 2–1), v Wales (won 3–0),
   v Scotland (won 1–0), v Czechoslovakia (1–1), v Poland (lost 0–2), v Austria (won 7–0)
   1 goal, v Poland (1–1), v Italy (lost 0–1)
1974 v Wales (won 2–0), v N. Ireland (won 1–0), v Scotland (lost 0–2), v Argentina (2–2),
   v E. Germany (1–1), v Bulgaria (won 1–0), v Yugoslavia (2–2), v Czechoslovakia (won 3–0)
   2 goals, v Portugal (0–0)
1975 v W. Germany (won 2–0) 1 goal, v Cyprus (won 5–0), v Cyprus (won 1–0),
   v N. Ireland (0–0), v Scotland (won 5–1) 1 goal, v Switzerland (won 2–1),
   v Czechoslovakia (lost 1–2)

COLIN BELL would have made more than his 48 appearances for England had it not been for a serious knee injury that brought his career to a premature end. Though he made his England debut in 1968, it wasn't until after the 1970 World Cup that he began to establish himself in Alf Ramsey's team. His non-stop running and enduring commitment in that infamous World Cup qualifying tie against Poland at Wembley in 1973 sadly wasn't enough to earn England a place in the finals.

Colin Bell beats Poland's Jerzy Gorgon to the ball during a World Cup qualifying match against Poland in 1973. England's draw with Poland resulted in their failure to qualify for the World Cup. (Getty Images)

Bell began his career with Horden Colliery Welfare, where his potential was spotted by Bury. Making his League debut for the Shakers shortly before his 18th birthday, he ended his first full campaign as the club's leading goalscorer, and in March 1966, after scoring 25 goals in 82 games for the Gigg Lane club, he signed for Manchester City for a fee of £45,000. He scored on his City debut in a 2–1 win at Derby County and went on to help the club clinch promotion to the top flight by winning the Second Division Championship. His form the following season was outstanding and led to him winning selection for a variety of representative matches.

For a midfield player whose primary talent was his prodigious running, he was also an outstanding finisher, netting two hat-tricks in his City career. Bell became the midfield mastermind of the young City side that won the First Division title, the FA Cup, the European Cup Winners' Cup and the League Cup in a four-year spell between the late 1960s and early 1970s. The injury to his knee forced him to miss the whole of the 1976/77 season, but there was still time for one further honour, a Central League Championship medal in 1977/78, before he reluctantly decided to retire in August 1979. Bell was a model professional, and his balance and athleticism earned him the nickname 'Nijinsky', after the racehorse.

Tommy WRIGHT

Position	Full-back
Born	Thomas James Wright, Liverpool, 21 October 1944
Height	5ft 8in
Weight	11st 3lb
Clubs	Everton
England Caps	11
	1968 v Soviet Union (won 2–0), v Romania (0–0)
	1969 v Romania (1–1), v Mexico (0–0), v Uruguay (won 2–1), v Brazil (lost 1–2), v Holland (won 1–0)
	1970 v Wales (1–1), v Romania (won 1–0), v Brazil (lost 0–1), v Belgium (won 3–1)

TOMMY WRIGHT was an inside-forward when he joined Everton, before being converted into a wing-half and finally a full-back, the position where he made his name. After making his debut as a replacement for Alex Parker in a 1–1 draw at Blackpool in October 1964, he was a virtual ever-present in the Everton side for the next nine seasons, including the League Championship winning season of 1969/70. He also won an FA Cup winners' medal in 1966 as the Blues beat Sheffield Wednesday 3–2, and in 1968 he won the first of 11 full caps for England when he played against the Soviet Union in the European Championships third-place play-off. He later represented his country in the 1970 World Cup Finals in Mexico.

Tommy Wright was one of the most constructive back-four players in the Football League and liked nothing better than to force his way down the flanks when the opportunity arose. One of football's natural gentlemen, he went on to play in 371 League and Cup games for Everton before hanging up his boots.

Bob McNAB

Position	Left-back
Born	Robert McNab, Huddersfield, 20 July 1943
Height	5ft 9in
Weight	11st 6lb
Clubs	Huddersfield Town, Arsenal, Wolverhampton Wanderers
England Caps	4
	1968 v Romania (0–0), v Bulgaria (1–1)
	1969 v Romania (1–1), v N. Ireland (won 3–1)

BOB McNAB joined Arsenal from his home-town club Huddersfield Town as a replacement for Billy McCullough in October 1966. The Gunners paid £50,000 for his services, which at the time was the highest fee ever paid for a full-back. He immediately won a place in the Arsenal side and was the club's first-choice left-back for the next nine seasons. During seasons 1967/68 and 1968/69 he played a major part in helping Arsenal reach two League Cup finals. In 1969/70 he won the first of his four England caps and helped the Gunners win the Inter Cities Fairs Cup Final. In the club's double-winning season of 1970/71, he played in 62 of the 64 first-team games, winning League and FA Cup winners' medals. There followed a spate of niggling injuries but by 1972/73 he was back to his best, helping the club finish as runners-up in the League Championship. Over the next couple of seasons, a succession of injuries and loss of form resulted in him losing his place to Sammy Nelson, and in June 1975, after appearing in 365 first-team games, he joined Wolverhampton Wanderers.

After one season at Molineux McNab went to the United States, where he finished his career. He became coach to the Vancouver Whitecaps and moved to California, to run his own executive recruitment agency.

Gordon WEST

Position	Goalkeeper
Born	Gordon West, Darfield, 24 April 1943
Height	6ft 1in
Weight	14st 0lb
Clubs	Blackpool, Everton, Tranmere Rovers
England Caps	3
	1968 v Bulgaria (1–1)
	1969 v Wales (won 2–1), v Mexico (0–0)

GORDON WEST made three appearances for England in the late sixties but he surprised the football world by declining to join the World Cup squad in Mexico in 1970.

West began his career with Blackpool as a 17-year-old, making his debut at Bolton Wanderers in January 1961. A little over a year later he was on his way to Everton after Blues manager Harry Catterick paid £27,500 to secure his services – then a record fee for a goalkeeper, but one that paid immediate dividends, as West replaced Albert Dunlop and helped the Blues take the League Championship in his first full season at Goodison Park. Over the next three seasons West occasionally lost his place to Andy Rankin, but when Everton won the FA Cup in 1966, beating Sheffield Wednesday 3–2, he was in goal. An instinctive performer and courageous at close-quarters, he was also breathtaking as a shot-stopper. If he had a weakness, it was a rather inadequate kick – a legacy of a long-standing thigh injury. He successfully fought off the challenge of Rankin, and went on to miss only a handful of games, picking up a second League Championship medal in 1969/70.

He eventually left Goodison Park in 1973 after appearing in 399 League and Cup games for Everton, but many believed the 30-year-old was retiring prematurely. They were proved right when, two years later, he was lured back to the game by Tranmere Rovers. Across the Mersey, Everton were not to find a truly satisfactory replacement for West until the arrival of Neville Southall.

Paul REANEY

Position	Right-back
Born	Paul Reaney, Fulham, 22 October 1944
Height	5ft 9in
Weight	11st 11lb
Clubs	Leeds United, Bradford City
England Caps	3
	1968 v Bulgaria (1–1)
	1969 v Portugal (won 1–0)
	1971 v Mexico (won 1–0)

ONLY JACK CHARLTON and Scottish international Billy Bremner have played more games for Leeds United than right-back Paul Reaney. He was an apprentice motor mechanic when he joined Leeds' groundstaff in October 1961 and within a year had made his Football League debut for the Yorkshire club in a 2–0 win at Swansea Town. He was virtually an ever-present in his time at Elland Road, but a broken leg suffered at West Ham towards the end of the 1969/70 season forced him out of Alf Ramsey's England squad for the 1970 World Cup Finals in Mexico.

Dubbed 'Speedy' for his quickness to overlap into attack and knock in teasing crosses for the United forwards, Reaney was also rated one of the top markers of his day, few top-flight performers getting the better of him. He collected two League Championship medals, an FA Cup winners' medal, a League Cup winners' medal, Inter Cities Fairs Cup medals and a Second Division Championship medal in his 17 years at Elland Road. Giving Leeds another eight seasons' service after recovering fully from his broken leg, he made 745 first-team appearances in all before joining Bradford City on a free transfer.

In the summer of 1978 Reaney went to play in Australia for Newcastle UB United and was voted Australia's Player of the Year. Now living in Knaresborough, he runs coaching courses at schools and holiday camps.

John RADFORD

Position	Forward
Born	John Radford, Hemsworth, 22 February 1947
Height	5ft 11in
Weight	11st 11lb
Clubs	Arsenal, West Ham United, Blackburn Rovers
England Caps	2
	1969 v Romania (1–1)
	1971 v Switzerland (won 3–2)

JOHN RADFORD began his career with Arsenal and soon secured a regular place in the club's youth side, scoring 42 goals in 38 games in his first season at Highbury. He maintained his terrific striking rate the following season, netting 49 goals in 69 games, resulting in him making his first-team debut towards the end of that 1963/64 campaign at West Ham United. Able to play in all the forward-line positions, he had early success in the right-wing position in 1968/69, scoring 19 goals and winning four England Under-23 caps. In 1969/70 he added a full England cap and an Inter Cities Fairs Cup winners' medal to his honours and again finished the season as the club's leading scorer, with 19 goals. In the Gunners' double-winning season, he reverted to centre-forward, where he enjoyed notable success alongside Ray Kennedy. He continued to find the net on a regular basis for the next few seasons, though, following a series of injuries, he eventually lost his place to the up-and-coming Frank Stapleton.

Radford scored 149 goals in 481 League and Cup games. After joining West Ham United he had a spell with Blackburn Rovers, before enjoying further success with non-League Bishop's Stortford.

Terry COOPER

Position	Left-back
Born	Terence Cooper, Castleford, 12 July 1944
Height	5ft 8in
Weight	10st 9lb
Clubs	Leeds United, Middlesbrough, Bristol City, Bristol Rovers, Doncaster Rovers
England Caps	20
	1969 v France (won 5–0), v Wales (won 2–1), v Scotland (won 4–1), v Mexico (0–0)
	1970 v Holland (0–0), v Belgium (won 3–1), v Colombia (won 4–0), v Ecuador (won 2–0), v Romania (won 1–0), v Brazil (lost 0–1), v Czechoslovakia (won 1–0), v W. Germany (lost 2–3 aet), v E. Germany (won 3–1)
	1971 v Malta (won 5–0), v N. Ireland (won 1–0), v Wales (0–0), v Scotland (won 3–1), v Switzerland (won 3–2), v Switzerland (1–1)
	1974 v Portugal (0–0)

TERRY COOPER played for England in the 1970 World Cup Finals in Mexico. He broke a leg shortly afterwards, but fought back to earn a recall from Don Revie and take his total of full international caps to 20.

Cooper made his Leeds United debut as a pacey winger on the day the Yorkshire club gained promotion to the First Division in 1963/64, but later switched to full-back with devastating effect and became a master of the attacking overlap. He had trials with Wolverhampton Wanderers but was playing for Ferrybridge Amateurs when he joined Leeds as an apprentice in the summer of 1961. After turning professional, he replaced Willie Bell, using his experience as a winger to make breathtaking runs that added weight to the Elland Road club's attack. Though his goals were few and far between, he did score against Arsenal in the 1968 League Cup Final to give United their first major trophy. He went on to play in 350 games for Leeds before joining Middlesbrough in March 1975, helping the Teeside club win the Second Division Championship.

Cooper later signed for Bristol City before moving across the city to become player-coach at Bristol Rovers. He then assisted Doncaster Rovers for a brief spell under Billy Bremner, before, in May 1982, returning to Bristol City as player-manager and becoming Britain's first player-director. He steered them to victory in the 1986 Freight Rover Trophy Final before leaving to take charge of Exeter City. After leading the Grecians to the Fourth Division title he was appointed manager of Birmingham City, but in January 1994 he rejoined Exeter as manager. Sadly, ill-health prompted him to quit football in the summer of 1995.

Francis LEE

Position	Forward
Born	Francis Henry Lee, Westhoughton, 29 April 1944
Height	5ft 8in
Weight	12st 2lb
Clubs	Bolton Wanderers, Manchester City, Derby County
England Caps	27 Goals 10

1968 v Bulgaria (1–1)

1969 v France (won 5–0) 1 goal, v N. Ireland (won 3–1) 1 goal, v Wales (won 2–1) 1 goal, v Scotland (won 4–1), v Mexico (0–0), v Uruguay (won 2–1) 1 goal, v Holland (won 1–0), v Portugal (won 1–0)

1970 v Holland (0–0), v Belgium (won 3–1), v Wales (1–1) 1 goal, v Colombia (won 4–0), v Ecuador (won 2–0) 1 goal, v Romania (won 1–0), v Brazil (lost 0–1), v W. Germany (lost 2–3 aet), v E. Germany (won 3–1) 1 goal

1971 v Greece (won 3–0) 1 goal, v Malta (won 5–0) 1 goal, v N. Ireland (won 1–0), v Wales (0–0), v Scotland (won 3–1), v Switzerland (won 3–2), v Switzerland (1–1), v Greece (won 2–0)

1972 v W. Germany (lost 1–3) 1 goal

....

FRANCIS LEE, who finished his international career with 10 goals in his 27 appearances, was a vital part of Alf Ramsey's England squad for the 1970 World Cup Finals in Mexico as the side tried to defend the trophy.

Lee made his Football League debut for Bolton Wanderers as a 16-year-old amateur in November 1960, partnering 35-year-old Nat Lofthouse on the right-wing in a 3–1

Francis Lee. (Lancashire Evening Post)

victory over Manchester City. It was an eventful debut for Lee as he both scored a goal and got booked. Lee's volatile temperament was to land him in trouble at Bolton on a number of occasions, not least when he refused to play after being dropped to the club's 'A' team. Things were patched up, however, and though a number of clubs were keen to sign him following a string of transfer requests, he stayed with Bolton until the beginning of the 1967/68 season. Then, in October 1967, having scored over 100 goals for the Wanderers and rarely been out of the headlines, he joined Manchester City.

A bustling, sturdy little striker, barrel-chested and slightly portly, Lee was one of the most tenacious and effective of strikers, scoring many goals, including a hat-trick in the Manchester derby win over United at Old Trafford in December 1970. He also won many penalties for City and wasn't really fussy how he won them. In fact, City won so many penalties during the early 1970s, many of them for fouls on Lee, that it became a topical talking point. In the European Cup Winners' Cup Final of 1970 against Gornik Zabrze of Poland, he hit the ball so hard and straight into the net that it needed a close study of an action-replay to check that the ball had not gone through Kostka the goalkeeper's body! In 1971/72 he topped the First Division scoring charts with 33 goals, including 15 from the penalty spot. For this achievement he was awarded the bronze boot in the Golden Boot competition.

In August 1974 Lee left Maine Road to join Derby County for £110,000, and in his first season at the Baseball Ground he helped the Rams win the League Championship. He retired a year later, by which time the paper business that he had started as a player with Bolton was thriving, eventually securing him millionaire status. In February 1994 he became chairman of Manchester City, before resigning during the 1997/98 season.

Jeff ASTLE

Position	Centre-forward
Born	Jeffrey Astle, Eastwood, 13 May 1942
Died	19 January 2002
Height	6ft 0in
Weight	11st 6lb
Clubs	Notts County, West Bromwich Albion
England Caps	5
	1969 v Wales (won 2–1), v Portugal (won 1–0)
	1970 v Scotland (0–0), v Brazil (lost 0–1), v Czechoslovakia (won 1–0)

JEFF ASTLE won five full caps for England but never managed to get on the scoresheet: he was unlucky not to do so, being forced to adapt to England manager Alf Ramsey's wingless style of 4–4–2 instead of the 4–2–4 system used by Albion and the majority of other top-flight clubs.

Astle began his Football League career at Notts County, where his heading ability was brought out by Tommy Lawton, and it was his power in the air that was to be his trademark as one of the most feared strikers in the game. Signed by West Bromwich

Albion manager Jimmy Hagan for a giveaway £25,000, he soon became the undisputed 'King of the Hawthorns'. In 1967/68, when he scored the only goal of the 1968 final – an extra-time winner against Everton – he joined the select band of players who have managed to score in every round of the FA Cup. That winner was just one of nine goals in the Cup run to add to the 26 he scored in Albion's First Division campaign. He went on to score over 20 goals a season in 1968/69 and 1969/70, after which the club's other great goalscorer of the time, Tony Brown, took over as Albion's main source of goals.

A number of injuries forced Astle's premature retirement from the first-class game. He went on to play non-League football for Dunstable Town, Weymouth, Atherstone and Hillingdon Borough, before later finding fame with his regular singing appearances on Frank Skinner's *Fantasy Football League* programme.

Emlyn HUGHES

Position	Defender
Born	Emlyn Walter Hughes, Barrow-in-Furness, 28 August 1947
Height	5ft 11in
Weight	11st 13lb
Clubs	Blackpool, Liverpool, Wolverhampton Wanderers, Rotherham United, Hull City, Swansea City

England Caps   62   Goals   1

1969 v Holland (won 1–0), v Portugal (won 1–0)

1970 v Belgium (won 3–1), v Wales (1–1), v N. Ireland (won 3–1), v Scotland (0–0), v E. Germany (won 3–1)

1971 v Malta (won 1–0), v Greece (won 3–0), v Malta (won 5–0), v Wales (0–0), v Switzerland (1–1), v Greece (won 2–0)

1972 v W. Germany (lost 1–3), v W. Germany (0–0), v Wales (won 3–0) 1 goal, v N. Ireland (lost 0–1), v Scotland (won 1–0), v Wales (won 1–0)

1973 v Wales (1–1), v Scotland (won 5–0), v Wales (won 3–0), v Scotland (won 1–0), v Poland (lost 0–2), v Soviet Union (won 2–1), v Italy (lost 0–2), v Austria (won 7–0), v Poland (1–1), v Italy (lost 0–1)

1974 v Wales (won 2–0), v N. Ireland (won 1–0), v Scotland (lost 0–2), v Argentina (2–2), v E. Germany (1–1), v Bulgaria (won 1–0), v Yugoslavia (2–2), v Czechoslovakia (won 3–0), v Portugal (0–0)

1975 v Cyprus (won 1–0), v N. Ireland (0–0)

1976 v Italy (lost 0–2)

1977 v Luxembourg (won 5–0), v Wales (lost 0–1), v Scotland (lost 1–2), v Brazil (0–0), v Argentina (1–1), v Uruguay (0–0), v Switzerland (0–0), v Luxembourg (won 2–0), v Italy (won 2–0)

1978 v W. Germany (lost 1–2), v N. Ireland (won 1–0), v Scotland (won 1–0), v Hungary (won 4–1), v Denmark (won 4–3), v Eire (1–1)

1979 v N. Ireland (won 4–0), v Wales (0–0), v Sweden (0–0)

1980 v Spain (won 2–0), v N. Ireland (1–1), v Scotland (won 2–0)

Honours	Footballer of the Year 1977

Emlyn Hughes in possession of the ball in an England v Argentina match, 29 May 1974.
(Getty Images)

THE SON OF a Welsh Rugby League star, Emlyn Hughes began his career with Blackpool, making his debut as an 18-year-old against Blackburn Rovers in May 1966. Liverpool manager Bill Shankly was watching the game and made an offer straight after the match, but had to wait ten months before making his signing for £65,000. Shanks predicted that one day Emlyn Hughes would lead England, and of course he was right. He was a natural for the job, his unbounded energy and infectious enthusiasm helping him to collect 62 caps.

Hughes arrived at Anfield in February 1967, making a few appearances at left-back for the injured Gerry Byrne, but it was at left-half, replacing Willie Stevenson, that he found a permanent position. His dynamic surges into the opposition's penalty box brought him his fair share of spectacular goals. He holds the record for the highest number of appearances in first-class matches over a season, having turned out 74 times for Liverpool in 1972/73. A versatile player, he moved in 1973/74 to the centre of the Reds' defence, replacing Tommy Smith as captain, and though perhaps not quite as popular as Tommy, he was a great motivator, leading by example. In his five seasons as captain, he led Liverpool to two League Championships, two European Cups, the FA Cup and the UEFA Cup. Loved by the Anfield crowd, he was voted Footballer of the Year in 1977 and won more international caps as a Liverpool player than anyone else.

In August 1979, having made 657 appearances for the Reds, Hughes moved to Wolverhampton Wanderers, helping them beat Nottingham Forest in the League Cup Final in his first season with the club. He then had a spell as player-manager with Rotherham United before playing for Hull City and Swansea. His personality later earned him a nationwide reputation as a television celebrity, as a team captain on the BBC's *A Question of Sport*.

1970-79

The Slipping Crown

E ngland went to Mexico in 1970 to defend their world crown, but before the squad even arrived a cloud hung over their challenge, since Bobby Moore was held by the Colombian authorities after an outlandish allegation that he had stolen a £625 bracelet. England had a rough ride in their opening game against Romania but won through with a Hurst goal. A sleepless night before the encounter with Brazil, as Mexican and Brazilian fans chanted outside the squad's hotel, did not augur well. Brazil won 1–0 but the match is remembered for Gordon Banks' spectacular save from Pele's header. England then beat Czechoslovakia to qualify for the quarter-final against West Germany, but when Banks succumbed to a mystery illness, his replacement, Peter Bonetti, was thrust into the spotlight. England relaxed their grip on the game and a two-goal lead was thrown away. Sir Alf Ramsey decided to rest Charlton and Peters for the semi-final and a double substitution ensued; however, it was the ring-rusty Bonetti who was blamed for two of the three goals that took Germany through.

In 1972 England reached the quarter-final stage of the European Championships, but once more the Germans put paid to their aspirations with a 3–1 aggregate result.

Failure to qualify for the 1974 World Cup came at the hands of Poland. Goalkeeper Jan Tomaszewski defied England almost single-handed and Alf

Ramsey was sacked. Joe Mercer had a brief spell as caretaker manager before the FA named Don Revie, the successful Leeds United boss, as England's new manager. The Revie era had few highlights beyond Malcolm Macdonald's five goals against Cyprus and the emphatic 5–1 won over Scotland, both in 1975. It ended in controversial circumstances when, in 1977, he departed under a cloak of secrecy for a Middle Eastern coaching job. His replacement was West Ham's Ron Greenwood, who, though he failed in the almost impossible task of getting England to the 1978 World Cup Finals, did eventually bring them back on to the right road.

Ian STOREY-MOORE

Position	Winger
Born	Ian Storey-Moore, Ipswich, 17 May 1945
Height	5ft 10in
Weight	12st 7lb
Clubs	Nottingham Forest, Manchester United
England Caps	1
	1970 v Holland (0–0)

THERE IS NO DOUBT that, but for Alf Ramsey's policy of not playing wingers, Ian Storey-Moore would have won more than the one England cap he gained against Holland in 1970.

He signed professional forms for Nottingham Forest in May 1961 after being spotted playing in Scunthorpe junior football. He made his League debut for Forest against his home-town team two years later but it took him a little longer than that for him to become a first-team regular at the City Ground. A brilliant, exciting player, Storey-Moore was a lethal finisher, ending up the club's top scorer in 1966/67, 1968/69, 1969/70 and 1970/71, and repeating the feat the following season even though he left the club in February 1971. His best season was 1966/67, when he scored 25 League and Cup goals, including a hat-trick in a 3–2 defeat of Everton in an FA Cup sixth-round tie.

After scoring 118 goals in 272 games for Forest, he joined Manchester United, although he almost moved instead to Derby County – the Rams even introduced him to the crowd as their new player!

An instant hit at Old Trafford, he had made only 39 appearances before injuries forced his retirement. He later made a number of appearances for Chicago Stings in the NASL, and played for and managed both Shepshed Charterhouse and Burton Albion.

Peter OSGOOD

Position	Centre-forward
Born	Peter Leslie Osgood, Windsor, 20 February 1947
Height	6ft 2in
Weight	12st 10lb
Clubs	Chelsea, Southampton, Norwich City
England Caps	4
	1970 v Belgium (won 3–1), v Romania (won 1–0), v Czechoslovakia (won 1–0)
	1973 v Italy (lost 0–1)

PETER OSGOOD was a brilliant individualist who graced the English game for a decade and most certainly should have won more than four full caps for England. He signed for Chelsea in September 1964, where his tremendous skills made him a great crowd favourite. He could put thousands on the gate at the height of his powers and he was an automatic first-team choice at Stamford Bridge until he had public rows with manager Dave Sexton. Ossie scored in every round of the FA Cup during the course of the 1969/70 season, plundering a hat-trick at Queen's Park Rangers and crowning it all with a superb diving header that left keeper David Harvey bewildered in the Cup Final replay against Leeds United at Old Trafford. He went on to score 150 goals in 380 games for Chelsea, including five against Jeunesse Hautcharge in the European Cup Winners' Cup.

Southampton manager Lawrie McMenemy splashed out a record £275,000 to bring Osgood to the Dell. Although he impressed in his early games for the club, he could not prevent them being relegated to the Second Division. He won a second FA Cup winners' medal in 1976 and then, after a month's loan spell with Norwich City, he left the Dell to play for Philadelphia Furies, before returning to Chelsea, where he ended his League career.

Since leaving the game, Osgood has been a Windsor licensee, a coach at holiday camps, a sports promotion manager and, more recently, a match-day host at Chelsea.

Ralph COATES

Position	Midfielder
Born	Ralph Coates, Hetton-le-Hole, 26 April 1946
Height	5ft 7in
Weight	11st 7lb
Clubs	Burnley, Tottenham Hotspur, Leyton Orient
England Caps	4
	1970 v N. Ireland (won 3–1)
	1971 v Greece (won 3–0), v Malta (won 5–0), v Wales (0–0)

IGNORED BY the professional clubs, Ralph Coates took a job at Eppleton Colliery and it was while playing for the colliery's Welfare side that he was noticed by Burnley. A tireless, bustling worker, who could be back defending one minute and looking to score the next, Coates quickly established a reputation as a more-than-promising midfielder-cum-winger. His performances soon earned him international recognition in the form of eight England Under-23 caps and selection four times to play for the Football League. He also won the first of his England caps while at Turf Moor, playing in the 3–1 win over Northern Ireland in April 1970. Having scored 32 goals in 261 games for the Clarets, he was eventually allowed to leave Turf Moor for economic reasons. He joined Tottenham Hotspur for £190,000 and his first appearances as a Spurs player were his third and fourth caps for England!

At White Hart Lane, Coates never truly completed the spectacular development that earned him star billing at Turf Moor. A member of the Spurs team that won the UEFA Cup in 1972 and 1974, his crowning glory came in the 1973 League Cup Final against Norwich City when, as a substitute, he thumped home the winning goal.

Coates left Spurs in 1978 to play for the old St George's club of Sydney, but later returned to play for Leyton Orient. He later played non-League football for Hertford Heath, Ware and Nazeing, before becoming the manager of a Hertfordshire leisure complex.

Brian KIDD

Position	Forward
Born	Brian Kidd, Manchester, 29 May 1949
Height	5ft 10in
Weight	11st 6lb
Clubs	Manchester United, Arsenal, Manchester City, Everton, Bolton Wanderers
England Caps	2 Goals 1
	1970 v N. Ireland (won 3–1), v Ecuador (won 2–0) 1 goal

AN EXHILARATING FORWARD when playing to the peak of his form, Brian Kidd hit the heights of his career when it had barely started. On his 19th birthday, in 1968, he lined up alongside such greats as Bobby Charlton and George Best to score a goal in Manchester United's famous European Cup Final victory over Portuguese club Benfica at Wembley. Kidd was speedy, had great attacking flair and was capable of scoring with either foot or with his head. He won two England caps before moving to Arsenal for £110,000 in 1974.

After two years at Highbury, during which he was top scorer in both campaigns, Kidd was anxious to return north, and in June 1976 he jumped at the chance of joining Manchester City for £100,000. He finished his first season at Maine Road as the club's top scorer with 21 goals and topped the charts 12 months later with 16. In March 1979 he was on the move again, this time to Everton for £150,000. With the Goodison club he had the unwelcome distinction of becoming only the second player since the Second World War to be dismissed in an FA Cup semi-final, when he was sent off against West Ham United. Shortly afterwards he signed for Bolton Wanderers, but his stay at Burnden Park was brief and he went to play in the NASL with Fort Lauderdale, Atlanta Chiefs and Minnesota Strikers.

Kidd returned to play non-League football as player-manager of Barrow before becoming assistant manager of Preston North End. He took over the reins when Tommy Booth left, before returning to Old Trafford as a member of the club's coaching staff. After a period as Alex Ferguson's assistant, he became manager of Blackburn Rovers and was subsequently assistant to Terry Venables at Leeds United.

Allan CLARKE

Position	Forward
Born	Allan John Clarke, Willenhall, 31 July 1946
Height	6ft 0in
Weight	10st 13lb
Clubs	Walsall, Fulham, Leicester City, Leeds United, Barnsley
England Caps	19 Goals 10
	1970 v Czechoslovakia (won 1–0) 1 goal, v E. Germany (won 3–1) 1 goal
	1971 v Malta (won 5–0) 1 goal, v N. Ireland (won 1–0) 1 goal, v Wales (0–0), v Scotland (won 3–1)
	1973 v Scotland (won 5–0) 2 goals, v Wales (won 3–0), v Scotland (won 1–0),

Allan Clarke. (Lancashire Evening Post)

v Czechoslovakia (1–1) 1 goal, v Poland (lost 0–2), v Soviet Union (won 2–1), v Italy (lost 0–2), v Austria (won 7–0) 2 goals, v Poland (1–1) 1 goal, v Italy (lost 0–1)

1974 v Portugal (0–0)

1975 v Czechoslovakia (lost 1–2), v Portugal (1–1)

....

NICKNAMED 'SNIFFER' in recognition of his clinical penalty-box skills, Allan Clarke scored in each of his first four internationals and went on to score ten goals in 19 appearances for England.

An instinctive goalscorer, Clarke came from a footballing family – brothers Wayne, Frank, Derek and Kelvin all played League football – but he was the pick of the crop. He joined Walsall as an apprentice in 1961, turning professional two years later. He soon began knocking in goals and in March 1966 he joined First Division Fulham for £35,000. In 1966/67 he was the Cottagers' leading scorer with 29 League and Cup goals, a total which included a hat-trick in a 5–1 win over Newcastle United. He topped the charts again the following season, scoring four times in a 6–2 League Cup defeat of Workington. Following Fulham's relegation in 1968, Clarke demanded a move and Leicester City paid a club-record £150,000 for his services. He soon ingratiated himself to the Leicester public with a hat-trick in a 3–0 win over Manchester City and the FA Cup semi-final winner against West Bromwich Albion. Voted Man-of-the-Match in Leicester's 1969 FA Cup Final defeat by Manchester City, he was soon on his way to Elland Road, after Leeds United manager Don Revie splashed out £165,000.

Clarke played in three FA Cup finals for the Yorkshire club – scoring the winning goal in 1972 – won a League Championship medal in 1974, and was also the scorer in their Inter Cities Fairs Cup Final victory of 1971. He had scored 151 goals in 366 games for Leeds when, in the summer of 1978, he left to become player-manager of Barnsley. After helping the Oakwell club out of the Fourth Division in his first season, he returned to Leeds as boss, subsequently also managing Scunthorpe United, Barnsley again and Lincoln City.

Peter SHILTON

Position	Goalkeeper
Born	Peter Leslie Shilton, Leicester, 18 September 1949
Height	6ft 0in
Weight	12st 10lb
Clubs	Leicester City, Stoke City, Nottingham Forest, Southampton, Derby County, Plymouth Argyle, Wimbledon, Bolton Wanderers, Coventry City, West Ham United, Leyton Orient
England Caps	125

1970 v E. Germany (won 3–1)

1971 v Wales (0–0), v Switzerland (1–1)

1972 v N. Ireland (lost 0–1), v Yugoslavia (1–1)

1973 v Scotland (won 5–0), v N. Ireland (won 2–1), v Wales (won 3–0), v Scotland (won 1–0), v Czechoslovakia (1–1), v Poland (lost 0–2), v Soviet Union (won 2–1), v Italy (lost 0–2), v Austria (won 7–0), v Poland (1–1), v Italy (lost 0–1)

1974 v Wales (won 2–0), v N. Ireland (won 1–0), v Scotland (lost 0–2), v Argentina (2–2)
1975 v Cyprus (won 5–0)
1977 v N. Ireland (won 2–1), v Wales (lost 0–1)
1978 v Wales (won 3–1), v Hungary (won 4–1), v Czechoslovakia (won 1–0)
1979 v Sweden (0–0), v Austria (lost 3–4), v N. Ireland (won 5–1)
1980 v Spain (won 2–0), v Italy (lost 0–1), v Norway (won 4–0), v Switzerland (won 2–1)
1981 v Romania (0–0), v Hungary (won 1–0)
1982 v Holland (won 2–0), v Scotland (won 1–0), v Finland (won 4–1), v France (won 3–1),
     v Czechoslovakia (won 2–0), v Kuwait (won 1–0), v W. Germany (0–0), v Spain (0–0),
     v Denmark (2–2), v W. Germany (lost 1–2), v Greece (won 3–0)
1983 v Wales (won 2–1), v Greece (0–0), v Hungary (won 2–0), v N. Ireland (0–0),
     v Scotland (won 2–0), v Australia (0–0), v Australia (won 1–0), v Australia (1–1),
     v Denmark (lost 0–1), v Hungary (won 3–0)
1984 v France (lost 0–2), v N. Ireland (won 1–0), v Wales (lost 0–1), v Scotland (1–1),
     v Soviet Union (lost 0–2), v Brazil (won 2–0), v Uruguay (lost 0–2), v Chile (0–0),
     v E. Germany (won 1–0), v Finland (won 5–0), v Turkey (won 8–0), v N. Ireland (won 1–0)
1985 v Romania (0–0), v Finland (1–1), v Scotland (lost 0–1), v Italy (lost 1–2),
     v W. Germany (won 3–0), v Romania (1–1), v Turkey (won 5–0), v N. Ireland (0–0)
1986 v Egypt (won 4–0), v Israel (lost 1–2), v Soviet Union (won 1–0), v Scotland (won 2–1),
     v Mexico (won 3–0), v Canada (won 1–0), v Portugal (lost 0–1), v Morocco (0–0),
     v Poland (won 3–0), v Paraguay (won 3–0), v Argentina (lost 1–2), v N. Ireland (won 3–0),
     v Sweden (lost 0–1)
1987 v Spain (won 4–2), v Brazil (1–1), v W. Germany (lost 1–3), v Turkey (won 8–0),
     v Yugoslavia (won 4–1)
1988 v Holland (2–2), v Scotland (won 1–0), v Colombia (1–1), v Switzerland (won 1–0),
     v Eire (lost 0–1), v Holland (lost 1–3)
1989 v Denmark (won 1–0), v Sweden (0–0), v Greece (won 2–1), v Albania (won 2–0),
     v Albania (won 5–0), v Chile (0–0), v Scotland (won 2–0), v Poland (0–0), v Denmark (1–1)
1990 v Sweden (0–0), v Poland (won 2–0), v Italy (0–0), v Yugoslavia (won 2–1), v Brazil
     (won 1–0), v Czechoslovakia (won 4–2), v Denmark (won 1–0), v Uruguay (lost 1–2),
     v Tunisia (1–1), v Eire (1–1), v Holland (0–0), v Egypt (won 1–0), v Belgium (won 1–0),
     v Cameroon (won 3–2), v W. Germany (1–1 aet, W. Germany won 4–3 on penalties),
     v Italy (lost 1–2)

Honours   Footballer of the Year 1978

UNDOUBTEDLY one of the greatest goalkeepers in the modern era, Peter Shilton trained as hard as any, and his dedication to fitness and technique ensured one of the longest careers in recent times. Indeed, other than Stanley Matthews no one can beat the length of Shilton's England career. He holds the English appearance record with 125 caps and was the most-capped keeper in the world until a few years ago, when he was overtaken by Swedish No. 1 Thomas Ravelli.

A schoolboy prodigy, Shilton began his career with his home-town team of Leicester City and became the club's youngest-ever First Division debutant at the age of 16 when, characteristically, he kept a clean sheet against Everton. He continued to make good progress, so much so that Gordon Banks moved on to Stoke City. In 1970/71, when Leicester won the Second Division Championship, Shilton helped to create the club's best-ever defensive record when he kept a record 23 clean sheets. He

Peter Shilton prepares to throw the ball during the 1988 European Championship game against Holland. England lost 3–1. (Getty Images)

was rarely out of the public eye – his adoption of an all-white playing kit and his long-distance scoring success at Southampton assured that!

Shilton had appeared in 339 games for Leicester when, in November 1974, he, like Banks before him, joined Stoke City, the fee of £325,000 setting a world record for a goalkeeper at the time. Following the Potters' relegation, Shilton was the subject of a typically shrewd business deal by Brian Clough, who paid £240,000 for his services. In terms of honours, he enjoyed his best years with Nottingham Forest, being selected as the PFA Player of the Year in 1978, and gaining a League Championship medal, League Cup medal and two European Cup winners' medals. He left Forest in August 1982, after playing in 272 games, to join Southampton for £300,000.

While at the Dell, Shilton became the most-capped England keeper of all time, skippered the national side on a number of occasions and was awarded the MBE in 1986. Then, after another big-money transfer to Derby County, he set about creating a further series of career landmarks. He passed Terry Paine's all-time record for the highest number of League appearances and overtook Bobby Moore's haul of England caps. After bowing out of the international scene in 1990, he was upgraded to OBE before taking the plunge into management with Plymouth Argyle. It wasn't for him, but, amazingly, he came back as a player, first with Wimbledon and then Bolton Wanderers. After spells with Coventry and West Ham, he joined Leyton Orient, where, four days before Christmas 1996, he made his 1,000th Football League appearance.

Roy McFARLAND

Position	Centre-half
Born	Roy Leslie McFarland, Liverpool, 5 April 1948
Height	5ft 11in
Weight	11st 2lb
Clubs	Tranmere Rovers, Derby County, Bradford City
England Caps	28

1971 v Malta (won 1–0), v Greece (won 3–0), v Malta (won 5–0), v N. Ireland (won 1–0), v Scotland (won 3–1), v Switzerland (won 3–2), v Greece (won 2–0)
1972 v W. Germany (0–0), v Wales (won 3–0), v Scotland (won 1–0), v Wales (won 1–0)
1973 v Wales (1–1), v N. Ireland (won 2–1), v Wales (won 3–0), v Scotland (won 1–0), v Czechoslovakia (1–1), v Poland (lost 0–2), v Soviet Union (won 2–1), v Italy (lost 0–2), v Austria (won 7–0), v Poland (1–1), v Italy (lost 0–1)
1974 v Wales (won 2–0), v N. Ireland (won 1–0)
1975 v Czechoslovakia (lost 1–2)
1976 v Scotland (lost 1–2), v Eire (1–1), v Italy (lost 0–2)

ROY McFARLAND played his early football for Tranmere Rovers but it wasn't long before Derby County manager Brian Clough snapped him up in the summer of 1967. Forming an excellent central defensive partnership with Dave Mackay, he helped the Rams win the Second Division title in 1968/69. His performances at the heart of the

Derby defence led to him winning the first of 28 international caps in England's 1–0 win over Malta in Valletta.

McFarland was an inspirational captain as the Rams won their first League Championship the following season. He missed out, however, on almost all of Derby's second League Championship-winning season of 1974/75 due to an Achilles tendon injury sustained while playing for England. A year earlier, in October 1973, he played in the England side that failed to beat Poland, meaning that he also missed out on the 1974 World Cup Finals. Skilful, consistent and uncompromising, McFarland made 530 appearances for Derby, scoring 48 goals, mainly from set-pieces.

In May 1981 McFarland moved to Valley Parade as player-manager of Bradford City, and in his first season in charge he took the Bantams to promotion to the Third Division. He later returned to the Baseball Ground and took over as caretaker boss when Peter Taylor resigned. He stayed at Derby as Arthur Cox's assistant until 1993, when he took over the reins himself. In June 1995 he left to manage Bolton Wanderers but was dismissed before the year was out following the Trotters' dismal run of results. He then took charge of Cambridge United, but despite leading them to promotion to the Second Division he lost his job in 2001.

Martin CHIVERS

Position	Centre-forward
Born	Martin Harcourt Chivers, Southampton, 27 April 1945
Height	6ft 1in
Weight	13st 13lb
Clubs	Southampton, Tottenham Hotspur, Servette Geneva, Norwich City, Brighton and Hove Albion
England Caps	24 Goals 13
	1971 v Malta (won 1–0), v Greece (won 3–0) 1 goal, v Malta (won 5–0) 2 goals, v N. Ireland (won 1–0), v Scotland (won 3–1) 2 goals, v Switzerland (won 3–2) 1 goal, v Switzerland (1–1), v Greece (won 2–0) 1 goal
	1972 v W. Germany (lost 1–3), v W. Germany (0–0), v N. Ireland (lost 0–1), v Scotland (won 1–0), v Wales (1–0)
	1973 v Wales (1–1), v Scotland (won 5–0) 1 goal, v N. Ireland (won 2–1) 2 goals, v Wales (won 3–0) 1 goal, v Scotland (won 1–0), v Czechoslovakia (1–1), v Poland (lost 0–2), v Soviet Union (won 2–1) 1 goal, v Italy (lost 0–2), v Austria (won 7–0) 1 goal, v Poland (1–1)

THOUGH HE COULD LOOK deceptively clumsy and casual, Martin Chivers scored some spectacular goals, including 13 in 24 full international games for England.

Beginning his League career with his home-town club Southampton, Chivers ended his first full season of 1963/64 as the club's joint-leading scorer. His 21 goals came from only 28 games and included a hat-trick in a 5–1 defeat of Swindon Town. That season also saw him win the first of 12 England Under-23 caps while at the Dell, when he played against France. In the Saints' promotion-winning season of 1965/66, Chivers scored 30 goals in his first 29 outings, including four in a 9–3 home win over

Martin Chivers. (Lancashire Evening Post)

Wolverhampton Wanderers and a hat-trick as Cardiff City were beaten 5–3 at Ninian Park. Chivers went on to score 107 goals in 189 games for the Saints, but then became restless. The Southampton board agreed to his transfer request and in January 1968 he moved to Tottenham Hotspur for a record fee of £125,000, with Frank Saul, valued at £45,000, moving in the opposite direction. He hadn't been at White Hart Lane long when he twisted his knee and was sidelined for a year. Eventually he returned to full fitness and, having scored both Spurs goals in the 1971 Football League Cup Final victory over Aston Villa, the goals kept coming. Against Wolves at Molineux in the first leg of the 1972 UEFA Cup Final, he hit home a stunning 25-yarder after beating two men, and followed this with a soaring header, while a 35-yard free kick of tremendous velocity provided a crucial away goal against Victoria Setubal in March 1973.

A player whose long throw-in was a powerful weapon, Chivers finally left Spurs in July 1976 to join Swiss club Servette Geneva. He later had short spells at Norwich and Brighton but was no longer up to the demands of League football.

Joe ROYLE

Position	Centre-forward
Born	Joseph Royle, Liverpool, 8 April 1949
Height	6ft 1in
Weight	12st 1lb
Clubs	Everton, Manchester City, Bristol City, Norwich City
England Caps	6 Goals 2
	1971 v Malta (won 1–0)
	1972 v Yugoslavia (1–1) 1 goal
	1976 v N. Ireland (won 4–0), v Italy (won 3–2), v Finland (won 2–1) 1 goal
	1977 v Luxembourg (won 5–0)

UNTIL RECENTLY, when Wayne Rooney made his League debut for Everton, Joe Royle, who won six full caps for England spread over six years, was the youngest-ever player to wear the famous royal blue of the Merseyside giants. In January 1966, at the age of 16 years 288 days, he played for the Blues at Blackpool. He had been called into the side to replace the axed Alex Young, but when furious fans attacked manager Harry Catterick for making that decision, Royle returned to the club's Central League side. He worked hard to improve his game and in 1968/69 finished as the club's leading scorer with 22 goals, a total that included a hat-trick in a 7–1 home win over Leicester City. Royle top-scored for Everton for the next three seasons, netting another hat-trick in a 4–2 win over Southampton in September 1969 and then four goals against the same opposition in November 1971 as the Saints were beaten 8–0.

Royle had scored 119 goals in 275 League and Cup games when, in December 1974, he was transferred to Manchester City for £200,000. Though not as prolific as before, he had three good years at Maine Road before spells with Bristol City and Norwich City, where his playing career came to a premature end because of injury.

Entering management with Oldham Athletic, he combined integrity, humour and sound judgement as the Latics won promotion to the top flight and reached the League Cup Final and FA Cup semi-final. In November 1994 he returned to Goodison as manager, but following clashes with chairman Peter Johnson he left the club. He took charge at Manchester City, leading the club into the Premiership after successive promotions, and then became manager of Ipswich Town.

Colin HARVEY

Position	Midfielder
Born	Colin James Harvey, Liverpool, 16 November 1945
Height	5ft 7in
Weight	11st 0lb
Clubs	Everton, Sheffield Wednesday
England Caps	1
	1971 v Malta (won 1–0)

COLIN HARVEY, who had every attribute demanded of a modern midfielder, only won one full cap for England and that was in 1971 as Malta were beaten 1–0 in a European qualifying match.

Harvey made his Everton debut in a European Cup tie at Inter Milan's San Siro Stadium, and neither smoke bombs and fireworks nor the baying of over 90,000 Italians intimidated the 18-year-old. He played with great maturity as the Blues lost by just a single goal to one of the best club sides in the world. Establishing himself as a first-team regular in 1964/65, he scored in his first-ever Merseyside derby as Everton beat Liverpool 4–0. He wasn't a prolific scorer, however, and even his best-remembered goal, the winner at Burnden Park in the 1966 FA Cup semi-final against Manchester United, was miss-hit, bobbling over Harry Gregg from 15 yards. He had played in 384 games for the Blues when, in October 1974, he joined Sheffield Wednesday. Sadly, a nagging hip injury caught up with him, and, just over a year after arriving at Hillsborough, he was forced to retire.

Harvey took up coaching and turned out to be a natural, deserving much of the credit for Everton's success in the mid-1980s. He was not, however, cut out to be a manager. Succeeding Howard Kendall as Everton boss in the summer of 1987, he knew deep down that it was not the right role for him and three years later he was dismissed. He returned just six days later as assistant manager to the reappointed Kendall, but later left to become assistant manager to Graeme Sharp at Oldham until both resigned their posts in February 1997.

Peter STOREY

Position	Defender
Born	Peter Edwin Storey, Farnham, 7 September 1945
Height	5ft 10in
Weight	11st 7lb
Clubs	Arsenal, Fulham
England Caps	19

1971 v Greece (won 3–0), v N. Ireland (won 1–0), v Scotland (won 3–1), v Switzerland (1–1)

1972 v W. Germany (0–0), v Wales (won 3–0), v N. Ireland (lost 0–1), v Scotland (won 1–0), v Yugoslavia (1–1), v Wales (won 1–0)

1973 v Wales (1–1), v Scotland (won 5–0), v N. Ireland (won 2–1), v Wales (won 3–0), v Scotland (won 1–0), v Czechoslovakia (1–1), v Poland (lost 0–2), v Soviet Union (won 2–1), v Italy (lost 0–2)

KNOWN AS one of the hardest tacklers in the game, Peter Storey established himself in the England side during the seasons 1971/72 and 1972/73, taking over from the popular Nobby Stiles. He made his Arsenal debut in October 1965 as a replacement for Billy McCullough in the game against Leicester City at Filbert Street. Thereafter he was a virtual ever-present in the Gunners side for the next 12 seasons, appearing in League Cup finals against Leeds and Swindon Town, and also being a member of the club's Inter Cities Fairs Cup-winning team. During the club's 'double' year of 1970/71, he equalled Bobby Smith's record of winning League Championship and FA Cup winners' medals and England caps in the same season. He also played for Arsenal in the 1972 FA Cup Final against Leeds. By this time he had switched from his original full-back position to a wing-half midfield defensive position.

Storey, who had played in 501 League and Cup games for Arsenal, left Highbury in March 1977 to play for Fulham, but his stay at Craven Cottage was brief. Since retiring from the game he has led a colourful life, running a market stall in London's West End after managing a number of public houses.

Chris LAWLER

Position	Right-back
Born	Christopher Lawler, Liverpool, 20 October 1943
Height	6ft 0in
Weight	12st 10lb
Clubs	Liverpool, Portsmouth, Stockport County
England Caps	4 Goals 1

1971 v Malta (won 5–0) 1 goal, v Wales (0–0), v Scotland (won 3–1), v Switzerland (won 3–2)

CHRIS LAWLER, nicknamed 'the Silent Knight', scored 61 goals for Liverpool in a playing career that spanned more than 14 years. His ability to pop up in the opposition's penalty area and tuck the ball away – he scored a remarkable 11 goals in 66 appearances in European football – made him one of the greatest full-backs in Liverpool's history. He became a regular choice in the Reds side in 1964/65, when he completed a successful season by winning an FA Cup winners' medal as Liverpool beat Leeds United 2–1 after extra time. Lawler was incredibly loyal to the Anfield club, even postponing his wedding when the Reds played Inter Milan in the 1965 European Cup semi-final! He made his international debut against Malta in a European Championship qualifier, four days after appearing in the FA Cup Final against Arsenal in May 1971, and scored in a 5–0 Wembley win, going on to gain three more caps, never playing on the losing side.

An ever-present in seasons 1971/72 and 1972/73, when Liverpool won the League Championship and UEFA Cup respectively, he was later hampered by a knee injury sustained in a match against Queen's Park Rangers. After turning down a move to Manchester City, he joined Portsmouth, before later ending his playing career back in the north-west with Stockport County. He then became a member of the famous boot-room at Anfield, coaching the club's youngsters, but he parted company with the club following the appointment of Kenny Dalglish as manager.

Paul MADELEY

Position	Defender
Born	Paul Edward Madeley, Leeds, 20 September 1944
Height	6ft 0in
Weight	12st 13lb
Clubs	Leeds United
England Caps	24
	1971 v N. Ireland (won 1–0), v Switzerland (won 3–2), v Switzerland (1–1), v Greece (won 2–0)
	1972 v W. Germany (lost 1–3), v W. Germany (0–0), v Wales (won 3–0), v Scotland (won 1–0)
	1973 v Scotland (won 5–0), v Czechoslovakia (1–1), v Poland (lost 0–2), v Soviet Union (won 2–1), v Italy (lost 0–2), v Austria (won 7–0), v Poland (1–1), v Italy (lost 0–1)
	1974 v Czechoslovakia (won 3–0), v Portugal (0–0)
	1975 v Cyprus (won 5–0), v Czechoslovakia (lost 1–2), v Portugal (1–1)
	1976 v Finland (won 4–1), v Eire (1–1)
	1977 v Holland (lost 0–2)

IGNORED AT UNDER-23 LEVEL, Paul Madeley represented the Football League before turning down the chance to go to Mexico with England for the 1970 World Cup Finals. He had been omitted from the original squad but got the chance to go when his team-mate Paul Reaney broke a leg. Thankfully, Alf Ramsey bore no grudge and Madeley won the first of 24 full caps against Northern Ireland in 1971.

Madeley played in every position except goal in a 17-year career with Leeds United. On leaving school he had begun work in an insurance broker's office and played in the Yorkshire League with Farsley Celtic, but, after being invited to Elland Road for

Paul Madeley of Leeds. (Lancashire Evening Post)

trials, he joined the club in May 1962. Originally groomed as Jack Charlton's successor, manager Don Revie soon realized that the young Madeley was a versatile performer – in one of his early seasons with the club he appeared in nine different positions! An integral member of a Leeds team noted for its 'hardmen', he was only cautioned twice in a career that saw him play in 726 games. He won two League Championship medals, an FA Cup winners' medal, a League Cup winners' medal and two Inter Cities Fairs Cup winners' medals.

On retiring in 1980 Madeley opened a sports shop in Leeds as well as keeping an interest in his family's successful home décor business, which was sold in a multi-million pound deal in December 1987.

Tommy SMITH

Position	Defender
Born	Thomas Smith, Liverpool, 6 April 1945
Height	5ft 11in
Weight	13st 0lb
Clubs	Liverpool, Swansea City
England Caps	1
	1971 v Wales (0–0)

TOMMY SMITH developed into one of the toughest defenders in the Football League and was an integral member of Bill Shankly's first great Liverpool side. He had two roles, at first playing midfield and then moving into the centre of defence. More skilful than generally recognized, he contributed greatly to Liverpool's FA Cup success of 1965 and the ensuing Championship campaign. Succeeding Ron Yeats as Liverpool captain, he was an inspiration, driving the team on to ever-greater efforts. He relished the job and its responsibilities, and in the 1970/71 season gave some of his best-ever performances, winning his only England cap as a result and only just being pipped as Footballer of the Year by Arsenal's Frank McLintock. In 1972/7 he led the Reds to the unique double of League Championship and UEFA Cup, following this with yet more trophies. In early 1977, troubled by knee problems, he announced his retirement, only to find himself hastily drafted back into the centre of defence following an injury to Phil Thompson. He had a superb season, facing Manchester United in the FA Cup Final, winning another League Championship medal and then making his 600th appearance in a Liverpool shirt in the European Cup Final against Borussia Moenchengladbach, where, to cap a wonderful year, he rose majestically to meet Heighway's corner and head home one of Liverpool's goals.

Smith later joined John Toshack at Swansea City before returning to Anfield for a brief spell as coach. Awarded the MBE for his services to the game, he was a player of great courage, toughness and determination.

Larry LLOYD

Position	Centre-half
Born	Laurence Valentine Lloyd, Bristol, 6 October 1948
Height	6ft 3in
Weight	14st 4lb
Clubs	Bristol Rovers, Liverpool, Coventry City, Nottingham Forest, Wigan Athletic
England Caps	4
	1971 v Wales (0–0), v Switzerland (1–1), v N. Ireland (lost 0–1)
	1980 v Wales (lost 1–4)

LARRY LLOYD won his fourth and last England cap nine years after his international debut, but it was to be in a match he would perhaps rather forget as Wales beat England 4–1 at the Racecourse Ground.

Lloyd began his League career with his home-town team Bristol Rovers before being signed by Liverpool manager Bill Shankly for £50,000. He was an immediate hit, the perfect replacement for Kop favourite Ron Yeats. Massive and powerful, inspired calm among those around him, winning both a League Championship medal and UEFA Cup winners' medal in 1973. Then, after Bob Paisley took over as Liverpool manager, he was surprisingly sold to Coventry City for a fee of £225,000. Unable to settle at Highfield Road, he joined Nottingham Forest on loan before the move was made permanent.

Forming a superb partnership with Kenny Burns in the heart of the Forest defence, Lloyd went on to win another League Championship medal, two League Cup winners' medals and two European Cup winners' medals. He left the City Ground in March 1981 to become player-manager of Wigan Athletic, guiding the then Springfield Park club to promotion to the Third Division. He later managed Notts County, leading them to the top of the First Division, but relegation and dismissal soon followed.

Tony BROWN

Position	Forward
Born	Anthony John Brown, Oldham, 3 October 1945
Height	5ft 7in
Weight	11st 6lb
Clubs	West Bromwich Albion, Torquay United
England Caps	1
	1971 v Wales (0–0)

TONY 'BOMBER' BROWN holds the West Bromwich Albion club record for the most League appearances, with a total of 574, and the most goals, 218, in a 20-year career at the Hawthorns. Though he appeared for Young England and the Football League XI during the early stages of his career, he had to wait until 1971 before making his long-overdue full international debut against Wales.

Originally a goalscoring wing-half, Brown made his Albion debut in September 1963, though it took him a couple of seasons to establish himself as a first-team regular. He was a first choice from 1965 to 1979, topping the club's scoring charts time after time and forming a prolific strike force with Jeff Astle. Brown was a versatile player and appeared in all the midfield and forward positions at the club, as well as being the Baggies' penalty-taker. In 1970/71 his 28 goals made him the First Division's leading scorer and helped him to win full honours. He went on to appear in almost 900 first-class games for Albion before leaving the Hawthorns in October 1981 to play for Torquay United. He later returned to the club as coach following the appointment of Johnny Giles as manager, but left after Giles resigned to take up the post of assistant manager at Birmingham City.

Rodney MARSH

Position	Forward
Born	Rodney William Marsh, Hatfield, 11 October 1944
Height	6ft 1in
Weight	13st 2lb
Clubs	Fulham, Queen's Park Rangers, Manchester City
England Caps	9 Goals 1
	1971 v Switzerland (1–1)
	1972 v W. Germany (lost 1–3), v W. Germany (0–0), v Wales (won 3–0) 1 goal,
	v N. Ireland (lost 0–1), v Scotland (won 1–0), v Yugoslavia (1–1), v Wales (won 1–0),
	v Wales (1–1)

RODNEY MARSH began his career with Fulham, scoring a superb volleyed goal on his debut as the Cottagers beat Aston Villa 1–0 in March 1963. After playing in just a handful of games over the next couple of seasons, he established himself in the Fulham side in 1964/65, scoring 17 goals in 41 games. During the course of that season, Marsh sustained a serious injury in the game at Leicester City, an injury that left him partially deaf. He subsequently seemed to lose form and was transferred to Queen's Park Rangers, the club with whom he was to win the first of his nine England caps. He played an important role in Rangers' rise from the Third to the First Division, winning a Third Division Championship winners' medal in 1966/67. He also won a League Cup winners' medal while at Loftus Road, scoring one of the goals in a 3–2 win over West Bromwich Albion.

In March 1972, Manchester City paid £200,000 to take Marsh to Maine Road, and with him in the side, City became a joy to watch, his imaginative play setting up a host of chances for his team-mates. Though not a prolific scorer, he did net a hat-trick in a 4–1 defeat of York City in the 1973/74 League Cup, going on to collect a runners-up medal as City reached the final, only to lose to Wolves.

Marsh later moved to the United States to play for Tampa Bay Rowdies before returning to Craven Cottage to team up with George Best, but, sadly, injury dogged his stay, and he was forced to retire.

Malcolm MacDONALD

Position	Centre-forward
Born	Malcolm Ian Macdonald, Fulham, 7 January 1950
Height	5ft 11in
Weight	13st 5lb
Clubs	Fulham, Luton Town, Newcastle United, Arsenal
England Caps	14 Goals 6

1972 v Wales (won 3–0), v N. Ireland (lost 0–1), v Scotland (won 1–0)
1973 v Soviet Union (won 2–1)
1974 v Portugal (0–0), v Scotland (lost 0–2), v Yugoslavia (2–2)
1975 v W. Germany (won 2–0) 1 goal, v Cyprus (won 5–0) 5 goals, v N. Ireland (0–0),
     v Switzerland (won 2–1), v Czechoslovakia (lost 1–2), v Portugal (1–1)

MALCOLM MACDONALD scored five goals in one match for England – against Cyprus – to equal the natinal team's individual scoring record. He began his career as a full-back with Tonbridge before joining Fulham in August 1968. Manager Bobby Robson switched him to centre-forward, but when he left Macdonald fell out of favour and moved to Luton Town. In two seasons with the Hatters he averaged well over a goal every other game, scoring 49 goals in 88 League outings. Eventually, Newcastle United signed him for £180,000 in May 1971. On Tyneside he became the greatest idol since the days of Jackie Milburn. In one of his first matches for the Magpies he scored a hat-trick against Liverpool and he finished each of his five seasons at St James' Park as the club's leading scorer. He also scored in every round of the FA Cup when Newcastle reached the FA Cup Final in 1974. Understandably then, when Arsenal paid £333,333 for his services in the summer of 1976, the whole of Tyneside was stunned.

In his first season at Highbury, Macdonald was the First Division's leading goalscorer. Then, in 1977/78, he helped Arsenal to the FA Cup Final against Ipswich Town, but, just four games into the following season he suffered a serious leg injury in a League Cup tie at Rotherham, and in July 1979, at the age of 29, he announced his retirement.

Macdonald returned to Craven Cottage as the club's marketing executive, later being appointed manager as successor to Bobby Campbell. In 1981/82 he led the club to promotion to the Second Division, but, though the club almost made it into the top flight the following season, he parted company mid-way through the 1983/84 campaign following revelations about his private life. He later returned to the game as manager of Huddersfield Town for the 1987/88 season.

Malcolm Macdonald in Newcastle strip. (Lancashire Evening Post)

Colin TODD

Position	Defender
Born	Colin Todd, Chester-le-Street 12 December 1948
Height	5ft 9in
Weight	11st 6lb
Clubs	Sunderland, Derby County, Everton, Birmingham City, Nottingham Forest, Oxford United, Luton Town
England Caps	27
	1972 v N. Ireland (lost 0–1)
	1974 v Portugal (0–0), v Wales (won 2–0), v N. Ireland (won 1–0), v Scotland (lost 0–2), v Argentina (2–2), v E. Germany (1–1), v Bulgaria (won 1–0), v Yugoslavia (2–2), v Portugal (0–0)
	1975 v W. Germany (won 2–0), v Cyprus (won 5–0), v Cyprus (won 1–0), v N. Ireland (0–0), v Wales (2–2), v Scotland (won 5–1), v Switzerland (won 2–1), v Czechoslovakia (lost 1–2), v Portugal (1–1)
	1976 v N. Ireland (won 4–0), v Scotland (lost 1–2), v Brazil (lost 0–1), v Finland (won 4–1), v Eire (1–1), v Finland (won 2–1)
	1977 v Holland (lost 0–2), v N. Ireland (won 2–1)
Honours	Footballer of the Year 1975

COLIN TODD, who won 27 caps for England, began his career with Sunderland, and in five seasons at Roker Park missed very few games before moving to Derby County for £180,000, a record fee for a defender in February 1971. At the Baseball Ground, he helped the Rams win two League Championships, the year of the second, 1974/75, being probably his greatest season, with Todd rarely making an error. At the end of the campaign he was voted the PFA's Footballer of the Year.

Todd moved to Everton for £330,000 in September 1978, switching to Birmingham City 12 months later in another £300,000 deal. He helped the St Andrew's club gain promotion to the First Division in 1979/80 before rejoining Brian Clough at Nottingham Forest, but his stay at the City Ground was brief and he moved on to Oxford United, whom he helped win the Third Division Championship in 1983/84. He then went to play for Vancouver Whitecaps before ending a fine playing career with Luton Town.

Todd, who had appeared in 747 League and Cup games for his seven clubs, entered management with non-League Whitley Bay before becoming Bruce Rioch's assistant at Middlesbrough. When Rioch joined Bolton Wanderers, Todd followed him to Burnden Park, playing an important role in the club's promotion to the Premiership and progression to the League Cup Final. Following Rioch's decision to leave to manage Arsenal, Todd took over the reins at Bolton and in his first full season in charge took them back to the Premiership. He later parted company with the club and had a spell managing Swindon Town.

Tony CURRIE

Position	Midfielder
Born	Anthony William Currie, Edgware, 1 January 1950
Height	5ft 11in
Weight	12st 10lb
Clubs	Watford, Sheffield United, Leeds United, Queen's Park Rangers, Torquay United
England Caps	17 Goals 3

1972 v N. Ireland (lost 0–1)

1973 v Soviet Union (won 2–1), v Italy (lost 0–2), v Austria (won 7–0) 1 goal, v Poland (1–1), v Italy (lost 0–1)

1975 v Switzerland (won 2–1)

1978 v Brazil (1–1), v Wales (won 3–1) 1 goal, v N. Ireland (won 1–0), v Scotland (won 1–0), v Hungary (won 4–1) 1 goal, v Czechoslovakia (won 1–0)

1979 v N. Ireland (won 4–0), v N. Ireland (won 2–0), v Wales (0–0), v Sweden (0–0)

....

ON LEAVING SCHOOL, Tony Currie began working for a building company, later signing amateur forms for Queen's Park Rangers. After a brief spell as an apprentice he was rejected by Chelsea, and then picked up by Watford. An England youth international, he had made just 17 appearances for the Hornets when Sheffield United, realizing his potential, paid £35,000 to take him to Bramall Lane. He was soon pushing for England recognition, even though the Blades were not a fashionable club at that time, and he went on to play for the Football League and the England Under-23s before winning his first full cap against Northern Ireland in 1972.

Sheffield United finally succumbed to a bid from a top-flight club when Leeds United paid £240,000 for Currie's services in the summer of 1976. He maintained his star status at Elland Road, adding consistency to his many talents. However, with his wife unsettled in Yorkshire he left Leeds and returned to London with Queen's Park Rangers, who paid £400,000 to take him back to Loftus Road. He helped Rangers to the 1982 FA Cup Final before injuries hampered his progress. After a couple of months playing with Toronto Nationals he returned to these shores to play as a non-contract player with Torquay United. In October 1984 he joined Tranmere Rovers but was released without making a senior appearance. Then, in 1988, he became full-time community organizer at Sheffield United.

Mick MILLS

Position	Full-back
Born	Michael Denis Mills, Godalming, 4 January 1949
Height	5ft 6in
Weight	10st 8lb
Clubs	Ipswich Town, Southampton, Stoke City
England Caps	42

1972 v Yugoslavia (1–1)

Mick Mills of Southampton in England strip. (Lancashire Evening Post)

1976 v Wales (won 2–1), v Wales (won 1–0), v N. Ireland (won 4–0), v Scotland (lost 1–2), v Brazil (lost 0–1), v Italy (won 3–2), v Finland (won 4–1), v Finland (won 2–1), v Italy (lost 0–2)

1977 v N. Ireland (won 2–1), v Wales (lost 0–1), v Scotland (lost 1–2)

1978 v W. Germany (lost 1–2), v Brazil (1–1), v Wales (won 3–1), v N. Ireland (won 1–0), v Scotland (won 1–0), v Hungary (won 4–1), v Denmark (won 4–f3), v Eire (1–1)

1979 v N. Ireland (won 4–0), v N. Ireland (won 2–0), v Scotland (won 3–1), v Bulgaria (won 3–0), v Austria (lost 3–4), v Denmark (won 1–0), v N. Ireland (won 5–1)

1980 v Spain (won 2–0), v Spain (won 2–1), v Switzerland (won 2–1)

1981 v Switzerland (lost 1–2), v Hungary (won 3–1), v Norway (lost 1–2), v Hungary (won 1–0)

1982 v Scotland (won 1–0), v Finland (won 4–1), v France (won 3–1), v Czechoslovakia (won 2–0), v Kuwait (won 1–0), v W. Germany (0–0), v Spain (0–0)

MICK MILLS made his England debut in 1972, though it was another four years before he won his second cap. It was a high personal honour when he captained his country for the first time against Wales in 1978 but his proudest moment was to lead England against Switzerland in a World Cup eliminator at Wembley in 1980.

Mills started out with Portsmouth but was released when the Fratton Park club abandoned their youth policy. Ipswich Town snapped him up and it was not long before he made his League debut against Wolverhampton Wanderers in May 1966. Just over three years later he became the first player in Ipswich history to make 100 League appearances before his 21st birthday. Following Bill Baxter's departure midway through the 1970/71 season, Mills was appointed the club's captain, and over the next 12 years he led the Suffolk club by example. He was ever-present for Ipswich in four successive seasons from 1972/73, appearing in 198 consecutive League games. The highlights of his career were the winning of the FA Cup in 1978, when Arsenal were beaten 1–0, and the defeat of AZ67 Alkmaar in the UEFA Cup Final of 1981.

Known as 'Captain Fantastic', Mills appeared in 741 games – a club record – and left Portman Road in November 1982 to join Southampton. He spent three seasons at the Dell before moving to Stoke City as player-manager. After some disappointing displays he was replaced by Alan Ball, whom he had recently appointed as his assistant. He also managed Colchester United and had a brief spell as assistant manager at Coventry City.

Frank LAMPARD senior

Position	Full-back
Born	Frank Richard George Lampard, West Ham, 20 September 1948
Height	5ft 10in
Weight	12st 1lb
Clubs	West Ham United, Southend United
England Caps	2
	1972 v Yugoslavia (1–1)
	1980 v Australia (won 2–1)

ONE OF THE GREATEST players in West Ham's post-war history, Frank Lampard senior broke his leg towards the end of the 1967/68 season, months after making his Football League debut. Thankfully he recovered from this major setback, and international recognition soon followed, with four England Under-23 caps before he won the first of his two full caps, against Yugoslavia in 1972. He had to wait another eight years for his second cap, former Hammers boss Ron Greenwood selecting him to play against Australia in Sydney in May 1980.

With West Ham, Lampard won two FA Cup winners' medals and in 1976 played in the European Cup Winners' Cup Final. In that match against Anderlecht, the Hammers were 1–0 up with just minutes remaining when Lampard suffered the second major setback of his career. Attempting to play the ball back to Mervyn Day, his studs got caught in the turf, causing him to suffer a serious stomach injury. To make matters worse, the Belgian side equalized from the incident and went on to win 4–2 after extra time. On a happier note, it was left-back Lampard who scored the semi-final winner against Everton to take West Ham through to the 1980 FA Cup Final. By then at the peak of his career, he won a League Cup runners-up medal in 1980/81 and helped the Hammers win the Second Division Championship.

The father of Chelsea's Frank Lampard, he went on to play in 660 first-team games before signing for Southend United, who were then managed by Bobby Moore. On hanging up his boots he returned to Upton Park as the club's assistant manager.

Jeff BLOCKLEY

Position	Central defender
Born	Jeffrey Paul Blockley, Leicester, 12 September 1949
Height	6ft 1in
Weight	12st 5lb
Clubs	Coventry City, Arsenal, Leicester City, Notts County
England Caps	1
	1972 v Yugoslavia (1–1)

JEFF BLOCKLEY was captain of Coventry City's youth team when they reached the FA Youth Cup Final of 1968, and the following season he made his first-team debut as a substitute at Southampton. Becoming a regular member of the Sky Blues' side in 1969/70, and missing very few games over the next four seasons, his performances at the heart of the Coventry defence led to him winning six England Under-23 caps and selection for the Football League. In October 1972, after appearing in 167 games for the Highfield Road club, he joined Arsenal for a fee of £200,000. Seven days after putting pen to paper, he made his only full international appearance for England in a 1–1 draw against Yugoslavia at Wembley.

Blockley's time at Highbury was not happy, and in January 1975 he left to join his home-town club, Leicester City, for half the price the Gunners had paid. At Filbert Street he had a loan spell with Derby County – without playing in the senior side – before moving to Notts County, where he ended his League career. He later played non-League football for Gloucester City before managing Leicester United.

Mick CHANNON

Position	Forward
Born	Michael Roger Channon, Orcheston, 28 November 1948
Height	6ft 1in
Weight	12st 4lb
Clubs	Southampton, Manchester City, Newcastle United, Bristol Rovers, Norwich City, Portsmouth
England Caps	46 Goals 20

1972 v Yugoslavia (1–1)

1973 v Scotland (won 5–0) 1 goal, v N. Ireland (won 2–1), v Wales (won 3–0), v Scotland (won 1–0), v Czechoslovakia (1–1), v Soviet Union (won 2–1), v Italy (lost 0–2), v Austria (won 7–0) 2 goals, v Poland (1–1), v Italy (lost 0–1)

1974 v Portugal (0–0), v Wales (won 2–0), v N. Ireland (won 1–0), v Scotland (lost 0–2), v Argentina (2–2) 1 goal, v E. Germany (1–1) 1 goal, v Bulgaria (won 1–0), v Yugoslavia (2–2) 1 goal, v Czechoslovakia (won 3–0) 1 goal, v Portugal (0–0)

1975 v W. Germany (won 2–0), v Cyprus (won 5–0), v Cyprus (won 1–0), v N. Ireland (0–0), v Wales (2–2), v Scotland (won 5–1), v Switzerland (won 2–1) 1 goal, v Czechoslovakia (lost 1–2) 1 goal, v Portugal (1–1) 1 goal

1976 v Wales (won 2–1), v N. Ireland (won 4–0) 2 goals, v Scotland (lost 1–2) 1 goal, v Brazil (lost 0–1), v Italy (won 3–2) 2 goals, v Finland (won 4–1) 1 goal, v Finland (won 2–1), v Italy (lost 0–2)

1977 v Luxembourg (won 5–0) 2 goals, v N. Ireland (won 2–1) 1 goal, v Wales (lost 0–1), v Scotland (lost 1–2) 1 goal, v Brazil (0–0), v Argentina (1–1), v Uruguay (0–0), v Switzerland (0–0)

....

MICK CHANNON was recognized as one of the top strikers in the First Division during the seventies and early eighties, finding the net over 300 times, including 20 times for England in an international career spanning five years.

One of the greatest forwards ever to play for Southampton, Channon scored more goals for the club than any other Saints player. He had made just a handful of first-team appearances when Southampton manager Ted Bates decided to sell Martin Chivers and give Channon a long run in the side. In 1969/70 he was the club's leading scorer and won the first of nine England Under-23 caps. He remained Southampton's leading goalscorer for the next six seasons, with a best of 21 in 1973/74. During that time he netted six hat-tricks and helped the Saints reach the 1976 FA Cup Final, where they upset all the odds by beating Manchester United 1–0. Sensing he had achieved all he could as a Southampton player, he asked for a transfer and in the summer of 1977 joined Manchester City. After two fairly disappointing seasons at Maine Road, Lawrie McMenemy brought him back to the Dell, but in the summer of 1982 he parted company with the club a second time, having scored a total of 215 goals for them in 580 League and Cup games. He then had brief spells with Newcastle United and Bristol Rovers before joining Norwich City, helping the Canaries win the League Cup in 1985, and ending his Football League career with Portsmouth.

Fans who were privileged to see Mick Channon play can fondly remember each goal being celebrated with his unique windmilling-arm action. He is now a racehorse trainer.

Mick Channon playing for Norwich City. (Lancashire Evening Post)

Ray CLEMENCE

Position	Goalkeeper
Born	Raymond Neal Clemence, Skegness, 5 August 1948
Height	6ft 0in
Weight	12st 9lb
Clubs	Scunthorpe United, Liverpool, Tottenham Hotspur
England Caps	61

1972 v Wales (won 1–0)

1973 v Wales (1–1)

1974 v E. Germany (1–1), v Bulgaria (won 1–0), v Yugoslavia (2–2), v Czechoslovakia (won 3–0), v Portugal (0–0)

1975 v W. Germany (won 2–0), v Cyprus (won 1–0), v N. Ireland (0–0), v Wales (2–2), v Scotland (won 5–1), v Switzerland (won 2–1), v Czechoslovakia (lost 1–2), v Portugal (1–1)

1976 v Wales (won 2–1), v Wales (won 1–0), v N. Ireland (won 4–0), v Scotland (lost 1–2), v Brazil (lost 0–1), v Finland (won 4–1), v Eire (1–1), v Finland (won 2–1), v Italy (lost 0–2)

1977 v Holland (lost 0–2), v Luxembourg (won 5–0), v Scotland (lost 1–2), v Brazil (0–0), v Argentina (1–1), v Uruguay (0–0), v Switzerland (0–0), v Luxembourg (won 2–0), v Italy (won 2–0)

1978 v W. Germany (lost 1–2), v N. Ireland (won 1–0), v Scotland (won 1–0), v Denmark (won 4–3), v Eire (1–1)

1979 v N. Ireland (won 4–0), v N. Ireland (won 2–0), v Scotland (won 3–1), v Bulgaria 3–0), v Austria (lost 3–4), v Denmark (won 1–0), v Bulgaria (won 2–0)

1980 v Eire (won 2–0), v Argentina (won 3–1), v Wales (lost 1–4), v Scotland (won 2–0), v Belgium (1–1), v Spain (won 2–1), v Romania (lost 1–2)

1981 v Spain (lost 1–2), v Brazil (lost 0–1), v Switzerland (lost 1–2), v Hungary (won 3–1), v Norway (lost 1–2)

1982 v N. Ireland (won 4–0), v Finland (won 4–1), v Luxembourg (won 9–0)

1983 v Luxembourg (won 4–0)

RAY CLEMENCE was unlucky to be around at the same time as Peter Shilton, for throughout his illustrious career at international level, in which he won 61 caps, he was always vying for the No. 1 jersey with Shilts.

Clemence was signed by Bill Shankly from Scunthorpe United for £18,000, the 19-year-old goalkeeper having made just 50 senior appearances for the Irons in the lower divisions.

He immediately impressed with his safe handling and sharp reflexes, getting down quickly to low shots, knowing when to come off his line and having great positional sense. In his first full season he conceded just 22 goals in 41 games, helping the Reds equal the First Division record of 24 wins in a season. In 1978/79 he went even better, only letting in 16 goals. He was one of the first goalkeepers to act as a sweeper behind his defence, leaving his penalty area to cut out the long through ball. His world-class saves were many, but perhaps there was none more important than that in the 1975/76 UEFA Cup away leg at Dynamo Dresden, when he saved a penalty by diving full length to his right to reach a hard low shot and keep the tie goalless after 90 minutes. During his time with Liverpool, Clemence won five League

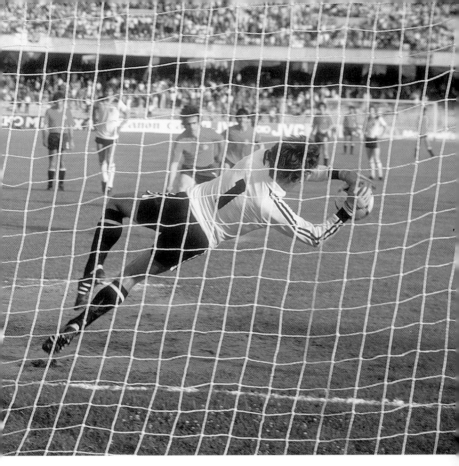

Ray Clemence saves a penalty during the European Championship match against Spain in Naples, June 1980. England won 2–1. (Getty Images)

Championship medals, three European Cup winners' medals, two UEFA Cup winners' medals, an FA Cup winners' medal and a League Cup winners' medal. He was also on the losing side in two FA Cup finals and one League Cup Final. Shankly's assessment of the man was that he was possibly the most important factor in Liverpool's continued success throughout the seventies. In 11 seasons, he missed a mere six League games, amassing over 650 appearances as Liverpool dominated British football.

In August 1981 Clemence announced he was looking for a new challenge and joined Tottenham Hotspur for a fee of £300,000. He made his Spurs debut in the FA Charity Shield, and in his first season at White Hart Lane he helped the club retain the FA Cup and reach the League Cup Final, where they lost to Liverpool!

Having completed 1,000 first-class games in 1985, Clemence was rewarded for his services to football with an MBE in the 1987 Birthday Honours list. Injury then forced him into retirement, and after a spell as manager of Barnet he became England's full-time goalkeeping coach.

Kevin KEEGAN

Position	Forward
Born	Kevin Joseph Keegan, Doncaster, 14 February 1951
Height	5ft 8in
Weight	10st 10lb
Clubs	Scunthorpe United, Liverpool, SV Hamburg, Southampton, Newcastle United
England Caps	63 Goals 20

1972 v Wales (won 1–0)

1973 v Wales (1–1)

1974 v Wales (won 2–0) 1 goal, v N. Ireland (won 1–0), v Argentina (2–2), v E. Germany (1–1), v Bulgaria (won 1–0), v Yugoslavia (2–2) 1 goal, v Czechoslovakia (won 3–0)

1975 v W. Germany (won 2–0), v Cyprus (won 5–0), v Cyprus (won 1–0) 1 goal, v N. Ireland (0–0), v Scotland (won 5–1), v Switzerland (won 2–1) 1 goal, v Czechoslovakia (lost 1–2), v Portugal (1–1)

1976 v Wales (won 2–1), v Wales (won 1–0), v N. Ireland (won 4–0), v Scotland (lost 1–2), v Brazil (lost 0–1), v Finland (won 4–1) 2 goals, v Eire (1–1), v Finland (won 2–1), v Italy (lost 0–2)

1977 v Holland (lost 0–2), v Luxembourg (won 5–0) 1 goal, v Wales (lost 0–1), v Brazil (0–0), v Argentina (1–1), v Uruguay (0–0), v Switzerland (0–0), v Italy (won 2–0) 1 goal

1978 v W. Germany (lost 1–2), v Brazil (1–1) 1 goal, v Hungary (won 4–1), v Denmark (won 4–3) 2 goals, v Eire (1–1), v Czechoslovakia (won 1–0)

1979 v N. Ireland (won 4–0) 1 goal, v Wales (0–0), v Scotland (won 3–1) 1 goal, v Bulgaria (won 3–0) 1 goal, v Sweden (0–0), v Austria (lost 3–4) 1 goal, v Denmark (won 1–0) 1 goal, v N. Ireland (won 5–1)

1980 v Eire (won 2–0) 2 goals, v Spain (won 2–0), v Argentina (won 3–1) 1 goal, v Belgium (1–1), v Italy (lost 0–1), v Spain (won 2–1)

1981 v Spain (lost 1–2), v Switzerland (lost 1–2), v Hungary (won 3–1) 1 goal, v Norway (lost 1–2), v Hungary (won 1–0)

1982 v N. Ireland (won 4–0), v Scotland (won 1–0), v Finland (won 4–1), v Spain (0–0)

Honours	Footballer of the Year 1976 and 1982

KEVIN KEEGAN'S England career, in which his first three appearances were all against Wales, had its ups and downs – he was proud to captain his country, yet he was also roughed up by the Belgrade police after walking out on England, having been dropped by Don Revie.

Signed from Scunthorpe United for just £35,000, Kevin Keegan hit Anfield like a tornado. Converted from a deep-lying winger to striker, he made his debut for the Reds against Notts County in the opening match of the 1971/72 season and scored after just seven minutes. Normally, an unknown player like Keegan would have spent an apprenticeship in the club's Central League side, but he had the kind of talent that was to turn him into a world-class star, his all-action approach winning over the fans and soon making him the idol of the Kop. Brave, quick and inexhaustible, he shared an understanding with John Toshack that bordered on the telepathic. There were numerous high spots in his Liverpool career, his performance in the 1974 FA Cup Final against Newcastle, when he scored two goals, perhaps being one of his best for the club, but there were odd turbulent times too, in particular the occasion he was sent off with Leeds' Billy Bremner at Wembley.

Kevin Keegan celebrates his goal during a match against Scotland at Wembley on 26 May 1979. England won 3–1. (Getty Images)

In 1977 Keegan answered the call of continental football and joined SV Hamburg of Germany for £500,000, having won three League Championship medals, two UEFA Cup medals and European and FA Cup winners' medals during his six years at Anfield. It made him England's most expensive and best-paid player. His three years at Hamburg enhanced his game further, teaching him to overcome man-to-man marking.

In February 1980, Southampton manager Lawrie McMenemy swooped to sign him, and in his first season at the Dell he netted 26 goals, sufficient to make Keegan the leading scorer in the First Division, for which he was awarded the Golden Boot. Sadly, he didn't play for England in the 1982 World Cup, despite having a lot to offer, as evidenced by a two-year successful spell at Newcastle when he led the Magpies back to the top flight.

Keegan became a folk hero on Tyneside and later returned to St James' Park as manager. In 1992/93 the Magpies won the First Division Championship, and they went on to finish runners-up in the Premiership on two occasions. Keegan later managed Fulham, whom he took to the Second Division title, before he took on the poisoned chalice of the England job. Resigning after a home defeat by Germany, he returned to club management with Manchester City.

David NISH

Position	Midfield/Left-back
Born	David John Nish, Burton-on-Trent, 26 September 1947
Height	5ft 11in
Weight	11st 3lb
Clubs	Leicester City, Derby County
England Caps	5
	1973 v N. Ireland (won 2–1)
	1974 v Portugal (0–0), v Wales (won 2–0), v N. Ireland (won 1–0), v Scotland (lost 0–2)

DAVID NISH was a teenage prodigy and was once chosen as a first-team substitute by Leicester City while still at school! Once established as a regular member of the Filbert Street club's first team, he showed amazing versatility, appearing as a creative midfielder and defensive wing-half before settling as an attacking left-back. After just a few seasons in the side he was appointed club captain, and when the Foxes reached Wembley in 1969 he was the youngest-ever Cup Final captain, at the age of 21. He rarely missed a game during his time with Leicester, picking up 10 England Under-23 caps and representing the Football League. He led the Foxes back to the First Division in 1971, but within a year reigning League champions Derby County paid a then British record fee of £225,000 to take him to the Baseball Ground. At Derby his displays won him five full caps and in 1974/75 he helped the Rams win another League Championship.

Nish subsequently suffered a series of knee injuries and left the Football League to play in the NASL for Tulsa Roughnecks. He later joined the coaching staff at Middlesbrough before rejoining Leicester as Youth Development Officer.

John RICHARDS

Position	Centre-forward
Born	John Peter Richards, Warrington, 9 November 1950
Height	5ft 10in
Weight	11st 5lb
Clubs	Wolverhampton Wanderers, Derby County, Martimo
England Caps	1
	1973 v N. Ireland (won 2–1)

FORMING A GREAT PARTNERSHIP with Derek Dougan, John Richards was one of the most prolific scorers in the history of Wolverhampton Wanderers. Though he made his debut in a 3–3 draw against local rivals West Bromwich Albion in February 1970, it was 1971/72 before he established himself as a first-team regular. That season he netted 16 goals and won a UEFA Cup runners-up medal. The following season he was the country's leading scorer with 33 League and Cup goals, including hat-tricks in the wins over Stoke City and Everton, leading to him winning his one and only international cap against Northern Ireland. In 1974 he scored the winning goal in

Wolves' 2–1 win over Manchester City and in 1976/77 he helped the club win the Second Division Championship. In 1980 he was a member of the Wolves side that beat Nottingham Forest 1–0 in the League Cup Final. The only player to have received two benefits at Molineux – 1982 and 1986, the second coming some three years after he had left the club – he went on to score 194 goals in 486 games before leaving Wolves in unhappy circumstances.

Richards joined Portuguese side Martimo in the summer of 1983 after a loan spell at Derby County, and spent three years there before returning to work for Wolverhampton Leisure Services Department. He is now the Molineux club's managing director.

Kevin HECTOR

Position	Forward
Born	Kevin James Hector, Leeds, 2 November 1944
Height	5ft 9in
Weight	10st 9lb
Clubs	Bradford Park Avenue, Derby County
England Caps	2
	1973 v Poland (1–1), v Italy (lost 0–1)

KEVIN HECTOR, who failed to score in either of his two international appearances, began his Football League career with Bradford Park Avenue, scoring 113 goals in 176 consecutive League appearances for the Yorkshire club. He topped the club's goalscoring charts in each season he was with them, with a best of 44 in 1965/66; his total included five in one 28-minute spell in a 7–2 win against Barnsley, three of which were produced in the space of nine minutes.

In September 1966, Hector joined Derby County and became an instant success. He was the Rams' leading scorer in each of his first three seasons, helping the club win promotion to the top flight as Second Division champions in 1968/69, and playing a major part in the Derby side that won two League Championships in 1971/72 and 1974/75. In setting a total of 589 appearances for the Rams in all matches, he created a club record that is unlikely to be broken. His goalscoring ability was never open to question and during the 1976/77 UEFA Cup competition he netted five of Derby's goals in a 12–0 win over Finn Harps.

Tommy Docherty sold Hector to Vancouver Whitecaps, and during his time with the club Hector also played non-League football for Boston United and Burton Albion, before being brought back to the Baseball Ground by Derby's new manager, Colin Addison. He continued where he'd left off, ending his career as one of only a few players to score over a hundred League goals for two separate clubs.

Phil PARKES

Position	Goalkeeper
Born	Phillip Benjamin Neil Frederick Parkes, Sedgley, 8 August 1950
Height	6ft 3in
Weight	14st 7lb
Clubs	Walsall, Queen's Park Rangers, West Ham United, Ipswich Town
England Caps	1
	1974 v Portugal (0–0)

PHIL PARKES began his career with Walsall before moving to Queen's Park Rangers in the summer of 1970. He stayed with the Loftus Road club for eight seasons, his performances helping the club win promotion to the First Division in 1974/75 and then the following season to the runners-up spot in the top flight behind Liverpool. Parkes, who represented England at Under-21 and Under-23 level, won his one and only full international cap in April 1974, when he kept a clean sheet in a goalless draw against Portugal.

In February 1979 Parkes moved to West Ham United for a fee of £525,000, at the time the highest fee ever paid for a goalkeeper. In May 1980 he won an FA Cup winners' medal as the Hammers beat Arsenal 1–0, and he was back at Wembley in March 1981 for the League Cup Final against Liverpool, which the club lost after a replay. Parkes was ever-present in four of his 12 seasons at Upton Park, and went on to appear in 436 games before making way for Czech international Ludek Miklosko. He later ended his career with Ipswich Town.

Mike PEJIC

Position	Left-back
Born	Michael Pejic, Chesterton, 25 January 1950
Height	5ft 7in
Weight	11st 0lb
Clubs	Stoke City, Everton, Aston Villa
England Caps	4
	1974 v Portugal (0–0), v Wales (won 2–0), v N. Ireland (won 1–0), v Scotland (lost 0–2)

ONE OF THE most competitive players ever to wear the red and white stripes of Stoke City, Mike Pejic made the first of his 336 appearances for the Potteries club at West Ham United in April 1969. Strong in defence and always eager to attack, he was a member of the Stoke side that won the League Cup at Wembley in 1972, going on to win four full caps for England, following eight appearances at Under-23 level.

In February 1977, Stoke's desperate financial situation saw him transferred to Everton for £135,000, a figure which the majority of Stoke supporters felt was well below his true worth. Sadly, his career was hampered by a persistent groin injury, and this restricted his appearances for the Goodison club. The popular left-back ended his first-class record with Aston Villa before trying his hand at farming and the life of a greengrocer, later returning to the game as coach and manager at Northwich Victoria, Leek Town and Port Vale. In June 1994 he was appointed manager of Chester City, but his stay at the Deva Stadium was short-lived, and after just seven months in charge he left the then struggling Second Division club.

Martin DOBSON

Position	Midfielder
Born	Martin John Dobson, Blackburn, 14 February 1948
Height	5ft 10in
Weight	11st 6lb
Clubs	Bolton Wanderers, Burnley, Everton, Bury
England Caps	5
	1974 v Portugal (0–0), v E. Germany (1–1), v Bulgaria (won 1–0), v Yugoslavia (won 2–0), v Czechoslovakia (won 3–0)

MARTIN DOBSON started his career as a centre-forward with Bolton Wanderers but in 1967 was given a free transfer. He was considering giving up the game, until his father persuaded Burnley manager Harry Potts to give him a trial. Eventually switched to midfield, Dobson soon won international recognition, being called up for the England Under-23s against Bulgaria at Plymouth. In 1972/73 he captained Burnley to the Second Division Championship and the following season led them to sixth place in the First Division and to the semi-finals of the FA Cup. Shortly after winning the first of five full caps he moved to Everton for a new British transfer record of £300,000.

In five years on Merseyside, Dobson was always a first-team regular. He played in two UEFA Cup campaigns, the 1977 FA Cup semi-final defeat by Liverpool, and the League Cup Final against Aston Villa, which the Midlands side won after three matches. It was something of a surprise when, in the summer of 1979, he moved back to Turf Moor after scoring 40 goals in 230 League and Cup games for Everton. In 1981/82 he led the Clarets to the Third Division Championship, but after taking his tally of goals to 76 in 499 games he moved to Bury as player-manager.

On hanging up his boots he managed Bristol Rovers, and then returned to his first club, Bolton Wanderers, as Youth Development Officer.

Dave WATSON

Position	Centre-half
Born	David Vernon Watson, Stapleford, 5 October 1946
Height	6ft 0in
Weight	11st 7lb
Clubs	Notts County, Rotherham United, Sunderland, Manchester City, Werder Bremen, Southampton, Stoke City, Derby County

England Caps   65   Goals   3

1974 v Portugal (0–0), v Scotland (lost 0–2), v Argentina (2–2), v E. Germany (1–1),
v Bulgaria (won 1–0), v Yugoslavia (2–2), v Czechoslovakia (won 3–0), v Portugal
(0–0)

1975 v W. Germany (won 2–0), v Cyprus (won 5–0), v Cyprus (won 1–0), v N. Ireland
(0–0), v Wales (2–2), v Scotland (won 5–1), v Switzerland (won 2–1), v Czechoslovakia
(lost 1–2), v Portugal (1–1)

1977 v Holland (lost 0–2), v Luxembourg (won 5–0), v N. Ireland (won 2–1), v Wales (lost
0–1), v Scotland (lost 1–2), v Brazil (0–0), v Argentina (1–1), v Uruguay (0–0),
v Switzerland (0–0), v Luxembourg (won 2–0), v Italy (won 2–0)

1978 v W. Germany (lost 1–2), v Brazil (1–1), v Wales (won 3–1), v N. Ireland (won 1–0),
v Scotland (won 1–0), v Hungary (won 4–1), v Denmark (won 4–3), v Eire (1–1),
v Czechoslovakia (won 1–0)

1979 v N. Ireland (won 4–0) 1 goal, v N. Ireland (won 2–0) 1 goal, v Wales (0–0), v Scotland
(won 3–1), v Bulgaria (won 3–0) 1 goal, v Sweden (0–0), v Austria (lost 3–4), v Denmark
(won 1–0), v N. Ireland (won 5–1), v Bulgaria (won 2–0)

1980 v Eire (won 2–0), v Spain (won 2–0), v Argentina (won 3–1), v N. Ireland (1–1),
v Scotland (won 2–0), v Belgium (1–1), v Italy (lost 0–1), v Spain (won 2–1), v Norway
(won 4–0), v Romania (lost 1–2), v Switzerland (won 2–1)

1981 v Romania (0–0), v Wales (0–0), v Scotland (lost 0–1), v Switzerland (lost 1–2),
v Hungary (won 3–1)

1982 v N. Ireland (won 4–0), v Iceland (1–1)

A CORNERSTONE OF the England side of the 1970s, Dave Watson won 65 caps and was an essential part of Ron Greenwood's England, being kept in the squad until the 1982 World Cup, by which time he was 35.

Watson began his Football League career with Notts County. Most of his games for the Meadow Lane club were at centre-forward, but, after moving to Rotherham United, Millers manager Tommy Docherty switched him to centre-half. One of the best headers of a ball and most accomplished centre-halves outside the top flight, he joined Sunderland in 1970, the first of a number of big-money transfers, winning an FA Cup winners' medal in 1976 when Sunderland beat Leeds United. A big-hearted player, he always seemed to have the strength to keep his balance and retain possession of the ball.

In the summer of 1975, Watson joined Manchester City, ending his first campaign at Maine Road with a League Cup winners' medal, and in 1976/77 he helped City to runners-up spot in the First Division. A virtual ever-present in his four seasons at Maine Road, he played briefly for Werder Bremen before returning to League action with Southampton. After a couple of seasons at the Dell he moved to Stoke City, where he enjoyed an Indian summer. He was released to go on an 'illegal' tour of South Africa, which never happened, but finally moved to Vancouver Whitecaps in the NASL. On his return, he linked up with Derby County, later playing for Fort Lauderdale, Notts County (again) and Kettering.

Dave Watson in Sunderland strip.
(Lancashire Evening Post)

Stan BOWLES

Position	Midfielder
Born	Stanley Bowles, Manchester, 24 December 1948
Height	5ft 10in
Weight	11st 4lb
Clubs	Manchester City, Bury, Crewe Alexandra, Carlisle United, Queen's Park Rangers, Nottingham Forest, Leyton Orient, Brentford
England Caps	5 Goals 1
	1974 v Portugal (0–0), v Wales (won 2–0) 1 goal, v N. Ireland (won 1–0)
	1976 v Italy (lost 0–2)
	1977 v Holland (lost 0–2)

WITH HIS FLAIR and ability, it was natural that Stan Bowles would eventually be selected by England, although he was capped only five times. His was a talent that did not fully blossom until he was in his mid-20s, by which time he had played for Manchester City, Bury, Crewe Alexandra and Carlisle United, moving on from most of these clubs in controversial circumstances. When he joined Queen's Park Rangers in September 1972, some football experts said that it was a high-risk expense at £112,000. How wrong they were! Stan Bowles went on to become one of the finest players ever to grace Loftus Road, his reputation growing in tandem with that of the Queen's Park Rangers side of the 1970s, built around quality players like Parkes, McLintock, Webb and Francis, besides, of course, Stan himself.

At the end of 1979, having scored 97 goals in 315 games, Bowles moved to Nottingham Forest, where he played for a short spell under Brian Clough. He then went to Orient and ultimately Brentford, where he ended his Football League career. Both on and off the field he was a colourful character, to say the least!

Trevor BROOKING

Position	Midfielder
Born	Trevor David Brooking, Barking, 2 October 1948
Height	6ft 1in
Weight	13st 8lb
Clubs	West Ham United
England Caps	47 Goals 5
	1974 v Portugal (0–0), v Argentina (2–2), v E. Germany (1–1), v Bulgaria (won 1–0), v Yugoslavia (2–2), v Czechoslovakia (won 3–0), v Portugal (0–0)
	1975 v Portugal (1–1)
	1976 v Wales (won 2–1), v Brazil (lost 0–1), v Italy (won 3–2), v Finland (won 4–1), v Eire (1–1), v Finland (won 2–1), v Italy (lost 0–2)
	1977 v Holland (lost 0–2), v N. Ireland (won 2–1), v Wales (lost 0–1), v Italy (won 2–0) 1 goal
	1978 v W. Germany (lost 1–2), v Wales (won 3–1), v Scotland (won 1–0), v Hungary (won 4–1), v Denmark (won 4–3), v Eire (1–1)
	1979 v N. Ireland (won 4–0), v Wales (0–0), v Scotland (won 3–1), v Bulgaria (won 3–0), v Sweden (0–0), v Austria (lost 3–4), v Denmark (won 1–0), v N. Ireland (won 5–1)

Trevor Brooking in action against Wales, 1980. Wales won 4–1. (Getty Images)

1980 v Argentina (won 3–1), v Wales (lost 1–4), v N. Ireland (1–1), v Scotland (won 2–0)
1 goal, v Belgium (1–1), v Spain (won 2–1) 1 goal, v Switzerland (won 2–1)
1981 v Spain (lost 1–2), v Romania (0–0), v Hungary (won 3–1) 2 goals, v Hungary (won 1–0)
1982 v Scotland (won 1–0), v Finland (won 4–1), v Spain (0–0)

CAPPED 47 TIMES by England, the international game that gave Trevor Brooking the greatest pleasure was the World Cup qualifying game in Hungary in 1981, when his two goals helped England to a 3–1 win and a place in the finals.

One of the greatest players ever to wear the claret and blue of West Ham United, Brooking grew up a Hammers supporter. He made his first-team debut in August 1967, but it took him a while to establish himself as a regular at Upton Park. It was only following the transfer of Martin Peters to Spurs that Brooking settled down as a left-sided midfield player, though when Ron Greenwood left him out of the side midway through the 1970/71 season, he went on the transfer list. He went on to win two FA Cup winners' medals, scoring the only goal of the game in the 1980 victory over Arsenal when he stooped low to guide Stuart Pearson's shot past Pat Jennings and into the net. He also won runners-up medals in the European Cup Winners' Cup of 1976 and the League Cup of 1981. In 1980/81 he won a Second Division Championship medal when he was probably at his peak. Also that year, he was awarded the MBE, an admirable reward for his loyalty to West Ham United. He had scored 102 goals in 635 games when he finally decided to quit at the end of the 1983/84 season.

Now the FA's Director of Football, Trevor Brooking was a true sportsman, one of football's gentlemen at a time when the game was becoming increasingly aggressive.

Keith WELLER

Position	Winger
Born	Keith Weller, Islington, 11 June 1946
Height	5ft 9in
Weight	12st 11lb
Clubs	Tottenham Hotspur, Millwall, Chelsea, Leicester City
England Caps	4 Goals 1
	1974 v Wales (won 2–0), v N. Ireland (won 1–0) 1 goal, v Scotland (lost 0–2), v Argentina (2–2)

IT WAS WITH his fourth and final League club, Leicester City, that Keith Weller began to flourish, playing for the Football League against the Scottish League in 1973 and making his England debut against Wales in May 1974.

Weller spent much of his time at White Hart Lane as cover for the first-choice wingers Jimmy Robertson and Cliff Jones, and so, unable to get a regular first-team spot, he left to play for Millwall. While at The Den he dropped back into midfield and formed a most effective partnership with Derek Possee. The excellent ball skills he had developed as a winger allowed him to run at opponents from deep positions. Impressive displays for the Lions alerted the top clubs to his potential, and in 1970 he joined Chelsea. Although he played in their triumphant European Cup Winners' Cup team of 1971, he did not really settle at Stamford Bridge, and after just one season he joined Leicester City for £100,000.

Weller's individual flair also had its temperamental side. At half-time in Leicester's game with Ipswich Town in December 1974 he went on 'strike', refusing to reappear for the second half in protest at Leicester's refusal to grant his transfer request! However, his unique style and shooting was an integral part of Jimmy Bloomfield's team and he stayed with the Foxes until the end of the 1977/78 season. He then went to the United States to play for New England Teamen and, later, Fort Lauderdale Strikers before moving into the American Indoor League with Tacoma Stars.

Frank WORTHINGTON

Position	Forward
Born	Frank Stewart Worthington, Halifax, 23 November 1948
Height	6ft 0in
Weight	12st 0lb
Clubs	Huddersfield Town, Leicester City, Bolton Wanderers, Birmingham City, Leeds United, Sunderland, Southampton, Brighton and Hove Albion, Tranmere Rovers, Preston North End, Stockport County
England Caps	8 Goals 2
	1974 v N. Ireland (won 1–0), v Scotland (lost 0–2), v Argentina (2–2) 1 goal, v E. Germany (1–1), v Bulgaria (won 1–0) 1 goal, v Yugoslavia (2–2), v Czechoslovakia (won 3–0), v Portugal (0–0)

A TALENTED FOOTBALLER and an extrovert character, Frank Worthington was rewarded with an England call-up in 1974, and he went on to make eight appearances at full international level. His elegant and effective centre-forward play should have brought him many more.

Worthington began his career with Huddersfield Town, and after helping them to win the Second Division Championship in 1970 the chance came for him to join Liverpool. A fee of £150,000 had been agreed but a medical examination revealed that he had high blood pressure. Leicester City seized their chance and a cut-price Worthington moved to Filbert Street for £80,000. He had scored 72 goals in 210 games for the Foxes when he joined Bolton on loan, manager Ian Greaves searching for some extra quality to lift the Wanderers into the First Division after two near misses. Soon signed on a permanent basis, Worthington became a footballing hero at Burnden Park in what was a relatively short career there. He swiftly rediscovered the style that had made him one of the best strikers in the game and in 1977/78 helped the Trotters win the Second Division title. The following season he proved his class as a target man and a finisher, topping the First Division scoring charts with 24 goals. His televised goal against Ipswich Town won him the 'Goal of the Season' competition. On leaving Bolton he joined Birmingham City, later having spells with Leeds United, Sunderland, Southampton, Brighton, Tranmere, Preston and Stockport County.

One of the game's most gifted and colourful strikers, Worthington made 757 League appearances in a career that saw him approaching his 40th birthday before he left the first-class game.

Alec LINDSAY

Position	Left-back
Born	Alec Lindsay, Bury, 27 February 1948
Height	5ft 10in
Weight	11st 0lb
Clubs	Bury, Liverpool, Stoke City
England Caps	4
	1974 v Argentina (2–2), v E. Germany (1–1), v Bulgaria (won 1–0), v Yugoslavia (2–2)

THERE IS LITTLE DOUBT that full-back Alec Lindsay was at the peak of his form when England caretaker-manager Joe Mercer awarded him the first of four caps in the 2–2 draw with Argentina in 1974.

Beginning his career with his home-town club Bury, Lindsay helped the Shakers win promotion to the Second Division in 1967/68, before joining Liverpool for a fee of £67,000 in March 1969. The Reds had watched him on a number of occasions but were never sure as to his best position, Lindsay having been used at Bury as a wing-half, inside-forward and even on the wing in a couple of games. After some disappointing displays in midfield, he was switched to the left-back berth that he was to grace so stylishly for the next seven seasons or so. A number of players had been tried in this problem area for the Anfield club, but Lindsay took to the role immediately and made the position his own. During his time at Anfield, he won a UEFA Cup winners' medal in 1973, League Championship-winning medals in 1973 and 1976, and an FA Cup winners' medal in 1974. In that 1974 Cup Final, against Newcastle United, he was in tremendous form. Prominent on the overlap, he drove a ferocious cross-shot past keeper Iam McFaul, only to have his joy cut short by an offside flag.

Unfortunately, because of personal problems, Lindsay's form began to deteriorate, and in August 1977 he joined Stoke City before trying his luck in the United States and Canada. His last club was Toronto Blizzards in 1979, after which he turned his back on football for good.

Gerry FRANCIS

Position	Midfielder
Born	Gerald Charles James Francis, Chiswick, 6 December 1951
Height	5ft 10in
Weight	12st 3lb
Clubs	Queen's Park Rangers, Crystal Palace, Coventry City, Exeter City, Cardiff City, Swansea City, Portsmouth, Bristol Rovers
England Caps	12 Goals 3
	1974 v Czechoslovakia (won 3–0), v Portugal (0–0)
	1975 v Wales (2–2), v Scotland (won 5–1) 2 goals, v Switzerland (won 2–1), v Czechoslovakia (lost 1–2), v Portugal (1–1)
	1976 v Wales (won 1–0), v N. Ireland (won 4–0) 1 goal, v Scotland (lost 1–2), v Brazil (lost 0–1), v Finland (won 4–1)

GERRY FRANCIS won his first full England cap in October 1974 and was made captain of the national side in 1975. The following year he suffered an injury that was to finish his international career and restrict his League football opportunities for the ensuing couple of seasons.

The product of the Queen's Park Rangers youth scheme that was so successful in the late 1960s, Francis made his debut as a substitute against Liverpool in March 1969, but it was 1970/71 before he established himself as a regular first-teamer. After his injury he fought back to become a regular again in 1978/79, but he never quite regained his form of earlier years. He subsequently moved through a number of transfer deals, going to Crystal Palace in 1979, returning to Shepherd's Bush the following year, moving to Coventry City in 1982 and later to Exeter City, before brief spells as a non-contract player with Cardiff, Swansea, Portsmouth and Bristol Rovers.

Francis moved into management with Exeter City before taking charge of Bristol Rovers and leading the then Eastville club into the old Second Division. In May 1991 he was appointed manager of Queen's Park Rangers, and in four seasons at Loftus Road he kept the club in the top half of the Premiership. He then moved across London to take charge at Tottenham Hotspur, but after parting company with the club he returned to Loftus Road for a second spell in charge of Queen's Park Rangers. He then took charge of Bristol Rovers for a second time, and now runs a successful antique shop in Chertsey.

Dave THOMAS

Position	Winger
Born	David Thomas, Kirkby, 5 October 1950
Height	5ft 8in
Weight	9st 13lb
Clubs	Burnley, Queen's Park Rangers, Everton, Wolverhampton Wanderers, Middlesbrough, Portsmouth
England Caps	8
	1974 v Czechoslovakia (won 3–0), v Portugal (0–0)
	1975 v Cyprus (won 5–0), v Cyprus (won 1–0), v Wales (2–2), v Scotland (won 5–1), v Czechoslovakia (lost 1–2), v Portugal (1–1)

ABLE TO PLAY on either flank, Dave Thomas, who won eight full caps for England during his time with Queen's Park Rangers, was very fast and an excellent crosser of the ball. He began his career with Burnley, where he became the Turf Moor club's youngest-ever top-flight player, appearing in the Clarets' 1–1 home draw against Everton on the final day of the 1966/67 season aged 16 years 220 days. The following season he helped Burnley win the FA Youth Cup before winning international recognition at Under-23 level, despite being well short of his 20th birthday. Surprisingly sold to Burnley's Second Division promotion rivals Queen's Park Rangers for £165,000, he was an important member of the Rangers team that won promotion to the First Division, and was subsequently a regular choice in 1975/76 when the club finished as runners-up to Liverpool.

Everton were one of a number of clubs interested in signing Thomas and in August 1977 they completed the transfer for a fee of £200,000. In his first season at Goodison, Thomas provided the crosses from which Bob Latchford scored the majority of his goals. He only stayed two seasons, however, before leaving to join Wolverhampton Wanderers. Never really settling at Molineux, he had a spell with Vancouver Whitecaps before returning to play for Middlesbrough. He ended his League career with Portsmouth, where he later became youth coach.

Steve WHITWORTH

Position	Right-back
Born	Stephen Whitworth, Ellistown, 20 March 1952
Height	6ft 0in
Weight	11st 9lb
Clubs	Leicester City, Sunderland, Bolton Wanderers, Mansfield Town
England Caps	7
	1975 v W. Germany (won 2–0), v Cyprus (won 1–0), v N. Ireland (0–0), v Wales (2–2), v Scotland (won 5–1), v Switzerland (won 2–1), v Portugal (1–1)

STEVE WHITWORTH made his name with Leicester City, helping the then Filbert Street club win the Second Division Championship in 1970–71. He missed only three games of Jimmy Bloomfield's reign as manager, appearing in 198 consecutive League games and creating a then club record. He won seven full caps for England to add to his six at Under-23 level, thus completing his representative set, following numerous school and youth selections.

A temporary loss of form in his testimonial season saw Whitworth transferred to Sunderland for £125,000, where he was ever-present as they won promotion to the First Division in 1979/80, but after a couple of years at Roker Park he was on the move again, this time to Bolton Wanderers. Though he made the right-back position his own in two seasons with the club, the Trotters were relegated and he moved on to Mansfield Town. He was a regular in the Stags side as they struggled in the Fourth Division, scoring his first-ever League goal when he converted a penalty against Hereford United in March 1985. On leaving Field Mill, he joined Barnet as player-coach and took the Underhill club close to becoming the first club to gain automatic elevation from the Vauxhall Conference to the Fourth Division.

Ian GILLARD

Position	Left-back
Born	Ian Terry Gillard, Hammersmith, 9 October 1950
Height	6ft 0in
Weight	12st 8lb
Clubs	Queen's Park Rangers, Aldershot
England Caps	3
	1975 v W. Germany (won 2–0), v Wales (2–2), v Czechoslovakia (lost 1–2)

IAN GILLARD joined Queen's Park Rangers straight from school, and after working his way up through the ranks he made his League debut in a 2–1 win over Nottingham Forest in November 1968. The attacking left-back was a permanent fixture in the Rangers side for the next 14 seasons, being ever-present in 1974/75 and 1980/81. His form led to him winning England Under-23 honours in March 1974, when he played in a 2–0 win over Scotland at St James' Park. He went on to win six caps at Under-23 level before being awarded the first of three full caps in a 2–0 defeat of West Germany in March 1975.

Gillard, who played in just eight games when Rangers won promotion to the First Division in 1972/73, missed just one game when the club finished runners-up to Liverpool in 1975/76. A member of the Rangers side that lost to Tottenham Hotspur in the FA Cup Final of 1982, he went on to appear in 484 League and Cup games before moving to Aldershot in July of that year. He was a regular at the Recreation Ground for a couple of seasons before hanging up his boots.

Alan HUDSON

Position	Midfielder
Born	Alan Anthony Hudson, Chelsea, 21 June 1951
Height	5ft 11in
Weight	12st 1lb
Clubs	Chelsea, Stoke City, Arsenal
England Caps	2
	1975 v W. Germany (won 2–0), v Cyprus (won 5–0)

ALAN HUDSON, who won just two caps for England, ranks alongside players such as Stan Bowles, Tony Currie, Rodney Marsh and Frank Worthington as one of the great enigmas of English football over recent decades. He started his football career with Chelsea, helping the Stamford Bridge club win the European Cup Winners' Cup in 1970/71. Ranked as the golden boy of English football, his short and controversial career at Chelsea ended in January 1974 when he left behind the bright lights of the King's Road and joined Stoke City for a fee of £240,000.

During his time at the Victoria Ground, Hudson was responsible in large part for the most exciting period in the club's history. However, after falling out with Stoke manager Tony Waddington over an injury, and with the Potters short of money following the collapse of the Butler Street Stand roof, he was sold to Arsenal for £200,000 in December 1976. He had some success at Highbury, picking up a losers' medal in the 1978 FA Cup Final, before moving to the United States to play for Seattle Sounders. In 1983 he rejoined Chelsea, but, unable to make the first team, he moved back to Stoke. New City manager Mick Mills made him captain but a nagging knee injury forced him to retire at the age of 34. After his football career he became a nightclub owner, but he now writes a controversial column for a local newspaper.

Kevin BEATTIE

Position	Defender
Born	Kevin Thomas Beattie, Carlisle, 18 December 1953
Height	5ft 10in
Weight	12st 2lb
Clubs	Ipswich Town, Colchester United, Middlesbrough
England Caps	9 Goals 1
	1975 v Cyprus (won 5–0), v Cyprus (won 1–0), v Scotland (won 5–1) 1 goal, v Switzerland (won 2–1), v Portugal (1–1)
	1976 v Finland (won 2–1), v Italy (lost 0–2)
	1977 v Holland (lost 0–2), v Luxembourg (won 2–0)

KEVIN BEATTIE was the first PFA Young Player of the Year, an award presented to him by Leeds United manager Don Revie. The following season the Leeds boss was appointed manager of England in succession to Joe Mercer. In his fourth match in charge, Revie selected Beattie in the centre of England's defence for their European Championship qualifier against Cyprus at Wembley. It was a game England won 5–0, with Malcolm Macdonald creating a post-war record by scoring all England's goals. The Ipswich player almost got his name on the scoresheet, but in the process of scoring he was adjudged to have fouled the goalkeeper. He went on to win nine caps, all but one under Revie's management.

Beattie was a product of Ipswich Town's youth policy masterminded by Bobby Robson. One of the game's creative forces, he was a huge favourite with the Ipswich crowd, soon establishing himself at the heart of the Portman Road club's defence. He was a member of the Ipswich team that beat Arsenal in the 1978 FA Cup Final, and could have become one of the all-time greats but for five operations on his right knee in the space of four years. After scoring 32 goals in 307 games for the Portman Road club, he played briefly for Colchester United and Middlesbrough before he was forced to retire in 1982.

Dennis TUEART

Position	Winger
Born	Dennis Tueart, Newcastle, 27 November 1949
Height	5ft 8in
Weight	11st 2lb
Clubs	Sunderland, Manchester City, Stoke City, Burnley, Derry City
England Caps	6 Goals 2
	1975 v Cyprus (won 1–0), v N. Ireland (0–0)
	1976 v Finland (won 2–1) 1 goal
	1977 v N. Ireland (won 2–1) 1 goal, v Wales (lost 0–1), v Scotland (lost 1–2)

IN MAY 1975, at the end of his first full season at Maine Road, Tueart, a goal-serving winger, was selected for England in a European Championship qualifier against

Cyprus in Limassol. He appeared as a substitute for Kevin Keegan, who had earlier scored England's goal in what proved to be a 1–0 victory. Tueart went on to win six full caps, scoring twice for his country.

A regular in the Sunderland team relegated from the top flight in 1970, Tueart spent the rest of his Roker Park career in the Second Division. The highlight was undoubtedly the Wearsiders' memorable victory over Leeds United in the FA Cup Final of 1973. During Sunderland's first-ever European campaign, in the Cup Winners' Cup of 1973/74, Tueart scored in both legs of the first-round tie against Vasas Budapest, but after the club were beaten in a later round by Sporting Lisbon he left Sunderland to join Manchester City for £275,000, then a record for both clubs. He made his City debut in the Manchester derby and shortly afterwards represented the Football League against the Scottish League, scoring in a 5–0 win. In December 1974 he was selected as an over-age player in England's Under-23 side to meet Scotland at Aberdeen and scored twice in a 3–0 win. He was City's top scorer in 1975/76 with 24 goals, including a hat-trick in a 6–1 League Cup win over Norwich City, the Blues going on to lift the trophy. In the final against Newcastle, Tueart clinched victory with a spectacular overhead kick, a goal that has rightly been endlessly replayed on television. He was also instrumental in City finishing the 1976/77 season as runners-up to Liverpool, while the following season he netted three hat-tricks.

In February 1978 Tueart was lured to America to join New York Cosmos before returning to Maine Road early in 1980. Though no longer an automatic choice, he won an FA Cup runners-up medal in the replayed final against Spurs before leaving City for a second time. He then had spells with Stoke and Burnley before turning out for Irish League club Derry City. He is now back at Maine Road as one of the club's directors.

Colin VILJOEN

Position	Midfielder
Born	Colin Viljoen, Johannesburg, 20 June 1948
Height	5ft 8in
Weight	10st 10lb
Clubs	Ipswich Town, Manchester City, Chelsea
England Caps	2
	1975 v N. Ireland (0–0), v Wales (2–2)

SOUTH AFRICAN-BORN COLIN VILJOEN made a remarkable debut for Ipswich Town against Portsmouth in March 1967. After finding themselves two goals down after quarter-of-an-hour, Town fought back to win 4–3, with Viljoen scoring a hat-trick. He endeared himself to the Ipswich fans even further the following season when he netted another hat-trick in the East Anglian derby against Norwich City, Town again coming back from two goals down to win 4–3. His form over the next few seasons eventually led to him winning two full caps for England, but shortly after his second appearance against Wales he began to suffer from Achilles tendon trouble and missed the entire 1976/77 campaign after undergoing three operations on the injury.

In the summer of 1978, after having scored 54 goals in 372 games for Ipswich, Viljoen left Portman Road to join Manchester City, where he was again hampered by injuries. He appeared in 38 games for the Maine Road club before ending his League career with Chelsea, whom he joined in March 1980. On hanging up his boots he became the licensee of a pub near Heathrow Airport.

David JOHNSON

Position	Centre-forward
Born	David Edward Johnson, Liverpool, 23 October 1951
Height	5ft 10in
Weight	11st 0lb
Clubs	Everton, Ipswich Town, Liverpool, Barnsley, Manchester City, Preston North End
England Caps	8 Goals 5
	1975 v Wales (2–2) 2 goals, v Scotland (won 5–1) 1 goal, v Switzerland (won 2–1)
	1980 v Eire (won 2–0), v Argentina (won 3–1) 2 goals, v N. Ireland (1–1), v Scotland (won 2–0), v Belgium (1–1)

DAVID JOHNSON began his Football League career with Everton, but despite his early successes, which included a hat-trick in an 8–0 romp over Southampton, he was transferred to Ipswich Town in October 1971. At Portman Road he matured into a useful centre-forward, winning eight England caps, the first against Wales in 1975 when he scored both England's goals in a 2–2 draw. In August 1976 he joined Liverpool for a club record of £200,000.

Johnson's courageous approach and his speed, skill and unselfishness instantly endeared him to the Kop. Despite being hampered by a series of niggling injuries during his early days at Anfield, he managed to collect a League Championship winners' medal and figured in the Wembley defeat by Manchester United, but he missed out on European glory. Just when it seemed Liverpool were going to discard him, his luck changed and, after striking up a good understanding with Kenny Dalglish, he won a European Cup winners' medal and four League Championship medals.

In August 1982 Johnson's colourful career came full circle when he rejoined Everton for £100,000. Unable to reproduce his form of old, he had a month's loan with Barnsley before joining Manchester City. He then had a brief spell with Tulsa Roughnecks in the NASL before being transferred to Preston North End, where he ended his first-class career. He occupies a unique place in Merseyside folklore, being the only player to have scored a derby winner for both Everton and Liverpool.

Brian LITTLE

Position	Forward
Born	Brian Little, Durham, 25 November 1953
Height	5ft 8in
Weight	11st 2lb
Clubs	Aston Villa
England Caps	1
	1975 v Wales (2–2)

BRIAN LITTLE won his only full cap in what was one of the briefest debuts for England. Replacing Mick Channon against Wales at Wembley with just ten minutes to play, he helped set up England's second goal for fellow debutant David Johnson in a 2–2 draw.

Only 17 when he made his Football League debut for Aston Villa, Little played an important part in the club's FA Youth Cup success when they beat Liverpool in the final, and was also influential in their Third Division Championship-winning campaign. He went on to win League Cup winners' tankards in 1975 and 1977, scoring two of Villa's goals in the 3–2 win over Everton in the second replay of that final at Old Trafford. In fact, his match-winner came in the dying seconds of injury time. He was the Second Division's leading scorer in 1974/75 with 20 goals, this form leading to his call-up by England. During the 1979/80 season a proposed £610,000 move to neighbours Birmingham City fell through on medical grounds and sadly, at the end of the following season, he was forced to give up the game. He had scored 82 goals in 301 games for Villa. He then had a spell working in Villa's promotions department before moving to Molineux as Wolves' first-team coach. After a spell coaching at Middlesbrough he was appointed manager of Darlington.

Little led the Quakers to the GM Vauxhall Conference title and back into the Football League, where they won the Fourth Division Championship. He then took charge of Leicester City and, after three successive seasons of reaching the Wembley play-off finals, the Foxes eventually won promotion to the Premiership. In November 1994 Little returned to Aston Villa as manager, but after leading the club to success in the League Cup he parted company with them in 1998. He later managed Hull City before making way for Jan Molby. Little is now manager of Second Division Tranmere Rovers.

Trevor CHERRY

Position	Defender
Born	Trevor John Cherry, Huddersfield, 23 February 1948
Height	5ft 10in
Weight	11st 6lb
Clubs	Huddersfield Town, Leeds United, Bradford City
England Caps	27

Trevor Cherry of Leeds United.
(Lancashire Evening Post)

1976 v Wales (won 2–1), v Scotland (lost 1–2), v Brazil (lost 0–1), v Finland (won 4–1),
v Eire (1–1), v Italy (lost 0–2)
1977 v Luxembourg (won 5–0), v N. Ireland (won 2–1), v Scotland (lost 1–2), v Brazil (0–0),
v Argentina (1–1), v Uruguay (0–0), v Switzerland (0–0), v Luxembourg (won 2–0), v Italy
(won 2–0)
1978 v Brazil (1–1), v Wales (won 3–1), v Czechoslovakia (won 1–0)
1979 v Wales (0–0), v Sweden (0–0)
1980 v Eire (won 2–0), v Argentina (won 3–1), v Wales (lost 1–4), v N. Ireland (1–1),
v Scotland (won 2–0), v Australia (won 2–1), v Spain (won 2–1)

TREVOR CHERRY won 27 caps for England but blotted his copybook when he was sent off in the match against Argentina in Buenos Aires in 1980. The incident in question saw him lose two teeth after being punched by an Argentinian player!

Cherry was captain of Huddersfield Town when they won the Second Division Championship in 1969/70, and by the time of his transfer to Leeds United in the summer of 1972 he had appeared in 208 games for the Terriers. He quickly settled into the left-back berth vacated by the injured Terry Cooper, but in subsequent years he operated in a variety of defensive positions and sometimes even in midfield. At Elland Road he won a League Championship medal and FA Cup and European Cup Winners' Cup runners-up medals, being voted the club's Player of the Year in 1981.

In December 1982, after appearing in 460 League and Cup games for Leeds, he left to join Bradford City as player-manager. He took them to promotion in 1984/85, winning the Third Division Manager of the Month award in the process. Controversially sacked in January 1987, he then became a director of a sports promotion firm and is now a director of Huddersfield Town.

Phil NEAL

Position	Right-back
Born	Philip George Neal, Irchester, 20 February 1951
Height	5ft 11in
Weight	12st 2lb
Clubs	Northampton Town, Liverpool, Bolton Wanderers
England Caps	50 Goals 3

1976 v Wales (won 2–1), v Italy (won 3–2)
1977 v Wales (lost 0–1), v Scotland (lost 1–2), v Brazil (0–0), v Argentina (1–1), v Uruguay
(0–0), v Switzerland (0–0), v Italy (won 2–0)
1978 v W. Germany (lost 1–2), v N. Ireland (won 1–0) 1 goal, v Scotland (won 1–0),
v Hungary (won 4–1) 1 goal, v Denmark (won 4–3) 1 goal, v Eire (1–1)
1979 v N. Ireland (won 4–0), v N. Ireland (won 2–0), v Scotland (won 3–1), v Bulgaria

(won 3–0), v Austria (lost 3–4), v Denmark (won 1–0), v N. Ireland (won 5–1)

1980 v Spain (won 2–0), v Argentina (won 3–1), v Wales (lost 1–4), v Belgium (1–1),
v Italy (lost 0–1), v Romania (lost 1–2), v Switzerland (won 2–1)

1981 v Spain (lost 1–2), v Brazil (lost 0–1), v Hungary (won 3–1), v Norway (lost 1–2),
v Hungary (won 1–0)

1982 v Wales (won 1–0), v Holland (won 2–0), v Iceland (1–1), v France (won 3–1),
v Kuwait (won 1–0), v Denmark (2–2), v Greece (won 3–0), v Luxembourg
(won 9–0)

1983 v Wales (won 2–1), v Greece (0–0), v Hungary (won 2–0), v N. Ireland (0–0),
v Scotland (won 2–0), v Australia (won 1–0), v Australia (1–1), v Denmark
(lost 0–1)

WHEN HE PLAYED the last of his 50 internationals, against Denmark in 1983, Phil Neal was the most-capped England right-back of all time. He began his career with Northampton Town and had made 206 appearances for the Cobblers when Bob Paisley paid £65,000 to take him to Anfield in October 1974. He was ever-present from his second appearance for the club in December 1974 until he missed the match against Sunderland in October 1983 – a run of 366 consecutive League matches, mainly in the No. 2 shirt.

An intelligent, positional player, Neal denied opposing wingers any space. Excellent in defence, his distribution was also immaculate. The majority of his goals came from the penalty spot, including the clincher in the 1977 European Cup Final, and he was on the mark again against AS Roma in 1984. He played in four European Cup finals, captaining the club in two of them. His masterly performances at full-back, week in, week out, were an integral part of the Reds' great defensive displays over the years. When he was forced to miss the second leg of a European Cup tie against Odense, it ended a club-record of 417 consecutive appearances. During his time with the club, Neal won almost every honour in the game, picking up eight League Championship medals, a UEFA Cup winners' medal, four European Cup winners' medals and four League Cup winners' medals. Only an FA Cup winners' medal eluded him. He went on to score 60 goals in 635 games for Liverpool before leaving Anfield to become player-manager of Bolton Wanderers.

Neal's first few years in management were quite eventful. The club reached the Freight Rover Trophy Final, only to lose to Bristol City, and were relegated to the Fourth Division for the first time in their history, but they bounced back immediately, winning promotion the following season. In 1989 the Wanderers returned to Wembley, beating Torquay United 4–1 in the Sherpa Van Trophy Final. On leaving Burnden Park, Neal had a brief period of involvement with the England management team before later taking charge at Coventry City, Cardiff City and Manchester City. He also spends his time working in the media.

Phil Neal of Liverpool in England strip.
(Lancashire Evening Post)

Phil THOMPSON

Position	Centre-back
Born	Philip Bernard Thompson, Liverpool, 21 January 1954
Height	6ft 0in
Weight	11st 8lb
Clubs	Liverpool, Sheffield United
England Caps	42 Goals 1

1976 v Wales (won 2–1), v Wales (won 1–0), v N. Ireland (won 4–0), v Scotland (lost 1–2),
  v Brazil (lost 0–1), v Italy (won 3–2) 1 goal, v Finland (won 4–1), v Finland (won 2–1)
1978 v Eire (1–1), v Czechoslovakia (won 1–0)
1979 v N. Ireland (won 2–0), v Scotland (won 3–1), v Bulgaria (won 3–0), v Sweden (0–0),
  v Austria (lost 3–4), v Denmark (won 1–0), v N. Ireland (won 5–1), v Bulgaria
  (won 2–0)
1980 v Eire (won 2–0), v Spain (won 2–0), v Argentina (won 3–1), v Wales (lost 1–4),
  v Scotland (won 2–0), v Belgium (1–1), v Italy (lost 0–1), v Spain (won 2–1), v Norway
  (won 4–0), v Romania (lost 1–2)
1981 v Hungary (won 3–1), v Norway (lost 1–2), v Hungary (won 1–0)
1982 v Wales (won 1–0), v Holland (won 2–0), v Scotland (won 1–0), v Finland (won 4–1),
  v France (won 3–1), v Czechoslovakia (won 2–0), v Kuwait (won 1–0), v W. Germany
  (0–0), v Spain (0–0), v W. Germany (lost 1–2), v Greece (won 3–0)

PHIL THOMPSON'S frail-looking frame gave the impression that he wouldn't make a top-class defender because he lacked the necessary physical attributes. This couldn't have been further from the truth, for his determination and skill earned him the captaincy of both Liverpool and England, for whom he won 42 caps.

Originally a midfielder, Thompson made his Liverpool debut as a substitute at Old Trafford in April 1972 before establishing himself in the Reds' side, albeit in a variety of roles. With regular centre-back Larry Lloyd injured, Bill Shankly tried Thompson alongside Emlyn Hughes at the heart of the Liverpool defence, and in 1974 he completely shackled Newcastle and England centre-forward Malcolm Macdonald as the Reds beat Newcastle United in the FA Cup Final. The Thompson–Hughes partnership played a great part in Liverpool's success as the trophies piled up during the second half of the 1970s. Thompson was a great reader of the game, often playing his way out of trouble in European style, keeping the ball and setting up attacks with superb distribution. Liverpool often attacked *en masse* and it was Thompson who was left at the back ready to deal with any possible breakaways – he was probably the most accomplished British defender in one-to-one situations. A great motivator, he eventually took the Liverpool captaincy, inspiring his team-mates to new heights. He led the Reds to two League Championships and to European Cup success over Real Madrid in 1981. Though he later lost the captaincy to Graeme Souness, he won a further two League titles before his Anfield career came to an abrupt end in 1985.

After being hit by a crop of injuries he moved to Sheffield United, but 18 months later he was back at Anfield on the club's coaching staff. Later a Sky TV pundit, he is now back at his beloved Anfield as assistant manager to Gerard Houllier.

Mike DOYLE

Position	Defender
Born	Michael Doyle, Manchester, 25 November 1946
Height	6ft 0in
Weight	11st 9lb
Clubs	Manchester City, Stoke City, Bolton Wanderers, Rochdale
England Caps	5
	1976 v Wales (won 2–1), v Scotland (lost 1–2), v Brazil (lost 0–1), v Italy (won 3–2)
	1977 v Holland (lost 0–2)

MIKE DOYLE, capped by England shortly after his appointment as Manchester City captain in 1975, was a very determined player in whatever position he was given. He made his Manchester City debut against Cardiff in March 1965 as a centre-forward before winning a regular place the following season when the club won the Second Division Championship. Though not a prolific scorer, he did net six goals in a four-match spell either side of Christmas 1965 to consolidate the club's position at the top of the division. When City won the League Championship in 1967/68, Doyle had an outstanding season and was rewarded with selection for both England Under-23s and Young England. There followed appearances for the Football League, the first against the Scottish League in 1972. Doyle seemed to save his goals for the European competitions or domestic trophy finals. He scored the equalizing goal in the 1970 League Cup Final after West Brom had gone a goal up, and in April 1970 he scored one of the goals in the European Cup Winners' Cup semi-final second leg against Schalke 04, City winning 5–1 after losing by the only goal in Germany. One of City's finest players under Mercer and Allison, and later Tony Book, he won two League Cup winners' medals, an FA Cup winners' medal, a European Cup Winners' Cup medal and a League Championship medal. In the summer of 1978, after struggling with injuries and having played in 568 games for City, Doyle left to join Stoke. After playing in over 100 games for the Potters he moved to Bolton, later playing for Rochdale before hanging up his boots.

Phil BOYER

Position	Forward
Born	Philip John Boyer, Nottingham, 25 January 1949
Height	5ft 8in
Weight	11st 2lb
Clubs	Derby County, York City, Bournemouth, Norwich City, Southampton, Manchester City
England Caps	1
	1976 v Wales (won 2–1)

AFTER BEING RELEASED by Brian Clough at Derby County, Phil Boyer signed for York City, where he found himself playing alongside Ted MacDougall. He scored 27 goals in 109 League games for York before joining Bournemouth. His form for the Dean

Court club, where he netted 46 goals in 141 League outings, led to Norwich City paying £145,000 for his services — a club-record fee at the time.

At Carrow Road he was capped by England, and with MacDougall alongside him again the Canaries enjoyed two exciting seasons. Boyer's best campaign was 1974/75, when he scored 21 goals in 54 League and Cup games and helped the Canaries finish third in the First Division. He had scored 34 goals in 116 games when, in August 1977, he joined Southampton to fill the gap left by the departure of Mick Channon. His intelligent forward play paid dividends, and the following season Boyer ended up as the Saints' leading goal scorer when they finished runners-up in the Second Division. In 1979/80, he was again Southampton's top scorer with 23 League goals, including three hat-tricks. The arrival of Kevin Keegan meant that he had to move on and in November 1980 he joined Manchester City, where, sadly, an injury curtailed his career. He went to play in Hong Kong before returning to become player-manager of Grantham Town.

Ray KENNEDY

Position	Midfielder
Born	Raymond Kennedy, Seaton Delaval, 28 July 1951
Height	5ft 11in
Weight	13st 4lb
Clubs	Arsenal, Liverpool, Swansea City, Hartlepool United
England Caps	17 Goals 3

1976 v Wales (won 2–1) 1 goal, v Wales (won 1–0), v N. Ireland (won 4–0), v Scotland (lost 1–2)
1977 v Luxembourg (won 5–0) 1 goal, v Wales (lost 0–1), v Scotland (lost 1–2), v Brazil (0–0), v Argentina (1–1), v Switzerland (0–0), v Luxembourg (won 2–0) 1 goal
1979 v Bulgaria (won 2–0)
1980 v Spain (won 2–0), v Argentina (won 3–1), v Wales (lost 1–4), v Belgium (1–1), v Italy (lost 0–1)

AN INTEGRAL MEMBER of the England side during the second half of the seventies, Ray Kennedy joined Arsenal as an apprentice after being rejected by Port Vale. He made his League debut for the Gunners against Sunderland in February 1970 and shot to fame after scoring one of Arsenal's goals in that season's two-legged Inter Cities Fairs Cup Final as they beat Anderlecht 4–3 on aggregate. He became a regular in the Arsenal side the following season, ending the campaign in which the club did the 'double' with 26 goals as well as winning the Rothman's Young Player of the Year award. He spent a further three seasons at Highbury, winning another FA Cup winners' medal in 1971/72.

Kennedy subsequently joined Liverpool as Bill Shankly's last signing, and when Shankly left the club he impressed new manager Bob Paisley in a deep-lying position behind the twin strike force of Keegan and Toshack. By November 1975 he had been installed on the left side of Liverpool's midfield and over the next six years or so he helped the Reds win ten major honours.

Though he was short of pace, he read the game well and could change the emphasis of a game with a sweeping crossfield pass, though his deadliest attribute was the ability to make a late run into the box to finish off a move at the far post. Ultimately squeezed out of the Liverpool side by Ronnie Whelan, he joined Swansea City.

The Swans were unbeaten in Kennedy's first nine games but midway through the following season he returned to his native north-east to play for Hartlepool United. It was later revealed that Ray Kennedy was suffering from Parkinson's Disease. Since then he has spent his time raising public awareness of the illness and dealing with his own health.

Dave CLEMENT

Position	Right-back
Born	David Thomas Clement, Battersea, 2 February 1948
Died	31 March 1982
Height	5ft 10in
Weight	11st 5lb
Clubs	Queen's Park Rangers, Bolton Wanderers, Fulham, Wimbledon
England Caps	5
	1976 v Wales (won 2–1), v Wales (won 1–0), v Italy (won 3–2), v Italy (lost 0–2)
	1977 v Holland (lost 0–2)

ONE OF THE GAME'S most talented full-backs, Dave Clement, who won five full caps for England, made his League debut for Queen's Park Rangers in a 5–1 home win over Scunthorpe United in April 1967. However, it was to be his only appearance that season, in which Rangers went on to win the Third Division Championship, having already won the League Cup. After winning a regular place in 1968/9, Clement missed very few games over the next 12 seasons, being ever-present in 1970/71 and 1971/72 when he appeared in 108 consecutive League games. In 1972/73 he was outstanding as Rangers won promotion to the First Division, while in 1975/76 his performances went a long way towards helping the club finish runners-up in the top flight to Liverpool.

Clement went on to appear in 476 League and Cup games for Rangers before, in June 1979, joining Bolton Wanderers for a fee of £150,000. His first season at Burnden Park saw the Trotters relegated, and midway through the following campaign he returned to London to play for Fulham. Twelve months later he left Craven Cottage to join Wimbledon, but in 1982 he committed suicide.

Peter TAYLOR

Position	Winger
Born	Peter John Taylor, Southend, 3 January 1953
Height	5ft 9in
Weight	11st 7lb
Clubs	Southend United, Crystal Palace, Tottenham Hotspur, Leyton Orient, Oldham Athletic, Exeter City
England Caps	4 Goals 2
	1976 v Wales (won 2–1) 1 goal, v Wales (won 1–0) 1 goal, v N. Ireland (won 4–0),
	v Scotland (lost 1–2)

REJECTED BY SPURS as a youngster, Peter Taylor began his career with his home-town club Southend United, where he stood out as a player of immense potential. He was transferred to Crystal Palace, rose to Under-23 status and became one of the few Third Division players to appear in a full international for England.

A fast-raiding winger, Taylor joined Spurs for £400,000 in September 1976 but was hampered with injuries during his time at White Hart Lane. He later moved to Orient and had a loan spell with Oldham Athletic before entering non-League football with Maidstone United. He then helped out former Palace team-mate Gerry Francis as a non-contract player with Exeter City before returning to Maidstone as player-manager. A member of the England semi-professional team, he managed a number of non-League clubs before taking over the reins at Southend United. Since then he has managed Gillingham, whom he took into the First Division, and Leicester City, before taking charge at the Withdean Stadium. Taylor, who also took charge of England for their game against Italy, led Brighton to the Second Division Championship before parting company with the club. He is currently manager of Hull City.

Tony TOWERS

Position	Midfielder
Born	Anthony Mark Towers, Manchester, 13 April 1952
Height	5ft 9in
Weight	11st 0lb
Clubs	Manchester City, Sunderland, Birmingham City, Rochdale
England Caps	3
	1976 v Wales (won 1–0), v N. Ireland (won 4–0), v Italy (won 3–2)

AN ENGLAND schoolboy international, Tony Towers began his career with his home-town club Manchester City, where he added England youth and Under-23 honours to his name. When City won the European Cup Winners' Cup in 1970, Towers was the substitute who scored in extra time to give the club victory over Academica de Coimbra in the second leg of the quarter-final. He went on to appear in 159 games for the Maine Road club before being transferred to Sunderland for £100,000 plus Mick Horswill, who made the switch to City.

Towers soon settled into the Sunderland side and was a big influence on the club's midfield as they won the Second Division Championship in 1975/76. He scored ten goals from 34 games, including the all-important winner against Bolton Wanderers in the penultimate home game of the season. Whenever Towers scored, the Wearsiders did not lose! His form led to him winning three full caps for England, but at the end of the club's first season back in the top flight he was on the move again, this time to Birmingham City for a fee of £140,000. Sadly, he was a huge disappointment at St Andrew's, his better games coming at the end of his spell there when he played as a sweeper. He later played for Montreal Manic, Tampa Bay Rowdies and Vancouver Whitecaps before turning out as a non-contract player with Rochdale.

Brian GREENHOFF

Position	Defender
Born	Brian Greenhoff, Barnsley, 28 April 1953
Height	5ft 10in
Weight	11st 8lb
Clubs	Manchester United, Leeds United, Rochdale
England Caps	18

1976 v Wales (won 1–0), v N. Ireland (won 4–0), v Eire (1–1), v Finland (won 2–1), v Italy (lost 0–2)

1977 v Holland (lost 0–2), v N. Ireland (won 2–1), v Wales (lost 0–1), v Scotland (lost 1–2), v Brazil (0–0), v Argentina (1–1), v Uruguay (0–0)

1978 v Brazil (1–1), v Wales (won 3–1), v N. Ireland (won 1–0), v Scotland (won 1–0), v Hungary (won 4–1)

1980 v Australia (won 2–1)

BRIAN GREENHOFF was a ballboy at Wembley when he saw his brother Jimmy win a 1968 League Cup winners' medal for Leeds. Brian later played in an FA Cup Final himself for Manchester United and trod the turf as an England player. The Greenhoffs' father was a professional footballer and Brian predated Jimmy at Old Trafford by six years. He made his League debut against Ipswich Town in September 1973 and his versatility made him an important member of the Old Trafford set-up – after Under-23 honours he won the first of 18 caps against Wales in 1976. He played in two FA Cup finals for Manchester United, gaining a winners' medal in 1977, and was a non-playing substitute in 1979. Two years after the Wembley victory he was sold to Leeds United for a fee of £350,000.

Brian's stay at Elland Road was disrupted by injuries and, after a loan period with Rochdale, managed by his brother Jimmy, he joined the Spotland club on a permanent basis. He later helped out Chadderton FC and worked as a sales representative for a sports goods wholesaler.

Brian Greenhoff playing for Leeds United.
(Lancashire Evening Post)

Stuart PEARSON

Position	Forward
Born	Stuart James Pearson, Hull, 21 June 1949
Height	5ft 9in
Weight	12st 7lb
Clubs	Hull City, Manchester United, West Ham United
England Caps	15 Goals 4

1976 v Wales (won 1–0), v N. Ireland (won 4–0) 1 goal, v Scotland (lost 1–2), v Brazil (lost 0–1), v Finland (won 4–1) 1 goal, v Eire (1–1) 1 goal

1977 v Holland (lost 0–2), v Wales (lost 0–1), v Scotland (lost 1–2), v Brazil (0–0), v Argentina (1–1) 1 goal, v Uruguay (0–0), v Italy (won 2–0), W. Germany (lost 1–0) 1 goal, v N. Ireland (won 1–0)

STUART PEARSON was a consistent goalscorer for his home-town club Hull City when, at the end of Manchester United's relegation season of 1973/74, Tommy Docherty paid out £200,000 to take him to Old Trafford. Seen as the player who could take the Reds back to the top flight, he didn't disappoint, responding with 17 goals as United won the Second Division Championship. Capped 15 times while with the Reds, he was a great favourite with the Old Trafford faithful. He scored in the 1977 FA Cup Final when United beat Liverpool 2–1, and went on to score 66 goals in 179 games for United before joining West Ham United for £220,000.

Pearson was back at Wembley in 1980 as a member of the Hammers' FA Cup-winning team as they beat Fulham. Surprisingly released by the Upton Park club at the end of the 1981/82 season, he went on Jimmy Hill's 'rebel' soccer tour of South Africa and played in the NASL before a knee injury, which had frequently threatened his career, forced his retirement from the professional game. He then turned to Rugby Union, occasionally playing on the wing for Sale, but later returned to soccer, first as manager of non-League Northwich Victoria and then as coach at West Bromwich Albion. He subsequently had a brief spell as assistant manager of Bradford City.

Jimmy RIMMER

Position	Goalkeeper
Born	James John Rimmer, Southport, 10 February 1948
Height	6ft 1in
Weight	13st 2lb
Clubs	Manchester United, Swansea City, Arsenal, Aston Villa
England Caps	1

1976 v Italy (won 3–2)

JIMMY RIMMER, who was capped by England against Italy on their American tour of 1976, began his career with Manchester United, graduating through the club's junior teams and winning an FA Youth Cup winners' medal in 1964. After impressing on United's tour of Australia in 1967, he was given his League debut towards the end of the following season. He was the substitute goalkeeper when United beat Benfica in

Stuart Pearson of Hull City, Manchester United and West Ham.
(Lancashire Evening Post)

the 1968 European Cup Final and spent most of his time as understudy to Alex Stepney before being loaned out to Swansea City.

Rimmer's displays for the Swans alerted a number of other top-flight clubs and in February 1974 he joined Arsenal. He impressed by keeping a clean sheet on his debut in an unexpected victory against Liverpool at Anfield, and with Bob Wilson retiring at the end of the season he grabbed his opportunity. During his three seasons at Highbury he showed great consistency, missing only three matches, but in 1977 he realized his Arsenal days were numbered following the signing of Pat Jennings.

Rimmer joined Aston Villa and served the Midlands club for six seasons, helping them win both the League Championship and the European Cup. He had played 285 games for Villa before losing his place to the up-and-coming Nigel Spink. He then returned to the Vetch Field to play for Swansea for a couple of seasons before becoming the Welsh club's youth-team coach.

Ray WILKINS

Position	Midfielder
Born	Raymond Colin Wilkins, Hillingdon, 14 September 1956
Height	5ft 8in
Weight	10st 11lb
Clubs	Chelsea, Manchester United, AC Milan, Paris St Germain, Glasgow Rangers, Queen's Park Rangers, Crystal Palace, Wycombe Wanderers, Hibernian, Millwall, Leyton Orient
England Caps	84 Goals 3

1976 v Italy (won 3–2), v Eire (1–1), v Finland (won 2–1)

1977 v N. Ireland (won 2–1), v Brazil (0–0), v Argentina (1–1), v Uruguay (0–0), v Switzerland (0–0), v Luxembourg (won 2–0), v Italy (won 2–0)

1978 v W. Germany (lost 1–2), v Wales (won 3–1), v N. Ireland (won 1–0), v Scotland (won 1–0), v Hungary (won 4–1), v Denmark (won 4–3), v Eire (1–1), v Czechoslovakia (won 1–0)

1979 v N. Ireland (won 2–0), v Wales (0–0), v Scotland (won 3–1), v Bulgaria (won 3–0), v Sweden (0–0), v Austria (lost 3–4) 1 goal, v Denmark (won 1–0), v N. Ireland (won 5–1), v Bulgaria (won 2–0), v Spain (won 2–0), v Argentina (won 3–1), v Wales (lost 1–4), v N. Ireland (1–1), v Scotland (won 2–0), v Belgium (1–1) 1 goal, v Italy (lost 0–1), v Spain (won 2–1)

1981 v Spain (lost 1–2), v Romania (0–0), v Brazil (lost 0–1), v Wales (0–0), v Scotland (lost 0–1), v Switzerland (lost 1–2), v Hungary (won 3–1)

1982 v N. Ireland (won 4–0) 1 goal, v Wales (won 1–0), v Holland (won 2–0), v Scotland (won 2–0), v Finland (won 4–1), v France (won 3–1), v Czechoslovakia (won 2–0), v Kuwait (won 1–0), v W. Germany (0–0), v Spain (0–0), v Denmark (2–2), v W. Germany (lost 1–2)

1983 v Denmark (lost 0–1)

1984 v N. Ireland (won 1–0), v Wales (lost 0–1), v Scotland (1–1), v Soviet Union (lost 0–2), v Brazil (won 2–0), v Uruguay (lost 0–2), v Chile (0–0), v E. Germany (won 1–0), v Finland (won 5–0), v Turkey (won 8–0)

1985 v N. Ireland (won 1–0), v Eire (won 2–1), v Romania (0–0), v Finland (1–1), v Scotland

Ray Wilkins. (Lancashire Evening Post)

(lost 0–1), v Italy (lost 1–2), v Mexico (lost 0–1), v Turkey (won 5–0), v N. Ireland (0–0)
1986 v Egypt (won 4–0), v Israel (won 2–1), v Soviet Union (won 1–0), v Scotland (won 2–1),
v Mexico (won 3–0), v Canada (won 1–0), v Portugal (lost 0–1), v Morocco (0–0),
v Sweden (lost 0–1), v Yugoslavia (won 2–0)

CAPTAIN OF the England youth team, 'Butch' Wilkins joined Chelsea straight from school, and at the age of 18 became the Stamford Bridge club's youngest-ever skipper. He led them to promotion to the First Division in 1976/77, but was unable to prevent their slide back to the Second Division in 1978/79. By then a regular choice for England, going on to win 84 caps, Wilkins moved to Manchester United in the summer of 1979 for a fee of £825,000. He spent five good years at Old Trafford but with only an FA Cup winners' medal (1983) to show for it, although he came close to winning the League Championship in his first season with the Reds.

In 1984 Wilkins joined the exodus to Italy, signing for AC Milan for £1.5 million. After three years he lost his place and moved to French club Paris St Germain. However, he hardly got a game in the French team and was rescued by Graeme Souness, who signed him for Glasgow Rangers in November 1987. He hardly missed a game in his two years at Ibrox, winning Scottish Premier League Championship and Skol Cup winners' medals. In November 1989 he returned to London to play for Queen's Park Rangers. After making 182 first-team appearances he moved to Crystal Palace, but after appearing in just one game he was back at Loftus Road as Queen's Park Rangers' player-manager. On resigning his post, he played in one game for Wycombe Wanderers before returning north of the border to play for Hibernian. Brought back to the English game on a weekly contract, he had brief spells with Millwall and Leyton Orient before finally hanging up his boots.

Gordon HILL

Position	Winger
Born	Gordon Alec Hill, Sunbury, 1 April 1954
Height	5ft 7in
Weight	10st 12lb
Clubs	Millwall, Manchester United, Derby County, Queen's Park Rangers
England Caps	6
	1976 v Italy (won 3–2), v Eire (1–1), v Finland (won 2–1)
	1977 v Luxembourg (won 5–0), v Switzerland (0–0), v Luxembourg (won 2–0)

GORDON HILL was playing Third Division football for Millwall when Manchester United manager Tommy Docherty paid £70,000 to bring him to Old Trafford. With Steve Coppell on the right wing and Gordon Hill on the left, United played some of the most attractive football seen for a good number of years. Within months of his arrival at Old Trafford, Hill was playing for England against Italy, which cost United a further £10,000. After scoring twice in the semi-final against Derby County, he stepped out at Wembley for the 1976 FA Cup Final against Southampton. United lost, but he collected a winners' medal the following year as United beat Liverpool 2–1. In both games he was replaced by David McCreery, the only instance of a player being substituted in two different Wembley finals.

A disagreement at Old Trafford led to Hill's departure when Tommy Docherty, by now in charge of Derby County, signed him for a second time. Queen's Park Rangers, who had once released Hill as a junior, bought him in November 1979 and once again the buying manager was none other than Tommy Docherty.

On leaving the English game, Hill had spells in the NASL with Chicago Sting and Montreal Manic before playing in the American indoor league. He then played for a number of foreign teams, including HJK Helsinki and Twente Enschede, before becoming player-manager of Northwich Victoria. He now lives in Tampa Bay, where he is a soccer coach.

Joe CORRIGAN

Position	Goalkeeper
Born	Joseph Thomas Corrigan, Manchester, 18 November 1948
Height	6ft 4in
Weight	14st 0lb
Clubs	Manchester City, Brighton and Hove Albion, Norwich City, Stoke City
England Caps	9
	1976 v Italy (won 3–2)
	1978 v Brazil (1–1)
	1979 v Wales (0–0)
	1980 v N. Ireland (1–1), v Australia (won 2–1)
	1981 v Wales (0–0), v Scotland (lost 0–1)
	1982 v Wales (won 1–0), v Iceland (1–1)

IN HIS EARLY DAYS at Maine Road, Joe Corrigan was always in the shadow of Harry Dowd and Ken Mulhearn, and when he did occasionally get a chance to play he was inconsistent. Despite this unimpressive start to his career, he fought hard to establish himself but faced another crisis of confidence when City signed Motherwell keeper Keith MacRae. Corrigan again buckled down and won back his place, going on to serve City for a further nine years. Manchester City have had three outstanding goalkeepers, Frank Swift, Bert Trautmann and Joe Corrigan, and it was unlucky for Corrigan to have been in the game at the same time as Peter Shilton and Ray Clemence. Corrigan won nine caps for England, the first in a 3–2 win over Italy in New York in 1976.

Corrigan's best season for City was 1976/77, when he conceded just 34 goals in his 42 League appearances, keeping 22 clean sheets. He won League Cup honours in 1970 and 1976, and a European Cup Winners' Cup medal in 1970 when City beat Gornik Zabrze of Poland 2–1. When City played Spurs at Wembley in the 1981 FA Cup Final, Corrigan was named 'Man-of-the-Match' after his heroics between the posts in the 1–1 draw. Spurs won the replay 3–2.

Corrigan played in 592 League and Cup games for Manchester City before joining Seattle Sounders in the NASL. He later returned to these shores to play for Brighton and Hove Albion, Norwich City and Stoke City before retiring. He is now full-time goalkeeping coach at Liverpool.

Charlie GEORGE

Position	Forward
Born	Charles Frederick George, Islington, 10 October 1950
Height	5ft 11in
Weight	11st 9lb
Clubs	Arsenal, Derby County, Southampton, Nottingham Forest, Dundee United, Bournemouth
England Caps	1
	1976 v Eire (1–1)

CHARLIE GEORGE will always be remembered as the long-haired 20-year-old who scored Arsenal's winning goal in the 1971 FA Cup Final, taking the 'double' to Highbury. He made his first-team debut for the Gunners against West Bromwich Albion on the opening day of the 1969/70 season, and in that campaign helped them win the Inter Cities Fairs Cup, their first major honour for 17 years. A vital member of Arsenal's double-winning side, he then only played in about half of the next four seasons' fixtures due to injuries, loss of form and disciplinary reasons. Having become disillusioned with the team he had supported as a boy, he left Highbury in the summer of 1975 to join Derby County.

George spent three-and-a-half seasons at the Baseball Ground and won an England cap before signing for Southampton for £400,000 in December 1978. However, shortly after joining the Saints it was revealed that he had a knee injury and would be out of action for some months. Although he subsequently showed flashes of his old brilliance, he could not be guaranteed a first-team place, and, after a loan spell at Nottingham Forest, he went to play in the United States and Hong Kong before coming home to try his luck with Dundee United and Bournemouth. He now helps out at Highbury as a match-day host and runs the club's museum.

Trevor FRANCIS

Position	Forward
Born	Trevor John Francis, Plymouth, 19 April 1954
Height	5ft 10in
Weight	11st 7lb
Clubs	Birmingham City, Nottingham Forest, Manchester City, Sampdoria, Atalanta, Glasgow Rangers, Queen's Park Rangers, Sheffield Wednesday
England Caps	52 Goals 12
	1977 v Holland (lost 0–2), v Luxembourg (won 5–0) 1 goal, v Scotland (lost 1–2), v Brazil (0–0), v Switzerland (0–0), v Luxembourg (won 2–0), v Italy (won 2–0)
	1978 v W. Germany (lost 1–2), v Brazil (1–1), v Wales (won 3–1), v Scotland (won 1–0), v Hungary (won 4–1) 1 goal
	1979 v Bulgaria (won 3–0), v Sweden (0–0), v Austria (lost 3–4), v N. Ireland (won 5–1) 2 goals, v Bulgaria (won 2–0)
	1980 v Spain (won 2–1) 1 goal
	1981 v Spain (lost 1–2), v Romania (0–0), v Scotland (lost 0–1), v Switzerland (lost 1–2), v Norway (lost 1–2)

Trevor Francis. (Lancashire Evening Post)

1982 v N. Ireland (won 4–0), v Wales (won 1–0) 1 goal, v Scotland (won 1–0), v Finland (won 4–1), v France (won 3–1), v Czechoslovakia (won 2–0) 1 goal, v Kuwait (won 1–0) 1 goal, v W. Germany (0–0), v Spain (0–0), v Denmark (2–2) 2 goals

1983 v Greece (0–0), v Hungary (won 2–0) 1 goal, v N. Ireland (0–0), v Scotland (won 2–0), v Australia (0–0), v Australia (won 1–0), v Australia (1–1) 1 goal, v Denmark (lost 0–1)

1984 v N. Ireland (won 1–0), v Soviet Union (lost 0–2), v E. Germany (won 1–0), v Turkey (won 8–0)

1985 v N. Ireland (won 1–0), v Romania (0–0), v Finland (1–1), v Scotland (lost 0–1), v Italy (lost 1–2), v Mexico (lost 0–1)

1986 v Scotland (won 2–1)

TREVOR FRANCIS made 52 England appearances, played in the 1982 World Cup in Spain and was unfortunate not to be in the squad for the 1986 World Cup in Mexico. The previous summer he had played against Italy and Mexico in a World Cup warm-up competition in Mexico City and looked the best of the England strikers in both games.

Francis began his career with Birmingham City, and in February 1971 he became the first 16-year-old to score four goals in a League game when Bolton were beaten 4–0 at St Andrew's. Forming a prolific goalscoring partnership with Bob Latchford, he helped the Blues win promotion to the First Division in 1971/72. He continued to score goals on a regular basis in the top flight, with a best of 25 in 1977/78. After scoring 133 goals in 330 games, he became Britain's first-ever seven-figure signing, when Nottingham Forest paid a reported £1.5 million for his services in February 1979. Despite being plagued by injuries at the City Ground, he scored the winning goal in the 1979 European Cup Final against Malmo.

Just one week into the 1981–82 season, Francis joined Manchester City, but a year later he was on his way to Sampdoria, where he won an Italian Cup winners' medal. After a spell with Atalanta, he signed for Glasgow Rangers. A Skol Cup winners' medal at Ibrox was followed by a return to League football with Queen's Park Rangers. After a year as player-manager at Loftus Road, he joined Sheffield Wednesday. After helping them win the League Cup in 1991 he replaced Ron Atkinson as manager. He helped the Owls finish third in the First Division in his first season in charge and in 1992/93 took the club to two domestic finals. He parted company with the Hillsborough club in 1995 and the following year took charge of Birmingham City. Though he came close to taking the Blues into the Premiership, it wasn't to be, and he is now manager of First Division Crystal Palace.

John GIDMAN

Position	Right-back
Born	John Gidman, Liverpool, 10 January 1954
Height	5ft 11in
Weight	11st 13lb
Clubs	Aston Villa, Everton, Manchester United, Manchester City, Stoke City, Darlington
England Caps	1
	1977 v Luxembourg (won 5–0)

AN ATTACKING FULL-BACK famed for his fearsome tackling, John Gidman joined Aston Villa after being discarded by Liverpool. An important member of Villa's FA Youth Cup-winning team of 1971/72, he also appeared regularly in the first team as they went on to win that season's Third Division Championship. Gidman also won two League Cup winners' medals while with Villa, in 1975 and 1977, his form in the latter year also winning him an England cap.

After making 242 appearances for Villa, Gidman left to join Everton, who paid a club-record fee of £650,000 in October 1979 to secure his services. He spent less than two years at Goodison before leaving in the summer of 1981 to join Manchester United in a deal that saw Mickey Thomas travel in the opposite direction. He immediately slotted into the Old Trafford club's defence but soon afterwards suffered a series of setbacks, almost losing an eye in a firework accident and then being plagued by a number of serious injuries. He fought his way back to win an FA Cup winners' medal against Everton in 1985, but at the end of the following season he was given a free transfer. He joined Manchester City and later signed for Stoke City. Following a brief spell with Darlington he was forced to retire from the game because of injury.

Paul MARINER

Position	Centre-forward
Born	Paul Mariner, Bolton, 22 May 1953
Height	6ft 0in
Weight	12st 2lb
Clubs	Plymouth Argyle, Ipswich Town, Arsenal, Portsmouth
England Caps	35 Goals 13

1977 v Luxembourg (won 5–0), v N. Ireland (won 2–1), v Luxembourg (won 2–0) 1 goal
1978 v Wales (won 3–1), v Scotland (won 1–0)
1980 v Wales (lost 1–4) 1 goal, v N. Ireland (1–1), v Scotland (won 2–0), v Australia (won 2–1) 1 goal, v Italy (lost 0–1), v Spain (won 2–1), v Norway (won 4–0) 1 goal, v Switzerland (won 2–1) 1 goal
1981 v Spain (lost 1–2), v Switzerland (lost 1–2), v Hungary (won 3–1), v Norway (lost 1–2), v Hungary (won 1–0)
1982 v Holland (won 2–0) 1 goal, v Scotland (won 1–0) 1 goal, v Finland (won 4–1) 2 goals, v France (won 3–1) 1 goal, v Czechoslovakia (won 2–0) 1 goal, v Kuwait (won 1–0), v W. Germany (0–0), v Spain (0–0), v Denmark (2–2), v W. Germany (lost 1–2), v Greece (won 3–0)
1983 v Wales (won 2–1), v Denmark (lost 0–1), v Hungary (won 3–0) 1 goal, v Luxembourg (won 4–0) 1 goal
1984 v E. Germany (won 1–0)
1985 v Romania (0–0)

PAUL MARINER began his footballing career with non-League Chorley before being transferred to Plymouth Argyle in July 1973. After working his way up through the ranks, he formed a prolific strike partnership with Billy Rafferty that did much to ensure Argyle's promotion to the Second Division in 1975/76. It also attracted the attention of First Division clubs Ipswich, West Bromwich Albion and West Ham, but it was Ipswich manager Bobby Robson who made the Home Park club an offer they could not refuse in October 1976. Robson left Ipswich to become manager of the national side shortly afterwards, but clearly still had a high opinion of Mariner, awarding him the first of his 35 caps some six months after his move to Portman Road.

Mariner ended the 1977/78 campaign as the club's top scorer with 22 goals, having also won an FA Cup winners' medal when Ipswich beat Arsenal 1–0 in the final. He led the scoring charts again in 1978/79 and 1979/80, and helped Town lift the UEFA Cup in 1981. Although his goalscoring achievements were less over his last three seasons at Portman Road, he had scored 131 goals in 339 games when he signed for Arsenal in February 1984.

Although hardly in the veteran stage, Mariner had seen his best years, and in August 1986, after scoring 17 goals in 70 games for the Gunners, he joined Portsmouth. In his first season at Fratton Park he helped Pompey gain promotion to the top flight. He later had a brief spell as commercial manager of Colchester United, but now spends most of his time coaching in the United States.

Brian TALBOT

Position	Midfielder
Born	Brian Ernest Talbot, Ipswich, 21 July 1953
Height	5ft 10in
Weight	12st 0lb
Clubs	Ipswich Town, Arsenal, Watford, Stoke City, West Bromwich Albion, Fulham, Aldershot
England Caps	6
	1977 v N. Ireland (won 2–1), v Scotland (lost 1–2), v Brazil (0–0), v Argentina (1–1), v Uruguay (0–0)
	1980 v Australia (won 2–1)

AFTER TURNING PROFESSIONAL with Ipswich Town, Brian Talbot had a two-year loan spell with Toronto Metros before making his League debut for the Portman Road club against Burnley in February 1974. He spent seven seasons at Ipswich, playing in 227 first-team games and winning five England caps. He was also a member of the Town side that beat Arsenal 1–0 in the 1978 FA Cup Final. In January 1979 the all-action midfielder joined the Gunners for £450,000, and at the end of his first season was a member of Arsenal's FA Cup-winning team against Manchester United. He thus became, and remains, the only player ever to play for different cup-winning teams in successive seasons. Talbot created an Arsenal club record in 1979/80 when he appeared in all of the club's 70 first-team games that season, which included defeats in the FA Cup Final against West Ham United and the European Cup Winners' Cup Final against Valencia. The driving force behind both Ipswich and Arsenal's midfield, his play was built around his great stamina. In just over six seasons at Highbury he played in a staggering 327 first-team games.

Following the signing of Steve Williams, Talbot realized his Arsenal days were over and in June 1985 he joined Watford. He later played for Stoke City, West Bromwich

Albion and Fulham, and after serving as chairman of the PFA he went into management with West Bromwich Albion and Aldershot before moving overseas to take charge of Hibernians in Malta. He is now back in the Football League as manager of Rushden and Diamonds.

Terry McDERMOTT

Position	Midfielder
Born	Terence McDermott, Kirkby, 8 December 1951
Height	5ft 9in
Weight	12st 13lb
Clubs	Bury, Newcastle United, Liverpool
England Caps	25 Goals 3
	1977 v Switzerland (0–0), v Luxembourg (won 2–0)
	1979 v N. Ireland (won 2–0), v Wales (0–0), v Sweden (0–0), v Denmark (won 1–0), v N. Ireland (won 5–1)
	1980 v Eire (won 2–0), v N. Ireland (1–1), v Scotland (won 2–0), v Belgium (1–1), v Spain (won 2–1), v Norway (won 4–0) 2 goals, v Romania (lost 1–2), v Switzerland (won 2–1)
	1981 v Romania (0–0), v Brazil (lost 0–1), v Switzerland (lost 1–2) 1 goal, v Hungary (won 3–1), v Norway (lost 1–2), v Hungary (won 1–0)
	1982 v Wales (won 1–0), v Holland (won 2–0), v Scotland (won 1–0), v Iceland (1–1)
Honours	Footballer of the Year 1980

MIDFIELDER TERRY McDERMOTT made 25 appearances for England between 1977 and 1982 but never made it onto the World Cup stage. Though Liverpool born, he began his footballing career with homely Bury before being transferred to Newcastle United in January 1973. Although on the losing side in the 1974 FA Cup Final against Liverpool, he had been particularly impressive for the Magpies, and shortly afterwards he moved to Anfield for a fee of £170,000.

Liverpool won the League Championship and the UEFA Cup in 1975/76 without McDermott's assistance. Left languishing in the reserves, it seemed only a matter of time before his purchase would be written off as an expensive mistake and he would be sold on. However, Bob Paisley kept faith with him and the following season saw McDermott firmly established, playing a memorable role in the run-in, which saw the League title and European Cup come to Anfield. McDermott was superb and dangerous when running from deep positions and arriving late in the penalty area, where his finishing could be deadly. In 1977/78, when Graeme Souness arrived at Anfield, he reached his peak. The Scot's style of play allowed the wiry McDermott the freedom he needed to express his talents fully, and in September 1978 he started and finished one of Anfield's best-ever goals in the televised 7–0 hammering of Spurs. In 1980 he became the first man to win awards from the Football Writers' Association and his fellow players in the same season.

Seeming to lose a little impetus, he returned to the north-east to team up with Kevin Keegan at Newcastle, helping the club return to the top flight. He later played for Cork City and Apoel of Cyprus before returning to St James' Park, where he enjoyed equal success, for a third time as Keegan's right-hand man.

Terry McDermott of Liverpool. (Lancashire Evening Post)

Trevor WHYMARK

Position	Forward
Born	Trevor John Whymark, Burston, 4 May 1950
Height	5ft 10in
Weight	10st 8lb
Clubs	Ipswich Town, Derby County, Sparta Rotterdam, Grimsby Town, Southend United, Peterborough United, Colchester United
England Caps	1
	1977 v Luxembourg (won 2–0)

HAVING SCORED 65 goals for Ipswich Town's youth and reserve sides in 1968/69, Trevor Whymark was given his Football League debut at the start of the following season. Yet it was 1972/73 before he established himself as a first-team regular at Portman Road. Proving to be a prolific goalscorer, he netted all four of the club's goals in a 4–0 win over Lazio in a UEFA Cup second-round match in 1973/74. He continued to score on a regular basis, netting another four in a 7–0 demolition of West Bromwich Albion – the first time an Ipswich player had scored four goals in a First Division match – and then a hat-trick in a 5–0 win over East Anglian rivals Norwich City. In 1977/78 he scored four goals in a match for the third time as Swedish side Landskrona Bois were beaten 5–0. That performance led to him winning his first full cap for England, when he came on as a substitute for Terry McDermott in a 2–0 win in Luxembourg. Sadly, Whymark damaged his knee ligaments in the Boxing Day match at Norwich and, though he played a few games the following season, he was allowed to leave the club after scoring 104 goals in 335 games.

Whymark later had a brief spell with Derby County before Grimsby Town broke their transfer record to sign him. After a couple of seasons at Blundell Park, he ended his first-class career with spells at Southend United, Peterborough and Colchester United.

Steve COPPELL

Position	Winger
Born	Stephen James Coppell, Liverpool, 9 July 1955
Height	5ft 8in
Weight	11st 11lb
Clubs	Tranmere Rovers, Manchester United
England Caps	42 Goals 7
	1977 v Italy (won 2–0)
	1978 v W. Germany (lost 1–2), v Brazil (1–1), v Wales (won 3–1), v N. Ireland (won 1–0), v Scotland (won 1–0) 1 goal, v Hungary (won 4–1), v Denmark (won 4–3), v Eire (1–1), v Czechoslovakia (won 1–0) 1 goal
	1979 v N. Ireland (won 4–0), v N. Ireland (won 2–0) 1 goal, v Wales (0–0), v Scotland (won 3–1) 1 goal, v Bulgaria (won 3–0), v Austria (lost 3–4) 1 goal, v Denmark (won 1–0), v N. Ireland (won 5–1)

1980 v Eire (won 2–0), v Spain (won 2–0), v Argentina (won 3–1), v Wales (lost 1–4),
    v Scotland (won 2–0) 1 goal, v Belgium (1–1), v Italy (lost 0–1), v Romania (lost 1–2),
    v Switzerland (won 2–1)
1981 v Romania (0–0), v Brazil (lost 0–1), v Wales (0–0), v Scotland (lost 0–1), v Switzerland
    (lost 1–2), v Hungary (won 3–1), v Hungary (won 1–0)
1982 v Scotland (won 1–0), v Finland (won 4–1), v France (won 3–1), v Czechoslovakia (won
    2–0), v Kuwait (won 1–0), v W. Germany (0–0)
1983 v Greece (0–0), v Luxembourg (won 9–0) 1 goal

STEVE COPPELL WAS noted for his all-action never-say-die attitude, but his career was brought to an early end by a tackle from the Hungarian defender Joseph Toth at Wembley in 1981. He struggled on for another 14 months, producing some of his best-ever football and undergoing three operations, but there was no way back. He was able to play in the first four games of the 1982 World Cup Finals but the problem flared up again in the match against West Germany, and though he played in a further two games for England he subsequently retired, on medical advice.

Coppell was studying economics at Liverpool University when Tranmere Rovers rated him highly enough to place him as an amateur in their Third Division side. After just 38 games for the Prenton Park club, his potential was spotted by Manchester United, then top of the Second Division, Reds manager Tommy Docherty paying £30,000 to take him to Old Trafford in February 1975.

Coppell swiftly established himself in United's first team and progressed to international level almost immediately, appearing once in the England Under-23 side before making his full debut against Italy in November 1977. Able to wriggle past defenders, race to the line and send over a perfect cross, he could also chase back and provide cover for his defenders. His efforts were rewarded with an FA Cup winners' medal in 1977, and he appeared in over 400 games for the Reds before his enforced retirement.

In June 1984 Coppell turned to management with Crystal Palace, showing the same enthusiasm that he had displayed as Chairman of the PFA. At 28, he was the youngest League manager. Now manager of Brighton and Hove Albion, he has also managed Brentford and had four different periods in charge at Selhurst Park!

Bob LATCHFORD

Position	Centre-forward
Born	Robert Dennis Latchford, Birmingham, 18 January 1951
Height	6ft 0in
Weight	12st 0lb
Clubs	Birmingham City, Everton, Swansea City, Coventry City, NAC Breda, Lincoln City, Newport County
England Caps	12 Goals 5
	1977 v Italy (won 2–0)
	1978 v Brazil (1–1), v Wales (won 3–1) 1 goal, v Denmark (won 4–3) 1 goal, v Eire (1–1) 1 goal, v Czechoslovakia (won 1–0)

1979 v N. Ireland (won 4–0) 2 goals, v N. Ireland (won 2–0), v Wales (0–0), v Scotland (won 3–1), v Bulgaria (won 3–0), v Austria (lost 3–4)

BOB LATCHFORD made his name with his home-town team Birmingham City, scoring 84 goals in 194 games, and helping them win promotion to the First Division in 1971/72. He signed for Everton in February 1974 for a fee of £350,000 and in his first four full seasons with the Merseyside club was the top League goalscorer. He reached his peak in 1977/78, when he won the first of 12 caps and became the first First Division player for six years to reach the 30-goal mark. Latchford's total included four in a 5–1 win at Queen's Park Rangers. He reached the final game of that season at home to Chelsea needing two goals to claim a national newspaper prize of £10,000. Everton won 6–0 and Latchford netted the goals necessary to win the money and carve a place for himself in Merseyside football folklore.

Latchford had scored 138 goals in 289 League and Cup games when, in 1981, he left to join Swansea City. He enjoyed mixed fortunes in South Wales, but scored 32 goals in 1982/83 before being given a free transfer and joining Dutch club NAC Breda. Within five months he had returned to England and signed for Coventry City. Twelve months later he left to play for Lincoln City, ending his first-class career with Newport County.

Peter BARNES

Position	Winger
Born	Peter Simon Barnes, Manchester, 10 June 1957
Height	5ft 10in
Weight	11st 0lb
Clubs	Manchester City, West Bromwich Albion, Leeds United, Real Betis, Coventry City, Manchester United, Bolton Wanderers, Port Vale, Hull City, Faranse, Sunderland
England Caps	22 Goals 3
	1977 v Italy (won 2–0)
	1978 v W. Germany (lost 1–2), v Brazil (1–1), v Wales (won 3–1) 1 goal, v Scotland (won 1–0), v Hungary (won 4–1), v Denmark (won 4–3), v Eire (1–1), v Czechoslovakia (won 1–0)
	1979 v N. Ireland (won 4–0), v N. Ireland (won 2–0), v Scotland (won 3–1) 1 goal, v Bulgaria (won 3–0) 1 goal, v Austria (lost 3–4), v Denmark (won 1–0)
	1980 v Wales (lost 1–4)
	1981 v Spain (lost 1–2), v Brazil (lost 0–1), v Wales (0–0), v Switzerland (lost 1–2), v Norway (lost 1–2)
	1982 v Holland (won 2–0)

THE SON OF former Manchester City wing-half and chief scout Ken Barnes, Peter Barnes won the first of his 22 caps for England when he played against Italy in a World Cup qualifier in November 1977. He had joined Manchester City straight from school and, after turning professional in 1974, won England youth honours. Though he made his City debut that year, it was the 1975/76 season before he won a regular place in the Blues' side. His dazzling displays on the wing earned him Under-21 caps, and in the League Cup Final of 1976 he scored in City's 2–1 win over Newcastle United. At the end of the season he was named as the Young Player of the Year.

An exciting winger, Barnes was, surprisingly, allowed to leave Maine Road and join West Bromwich Albion for a fee of £650,000 in 1979. He ended his first season at the Hawthorns as the Baggies' leading scorer with 15 goals, but midway through the following campaign he was sold to Leeds United for £930,000. While at Elland Road he was loaned to Spanish club Real Betis, but in October 1984 he was transferred to Coventry City after a brief loan spell with Manchester United. In January 1987 he rejoined Manchester City, but, after taking his tally of goals in his two spells to 22 in 161 games, he joined Hull City following loan spells with Bolton Wanderers and Port Vale. He later ended his first-class career with Sunderland before playing non-League football for Northwich Victoria, Radcliffe Borough and Mossley.

Tony WOODCOCK

Position	Forward
Born	Anthony Stewart Woodcock, Nottingham, 6 December 1955
Height	5ft 10in
Weight	11st 0lb
Clubs	Nottingham Forest, Lincoln City, Doncaster Rovers, FC Cologne, Arsenal, Fortuna Dusseldorf
England Caps	42 Goals 16

1978 v N. Ireland (won 1–0), v Eire (1–1), v Czechoslovakia (won 1–0)
1979 v Bulgaria (won 3–0), v Sweden (0–0), v N. Ireland (won 5–1) 2 goals, v Bulgaria (won 2–0)
1980 v Eire (won 2–0), v Spain (won 2–0) 1 goal, v Argentina (won 3–1), v Belgium (1–1), v Italy (lost 0–1), v Spain (won 2–1) 1 goal, v Norway (won 4–0) 1 goal, v Romania (lost 1–2) 1 goal, v Switzerland (won 2–1)
1981 v Romania (0–0), v Wales (0–0), v Scotland (lost 0–1)
1982 v N. Ireland (won 4–0), v Holland (won 2–0) 1 goal, v Finland (won 4–1), v W. Germany (0–0), v Spain (0–0), v W. Germany (lost 1–2) 1 goal, v Greece (won 3–0) 2 goals, v Luxembourg (won 9–0) 1 goal
1983 v Greece (0–0), v Luxembourg (won 4–0)
1984 v France (lost 0–2), v N. Ireland (won 1–0) 1 goal, v Wales (lost 0–1), v Scotland (1–1) 1 goal, v Brazil (won 2–0), v Uruguay (lost 0–2), v E. Germany (won 1–0), v Finland (won 5–0) 1 goal, v Turkey (won 8–0) 2 goals, v N. Ireland (won 1–0), v Romania (1–1), v Turkey (won 5–0)
1986 v Israel (won 2–1)

AFTER MAKING his League debut for Nottingham Forest against Aston Villa in April 1974, Tony Woodcock was given little opportunity in the first team, and in 1976 had loan spells at Lincoln City and Doncaster Rovers. In November of that year Brian Clough called him into the first team for the Anglo-Scottish Cup match against Ayr United. He scored one of the goals in Forest's 2–0 second-leg win and went on to become an important member of the Reds' promotion squad, scoring 11 goals in 30 games. He proved the perfect foil to Peter Withe in 1977/78 when Forest won the League Championship, both strikers scoring 19 goals. This led to him winning the first of his 42 caps when he played in the 1–0 win over Northern Ireland. Following Withe's departure, Woodcock linked well with Garry Birtles and continued scoring goals, including a hat-trick in a 3–1 win over Middlesbrough at Ayresome Park in September 1979. Shortly afterwards he was transferred to German club Cologne, where he spent three successful seasons before returning home to play for Arsenal.

As lethal as any striker in the country on his day – he was Arsenal's leading scorer in each of his four seasons at Highbury – Woodcock also created a number of goalscoring opportunities for his team-mates. His best performance for Arsenal was in the game against Aston Villa in October 1983, when he scored five times. In July 1986 he returned to Germany to resume his career with Cologne. He later spent a season with Fortuna Dusseldorf, then managed VFV Leipzig, before making Germany his adopted home.

Viv ANDERSON

Position	Right-back
Born	Vivian Alexander Anderson, Nottingham, 29 August 1956
Height	5ft 11in
Weight	10st 4lb
Clubs	Nottingham Forest, Arsenal, Manchester United, Sheffield Wednesday, Barnsley, Middlesbrough
England Caps	30 Goals 2

1978 v Czechoslovakia (won 1–0)
1979 v Sweden (0–0), v Bulgaria (won 2–0)
1980 v Spain (won 2–1), v Norway (won 4–0)
1981 v Romania (0–0), v Wales (0–0), v Scotland (lost 0–1)
1982 v N. Ireland (won 4–0), v Iceland (1–1)
1984 v N. Ireland (won 1–0), v Turkey (won 8–0) 1 goal
1985 v N. Ireland (won 1–0), v Eire (won 2–1), v Romania (0–0), v Finland (1–1), v Scotland (lost 0–1), v Mexico (lost 0–1), v United States (won 5–0)
1986 v Soviet Union (won 1–0), v Mexico (won 3–0), v Sweden (lost 0–1), v N. Ireland (won 3–0), v Yugoslavia (won 2–0) 1 goal
1987 v Spain (won 4–2), v Turkey (won 2–0), v N. Ireland (won 2–0), v W. Germany (lost 1–3)
1988 v Hungary (0–0), v Colombia (1–1)

THE FIRST black footballer to play for England, Viv Anderson began his career with his home-town club, Nottingham Forest. Though he made his League debut for the Reds against Sheffield Wednesday at Hillsborough in September 1974, it wasn't until 1976/77 that he established himself as a first-team regular. Nicknamed 'Spider' because of his long legs, he made his England debut against Czechoslovakia in 1978, winning the last of his 30 caps some ten years later.

Viv Anderson playing for Nottingham Forest.
(Lancashire Evening Post)

A most popular player at the City ground, Anderson made 430 League and Cup appearances for Forest, winning a League Championship medal and two League Cup winners' medals, as well as being a member of two European Cup-winning sides. He remained the club's regular right-back until the end of the 1983/84 season, when he was transferred to Arsenal for £250,000.

In 1987, after appearing in 150 games for the Gunners, he moved to Manchester United, again for £250,000, the fee being fixed by an independent tribunal. Plagued by injuries during his time at Old Trafford, he appeared in 69 games before being given a free transfer and joining Sheffield Wednesday. On leaving Hillsborough, he had a brief spell with Barnsley before joining Middlesbrough, where he was Bryan Robson's assistant manager for seven seasons.

Kenny SANSOM

Position	Left-back
Born	Kenneth Graham Sansom, Camberwell, 26 September 1958
Height	5ft 6in
Weight	11st 8lb
Clubs	Crystal Palace, Arsenal, Newcastle United, Queen's Park Rangers, Coventry City, Everton, Brentford, Watford
England Caps	86 Goals 1

1979 v Wales (0–0), v Bulgaria (won 2–0)

1980 v Eire (won 2–0), v Argentina (won 3–1), v Wales (lost 1–4), v N. Ireland (1–1), v Scotland (won 2–0), v Belgium (1–1), v Italy (lost 0–1), v Norway (won 4–0), v Romania (lost 1–2), v Switzerland (won 2–1)

1981 v Spain (lost 1–2), v Romania (0–0), v Brazil (lost 0–1), v Wales (0–0), v Scotland (lost 0–1), v Switzerland (lost 1–2)

1982 v N. Ireland (won 4–0), v Wales (won 1–0), v Holland (won 2–0), v Scotland (won 1–0), v Finland (won 4–1), v France (won 3–1), v Czechoslovakia (won 2–0), v W. Germany (0–0), v Spain (0–0), v Denmark (2–2), v W. Germany (lost 1–2), v Greece (won 3–0), v Luxembourg (won 9–0)

1983 v Greece (0–0), v Hungary (won 2–0), v N. Ireland (0–0), v Scotland (won 2–0), v Denmark (lost 0–1), v Hungary (won 3–0), v Luxembourg (won 4–0)

1984 v France (lost 0–2), v Scotland (1–1), v Soviet Union (lost 0–2), v Brazil (won 2–0), v Uruguay (lost 0–2), v Chile (0–0), v E. Germany (won 1–0), v Finland (won 5–0) 1 goal, v Turkey (won 8–0)

1985 v N. Ireland (won 1–0), v Eire (won 2–1), v Romania (0–0), v Finland (1–1), v Scotland (lost 0–1), v Italy (lost 1–2), v Mexico (lost 0–1), v W. Germany (won 3–0), v United States (won 5–0), v Romania (1–1), v Turkey (won 5–0), v N. Ireland (0–0)

1986 v Egypt (won 4–0), v Israel (won 2–1), v Soviet Union (won 1–0), v Scotland (won 2–1), v Mexico (won 3–0), v Canada (won 1–0), v Portugal (lost 0–1), v Morocco (0–0), v Poland (won 3–0), v Paraguay (won 3–0), v Argentina (lost 1–2), v Sweden (lost 0–1),

Kenny Sansom is chased by a Moroccan defender during the World Cup Group F match at Monterrey, Mexico on 6 June 1986. The match ended as a 0–0 draw. (Getty Images)

v N. Ireland (won 3–0), v Yugoslavia (won 2–0)

1987 v Spain (won 4–2), v N. Ireland (won 2–0), v Turkey (0–0), v W. Germany (lost 1–3),
v Turkey (won 8–0), v Yugoslavia (won 4–1)

1988 v Holland (2–2), v Scotland (won 1–0), v Colombia (1–1), v Switzerland (won 1–0),
v Eire (lost 0–1), v Holland (lost 1–3), v Soviet Union (lost 1–3)

THE MOST-CAPPED full-back in England's history, Kenny Sansom began his long and illustrious career with Crystal Palace, signing professional forms in December 1975 and over the course of the next five years playing in nearly 200 first-team games for the club, helping them win the Second Division Championship in 1978/79. The following season he started a remarkable record, when he was voted for the first of his eight consecutive left-back Division One PFA awards, a sequence that no other top-flight outfield player has come remotely close to emulating. He was regarded as the best left-back in the country when Arsenal paid £1.25 million for his services in August 1980, and in his eight seasons at Highbury he became the club's most-capped player with 77 call-ups. He also captained Arsenal in a League Cup Final against Liverpool in 1987.

A player who showed great consistency, being ever-present in his first two seasons and missing just five League games over the next campaign, he had appeared in 394 games for the Gunners when, after being replaced by Nigel Winterburn, he joined Newcastle United.

However, his stay on Tyneside was brief and in June 1989 he returned to London to play for Queen's Park Rangers. He played for Coventry City before joining Watford as player-coach, after short spells with Everton and Brentford. He later returned to Vicarage Road as the club's assistant manager.

Laurie CUNNINGHAM

Position	Winger
Born	Lawrence Paul Cunningham, Archway, 8 March 1956
Died	Madrid, 15 July 1989
Height	5ft 8in
Weight	10st 13lb
Clubs	Leyton Orient, West Bromwich Albion, Real Madrid, Olympique Marseille, RSC Charleroi, Real Betis, Manchester United, Leicester City, Wimbledon
England Caps	6
	1979 v Wales (0–0), v Sweden (0–0), v Austria (lost 3–4)
	1980 v Eire (won 2–0), v Spain (won 2–0), v Romania (lost 1–2)

THOUGH HE NEVER reproduced his club form at international level, Laurie Cunningham did go on to win six full caps, after becoming the first black player to be capped at any level when he represented the England Under-21s.

Fast, skilful and confident, Cunningham broke into League football with Leyton Orient before West Bromwich Albion manager Johnny Giles brought him to the Hawthorns in March 1977 in a £110,000 deal that saw both Joe Mayo and Alan

Glover go in the opposite direction. His skill almost earned the Baggies a place in the UEFA Cup, Cunningham scoring six goals in 13 appearances. In 1977/78 he helped take Albion to the FA Cup semi-finals and the following season they finished third in the First Division, their highest placing for over 25 years. Though he only spent two years at the Hawthorns, he was one of the best wingers in the country during that time.

In June 1979 Cunningham took advantage of the new freedom of contract laws and joined Real Madrid in a £995,000 deal. Though he had injury problems, he helped them win the Spanish League Championship in his first season with them. He spent eight years on the continent, playing for Olympique Marseille, RSC Charleroi and Real Betis, before returning to England to play for Manchester United. He later had spells with Leicester City and Wimbledon, with whom he won an FA Cup winners' medal as a non-playing substitute. He had just returned to Spain to play for Rayo Vallecano when he was tragically killed in a car accident near Madrid.

Kevin REEVES

Position	Forward
Born	Kevin Philip Reeves, Burley, 20 October 1957
Height	5ft 10in
Weight	11st 4lb
Clubs	Bournemouth, Norwich City, Manchester City, Burnley
England Caps	2
	1979 v Bulgaria (won 2–0)
	1980 v N. Ireland (1–1)

KEVIN REEVES was Bournemouth's top scorer in his first season of League football in 1975/76, before leaving Dean Court in January 1977 to play for Norwich City. The Canaries were managed by John Bond, his former boss at Bournemouth, and it was under him that Reeves' career at the top level blossomed. After winning a number of England Under-21 caps, he pulled on a full England shirt for the first time against Bulgaria in the European Championships at Wembley in November 1979.

In March 1980 Reeves moved to Manchester City in exchange for £1 million as Malcolm Allison desperately tried to revive the Maine Road club's flagging fortunes. It didn't work, and after Allison's dismissal in came new manager John Bond! Reeves again thrived under his mentor, winning a second England cap and top-scoring in each of his first two full seasons. He also netted from the penalty spot for City in the 1981 FA Cup Final replay against Spurs, the North London club edging home by the odd goal in five in a thrilling contest.

Predictably, Reeves followed Bond when the latter took over at Burnley, but, sadly, he had to retire at the age of 26 after a spate of injuries. After coaching stints at Burnley and Birmingham City, he teamed up with Brian Flynn at Wrexham as the Robins' assistant manager. The pair of them are now in similar capacities with Swansea City.

Glenn HODDLE

Position   Midfielder
Born   Glenn Hoddle, Hayes, 27 October 1957
Height   6ft 0in
Weight   11st 6lb
Clubs   Tottenham Hotspur, AS Monaco, Swindon Town, Chelsea
England Caps   53   Goals   8

Glenn Hoddle. (David Cannon/Getty Images)

1979 v Bulgaria (won 2–0) 1 goal
1980 v Wales (lost 1–4), v Australia (won 2–1) 1 goal, v Spain (won 2–1)
1981 v Spain (lost 1–2) 1 goal, v Wales (0–0), v Scotland (lost 0–1), v Norway (lost 1–2),
    v N. Ireland (won 4–0) 1 goal
1982 v Wales (won 1–0), v Iceland (1–1), v Czechoslovakia (won 2–0), v Kuwait (won 1–0),
    v Luxembourg (won 9–0) 1 goal, v N. Ireland (0–0)
1983 v Scotland (won 2–0), v Hungary (won 3–0) 1 goal, v Luxembourg (won 4–0)
1984 v France   (lost 0–2)
1985 v Eire (won 2–1), v Scotland (lost 0–1), v Italy (lost 1–2), v Mexico (lost 0–1),
    v W. Germany (won 3–0), v United States (won 5–0), v Romania (1–1) 1 goal, v Turkey
    (won 5–0), v N. Ireland (0–0)
1986 v Israel (won 2–1), v Soviet Union (won 1–0), v Scotland (won 2–1) 1 goal, v Mexico
    (won 3–0), v Canada (won 1–0), v Portugal (lost 0–1), v Morocco (0–0), v Poland (won
    3–0), v Paraguay (won 3–0), v Argentina (lost 1–2), v Sweden (lost 0–1), v N. Ireland
    (won 3–0), v Yugoslavia (won 2–0)
1987 v Spain (won 4–2), v Turkey (0–0), v Scotland (0–0), v W. Germany (lost 1–3),
    v Turkey (won 8–0), v Yugoslavia (won 4–1)
1988 v Holland (2–2), v Hungary (0–0), v Colombia (1–1), v Eire (lost 0–1), v Holland (lost
    1–3), v Soviet Union (lost 1–3)

GLEN HODDLE was one of the most gifted footballers ever to have played for Tottenham Hotspur. His first full season in the White Hart Lane side was marred by relegation, but he soon helped them back into the top flight. Having won his first England Under-21 cap against Wales in December 1976, he won seven more and played twice for the England 'B' team before marking his full international debut with a goal against Bulgaria. In 1979/80 he netted 22 goals for Spurs, and at the end of the season he was named as the PFA Young Player of the Year. He won FA Cup winners' medals in 1981 (when his free-kick resulted in an equalizer) and 1982 (when he scored in both games), and played in the losing team of 1987.

In the summer of 1987 Hoddle signed for French League club AS Monaco, helping them to the French title in 1987/88, when he was voted the best foreign player in French football. Unfortunately, he was subsequently troubled by persistent knee injuries, which all but ended his career. In December 1990 he bought up his contract and returned to England to sign for Chelsea on a non-contract basis. Without playing a game, he left in March 1991 to embark on a career in management.

Succeeding Ossie Ardiles at Swindon Town, he took the club to promotion in 1993 via the play-offs, but then left the County Ground to manage Chelsea. He took them to the FA Cup Final in 1994, where they lost 4–0 to Manchester United, before succeeding Terry Venables as manager of England. After 30 months in charge of the national team, his contract was terminated by the FA. He then took charge of Southampton, before returning to his beloved White Hart Lane in the hope of bringing success to his former club. Sadly for Hoddle, the expected success did not come, and he was dismissed in September 2003 following a disappointing start to the season.

1980–89

Fighting the Hand
of God

Ron Greenwood guided the national team to the 1980 European Championships, but crowd violence and a disappointing 1–1 draw against Belgium marred England's return to the world stage in their first game. The ensuing 1–0 defeat to Italy put them out of the tournament, but as a saving grace England beat Spain 2–1 in their remaining group game.

In 1981 England overcame a shock World Cup qualifying defeat against Switzerland to reach the 1982 Finals in Spain. Though England had lost the services of Brooking and Keegan, they started well with a 3–1 win over France, Bryan Robson scoring the fastest-ever World Cup goal after 27 seconds. England beat Czechoslovakia 2–0 in their next game to secure their second-phase place, and a single Trevor Francis goal beat Kuwait in the final group game to give England maximum points. Against West Germany and Spain in the second phase, England disappointed with two goalless draws.

Greenwood left as England manager, to be succeeded by Bobby Robson. Though Robson failed in his first task of qualifying for the 1984 European Championships, he did take England to the 1986 World Cup Finals in Mexico. On the way his team inflicted a 2–0 defeat on Brazil at their

Maracana Stadium, with Watford's outstanding young winger, John Barnes, scoring a magnificent individual goal.

England started badly in Mexico, losing 1–0 to Portugal, and, to make matters worse, in the next game, against Morocco, captain Bryan Robson dislocated his suspect shoulder and Ray Wilkins was sent off. However, Lineker netted a hat-trick against Poland to take England through to the knockout stage, where they beat Paraguay 3–0. Argentina beckoned in the quarter-finals. Two goals from Diego Maradona put England out: the first was scored with the help of the now infamous 'hand of God'; the second was probably the greatest ever seen on the world stage.

This England side then flattered to deceive, qualifying with ease for the 1988 European Championships but losing all three games they played in the finals in Germany – the Republic of Ireland, Holland and the Soviet Union all beat Bobby Robson's side. The Republic's 1–0 win was bemoaned by the press (at least partly because of the presence of Jack Charlton as manager), but it should be pointed out that the other two sides were the eventual finalists.

Bryan ROBSON

Position	Midfielder
Born	Bryan Robson, Chester-le-Street, 11 January 1957
Height	5ft 11in
Weight	11st 12lb
Clubs	West Bromwich Albion, Manchester United, Middlesbrough
England Caps	90 Goals 26

1980 v Eire (won 2–0), v Australia (won 2–1), v Norway (won 4–0), v Romania (lost 1–2), v Switzerland (won 2–1)

1981 v Spain (lost 1–2), v Romania (0–0), v Brazil (lost 0–1), v Wales (0–0), v Scotland (lost 0–1), v Switzerland (lost 1–2), v Hungary (won 3–1), v Norway (lost 1–2) 1 goal, v Hungary (won 1–0)

1982 v N. Ireland (won 4–0) 1 goal, v Wales (won 1–0), v Holland (won 2–0), v Scotland (won 1–0), v Finland (won 4–1) 2 goals, v France (won 3–1) 2 goals, v Czechoslovakia (won 2–0), v W. Germany (0–0), v Spain (0–0), v Denmark (2–2), v Greece (won 3–0), v Luxembourg (won 9–0)

1983 v Scotland (won 1–0) 1 goal, v Hungary (won 3–0), v Luxembourg (won 4–0) 2 goals

1984 v France (lost 0–2), v N. Ireland (won 1–0), v Scotland (2–2), v Soviet Union (lost 0–2), v Brazil (won 2–0), v Uruguay (lost 0–2), v Chile (0–0)

1985 v E. Germany (won 1–0) 1 goal, v Finland (won 5–0) 1 goal, v Turkey (won 8–0) 3 goals, v Eire (won 2–1), v Romania (0–0), v Finland (1–1), v Scotland (lost 0–1), v Mexico (lost 0–1), v Italy (lost 1–2), v W. Germany (won 3–0) 1 goal, v United States (won 5–0)

1986 v Romania (1–1), v Turkey (won 5–0) 1 goal, v Israel (won 2–1) 2 goals, v Mexico (won 3–0), v Portugal (lost 0–1), v Morocco (0–0)

1987 v N. Ireland (won 3–0), v Spain (won 4–2), v N. Ireland (won 2–0) 1 goal, v Turkey (0–0), v Brazil (1–1), v Scotland (0–0)

1988 v Turkey (won 8–0) 1 goal, v Yugoslavia (won 4–1) 1 goal, v Holland (2–2), v Hungary (0–0), v Scotland (won 1–0), v Colombia (1–1), v Switzerland (won 1–0), v Eire (lost 0–1), v Holland (lost 1–3) 1 goal, v Soviet Union (lost 1–3)

1989 v Scotland (won 1–0), v Sweden (0–0), v Saudi Arabia (1–1), v Greece (won 2–1) 1 goal, v Albania (won 2–0) 1 goal, v Albania (won 5–0), v Chile (0–0), v Scotland (won 2–0), v Poland (won 3–0), v Denmark (1–1)

1990 v Poland (0–0), v Italy (0–0), v Yugoslavia (won 2–1) 2 goals, v Czechoslovakia (won 4–2), v Uruguay (lost 1–2), v Tunisia (1–1), v Eire (1–1), v Holland (0–0)

1991 v Cameroon (won 2–0), v Eire (1–1)

1992 v Turkey (won 1–0)

INITIALLY a back-four player, Bryan Robson developed the attacking side of his game to such an extent that his powerful surges from midfield into the penalty area became his trademark. His midfield brilliance earned him a place in England's 1982 World Cup squad, and he scored his country's first goal in the opening game against France after only 27 seconds. Capped 90 times in all, Robson took into the international game all the physical aggression needed to withstand the pressures of the English Football League, yet he also had a natural class that would impress in any of the World XIs of the past.

Bryan Robson in action during a friendly match against Chile in Santiago, June 1984. The game was a goalless draw. (David Cannon/Getty Images)

Robson began his career with West Bromwich Albion, where his skills were best expressed in midfield as he provided the ideal service for Regis and Cunningham. He suffered a major setback during the course of the 1976/77 season when he broke his leg no fewer than three times, but he doggedly fought back, and when Albion boss Ron Atkinson took charge at Manchester United he returned to the Hawthorns and broke the existing transfer record by paying £1.5 million to take Robson to Old Trafford.

It is perhaps as captain that Robson made his greatest impression, both for Manchester United and England. He led United to FA Cup Final victories, scoring two goals in their 1983 4–0 win over Brighton. In 1991 he led United to victory over Barcelona in the European Cup Winners' Cup Final in Rotterdam, and he went on to score a total of 100 goals in 465 games for the Red Devils before being appointed player-manager of Middlesbrough in May 1994.

Robson steered Boro into the Premiership as First Division champions in his first season at the club, and though they were relegated the next season they managed to reach both FA and League Cup finals, only to lose to Chelsea and Leicester City respectively. In 1997/98 Robson again inspired Boro to promotion and to another League Cup Final, but he parted company with the club in 2001.

Garry BIRTLES

Position	Forward
Born	Garry Birtles, Nottingham, 27 July 1956
Height	5ft 11in
Weight	10st 12lb
Clubs	Nottingham Forest, Manchester United, Notts County, Grimsby Town
England Caps	3
	1980 v Argentina (won 3–1), v Italy (lost 0–1), v Romania (lost 1–2)

A CARPET-FITTER by trade, Garry Birtles joined Nottingham Forest from Long Eaton in December 1976. Though he made his debut in a 2–0 win over Hull City in March 1977, he didn't play again until the club were in the First Division. Replacing Peter Withe in that 1978/79 season, he ended the campaign as the club's top scorer with 26 League and Cup goals. He won the first of three England caps in May 1980 and played in the European Championships later that summer.

At the beginning of the following season Birtles signed for Manchester United for a fee of £1.25 million, but the move was not a success and after just 64 first-team appearances he was back at the City Ground for a cut-price fee of £250,000. Hampered by injuries, it wasn't until 1986/87 that he again emerged as a goalscorer, linking well with Nigel Clough to score 15 goals in 33 games. Most Forest fans were surprised at the end of the season when he was given a free transfer and joined Notts County. He later played for Grimsby Town, starring in a back-four role for the Mariners.

Alan DEVONSHIRE

Position	Midfielder
Born	Alan Ernest Devonshire, Park Royal, 13 April 1956
Height	5ft 11in
Weight	11st 0lb
Clubs	West Ham United, Watford
England Caps	8
	1980 v N. Ireland (1–1), v Australia (won 2–1)
	1982 v Holland (won 2–0), v Iceland (1–1), v W. Germany (lost 1–2)
	1983 v Wales (won 2–1), v Greece (0–0), v Luxembourg (won 4–0)

ALAN DEVONSHIRE, capped eight times by England, had the confidence to carry the ball, his seemingly frail physique withstanding a fair amount of punishment. He joined West Ham from Isthmian League club Southall in October 1976 and established himself in the Hammers side soon after signing professional forms. One of the most skilful players in the club's history, he enjoyed an almost telepathic understanding with fellow midfield player Trevor Brooking. He played an outstanding part in the Hammers' FA Cup success of 1980, scoring a brilliant individual goal in the semi-final win over Everton at Elland Road and providing the cross from which Brooking headed the winning goal against Arsenal at Wembley.

In a third-round FA Cup tie against Wigan Athletic in January 1984, Devonshire snapped three ligaments in his right knee and, with the exception of a couple of FA Cup matches against Wimbledon, was out of action for 19 months, including missing the entire 1984/85 season. In 1986/87 he was back to his best, helping the club finish third in the First Division. Sadly, in the opening game of the following season he snapped the Achilles' tendon and didn't play again until midway through the 1988/89 campaign. He went on to appear in 446 games for the Hammers, after which the classy midfielder, who had given the Upton Park club 15 years' service, moved to Watford, where he ended his career.

Russell OSMAN

Position	Centre-back
Born	Russell Charles Osman, Repton, 14 February 1959
Height	6ft 0in
Weight	11st 10lb
Clubs	Ipswich Town, Leicester City, Southampton, Bristol City, Brighton and Hove Albion, Cardiff City
England Caps	11
	1980 v Australia (won 2–1)
	1981 v Spain (lost 1–2), v Romania (0–0), v Switzerland (lost 1–2), v Norway (lost 1–2)
	1982 v Iceland (1–1), v Denmark (2–2)
	1983 v Australia (0–0), v Australia (won 1–0), v Australia (1–1), v Denmark (lost 0–1)

RUSSELL OSMAN started out with Ipswich Town, where, under the management of Bobby Robson, he formed an excellent central defensive partnership with Terry Butcher. In 1975 he won an FA Youth Cup winner's medal, though he had to wait until September 1977 before making his first-team debut at Chelsea. In May 1980 he won the first of 11 full caps for England when he played against Australia.

Osman twice went close to a League Championship medal, the club finishing runners-up in the First Division in 1980/81 and 1981/82. He also helped them win the UEFA Cup in 1981 when they beat AZ67 Alkmaar 5–4 on aggregate. Osman was ever-present in seasons 1979/80 and 1980/81, and had played in 384 first-team games when he left Portman Road in the summer of 1985 to join Leicester City for a fee of £240,000. He made 108 appearances for the Foxes before signing for Southampton for £325,000 in June 1988.

Osman's first managerial role was with Bristol City, where he was initially caretaker-manager, but in 1994 he lost his job. He became manager of Cardiff City in November 1996 but midway through the following season he was replaced by Frank Burrows. He then returned to Ashton Gate as Bristol City's coach.

Terry BUTCHER

Position	Centre-back
Born	Terence Ian Butcher, Singapore, 28 December 1958
Height	6ft 4in
Weight	14st 5lb
Clubs	Ipswich Town, Glasgow Rangers, Coventry City, Sunderland
England Caps	77 Goals 3

1980 v Australia (won 2–1)

1981 v Spain (lost 1–2)

1982 v Wales (won 1–0), v Scotland (won 1–0), v France (won 3–1), v Czechoslovakia (won 2–0), v W. Germany (0–0), v Spain (0–0)

1983 v Denmark (2–2), v W. Germany (lost 1–2), v Luxembourg (won 9–0), v Wales (won 2–1) 1 goal, v Greece (0–0), v Hungary (won 2–0), v N. Ireland (0–0), v Scotland (won 2–0), v Australia (0–0), v Australia (won 1–0), v Australia (1–1)

1984 v Denmark (lost 0–1), v Finland (won 5–0), v Luxembourg (won 4–0) 1 goal, v France (lost 0–2), v N. Ireland (won 1–0)

1985 v E. Germany (won 1–0), v Finland (won 5–0), v Turkey (won 8–0), v N. Ireland (won 1–0), v Eire (won 2–1), v Romania (0–0), v Finland (1–1), v Scotland (lost 0–1), v Italy (lost 1–2), v W. Germany (won 3–0), v United States (won 5–0)

1986 v Israel (won 2–1), v Soviet Union (won 1–0), v Scotland (won 2–1) 1 goal, v Mexico (won 3–0), v Canada (won 1–0), v Portugal (lost 0–1), v Morocco (0–0), v Poland (won 3–0), v Paraguay (won 3–0), v Argentina (lost 1–2)

1987 v Sweden (lost 0–1), v N. Ireland (won 3–0), v Yugoslavia (won 2–0), v Spain (won 4–2), v N. Ireland (won 2–0), v Brazil (1–1), v Scotland (0–0)

1988 v Turkey (won 8–0), v Yugoslavia (won 4–1)

1989 v Denmark (won 1–0), v Sweden (0–0), v Greece (won 2–1), v Albania (won 2–0), v Albania (won 5–0), v Chile (0–0), v Scotland (won 2–0), v Poland (won 3–0), v Denmark (1–1)

Terry Butcher during the Mexico World Cup match against Portugal in Monterrey, 3 June 1986. Portugal won 1–0. (David Cannon/Getty Images)

1990 v Sweden (0–0), v Poland (0–0), v Italy (0–0), v Yugoslavia (won 2–1), v Brazil (won 1–0), v Czechoslovakia (won 4–2), v Denmark (won 1–0), v Uruguay (lost 1–2), v Tunisia (1–1), v Eire (1–1), v Holland (0–0), v Belgium (won 1–0), v Cameroon (won 3–2), v W. Germany (1–1 aet, W. Germany won 4–3 on penalties)

TERRY BUTCHER, who won 77 international caps, played in three World Cup Finals, including skippering England to the semi-finals against West Germany in 1990.

Born in Singapore, where his father was in the Royal Navy, Butcher was a competitive and commanding central defender. He made his Ipswich Town debut against Everton in April 1978, establishing himself as a first-team regular the following season. In 1980, he made his international debut against Australia, and later that season he helped Ipswich to a UEFA Cup Final victory over AZ67 Alkmaar and to runners-up spot in the First Division. He continued to be the mainstay of the Ipswich defence, and when Mick Mills left to join Southampton he became captain; he was the club's Player of the Year in 1984/85. He went on to make 344 first-team appearances before being transferred to Glasgow Rangers for a fee of £725,000.

At Ibrox Butcher won three Scottish Premier League Championship medals, three Skol Cup winners' medals and a Scottish Cup runners-up medal. After falling out with Rangers manager Graeme Souness, he joined Coventry City as player-manager. Forced to sack his one-time Ipswich Town colleague Mick Mills, he too lost his job when he refused to negotiate a new 'manager only' contract. Following the sacking of Malcolm Crosbie, Butcher became player-manager of Sunderland in February 1993 but was dismissed after the club just avoided relegation to the Second Division. After a spell as a Sky TV commentator, Butcher is now back in the game as manager of Motherwell.

Alan SUNDERLAND

Position	Forward
Born	Alan Sunderland, Mexborough, 1 July 1953
Height	5ft 9in
Weight	11st 7lb
Clubs	Wolverhampton Wanderers, Arsenal, Ipswich Town
England Caps	1
	1980 v Australia (won 2–1)

DURING HIS SEVEN SEASONS with Wolverhampton Wanderers Sunderland appeared in a number of different positions. By the end of 1971/72, his first season with the club, he had helped them reach the UEFA Cup Final, where they lost to Tottenham Hotspur. A member of the Wolves side that won the 1974 League Cup Final, he top-scored for the Molineux club during their 1976/77 Second Division Championship winning season with 16 goals in 41 games. Then, having scored 35 goals in 198 games for Wolves, he joined Arsenal for £220,000 in November 1977.

At the end of his first season with the Gunners, Sunderland played in the FA Cup Final against Ipswich, and in 1978/79 he scored six goals in the club's victorious FA Cup campaign, including the winner in the final against Manchester United. Also collecting a

UEFA Cup winners' medal that season, he went on to score 92 goals in 281 first-team outings for the Gunners before leaving to see out his first-class career with Ipswich Town. Sunderland appeared in his only international match against Australia at Sydney in 1980 and was substituted by Brighton's Peter Ward.

David ARMSTRONG

Position	Midfielder
Born	David Armstrong, Durham, 26 December 1954
Height	5ft 8in
Weight	11st 3lb
Clubs	Middlesbrough, Southampton, Bournemouth
England Caps	3
	1980 v Australia (won 2–1)
	1982 v W. Germany (lost 1–2)
	1984 v Wales (lost 0–1)

AFTER BECOMING a regular in the Middlesbrough side midway through the 1972/73 season, David Armstrong went on to be ever-present in seven seasons, appearing in 305 consecutive League games – still a club record. He won a Second Division Championship medal in 1973/74 and towards the end of his Boro career was awarded a testimonial game against that Championship-winning side. His best season in terms of goals scored was 1979/80, when he topped the club's scoring charts with 14. Having already won England Under-23 and 'B' international honours, he gained his first full cap against Australia in May 1980.

Armstrong had scored 73 goals in 416 games for Boro when he was transferred to Southampton in the summer of 1981 for a record £600,000. He quickly fitted into the Saints' midfield, and in the face of some ultra-defensive football netted 15 goals in his first season at the Dell. Although naturally a left-sided player, his reading of the game allowed him to play in a variety of positions. He was an obvious choice as club captain and his performances led to him winning a further two caps. He had appeared in 262 games for the south coast club when a contractual dispute led to him joining Bournemouth.

Armstrong later became general manager of Waterlooville, having spent a number of years as an officer for Football in the Community, latterly with Reading.

Peter WARD

Position	Forward
Born	Peter David Ward, Derby, 27 July 1955
Height	5ft 7in
Weight	10st 3lb
Clubs	Brighton and Hove Albion, Nottingham Forest
England Caps	1
	1980 v Australia (won 2–1)

SIGNED FROM non-League Burton Albion, Peter Ward, who won a full England cap with a brief appearance as a substitute against Australia, scored six goals in the last eight games of the 1975/76 season as Brighton just missed out on promotion from the Third Division. In 1976/77, when Albion finished runners-up to Mansfield Town and thus secured promotion to the Second Division, Ward established a new club scoring record with 32 League goals. Included in this total were four goals in the 7–0 home win over Walsall. In fact, including Cup games, Ward's total was 36, eclipsing both Hugh Vallance and Arthur Attwood. He was the leading scorer in the entire Football League and, not surprisingly, was named the club's Player of the Season. Ward led the way again over the next couple of seasons, helping the club win promotion to the First Division in 1978/79 as runners-up to Crystal Palace. After struggling with injuries during the latter stages of that season, he was back to full fitness for the club's first-ever season of top-flight football, leading the way with 18 goals, including a hat-trick in a 3–1 defeat of Wolves.

In October 1980, Ward was transferred to Nottingham Forest, but he never really settled at the City Ground and two years later he rejoined the Seagulls on loan, taking his tally of goals to 95 in 227 appearances before hanging up his boots.

Eric GATES

Position	Forward
Born	Eric Lazenby Gates, Ferryhill, 28 June 1955
Height	5ft 6in
Weight	10st 4lb
Clubs	Ipswich Town, Sunderland, Carlisle United
England Caps	2
	1980 v Norway (won 4–0), v Romania (lost 1–2)

ALL OF ERIC GATES' football with Ipswich Town was played in the First Division, although it was 1977/78 before he established himself as a first-team regular, having made his League debut against Wolves in October 1973. In November 1979 Gates netted his first hat-trick for the Portman Road club in a 4–0 win over Manchester City, his strike the previous week against Southampton having been selected as *Match of the Day*'s 'Goal of the Month'. Gates continued to find the net over the next two seasons, Town finishing runners-up on both occasions. His form led to him winning two England caps but then injuries began to hamper his progress. He eventually returned to his goalscoring ways, ending the 1983/84 and 1984/85 seasons as the club's leading scorer. However, at the end of the latter season, having scored 96 goals in 384 first-team outings, he left Portman Road to join Sunderland.

At Roker Park, Gates scored 43 goals in 181 League games before leaving the Wearsiders to end his first-class career with Carlisle United.

Graham Rix of Arsenal. (Lancashire Evening Post)

Graham RIX

Position	Midfielder
Born	Graham Rix, Doncaster, 23 October 1957
Height	5ft 9in
Weight	11st 0lb
Clubs	Arsenal, Brentford, Caen, Le Havre, Dundee, Chelsea
England Caps	17
	1980 v Norway (won 4–0), v Romania (lost 1–2), v Switzerland (won 2–1)
	1981 v Brazil (lost 0–1), v Wales (0–0), v Scotland (lost 0–1)
	1982 v Holland (won 2–0), v Finland (won 4–1), v France (won 3–1), v Czechoslovakia (won 2–0), v Kuwait (won 1–0), v W. Germany (0–0), v Spain (0–0), v Denmark (2–2), v W. Germany (lost 1–2)
	1983 v Greece (0–0)
	1984 v N. Ireland (won 1–0)

WHEN HE WON the first of 17 full caps for England, against Norway during the course of the 1980/81 season, Graham Rix made club history by becoming Arsenal's first player to win caps at four different levels.

Rix, who was also a member of England's 1982 World Cup squad, replaced George Armstrong as Arsenal's left-sided midfield player midway through the 1977/78 season and came on as a substitute in that season's FA Cup Final against Ipswich Town. The following season, he and Liam Brady were the major influences behind the Gunners' successful campaign and it was Rix's excellent cross that was turned in by Alan Sunderland for Arsenal's winning goal in the final minute of the 1979 FA Cup Final against Manchester United. In 1980 he played in his third consecutive FA Cup Final as the Gunners went down to West Ham United. He was also the unfortunate Arsenal player who missed the final spot-kick in the penalty shoot-out against Valencia in that season's European Cup Winners' Cup Final.

Later appointed Arsenal captain, Rix was troubled by an Achilles tendon injury, which continued to flare up again subsequently. He went on loan to Brentford for a month before becoming player-coach at Chelsea. His career was a long and successful one but could perhaps have been even more notable had he not been compared to Liam Brady quite so often.

Alvin MARTIN

Position	Central defender
Born	Alvin Edward Martin, Bootle, 29 July 1958
Height	6ft 1in
Weight	13st 3lb
Clubs	West Ham United, Leyton Orient
England Caps	17
	1981 v Brazil (lost 0–1), v Scotland (lost 0–1), v Hungary (won 1–0)
	1982 v Greece (won 3–0), v Finland (won 4–1), v Luxembourg (won 9–0)

1983 v Wales (won 2–1), v Greece (0–0), v Hungary (won 2–0), v Hungary (won 3–0),
  v Luxembourg (won 4–0)
1984 v Wales (lost 0–1)
1985 v N. Ireland (won 1–0)
1986 v Israel (won 2–1), v Canada (won 1–0), v Paraguay (won 3–0), v Sweden (lost 0–1)

ALVIN MARTIN joined West Ham United as a schoolboy star after being turned down by his local club, Everton. A star of the Hammers' FA Youth Cup side of 1975 that lost to Ipswich Town in the final, he turned professional shortly afterwards but had to wait until March 1978 before making his first-team debut. He established himself at the heart of the West Ham defence midway through the following season and won his first major honour when the Hammers, a Second Division club, surprisingly beat Arsenal in the 1980 FA Cup Final. He helped West Ham win the Second Division Championship in 1980/81, when his displays led to him winning the first of 17 full caps for England. He appeared for England in the 1986 World Cup Finals in Mexico, having an outstanding game in the 3–0 defeat of Paraguay.

Taking over the club captaincy at Upton Park, Martin formed a formidable central defensive partnership with Tony Gale, and in 1985/86 the club finished third in the First Division, just four points behind champions Liverpool. During that season he scored a most unusual hat-trick in an 8–1 thrashing of Newcastle United, scoring against three different goalkeepers! Problems with his instep resulted in a number of operations, though he went on to play in 596 games before leaving to end his playing career with Leyton Orient. He later managed Sutherland United.

Peter WITHE

Position	Forward
Born	Peter Withe, Liverpool, 30 August 1951
Height	6ft 2in
Weight	12st 1lb
Clubs	Southport, Barrow, Wolverhampton Wanderers, Birmingham City, Nottingham Forest, Newcastle United, Aston Villa, Sheffield United, Huddersfield Town
England Caps	11 Goals 1
	1981 v Brazil (lost 0–1), v Wales (0–0), v Scotland (lost 0–1), v Norway (lost 1–2)
	1982 v Wales (won 1–0), v Iceland (1–1)
	1983 v Hungary (won 2–0) 1 goal, v N. Ireland (0–0), v Scotland (won 2–0), v Hungary (won 3–0)
	1984 v Turkey (won 8–0)

CAPPED 11 TIMES by England, the much-travelled Peter Withe played his early football with Southport before having a brief spell with Barrow. He then went abroad to play for Portland Timbers in the United States, and Port Elizabeth and Arcadia Shepherds in South Africa, before returning to these shores. He then made a few appearances for Wolves before joining Birmingham City in 1975. A year later, Withe joined Nottingham Forest, where he linked well with Tony Woodcock. After helping the club win promotion from the Second Division, he continued terrorizing defences

Peter Withe. (Lancashire Evening Post)

in the top flight, netting all four goals for Forest in a 4–0 defeat of Ipswich Town. On leaving the City Ground, the 'happy wanderer' played for Newcastle United before signing for Aston Villa.

It was at Villa Park that Peter Withe had the best years of his career, helping them win the League Championship in 1981 and the European Cup in 1982, when he scored the winner in the final against Hamburg.

Withe later played for Sheffield United and Birmingham City (again) before being appointed assistant manager of Huddersfield Town. He then managed Wimbledon before returning to Villa Park as the club's chief scout. Withe is currently coach of the Thailand national team.

Tony MORLEY

Position	Left-winger
Born	Anthony William Morley, Ormskirk, 26 August 1954
Height	5ft 8in
Weight	11st 9lb
Clubs	Preston North End, Burnley, Aston Villa, West Bromwich Albion, Birmingham City, Den Haag
England Caps	6
	1981 v Hungary (won 1–0)
	1982 v N. Ireland (won 4–0), v Wales (won 1–0), v Iceland (1–1), v Denmark (2–2), v Greece (won 3–0)

NEVER ON the losing side in his six international appearances, Tony Morley was both fast and comfortable on the ball. He also scored his fair share of spectacular goals. He began his career with Third Division Preston North End, where his wing displays brought him to the attention of the England Under-23 selectors. In February 1976 he left Deepdale to join Burnley, who were fighting at the time to stay in the First Division. It was a lost cause, however, and the Clarets were relegated.

Unable to create much of an impact during his stay at Turf Moor, Morley joined Aston Villa in the summer of 1979 for a fee of £200,000. He helped Villa win the League Championship in 1981, having enjoyed the best season of his career. He continued to perform with pace and style, and the following season scored four goals in the club's triumphant European campaign.

Following the emergence of Mark Walters, Morley left Villa Park to play for neighbours West Bromwich Albion before having a brief spell in Hong Kong. He returned to the Hawthorns before loan spells with Birmingham City and Burnley. Finally, he went abroad, helping Den Haag to runners-up spot in the Dutch Second Division and to the Netherlands Cup Final.

Steve FOSTER

Position	Central defender
Born	Stephen Brian Foster, Portsmouth, 24 September 1957
Height	6ft 0in
Weight	12st 8lb
Clubs	Portsmouth, Brighton and Hove Albion, Aston Villa, Luton Town, Oxford United
England Caps	3
	1982 v N. Ireland (won 4–0), v Holland (won 2–0), v Kuwait (won 1–0)

A PRODUCT OF the Portsmouth youth side, Steve Foster had arrived at Fratton Park as a centre-forward, but manager Ian St John suggested a switch of position and he soon established himself at the heart of the Pompey defence.

In the summer of 1979 he was transferred to Brighton, where his form led to him winning full international honours for England. He played in three games for England – all won and without a goal being conceded! He continued to turn in consistent performances for the Seagulls and led them to the 1983 FA Cup Final. Unfortunately he was suspended and missed the first match but he returned for the replay, which Albion lost 4–0 to Manchester United. In March 1984 he joined Aston Villa, but by the end of the year he had left Villa Park to sign for Luton Town.

Foster was the Hatters' first-choice centre-half for the next four years, winning a League Cup winners' medal in 1988 as Luton beat Arsenal 3–2 in the final. He then joined Oxford United before returning to the Goldstone Ground for a second spell in the summer of 1992. Sadly, his first-class career ended when knee ligament damage – which required surgery – didn't heal properly.

Cyrille REGIS

Position	Forward
Born	Cyrille Regis, Maripiasoula, French Guyana, 9 February 1958
Height	6ft 0in
Weight	13st 4lb
Clubs	West Bromwich Albion, Coventry City, Aston Villa, Wolverhampton Wanderers, Wycombe Wanderers, Chester City
England Caps	5
	1982 v N. Ireland (won 4–0), v Wales (won 1–0), v Iceland (1–1), v W. Germany (lost 1–2)
	1987 v Turkey (won 8–0)

WINNING THE FIFTH of his international caps five years after his previous appearance, Cyrille Regis was initially spotted playing for non-League Hayes by West Bromwich Albion's then chief scout, Ronnie Allen, who convinced the Baggies board that the young black forward was well worth £5,000. Six months later, with Allen now Albion's manager, Regis made a spectacular start to his career by scoring twice on his debut against Rotherham United and going on to score a number of sensational goals in that 1977/78 season. By the time Ron Atkinson took over the reins, Regis was part of an Albion side that went close to winning the League in 1979. Fast, skilful and powerfully built, he was Albion's leading scorer for three consecutive seasons.

After turning down a £750,000 bid from French side St Etienne, Albion surprisingly allowed Regis to join Coventry City in 1984. He had scored 140 goals in almost 400 games for Albion, going on to win an FA Cup winners' medal with the Sky Blues as they beat Tottenham Hotspur 3–2 in the 1987 FA Cup Final.

Regis later played for Aston Villa, Wolves, Wycombe Wanderers and Chester City before deciding to hang up his boots.

Steve PERRYMAN

Position	Midfielder/Defender
Born	Stephen John Perryman, Ealing, 21 December 1951
Height	5ft 8in
Weight	10st 10lb
Clubs	Tottenham Hotspur, Oxford United, Brentford
England Caps	1
	1982 v Iceland (1–1)
Honours	Footballer of the Year 1982

IN THE SEASON when he won his only full cap as a substitute against Iceland, Steve Perryman was voted the Football Writers' Association Player of the Year.

One of the most consistent and loyal players Spurs have ever had, Perryman holds the appearance record for the White Hart Lane club. He was already a first-team player when he played in Spurs' 1970 FA Youth Cup-winning side. Originally a midfield player, he dropped into the back four in 1977 and later played as a full-back. He played in over 1,000 first-team games in his 17 years with the club, winning more honours than any other player.

Perryman was awarded a testimonial in April 1979 and the MBE in the Queen's 1986 Birthday Honours List. A truly great professional and loyal club man, he finally left Spurs in March 1986 to join Oxford United. He later moved to Brentford as player-manager and led the Bees to the sixth round of the FA Cup and the Third Division play-offs in 1989. Surprisingly, he resigned in August 1990, but three months later took over as manager of Watford following the dismissal of former Spurs' team-mate Colin Lee. After steering the Hornets clear of relegation, he returned to White Hart Lane as assistant to Ossie Ardiles. He later followed the Argentinian to Japan, where he was his assistant at Shimizu-S-Pulse.

Paul GODDARD

Position	Forward
Born	Paul Goddard, Harlington, 12 October 1959
Height	5ft 9in
Weight	11st 5lb
Clubs	Queen's Park Rangers, West Ham United, Newcastle United, Derby County, Millwall, Ipswich Town
England Caps	1 Goals 1
	1982 v Iceland (1–1) 1 goal

ON 2 JUNE 1982, Paul Goddard made his full international debut for England, scoring in the 69th minute of a 1–1 draw with Iceland. In doing so, he became the first England player to score while playing less than a full match.

Goddard started his career with Queen's Park Rangers, where he first made an impact in 1979/80. Playing alongside Clive Allen, he scored 16 League goals, his form attracting the attention of a number of top clubs. On the basis of that form, West Ham United paid £800,000 for his services in the summer of 1980. He proved the perfect foil for David Cross, and in his first season at Upton Park he won a Second Division Championship medal and helped the Hammers reach the League Cup Final. Although he scored in the replay, West Ham were beaten 2–1 by Liverpool.

Following the arrival of Frank McAvennie, Goddard's first-team appearances became limited and in November 1986, after scoring 69 goals in 213 games, he joined Newcastle United. His family were soon homesick, however, so he was allowed to join Derby County. He quickly formed a good partnership with Dean Saunders, but 18 months later he was back in London as Millwall splashed out £800,000 for the 30-year-old striker. Two years later the Lions released him on a free transfer and he ended his career with Ipswich Town.

Ricky HILL

Position	Midfielder
Born	Ricky Anthony Hill, London, 5 March 1959
Height	5ft 11in
Weight	13st 0lb
Clubs	Luton Town, Le Havre, Leicester City
England Caps	3
	1982 v Denmark (2–2), v W. Germany (lost 1–2)
	1986 v Egypt (won 4–0)

RICKY HILL made a goalscoring debut for Luton Town when he was just 17, going on to be a first-team regular at Kenilworth Road for 12 seasons. Though not a prolific scorer, he reached double figures in 1982/83, while a season earlier he had helped the Hatters win the Second Division Championship – eight points ahead of rivals Watford – and won the first of his three international caps.

Hill was a member of the Luton side that reached the 1984/85 FA Cup semi-finals, but though he scored in the Villa Park encounter with Everton, the Toffees won 2–1. Despite injuries hampering his progress in 1987–88, he lined up to face Arsenal in that season's League Cup Final, a match the Hatters won 3–2. He had scored 65 goals in 507 games when he left Kenilworth Road to play for French club Le Havre, but after they had failed in their promotion bid, Hill was replaced by Cameroonian World Cup star Kana Biyik and returned to Football League action with Leicester City.

Hill spent just over a year at Filbert Street before playing in the NASL with Tampa Bay Rowdies. On his return he played non-League football for Hitchin Town and Chertsey Town before, in July 2000, taking over as manager of Luton Town. However, as the Hatters began to struggle, he was replaced by Joe Kinnear.

Luther BLISSETT

Position	Forward
Born	Luther Loide Blissett, Jamaica, 1 February 1958
Height	5ft 11in
Weight	11st 13lb
Clubs	Watford, AC Milan, Bournemouth, West Bromwich Albion, Bury, Mansfield Town
England Caps	14 Goals 3

1982 v W. Germany (lost 1–2), v Luxembourg (won 9–0) 3 goals
1983 v Wales (won 2–1), v Greece (0–0), v Hungary (won 2–0), v N. Ireland (0–0),
     v Scotland (won 2–0), v Australia (0–0), v Australia (1–1), v Denmark (lost 0–1),
     v Hungary (won 3–0)
1984 v Wales (lost 0–1), v Scotland (1–1), v Soviet Union (lost 0–2)

AN EXCITING and brave player, Luther Blissett netted a hat-trick on his second international appearance as England beat Luxembourg 9–0: they proved to be his only goals in 14 full appearances.

Blissett was playing football in the Brent Sunday League when Watford persuaded him to join them in the summer of 1975. Unsurpassed in popularity at Vicarage Road, he epitomized Graham Taylor's Watford with a combination of athleticism and attacking flair that helped the Hornets' rapid rise to the top flight. Although not always used as an outright striker, he set a string of goalscoring and appearance records both for Watford and among black players in English football.

In June 1983 Italian giants AC Milan paid £1 million for Blissett's services, but the following year he was back at Vicarage Road, the Hornets paying £550,000 to secure his services again – both incoming and outgoing transfer fees being club records. Four years later he was on the move again, this time to Bournemouth, but, another two years on he joined the Hornets for a third spell. Following a loan period with West Bromwich Albion, he had brief stints with Bury and Mansfield Town before entering non-League football with Southport. He later returned to his beloved Vicarage Road as the club's marketing assistant before becoming coach and then assistant manager.

Luther Blissett of Watford. (Lancashire Evening Post)

Sammy LEE

Position	Midfielder
Born	Samuel Lee, Liverpool, 7 February 1959
Height	5ft 5in
Weight	10st 11b
Clubs	Liverpool, Queen's Park Rangers, Osasuna, Southampton, Bolton Wanderers
England Caps	14 Goals 2
	1982 v Greece (won 3–0) 1 goal, v Luxembourg (won 9–0)
	1983 v Wales (won 2–1), v Greece (0–0), v Hungary (won 2–0), v Scotland (won 2–0), v Australia (1–1), v Denmark (lost 0–1), v Hungary (won 3–0) 1 goal, v Luxembourg (won 4–0)
	1984 v France (lost 0–2), v N. Ireland (won 1–0), v Wales (lost 0–1), v Chile (0–0)

THOUGH HIS STRIKE-RATE for Liverpool was disappointing, Sammy Lee, who won 14 full caps for England, scored on his debut against Greece from a powerfully hit free kick.

At first sight, Sammy Lee didn't appear to have the build of a footballer, but looks were deceptive, for he was as fast, resilient and determined as any man on the pitch. A driving force in the Liverpool team, he was forever urging the side forward with boyish enthusiasm, but he was just as ready to sprint back into defence. It was midway through the 1980/81 season that he finally displaced Jimmy Case on the right side of Liverpool's midfield, and he went on to become a fixture in the Reds' side that won three successive League Championships, two European Cups and four League Cups.

At the start of the 1984/85 season, Lee seemed set for many more campaigns at the top, but fitness problems and a loss of form sadly conspired to shatter the midfielder's confidence. In August 1986 he left Anfield to join Queen's Park Rangers, but failed to settle at Loftus Road and went to Spain to play for Osasuna. After performing creditably in the Spanish League, he returned to these shores to play for Southampton. Injuries prevented him from making much of an impression and he signed for his former team-mate Phil Neal, who was then manager of Bolton Wanderers. Again injuries hampered his progress and in 1992 he returned to Anfield as a member of the club's coaching staff – a position which he now holds with the senior England team.

Gary MABBUTT

Position	Central defender
Born	Gary Vincent Mabbutt, Bristol, 23 August 1961
Height	5ft 9in
Weight	10st 10lb
Clubs	Bristol Rovers, Tottenham Hotspur
England Caps	16 Goals 1
	1982 v W. Germany (lost 1–2)

Gary Mabbutt of Spurs. (Lancashire Evening Post)

1983 v Greece (won 3–0), v Luxembourg (won 9–0), v Wales (won 2–1), v Greece (0–0),
   v Hungary (won 2–0), v N. Ireland (0–0), v Scotland (won 2–0)
1984 v Hungary (won 3–0)
1987 v Yugoslavia (won 2–0) 1 goal, v N. Ireland (won 2–0), v Turkey (0–0)
1988 v W. Germany (1–1)
1992 v Turkey (won 1–0), v Poland (1–1), v Czechoslovakia (2–2)

CAPPED 16 TIMES over a nine-year period, Gary Mabbutt was one of a footballing family, his father Ray having turned out for Bristol Rovers and Newport County, and elder brother Kevin playing for Bristol Rovers and Crystal Palace. He followed in his father's footsteps and signed for Bristol Rovers, making his League debut while still an apprentice. During his four years at Eastville, he showed great character as well as great ability, occupying every outfield position despite suffering from diabetes.

In August 1982 Mabbutt signed for Tottenham Hotspur, making his first senior appearance against Liverpool in the FA Charity Shield. Going on to play in a variety of positions for both club and country, he led Spurs in the 1987 FA Cup Final, where, after putting his side 2–1 up, he deflected a Lloyd McGrath cross into his own goal. Four years later he ended with a winners' medal after leading Spurs to victory over Nottingham Forest. At one time he looked to be out of favour with the England management but his consistency and reliability saw him recalled to the national side during the early stages of the 1991/92 season. Despite breaking his leg and missing the entire 1996/97 season bar one game, he went on to play in 619 games for the North London club.

Mark CHAMBERLAIN

Position	Winger
Born	Mark Valentine Chamberlain, Stoke-on-Trent, 19 November 1961
Height	5ft 9in
Weight	10st 7lb
Clubs	Port Vale, Stoke City, Sheffield Wednesday, Portsmouth, Brighton and Hove Albion, Exeter City
England Caps	8 Goals 1
	1982 v Luxembourg (won 9–0) 1 goal
	1983 v Denmark (lost 0–1)
	1984 v Scotland (1–1), v Soviet Union (lost 0–2), v Brazil (won 2–0), v Uruguay (lost 0–2), v Chile (0–0), v Finland (won 5–0)

WINGER MARK CHAMBERLAIN, the younger brother of Neville, began his career with Port Vale, where, after establishing himself halfway through the 1980/81 season, he missed very few games. The following season his performances led to him being chosen for the PFA Fourth Division team, but during the early part of the 1982/83 season he was sold to neighbours and rivals Stoke City for £150,000. While at the Victoria ground, he won the first of eight full caps for England, scoring in a 9–0 win over Luxembourg at Wembley.

Chamberlain later moved to Sheffield Wednesday for twice the amount the Potters had paid for him but never really settled at Hillsborough, over half his appearances coming as a substitute. He then joined Portsmouth, where he was a most popular player, appearing in 188 games before joining Brighton and Hove Albion on a free transfer. He later ended his first-class career with Exeter City.

Derek STATHAM

Position	Left-back
Born	Derek James Statham, Wolverhampton, 24 March 1959
Height	5ft 6in
Weight	11st 2lb
Clubs	West Bromwich Albion, Southampton, Stoke City, Walsall
England Caps	3
	1983 v Wales (won 2–1), v Australia (0–0), v Australia (won 1–0)

PLAYING AT LEFT-BACK for West Bromwich Albion at the Victoria Ground against Stoke City in December 1976, Derek Statham made a wonderful start to his Football League career by scoring a brilliant solo goal past England keeper Peter Shilton. His all-action approach to the game, ability to outjump much taller opponents, and runs down the left flank made him one of the best backs in the League at this time. High-priced moves to both Liverpool and Glasgow Rangers, however, were called off because the Albion defender was injury prone. As a result, he made just three full international appearances, despite his ability, which warranted many more.

One of Albion's most consistent post-war players, Statham left the Hawthorns in August 1987 when Southampton paid £100,000 to take him to the Dell. He later had spells with both Stoke City and Walsall before leaving the first-class game to play non-League football for Telford United.

Gordon COWANS

Position	Midfielder		
Born	Gordon Sidney Cowans, Durham, 27 October 1958		
Height	5ft 8in		
Weight	10st 6lb		
Clubs	Aston Villa, Bari, Blackburn Rovers, Derby County, Wolverhampton Wanderers, Sheffield United, Bradford City, Stockport County, Burnley		
England Caps	10	Goals	2
	1983 v Wales (won 2–1), v N. Ireland (0–0), v Scotland (won 2–0) 1 goal, v Australia (0–0), v Australia (won 1–0), v Australia (1–1), v Hungary (won 2–0)		
	1986 v Egypt (won 4–0) 1 goal, v Soviet Union (won 1–0)		
	1991 v Eire (1–1)		

ONE OF THE GAME'S most skilful players, Gordon Cowans began his career with Aston Villa, where from 1979 to 1983 he was ever-present, appearing in 168 consecutive League games. In 1980 he was voted Young Player of the Year and the following season he inspired Villa to the League Championship. Linking well with Dennis Mortimer and Des Bremner, he helped Villa lift the European Cup in 1982 and the European Super Cup the following year. He graduated to full England honours when he made his debut against Wales at Wembley in February 1983, the first of ten caps.

In August 1983 he suffered a double fracture of the right leg, which kept him sidelined for the entire 1983/84 season. He returned in 1984/85 but failed to re-capture his pre-injury form, and at the end of the season he moved to Italian First Division club Bari for £500,000. After three years in Italy he returned to Villa Park, but after just one season he was transferred to Blackburn Rovers. He helped the Ewood Park club win promotion via the play-offs but at the end of the 1992/93 season he joined Villa for a third time. He took his tally of first-team appearances to 527 before joining Derby County and later playing for Wolverhampton Wanderers, Sheffield United, Bradford City, Stockport County and Burnley.

Graham ROBERTS

Position	Central defender
Born	Graham Paul Roberts, Southampton, 3 July 1959
Height	5ft 10in
Weight	12st 12lb
Clubs	Portsmouth, Tottenham Hotspur, Glasgow Rangers, Chelsea, West Bromwich Albion
England Caps	6
	1983 v N. Ireland (0–0), v Scotland (won 2–0)
	1984 v France (lost 0–2), v N. Ireland (won 1–0), v Scotland (1–1), v Soviet Union (lost 0–2)

HAVING BEEN REJECTED by Southampton, Bournemouth and Portsmouth, Graham Roberts played part-time for Weymouth while working as a fitter's mate in a shipyard. By the end of the 1979/80 season, Spurs and West Bromwich Albion wanted to buy him. Roberts chose Spurs, signing for £35,000 in May 1980, a record fee for a non-League player. Within 12 months he had established himself at centre-half and helped his club to victory over Manchester City in the 100th FA Cup Final. A hard-tackling, aggressive player, he soon became a folk hero with the Spurs crowd. The following season he earned a second FA Cup winners' medal, his long attacking run early in the replay bringing about the penalty from which Glenn Hoddle scored the winning goal. He won his first England cap in May 1983 when he appeared against Northern Ireland, and he went on to win six full caps and one 'B' cap in his time at White Hart Lane. In 1984 he captained Spurs in Steve Perryman's absence and led the side to victory over Anderlecht in the UEFA Cup Final, scoring the crucial late equalizing goal that took the final into extra time and the ensuing penalty shoot-out.

In December 1986, soon after David Pleat's arrival, Roberts was transferred to Glasgow Rangers for £450,000. In his first season at Ibrox he helped the club win the Scottish Premier League and the Skol Cup. He later moved to Chelsea before joining West Bromwich Albion in November 1990. Roberts later had a spell as manager of non-League Enfield.

John BARNES

Position	Forward
Born	John Charles Bryan Barnes, Jamaica, 7 November 1963
Height	5ft 11in
Weight	12st 0lb
Clubs	Watford, Liverpool, Newcastle United, Charlton Athletic
England Caps	79 Goals 11

1983 v N. Ireland (0–0), v Australia (0–0), v Australia (won 1–0), v Australia (1–1)

1984 v Denmark (lost 0–1), v Luxembourg (won 4–0), v France (lost 0–2), v Scotland (1–1), v Soviet Union (lost 0–2), v Brazil (won 2–0) 1 goal, v Uruguay (lost 0–2), v Chile (0–0)

1985 v E. Germany (won 1–0), v Finland (won 5–0), v Turkey (won 8–0) 2 goals, v N. Ireland (won 1–0), v Romania (0–0), v Finland (1–1), v Scotland (lost 0–1), v Italy (lost 1–2), v Mexico (lost 0–1), v W. Germany (won 3–0), v United States (won 5–0)

1986 v Romania (1–1), v Israel (won 2–1), v Mexico (won 3–0), v Canada (won 1–0), v Argentina (lost 1–2)

1987 v Sweden (lost 0–1), v Turkey (0–0), v Brazil (1–1)

1988 v W. Germany (lost 1–3), v Turkey (won 8–0) 2 goals, v Yugoslavia (won 4–1) 1 goal, v Israel (0–0), v Holland (2–2), v Scotland (won 1–0), v Colombia (1–1), v Switzerland (won 1–0), v Eire (lost 0–1), v Holland (lost 1–3), v Soviet Union (lost 1–3)

1989 v Sweden (0–0), v Greece (won 2–1) 1 goal, v Albania (won 2–0) 1 goal, v Poland (won 3–0) 1 goal, v Denmark (1–1)

1990 v Sweden (0–0), v Italy (0–0), v Brazil (won 1–0), v Denmark (won 1–0), v Uruguay (lost 1–2) 1 goal, v Tunisia (1–1), v Eire (1–1), v Holland (0–0), v Egypt (won 1–0), v Belgium (won 1–0), v Cameroon (won 3–2)

1991 v Hungary (won 1–0), v Poland (won 2–0), v Cameroon (won 2–0), v Eire (1–1), v Turkey (won 1–0), v Soviet Union (won 3–1), v Argentina (2–2)

1992 v Czechoslovakia (2–2), v Finland (won 2–1)

1993 v San Marino (won 6–0), v Turkey (won 2–0), v Holland (2–2) 1 goal, v Poland (1–1), v United States (lost 0–2), v Germany (lost 1–2)

1995 v United States (won 2–0), v Romania (1–1), v Nigeria (won 1–0), v Uruguay (0–0), v Sweden (3–3)

1996 v Colombia (0–0)

Honours	Footballer of the Year 1988 and 1990

A PLAYER RENOWNED for his dazzling dribbling and finishing, John Barnes confirmed his World Cup potential 12 months after making his international debut with a brilliant solo goal against Brazil. He ran through the entire Brazilian defence and dribbled round the goalkeeper to score the opening goal in England's 2–0 win.

Jamaican-born Barnes came to live in England in 1976 when his father was posted to London as Jamaica's military attaché. When his parents returned to the Caribbean, he stayed to begin a career in football with Watford. While at Vicarage Road, he helped the Hornets win promotion to the First Division and reach the 1984 FA Cup Final, where they lost 2–0 to Everton. For six successive seasons he reached double figures in terms of goals scored – the only player in Watford's history to achieve this feat. He went on to score 84 goals in 286 games before, in June 1987, joining Liverpool for a fee of £900,000.

John Barnes. (Lancashire Evening Post)

The Liverpool fans soon took to him, naming him 'Tarmac' – the black Heighway! Although not a great goalscorer, he was a scorer of great goals. He could score with his head or either foot, his speciality being the ability to bend a ball at free kicks to make spectacular strikes. A fabulous player, he was voted Player of the Year in his first season at Anfield and won the honour again in 1990, so joining an elite band of players who have managed to win this award twice. One of the most brilliant entertainers to grace British football since the Second World War, he scored 108 goals in 407 games for Liverpool before joining Newcastle United in the summer of 1997. Awarded the MBE in October 1998, he later played for Charlton Athletic before becoming assistant manager to Kenny Dalglish at Celtic.

Danny THOMAS

Position	Full-back
Born	Daniel Joseph Thomas, Worksop, 12 November 1961
Height	5ft 7in
Weight	11st 0lb
Clubs	Coventry City, Tottenham Hotspur
England Caps	2
	1983 v Australia (0–0), v Australia (1–1)

A VERY POPULAR and friendly player, Danny Thomas made his Football League debut for Coventry City in September 1979. He soon established himself at full-back in a young and talented Sky Blues team and earned a place in the England Under-21 side. A top-class full-back who could play on either flank, he played twice for the full England team on their 1983 summer tour of Australia before Spurs manager Keith Burkinshaw paid £250,000 to take him to White Hart Lane.

Thomas played in both legs of the UEFA Cup Final victory over Anderlecht in 1984 and was a regular in the Spurs side up until 1987, when a serious injury sustained in the match against Queen's Park Rangers brought his career to an end in January 1988. He announced his retirement after fighting a losing battle to regain full fitness. He then qualified as a physiotherapist, and in May 1992 returned to the game in that capacity at West Bromwich Albion.

Steve WILLIAMS

Position	Midfielder
Born	Steven Charles Williams, London, 12 July 1958
Height	5ft 11in
Weight	10st 11lb
Clubs	Southampton, Arsenal, Luton Town, Exeter City
England Caps	6
	1983 v Australia (0–0), v Australia (won 1–0)
	1984 v France (lost 0–2), v E. Germany (won 1–0), v Finland (won 5–0), v Turkey (won 8–0)

ONE OF THE BEST midfield players Southampton have ever produced, Steve Williams went straight into the Saints' first team without appearing previously for the club's reserve side. He made his debut in the south coast derby against Portsmouth in April 1987, and over the next nine seasons went on to play in 335 League and Cup games. He helped the club to the 1979 League Cup Final and to runners-up spot in the First Division in 1983/84. He also won six full caps, four 'B' caps and 14 Under-21 caps. There is no doubt that he would have won many more at full international level had it not been for his temperament, which let him down on many occasions. Lawrie McMenemy managed to curb most of his aggression and even made him team captain, but in December 1984 he left the Dell to join Arsenal – the team he had supported as a boy – for £550,000.

Williams' early days at Highbury were hampered by injuries, but in 1986/87 he helped the Gunners to Littlewoods Cup victory over Liverpool. Unfortunately a rift developed between Williams and Arsenal manager George Graham, and in July 1988 he was transferred to Luton Town. He spent two seasons at Kenilworth Road before finishing his career with ex-Saints team-mate Alan Ball at Exeter City.

Mark BARHAM

Position	Right-winger
Born	Mark Francis Barham, Folkestone, 12 July 1962
Height	5ft 7in
Weight	11st 0lb
Clubs	Norwich City, Huddersfield Town, Middlesbrough, West Bromwich Albion, Brighton and Hove Albion, Shrewsbury Town
England Caps	2
	1983 v Australia (0–0), v Australia (won 1–0)

CAPTAIN OF the Norwich City youth side that won the South East Counties League title in 1979/80, Mark Barham made his League debut as a substitute in a 5–0 defeat at Manchester United towards the end of that campaign. By the start of the following season he had established himself in the Canaries' first team but couldn't prevent the club from losing their top-flight status. In 1981/82 he was instrumental in the club returning to the First Division as they finished third in the Second Division. His exciting wing play began to attract the attention of the England selectors and he won two full caps on the tour to Australia in 1983.

Barham went on to help the Canaries win the League Cup in 1985 and the Second Division Championship the following season, but then a serious knee injury threatened to end his career. He recovered from this, only to face stiff competition for his place from both Ruel Fox and Dale Gordon, so, having scored 25 goals for Norwich in 218 games, he joined Huddersfield Town. He later played League football for Middlesbrough, West Bromwich Albion, Brighton and Hove Albion and Shrewsbury Town before playing non-League football for Sittingbourne.

John GREGORY

Position	Midfielder
Born	John Charles Gregory, Scunthorpe, 11 May 1954
Height	6ft 1in
Weight	11st 5lb
Clubs	Northampton Town, Aston Villa, Brighton and Hove Albion, Queen's Park Rangers, Derby County, Portsmouth, Plymouth Argyle, Bolton Wanderers
England Caps	6
	1983 v Australia (0–0), v Australia (won 1–0), v Australia (1–1), v Denmark (lost 0–1), v Hungary (won 3–0)
	1984 v Wales (lost 0–1)

MUCH-TRAVELLED MIDFIELDER John Gregory, who made six full international appearances for England, began his career with Northampton Town, turning professional in May 1972 and going on to make 187 League appearances for the Cobblers. In June 1977 he joined Aston Villa, but after two seasons in the Midlands Brighton paid £250,000 to take him to the Goldstone Ground and he helped the club retain their First Division status while there. His first League success came at Queen's Park Rangers, who signed him for £300,000 in June 1981. He made an FA Cup Final appearance in 1982 and was ever-present in the run that secured the Second Division Championship in 1983. He then moved to Derby County and was again ever-present in a Second Division Championship-winning side, this time in 1987.

In July 1989 Gregory took over as player-manager of Portsmouth, but after they struggled he left Fratton Park at the end of the year. He then had two brief non-contract spells with Plymouth Argyle and Bolton Wanderers before later becoming coach at Leicester City and then Aston Villa. He returned to management with Wycombe Wanderers before taking charge of Premier League Aston Villa and, subsequently, First Division Derby County, which he left, in controversial circumstances.

John Gregory. (Lancashire Evening Post)

Paul WALSH

Position	Forward
Born	Paul Anthony Walsh, Plumstead, 1 October 1962
Height	5ft 8in
Weight	10st 1lb
Clubs	Charlton Athletic, Luton Town, Liverpool, Tottenham Hotspur, Queen's Park Rangers, Portsmouth, Manchester City
England Caps	5 Goals 1
	1983 v Australia (0–0), v Australia (won 1–0) 1 goal, v Australia (1–1)
	1984 v France (lost 0–2), v Wales (lost 0–1)

A SKILFUL ball-playing forward, Paul Walsh's natural talent was clear at an early age. He began his career with Charlton Athletic but in July 1982 moved to Luton Town for a fee of £250,000. Just 19 years old at the time, he had played in 87 Second Division games for the Addicks. He was an instant success at Kenilworth Road, netting three hat-tricks in his first season with the Hatters and winning full international honours to add to the England Under-21 honours gained with Charlton.

At the end of the following season, Walsh, who had scored 28 goals in 89 games, was transferred to Liverpool for £750,000. The PFA's Young Player of the Year, he was expected to succeed Kenny Dalglish but, despite a European Cup Final in 1985, a League title in 1986 and a League Cup Final in 1987, he was too often left on the fringes. In February 1988 he joined Tottenham Hotspur for £500,000, but though he became a great favourite at White Hart Lane he was unable to deliver the quantity of goals his talents deserved. After a loan spell with Queen's Park Rangers, he joined Portsmouth, playing an integral part in Pompey's spirited bid for promotion to the Premier League. He subsequently signed for Manchester City in what proved to be an inspired move, Walsh scoring some vital goals to lift the Maine Road club clear of relegation. He later returned to Fratton Park, where a knee ligament injury curtailed his career.

Nick PICKERING

Position	Midfielder
Born	Nicholas Pickering, Newcastle-upon-Tyne, 4 August 1963
Height	6ft 1in
Weight	11st 11lb
Clubs	Sunderland, Coventry City, Derby County, Darlington, Burnley
England Caps	1
	1983 v Australia (1–1)

NICK PICKERING made his League debut for Sunderland against Ipswich Town on the opening day of the 1981/82 season. During that campaign, his consistent performances brought him to the attention of the international selectors and in

September 1982 he won the first of 15 England Under-21 caps. The following summer, while still only 19, he won his only full cap when he played in a 1–1 draw against Australia in Melbourne.

During the 1984/85 season, Pickering, at the age of 21, captained Sunderland in the League Cup Final clash with Norwich City at Wembley. The Wearsiders lost 1–0 and just weeks later were relegated to the Second Division. After making 211 first-team appearances for the Black Cats, Pickering was transferred to Coventry City for £120,000, and at the end of his first full season with the Sky Blues he won an FA Cup winners' medal as they beat Tottenham Hotspur 3–2. A fee of £250,000 took him to Derby County in the summer of 1988, but he was never an automatic choice at the Baseball Ground, and in October 1991 he joined Darlington, later ending his League career with Burnley.

Nigel SPINK

Position	Goalkeeper
Born	Nigel Philip Spink, Chelmsford, 8 August 1958
Height	6ft 1in
Weight	13st 10lb
Clubs	Aston Villa, West Bromwich Albion, Millwall
England Caps	1
	1983 v Australia (1–1)

NIGEL SPINK worked as an apprentice plasterer on leaving school and joined his home-town team Chelmsford City as a part-time professional. His displays in the Southern League attracted the attention of a number of top clubs, including Crystal Palace, Nottingham Forest and West Ham United. However, in January 1977 the powerfully built goalkeeper signed a five-year contract with Aston Villa, despite being fourth choice at the time behind Jimmy Rimmer, John Burridge and Jake Findlay.

Spink made his League debut for Villa against Nottingham Forest on Boxing Day 1979, but, remarkably, his next first-team appearance was in the 1982 European Cup Final against Bayern Munich in Rotterdam. He had been named substitute keeper, but after just ten minutes' play he was plunged into the deep end as Jimmy Rimmer left the field with a damaged neck. Spink played superbly and stepped up to collect his winners' medal after Villa had won 1–0. He eventually replaced Rimmer on a permanent basis midway through the 1982/83 season and won full international honours on the 1983 close season tour of Australia. He went on to help Villa win promotion back to the top flight in 1987/88, and when Villa were runners-up to Liverpool in 1989/90 Spink was not only ever-present but conceded just 38 goals. He went on to play in 461 games for Villa before leaving to join neighbours West Bromwich Albion in January 1996. In doing so he became, at 37 years 176 days, the oldest player ever to join the Baggies' ranks. His vast experience and presence between the posts was a great confidence booster to the Albion defence. He later acted as the club's goalkeeping coach, before ending his career with Millwall.

Mike DUXBURY

Position	Defender
Born	Michael Duxbury, Blackburn, 1 September 1959
Height	5ft 10in
Weight	11st 2lb
Clubs	Manchester United, Blackburn Rovers, Bradford City
England Caps	10
	1983 v Luxembourg (won 4–0)
	1984 v France (lost 0–2), v Wales (lost 0–1), v Scotland (1–1), v Soviet Union (lost 0–2),
	v Brazil (won 2–0), v Uruguay (lost 0–2), v Chile (0–0), v E. Germany (won 1–0),
	v Finland (won 5–0)

MIKE DUXBURY MADE nine full international appearances for England within the space of 12 months, after he won his first against Luxembourg in November 1983.

Duxbury had spent five years languishing in Manchester United's Central League side before making his Football League debut against Birmingham City in August 1980. Over the next couple of seasons he spent his time playing in a variety of positions, before in 1982 establishing himself as United's first-choice right-back. It was in this position that he won his ten full caps, adding to his seven appearances at Under-21 level. Though he lost his right-back spot to John Gidman, Duxbury maintained a first-team place because of his versatility, winning FA Cup winners' medals in 1983 and 1985. Tough and skilful, he went on to appear in 376 League and Cup games for Manchester United before being given a free transfer and joining his home-town club Blackburn Rovers. He spent just 18 months at Ewood Park before moving across the Pennines to end his first-class career with Bradford City.

Brian STEIN

Position	Forward
Born	Brian Stein, Cape Town, 19 October 1957
Height	5ft 10in
Weight	11st 8lb
Clubs	Luton Town, Annecy, Barnet
England Caps	1
	1984 v France (lost 0–2)

BRIAN STEIN was one of nine children. His father was put under house arrest because of his political opposition to apartheid, and Brian was only eight when his family left South Africa for England. By the time he was in his mid-teens, he was a regular goalscorer in North London football. Soon after joining Edgware Town, he was spotted by Luton Town. He made his Hatters debut in a League Cup third-round second replay against Manchester City at Old Trafford midway through the

1977/78 season, before winning a regular place the following campaign. Over the next few seasons, he found the net with great regularity, with his best season in terms of goals scored coming in the club's Second Division Championship-winning season of 1981/82, when he netted 21 goals. In the top flight he formed a deadly strike partnership with Paul Walsh, and 12 months after sitting on the substitutes' bench for England's match against Wales he made his full international debut alongside Walsh against France.

Stein scored two of Luton's goals when they beat Arsenal 3–2 to win the 1988 League Cup Final. He left Kenilworth Road shortly afterwards to play for French club Annecy, but rejoined Luton in 1991, taking his total of goals to 154 in 496 games, before seeing out his career with Barnet.

Alan KENNEDY

Position	Left-back
Born	Alan Philip Kennedy, Sunderland, 31 August 1954
Height	5ft 9in
Weight	10st 7lb
Clubs	Newcastle United, Liverpool, Sunderland, Hartlepool United, Beerschot, Wigan Athletic, Wrexham
England Caps	2
	1984 v N. Ireland (won 1–0), v Wales (lost 0–1)

AFTER ONLY A HANDFUL of senior outings for Newcastle United, Alan Kennedy appeared for the Magpies in the 1974 FA Cup Final against Liverpool, before going on to win Under-23 and 'B' international honours while at St James' Park. He was also selected for a full England place in 1975 but a knee injury prevented his appearance. He didn't get another chance to play for his country for almost a decade, by which time he had left the Magpies following their relegation in 1978, and joined Liverpool for a fee of £300,000.

Kennedy started in the Reds' side as an out-and-out winger, but after being switched to left-back he never looked back, helping the club win the League Championship in his first two seasons at Anfield. In the 1981 European Cup Final against Real Madrid, the most memorable game of Kennedy's career, he scored the game's only goal, in the 84th minute. He went on to help the Reds win three more League Championships and in the 1984 European Cup Final he helped the club secure the 'treble' by scoring the deciding penalty in a shoot-out with Roma. His performances led to him being selected for England by Bobby Robson later that summer, but the following season he lost his place to Jim Beglin and joined his home-town club Sunderland.

Kennedy later had a spell playing for Hartlepool United before trying his luck with the Belgian club Beerschot. On his return he played for Wigan Athletic and non-League Colne Dynamoes before returning to League action with Wrexham. Then, after a brief spell with Morecambe, he became player-manager of Netherfield before ending his career with Barrow.

Mark WRIGHT

Position	Central defender
Born	Mark Wright, Dorchester, 1 August 1963
Height	6ft 3in
Weight	12st 1lb
Clubs	Oxford United, Southampton, Derby County, Liverpool
England Caps	45 Goals 1

1984 v Wales (lost 0–1)
1985 v E. Germany (won 1–0), v Finland (won 5–0), v Turkey (won 8–0), v Eire (won 2–1), v Romania (0–0), v Italy (lost 1–2), v W. Germany (won 3–0)
1986 v Romania (1–1), v Turkey (won 5–0), v N. Ireland (0–0), v Egypt (won 4–0), v Soviet Union (won 1–0)
1987 v Yugoslavia (won 2–0), v N. Ireland (won 2–0), v Scotland (0–0)
1988 v Israel (0–0), v Holland (2–2), v Colombia (1–1), v Switzerland (won 1–0), v Eire (lost 0–1), v Holland (lost 1–3)
1990 v Czechoslovakia (won 4–2), v Tunisia (1–1), v Holland (0–0), v Egypt (won 1–0) 1 goal, v Belgium (won 1–0), v Cameroon (won 3–2), v W. Germany (1–1 aet, W. Germany won 4–3 on penalties), v Italy (lost 1–2)
1991 v Hungary (won 1–0), v Poland (won 2–0), v Eire (1–1), v Eire (1–1), v Cameroon (won 2–0), v Soviet Union (won 3–1), v Argentina (2–2), v Australia (won 1–0), v New Zealand (won 2–0), v Malaysia (won 4–2)
1992 v France (won 2–0), v Finland (won 2–1)
1993 v Spain (lost 0–1)
1996 v Croatia (0–0), v Hungary (won 3–0)

AFTER JUST 11 first-team games for Oxford United, Mark Wright was used as a 'make-weight' in a complicated deal that took him and Keith Cassells to Southampton in exchange for Trevor Hebberd and George Lawrence. He soon became a fixture at the heart of the Saints' defence, and in 1982/83, his first full season with the club, he was selected for the England Under-21 side. The following season he graduated to the national side, winning his first full cap against Wales at Wrexham in May 1984. Sadly, a broken leg suffered in the FA Cup semi-final against Liverpool forced him to miss the 1986 World Cup Finals in Mexico, although he did appear in the Finals four years later.

After five seasons on the south coast Wright joined Peter Shilton in moving to Derby County as part of Robert Maxwell's drive to establish the Rams as a First Division force. Derby, however, sank to the foot of the First Division, and in the summer of 1991 Wright was sold to Liverpool for £2.2 million. Injured in only his second game for the Reds, he missed three months of the campaign but ended the season with an FA Cup winners' medal after captaining Liverpool to a 2–0 FA Cup Final win. He spent much of the next couple of seasons in the reserves but eventually forced his way back into Roy Evans' plans and won a recall to the England side after four years' absence. Injuries then began to take their toll, and though he always looked a class act when wearing the red of Liverpool, he was forced into retirement.

Wright later managed non-League Southport before leaving to take charge of his first club, Oxford United, albeit briefly. He then moved on to manage Chester City.

Terry FENWICK

Position	Defender
Born	Terence William Fenwick, Durham, 17 November 1959
Height	5ft 11in
Weight	11st 1lb
Clubs	Crystal Palace, Queen's Park Rangers, Tottenham Hotspur, Leicester City, Swindon Town
England Caps	20
	1984 v Wales (lost 0–1), v Scotland (1–1), v Soviet Union (lost 0–2), v Brazil (won 2–0), v Uruguay (lost 0–2), v Chile (0–0)
	1985 v Finland (1–1), v Scotland (lost 0–1), v Mexico (lost 0–1), v United States (won 5–0), v Romania (1–1), v Turkey (won 5–0), v N. Ireland (0–0)
	1986 v Egypt (won 4–0), v Mexico (won 3–0), v Portugal (lost 0–1), v Morocco (0–0), v Portugal (won 3–0), v Argentina (lost 1–2), v Israel (0–0)

TERRY FENWICK began his career with Crystal Palace, where, after winning three England Under-21 caps and helping the club win the 1978/79 Second Division Championship, he was regarded as a defender with a bright future. Capable of playing in any of the defensive positions, he left Selhurst Park to join Queen's Park Rangers. At Loftus Road he won a further eight Under-21 caps and played in the 1982 FA Cup Final against Spurs. It was Fenwick's headed goal that forced a replay, which Spurs won to retain the trophy. He was also a member of Rangers' 1982/83 Second Division Championship-winning side and played in the 1986 League Cup Final defeat by Oxford United. While with Rangers, Fenwick became the club's most-capped England player, collecting 19 of his 20 caps there.

In December 1987 Fenwick joined Terry Venables for a third time, moving to Tottenham Hotspur for £550,000. His versatility saw him play at full-back, in central defence, in midfield and in a continental sweeper's role. Just when it seemed he had found his best position, having settled at right-back, he broke a leg. On his return to full fitness he had a loan spell with Leicester City, but then on his return to White Hart Lane he broke his ankle in the warm-up before a match against Portsmouth.

In February 1995 Fenwick became manager of Portsmouth, but after leading the club to the verge of the First Division play-offs in 1996/97 he was sacked, control of the Fratton Park club passing over to Martin Gregory.

Gary LINEKER

Position	Forward		
Born	Gary Winston Lineker, Leicester, 30 November 1960		
Height	5ft 10in		
Weight	12st 5lb		
Clubs	Leicester City, Everton, Barcelona, Tottenham Hotspur, Grampus Eight		
England Caps	80	Goals	48
	1984 v Scotland (1–1)		
	1985 v Eire (won 2–1) 1 goal, v Romania (0–0), v Scotland (lost 0–1), v Italy (lost 1–2), v W. Germany (won 3–0), v United States (won 5–0) 2 goals		

Gary Lineker in action during the Italy World Cup match against Egypt in Cagliari on 21 June 1990. England won 1–0. (David Cannon/Getty Images)

1986 v Romania (1–1), v Turkey (won 5–0) 3 goals, v N. Ireland (0–0), v Egypt (won 4–0),
   v Soviet Union (won 1–0), v Canada (won 1–0), v Portugal (lost 0–1), v Mexico (0–0),
   v Poland (won 3–0) 3 goals, v Paraguay (won 3–0) 2 goals, v Argentina (lost 1–2) 1 goal
1987 v N. Ireland (won 3–0) 2 goals, v N. Ireland (won 2–0), v Yugoslavia (won 2–0),
   v Spain (won 4–2) 4 goals, v Turkey (0–0), v Brazil (1–1) 1 goal
1988 v W. Germany (lost 1–3) 1 goal, v Turkey (won 8–0) 3 goals, v Yugoslavia (won 4–1)
   1 goal, v Holland (2–2) 1 goal, v Hungary (0–0), v Scotland (won 1–0), v Colombia (1–1)
   1 goal, v Switzerland (won 1–0) 1 goal, v Eire (lost 0–1), v Holland (lost 1–3), v Soviet
   Union (lost 1–3)
1989 v Sweden (0–0), v Saudi Arabia (1–1), v Greece (won 2–1), v Albania (won 2–0),
   v Albania (won 5–0) 1 goal, v Poland (won 3–0) 1 goal, v Denmark (1–1)
1990 v Sweden (0–0), v Poland (0–0), v Italy (0–0), v Yugoslavia (won 2–1), v Brazil (won
   1–0) 1 goal, v Czechoslovakia (won 4–2), v Denmark (won 1–0) 1 goal, v Uruguay (lost
   1–2), v Tunisia (1–1), v Eire (1–1) 1 goal, v Holland (0–0), v Egypt (won 1–0), v Belgium
   (won 1–0), v Cameroon (won 3–2) 2 goals, v W. Germany (1–1 aet, W. Germany won 4–3
   on penalties) 1 goal, v Italy (lost 1–2)
1991 v Hungary (won 1–0) 1 goal, v Poland (won 2–0) 1 goal, v Eire (1–1), v Cameroon (won
   2–0) 2 goals, v Eire (1–1), v Turkey (won 1–0), v Argentina (2–2) 1 goal, v Australia (won
   1–0), v New Zealand (won 1–0) 1 goal, v Malaysia (won 4–2) 4 goals
1992 v Germany (lost 0–1), v Turkey (won 1–0), v Poland (1–1) 1 goal, v France (won 2–0)
   1 goal, v Czechoslovakia (2–2), v CIS (2–2) 1 goal, v Hungary (won 1–0), v Brazil (1–1),
   v Finland (won 2–1), v Denmark (0–0), v France (0–0), v Sweden (lost 1–2)

Honours   Footballer of the Year 1986 and 1992

GARY LINEKER was desperately unlucky not to surpass Bobby Charlton's record of 49
goals, falling just one short of equalling the Manchester United player's record. His
total of 48 goals included four in the defeats of Spain and Malaysia, two hat-tricks
against Turkey and another hat-trick against Poland.

A member of Leicester City's Second Division Championship-winning team,
earning promotion again in 1983, Gary Lineker's greatest asset in his early days was
his blistering pace. He top-scored in four successive seasons at Filbert Street, and with
103 League and Cup goals for the Foxes a move was inevitable. In the summer of
1985, following an independent tribunal, Lineker joined Everton for a fee of
£800,000 plus a percentage of any future fee. He soon struck up a superb attacking
partnership with Graeme Sharp and went on to score 38 goals in 52 outings,
including three hat-tricks. He tormented defences the length and breadth of the
country, and as the season neared its climax the Blues looked a reasonable bet to
clinch the League and FA Cup double. Lineker's contribution was recognized by
awards from the PFA and Football Writers' Association, who both voted him their
Player of the Year. The Blues eventually finished runners-up in both the League and
the FA Cup, Lineker scoring the opening goal of the historic all-Merseyside FA Cup
Final.

Lineker was a key figure in England's 1986 World Cup campaign, ending it as the
leading scorer in the Finals with six goals. Four weeks after arriving home from
Mexico, he joined Spanish giants Barcelona, who paid £2.5 million for his services.
After helping them win the Spanish Cup in 1988 and the European Cup Winners' Cup
the following year, he returned to Football League action with Tottenham Hotspur in

1989. Top scorer in each of his three seasons at White Hart Lane, he helped Spurs win the FA Cup in 1991 before leaving to join Japanese club Grampus Eight.

Never booked during his entire career, Lineker's services to football were rewarded in the 1992 New Year's Honours List with the OBE.

Steve HUNT

Position	Midfielder
Born	Stephen Kenneth Hunt, Witton, 4 August 1956
Height	5ft 7in
Weight	10st 10lb
Clubs	Aston Villa, New York Cosmos, Coventry City, West Bromwich Albion
England Caps	2
	1984 v Scotland (1–1), v Soviet Union (lost 0–2)

STEVE HUNT began his career with local club Aston Villa, but on being unable to win a place on a regular basis he left Villa Park to play for New York Cosmos in the NASL. He helped Cosmos win the NASL Championships in 1977 and again in 1978, but in September of that year he returned to England to play for Coventry City. He was a regular in the Sky Blues side for almost six years, his best season being 1981/82 when he netted 12 goals from midfield. However, in March 1984, after scoring 34 goals from 216 games, he left to join West Bromwich Albion for £80,000.

Hunt won two caps for England while with the Baggies, but when Ron Saunders arrived to manage Albion his face did not fit and he rejoined Villa in a deal involving Darren Bradley plus £90,000. He was a regular in the Villa side until the appointment of Graham Taylor, after which his appearances were restricted. Sadly, in November 1987 injury forced his retirement from the game.

Mark HATELEY

Position	Forward		
Born	Mark Wayne Hateley, Liverpool, 7 November 1961		
Height	6ft 1in		
Weight	11st 8lb		
Clubs	Coventry City, Portsmouth, AC Milan, Monaco, Glasgow Rangers, Queen's Park Rangers, Leeds United, Hull City		
England Caps	32	Goals	9
	1984 v Soviet Union (lost 0–2), v Brazil (won 2–0) 1 goal, v Uruguay (lost 0–2), v Chile (0–0)		
	1985 v E. Germany (won 1–0), v Finland (won 5–0) 2 goals, v N. Ireland (won 1–0) 1 goal, v Eire (won 2–1), v Finland (1–1) 1 goal, v Scotland (lost 0–1), v Italy (lost 1–2) 1 goal, v Mexico (lost 0–1)		
	1986 v Romania (1–1), v Turkey (won 5–0), v Egypt (won 4–0), v Scotland (won 2–1), v Mexico (won 3–0) 2 goals, v Canada (won 1–0) 1 goal, v Portugal (lost 0–1), v Morocco (0–0), v Paraguay (won 3–0)		
	1987 v Turkey (0–0), v Brazil (1–1), v Scotland (0–0)		

Mark Hateley. (Lancashire Evening Post)

1988 v W. Germany (lost 1–3), v Holland (2–2), v Hungary (0–0), v Colombia (1–1), v Eire (lost 0–1), v Holland (lost 1–3), v Soviet Union (lost 1–3)
1992 v Czechoslovakia (2–2)

....

MARK HATELEY, who scored against Brazil in the Maracana Stadium in what was only his second international appearance, began his career with Coventry City. He made his debut against Wolves in May 1979, but had to wait until the 1981/82 season before winning a regular place in the Sky Blues side. His performances in the Coventry attack led to him winning international recognition and he scored twice on his debut for the England Under-21s. He went on to score 34 goals in 111 games for Coventry before he was transferred to Portsmouth for £190,000 – a fee set by an independent tribunal.

Hateley spent just one season at Fratton Park, scoring 25 goals in 44 games – a total that included hat-tricks against Cambridge United and Grimsby Town in the space of four days. He joined AC Milan for £1 million but after three years at the San Siro he moved to Monaco before, in 1990, joining Glasgow Rangers. After winning numerous League and Cup honours and appearing in 216 games for the Ibrox club, he returned south of the border to play for Queen's Park Rangers. Then, following a loan spell at Leeds United, he rejoined the Scottish giants for a second spell. In the summer of 1997 he joined struggling Hull City as their player-manager, but, sadly, things didn't work out for him.

Dave WATSON

Position	Central defender
Born	David Watson, Liverpool, 20 November 1960
Height	6ft 0in
Weight	13st 0lb
Clubs	Liverpool, Norwich City, Everton
England Caps	12

1984 v Brazil (won 2–0), v Uruguay (lost 0–2), v Chile (0–0)
1985 v Mexico (lost 0–1), v United States (won 5–0)
1986 v Scotland (won 2–1)
1987 v N. Ireland (won 3–0)
1988 v Israel (0–0), v Holland (2–2), v Scotland (won 1–0), v Switzerland (won 1–0), v Soviet Union (lost 1–3)

....

DAVE WATSON began his career with Liverpool, but unable to make the grade he moved to Norwich City in November 1980 for an initial fee of £50,000, a similar sum after he had made 25 senior appearances and a further £100,000 after he had collected his first full England cap, which he did in June 1984 against Brazil.

In the summer of 1986, Everton manager Howard Kendall splashed out £900,000, a club record, to bring Watson to Goodison Park. Despite initially appearing indecisive and clumsy, he soon won over the hearts of the Blues fans as Everton went on to win the League Championship in his first season with the club. He gradually became much more positive in attack, acquiring the welcome knack of chipping in with priceless goals, and he was eventually handed the job of skipper.

Charlie Nicholas of Scotland pursues Dave Watson during a game at Wembley in April 1986. England won the match 2–1. (Getty Images)

He stepped up to become caretaker manager after Joe Royle's departure and steered the club safely through a relegation dogfight in the spring of 1997. After suffering with knee and back problems he had to undergo a cartilage operation, but he returned to end his Everton career just three matches short of the outfield appearance record at the club, held by Brian Labone.

Though a considerable influence in a coaching capacity, Dave Watson finally severed his links with the Blues, crossing the Mersey to manage Tranmere Rovers.

Clive ALLEN

Position	Forward
Born	Clive Darren Allen, London, 20 May 1961
Height	5ft 10in
Weight	12st 3lb
Clubs	Queen's Park Rangers, Arsenal, Crystal Palace, Tottenham Hotspur, Bordeaux, Manchester City, Chelsea, West Ham United, Millwall, Carlisle United
England Caps	5
	1984 v Brazil (won 2–0), v Uruguay (lost 0–2), v Chile (0–0)
	1987 v Turkey (0–0)
	1988 v Israel (0–0)
Honours	Footballer of the Year 1987

CLIVE ALLEN started out with Queen's Park Rangers, making his Football League debut against Chelsea in November 1978, and after scoring in his fourth substitute appearance he grabbed a hat-trick in his first full match as Rangers won 5–1 at Coventry City. After ending the season as the club's top scorer with 28 goals from 39 League games, he was signed by Arsenal for £1.25 million but passed on to Crystal Palace before the new season even started, in part-exchange for Kenny Sansom. Despite a good start at Selhurst Park, with a hat-trick in his third game, he didn't settle and returned to Loftus Road in the summer of 1981. After impressing towards the end of the 1983/84 season, he was included in Bobby Robson's England squad for the tour of South America and made his full England debut in a 2–0 win against Brazil. That summer he joined Tottenham Hotspur, but in each of his first two seasons at White Hart Lane his appearances were restricted by injury.

It was only in 1986/87, when operating as a lone striker, that Allen showed the full depth of his clinical finishing, scoring 49 goals (33 in the League and 16 in the two Cup competitions) as Spurs finished third in the League and reached the FA Cup Final, where they lost 3–2 to Coventry City. He was voted Player of the Year in the annual PFA awards and Footballer of the Year by the Football Writers' Association.

At the end of the following season Allen signed for French champions Bordeaux, but after one season returned to England to play for Manchester City. Moving to Chelsea in December 1991, he later had spells with West Ham United and Millwall before ending his playing days with Carlisle United.

Gary STEVENS

Position	Defender/Midfielder
Born	Gary Andrew Stevens, Hillingdon, 30 March 1962
Height	6ft 0in
Weight	12st 0lb
Clubs	Brighton and Hove Albion, Tottenham Hotspur, Portsmouth
England Caps	7
	1984 v Finland (won 5–0), v Turkey (won 8–0)
	1985 v N. Ireland (won 1–0)
	1986 v Scotland (won 2–0), v Mexico (won 3–0), v Morocco (0–0), v Paraguay (won 3–0)

PLAYING FOR Brighton and Hove Albion against Manchester United in the 1983 FA Cup Final, Gary Stevens defended brilliantly and scored a late equalizer that took the game into extra time and eventually a replay, which the Seagulls lost. Joining Spurs for £300,000 later that summer, he failed to establish himself as a central defender and was switched to full-back. However, it was as a midfield player that he proved highly successful in both legs of the 1984 UEFA Cup Final and on his seven appearances for England – six wins and a draw and not one goal conceded! His defensive experience helped him to win the ball in midfield and he showed a willingness to join the attack that had not been apparent when he played at the back.

In March 1985, just as he seemed set to become an England regular, Stevens suffered damaged knee ligaments which kept him out of the team for six months. Thereafter his career was plagued with injury, notably a broken shoulder sustained in an aerial challenge with Wimbledon's John Fashanu in November 1986 and further knee trouble following a notorious Vinny Jones challenge two years later.

In March 1990 Stevens was loaned to Portsmouth in an effort to prove his fitness, the transfer later being made permanent. However, injuries continued to blight his career and in February 1992 he was forced to retire.

Trevor STEVEN

Position	Midfielder		
Born	Trevor McGregor Steven, Berwick, 21 September 1963		
Height	5ft 8in		
Weight	10st 9lb		
Clubs	Burnley, Everton, Glasgow Rangers, Marseille		
England Caps	36	Goals	4
	1985 v N. Ireland (won 1–0), v Eire (won 2–1) 1 goal, v Romania (0–0), v Finland (1–1), v Italy (lost 1–2), v United States (won 5–0) 1 goal		
	1986 v Turkey (won 5–0), v Egypt (won 4–0) 1 goal, v Soviet Union (won 1–0), v Mexico (won 3–0), v Poland (won 3–0), v Paraguay (won 3–0), v Argentina (lost 1–2)		
	1987 v Sweden (0–0), v Yugoslavia (won 2–0), v Spain (won 4–2)		
	1988 v Turkey (won 8–0), v Yugoslavia (won 4–1), v Holland (2–2), v Hungary (0–0), v Scotland (won 1–0), v Switzerland (won 1–0), v Holland (lost 1–3), v Soviet Union (lost 1–3)		

Murdo McLeod of Scotland takes on Trevor Steven during the Rous Cup match at Wembley on 21 May 1988. England won 1–0. (Simon Bruty/Getty Images)

1989 v Scotland (won 2–0)
1990 v Czechoslovakia (won 4–2), v Cameroon (won 3–2), v W. Germany (1–1 aet, W. Germany won 4–3 on penalties), v Italy (lost 1–0)
1991 v Cameroon (won 2–0)
1992 v Germany (0–0), v CIS (2–2) 1 goal, v Brazil (1–1), v Finland (won 2–1), v Denmark (0–0), v France (0–0)

TREVOR STEVEN, who represented England in the 1986 World Cup Finals in Mexico, began his career with Burnley, where his outstanding displays on the wing soon had the bigger clubs tracking his progress. Everton manager Howard Kendall carefully monitored the Clarets' starlet for two years before splashing out £325,000 for his services in the summer of 1983. Although he wasn't a regular in his first season with the Blues, he collected an FA Cup winners' medal in 1984 as Everton beat Watford 2–0 in the final. The following year Everton secured the League Championship, with Steven's silky skills and tight control complementing the more aggressive combative style of Peter Reid. In addition, the Toffees won the European Cup Winners' Cup, defeating Rapid Vienna 3–1 in the final in Rotterdam. Steven chipped in with a goal as he had done in the deciding leg of the semi-final against Bayern Munich. Subsequently, having helped Everton win the League title again in 1986/87 and played against Liverpool in the 1989 FA Cup Final, Steven, who had scored 58 goals in 283 games, refused to sign a new contract and joined Glasgow Rangers for £1.5 million.

With the Ibrox club Steven won two League Championship medals and a League Cup winners' medal, but in August 1991 he was surprisingly sold to Marseille for £5.5 million. In his only season on the Riviera, the French club won the Championship, then sold Steven back to Rangers for £2.4 million. He won two more League Championship medals before, no longer being an automatic choice, he decided to retire.

Gary BAILEY

Position	Goalkeeper
Born	Gary Richard Bailey, Ipswich, 9 August 1958
Height	6ft 1in
Weight	13st 2lb
Clubs	Manchester United
England Caps	2
	1985 v Eire (won 2–1), v Mexico (lost 0–1)

THE SON OF ROY Bailey, the former Ipswich Town goalkeeper, Gary was living in South Africa and playing for Witts University when, following a trial with Manchester United, he was offered terms. Early in his career, when United played West Bromwich Albion, Tony Brown the Albion forward netted twice against him in a 5–3 win for the Baggies and, in doing so, created a piece of Football League history – it was the only known instance of the same player scoring past both father and son, Brown having netted past Roy during Ipswich Town's League Championship winning season of 1961/62.

Bailey ended his first season at Old Trafford with an FA Cup Final appearance but was on the losing side. Successful Cup Final appearances followed, however, as United beat Brighton and Hove Albion in 1983 and Everton in 1985.

After 14 appearances for the England Under-21 side, Bailey was rewarded with his first full cap against Eire in March 1985. However, he sustained a bad knee injury while training with the England squad in February 1986 and, at the age of 29, he was forced to retire from the game, having made 373 appearances for Manchester United. He returned to South Africa and later resumed his playing career with Kaiser Chiefs, before becoming a television commentator.

Chris WADDLE

Position	Winger
Born	Christopher Roland Waddle, Hepworth, 14 December 1960
Height	6ft 0in
Weight	11st 6lb
Clubs	Newcastle United, Tottenham Hotspur, Marseille, Sheffield Wednesday, Falkirk, Bradford City, Sunderland, Burnley
England Caps	62 Goals 6

1985 v Eire (won 2–1), v Romania (0–0), v Finland (1–1), v Scotland (lost 0–1), v Italy (lost 1–2), v Mexico (lost 0–1), v W. Germany (won 3–0), v United States (won 5–0)

1986 v Romania (1–1), v Turkey (won 5–0) 1 goal, v. N. Ireland (0–0), v Israel (won 2–1), v Soviet Union (won 1–0) 1 goal, v Scotland (won 2–1), v Mexico (won 3–0), v Canada (won 1–0), v Portugal (lost 0–1), v Morocco (0–0), v Poland (won 3–0), v Argentina (lost 1–2)

1987 v Sweden (lost 0–1), v N. Ireland (won 3–0) 1 goal, v Yugoslavia (won 2–0), v Spain (won 4–2), v N. Ireland (won 2–0) 1 goal, v Turkey (0–0), v Brazil (1–1), v Scotland (0–0)

1988 v W. Germany (lost 1–3), v Israel (0–0), v Hungary (0–0), v Scotland (won 1–0), v Colombia (1–1), v Switzerland (won 1–0), v Eire (lost 0–1), v Holland (lost 1–3)

1989 v Sweden (0–0), v Saudi Arabia (1–1), v Albania (won 2–0), v Albania (won 5–0) 1 goal, v Chile (0–0), v Scotland (won 2–0) 1 goal, v Poland (won 3–0), v Denmark (1–1)

1990 v Sweden (0–0), v Poland (0–0), v Italy (0–0), v Yugoslavia (won 2–1), v Brazil (won 1–0), v Denmark (won 1–0), v Uruguay (lost 1–2), v Tunisia (1–1), v Eire (1–1), v Holland (0–0), v Egypt (won 1–0), v Belgium (won 1–0), v Cameroon (won 3–2), v W. Germany (1–1 aet, W. Germany won 4–3 on penalties), v Italy (lost 1–2)

1991 v Hungary (won 1–0), v Poland (won 2–0)

1992 v Turkey (won 1–0)

Honours	Footballer of the Year 1993

ONE OF THE MOST skilful of modern-day players, Chris Waddle began his career with Newcastle United, who picked him up from local Northern League club Tow Law Town in the summer of 1980. Under the guidance of Arthur Cox, he made rapid progress at St James' Park, helping the Magpies win promotion to the First Division in 1983/84. Called up for England the following season, he remained a member of the squad for the next six seasons, winning 62 caps and appearing in two World Cup Finals.

Spurs signed Waddle in July 1985 for £590,000, and after scoring twice on his debut in a 4–0 win over Watford he began to strike up a fine understanding with Glenn Hoddle. In 1986/87 Spurs finished third in the First Division and reached the FA Cup Final, where they lost 3–2 to Coventry City. Waddle spent much of the following season sidelined with heel and hernia problems but came back strongly in 1988/89 in a new creative role to top-score with 14 goals. That summer, Spurs accepted an offer of £4.25 million from French champions, Marseille.

In three seasons with the French club Waddle won three League Championships and reached the final of the 1991 European Cup, where Marseille lost to Red Star Belgrade on penalties. On being released, he joined Sheffield Wednesday, and at the

Chris Waddle playing for Spurs. (Lancashire Evening Post)

end of his first season with the Hillsborough club he was voted the Football Writers' Association Player of the Year. On leaving the Owls, he moved north of the border to play for Falkirk, before having a spell with Sunderland prior to taking over the player-manager's position at Burnley.

Peter DAVENPORT

Position	Forward
Born	Peter Davenport, Birkenhead, 24 March 1961
Height	5ft 11in
Weight	11st 3lb
Clubs	Nottingham Forest, Manchester United, Middlesbrough, Sunderland, St Johnstone, Stockport County, Macclesfield
England Caps	1
	1985 v Eire (won 2–1)

PETER DAVENPORT began his footballing career as an amateur with Everton but in 1980 he was released after making little impact. He went to play for Cammel Laird FC, where his prolific goalscoring feats attracted the attention of Nottingham Forest. He made a sensational start to his Forest career, scoring four goals in his five appearances at the end of the 1981/82 season, including a hat-trick against Ipswich Town. He was hampered by injuries the following year but soon became Forest's No. 1 striker, topping the club's scoring charts for the next two seasons. During the course of the 1984/85 season he netted his second hat-trick for the club in a 3–1 defeat of Sunderland and won an England cap against Eire. He scored another treble for Forest against Arsenal midway through the following season but was then sold to Manchester United for £570,000.

The move didn't work out and two years later Davenport moved to Middlesbrough for £700,000. In 1990/91 he was back in the top flight with Sunderland but later had spells with St Johnstone, Stockport County, Southport and Macclesfield, later becoming the latter club's manager.

Gary STEVENS

Position	Right-back
Born	Gary Michael Stevens, Barrow, 27 March 1963
Height	5ft 11in
Weight	10st 11lb
Clubs	Everton, Glasgow Rangers, Tranmere Rovers
England Caps	46
	1985 v Italy (lost 1–2), v W. Germany (won 3–0)
	1986 v Romania (1–1), v Turkey (won 5–0), v N. Ireland (0–0), v Egypt (won 4–0), v Israel (won 2–1), v Scotland (won 2–1), v Canada (won 1–0), v Portugal (lost 0–1), v Morocco (0–0), v Poland (won 3–0), v Paraguay (won 3–0), v Argentina (lost 1–2)
	1987 v Brazil (1–1), v Scotland (0–0)

Gary Stevens of Everton. (Lancashire Evening Post)

1988 v Turkey (won 8–0), v Yugoslavia (won 4–1), v Israel (0–0), v Holland (2–2), v Hungary (0–0), v Scotland (won 1–0), v Switzerland (won 1–0), v Eire (lost 0–1), v Holland (lost 1–3), v Soviet Union (lost 1–3)
1989 v Denmark (won 1–0), v Sweden (0–0), v Greece (won 2–1), v Albania (won 2–0), v Albania (won 5–0), v Scotland (won 2–0), v Poland (won 3–0)
1990 v Sweden (0–0), v Poland (0–0), v Italy (0–0), v Brazil (won 1–0), v Denmark (won 1–0), v Tunisia (1–1), v Eire (1–1), v Italy (lost 1–2)
1991 v Soviet Union (won 3–1)
1992 v CIS (2–2), v Hungary (won 1–0), v Brazil (1–1), v Finland (won 2–1)

THE EVERTON FULL-BACK Gary Stevens' great composure on the ball, allied to his natural sprinting ability, led to him winning full international honours for England shortly after establishing himself as a first-team regular. He was a member of the England team that reached the 1986 World Cup quarter-finals, going on to appear in 46 games for his country. For Everton he won two League Championship winners' medals, an FA Cup winners' medal and a European Cup Winners' Cup medal. He was a virtual ever-present in the Everton side for seven seasons, scoring 12 goals in 284 games before leaving Goodison in the summer of 1988 to join Glasgow Rangers for £1.25 million.

At Ibrox Stevens won six Scottish Premier Division Championship medals, a Scottish Cup winners' medal and three Scottish League Cup medals. In September 1994, after appearing in 245 first-team games for the Scottish giants, he returned to Merseyside to play for Tranmere Rovers, where his versatility and experience proved an invaluable asset; he went on to clock up 150 appearances at Prenton Park.

Peter REID

Position	Midfielder
Born	Peter Reid, Huyton, 20 June 1956
Height	5ft 8in
Weight	10st 7lb
Clubs	Bolton Wanderers, Everton, Queen's Park Rangers, Manchester City, Southampton, Notts County, Bury
England Caps	13
	1985 v Mexico (lost 0–1), v W. Germany (won 3–0), v United States (won 5–0), v Romania (1–1)
	1986 v Scotland (won 2–1), v Canada (won 1–0), v Poland (won 3–0), v Paraguay (won 3–0), v Argentina (lost 1–2)
	1987 v Brazil (1–1), v W. Germany (lost 1–3), v Yugoslavia (won 4–1)
	1988 v Switzerland (won 1–0)
Honours	Footballer of the Year 1985

REPLACING THE INJURED Bryan Robson in the 1986 World Cup Finals, Peter Reid, who went on to win 13 caps for England, was a member of the Huyton Boys' team that caused something of an upset when they won the English Schools Trophy in 1970.

Reid began his Football League career with Bolton Wanderers, where his cultured midfield play and intense desire to be involved at all times were features of the

Wanderers' Second Division Championship-winning team of 1977/78. Injury forced him to miss Bolton's opening games in the top flight but he soon recovered to take his place in the side. Then, on New Year's Day 1979, he collided with Everton goalkeeper George Wood on an icy Burnden Park and broke his leg. Out of the game for over 12 months, contractual problems subsequently prevented him from playing, until he was placed on a weekly contract. He suffered another broken leg, this time at Barnsley, but again won his fight for fitness, and in December 1982 he became one of the bargain buys of all time when he joined Everton for just £60,000.

In 1984/85, his most injury-free term, Everton won the League Championship and European Cup Winners' Cup and Reid was voted the players' Player of the Year. He helped the Blues win their second League title in three years in 1987, and then, following the departure of Howard Kendall, he became Everton's player-coach. He later left to continue his playing career with Queen's Park Rangers before becoming player-coach at Manchester City. Later appointed the Maine Road club's manager, he left to spend seven years in charge of Sunderland, taking the Black Cats into the Premiership as runaway First Division leaders, before losing his job in October 2002. He then managed Leeds united before parting company with the Yorkshire club in November 2003.

Kerry DIXON

Position	Forward
Born	Kerry Michael Dixon, Luton, 24 July 1961
Height	6ft 0in
Weight	13st 0lb
Clubs	Reading, Chelsea, Southampton, Luton Town, Millwall, Watford, Doncaster Rovers
England Caps	8 Goals 4
	1985 v Mexico (lost 0–1), v W. Germany (won 3–0) 2 goals, v United States (won 5–0) 2 goals, v N. Ireland (0–0)
	1986 v Israel (won 2–1), v Mexico (won 3–0), v Poland (won 3–0), v Sweden (lost 0–1)

KERRY DIXON began his career with Reading, where he soon gained a reputation as a prolific goalscorer, and though the Royals eventually lost their Third Division status in 1978/79, Dixon was the divisional top scorer with 26 goals. On joining Chelsea, he scored twice on his debut and began to form a lethal strike partnership with David Speedie, notching 28 goals as the club won the Second Division Championship in 1983/84. He topped the First Division scoring charts in his first season in the top flight but despite a great start at international level – scoring a goal every other game – he was never given an extended England run.

In 1988/89 after just one season in Division Two, Dixon's goals were a major factor in Chelsea winning the Second Division title. However, in the summer of 1992, after losing his place to Tony Cascarino, he joined Southampton for £575,000. Injuries hampered his progress at the Dell and in February 1993 he was loaned out to Luton Town. The move later became permanent but it wasn't long before he was on the move again, this time to Millwall. Despite outscoring the Lions' big-money signings, Dixon later joined Watford before being appointed player-manager of Doncaster Rovers.

Paul BRACEWELL

Position	Midfielder
Born	Paul William Bracewell, Stoke-on-Trent, 19 July 1962
Height	5ft 8in
Weight	10st 9lb
Clubs	Stoke City, Sunderland, Everton, Newcastle United, Fulham
England Caps	3
	1985 v W. Germany (won 3–0), v United States (won 5–0), v N. Ireland (0–0)

PAUL BRACEWELL spent three seasons with his home-town club Stoke City before following manager Alan Durban to Sunderland for £250,000. Things didn't work out for him at Roker Park and after just one season he moved to Everton. He had the rare distinction of making his Everton debut at Wembley, when he played in the Charity Shield showpiece against Liverpool in August 1984. Forming a good understanding with Peter Reid in the Everton midfield, he won his first England cap when he replaced Bryan Robson against West Germany on the summer tour to Mexico.

On New Year's Day 1986, Bracewell suffered a serious ankle injury at Newcastle United and was out of action for more than 20 months. During this time he underwent five operations and then, after returning to first-team action towards the end of the 1987/88 season, he had to undergo more surgery on his right ankle. Finally, having won League Championship and European Cup Winners' Cup medals with Everton, he left Goodison in the summer of 1989 to rejoin Sunderland for a fee of £250,000.

Bracewell played for the Wearsiders in the 1992 FA Cup Final before joining Newcastle United. He made a telling contribution to the Magpies' promotion to the Premiership before returning in 1995 for a third spell with Sunderland. His experience proved vital as the Black Cats won the First Division Championship. He later managed Fulham before taking over the reins at Halifax Town.

Chris WOODS

Position	Goalkeeper
Born	Christopher Charles Eric Woods, Boston, 14 November 1959
Height	6ft 2in
Weight	12st 8lb
Clubs	Nottingham Forest, Queen's Park Rangers, Norwich City, Glasgow Rangers, Sheffield Wednesday, Reading, Southampton, Sunderland, Burnley
England Caps	43
	1985 v United States (won 5–0)
	1986 v Egypt (won 4–0), v Israel (won 2–1), v Canada (won 1–0)
	1987 v Yugoslavia (won 4–1), v Spain (won 4–2), v N. Ireland (won 2–0), v Turkey (won 8–0), v Scotland (0–0)
	1988 v Israel (0–0), v Hungary (0–0), v Switzerland (won 1–0), v Soviet Union (lost 1–3)
	1989 v Denmark (1–1)
	1990 v Brazil (won 1–0), v Denmark (won 1–0)

1991 v Hungary (won 1–0), v Poland (1–1), v Eire (1–1), v Soviet Union (won 3–1),
  v Australia (won 1–0), v New Zealand (won 1–0), v New Zealand (won 2–0), v Malaysia
  (won 4–2)
1992 v Germany (lost 1–2), v Turkey (won 1–0), v Poland (1–1), v France (won 2–0), v CIS
  (2–2), v Brazil (1–1), v Poland (won 2–1), v Denmark (0–0), v France (0–0), v Sweden (lost
  1–2)
1993 v Spain (lost 0–1), v Norway (1–1), v Turkey (won 4–0), v San Marino (won 7–1),
  v Turkey (won 2–0), v Holland (2–2), v Poland (won 3–0), v Norway (lost 0–2), v United
  States (lost 0–2)

CHRIS WOODS was only on the losing side in six of his 43 appearances for England, keeping a clean sheet in 22 of those games. He sprang to fame in 1977/78, the season in which Nottingham Forest, newly promoted to the First Division, ran away with the League Championship. Though he played no part in that particular triumph, he starred in the club's first-ever League Cup victory. Peter Shilton was ineligible to play and so Woods played in every match from the third round to the final. One of the youngest keepers to appear in a major final, he performed heroics to help Forest win 1–0 in a replay after a goalless draw at Wembley. The following season he was selected for the England Under-21 side – the first player to be so honoured without a Football League appearance to his name. Too good a player to be Peter Shilton's understudy, he was allowed to join Queen's Park Rangers in the summer of 1979 and was the club's first-choice keeper until losing his place to John Burridge in 1981. Sold to Norwich City, he won another League Cup winners' medal in 1985 when the Canaries beat Sunderland 1–0. While at Carrow Road, Woods won the first of his 43 caps and became one of the first England internationals to join the exodus to Graeme Souness' Glasgow Rangers team.

In five years at Ibrox Park, Woods won four Scottish Premier League Championship medals and four Skol League Cup winners' medals. However, in 1991 Rangers reduced their contingent of English players to avoid problems with the UEFA ruling on 'foreigners' and he was sold to Sheffield Wednesday for £1.2 million. In his first season at Hillsborough the Owls finished third in the First Division, and in 1992/93 he helped them reach both the FA and League Cup finals. He then had a brief loan spell with Reading before joining Southampton, while playing for whom he broke a leg in a match at Blackburn. On recovering from the injury he joined Sunderland, before finishing his career with Burnley.

Danny WALLACE

Position	Forward
Born	David Lloyd Wallace, Greenwich, 21 January 1964
Height	5ft 4in
Weight	9st 13lb
Clubs	Southampton, Manchester United, Millwall, Birmingham City, Wycombe Wanderers
England Caps	1 Goals 1
	1986 v Egypt (won 4–0) 1 goal

AT 16 YEARS 313 DAYS OLD, Danny Wallace became Southampton's youngest-ever player when he made his Football League debut while still an apprentice in a 1–1 draw at Manchester United in November 1980. Elder brother of twins Ray and Rod, he won a regular place in the Saints side on the left wing from October 1982, and finished his first full season as the club's leading scorer with 12 goals. In 1983/84 he missed just one game as Southampton achieved their highest-ever League placing when they finished runners-up to champions Liverpool. Although he won 14 England Under-21 caps, he made just one appearance at full international level, scoring a goal in a 4–0 win over Egypt.

Eventually overshadowed by the exploits of younger brother Rod, Danny left the Dell after scoring 74 goals in 311 games to join Manchester United for £1.2 million. It was not a happy move, for even though he won an FA Cup winners' medal after the Reds had beaten Crystal Palace, he could not win a regular place in the club's starting line-up. In October 1993 he joined Birmingham City for £250,000, but after just 16 League appearances he moved to Wycombe Wanderers, where he ended his first-class career.

Peter BEARDSLEY

Position	Forward
Born	Peter Andrew Beardsley, Newcastle, 18 January 1961
Height	5ft 8in
Weight	11st 7lb
Clubs	Carlisle United, Vancouver Whitecaps, Manchester United, Newcastle United, Liverpool, Everton, Bolton Wanderers, Manchester City, Fulham, Hartlepool United
England Caps	59 Goals 9

1986 v Egypt (won 4–0), v Israel (won 2–1), v Soviet Union (won 1–0), v Mexico (won 3–0) 1 goal, v Canada (won 1–0), v Portugal (lost 0–1), v Poland (won 3–0), v Paraguay (won 3–0) 1 goal, v Argentina (lost 1–2)

1987 v N. Ireland (won 3–0), v Yugoslavia (won 2–0), v Spain (won 4–2), v N. Ireland (won 2–0), v Brazil (1–1), v Scotland (0–0)

1988 v W. Germany (lost 1–3), v Turkey (won 8–0) 1 goal, v Yugoslavia (won 4–1) 1 goal, v Israel (0–0), v Holland (2–2), v Hungary (0–0), v Scotland (won 1–0) 1 goal, v Colombia (1–1), v Switzerland (won 1–0), v Eire (lost 0–1), v Holland (lost 1–3)

1989 v Denmark (won 1–0), v Sweden (0–0), v Saudi Arabia (1–1), v Greece (won 2–1), v Albania (won 2–0), v Albania (won 5–0) 2 goals, v Poland (won 3–0), v Denmark (1–1)

1990 v Sweden (0–0), v Poland (0–0), v Italy (0–0), v Brazil (1–1), v Uruguay (lost 1–2), v Tunisia (1–1), v Eire (1–1), v Egypt (won 1–0), v Cameroon (won 3–2), v W. Germany (1–1 aet, W. Germany won 4–3 on penalties), v Italy (lost 1–2)

1991 v Poland (won 2–0) 1 goal, v Eire (1–1), v Soviet Union (won 3–1), v Eire (1–1)

1994 v Denmark (won 1–0), v Greece (won 5–0) 1 goal, v Norway (0–0)

1995 v Nigeria (won 1–0), v Eire (lost 0–1), v Uruguay (0–0), v Japan (won 2–1), v Sweden (3–3)

1996 v Portugal (1–1), v China (won 3–0)

PETER BEARDSLEY, who was a late and unexpected inclusion for England's 1986 World Cup squad for the finals in Mexico, struck up an inspired partnership with Gary Lineker, which revived a flagging campaign. The pair of them were still important members of the England side four years later in the World Cup Finals in Italy.

A quick-thinking, skilful striker, Beardsley began his career with Carlisle United before trying his luck in North America with Vancouver Whitecaps. His success in Canada alerted Manchester United and they brought him back to these shores. A year later, Newcastle United manager Arthur Cox signed him as a strike partner for Kevin Keegan and in 1983/84, his first season with the club, he scored 20 goals as the Magpies won promotion to the First Division.

In the summer of 1987, Beardsley joined Liverpool, winning a League Championship medal in his first season at Anfield. This was followed by an FA Cup winners' medal in 1989 and another League title triumph the following season. It was a shock when Liverpool manager Graeme Souness sold him to Everton in the summer of 1991. Unsurprisingly, he was the mainstay of the Everton side in two disappointing seasons but, with the club desperately needing money, he was sold to Newcastle United for £1.4 million.

One of the Magpies' all-time greats, he scored 118 goals in 319 games in his two spells with the club and was awarded the MBE in the 1995 Queen's Birthday Honours List. He joined Bolton Wanderers in the summer of 1997, later having loan spells with Manchester City and Fulham before ending his playing career back in the north-east with Hartlepool United.

Steve HODGE

Position	Midfielder
Born	Stephen Brian Hodge, Nottingham, 25 October 1962
Height	5ft 8in
Weight	9st 11lb
Clubs	Nottingham Forest, Aston Villa, Tottenham Hotspur, Leeds United, Derby County, Queen's Park Rangers, Watford, Leyton Orient
England Caps	24
	1986 v Soviet Union (won 1–0), v Scotland (won 2–1), v Canada (won 1–0), v Portugal (lost 0–1), v Morocco (0–0), v Poland (won 3–0), v Paraguay (won 3–0), v Argentina (lost 1–2)
	1987 v Sweden (lost 0–1), v N. Ireland (won 3–0), v Yugoslavia (won 2–0), v Spain (won 4–2), v N. Ireland (won 2–0), v Turkey (0–0), v Scotland (0–0)
	1989 v Denmark (1–1)
	1990 v Italy (0–0), v Yugoslavia (won 2–1), v Czechoslovakia (won 4–2), v Denmark (won 1–0), v Uruguay (lost 1–2), v Tunisia (1–1)
	1991 v Cameroon (won 2–0), v Turkey (won 1–0)

A BUSY left-sided midfield player, Steve Hodge made his League debut for Nottingham Forest in the final game of the 1981/82 season. His performances during the first half of the following campaign led to him winning England Under-21 honours, and he had won five caps at that level by the time of his £450,000 move to

Aston Villa in August 1985. At Villa Park he won 11 full caps and was a regular member of England's 1986 World Cup team. However, with Villa struggling at the wrong end of the table, he took the chance of a £650,000 move to Tottenham Hotspur. Despite helping Spurs to that season's FA Cup Final, he never really settled in London and in August 1988 he rejoined Nottingham Forest.

Back at the City Ground, Hodge won League Cup winners' medals in 1989 and 1990, and came on as a substitute in the 1991 FA Cup Final against Spurs. Brian Clough sold him to Leeds United in the summer of 1991 for £900,000. Despite being hampered by injury problems, he scored some vital goals and made enough appearances to help Leeds win the League Championship in 1991/92. Then, following a short loan spell with Derby County, he joined Queen's Park Rangers before playing for Watford and finally Leyton Orient.

Tony COTTEE

Position	Forward
Born	Anthony Richard Cottee, West Ham, 11 July 1965
Height	5ft 8in
Weight	11st 4lb
Clubs	West Ham United, Everton, Leicester City, Birmingham City, Barnet, Millwall
England Caps	7
	1987 v Sweden (lost 0–1), v N. Ireland (won 3–0)
	1988 v Hungary (0–0)
	1989 v Denmark (won 1–0), v Sweden (0–0), v Chile (0–0), v Scotland (won 2–0)

TONY COTTEE made a sensational debut for his boyhood favourites West Ham United, scoring after 26 minutes in the London derby against Tottenham Hotspur, aged just 17. Two seasons later he was capped by England at Under-21 level and was voted the PFA Young Player of the Year. After winning full international honours against Sweden, he returned to Upton Park and three days later netted his first hat-trick for the club against Coventry City.

In the summer of 1988 he joined Everton for a fee of £2.3 million and marked his debut with a magnificent hat-trick in a 4–0 win over Newcastle United – his first goal coming after just 34 seconds! Although he ended his first season on Merseyside as the Blues' leading scorer and helped the team reach the FA Cup Final, his team-mates were guilty of not playing to his particular strengths. Top scorer in five of his six seasons at Goodison, he rejoined the Hammers in September 1994. The most prolific West Ham striker since Geoff Hurst, he was surprisingly allowed to join Selengor of Malaysia before returning to the UK to play for Leicester City. He helped the Foxes reach the League Cup Final of 1999, where they lost to Spurs, but achieved his ambition of collecting a winners' medal the following season as Leicester beat Tranmere Rovers to lift the League Cup.

Later appointed player-manager of Barnet, Cottee completed his trip around the divisions by joining Second Division promotion candidates Millwall, before being released in the summer of 2001.

Tony ADAMS

Position	Central defender
Born	Tony Alexander Adams, Romford, 10 October 1966
Height	6ft 3in
Weight	13st 11lb
Clubs	Arsenal
England Caps	66 Goals 5

1987 v Spain (won 4–2), v Turkey (0–0), v Brazil (1–1)

1988 v W. Germany (lost 1–3), v Turkey (won 8–0), v Yugoslavia (won 4–1) 1 goal, v Holland (2–2) 1 goal, v Hungary (0–0), v Scotland (won 2–0), v Colombia (1–1), v Switzerland (won 1–0), v Eire (lost 0–1), v Holland (lost 1–3), v Soviet Union (lost 1–3) 1 goal

1989 v Denmark (won 1–0), v Sweden (0–0), v Saudi Arabia (1–1) 1 goal

1991 v Eire (1–1), v Eire (1–1)

1993 v Norway (lost 0–2), v Turkey (won 4–0), v San Marino (won 7–1), v Turkey (won 2–0), v Holland (2–2), v Poland (1–1), v Norway (0–0)

1994 v Poland (won 3–0), v Holland (lost 0–2), v Denmark (won 1–0), v Greece (won 5–0), v Norway (0–0)

1995 v United States (won 2–0), v Romania (1–1), v Eire (lost 0–1), v Uruguay (0–0)

1996 v Colombia (0–0), v Norway (0–0), v Switzerland (1–1), v Portugal (1–1), v China (won 3–0), v Switzerland (1–1), v Scotland (won 2–0), v Holland (won 4–1), v Spain (0–0 aet, England won 4–3 on penalties), v Germany (1–1 aet, Germany won 6–5 on penalties)

1997 v Georgia (won 2–0), v Georgia (won 2–0)

1998 v Italy (0–0), v Chile (lost 0–2), v Portugal (won 3–0), v Saudi Arabia (0–0), v Tunisia (won 2–0), v Romania (lost 1–2), v Colombia (won 2–0), v Argentina (2–2 aet, Argentina won 4–3 on penalties)

1999 v Sweden (0–0), v France (lost 0–2)

2000 v Luxembourg (won 6–0), v Poland (0–0), v Belgium (won 2–1), v Scotland (won 2–0), v Scotland (lost 0–1), v Ukraine (won 2–0) 1 goal, v Portugal (lost 2–3)

2001 v France (1–1), v Germany (lost 0–1)

AN INSPIRATIONAL LEADER for both Arsenal and England, Tony Adams was an integral part of both teams' defences for well over a decade, going on to win 66 caps for England. An imposing central defender, strong in the tackle and hugely effective in the air, he became the second-youngest player in Arsenal's history when in November 1983, at the age of 17 years 26 days, he played against Sunderland. During the next couple of seasons he admirably covered for the likes of David O'Leary and Tommy Caton before, in 1986/87, forming a formidable central defensive partnership at the heart of the Gunners' defence with O'Leary. Then aged 20, he made his full England debut against Spain as well as helping Arsenal beat Liverpool in the League Cup Final. That day he was also named as the PFA Young Player of the Year.

In March 1988 George Graham handed Adams the Arsenal captaincy. The following season he led from the front as the Gunners won the League title. Despite

his heroic performances for Arsenal, he was omitted from England's 1990 World Cup squad and six months later he was given a three-month prison sentence for a well-publicized drink-drive offence. However, on his return to the side, he guided Arsenal to their second League Championship in three seasons. During the course of the 1992/93 season he became the first captain to lift both the FA Cup and League Cup trophies in the same season. The following campaign saw him lead the Gunners to success in the European Cup Winners' Cup, and though injuries often restricted his appearances over the following seasons, he continued to represent both Arsenal and England, captaining Arsenal to the 'double' in 2001/02 and providing great inspiration to the side. Arsene Wenger's plans to reduce the average age of the Gunners' back line led to Adams finally deciding to hang up his boots at the end of that memorable season, having appeared in 672 games for the Gunners. He went on to manage Wycombe Wanderers.

Stuart PEARCE

Position	Left-back
Born	Stuart Pearce, Hammersmith, 24 April 1962
Height	5ft 10in
Weight	12st 9lb
Clubs	Coventry City, Nottingham Forest, Newcastle United, West Ham United, Manchester City
England Caps	78 Goals 5

1987 v Brazil (1–1), v Scotland (0–0)

1988 v W. Germany (lost 1–3), v Israel (0–0), v Hungary (0–0)

1989 v Denmark (won 1–0), v Sweden (0–0), v Saudi Arabia (1–1), v Greece (won 2–1), v Albania (won 2–0), v Albania (won 5–0), v Chile (0–0), v Scotland (won 2–0), v Poland (won 3–0), v Denmark (1–1)

1990 v Sweden (0–0), v Poland (0–0), v Italy (0–0), v Yugoslavia (won 2–1), v Brazil (won 1–0), v Czechoslovakia (won 4–2) 1 goal, v Denmark (won 1–0), v Uruguay (lost 1–2), v Tunisia (1–1), v Eire (1–1), v Holland (0–0), v Egypt (won 1–0), v Belgium (won 1–0), v Cameroon (won 3–2), v W. Germany (1–1 aet, W. Germany won 4–3 on penalties)

1991 v Hungary (won 1–0), v Poland (won 2–0), v Eire (1–1), v Cameroon (won 2–0), v Eire (1–1), v Turkey (won 1–0), v Argentina (2–2), v Australia (won 1–0), v New Zealand (won 1–0), v New Zealand (won 2–0) 1 goal, v Malaysia (won 4–2)

1992 v Turkey (won 1–0), v Poland (1–1), v France (won 2–0), v Czechoslovakia (2–2), v Brazil (1–1), v Finland (won 2–1), v Denmark (0–0), v France (0–0), v Sweden (lost 1–2)

1993 v Spain (lost 0–1), v Norway (1–1), v Turkey (won 4–0) 1 goal

1994 v Poland (won 3–0) 1 goal, v San Marino (won 7–1), v Greece (won 5–0)

1995 v Romania (1–1), v Japan (won 2–1), v Brazil (lost 1–3)

1996 v Norway (0–0), v Switzerland (won 3–1) 1 goal, v Portugal (1–1), v Bulgaria (won 1–0), v Croatia (0–0), v Hungary (won 3–0), v Switzerland (1–1), v Scotland (won 2–0), v Holland (won 4–1), v Spain (0–0 aet, England won 4–3 on penalties), v Germany (1–1 aet, Germany won 6–5 on penalties)

1997 v Moldova (won 4–0), v Poland (won 2–0), v Italy (lost 0–1), v Mexico (won 2–0), v S. Africa (won 2–1), v Italy (won 2–0)

2000 v Luxembourg (won 6–0), v Poland (0–0)

Stuart Pearce celebrates after scoring his penalty during the European Championship match with Spain at Wembley on 22 June 1996. England won the match in a penalty shoot-out after extra time. (Ben Radford/Getty Images)

THOUGH HE WILL be remembered for failing from the 12-yard mark in the semi-final shoot-out against West Germany in the 1990 World Cup, Stuart Pearce had a superb Euro '96 and laid the ghost to rest by scoring twice from the spot in penalty shoot-outs.

Pearce was spotted playing non-League football for Wealdstone United by Coventry City manager Bobby Gould. He had played in 51 games for the Sky Blues before joining Nottingham Forest in a double deal involving Ian Butterworth in the summer of 1985. He soon became a firm favourite with the Forest fans for his aggressive tackling and wholehearted determination. In 1987 he was awarded the first of his 78 caps and became Forest's captain. Then, in 1988/89, he skippered Forest to League Cup and Simod Cup success. Playing in 522 games for Forest, he scored 88 goals, many of them spectacular efforts from outside the penalty area. A number of his goals also came from the penalty spot.

Pearce, who announced his retirement from international football at the end of Euro '96, was later appointed Forest's player-manager following Frank Clark's departure. He then became the first manager to represent his country as a player when he was persuaded to play in England's World Cup qualifiers in 1996/97. One of the most popular players ever to wear the red of Nottingham Forest, he left the City Ground in 1997 to join Newcastle United, later having spells with both West Ham United and Manchester City.

Neil WEBB

Position	Midfielder
Born	Neil John Webb, Reading, 30 July 1963
Height	6ft 0in
Weight	13st 0lb
Clubs	Reading, Portsmouth, Nottingham Forest, Manchester United, Swindon Town, Grimsby Town
England Caps	26 Goals 4
	1988 v W. Germany (lost 1–3), v Turkey (won 8–0) 1 goal, v Yugoslavia (won 4–1), v Israel (0–0), v Holland (2–2), v Scotland (won 1–0), v Switzerland (won 1–0), v Eire (lost 0–1), v Soviet Union (lost 1–3)
	1989 v Denmark (won 1–0) 1 goal, v Sweden (0–0), v Greece (won 2–1), v Albania (won 2–0), v Albania (won 5–0), v Chile (0–0), v Scotland (won 2–0), v Poland (won 3–0) 1 goal, v Denmark (1–1)
	1990 v Sweden (0–0), v Italy (0–0)
	1992 v France (won 2–0), v Hungary (won 1–0) 1 goal, v Brazil (1–1), v Finland (won 2–1), v Denmark (0–0), v Sweden (lost 1–2)

THE SON OF former Reading forward Dougie Webb, Neil followed his father to Elm Park before joining Portsmouth, where he began to produce some impressive midfield displays. After appearing in 123 games for the Fratton Park club he signed for Nottingham Forest in the summer of 1985, making his debut on the opening day of the 1985/86 season. He became an important member of Forest's midfield as well as a regular goalscorer, netting hat-tricks in the wins over Coventry City in January 1986 and Chelsea in September of the same year. His performances led to him winning the first of his 26 full caps for England against West Germany in 1988, but when his contract expired in 1989 a tribunal set a fee of £1.5 million, which Manchester United were more than happy to meet.

Hampered by injuries in his first season at Old Trafford, he came back to gain an FA Cup winners' medal in 1990 and to make an appearance in that year's World Cup Finals. He returned to the City Ground for a second spell in October 1992 before, following a loan spell at Swindon Town, he joined Grimsby Town, subsequently playing non-League football with Aldershot.

Mick HARFORD

Position	Forward
Born	Michael Gordon Harford, Sunderland, 12 February 1959
Height	6ft 2in
Weight	12st 9lb
Clubs	Lincoln City, Newcastle United, Bristol City, Birmingham City, Luton Town, Derby County, Chelsea, Sunderland, Coventry City, Wimbledon
England Caps	2
	1988 v Israel (0–0)
	1989 v Denmark (won 1–0)

MUCH-TRAVELLED STRIKER Mick Harford, who appeared in two full internationals for England, began his career with Lincoln City. After topping the club's scoring charts in his first two seasons with the Imps, he left to join Newcastle United for £180,000, still the record fee received by the Sincil Bank club.

Harford failed to settle at St James' Park and joined Bristol City, but the Robins were on the verge of bankruptcy and could not meet the instalments on his transfer fee. Newcastle appealed to the Football League, who ordered Bristol City to return Harford to the Magpies on a free transfer. The Ashton Gate club immediately sold him to Birmingham City, the fee of £100,000 being paid to Newcastle rather than Bristol. His goals helped the Blues stave off relegation to the Second Division but he was soon on the move again, this time to Luton Town, where he enjoyed the best years of his career. In 1988 he won a League Cup winners' medal but, after scoring 81 goals in 186 games for the Hatters, he made a surprise move to Derby County. Unable to prevent the Rams' relegation in 1990/91, he returned to Kenilworh Road for a second spell before signing for Chelsea. He later played for his home-town club Sunderland, and then Coventry City, before joining Wimbledon, where he also had a spell as coach.

Steve McMAHON

Position	Midfielder
Born	Stephen McMahon, Liverpool, 20 August 1961
Height	5ft 9in
Weight	11st 8lb
Clubs	Everton, Aston Villa, Liverpool, Manchester City, Swindon Town
England Caps	17
	1988 v Israel (0–0), v Hungary (0–0), v Colombia (1–1), v Soviet Union (lost 1–3)
	1989 v Denmark (won 1–0)
	1990 v Sweden (0–0), v Poland (0–0), v Italy (0–0), v Yugoslavia (won 2–1), v Brazil (won 1–0), v Czechoslovakia (won 4–2), v Denmark (won 1–0), v Eire (1–1), v Egypt (won 1–0), v Belgium (won 1–0), v Italy (lost 1–2)
	1991 v Eire (1–1)

A FORMER Goodison Park ballboy, Steve McMahon joined Everton, where his honest endeavour and total commitment was much appreciated by the Blues' supporters. A bright future seemed assured when he was selected to play for the England Under-21 side against the Republic of Ireland, and, though he wasn't playing in a particularly good Everton side, he continued to perform at a consistently high level. When his contract ended in 1983 he refused to sign another, instead joining Aston Villa for a fee of £250,000, but, unable to settle in the Midlands, he became Kenny Dalglish's first signing when he moved to Anfield for £350,000. It was only after he joined Liverpool that he won full international honours and a place in Bobby Robson's 1990 World Cup squad.

McMahon's abrasive ball-winning qualities, fine distribution and powerful shooting were soon in evidence at Liverpool, and, ironically, his first goal for the club was the winner in the Merseyside derby. However, it was only after the arrival of John Barnes and Peter Beardsley that McMahon began to realize his full potential. His success at Liverpool brought him 17 caps, but after six seasons at Anfield in which he won three League Championship and two FA Cup winners' medals, he moved to Manchester City for £900,000.

In November 1994 McMahon was appointed player-manager of Swindon Town, and though the club suffered successive relegations he inspired the Robins to win the Second Division Championship in 1995/96. Later relieved of his duties, he is now manager of Blackpool, whom he helped to promotion to the Second Division via the play-offs in 2000/01.

Steve BULL

Position	Forward		
Born	Stephen George Bull, Tipton, 28 March 1965		
Height	5ft 11in		
Weight	11st 4lb		
Clubs	West Bromwich Albion, Wolverhampton Wanderers		
England Caps	13	Goals	4

1988 v Scotland (won 2–0) I goal
1989 v Denmark (I–I)
1990 v Yugoslavia (won 2–1), v Czechoslovakia (won 4–2) 2 goals, v Denmark (won 1–0),
   v Uruguay (lost 1–2), v Tunisia (I–I) I goal, v Eire (I–I), v Holland (0–0), v Egypt (won
   1–0), v Belgium (won 1–0)
1991 v Hungary (won 1–0), v Poland (won 2–0)

STEVE BULL's goalscoring achievements brought him international recognition. After Under-21 and 'B' matches, he made a goalscoring full international debut in a 2–0 win over Scotland.

Originally with West Bromwich Albion, Bull was given permission to leave the Hawthorns by Baggies manager Ron Atkinson in November 1986 for a mere £65,000, a deal which also involved Andy Thompson. He soon struck up a good understanding with Andy Mutch and in 1987/88 he helped Wolves win the Fourth Division Championship. It was his first full season and he scored the remarkable total of 52 goals. He also scored in every round of the Sherpa Van Trophy leading up to the final, where Wolves beat Burnley. In 1988/89 Bull scored 50 goals to become the first player for over 60 years to score over 100 goals in consecutive English seasons, as Wolves won the Third Division title.

He continued to top the goalscoring charts for Wolves and on the opening day of the 1996/97 season, set a new club record by scoring the 17th hat-trick of his career against Grimsby Town. Despite suffering from a series of injuries, he went on to score a remarkable 300 goals in 544 first-team games before announcing his retirement.

Gary PALLISTER

Position	Central defender
Born	Gary Andrew Pallister, Ramsgate, 30 June 1965
Height	6ft 4in
Weight	13st 0lb
Clubs	Middlesbrough, Darlington, Manchester United
England Caps	22
	1988 v Hungary (0–0)
	1989 v Saudi Arabia (I–I)
	1991 v Cameroon (won 2–0), v Turkey (won 1–0)
	1992 v Germany (lost 0–1)
	1993 v Norway (lost 0–2), v United States (lost 0–2), v Brazil (I–I), v Germany (lost 1–2)
	1994 v Poland (won 3–0), v Holland (lost 0–2), v San Marino (won 7–1), v Denmark (won 1–0)
	1995 v United States (won 2–0), v Romania (I–I), v Eire (lost 0–1), v Uruguay (0–0), v Sweden (3–3)
	1996 v Norway (0–0), v Switzerland (won 3–1)
	1997 v Moldova (won 3–0), v Poland (won 2–1)
Honours	Footballer of the Year 1992

Gary Pallister takes on Karl-Heinz Riedle of Germany during a friendly match at Wembley in September 1991. Germany won 1–0. (Bob Martin/Getty Images)

GARY PALLISTER played his early football for Billingham Town in the Northern League before joining Middlesbrough. Shortly after making his League debut he went on loan to Darlington, before returning to Ayresome Park to form a formidable central defensive partnership with Tony Mowbray. He became the first player from the Second Division to be selected by Bobby Robson for the full England squad, but Boro manager Bruce Rioch had to pull him out of the party so that he could play for the club in the end of season play-offs. He eventually won the first of 22 full caps for England against Hungary in 1988.

Following Boro's relegation in 1989, Pallister joined Manchester United for £2.3 million. Though he didn't look too comfortable at the start, as time progressed he began to look more confident, and by 1992 he was impressing his colleagues enough to be named PFA Player of the Year. He helped United win their first League Championship since 1967 when they won the Premiership in 1992/93, and then went on to win four League Championship medals, three FA Cup winners' medals, a League Cup winners' medal and a European Cup Winners' Cup winners' medal.

Pallister went on to appear in 437 games for the Reds before rejoining Middlesbrough in the summer of 1998. A towering presence in the air, injuries finally forced the likeable defender to leave the game.

Paul GASCOIGNE

Position	Midfielder
Born	Paul John Gascoigne, Gateshead, 27 May 1967
Height	5ft 10in
Weight	11st 12lb
Clubs	Newcastle United, Tottenham Hotspur, Lazio, Glasgow Rangers, Middlesbrough, Everton, Burnley
England Caps	57 Goals 10

1989 v Denmark (0–0), v Saudi Arabia (1–1), v Albania (won 5–0) 1 goal, v Chile (0–0), v Scotland (won 2–0)

1990 v Sweden (0–0), v Brazil (won 1–0), v Czechoslovakia (won 4–2) 1 goal, v Denmark (won 1–0), v Uruguay (lost 1–2), v Tunisia (1–1), v Eire (1–1), v Holland (0–0), v Egypt (won 1–0), v Belgium (won 1–0), v Cameroon (won 3–2), v W. Germany (1–1 aet, W. Germany won 4–3 on penalties)

1991 v Hungary (won 1–0), v Poland (won 2–0), v Cameroon (won 2–0)

1993 v Norway (1–1), v Turkey (won 4–0) 2 goals, v San Marino (won 6–0), v Turkey (won 2–0) 1 goal, v Holland (2–2), v Poland (1–1), v Norway (lost 0–2)

1994 v Poland (won 3–0) 1 goal, v Denmark (won 1–0)

1995 v Japan (won 2–1), v Sweden (3–3), v Brazil (lost 1–3)

1996 v Colombia (0–0), v Switzerland (won 3–1), v Portugal (1–1), v Bulgaria (won 1–0), v Croatia (0–0), v China (won 3–0) 1 goal, v Switzerland (1–1), v Scotland (won 2–0) 1 goal, v Holland (won 4–1), v Spain (0–0 aet, England won 4–3 on penalties), v Germany (1–1 aet, Germany won 6–5 on penalties)

1997 v Moldova (won 3–0) 1 goal, v Poland (won 2–1), v Georgia (won 2–0), v S. Africa (won 2–1), v Poland (won 2–0), v Italy (won 2–0), v France (won 1–0), v Brazil (lost 0–1)

1998 v Moldova (won 4–0) 1 goal, v Italy (0–0), v Cameroon (won 2–0), v Saudi Arabia (0–0), v Morocco (won 1–0), v Belgium (0–0)

PAUL GASCOIGNE was hailed as the player around whom England should build its team for the 1990 World Cup. He was the undoubted star in England's march to the semi-finals, and his televised tears when he realized that a booking in the semi-final would rule him out of the final, were England to progress, endeared him to the nation.

Gascoigne progressed through the ranks at Newcastle United to make his League debut a month before turning professional. Quickly establishing himself as the most exciting talent of his generation, he was voted Young Player of the Year by the PFA in 1988. His sense of humour occasionally got him into trouble but in the summer of 1988, after scoring 25 goals in 107 games for the Magpies, Spurs manager Terry Venables signed Gazza for a British record fee of £2 million. Within 11 days of his Spurs debut at Newcastle, when the Geordie fans pelted him with Mars bars, he won his first full England cap, playing as a substitute against Denmark.

Following the 1990 World Cup, Gascoigne continued where he had left off, steering Spurs almost single-handedly to the 1991 FA Cup Final. His day was ruined after only 15 minutes by a serious ligament injury caused by a rash challenge on his part, and he was carried off. The career-threatening damage to his cruciate ligament

Paul Gascoigne bursts into tears after the World Cup Finals 1990 semi-final with West Germany in Turin. The match ended 1–1 after extra time and West Germany went on to win 4–3 on penalties. (David Cannon/Getty Images)

put his record £8.5 million move to Lazio in jeopardy but, after taking a year to recover, he eventually moved for £5 million to show the Italians what he could do.

In the summer of 1995 Gascoigne joined Glasgow Rangers for £4.3 million, helping the Scottish club to two Premier League titles and success in both cup competitions before joining Middlesbrough for £3.45 million in March 1998. He became the first player to make his debut for a club in a Wembley cup final when he came off the bench in the League Cup Final against Chelsea. His charisma both off and on the field contributed to Boro's late successful promotion bid to the Premiership, but sadly he was not part of the World Cup squad for France '98 following a well-documented argument with manager Glenn Hoddle. On leaving the north-east, Gascoigne had spells with Everton and Burnley before the next twists in his career took him briefly to China and then to a trial with Wolverhampton Wanderers.

David ROCASTLE

Position	Midfielder
Born	David Carlyle Rocastle, Lewisham, 2 May 1967
Died	31 March 2001
Height	5ft 9in
Weight	12st 10lb
Clubs	Arsenal, Leeds United, Manchester City, Chelsea, Norwich City, Hull City
England Caps	14
	1989 v Denmark (0–0), v Saudi Arabia (1–1), v Greece (won 2–1), v Albania (won 2–0), v Albania (won 5–0), v Poland (won 3–0), v Denmark (1–1)
	1990 v Sweden (0–0), v Poland (0–0), v Yugoslavia (won 2–1), v Denmark (won 1–0)
	1992 v Poland (1–1), v Czechoslovakia (2–2), v Brazil (1–1)

ONE OF ARSENAL'S most popular players of recent years, David 'Rocky' Rocastle soon became known throughout the length and breadth of the country as someone with great footballing skills, occasionally overshadowed by his sometimes temperamental behaviour. But this did not distract from the fact that, during the late 1980s and early 1990s, Rocastle was one of the most talented players in English football. Beautifully balanced and possessing the instinct of knowing when to release the ball, he scored a number of vital goals for the Gunners, perhaps none more important than the last-minute extra-time goal against Spurs that took Arsenal through to the 1987 League Cup Final against Liverpool. He was ever-present in Arsenal's League Championship-winning side of 1988/89, and his form led to the first of 14 caps for England.

Later during his time at Highbury Rocastle was switched to a more central midfield position but in August 1992, after playing in 287 games, he was sold to Leeds

United for £2 million. Injuries hampered his progress at Elland Road and after some 16 months he was transferred to Manchester City for a similar fee. Again his stay was brief and he soon moved to Chelsea, following which, after loan spells with Norwich City and Hull City, he decided to retire. In March 2001, aged just 33, this most popular of players lost his battle against cancer.

Des WALKER

Position	Central defender
Born	Desmond Sinclair Walker, Hackney, 26 November 1965
Height	5ft 11in
Weight	11st 13lb
Clubs	Nottingham Forest, Sampdoria, Sheffield Wednesday
England Caps	59

1989 v Denmark (won 1–0), v Sweden (0–0), v Greece (won 2–1), v Albania (won 2–0), v Albania (won 5–0), v Chile (0–0), v Scotland (won 2–0), v Poland (won 3–0), v Denmark (1–1)

1990 v Sweden (0–0), v Poland (0–0), v Italy (0–0), v Yugoslavia (won 2–1), v Brazil (won 1–0), v Czechoslovakia (won 4–2), v Denmark (won 1–0), v Uruguay (lost 1–2), v Tunisia (1–1), v Eire (1–1), v Holland (0–0), v Egypt (won 1–0), v Belgium (won 1–0), v Cameroon (won 3–2), v W. Germany (1–1 aet, W. Germany won 4–3 on penalties), v Italy (lost 1–2)

1991 v Hungary (won 1–0), v Poland (won 2–0), v Eire (1–1), v Cameroon (won 2–0), v Eire (1–1), v Turkey (won 1–0), v Argentina (2–2), v Australia (won 1–0), v New Zealand (won 1–0), v New Zealand (won 2–0), v Malaysia (won 4–2)

1992 v Turkey (won 1–0), v Poland (1–1), v France (won 2–0), v Czechoslovakia (2–2), v CIS (2–2), v Hungary (won 1–0), v Brazil (1–1), v Finland (won 2–1), v Denmark (0–0), v France (0–0), v Sweden (lost 1–2)

1993 v Spain (lost 0–1), v Norway (1–1), v Turkey (won 4–0), v San Marino (won 6–0), v Turkey (won 2–0), v Holland (2–2), v Poland (1–1), v Norway (lost 0–2), v United States (lost 0–2), v Brazil (1–1), v Germany (lost 1–2)

1994 v San Marino (won 7–1)

REJECTED BY TOTTENHAM HOTSPUR, Aston Villa and Birmingham City, Des Walker signed professional forms for Nottingham Forest in December 1983. Following his League debut against Everton in March 1984, he was selected for the England Under-21 side and thereafter was a fixture in the Forest side. Exceedingly fast, he displayed a maturity beyond his years and a coolness even in the most desperate of situations. He made the first of his 59 international appearances against Denmark in 1989, coming on as a substitute for Arsenal's Tony Adams.

After appearing in 345 League and Cup games for Forest with just one goal, scored in the 1–1 home draw against Luton Town on New Year's Day 1992, he signed for Italian club Sampdoria in May of that year. Following only 30 League games for the Italian side, however, he returned to England to sign for Sheffield Wednesday.

Still a class player – and one of the Owls' best-ever signings – his decisive tackling, timely interceptions and ability to read the game make him a formidable opponent. Captain during his latter years at Hillsborough, he went on to appear in 372 games for the Yorkshire club before returning to the City Ground in the summer of 2002, when he was immediately appointed captain. His calming influence and experience were a great help to his young team-mates.

Brian MARWOOD

Position	Winger
Born	Brian Marwood, Seaham, 5 February 1960
Height	5ft 7in
Weight	9st 13lb
Clubs	Hull City, Sheffield Wednesday, Arsenal, Sheffield United, Middlesbrough, Swindon Town, Barnet
England Caps	1
	1989 v Saudi Arabia (1–1)

A SKILFUL RIGHT-WINGER with a good goalscoring record at Hull City, where he began his League career, Brian Marwood soon attracted the attention of bigger clubs and in August 1984 he joined Sheffield Wednesday for £115,000. He quickly made his mark in the top flight, and in his second season with the club, 1985/86, he was the Owls' leading goalscorer. Midway through the following season he missed a number of games through injury and when he finally returned he seemed to have lost some of his confidence. In March 1988, after scoring 35 goals in 160 games for Wednesday, he was transferred to Arsenal for £600,000. At Highbury he won a League Championship medal and his one and only England cap when he came on as a substitute against Saudi Arabia.

Following the Gunners' recruitment of Anders Limpar, Marwood returned to Sheffield, but this time to United. By then, he had been appointed to the PFA and his appearances dwindled. After an unsuccessful loan spell at Middlesbrough, he joined Swindon Town as a non-contract player before ending his first-class career with Barnet.

David SEAMAN

Position	Goalkeeper
Born	David Andrew Seaman, Rotherham, 19 September 1963
Height	6ft 4in
Weight	14st 10lb
Clubs	Leeds United, Peterborough United, Birmingham City, Queen's Park Rangers, Arsenal, Manchester City
England Caps	75
	1989 v Saudi Arabia (1–1), v Denmark (1–1)
	1990 v Czechoslovakia (won 4–2)
	1991 v Cameroon (won 2–0), v Eire (1–1), v Turkey (won 1–0), v Argentina (2–2)
	1992 v Czechoslovakia (2–2), v Hungary (won 1–0)
	1994 v Poland (won 3–0), v Holland (lost 0–2), v San Marino (won 7–1), v Denmark (won 1–0), v Norway (0–0)

1995 v United States (won 2–0), v Romania (1–1), v Eire (lost 0–1)
1996 v Colombia (0–0), v Norway (0–0), v Switzerland (won 3–1), v Poland (won 2–0),
     v Bulgaria (won 1–0), v Croatia (0–0), v Hungary (won 3–0), v Switzerland (1–1),
     v Scotland (won 2–0), v Holland (won 4–1), v Spain (0–0 aet, England won 4–3 on
     penalties), v Germany (1–1 aet, Germany won 6–5 on penalties)
1997 v Moldova (won 3–0), v Poland (won 2–1), v Georgia (won 2–0), v georgia (won 2–0),
     v Poland (won 2–0), v France (won 1–0), v Brazil (lost 0–1)
1998 v Moldova (won 4–0), v Italy (0–0), v Portugal (won 3–0), v Saudi Arabia (0–0),
     v Tunisia (won 2–0), v Romania (lost 1–2), v Colombia (won 2–0), v Argentina (2–2 aet,
     Argentina won 4–3 on penalties)
1999 v Sweden (0–0), v Bulgaria (0–0), v Luxembourg (won 3–0), v France (lost 0–2),
     v Poland (won 3–1), v Hungary (1–1), v Sweden (0–0), v Bulgaria (1–1)
2000 v Belgium (won 2–1), v Scotland (won 2–0), v Scotland (lost 0–1), v Argentina (0–0),
     v Brazil (1–1), v Portugal (lost 2–3), v Germany (won 1–0)
2001 v France (1–1), v Germany (lost 0–1), v Finland (0–0), v Finland (won 2–1), v Albania
     (won 3–1), v Greece (won 2–0)
2002 v Germany (won 5–1), v Albania (won 2–0), v Paraguay (won 4–0), v Sweden (1–1),
     v Argentina (won 1–0), v Nigeria (0–0), v Denmark (won 3–0), v Brazil (lost 1–2),
     v Slovakia (won 2–1), v Macedonia (2–2)

DAVID SEAMAN took the steady and unspectacular route to international status, which parallel his solid and reliable goalkeeping style.

Unable to break into the Leeds United side because of the consistency of John Lukic, David Seaman joined Peterborough United in the summer of 1982. His brilliant form for The Posh was noted by Birmingham City manager Jim Smith, who paid £100,000 for his services in October 1984. Having helped the Blues win promotion to the First Division with a series of outstanding displays, he could not save the club from relegation after just one season in the top flight. In order to remain playing at the highest level, he joined Queen's Park Rangers for £225,000 in August 1986, and in four seasons at Loftus Road he was a first-team fixture. He won his first England cap in 1988/89, against Saudi Arabia.

In May 1990, after he had appeared in 175 games for Rangers, Arsenal paid out a record British fee for a goalkeeper of £1.3 million to obtain Seaman's services. No Gunners supporter could have realized the impact David Seaman would have on the Arsenal side. In the League Championship-winning season of 1990/91, when he was ever-present, he broke two records, conceding only 18 League goals and keeping 24 clean sheets! Very relaxed and composed both on and off the field of play, in 1992/93 he helped the club to the FA and League Cup double, while the following season he was a member of the Arsenal side that beat Parma to win the European Cup Winners' Cup. He enhanced his reputation even more during Euro '96 with two superb penalty saves, including one against Spain that was instrumental in England reaching the semi-final stage.

In 1997/98, after a series of niggling injuries, he helped Arsenal complete the League and Cup double and then appeared in all four of England's World Cup games

in France '98. He was instrumental in Arsenal completing another League and FA Cup double in 2001/02, he was England's first-choice keeper for the 2002 World Cup Finals in Japan and Korea. Though he was at fault for Ronaldinho's winner in the quarter-final against Brazil, he remained a model of consistency behind Arsenal's back four, maintaining a high percentage of clean sheets in his 552 first-team appearances.

In 2003, recognizing that his days as first-choice keeper at Arsenal were over, Seaman joined Manchester City before retiring midway through the 2003/04 season.

Mel STERLAND

Position	Right-back
Born	Melvyn Sterland, Sheffield, 1 October 1961
Height	5ft 11in
Weight	13st 2lb
Clubs	Sheffield Wednesday, Glasgow Rangers, Leeds United
England Caps	1
	1989 v Saudi Arabia (1–1)

AFFECTIONATELY KNOWN AS 'ZICO' because of his tremendous ability in dead-ball situations, Mel Sterland originally started his career at Hillsborough as a midfielder but was converted to right-back in 1981/82. A member of the Owls side that won promotion to the First Division in 1983/84, he scored a number of vital goals for the club, netting 11 times in 1985/86 – a great return for a full-back. His exciting displays eventually led to international recognition when he was selected to play for England against Saudi Arabia.

Sterland would probably have remained with Wednesday for the rest of his career, but after inexplicably being relieved of the captaincy he asked for a transfer and in March 1989 joined Glasgow Rangers for £800,000. In his brief stay at Ibrox he helped Rangers win the Scottish Premier League Championship, after which he moved on to Leeds United. Reunited with Howard Wilkinson, he helped Leeds win the Second Division title in 1989/90 and the League Championship two seasons later. Injuries then forced him to have a nine-month lay-off from the game, and when he finally returned he managed only five games before having to have a fourth operation on his ankle. Midway through the 1993/94 season, Leeds terminated his contract.

Michael THOMAS

Position	Midfielder
Born	Michael Lauriston Thomas, Lambeth, 24 August 1967
Height	5ft 10in
Weight	12st 4lb
Clubs	Arsenal, Portsmouth, Liverpool, Benfica, Middlesbrough, Wimbledon
England Caps	2
	1989 v Saudi Arabia (1–1)
	1990 v Yugoslavia (won 2–1)

MICHAEL THOMAS wrote himself into the Arsenal record books on 26 May 1989 when his injury-time goal in the last game of the season against Liverpool at Anfield decided the League Championship.

A former England youth captain, he started his career with a loan spell at Portsmouth before returning to Highbury to make his first-team debut in a League Cup semi-final home leg against Spurs. Within a season he had won England Under-21 honours, and when he played against Saudi Arabia to win his first full cap he became the first Arsenal player to have represented England at five different levels – schoolboy, youth, Under-21, 'B' and full international.

In December 1991, after appearing in 220 games for the Gunners, Thomas was transferred to Liverpool for £1.5 million. Though plagued by injuries, he repaid most of his transfer fee when he scored a stunning goal in the 1992 FA Cup Final win over Sunderland. He continued to be troubled by niggling injuries throughout his stay at Anfield but still managed to appear in 163 games before joining Benfica on a free transfer. He returned to England in the summer of 2000 and spent the following season playing for Wimbledon before leaving the first-class game.

Alan SMITH

Position	Forward
Born	Alan Martin Smith, Bromsgrove, 21 November 1962
Height	6ft 3in
Weight	12st 0lb
Clubs	Leicester City, Arsenal
England Caps	13 Goals 2
	1989 v Saudi Arabia (1–1), v Greece (won 2–1), v Albania (won 2–0), v Poland (won 3–0)
	1991 v Turkey (won 1–0), v Soviet Union (won 3–1) 1 goal, v Argentina (2–2)
	1992 v Germany (lost 0–1), v Turkey (won 1–0) 1 goal, v Poland (1–1), v Hungary (won 1–0), v Denmark (0–0), v Sweden (lost 1–2)

WHILE PLAYING FOR non-League Alvechurch, Alan Smith represented the English semi-professional side. His form soon drew the attention of Leicester City and he joined them for £22,000 in June 1982. In his first season at Filbert Street, his 13 goals when partnering the up-and-coming Gary Lineker helped the Foxes win promotion to the First Division. He continued to be a prolific scorer during his stay at Leicester, netting 84 goals in 217 games before his transfer to Arsenal. It was a strange affair, for he signed after the transfer deadline in March 1987. This resulted in his being loaned back to Leicester City for the rest of that season!

Smith ended his first season with the Gunners as the club's top scorer, but it was his goal-burst at the start of the 1988/89 season that elevated him into the England squad. He scored one and made another of the goals at Anfield that brought Arsenal the 1989 League Championship by the narrowest possible margin. His 23 First Division strikes also brought him the Golden Boot for 1989. He went on to help Arsenal win another League Championship in 1991 and the FA Cup two years later before, in 1994, volleying the winning goal in the 1994 European Cup Winners' Cup Final. On medical advice he retired from the game at the age of only 32.

Paul PARKER

Position	Defender
Born	Paul Andrew Parker, West Ham, 4 April 1964
Height	5ft 7in
Weight	11st 11lb
Clubs	Fulham, Queen's Park Rangers, Manchester United, Derby County, Sheffield United, Chelsea
England Caps	19

1989 v Albania (won 5–0), v Chile (0–0), v Denmark (1–1)
1990 v Yugoslavia (won 2–1), v Uruguay (lost 1–2), v Holland (0–0), v Egypt (won 1–0),
   v Belgium (won 1–0), v Cameroon (won 3–2), v W. Germany (1–1 aet, W. Germany won
   4–3 on penalties), v Italy (lost 1–2)
1991 v Hungary (won 1–0), v Poland (won 2–0), v Soviet Union (won 3–1), v Australia
   (won 1–0), v New Zealand (won 1–0)
1992 v Germany (lost 0–1)
1994 v Holland (lost 0–2), v Denmark (won 1–0)

PAUL PARKER, who won 19 caps for England and had an impressive World Cup in 1990, made his Football League debut for Fulham while still an apprentice and went on to win England youth and Under-21 honours during his time at Craven Cottage. Following Fulham's relegation to the Third Division in 1985/86, it was clear that he deserved a higher class of football and in June 1987 he joined Queen's Park Rangers for £300,000. He was rewarded for his consistent displays in Rangers' back four with his first full cap against Albania, but after one more season with the Loftus Road club he joined Manchester United for £2 million.

During his stay at Old Trafford, Parker won two Premier League Championship medals, an FA Cup winners' medal and a League Cup winners' medal. Sadly, injuries restricted his number of appearances and in five years with the club he only played in 135 games. After being given a free transfer, he had spells with Derby County and Sheffield United before rejoining Fulham and later ending his first-class career with Chelsea.

Nigel CLOUGH

Position	Forward
Born	Nigel Howard Clough, Sunderland, 19 March 1966
Height	5ft 10in
Weight	12st 3lb
Clubs	Nottingham Forest, Liverpool, Manchester City, Sheffield Wednesday
England Caps	14

1989 v Chile (0–0)
1991 v Argentina (2–2), v Australia (won 1–0), v Malaysia (won 4–2)
1992 v France (won 2–0), v Czechoslovakia (2–2), v CIS (2–2)
1993 v Spain (lost 0–1), v Turkey (won 4–0), v Poland (1–1), v Norway (lost 0–2), v United
   States (lost 0–2), v Brazil (1–1), v Germany (lost 1–2)

Nigel Clough of Nottingham Forest. (Lancashire Evening Post)

THE SON OF former Nottingham Forest manager Brian Clough, Nigel soon made a name for himself as a creative player with excellent passing ability. However, he was also a prolific scorer, topping Forest's scoring charts in six of the full eight seasons he was at the City Ground. He scored two hat-tricks for Forest, the first against Queen's

Park Rangers in December 1987 and the second in a 5–4 win in the League Cup at Coventry City in November 1990. He made the first of his 14 full international appearances for England while with Forest when he played against Chile at the end of the 1988/89 season.

He went on to help the Reds win the League Cup in 1989 and 1990, but before the start of the 1993/94 season he left the City Ground to join Liverpool for a fee of £2.75 million.

Hampered by injuries at Anfield, Clough made just 44 appearances before moving to Manchester City in January 1996. While at Maine Road he returned to the City Ground on loan and took his total of goals for Forest to 131 in 412 first-team appearances. There followed another loan spell, this time with Sheffield Wednesday, before he left Maine Road to become manager of non-League Burton Albion.

John FASHANU

Position	Forward
Born	John Fashanu, Kensington, 18 September 1962
Height	6ft 1in
Weight	11st 2lb
Clubs	Norwich City, Crystal Palace, Lincoln City, Millwall, Wimbledon, Aston Villa
England Caps	2
	1989 v Chile (0–0), v Scotland (won 2–0)

THE YOUNGER BROTHER of the late Justin Fashanu, John turned professional with Norwich City after being an associated schoolboy at Cambridge United. After receiving few opportunities in four years at Carrow Road, during which time he had a loan spell with Crystal Palace, he was transferred to Lincoln City. He made an immediate impact at Sincil Bank and was soon on his way to Millwall. At The Den he teamed up with Steve Lovell, their goalscoring partnership helping the Lions win promotion to the Second Division.

In March 1986, Wimbledon manager Dave Bassett paid £125,000 to take the gangling Fashanu to Wimbledon. His four goals in the last nine matches of the season helped the Dons win promotion to the top flight. In 1988 he collected an FA Cup winners' medal after Wimbledon defeated Liverpool 1–0, and his consistent displays were rewarded when he was chosen to play for England against Chile in 1989.

Despite suffering more than his fair share of injuries, he was Wimbledon's top scorer from 1986/87 to 1991/92. Forming a good understanding with Dean Holdsworth, he went on to score 126 goals in 326 games for the Dons. He joined Aston Villa for £1.3 million in the summer of 1994, despite Wimbledon chairman Sam Hammam offering him the club presidency in an attempt to get him to stay.

Sadly, Fashanu, who has many charitable interests in the poorest parts of Africa, was soon lost to the game through injury.

1990–99

On Penalties

Despite a mauling from the critics following England's performances in the 1988 European Championship, Bobby Robson survived to justify the FA's faith in him during World Cup 1990 in Italy. Seven games (three going into extra time) saw England make it into the semi-finals. As in 1966 and 1970, their opponents were West Germany. The tie was decided on penalties, but, with Pearce and Waddle unable to convert, the campaign ended on a low note after England lost to Italy 2–1 in the third-place play-off. England did go home with a trophy though – the Fair Play Trophy, awarded to the team incurring the fewest cautions and committing the fewest fouls.

Bobby Robson bowed out with dignity, to be replaced by Aston Villa manager Graham Taylor. Few games were won convincingly during his time in charge but a hard-fought draw in Poland took England to the 1992 European Championship Finals, a tournament chiefly remembered for Taylor's decision to withdraw captain Gary Lineker when he stood just one goal short of Bobby Charlton's record tally of 49.

Following England's failure to qualify for the 1994 World Cup Finals in America, Taylor was replaced by the charismatic Terry Venables. As hosts, England were assured of qualification for the 1996 European

Championship. When they drew 1–1 with Switzerland in their opening match, the tabloids went into overdrive. However, the next game saw England beat Scotland 2–0, with David Seaman brilliantly saving a McAllister penalty and Paul Gascoigne scoring a virtuoso goal. In the next round, Holland, one of the favourites, were beaten 4–1, with Alan Shearer and Teddy Sheringham each scoring twice. England then defeated Spain in the quarter-finals, Seaman again saving brilliantly, this time from Miguel Nadal in the penalty shoot-out. The semi-final saw England paired with Germany and after 90 minutes the score was 1–1. No goals were scored in extra time and the game went to penalties. Gareth Southgate missed his spot kick, Moller scored his, and Germany were through 6–5.

Terry Venables' shock decision to quit after the tournament was followed by the appointment of Glenn Hoddle. After weeks of hype England qualified for the 1998 World Cup finals after achieving a momentous 0–0 draw in Rome against Italy. The game was marred by scenes of violence on the terraces with baton-wielding police wading into a section of England fans.

In the 1998 World Cup in France, England made a solid start, beating Tunisia 2–0, but then went down to Romania. A 2–0 win over Colombia sent them into the quarter-finals against Argentina. Reduced to 10 men for 73 minutes after Beckham's dismissal, England held the Argentinians to a 2–2 draw after extra time. The game went to penalties but, with the score at 4–3 to Argentina, David Batty's spot kick was saved. Hoddle's contract was subsequently terminated by the FA, which then appointed Howard Wilkinson as caretaker coach. Shortly afterwards, Kevin Keegan agreed to take on the job full time.

Dave BEASANT

Position	Goalkeeper
Born	David John Beasant, Willesden, 20 March 1959
Height	6ft 4in
Weight	14st 3lb
Clubs	Wimbledon, Newcastle United, Chelsea, Grimsby Town, Wolverhampton Wanderers, Southampton, Nottingham Forest, Portsmouth, Wigan Athletic, Brighton and Hove Albion
England Caps	2
	1990 v Italy (0–0), v Yugoslavia (won 2–1)

DAVE BEASANT'S last appearance for Wimbledon was in the 1988 FA Cup Final, which saw him save John Aldridge's penalty. It was the first spot kick saved in a cup final at Wembley – and the Dons held on to take the trophy back to South London.

Beasant joined Wimbledon from non-League Edgware Town and, after making his debut in January 1979, did not miss a League game from the beginning of the 1981/82 season until he left for Newcastle United in the summer of 1988, a total of 304 consecutive Football League matches. During this time he won both Second and Fourth Division League Championship medals and was ever-present in seven seasons, playing in 388 games for the club. During his short stay at St James' Park, he had little opportunity to further his reputation, and after just six months on Tyneside he was rescued by Chelsea. There his form led to international recognition, Beasant coming on as a substitute goalkeeper against Italy. Following a disastrous match for Chelsea against Norwich City, he had loan spells at Grimsby and Wolves before joining Southampton in November 1993. He was later loaned to Nottingham Forest before joining the club on a permanent basis and helping them win promotion to the Premier League. Following his release from the City Ground, he joined Portsmouth on a three-month contract. He later appeared for Wigan Athletic before joining Brighton and Hove Albion, taking his total of first-class appearances for his ten clubs to 888.

Mike PHELAN

Position	Midfielder
Born	Michael Christopher Phelan, Nelson, 24 September 1962
Height	5ft 10in
Weight	12st 0lb
Clubs	Burnley, Norwich City, Manchester United, West Bromwich Albion
England Caps	1
	1990 v Italy (0–0)

MIKE PHELAN made his League debut for Burnley in February 1981 in the same week as he won his first England youth cap. The following season he won a Third Division Championship medal, but in 1982/83 he experienced relegation as the Clarets slid back into Division Three. That season, however, he was voted both Player and Young

Player of the Year for Burnley. Following the club's relegation to the Fourth Division in 1985, Phelan left Turf Moor to join Norwich City for £60,000, and in his first season at Carrow Road he helped the Canaries win the Second Division Championship. Over the next four seasons he rarely missed a game, and was captain when Norwich finished fourth in the First Division in 1988/89.

In the summer of 1989, Phelan followed Steve Bruce to Old Trafford. Winning an FA Cup winners' medal in his first season with Manchester United, he also earned his one and only England cap against Italy at this time. Another memorable season followed as the Reds won the European Cup Winners' Cup and then, in 1992, he won another FA Cup winners' medal. In 1992/93 he was a member of the United side that won the first Premier League Championship, going on to win the FA Cup again in 1994.

Given a free transfer, Phelan joined West Bromwich Albion, where he ended his playing days. After a spell coaching at Carrow Road, returned to Old Trafford as coach with Manchester United.

David PLATT

Position	Midfield/Forward
Born	David Andrew Platt, Oldham, 10 June 1966
Height	5ft 10in
Weight	11st 12lb
Clubs	Manchester United, Crewe Alexandra, Aston Villa, Bari, Sampdoria, Arsenal
England Caps	62 Goals 27

1990 v Italy (0–0), v Yugoslavia (won 2–1), v Brazil (won 1–0), v Denmark (won 1–0), v Tunisia (1–1), v Holland (0–0), v Egypt (won 1–0), v Belgium (won 1–0) 1 goal, v Cameroon (won 3–2) 1 goal, v W. Germany (1–1 aet, W. Germany won 4–3 on penalties), v Italy (lost 1–2) 1 goal

1991 v Hungary (won 1–0), v Poland (won 2–0), v Eire (1–1) 1 goal, v Eire (1–1), v Turkey (won 1–0), v Soviet Union (won 3–1) 2 goals, v Argentina (2–2) 1 goal, v Australia (won 1–0), v New Zealand (won 1–0), v New Zealand (won 2–0), v Malaysia (won 4–2)

1992 v Germany (lost 0–1), v Turkey (won 1–0), v Poland (1–1), v Czechoslovakia (2–2), v CIS (2–2), v Brazil (1–1) 1 goal, v Finland (won 2–1) 2 goals, v Denmark (0–0), v France (0–0), v Sweden (lost 1–2) 1 goal

1993 v Spain (lost 0–1), v Norway (1–1) 1 goal, v Turkey (won 4–0), v San Marino (won 6–0) 4 goals, v Turkey (won 2–0) 1 goal, v Holland (2–2) 1 goal, v Poland (1–1), v Norway (lost 0–2), v Brazil (1–1) 1 goal, v Germany (lost 1–2) 1 goal

1994 v Poland (won 3–0), v Holland (lost 0–2), v San Marino (won 7–1), v Denmark (won 1–0) 1 goal, v Greece (won 5–0) 2 goals, v Norway (0–0)

1995 v United States (won 2–0), v Nigeria (won 1–0) 1 goal, v Eire (lost 0–1), v Uruguay (0–0), v Japan (won 2–1) 1 goal, v Sweden (3–3) 1 goal, v Brazil (lost 1–3)

1996 v Bulgaria (won 1–0), v Croatia (0–0), v Hungary (won 3–0) 1 goal, v Switzerland (1–1), v Holland (won 4–1), v Spain (0–0 aet, England won 4–3 on penalties), v Germany (1–1 aet, Germany won 6–5 on penalties)

Honours	Footballer of the Year 1990

David Platt on the ball in an Umbro Cup match against Japan in 1995. (Getty Images)

FEW PLAYERS have embodied England's hopes in the way David Platt did during the 1990s. He helped England to the semi-final of the 1990 World Cup with an extra-time strike against Belgium and a goal in the quarter-final against Cameroon. Six years later he captained England to the semi-finals of Euro '96.

Though he signed professional forms for Manchester United, David Platt never made the first team and was allowed to join Crewe Alexandra on a free transfer. At Gresty Road he made rapid progress, and after scoring 61 goals in 152 first-team appearances he moved to Aston Villa for £200,000. He scored in each of his first three games for Villa and proved to be a regular marksman from midfield in his three-and-a-half-seasons with the club. He was top scorer in seasons 1989/90 and 1990/91, with 24 goals in each campaign. After his impressive displays in the World Cup Finals of 1990, he became the target for a number of top European clubs. At the end of the 1990/91 season, in which he had scored 68 goals in 155 games, he left Villa for Italian Serie A club Bari in a £5.5 million transfer deal. He had a disappointing first season with the Italian club, for they were relegated, and he left to play for Sampdoria.

He returned to England in the summer of 1995 to play for Arsenal but picked up a knee injury and didn't play again until towards the end of the season. He remained at Highbury until 1998, when he decided to retire from the game to learn the ropes before embarking on a career in management. In 1999 he took over the reins at Nottingham Forest but two years later left to take charge of the England Under-21 team.

Nigel WINTERBURN

Position	Left-back
Born	Nigel Winterburn, Nuneaton, 11 December 1963
Height	5ft 9in
Weight	11st 4lb
Clubs	Birmingham City, Wimbledon, Arsenal, West Ham United
England Caps	2
	1990 v Italy (0–0)
	1993 v Germany (lost 1–2)

THOUGH HE WON England youth honours while an apprentice with Birmingham City, Nigel Winterburn failed to make a single first-team appearance for the St Andrew's club during two years as a professional. Following an unsuccessful trial with Oxford United he joined Wimbledon, helping the Dons win promotion to the Second Division in his first season with the club. He was voted Wimbledon's Player of the Year for four consecutive seasons from 1983/84, and his form led to international recognition when he represented the England Under-21 side. He helped the Dons win promotion to the top flight in 1985/86 but a year later he was transferred to Arsenal for £400,000.

Initially he had to play second fiddle to Kenny Sansom at Arsenal, but at the start of the 1988/89 season he won a regular place and played in every game of the Gunners' triumphant League Championship campaign. He won his first England cap against Italy and then helped Arsenal win another League title in 1990/91. In 1992/93 he won League Cup and FA Cup winners' medals, following the victories over Sheffield Wednesday. He later helped the Gunners to two European Cup Winners' Cup finals but was then hampered by a series of injuries. Under new manager Arsene Wenger he helped Arsenal win the 'double' in 1998. In the summer of 2000, after appearing in 587 games for the Gunners, he left to play for West Ham United. A model of consistency in his three seasons with the Hammers, he was released in the summer of 2003.

Tony DORIGO

Position	Left-back
Born	Anthony Robert Dorigo, Melbourne, Australia, 31 December 1965
Height	5ft 9in
Weight	10st 7lb
Clubs	Aston Villa, Chelsea, Leeds United
England Caps	15

1990 v Yugoslavia (won 2–1), v Czechoslovakia (won 4–2), v Denmark (won 1–0),
   v Italy (lost 1–2)
1991 v Hungary (won 1–0), v Soviet Union (won 3–1)
1992 v Germany (lost 0–1), v Czechoslovakia (2–2), v Hungary (won 1–0),
   v Brazil (1–1)
1993 v San Marino (won 6–0), v Poland (1–1), v United States (lost 0–2),
   v Brazil (1–1)
1994 v Holland (lost 0–2)

TONY DORIGO won 15 caps for England over a four-year period. He had emigrated from Australia to sign associated schoolboy forms for Aston Villa in January 1982 before being apprenticed eight months later. After making his League debut for Villa against Ipswich Town in the final game of the 1983/84 season, he established himself as the club's first-choice left-back. When the Midlands club were relegated from the top flight at the end of the 1986/87 season, he joined Chelsea for £475,000, but at the end of his first season at Stamford Bridge they too were relegated!

When Chelsea won the Zenith Data Systems Cup Final, beating Middlesbrough in 1990, Dorigo scored the game's only goal. However, a year later the talented defender was on his way to Elland Road, joining Leeds United for £1.3 million. He played an outstanding role in the Yorkshire club's unexpected League Championship success in 1991/92, and though much of the rest of his time with the club was spent fighting against a series of injuries, he managed to take his total of first-team appearances for Leeds to 219 before he left Elland Road in 1997.

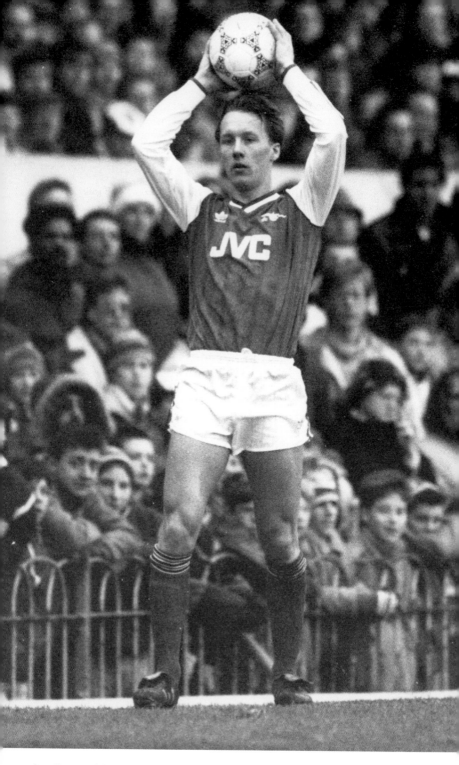

Lee Dixon of Arsenal. (Lancashire Evening Post)

Lee DIXON

Position	Right-back
Born	Lee Michael Dixon, Manchester, 17 March 1964
Height	5ft 9in
Weight	11st 8lb
Clubs	Burnley, Chester City, Bury, Stoke City, Arsenal
England Caps	22 Goals 1

1990 v Czechoslovakia (won 4–2)

1991 v Hungary (won 1–0), v Poland (won 2–0), v Eire (1–1), v Eire (1–1) 1 goal,
v Cameroon (won 3–2), v Turkey (won 1–0), v Argentina (2–2)

1992 v Germany (lost 0–1), v Turkey (won 1–0), v Poland (1–1), v Czechoslovakia
(2–2)

1993 v Spain (lost 0–1), v Norway (1–1), v Turkey (won 4–0), v San Marino (won 6–0),
v Turkey (won 2–0), v Holland (2–2), v Norway (lost 0–2), v United States
(lost 0–2)

1994 v San Marino (won 7–1)

1999 v France (lost 0–2)

LEE DIXON'S CONSISTENCY in the Arsenal back four was rewarded when Bobby
Robson gave him his first England cap. Though the 1990 World Cup passed him by,
he became a regular in Graham Taylor's England side, going on to win 22 caps, the
last of these five years after his previous appearance.

After beginning his career with Burnley, Dixon was just getting into his stride in
the game when he was shown the door by the Clarets' new manager John Bond. He
joined Chester City but was unable to inspire the team to new heights after they had
finished bottom of the Fourth Division. Martin Dobson had been Dixon's captain at
Turf Moor and it was Dobson, by then player-manager at Bury, who persuaded him
to move to Gigg Lane. After just one season with the Shakers, he was on the move
again, this time to Stoke City. His impressive displays at full-back alerted a number of
the top clubs, and in January 1988 Arsenal manager George Graham paid £380,000
to take him to the marble halls of Highbury.

At the end of his first season with the Gunners, Dixon had won a League
Championship medal. He continued to win honours at club level, including his first
European medal as Arsenal beat Parma in the Cup Winners' Cup Final in Copenhagen
in May 1994. Dixon went on to appear in 621 games for Arsenal before retiring at
the end of the 2001/02 season. With England caps, as well as domestic and European
medals, in the trophy cabinet he emphatically proved a number of people wrong in
their assessment of his abilities.

Ian WRIGHT

Position	Forward
Born	Ian Edward Wright, Woolwich, 3 November 1963
Height	5ft 10in
Weight	11st 8lb
Clubs	Crystal Palace, Arsenal, West Ham United, Nottingham Forest, Glasgow Celtic, Burnley
England Caps	33 Goals 9

1991 v Cameroon (won 2–0), v Eire (1–1), v Soviet Union (won 3–1), v New Zealand (won 1–0)

1992 v Hungary (won 1–0)

1993 v Norway (won 1–0), v Turkey (won 4–0), v Turkey (won 2–0), v Poland (1–1) 1 goal, v Norway (lost 0–2), v United States (lost 0–2), v Brazil (1–1), v Germany (lost 1–2)

1994 v Poland (won 3–0), v Holland (lost 0–2), v San Marino (won 7–1) 4 goals, v Greece (won 5–0), v Norway (0–0)

1995 v United States (won 2–0), v Romania (1–1)

1997 v Georgia (won 2–0), v Italy (lost 0–1), v Mexico (won 2–0), v S. Africa (won 2–1) 1 goal, v Italy (won 2–0) 1 goal, v France (won 1–0), v Brazil (lost 0–1)

1998 v Moldova (won 4–0) 2 goals, v Italy (0–0), v Saudi Arabia (0–0), v Morocco (won 1–0)

1999 v Luxembourg (won 3–0), v Czech Republic (won 2–0)

ONE OF THE GAME'S natural goalscorers, Ian Wright was capped 33 times by England and scored four goals in the 7–1 defeat of San Marino.

He began his League career with Crystal Palace after being spotted by Eagles manager Steve Coppell playing for Greenwich Borough. In his six seasons at Selhurst Park he formed a prolific goalscoring partnership with Mark Bright, but in 1989/90 he broke a leg twice. He recovered in time to be selected as a substitute for the 1990 FA Cup Final against Manchester United, and when he came on he scored two stunning goals to take the game to a replay. Then, in September 1991, after scoring 118 goals in 277 first-team games for Palace, he joined Arsenal for £2.5 million.

Wright scored a hat-trick on his League debut for the Gunners at Southampton and ended the season as the First Division's leading scorer with 29 goals. He also won the Golden Boot as Europe's top scorer. In 1992/93 he was instrumental in helping the Highbury club win the FA and League Cups. In 1994/95 he broke all European club goalscoring records when he scored in each tie of every round up to the final of the European Cup Winners' Cup. When the Gunners played Bolton Wanderers at the start of the 1997/98 season, he hit a hat-trick in a 4–1 win to make him Arsenal's greatest goalscorer of all time, overtaking Cliff Bastin's record of 178 League and Cup goals. Wright also won FA and League Championship medals that season but was kept out of the World Cup by a hamstring injury. He had scored 185 goals in 288 games for Arsenal when, in July 1998, he was transferred to West Ham United for £750,000.

Midway through his first season at Upton Park, Wright went to Nottingham Forest on loan but he was soon on his way to Glasgow Celtic on a permanent basis. His stay north of the border was brief, however, and he returned to Football League action with Burnley. Retiring from the game in the summer of 2000, he is now a hugely popular TV celebrity.

Ian Wright during the US Cup match against Brazil in 1993. The game ended as a 1–1 draw. (Shaun Botterill/Getty Images)

Lee SHARPE

Position	Left-winger
Born	Lee Stuart Sharpe, Halesowen, 27 May 1971
Height	6ft 0in
Weight	12st 12lb
Clubs	Torquay United, Manchester United, Leeds United, Bradford City, Portsmouth, Exeter City
England Caps	8
	1991 v Eire (1–1)
	1993 v Turkey (won 2–0), v Norway (lost 0–2), v United States (lost 0–2), v Brazil (1–1), v Germany (lost 1–2)
	1994 v Poland (won 3–0), v Holland (lost 0–2)

IN MARCH 1991 Lee Sharpe became the youngest player since Duncan Edwards to represent England, when he played against the Republic of Ireland still two months short of his 20th birthday.

His career was to be blighted by a series of injuries and illnesses. He was given his first chance in football as a YTS apprentice at Torquay United when he was just 16, but Manchester United quickly spotted his potential, and in May 1988, after only nine starts, he was on his way to Old Trafford for a fee of £185,000. Determined to make it to the top in the shortest time possible, Sharpe soon became the club's second most-capped player at Under-21 level behind former United keeper Gary Bailey. But whereas Bailey won most of his caps as an over-age player, Sharpe had won his eight prior to his 20th birthday. In 1991 he helped United reach the League Cup Final, where he scored against Liverpool, having netted three of the goals that beat Leeds in the semi-final as well as a stunning hat-trick at Arsenal in an earlier round.

Voted the PFA's Young Player of the Year in 1991, Sharpe played in 265 games for the Reds before being transferred to Leeds United for £4.5 million in August 1996. Hampered by injuries during his time at Elland Road, he later moved to Bradford City for a cut-price £200,000. While at Valley Parade, he had a loan spell with Portsmouth, but injuries continued to plague him, and he joined Exeter City on a non-contract basis, before signing for Icelandic club Grindourink in March 2003.

Geoff THOMAS

Position	Midfielder
Born	Geoffrey Robert Thomas, Manchester, 5 August 1964
Height	6ft 1in
Weight	13st 2lb
Clubs	Rochdale, Crewe Alexandra, Crystal Palace, Wolverhampton Wanderers, Nottingham Forest, Barnsley, Notts County
England Caps	9
	1991 v Turkey (won 1–0), v Soviet Union (won 3–1), v Argentina (2–2), v Australia (won 1–0), v New Zealand (won 1–0), v New Zealand (won 2–0), v Malaysia (won 4–2)
	1992 v Poland (1–1), v France (won 2–0)

AFTER A HANDFUL of games for Rochdale, midfielder Geoff Thomas joined Crewe Alexandra, where he soon made a name for himself with a series of consistent displays for the Gresty Road club. He was never on the losing side during the nine international appearances he made while with his next club, Crystal Palace.

In June 1987 Thomas joined Crystal Palace for a fee of just £50,000, and it wasn't long before his powerful running, strength and cultured style made him a great favourite with the Palace fans. Within a year he had succeeded Jim Cannon as the club captain and had led the Eagles back to the First Division. He was outstanding during the club's run to the 1990 FA Cup Final, and he scored the opening goal in the defeat of Everton when the club won the Zenith Data Systems Cup in 1991. Then in 1993, after scoring 35 goals in 249 games for Palace, he joined Wolves for £800,000. Injuries hampered his progress at Molineux and he subsequently played for a succession of clubs – Nottingham Forest, Barnsley and Notts County. Finally, in August 2001, after a 15-year absence, he returned to Crewe Alexandra but hung up his boots in the summer of 2002.

Dennis WISE

Position	Midfielder
Born	Dennis Frank Wise, Kensington, 15 December 1966
Height	5ft 6in
Weight	10st 10lb
Clubs	Wimbledon, Chelsea, Leicester City, Millwall
England Caps	21 Goals 1

1991 v Turkey (won 1–0) 1 goal, v Soviet Union (won 3–1), v Australia (won 1–0), v New Zealand (won 1–0), v New Zealand (won 2–0)
1994 v Norway (0–0)
1995 v Romania (1–1), v Nigeria (won 1–0)
1996 v Colombia (0–0), v Norway (0–0), v Portugal (1–1), v Hungary (won 3–0)
2000 v Belgium (won 2–1), v Argentina (0–0), v Brazil (1–1), v Malta (won 2–1), v Portugal (lost 2–3), v Germany (won 1–0), v Romania (lost 2–3)
2001 v France (1–1), v Finland (0–0)

DENNIS WISE was called up by Graham Taylor for his England debut in a vital European Championship match against Turkey and scored the only goal of the game to give England two vital points.

Having been released by Southampton as a youngster without being offered professional terms, Wise was snapped up by Wimbledon, making his League debut against Cardiff City in the final match of the 1984/85 campaign. He rose to national fame in 1987/88 during the Dons' FA Cup run, scoring the winner against Luton Town in the semi-final and then cleverly flighting a free kick from which Lawrie Sanchez headed the only goal to defeat Liverpool in the final. Many of his Cup Final colleagues left Plough Lane but Wise stayed with the Dons for a further two years, taking his tally of goals to 30 in 165 games before leaving to join neighbours Chelsea for £1.6 million.

Dennis Wise in action during a friendly at Wembley against Brazil in May 2000. The match was drawn 1–1. (David Cannon/Getty Images)

In 1991/92 Wise was Chelsea's leading scorer with 14 goals, but the next couple of seasons were marred by injuries and disciplinary problems. He bounced back, however, to become a great favourite at Stamford Bridge. An inspirational captain, he became the first Chelsea skipper to lift the FA Cup at Wembley, the first of three trophies the Blues won under his leadership. There is no doubt that the foreign influx in the Premier League added another dimension to his game.

In June 2001, after appearing in 445 games for Chelsea, Wise left to join Leicester City. After an indifferent start to his career with the Foxes, a long-term injury ruled him out of the second half of the season and, after a pre-season altercation involving Callum Davidson, he subsequently joined Millwall. When he eventually donned the captain's armband, his experience and skill helped considerably in bringing on the talented youngsters of the New Den.

David BATTY

Position	Midfielder
Born	David Batty, Leeds, 2 December 1968
Height	5ft 8in
Weight	12st 0lb
Clubs	Leeds United, Blackburn Rovers, Newcastle United
England Caps	42

1991 v Soviet Union (won 3–1), v Argentina (2–2), v Australia (won 1–0), v New Zealand (won 2–0), v Malaysia (won 4–2)
1992 v Germany (lost 0–1), v Turkey (won 1–0), v Hungary (won 1–0), v France (0–0), v Sweden (lost 1–2)
1993 v Norway (1–1), v San Marino (won 6–0), v United States (lost 0–2), v Brazil (1–1)
1994 v Denmark (won 1–0)
1995 v Japan (won 2–1), v Brazil (lost 1–3)
1997 v Moldova (won 3–0), v Georgia (won 2–0), v Italy (lost 0–1), v Mexico (won 2–0), v Georgia (won 2–0), v S. Africa (won 2–1), v Poland (won 2–0), v France (won 1–0)
1998 v Moldova (won 4–0), v Italy (0–0), v Chile (lost 0–2), v Switzerland (1–1), v Portugal (won 3–0), v Saudi Arabia (0–0), v Tunisia (won 2–0), v Romania (lost 1–2), v Colombia (won 2–0), v Argentina (2–2 aet, Argentina won 4–3 on penalties)
1999 v Bulgaria (0–0), v Luxembourg (won 3–0), v Hungary (1–1), v Sweden (0–0), v Bulgaria (1–1)
2000 v Luxembourg (won 6–0), v Poland (0–0)

IMPRESSING WITH his speed and tackling during his early days at Elland Road, David Batty soon won England Under-21 honours, despite less than half a season of League experience. He progressed during Leeds' Second Division Championship-winning season of 1989/90, representing England at international 'B' level. A superb ball-winner and passer, he became an established England midfielder under Graham Taylor.

In October 1993 Batty was surprisingly transferred to Blackburn Rovers for £2.75 million and finished the season as the Ewood Park club's Player of the Year. The following campaign, he collected a Premier League Championship medal with the

David Batty in a Euro 2000 qualifying match with Luxembourg at Wembley in September 1999. England won 6–0. (Gary M. Prior/Getty Images)

Lancashire club to go with the League Championship medal he had won with Leeds in 1991/92. Injuries restricted his appearances towards the end of his time at Blackburn, and in February 1996 Kevin Keegan signed Batty for Newcastle United. During the latter part of that season, the Geordies faltered in the final run-in and he missed out on a third Championship medal in the top flight.

In December 1998 Batty returned to his home-town club and took his total of appearances in his two spells with Leeds to 347. He looked unlikely to add to that total under new manager Terry Venables, who seemed reluctant to play him, but after the appointments of Peter Reid and, more recently, Eddie Gray, he again featured in the Leeds first team. However, he was unexpectedly released before his contract expired in the summer of 2004.

David HIRST

Position	Forward
Born	David Eric Hirst, Cudworth, 7 December 1967
Height	5ft 11in
Weight	13st 10lb
Clubs	Barnsley, Sheffield Wednesday, Southampton
England Caps	3 Goals 1
	1991 v Australia (won 1–0), v New Zealand (won 2–0) 1 goal
	1992 v France (won 2–0)

FOLLOWING A METEORIC RISE with Barnsley, where he made his League debut in August 1985, three months before turning professional, David Hirst signed for Sheffield Wednesday at the end of that season for £200,000. His first three seasons at Hillsborough were disappointing but in 1989/90 he began to make his mark, scoring 14 goals despite Wednesday being relegated to the Second Division. In 1990/91 he scored 24 goals to help the Owls win promotion at the first time of asking. He also won a League Cup winners' medal as a result of Wednesday's 1–0 win over Manchester United. At the end of that successful season he was called up by England manager Graham Taylor for the tour of Australasia, where he made his international debut.

In 1991/92 Hirst scored three minutes into the new campaign against Aston Villa and continued in similar vein, ending the season with 21 goals. He scored his 100th goal for the club to take the 1993 FA Cup Final to a replay, but he couldn't repeat the feat in the second game and had to settle for a losers' medal. He then suffered a series of injuries and, in consequence, his first-team appearances became limited. In October 1997, after scoring 128 League and Cup goals for the Owls, he was transferred to Southampton for £2 million, but at the end of his first season at the Dell he suffered a freak fall on a training run, resulting in a badly damaged knee that eventually forced him to quit the first-class scene.

John SALAKO

Position	Left-winger
Born	John Akin Salako, Nigeria, 11 February 1969
Height	5ft 10in
Weight	12st 8lb
Clubs	Crystal Palace, Swansea City, Coventry City, Bolton Wanderers, Fulham, Charlton Athletic, Reading
England Caps	5
	1991 v Australia (won 1–0), v New Zealand (won 1–0), v New Zealand (won 2–0), v Malaysia (won 4–2)
	1992 v Germany (lost 0–1)

JOHN SALAKO'S CONSISTENTLY exciting wing play eventually won him international recognition when he was chosen to tour Australasia with Graham Taylor's party at the end of the 1990/91 season. Featuring prominently in all four matches, he staked a claim for regular inclusion in the national side but eventually added just one more cap to his name.

Nigerian-born Salako worked his way up through Crystal Palace's junior ranks and went on to become a valued member of the Eagles side, though over half of his first 100 appearances for the club were as a substitute. It was the autumn of 1990 before he established himself as a regular member of the Palace side. He had scored 33 goals in 273 games for Palace when, in the summer of 1995, he joined Coventry City for £1.5 million. He failed, however, to make the most of his opportunities at Highfield Road and there followed brief spells with Bolton Wanderers and Fulham before he signed for Charlton Athletic in August 1999. At the Valley, Salako rediscovered some of his old magic, helping the Addicks win the First Division Championship at the end of his first season with the club. Later, frustrated by the lack of first-team opportunities, he joined Reading on loan before making the move permanent and helping the club win promotion to the First Division. Though still involved on the playing side he has begun to establish a media career in preparation for life after football.

Gary CHARLES

Position	Full-back
Born	Gary Andrew Charles, Newham, 13 April 1970
Height	5ft 9in
Weight	11st 8lb
Clubs	Nottingham Forest, Leicester City, Derby County, Aston Villa, Benfica
England Caps	2
	1991 v New Zealand (won 2–0), v Malaysia (won 4–2)

GARY CHARLES began his career with Nottingham Forest, but after just a handful of games Brian Clough allowed the young full-back to join Leicester City on loan. On his arrival at Filbert Street he displayed a maturity and confidence beyond his years, and earned himself an extension to his month's loan period until the end of the season.

Indeed, his form was such that he was called up to the England Under-21 squad, going on to win four caps. After rejoining Forest, he won full international honours on England's tour of Australasia.

Charles earned a runners-up medal in the 1991 FA Cup Final when he was the victim of a notorious Paul Gascoigne tackle. He also picked up a Wembley winners' medal from the Zenith Data Systems Cup Final in 1992, but when Forest suffered relegation a year later he experienced a crisis of confidence. He was transferred to Derby County but his first season at the Baseball Ground ended in a play-off defeat at the hands of Leicester City. Charles became a transfer target for Leicester's Brian Little but no deal transpired until Little had departed to Villa Park. He took both the full-back and Tommy Johnson there in a joint £2.9 million deal. Towards the end of the 1995/96 season, Charles suffered an horrendous ankle injury, which caused him to miss the whole of the following campaign. He went on to spend four years at Villa Park before, in January 1999, being transferred to Portuguese giants Benfica for £1.5 million.

Earl BARRETT

Position	Defender
Born	Earl Delisser Barrett, Rochdale, 28 April 1967
Height	5ft 10in
Weight	11st 7lb
Clubs	Manchester City, Chester City, Oldham Athletic, Aston Villa, Everton, Sheffield United, Sheffield Wednesday
England Caps	3
	1991 v New Zealand (won 1–0)
	1993 v Brazil (1–1), v Germany (lost 1–2)

AFTER FAILING to make progress at Manchester City, Earl Barrett was loaned out to Chester City, where he gained valuable League experience before being transferred to Oldham Athletic. In 1989/90 he moved from his usual full-back position to centre-back, and was an ever-present as the Latics, losing League Cup finalists, progressed to the semi-finals of the FA Cup. He also appeared in every match the following season and hardly put a foot wrong as the club won the Second Division Championship. He was then selected for England's tour of Australasia in the summer of 1991, making his international debut against New Zealand.

Barrett joined Aston Villa in February 1992 for £1.7 million and the following season was an ever-present for his new club, going from strength to strength. He had missed very few games for Villa when, in January 1995, he was unexpectedly transferred to Everton for the same fee he had cost the Midlands club. After impressing the Goodison faithful with some sterling displays, he was unlucky to sustain a bad knee injury against Feyenoord, but he later bounced back to become one of the club's most reliable defensive performers. When Howard Kendall took over the reins Barrett was allowed to go on loan to Sheffield United, and was just about to sign on a permanent basis for the Blades when rivals Sheffield Wednesday rushed through a deal for him. After just one season at Hillsborough, however, he decided to retire and parted company with the club.

Brian DEANE

Position	Forward
Born	Brian Christopher Deane, Leeds, 7 February 1968
Height	6ft 3in
Weight	12st 7lb
Clubs	Doncaster Rovers, Sheffield United, Leeds United, Benfica, Middlesbrough, Leicester City
England Caps	3
	1991 v New Zealand (won 1–0), v New Zealand (won 2–0)
	1993 v Spain (lost 0–1)

A TRADITIONAL target-man striker, Brian Deane proved highly popular at his first club, Doncaster Rovers, and his powerful displays saw him move to Sheffield United in July 1988 for £30,000. In his first season at Bramall Lane, he struck up a devastating partnership with Tony Agana, the pair netting 46 goals between them as the Blades earned promotion to the Second Division. Deane was chosen for England's tour of Australasia, earning two caps against New Zealand. A third against Spain followed later.

In the summer of 1993, Deane became Leeds United's record signing when the Elland Road club paid £2.9 million for his services. Despite scoring a last-minute equalizer on his Leeds debut, he struggled to live down his big price tag and it was only when Tony Yeboah arrived that he performed at his best. He went on to score 38 goals in 165 games before rejoining Sheffield United. Though he played for the Blades as though he had never been away, he had only agreed to sign on the understanding that, if a top European club came in for him, he would be allowed to leave. The lure of Benfica proved too great, but after just nine months in Portugal he returned to Premiership action with Middlesbrough when the Teesside club paid £3 million for his services. Injuries restricted the powerful striker's appearances during the early stages of his Riverside career, and he never really settled. He subsequently joined Leicester City where he netted the first goal at the Walker Stadium and reached double figures in the club's promotion-winning season of 2002/03.

Paul MERSON

Position	Forward
Born	Paul Charles Merson, Harlesden, 20 March 1968
Height	6ft 0in
Weight	13st 2lb
Clubs	Arsenal, Brentford, Middlesbrough, Aston Villa, Portsmouth, Walsall
England Caps	21 Goals 3
	1992 v Germany (lost 0–1), v Czechoslovakia (2–2) 1 goal, v Hungary (won 1–0), v Brazil (1–1), v Finland (won 2–1), v Denmark (0–0), v Sweden (lost 1–2)
	1993 v Spain (lost 0–1), v Norway (1–1), v Holland (2–2), v Brazil (1–1), v Germany (lost 1–2)

Paul Merson during a friendly against Portugal at Wembley in April 1998. England won 3–0. (Laurence Griffiths/Getty Images)

1994 v Holland (lost 0–2), v Greece (won 5–0)
1997 v Italy (lost 0–1)
1998 v Switzerland (1–1) 1 goal, v Portugal (won 3–0), v Belgium (0–0), v Argentina (2–2
    aet, Argentina won 4–3 on penalties)
1999 v Sweden (lost 1–2), v Czech Republic (won 2–0) 1 goal

AFTER WORKING HIS WAY UP through the ranks at Arsenal and making his Gunners debut against Manchester City in November 1986, Paul Merson was loaned out to Brentford in January 1987, to help him gain valuable League experience. On his return, he helped Arsenal win the League Championship in 1988/89, scoring 10 goals in 37 appearances and winning the first of four England Under-21 caps. Not surprisingly, he was voted the PFA Young Player of the Year. His progress was marred, though, by various altercations with Arsenal manager George Graham and it seemed for a time that certain sections of the press were hell-bent on destroying his career. He bounced back, however, to win another League Championship medal in 1990/91, and the following season was probably his best ever in the top flight, seeing him score a hat-trick against Crystal Palace and win the first of his 21 full England caps. In 1992/93 he was an important member of the team that won the FA and League Cup, scoring the first goal in the League Cup Final victory over Sheffield Wednesday. Then in November 1994 he courageously announced to the outside world that he was going to seek professional help for his off-the-field problems.

Merson went on to score 98 goals in 427 games for the Gunners' before joining Middlesbrough in the summer of 1997 for a fee of £4.5 million. In his first season in the north-east he helped Boro win promotion to the Premiership, scoring some fantastic goals along the way. His captaincy of the England 'B' team and inclusion in the 1998 World Cup squad merely confirmed the resurrection of his career. After the World Cup he left the Riverside to join Aston Villa in a £6.75 million deal.

Injuries hampered his progress in his first season at Villa Park but in 1999/2000 he helped the Villains reach the FA Cup Final, where they lost to Chelsea. Merson, who then took over the Villa captaincy, began to play some of the best football of his career. He subsequently moved on to Portsmouth, helping the Fratton Park club to achieve promotion to the Premiership as First Division Champions before signing in 2003 for Walsall.

Paul STEWART

Position	Forward
Born	Paul Andrew Stewart, Manchester, 7 October 1964
Height	5ft 11in
Weight	12st 4lb
Clubs	Blackpool, Manchester City, Tottenham Hotspur, Liverpool, Crystal Palace, Wolverhampton Wanderers, Burnley, Sunderland, Stoke City
England Caps	3
	1992 v Germany (lost 0–1), v Czechoslovakia (2–2), v CIS (2–2)

PAUL STEWART, who won his three international caps in a midfield role, established himself in Blackpool's Fourth Division side during 1982/83 – a season in which the Bloomfield Road club experienced its darkest days, having to apply for re-election to the Football League at its close. He was a regular in the Seasiders' promotion side of 1984/85 but it was two seasons later that the goals really started to flow. It came as no surprise when he left Blackpool to join Manchester City, who paid a quarter of a million pounds for his services. After City were relegated in 1986/87, Stewart scored 24 goals in the 1987/88 Second Division campaign, the best return of his career. He won his only England Under-21 cap in April 1988, scoring in a 4–2 defeat by France, before moving on to Tottenham Hotspur that summer for £1.7 million and enjoying four successful years at White Hart Lane. He won five England 'B' caps and scored Spurs' equalizer in the 1991 FA Cup Final at Wembley, going on to collect a winners' medal after the 2–1 victory over Nottingham Forest.

In July 1992 Stewart joined Liverpool for £2 million but injuries and competition for places were to dog his Anfield career. Loaned out to Crystal Palace, he helped the Eagles win the First Division Championship. (This followed the formation of the Premiership.) After loan spells at Wolves and Burnley, he joined Sunderland on a similar basis and helped the Wearsiders win the First Division. He ended his first-class career with Stoke City before going to play non-League football for Workington.

Tony DALEY

Position	Winger
Born	Anthony Mark Daley, Birmingham, 18 October 1967
Height	5ft 8in
Weight	11st 7lb
Clubs	Aston Villa, Wolverhampton Wanderers, Watford, Walsall
England Caps	7
	1992 v Poland (1–1), v CIS (2–2), v Hungary (won 1–0), v Brazil (1–1), v Finland (won 2–1), v Denmark (0–0), v Sweden (lost 1–2)

ON HIS DAY, Tony Daley was one of the most exciting wingers in the Football League. An instant hit with the Villa fans, he suffered the disappointment of relegation to the Second Division at the end of his first full season with the club. Injuries and a loss of form kept him out of the side until midway through the 1987/88 season, when he returned to score three vital goals as Villa climbed back into the top flight. Injuries again disrupted his career in 1990/91, but the following season under Ron Atkinson, he held down a regular place and won his first England cap. He was capped seven times and his last appearance came against Sweden in the European Championship Finals of 1992.

Daley's injuries and loss of form during the following two seasons saw him out of the Villa side and, after playing in 290 games, he joined neighbours Wolverhampton Wanderers for £1.25 million. Sadly, however, a serious cruciate ligament injury meant that he had to wait a year before making his debut for the Molineux club and the legacy of that injury prevented him from making much of an impression. He joined Watford on a free transfer, but was released after just a handful of appearances. He then returned to the Midlands to end his first-class career with Walsall before trying his luck in non-League football with Conference club Forest Green Rovers.

Andy GRAY

Position	Midfielder
Born	Andrew Arthur Gray, Lambeth, 22 February 1964
Height	5ft 11in
Weight	13st 3lb
Clubs	Crystal Palace, Aston Villa, Queen's Park Rangers, Tottenham Hotspur, Marbella, Swindon Town, Falkirk, Bury, Millwall
England Caps	1
	1992 v Poland (1–1)

ANDY GRAY made a late entry into the professional game, showing it is possible to bridge the gap between non-League football and the international arena. He had played for Corinthian Casuals and Dulwich Hamlet before joining Crystal Palace in November 1984. His impressive displays prompted Aston Villa to pay £150,000 for his services in November 1987, and not long after his arrival at Villa Park he won two England Under-21 caps as he helped the Midland side regain their place in the top flight. Shortly afterwards he returned to the capital to play for Queen's Park Rangers but he couldn't settle in West London and was soon back with Palace, where his talents were more suited to their aggressive long-ball game. During his second spell at Selhurst Park, his qualities received international recognition with a game for England against Poland.

After falling out of favour at Palace, Gray joined Spurs in February 1992 for a fee of £900,000 but failed to establish himself as a first-team regular and two years later went abroad to play Spanish League football for Marbella. On his return to these shores he joined Scottish club Falkirk, before spells with Bury and Millwall. He then decided to hang up his boots.

Andy SINTON

Position	Left-winger
Born	Andrew Sinton, Cramlington, 19 March 1966
Height	5ft 8in
Weight	11st 5lb
Clubs	Cambridge United, Brentford, Queen's Park Rangers, Sheffield Wednesday, Tottenham Hotspur, Wolverhampton Wanderers
England Caps	12
	1992 v Poland (1–1), v CIS (2–2), v Hungary (won 1–0), v Brazil (1–1), v France (0–0), v Sweden (lost 1–2)

1993 v Spain (lost 0–1), v Turkey (won 2–0), v Brazil (1–1), v Germany (lost 1–2)
1994 v Holland (lost 0–2), v San Marino (won 7–1)

ANDY SINTON began his career with Cambridge United before moving to Brentford, but it was with Queen's Park Rangers that he developed his full potential and eventually earned international recognition with England. At Loftus Road he proved himself highly adaptable, playing most of his matches as a winger but also turning out in central midfield and at left-back. Fast, skilful and capable of thunderous shooting, he went on to score 25 goals in 190 games for Rangers before a £2.75 million transfer to Sheffield Wednesday, but, due to a catalogue of injuries, he was unable to get a decent run in the Wednesday side and lost his place in the England line-up.

Sinton's career was rescued by former Queen's Park Rangers manager Gerry Francis, who was in charge of Spurs at the time, and signed him for £1.5 million. He became a firm favourite at White Hart Lane, where his accuracy in crossing and intelligent passing of the ball continued to be a feature of his game. More injuries, however, coupled with the arrival of David Ginola, restricted his first-team appearances, and in the summer of 1999 he moved to Wolverhampton Wanderers. After four seasons at Molineux he left to play non-league football for Burton Albion.

Rob JONES

Position	Right-back
Born	Robert Marc Jones, Wrexham, 5 November 1971
Height	5ft 10in
Weight	11st 0lb
Clubs	Crewe Alexandra, Liverpool
England Caps	8
	1992 v France (0–0)
	1994 v Poland (won 3–0), v Greece (won 5–0), v Norway (0–0)
	1995 v United States (won 2–0), v Romania (1–1), v Nigeria (won 1–0), v Uruguay (0–0)

THE GRANDSON OF the stalwart Liverpool defender Bill Jones, Wrexham-born Rob Jones represented Wales as a schoolboy before opting to change allegiance while at youth level. He was discovered by Graeme Souness when the latter was weighing up the talents of another Crewe Alexandra player – Jones had broken into the Railwaymen's side as the club's youngest-ever outfield player. He joined Liverpool in October 1991 and enjoyed a breathtaking rise to fame. Two days after putting pen to paper, he made his debut for the Reds in a goalless draw against Manchester United. He won the first of eight England caps four months later, and at the end of the season gained an FA Cup winners' medal as Liverpool beat Sunderland at Wembley.

The 1992/93 season saw the first signs of the injury problems that were eventually to wreck Jones' career. He developed shin splints, an agonizing condition that left him barely able to walk after most games and forced him to miss most of that season. Following Souness' departure from Liverpool, Jones – sufficiently recovered by then – was switched by Roy Evans to attacking wing-back, a transition he made with ease. In

1995 he picked up a League Cup winners' medal after Liverpool had beaten Bolton Wanderers. He showed his versatility by playing at left-back in the 1996 FA Cup Final defeat by Manchester United, but shortly afterwards he developed back trouble and was told to rest for six months or risk permanent disability.

On his day, Rob Jones was the complete full-back – decisive in the tackle, winning balls cleanly, and able to pass quickly and accurately over both short and long distances. Sadly though, after missing the entire 1998/99 season through injury, he was forced to retire.

Martin KEOWN

Position	Central defender
Born	Martin Raymond Keown, Oxford, 24 July 1966
Height	6ft 1in
Weight	12st 4lb
Clubs	Arsenal, Brighton and Hove Albion, Aston Villa, Everton
England Caps	43 Goals 2

1992 v France (won 2–0), v Czechoslovakia (2–2) 1 goal, v CIS (2–2), v Hungary (won 1–0), v Brazil (1–1), v Finland (won 2–1), v Denmark (0–0), v France (0–0), v Sweden (lost 1–2)
1993 v Holland (2–2), v Germany (lost 1–2)
1997 v Mexico (won 2–0), v South Africa (won 2–1), v Italy (won 2–0), v Brazil (lost 0–1)
1998 v Switzerland (1–1), v Morocco (won 1–0), v Belgium (0–0)
1999 v Czech Republic (won 2–0), v France (lost 0–2), v Poland (won 3–1), v Hungary (1–1), v Sweden (0–0)
2000 v Luxembourg (won 6–0), v Poland (0–0), v Belgium (won 2–1), v Scotland (lost 0–1), v Argentina (0–0), v Brazil (1–1), v Malta (won 2–1) 1 goal, v Portugal (lost 2–3), v Germany (won 1–0), v Romania (lost 2–3)
2001 v France (1–1), v Germany (lost 0–1), v Finland (0–0), v Mexico (won 4–0), v Greece (won 2–0)
2002 v Holland (lost 0–2), v Greece (2–2), v Paraguay (won 4–0), v S. Korea (1–1), v Cameroon (2–2)

THOUGH A MEMBER of the 1998 and 2002 England World Cup squads, Martin Keown failed to get a game in either tournament. However, he went on to win 43 caps spread over a period of 10 years.

After turning professional with Arsenal, Keown found his chances limited and went on loan to Brighton and Hove Albion, for whom he made his Football League debut. He returned to Highbury midway through the 1985/86 season and won a place at the heart of the Gunners' defence. However, during the close season he was transferred to Aston Villa and, despite his efforts, Villa were relegated to the Second Division. Keown, though, was an important member of the Villa side that regained their top-flight status at the first attempt. In August 1989 he joined Everton for £750,000 and, despite the presence of Ratcliffe and Watson, he was soon firmly established in the Toffees' back four, going on, in February 1992, to win the first of his many

Martin Keown during a friendly against Mexico at Derby County's Pride Park in May 2001. (Clive Brunskill/Getty Images)

international caps. Twelve months later, however, the Goodison favourite returned to Arsenal for a fee of £2 million.

In his second spell at Highbury, Keown developed into the best man-marker in the country. A commanding player who reads the game well, he is good in the air, strong in the tackle and has fair pace. He was an important member of the Arsenal side that completed the League and FA Cup double in seasons 1997/98 and 2001/02, and, despite several lay-offs through injury, he has appeared in over 400 League and Cup games for the Gunners.

Alan SHEARER

Position	Forward
Born	Alan Shearer, Newcastle, 13 August 1970
Height	6ft 0in
Weight	12st 6lb
Clubs	Southampton, Blackburn Rovers, Newcastle United
England Caps	63 Goals 30

1992 v France (won 2–0) 1 goal, v CIS (2–2), v France (0–0)

1993 v Spain (lost 0–1), v Norway (1–1), v Turkey (won 4–0) 1 goal

1994 v Holland (lost 0–2), v Denmark (won 1–0), v Greece (won 5–0) 1 goal, v Norway (0–0)

1995 v United States (won 2–0) 2 goals, v Romania (1–1), v Nigeria (won 1–0), v Eire (lost 0–1), v Japan (won 2–1), v Sweden (3–3), v Brazil (lost 1–3)

1996 v Colombia (0–0), v Norway (0–0), v Switzerland (won 3–1), v Portugal (1–1), v Hungary (won 3–0), v China (won 3–0), v Switzerland (1–1) 1 goal, v Scotland (won 2–0) 1 goal, v Holland (won 4–1) 2 goals, v Spain (0–0 aet, England won 4–3 on penalties), v Germany (1–1 aet, Germany won 6–5 on penalties) 1 goal

1997 v Moldova (won 3–0) 1 goal, v Poland (won 2–1) 2 goals, v Italy (lost 0–1), v Georgia (won 2–0) 1 goal, v Poland (won 2–0) 1 goal, v France (won 1–0) 1 goal, v Brazil (lost 0–1)

1998 v Chile (lost 0–2), v Switzerland (1–1), v Portugal (won 3–0) 2 goals, v Saudi Arabia (0–0), v Tunisia (won 2–0) 1 goal, v Romania (lost 1–2), v Colombia (won 2–0), v Argentina (2–2 aet, Argentina won 4–3 on penalties) 1 goal

1999 v Sweden (lost 1–2) 1 goal, v Bulgaria (0–0), v Luxembourg (won 3–0) 1 goal, v France (lost 0–2), v Poland (won 3–1), v Hungary (1–1) 1 goal, v Sweden (0–0), v Bulgaria (1–1) 1 goal

2000 v Luxembourg (won 6–0) 3 goals, v Poland (0–0), v Belgium (won 2–1) 1 goal, v Scotland (won 2–0), v Scotland (lost 0–1), v Argentina (0–0), v Brazil (1–1), v Ukraine (won 2–0), v Malta (won 2–1), v Portugal (lost 2–3), v Germany (won 1–0) 1 goal, v Romania (lost 2–3) 1 goal

Honours	Footballer of the Year 1994 and 1995

ALAN SHEARER, who made his last international appearance as captain of England in the Euro 2000 Championships, scored 30 goals in 63 games for his country, often playing as the lone striker with the brief to shield the ball and wait for support.

Captain Alan Shearer celebrates scoring England's second goal in the Euro 2000 qualifying match against Luxembourg in September 1999. Shearer scored a hat-trick and England won 6–0. (Ben Radford/Getty Images)

Shearer made his Football League debut for Southampton against Chelsea as a substitute, a month before turning professional. In his first full League game he caused a sensation, netting a hat-trick in a 4–2 win over Arsenal and becoming the youngest player to score three times in a top-flight match. Though he wasn't the most prolific of scorers during his time at the Dell, his record with the England Under-21 side was sensational – 13 goals in 11 games – and earned him a call-up to the full England side against France in February 1992. He represented England in the European Championship Finals in Sweden and then, on arriving home, signed for Blackburn Rovers for £3.6 million. Many felt that the British record fee paid for the striker was a little excessive, but by Boxing Day 1992 Shearer proved it was a bargain, scoring 22 goals in 25 games. Injuries – first a cartilage operation and then an operation to remove ligaments – meant that he missed the start of the 1993/94 season, but on his return he went on to score 34 League and Cup goals. By then the best striker in the country, he bettered this tally during the following campaign, netting 37 times to help Rovers win the Premier League title. In 1995/96 he repeated the feat, again scoring 37 goals and, in doing so, becoming the first player to reach 100 Premier League goals, also setting a new record with five hat-tricks.

Shearer had scored 128 goals in 162 League and Cup games for Rovers when in July 1996, after a superb Euro '96 tournament, he joined Newcastle United for a then world-record fee of £15 million. Despite being hindered by injury, he duly lived up to expectations, finishing the next season as the Premier League's leading scorer.

Awarded the OBE for services to football, he became the first player to score 100 times for two Premiership clubs and was voted by the PFA as the 'Player of the Decade' in the Premiership.

Keith CURLE

Position	Central defender
Born	Keith Curle, Bristol, 14 November 1963
Height	6ft 1in
Weight	12st 12lb
Clubs	Bristol Rovers, Torquay United, Bristol City, Reading, Wimbledon, Manchester City, Wolverhampton Wanderers, Sheffield United, Barnsley, Mansfield Town
England Caps	3
	1992 v CIS (2–2), v Hungary (won 1–0), v Denmark (0–0)

AFTER FAILING TO COMMAND a regular place in the Bristol Rovers side, Keith Curle, was transferred to Torquay United, but after just four months at Plainmoor left to sign for Bristol City. At Ashton Gate, Curle was converted from midfield to central defence, helping the Robins beat Bolton Wanderers in the 1986 Freight Rover Trophy Final. He then joined Reading, where his commanding displays at the heart of the Royals' defence alerted Wimbledon, and in October 1988 the Dons paid £500,000 to secure his services.

Appointed club captain, he soon established himself alongside Eric Young in the Wimbledon back four, and in his time with the Dons missed very few games. In the summer of 1991 he was unexpectedly sold to Manchester City for £2.5 million and while at Maine Road he won full international honours.

Curle captained City during the first Premier League season, 1992/93, and made 204 appearances before leaving to join Wolves for £650,000 in August 1996. Despite his debut for the Molineux club being delayed by injury, he went on to become a great favourite in the Wolves side, his organizational skills much in evidence. Later having a spell with Sheffield United as the Blades' player-coach, he joined Barnsley on a three-month contract before being appointed player-manager of Mansfield Town.

Nigel MARTYN

Position	Goalkeeper
Born	Nigel Anthony Martyn, St Austell, 11 August 1966
Height	6ft 2in
Weight	14st 7lb
Clubs	Bristol Rovers, Crystal Palace, Leeds United, Everton
England Caps	23
	1992 v CIS (2–2), v Hungary (won 1–0)
	1993 v Germany (lost 1–2)
	1997 v South Africa (won 2–1)
	1998 v Cameroon (won 2–0), v Chile (lost 0–2), v Belgium (0–0)
	1999 v Czech Republic (won 2–0), v France (lost 0–2)
	2000 v Luxembourg (won 6–0), v Poland (0–0), v Belgium (won 2–1), v Ukraine (won 2–0), v Romania (lost 2–3)
	2001 v Spain (won 3–0), v Mexico (won 4–0)
	2002 v Holland (lost 0–2), v Greece (2–2), v Sweden (1–1), v Holland (1–1), v Italy (lost 1–2), v S. Korea (1–1), v Cameroon (2–2)

NIGEL MARTYN began his League career with Bristol Rovers, whom he joined from St Blazey in the Duchy League in the summer of 1987. During his first season with the Pirates, he kept 12 clean sheets in a 13-match spell and, after proving himself to be one of the best keepers in the Third Division, won the first of 11 caps for the England Under-21 side. In November 1989, First Division Crystal Palace paid £1 million for the highly rated goalkeeper. In his second season at Selhurst Park the Eagles finished third in the First Division, their highest-ever finish in the Football League. Not surprisingly, his form led to international honours: Martyn came on as a substitute goalkeeper for Chris Woods in the 2–2 draw against the CIS in Moscow, having proven himself one of the most consistent goalkeepers in England. After a 6–1 defeat at Liverpool, he conceded just 29 goals, keeping 13 clean sheets, before a broken index finger brought to an end his run of 150 consecutive first-team appearances. Despite appearing on the transfer list, he continued to produce outstanding displays, helping Palace to the First Division play-off final, where he was beaten in the last minute of extra time by Leicester City's Steve Claridge.

Nigel Martyn during a friendly against Spain at Villa Park in February
2001. England won 3–0. (Ben Radford/Getty Images)

Martyn had appeared in 349 games for Crystal Palace when, in July 1996, he joined Premier League Leeds United for £2.25 million. In his first season at Elland Road he kept more clean sheets than any other Premier League keeper and, following an injury to David Seaman, he began to establish himself as England's clear second-choice keeper. One of the Yorkshire club's most consistent performers, he later found himself the club's second-choice behind the up-and-coming Paul Robinson, so in 2003, after offers from various clubs, he moved on to Everton.

Carlton PALMER

Position	Defender/Midfielder
Born	Carlton Lloyd Palmer, Rowley Regis, 5 December 1965
Height	6ft 2in
Weight	13st 3lb
Clubs	West Bromwich Albion, Sheffield Wednesday, Leeds United, Southampton, Nottingham Forest, Coventry City, Watford, Stockport County
England Caps	18 Goals 1
	1992 v CIS (2–2), v Hungary (won 1–0), v Brazil (1–1), v Finland (won 2–1), v Denmark (0–0), v France (0–0), v Sweden (lost 1–2)
	1993 v Spain (lost 0–1), v Norway (1–1), v Turkey (won 4–0), v San Marino (won 6–0) 1 goal, v Turkey (won 2–0), v Holland (2–2), v Poland (1–1), v Norway (lost 0–2), v United States (lost 0–2), v Brazil (1–1)
	1994 v Holland (lost 0–2)

HAVING MADE his League debut for West Bromwich Albion in September 1985, Carlton Palmer continued to hold down a regular place until his former boss Ron Atkinson signed him for Sheffield Wednesday for £750,000 in February 1989. Despite settling down well at Hillsborough in his first season, he couldn't prevent the Owls from being relegated to the Second Division, but his continued good form helped Wednesday return to the top-flight at the first time of asking. Unfortunately injury ruled him out of the Owls side that won the League Cup that season, but in 1991/92 he returned and scored his first-ever hat-trick in a 4–1 win at Queen's Park Rangers. Also that season he won the first of his 18 full caps for England, against the CIS in Moscow.

Palmer had made 263 appearances for the Owls when, in June 1994, he joined rivals Leeds United for a fee of £2.6 million. A wholehearted member of the Elland Road side, he appeared in over 100 games before £1 million moves took him to Southampton and later Nottingham Forest. His next port of call was Coventry City. While there he was unable to hold down a regular place and he had loan spells with Watford and Sheffield Wednesday. Palmer then became player-manager of Second Division Stockport County and later retired from the playing side in order to focus more fully on his managerial role. However, he has since been replaced by Sammy McIlroy.

Tim FLOWERS

Position	Goalkeeper
Born	Timothy David Flowers, Kenilworth, 3 February 1967
Height	6ft 2in
Weight	14st 0lb
Clubs	Wolverhampton Wanderers, Southampton, Swindon Town, Blackburn Rovers, Leicester City, Stockport County, Coventry City
England Caps	11
	1993 v Brazil (1–1)
	1994 v Greece (won 5–0)
	1995 v Nigeria (won 1–0), v Uruguay (0–0), v Japan (won 2–1), v Sweden (3–3), v Brazil (lost 1–3)
	1996 v China (won 3–0)
	1997 v Italy (lost 0–1)
	1998 v Switzerland (1–1), v Morocco (won 1–0)

TIM FLOWERS made his international debut against Brazil in Washington in June 1993 and conceded just a single goal, which was down to poor marking. Indeed, it took one of Flowers' specialities, a brilliant reflex save in the final minute, to ensure England didn't come away empty-handed.

Manager Tommy Docherty gave him his baptism for Wolverhampton Wanderers on the opening day of the 1984/85 season in a 2–2 draw against Sheffield United. He went on to miss very few games that season but couldn't prevent the club from being relegated to the Third Division, and in 1985/86 they were relegated yet again, this time to the Fourth Division.

Flowers had a loan spell at Southampton without playing a match for the Saints before eventually joining the south coast club on a permanent basis as Peter Shilton's understudy. He made a less than auspicious start, conceding five goals on his First Division debut at Old Trafford. In his second game, he fractured a cheekbone and had two loan spells at Swindon Town before finally breaking into the Southampton side on a regular basis. A good shot-stopper and possessing great concentration, he made 234 appearances for Southampton before joining Blackburn Rovers for £2.4 million in November 1993.

Flowers helped the Ewood Park club win the Premier League title in 1994/95, a season when he was one of six Blackburn players elected to the PFA Premier League 'Team of the Year'. He went on to play in 203 games for Rovers before joining Leicester City. Coming under pressure from Ian Walker, he had loan spells at both Stockport and Coventry, before long-term arthritic problems forced his retirement. A permanent move into coaching beckons.

David BARDSLEY

Position	Right-back
Born	David John Bardsley, Manchester, 11 September 1964
Height	5ft 10in
Weight	11st 7lb
Clubs	Blackpool, Watford, Oxford United, Queen's Park Rangers
England Caps	2
	1993 v Spain (lost 0–1), v Poland (1–1)

DAVID BARDSLEY'S impressive performances for Blackpool prompted a number of other to cast envious eyes in his direction, and in November 1983 he moved to Watford for a fee of £150,000. In his first season at Vicarage Road he helped the Hornets to their first FA Cup Final, but they were beaten 2–0 by Everton. Three years later, Oxford United, looking for a replacement for David Langan, were surprised to find Bardsley available and signed him for a club-record fee of £265,000.

His time with the club proved disappointing as they were relegated to the Second Division, although they had earlier reached the League Cup semi-finals. After beginning the 1989/90 season in Oxford colours, he joined Queen's Park Rangers for £500,000 plus Mark Stein. Awarded his first England cap against Spain, he was unfortunate to pick up an injury which kept him out of the Rangers side for a number of matches. He returned to help the club finish fifth in the top flight, and gained a further cap in a World Cup qualifier in Poland.

Bardsley went on to appear in 295 games for Rangers before returning to his first club, Blackpool, in July 1998. There he put his vast experience to good effect before hanging up his boots.

Paul INCE

Position	Midfielder
Born	Paul Emerson Carlyle Ince, Ilford, 21 October 1967
Height	5ft 11in
Weight	12st 2lb
Clubs	West Ham United, Manchester United, Inter Milan, Liverpool, Middlesbrough, Wolverhampton Wanderers
England Caps	53 Goals 2
	1993 v Spain (lost 0–1), v Norway (1–1), v Turkey (won 4–0), v Turkey (won 2–0), v Holland (2–2), v Poland (1–1), v United States (lost 0–2), v Brazil (1–1), v Germany (lost 1–2)
	1994 v Poland (won 3–0), v Holland (lost 0–2), v San Marino (won 7–1) 2 goals, v Denmark (won 1–0), v Norway (0–0)
	1995 v Romania (1–1), v Eire (lost 0–1)
	1996 v Bulgaria (won 1–0), v Croatia (0–0), v Hungary (won 3–0), v Switzerland (1–1), v Scotland (won 2–0), v Holland (won 4–1), v Germany (1–1 aet, Germany won 6–5 on penalties)

Paul Ince during the England v Scotland Euro 2000 play-off at Wembley in November 1999. Scotland won the game 1–0 but England went through on an aggregate score of 2–1. (Clive Brunskill/Getty Images)

1997 v Moldova (won 3–0), v Poland (won 2–1), v Georgia (won 2–0), v Italy (lost 0–1),
   v Mexico (won 2–0), v Georgia (won 2–0), v Poland (won 2–0), v Italy (won 2–0),
   v France (won 1–0), v Brazil (lost 0–1)
1998 v Italy (0–0), v Cameroon (won 2–0), v Chile (lost 0–2), v Switzerland (1–1),
   v Portugal (won 3–0), v Morocco (won 1–0), v Tunisia (won 2–0), v Romania (lost 1–2),
   v Colombia (won 2–0), v Argentina (2–2 aet, Argentina won 4–3 on penalties)
1999 v Sweden (lost 1–2), v France (lost 0–2)
2000 v Belgium (won 2–1), v Scotland (won 2–0), v Scotland (lost 0–1), v Brazil (1–1),
   v Malta (won 2–1), v Portugal (lost 2–3), v Germany (won 1–0), v Romania (lost 2–3)

| Honours | Footballer of the Year 1993 |

PAUL INCE, whose international career seemed to be over after his move to Inter Milan in 1995, earned the respect of a succession of English managers and went on to win 53 caps in a period spanning seven years.

Ince joined the Hammers on a YTS scheme in the summer of 1984, before signing professional forms in the summer of 1985. After working his way up through the ranks, he made his League debut in the London derby against Chelsea in November 1986, but it was 1988/89 when he really came to the fore. That season he scored a number of spectacular goals, including two in a 4–1 win over Liverpool, but he couldn't prevent the club from falling into the Second Division. Having declared a wish to leave Upton Park, he finally signed for Manchester United in September 1989, though at one stage it looked as though the transfer would fall through after he failed his medical. Two weeks later, however, an independent medical panel reported that his pelvic problems were not as serious as had initially been diagnosed. The transfer fee was duly reduced from £2 million to £1 million, and Ince went on to win two League Championships, two FA Cup winners' medals, a League Cup and European Cup Winners' Cup medal with Manchester United, as well as being voted Footballer of the Year in 1993.

In 1995, after appearing in 273 games for the Reds, he left Old Trafford to join Inter Milan, who paid £8 million for his services. Shortly afterwards, he threatened to quit Italian football after Cremonese supporters hurled racist abuse at him. He later returned to the UK to play for Liverpool, who paid £2 million for him, but he never hit peak form at Anfield. He left to continue his Premiership career at the Riverside with Middlesbrough, where his inspirational midfield displays helped the north-east club retain its top-flight status. Ince then moved to Wolverhampton Wanderers and helped the Molineux club achieve their aim of Premier League football.

David WHITE

Position	Winger/Forward
Born	David White, Manchester, 30 October 1967
Height	6ft 1in
Weight	12st 9lb
Clubs	Manchester City, Leeds United, Sheffield United
England Caps	1
	1993 v Spain (lost 0–1)

DISCOVERED ON THE DOORSTEP of Manchester City, David White did well to hold down a regular place on the right wing for short spells during his early days at Maine Road. Despite the club's relegation to the Second Division, he sprung to fame during the course of the 1987/88 season in a City team brimming with brilliant youngsters, scoring a hat-trick in the 10–1 demolition of Huddersfield Town. Promotion was achieved the following season, with White playing in all but one game, as he did again in 1989/90. Noted for his surging runs and powerful shooting, he was switched from the wing to central striker by manager Peter Reid, and during the course of the 1989/90 season he netted four goals in a 5–1 win at Aston Villa. He scored his third hat-trick for the club against Oldham Athletic the following season. Making his only full international appearance against Spain at Santander, he went on to score 96 goals in 342 games for City before joining Leeds United in December 1993 for a fee of £2 million.

Sadly, White struggled at Leeds with injury and with the burden of replacing Gordon Strachan, and in January 1996 he moved on to Sheffield United for £500,000. Again a series of niggling injuries, coupled with a long spell of recuperation following an operation, limited his first-team opportunities, and he eventually decided to retire.

Les FERDINAND

Position	Forward
Born	Leslie Ferdinand, Acton, 8 December 1966
Height	5ft 11in
Weight	13st 5lb
Clubs	Queen's Park Rangers, Brentford, Besiktas, Newcastle United, Tottenham Hotspur, West Ham United, Leicester City
England Caps	17 Goals 5
	1993 v San Marino (won 6–0) 1 goal, v Holland (2–2), v Norway (lost 0–2), v United States (lost 0–2)
	1994 v Poland (won 3–0) 1 goal, v San Marino (won 7–1) 1 goal
	1995 v United States (won 2–0)
	1996 v Portugal (1–1), v Bulgaria (won 1–0) 1 goal, v Hungary (won 3–0)
	1997 v Poland (won 2–1), v Georgia (won 2–0) 1 goal, v Italy (won 2–0)
	1998 v Moldova (won 4–0), v Saudi Arabia (0–0), v Morocco (won 1–0), v Belgium (0–0)
Honours	Footballer of the Year 1996

LES FERDINAND'S international career began under Graham Taylor, his most successful spell seeing two goals in as many games in 1993/94. His subsequent chances were limited because of Terry Venables' ploy of playing Alan Shearer as a lone striker.

Ferdinand was signed by Queen's Park Rangers after he was spotted playing in the Vauxhall Opel League with Hayes, and he was immediately given his debut as a substitute against Coventry City in April 1987. With opportunities at Loftus Road scarce, he was loaned out to both Brentford and Turkish club Besiktas, who were then managed by Gordon Milne. Ferdinand made a huge impact in Turkey, scoring 21 goals in 33 games, including the winning strike in the Turkish Cup Final against Fenerbahce. Once he was back in London, the goals began to flow and in 183 games for Rangers he scored 90 times. His form led to full international honours, and he scored on his debut in a 6–0 win over San Marino.

In 1995 Newcastle United manager Kevin Keegan signed Ferdinand for a fee of £8 million as a replacement for Andy Cole, who had joined Manchester United. The spearhead of the Magpies' title challenge in 1995/96, he scored 29 goals and landed the PFA Player of the Year award. Then, in the summer of 1997, he left St James' Park to return to London to play for Tottenham Hotspur. Though he was a huge favourite with the crowd, his time at White Hart Lane saw him suffer a succession of injuries that curtailed his appearances. The 2001/02 season was his best, with 15 goals in all competitions as he formed a deadly strike force with Teddy Sheringham. Midway through the 2002/03 season, Ferdinand left White Hart Lane to join Premiership strugglers West Ham United, but was unable to prevent them slipping into relegation. He subsequently signed for newly promoted Leicester City, starting the 2003/04 season doing what he does best – scoring goals.

Teddy SHERINGHAM

Position	Forward
Born	Edward Paul Sheringham, Highams Park, 2 April 1966
Height	5ft 11in
Weight	12st 5lb
Clubs	Millwall, Aldershot, Nottingham Forest, Tottenham Hotspur, Manchester United, Portsmouth
England Caps	51 Goals 11

1993 v Poland (1–1), v Norway (lost 0–2)
1995 v United States (won 2–0), v Romania (1–1), v Nigeria (won 1–0), v Uruguay (0–0), v Japan (won 2–1), v Sweden (3–3) 1 goal, v Brazil (lost 1–3)
1996 v Colombia (0–0), v Norway (0–0), v Switzerland (won 3–1) 1 goal, v Bulgaria (won 1–0), v Croatia (0–0), v Hungary (won 3–0), v Switzerland (1–1), v Scotland (won 2–0), v Holland (won 4–1) 2 goals, v Spain (0–0 aet, England won 4–3 on penalties), v Germany (1–1 aet, Germany won 6–5 on penalties)
1997 v Georgia (won 2–0) 1 goal, v Mexico (won 2–0) 1 goal, v Georgia (won 2–0) 1 goal, v S. Africa (won 2–1), v Poland (won 2–0) 1 goal, v Italy (won 2–0), v France (won 1–0), v Brazil (lost 0–1)
1998 v Italy (0–0), v Chile (lost 0–2), v Switzerland (1–1), v Portugal (won 3–0) 1 goal, v Saudi Arabia (0–0), v Tunisia (won 2–0), v Romania (lost 1–2)
1999 v Sweden (lost 1–2), v Bulgaria (0–0), v Bulgaria (1–1)
2001 v Finland (won 2–1), v Albania (won 3–1), v Mexico (won 4–0) 1 goal
2002 v Greece (2–2) 1 goal, v Sweden (1–1), v Italy (lost 1–2), v Paraguay (won 4–0), v S. Korea (1–1), v Cameroon (2–2), v Argentina (won 1–0), v Nigeria (0–0), v Denmark (won 3–0), v Brazil (lost 1–2)

Honours	Footballer of the Year 2001

Teddy Sheringham in action during the World Cup Group 9 qualifier against Greece in October 2001. England sealed qualification with a score of 2–2. (Gary M. Prior/Getty Images)

TEDDY SHERINGHAM, who had an outstanding Euro '96, scored the all-important goal against Greece that saw England qualify for the 2002 World Cup Finals.

After graduating through Millwall's junior sides, Sheringham made his League debut for the Lions against Brentford in January 1984. Following a spell on loan at Aldershot, he returned to Millwall and, in 1986/87, was ever-present, netting 18 goals. Following two seasons in the top flight, Millwall found themselves back in the Second Division for the 1990/91 campaign. Although the Lions failed at the play-off stage, Sheringham had a magnificent season, scoring 33 League goals, including all four in a 4–1 defeat of Plymouth Argyle. He ended the season as the highest goalscorer in the club's history. In the summer of 1991 he joined Nottingham Forest for £2 million, ending the season as the club's leading scorer, but his time there was not entirely happy and he returned to London early the following season, signing for Spurs. He ended his first season at White Hart Lane with 29 goals and won the Premier League Golden Boot award as well as his first cap.

Continuing to demonstrate his intelligence, quick thinking and unselfishness for both club and country, Sheringham eventually left Spurs in June 1997 to join Manchester United for a fee of £3.5 million as a direct replacement for Eric Cantona. He later struggled to hold down a regular first-team spot due to the fine form of Dwight Yorke and Andy Cole, but returned to first-team action towards the end of the 1998/99 season, coming off the bench against Bayern Munich in the Champion's League Final to score the equalizer before setting up Ole Gunnar Solskjaer for the winner. However, his best season at Old Trafford came in 2000/01, when he finished the campaign with many awards, including the Footballer of the Year and the PFA Player of the Year.

In order to secure regular first-team football and keep his place in the national squad, Sheringham finally returned to White Hart Lane. He scored a total of 111 goals in 239 games in his two spells with the North London club. Shortly before the start of the 2003/04 season he signed for Portsmouth.

Stuart RIPLEY

Position	Winger
Born	Stuart Edward Ripley, Middlesbrough, 20 November 1967
Height	5ft 11in
Weight	13st 0lb
Clubs	Middlesbrough, Bolton Wanderers, Blackburn Rovers, Southampton, Barnsley, Sheffield Wednesday
England Caps	2
	1994 v San Marino (won 7–1)
	1998 v Moldova (won 4–0)

STUART RIPLEY, who won his second cap for England four years after his first, was a member of the Middlesbrough Boys' team that shared the English Schools FA Trophy with Sunderland. He then joined the Ayresome Park club as an apprentice professional before making his Boro debut against Oldham Athletic in February 1985. The following season he was loaned out to Bolton Wanderers, where he scored in his first game for the club. It was 1986/87 before he established himself in the Middlesbrough side, helping them win promotion from the Third Division. The following season he netted his first hat-trick for the club in a 6–0 win over Sheffield United as the Boro entered the top flight via the play-offs. Following their relegation in 1988/89, Ripley stayed loyal to the club and in 1991/92 helped them win promotion to the newly formed Premier League.

In July 1992 Blackburn manager Kenny Dalglish paid £1.3 million to take Ripley to Ewood Park and in 1994/95 he helped Rovers win the Premier League title. Often hampered by injuries during his six seasons in the north-west, Ripley was transferred to Southampton for £1.5 million in the summer of 1998.

Again injuries restricted his number of first-team appearances and he had successful loan spells with both Barnsley and Sheffield Wednesday. Finding it hard to break into Gordon Strachan's side, Ripley decided to retire at the end of the 2001/02 season.

Darren ANDERTON

Position	Winger
Born	Darren Robert Anderton, Southampton, 3 March 1972
Height	6ft 1in
Weight	12st 5lb
Clubs	Portsmouth, Tottenham Hotspur
England Caps	30 Goals 7

1994 v Denmark (won 1–0), v Greece (won 5–0) 1 goal, v Norway (0–0)
1995 v United States (won 2–0), v Eire (lost 0–1), v Uruguay (0–0), v Japan (won 2–1) 1 goal, v Sweden (3–3) 1 goal, v Brazil (lost 1–3)
1996 v Hungary (won 3–0) 2 goals, v China (won 3–0), v Switzerland (1–1), v Scotland (won 2–0), v Holland (won 4–1), v Spain (0–0 aet, England won 4–3 on penalties), v Germany (1–1 aet, Germany won 6–5 on penalties)
1998 v Saudi Arabia (0–0), v Morocco (won 1–0), v Tunisia (won 2–0), v Romania (lost 1–2), v Colombia (won 2–0) 1 goal, v Argentina (2–2 aet, Argentina won 4–3 on penalties)
1999 v Sweden (lost 1–2), v Bulgaria (0–0), v Luxembourg (won 3–0), v Czech Republic (won 2–0) 1 goal, v France (lost 0–2)
2001 v France (1–1), v Italy (lost 0–1)
2002 v Sweden (1–1)

DARREN ANDERTON made an important contribution to England's performance in Euro '96 and appeared in all five of their matches in the 1998 World Cup in France. But for injuries he would probably have appeared in many more than the 30 international matches he has played.

Darren Anderton during a friendly with Sweden on 10 November 2001. (Ross Kinnaird/Getty Images)

Winger Anderton first hit the headlines during Portsmouth's long FA Cup run of 1991/92, though in fact he had already showed such good form that he was the subject of transfer speculation even before the club started their run. He scored both goals in Portsmouth's fourth-round victory over Leyton Orient and another couple in the club's 4–2 win over Middlesbrough. In the semi-final he scored a breakaway goal in extra time against Liverpool, which seemed certain to take Portsmouth to Wembley until the Reds' last-gasp equalizer. In May 1992 he signed for Spurs for £1.75 million. Initially he struggled to regain the form that prompted the club to buy him, but then he rediscovered his touch and won a call-up into the full England team. He is one of the best crossers of a ball in the Premier League, and his ability to deliver long balls and corners into opponents' 18-yard boxes created many of the club's goals over the next ten seasons. Sadly, for much of that time he was dogged by injuries, the 1998/99 season being his most successful in terms of fewest matches missed.

At his best, Darren Anderton is an international-class midfielder with great vision and accuracy.

Graham LE SAUX

Position	Left-back
Born	Graham Pierre Le Saux, Jersey, 17 October 1968
Height	5ft 10in
Weight	12st 2lb
Clubs	Chelsea, Blackburn Rovers, Southampton
England Caps	36 Goals 1

1994 v Denmark (won 1–0), v Greece (won 5–0), v Norway (0–0)
1995 v United States (won 2–0), v Romania (1–1), v Nigeria (won 1–0), v Eire (lost 0–1),
   v Uruguay (0–0), v Sweden (3–3), v Brazil (lost 1–3) 1 goal
1996 v Colombia (0–0), v Portugal (1–1)
1997 v Italy (lost 0–1), v Mexico (won 2–0), v Georgia (won 2–0), v S. Africa (won 2–1),
   v Poland (won 2–0), v Italy (won 2–0), v France (won 1–0), v Brazil (lost 0–1)
1998 v Italy (0–0), v Chile (lost 0–2), v Portugal (won 3–0), v Morocco (won 1–0), v Belgium
   (0–0), v Tunisia (won 2–0), v Romania (lost 1–2), v Colombia (won 2–0), v Argentina (2–2
   aet, Argentina won 4–3 on penalties)
1999 v Sweden (lost 1–2), v Bulgaria (0–0), v Czech Republic (won 2–0), v France (lost 0–2),
   v Poland (won 3–1), v Sweden (0–0)
2001 v Germany (lost 0–1)

A MEMBER OF the heroic England side that clinched World Cup qualification in Rome, Graham Le Saux went on to appear in all four of the team's 1998 World Cup Final matches in France. Sadly, since then he has suffered more than his fair share of injuries, which have restricted his international appearances to 36.

Spotted by Chelsea when playing for a local Jersey side, St Pauls, Le Saux signed professional forms without any further ado and made his debut against Portsmouth in

Graeme Le Saux during the Euro 2000 qualifier against Sweden in Stockholm. Sweden won the match 2–1. (Ben Radford/Getty Images)

May 1989, the Blues having already been confirmed as Second Division champions. However, it was 1991/92 before he won a regular place in the Chelsea side, and then he was unexpectedly sold to Blackburn Rovers in March 1993 for £500,000. Taking over from Alan Wright, he was a huge favourite with the Ewood Park faithful, with his forceful forward running, aggressive tackling and sheer enthusiasm. He went on to help Rovers win the Premier League Championship in 1994/95, before a well-documented onfield argument with team-mate David Batty. He had scarcely lived that down when an horrific injury, which saw him break his ankle and rupture tendons, curtailed his 1995/96 season. Out of action for over a year, he was able on his return to full fitness to reclaim both his old form and his international spot.

In the summer of 1997, Le Saux returned to Stamford Bridge for a fee of £5 million, the London club beating off opposition from Arsenal, Juventus and Barcelona for the defender's signature. He appeared in 312 games in his two spells with Chelsea before joining Southampton in the summer of 2003.

Matt LE TISSIER

Position	Forward
Born	Matthew Paul Le Tissier, St Peter Port, Guernsey, 14 October 1968
Height	6ft 1in
Weight	13st 8lb
Clubs	Southampton
England Caps	8
	1994 v Denmark (won 1–0), v Greece (won 5–0), v Norway (0–0)
	1995 v Romania (1–1), v Nigeria (won 1–0), v Eire (lost 0–1)
	1997 v Moldova (won 3–0), v Italy (lost 0–1)

MATT LE TISSIER was the youngest player to score a hat-trick for Southampton, which he did in his debut season of 1986/87. He was a prolific scorer for the Saints in his early days with the club, netting 24 League and Cup goals in 1989/90 and 23 the following season. At about this time he declined an offer to become part of the French international set-up, preferring to take his chances with England. In 1991/92 the Saints changed their playing style under new manager Ian Branfoot and goals became very scarce, although Le Tissier played and scored in the Zenith Data Systems Cup Final defeat by Nottingham Forest. He took over the mantle of the club's leading scorer again in 1992/93, and the following season scored enough spectacular goals to warrant a one-man goal of the year contest.

It seems rather unfair to say Le Tissier kept Southampton in the Premier League single-handedly, but without him and his goals it is likely that the club would have been relegated. He continued in 1994/95 to prove himself to be the most gifted Englishman in the Premier League but was consistently overlooked at international level. The cry of 'Le Tissier for England' was never heard louder than when he scored twice in a 3–2 defeat at Blackburn, including a stupendous 35-yard volley past former Saints keeper Tim Flowers. He ended the season with 30 goals, including all four in a League Cup win at Huddersfield Town.

During his last few seasons in the game, Le Tissier failed to score as regularly, missing quite a number of games through injury. His eventual tally was 210 goals in 540 games. Though he has now retired from first-class football his services are not lost to Southampton, for he remains involved at St Mary's as an ambassador for the club.

Steve BOULD

Position	Central defender
Born	Stephen Andrew Bould, Stoke, 16 November 1962
Height	6ft 4in
Weight	14st 2lb
Clubs	Stoke City, Torquay United, Arsenal, Sunderland
England Caps	2
	1994 v Greece (won 5–0), v Norway (0–0)

STEVE BOULD began his career with his home-town club Stoke City, and in his first four seasons at the Victoria Ground he could usually be found playing at right-back. However, in October 1982, still not able to command a regular place at the club, he was loaned out to Torquay United. He was later converted to centre-back, only for a severe back injury in a match at Blackburn to threaten his career. After an operation and seven months out of the game, he fully recovered and, in the summer of 1988, he followed his team-mate Lee Dixon to Arsenal, the Gunners paying £390,000 for his services.

After an injury-hit first season, Bould was ever-present at the heart of the Arsenal defence during the 1990/91 season, when the Gunners created a new club record by conceding just 18 goals. Cool, efficient, reliable and virtually unbeatable in the air, he was unfortunately troubled by injuries during his time at Highbury – in 1992/93 he missed both the FA and League Cup finals. He was 31 when he was eventually capped by England. Bould appeared in 373 games for Arsenal before joining Sunderland for a fee of £500,000 in July 1999. His contribution at the Stadium of Light was immense, helping the Black Cats find their feet in the Premiership, but, after just over a year in the north-east, injuries forced his retirement from the game.

Kevin RICHARDSON

Position	Midfielder
Born	Kevin Richardson, Newcastle, 4 December 1962
Height	5ft 9in
Weight	12st 0lb
Clubs	Everton, Watford, Arsenal, Real Sociedad, Aston Villa, Coventry City, Southampton, Barnsley, Blackpool
England Caps	1
	1994 v Greece (won 5–0)

AFTER MAKING his League debut for Everton in November 1981, Kevin Richardson appeared the following season in both the League Cup and FA Cup finals for the Toffees. He won League Championship and European Cup Winners' Cup medals in 1984/85, but at the beginning of the 1986/87 campaign he left Goodison to join Watford. An influential and versatile member of the Vicarage Road club's side, he was instrumental in Watford's 3–1 FA Cup sixth-round victory over Arsenal, prompting the Gunners to sign him in the summer of 1987.

He won another League Championship medal in 1988/89, but at the end of the following season, after a bad injury, he signed for Spanish team Real Sociedad of San Sebastian, linking up with John Aldridge and Dalian Atkinson. In August 1991 he joined Atkinson at Villa Park and played in every one of Villa's 51 games without once being substituted. He was made Villa team captain and played in 102 consecutive League games before injury forced him to miss a match.

Richardson left Aston Villa in February 1995 to sign for Coventry City, and two years later moved to Southampton. He spent just one season on the south coast before joining Barnsley. Appointed the Oakwell club's captain, he lost his place on the appointment of new manager Dave Bassett, and after a loan spell at Blackpool he joined the Seasiders on a permanent basis. Finally, after being unable to prevent the Bloomfield Road club's relegation, he decided to hang up his boots.

Barry VENISON

Position	Right-back
Born	Barry Venison, Consett, 16 August 1964
Height	5ft 10in
Weight	12st 3lb
Clubs	Sunderland, Liverpool, Newcastle United, Galatasaray, Southampton
England Caps	2
	1995 v United States (won 2–0), v Uruguay (0–0)

BARRY VENISON made his League debut for Sunderland against Notts County in October 1981, just a couple of months after his 17th birthday, and by the time he turned professional he had appeared in a further nine League games. His first two seasons with the Wearsiders saw him alternate between right-back and midfield but subsequently he became firmly established at right-back. At this time, Venison was a regular member of the England Under-21 side, winning ten caps at this level. He became the youngest Wembley Cup Final captain at the age of 20, leading Sunderland to the 1985 League Cup Final against Norwich City. At the end of that season, Sunderland were relegated and, after just one season playing in the Second Division, he left to join Liverpool for £200,000.

Venison arrived on Merseyside as a replacement for Phil Neal, but though he spent six seasons at Anfield he never truly established himself as a first-team regular. Nevertheless, he shared in the Liverpool success story, winning League Championship medals in 1987/88 and 1989/90, and an FA Cup winners' medal in 1989. After losing his place to Rob Jones, Venison returned to the north-east with Newcastle

United, helping the Magpies return to the top flight as champions of the new First Division. While with United he was capped twice by England but later left to play for Turkish side Galatasaray, who were then managed by Graeme Souness. In October 1995 he returned to the Premier League with Southampton, but a continuing back problem forced his retirement from the game.

Rob LEE

Position	Midfielder
Born	Robert Martin Lee, West Ham, 1 February 1966
Height	5ft 11in
Weight	11st 13lb
Clubs	Charlton Athletic, Newcastle United, Derby County
England Caps	21 Goals 2

1995 v Romania (1–1) 1 goal, v Nigeria (won 1–0)
1996 v Colombia (0–0), v Norway (0–0), v Switzerland (won 3–1), v Bulgaria (won 1–0), v Hungary (won 3–0)
1997 v Mexico (won 2–0), v Georgia (won 2–0), v S. Africa (won 2–1) 1 goal, v Poland (won 2–0), v France (won 1–0), v Brazil (lost 0–1)
1998 v Cameroon (won 2–0), v Chile (lost 0–2), v Switzerland (1–1), v Belgium (0–0), v Colombia (won 2–0)
1999 v Sweden (0–0), v Bulgaria (1–1), v Luxembourg (won 6–0)

FULL OF ENERGY and with a tremendous work-rate, Rob Lee turned in performances that led to 21 caps for England. The talented midfielder scored on his international debut against Romania.

After appearing in 343 League and Cup games for Charlton Athletic, in which he had netted 65 goals, Lee was rated one of the best midfield performers outside the top flight. In September 1992 he joined Newcastle United for a fee of £700,000 and very quickly became one of the top players in the Premier League. For Kevin Keegan's promotion-winning side, Lee played the majority of his games on the right wing, showing match-winning ability on the touchline. Strong in possession and able to withstand the hardest of tackles, he switched to a more conventional midfield role as the Magpies began life in the Premier League. He netted a hat-trick against Antwerp in a UEFA Cup game in 1994, and was an influential figure in the Magpies' resurgence, it often being said that when Rob Lee played well, Newcastle played well too. Though injuries restricted his appearances in later years, he went on to score 56 goals in 381 games before joining Derby County in February 2002. He figured regularly for the Rams, but was unable to prevent their relegation. At the end of the 2001/02 season his contract was not renewed.

Steve HOWEY

Position	Central defender
Born	Stephen Norman Howey, Sunderland, 26 October 1971
Height	6ft 2in
Weight	11st 12lb
Clubs	Newcastle United, Manchester City, Leicester City, Bolton Wanderers
England Caps	4
	1995 v Nigeria (won 1–0)
	1996 v Colombia (0–0), v Portugal (1–1), v Bulgaria (won 1–0)

STEVE HOWEY began his Newcastle United career as an out-and-out striker, but in 1991 he was switched to the heart of the Magpies' defence, initially by Ossie Ardiles but more positively by Kevin Keegan. Thereafter, his career took off and in 1992/93 he was an important member of the club's First Division Championship-winning team. His ability to move forward and distribute the ball with pinpoint accuracy fitted smoothly into Keegan's tactical plan.

After being selected on several occasions for the Under-21 side, he became a regular in Terry Venables' England squad, but had to withdraw on several occasions because of injury before finally making his debut in a 1–0 win over Nigeria in 1995.

Possessing pace, aggression and ball skills – perfect qualities for his position – Howey went on to appear in 242 games for the Magpies before joining Manchester City for a fee of £2 million in August 2000. Forming a strong defensive partnership with Richard Dunne, following the latter's arrival from Everton, he was a strong commanding player, hugely popular with the City faithful. He was rarely absent during his time at Maine Road. Howey left City, now managed by his former boss, Keegan, with one year of his Blues contract remaining and joined newly promoted Leicester City, but failed to settle and joined Bolton Wanderers in January 2004.

Neil RUDDOCK

Position	Central defender
Born	Neil Ruddock, Wandsworth, 9 May 1968
Height	6ft 2in
Weight	12st 12lb
Clubs	Millwall, Tottenham Hotspur, Southampton, Liverpool, Queen's Park Rangers, West Ham United, Crystal Palace, Swindon Town
England Caps	1
	1995 v Nigeria (won 1–0)

THOUGH HE TURNED PROFESSIONAL with Millwall in March 1986, a month later Neil Ruddock joined Tottenham Hotspur without having made a single League appearance for the Lions. Yet, in the summer of 1988, he returned to The Den, having appeared in only four games for Spurs! Millwall paid £300,000 for his services, but Ruddock did not get to play a full 90 minutes that season as the Lions returned to the top flight. In

February 1989 he was on the move again, this time to Southampton, where he soon established himself as a first-team regular. In 1991/92 he was sent off twice and booked in every other game up to Christmas. Then, after appearing in 132 games for the Saints, there was another strange twist to his career as he returned to Tottenham Hotspur. Unhappy with the set-up at White Hart Lane, however, he informed manager Ossie Ardiles that he no longer wanted to play for the club, and when Liverpool met the London club's asking price of £2.5 million, he was happy to sign with them.

With the Reds Ruddock won a League Cup winners' medal and was capped by England, but he was still unable to win a regular place in the side. Following a loan spell with Queen's Park Rangers, he joined West Ham United before later playing for Crystal Palace. Then, in the summer of 2001 he joined Swindon Town as the Wiltshire club's player-coach. He was a cult figure with the club, but injuries restricted his first-team appearances and he retired in 2002.

Steve McMANAMAN

Position	Forward
Born	Steven McManaman, Bootle, 11 February 1972
Height	6ft 0in
Weight	10st 6lb
Clubs	Liverpool, Real Madrid, Manchester City
England Caps	37 Goals 3

1995 v Nigeria (won 1–0), v Uruguay (0–0), v Japan (won 2–1)
1996 v Colombia (0–0), v Norway (0–0), v Switzerland (won 3–1), v Portugal (1–1),
    v Bulgaria (won 1–0), v Croatia (0–0), v China (won 3–0), v Switzerland (1–1), v Scotland
    (won 2–0), v Holland (won 4–1), v Spain (0–0 aet, England won 4–3 on penalties),
    v Germany (1–1 aet, Germany won 6–5 on penalties)
1997 v Poland (won 2–1), v Italy (lost 0–1), v Mexico (won 2–0)
1998 v Cameroon (won 2–0), v Switzerland (1–1), v Morocco (won 1–0), v Colombia
    (won 2–0)
1999 v Poland (won 3–1), v Hungary (1–1)
2000 v Luxembourg (won 6–0) 2 goals, v Poland (0–0), v Ukraine (won 2–0), v Malta
    (won 2–1), v Portugal (lost 2–3) 1 goal
2001 v France (1–1), v Finland (0–0), v Finland (won 2–1), v Albania (won 3–1), v Greece
    (won 2–0)
2002 v Germany (won 5–1), v Albania (won 2–0), v Greece (2–2)

STEVE McMANAMAN, who had an excellent Euro '96 for England, was called upon just once during World Cup '98 in France and not considered at all for the 2002 World Cup Finals in Japan and Korea.

McManaman was the first product of Liverpool's modern youth system to break through into the big time, and by the age of 23 he had been capped by England and secured both winners' medals and 'Man-of-the-Match' awards from FA and League Cup finals. He immediately impressed with his speed, skill and trickery, and made a telling contribution to the 1992 FA Cup triumph over Sunderland. When he was handed a free role in Roy Evans' new-look formation of 1994/95, he quickly matured

Steve McManaman during the World Cup Group 9 qualifier against Greece in October 2001. England qualified after the match ended 2–2. (Gary M. Prior/Getty Images)

into the most dangerous attacker in English football, showing intelligence, awareness and tactical appreciation. His brace of goals against Bolton Wanderers in the 1995 Coca Cola Cup Final were among the finest ever seen at Wembley. The only factor that appeared to pose any threat to his continued rise was his inconsistency, a performance of sheer brilliance one day being followed by another in which little went right.

In July 1999 McManaman left Anfield to play for Real Madrid. The following May he scored the goal of his life, his 67th-minute strike making him the first Englishman to score for a foreign side in a European final, and helping the Spanish club capture the European Cup for the eighth time, beating Valencia 3–0. He followed this up in 2001 by appearing in Real's triumph against Bayer Leverkusen at Hampden Park.

Increasingly unsure of a first-team place following Real's signing of David Beckham in July 2003, McManaman left shortly afterwards to become part of Kevin Keegan's Manchester City.

Warren BARTON

Position	Right-back
Born	Warren Dean Barton, Stoke Newington, 19 March 1969
Height	6ft 0in
Weight	12st 0lb
Clubs	Maidstone United, Wimbledon, Newcastle United, Derby County
England Caps	3
	1995 v Eire (lost 0–1), v Sweden (3–3), v Brazil (lost 1–3)

WARREN BARTON SIGNED for Maidstone United from Vauxhall League side Leytonstone and Ilford before the club embarked on its first Football League campaign. He made his League debut at Peterborough in August 1989 and helped the Stones reach a play-off position at the end of his first season with the club. Suitably impressed by his performances, Wimbledon paid £300,000 to take him to Plough Lane. Initially, he established himself in the Dons' midfield, his performances leading to international 'B' honours for England, but, following the signing of Vinnie Jones from Chelsea, he moved to right-back, where he continued to show good form, winning the first of three full caps against the Republic of Ireland.

Barton had appeared in 209 games for Wimbledon when Newcastle United paid £4.5 million for his services in the summer of 1995. He missed very few games during his time on Tyneside, playing a midfield holding role following the appointment of Kenny Dalglish as manager, and it was while fulfilling that role that he scored against his former club Wimbledon during the 1997/98 campaign. He went on to play in 220 games for the Magpies before, in February 2002, joining Derby County. An exemplary captain, he needed all his experience to cope with the Rams' depressing season of 2002/03.

Nick BARMBY

Position	Midfielder
Born	Nicholas Jonathan Barmby, Hull, 11 February 1974
Height	5ft 7in
Weight	11st 3lb
Clubs	Tottenham Hotspur, Middlesbrough, Everton, Liverpool, Leeds United
England Caps	23 Goals 4
	1995 v Uruguay (0–0), v Sweden (3–3)
	1996 v Colombia (0–0), v Norway (0–0), v Portugal (1–1), v China (won 3–0) 2 goals, v Switzerland (1–1), v Holland (won 4–1), v Spain (0–0 aet, England won 4–3 on penalties)
	1997 v Moldova (won 3–0) 1 goal
	2000 v Brazil (1–1), v Ukraine (won 2–0), v Malta (won 2–1), v Germany (won 1–0), v Romania (lost 2–3)
	2001 v France (1–1), v Germany (lost 0–1), v Italy (lost 0–1), v Spain (won 3–0) 1 goal
	2002 v Holland (lost 0–2), v Germany (won 5–1), v Albania (won 2–0), v Greece (2–2)

CRITICS WERE QUICK to link Nick Barmby's remarkable international advancement to his previous acquaintance with England's national manager Terry Venables at Tottenham Hotspur, but the much-travelled midfielder went on to win 23 caps and but for injury would have won many more.

The son of former Hull City player Jeff Barmby, Nick joined Tottenham Hotspur after spending some time at the Lilleshall Centre of Excellence. He was at the centre of a club versus country row when he was selected for the England youth side to compete in the World Cup Finals in Australia. Spurs wanted him to stay and take part in their FA Cup campaign, but the FA got their way and he went to Australia. After helping England to third place, he returned to White Hart Lane in time to play in Spurs' losing FA Cup semi-final against Arsenal.

In the summer of 1995 Barmby was allowed to join Middlesbrough for £5.25 million. He quickly established himself as a firm favourite at the new Holgate End but, with Bryan Robson seeking to strengthen his defence, he was sold to Everton for £5.75 million in October 1996, having scored 10 goals in 49 games. At Goodison Park he suffered a recurrence of a long-standing groin injury but bounced back to become an important member of the Everton side. Then, having scored 21 goals in 133 games, he moved across the city to rivals Liverpool for £6 million in the summer of 2000. A revelation in the Reds side, he helped them to win both the League and UEFA cups, but sadly injuries hampered his progress in his second season at Anfield, and during the summer of 2002 he was allowed to join Leeds United. He soon won over the fans before a serious injury in a pre-match warm-up at Tottenham kept him out of the side for four months.

Nick Barmby during a friendly against Spain at Villa Park in February 2001. England won 3–0. (Craig Prentis/Getty Images)

Andy COLE

Position	Forward
Born	Andrew Alexander Cole, Nottingham, 15 October 1971
Height	5ft 11in
Weight	11st 12lb
Clubs	Arsenal, Fulham, Bristol City, Newcastle United, Manchester United, Blackburn Rovers
England Caps	15 Goals 1

1995 v Uruguay (0–0)
1997 v Italy (lost 0–1)
1999 v France (lost 0–2), v Poland (won 3–1), v Sweden (0–0)
2000 v Scotland (won 2–0), v Argentina (0–0)
2001 v France (1–1), v Germany (lost 0–1), v Finland (0–0), v Spain (won 3–0), v Finland (won 2–1), v Albania (won 3–1) 1 goal
2002 v Holland (lost 0–2), v Greece (2–2)

ANDY COLE began his Football League career with Arsenal. Unable to hold down a regular place in the Gunners' side, he went on loan to Fulham before representing England at Under-21 level. Just two months later he was allowed to join Bristol City, and it was at Ashton Gate that his career took off as he scored 21 goals in 40 games. This form attracted the attention of Newcastle United manager Kevin Keegan who paid £1.75 million for his services in March 1993, and two months later he promptly picked up a First Division Championship medal. His next campaign was nothing short of sensational – Cole became the first player to score 40 League goals in a season for the Magpies. As well as ending the season as the country's leading goalscorer, he was also voted the PFA Young Player of the Year.

In January 1995, Cole was allowed to join Manchester United in exchange for Keith Gillespie and a fee of £6 million. He was to become the first United player to score five times in a League game, performing this feat against Ipswich Town, and soon afterwards he secured his first England cap, against Uruguay. Eventually forming a deadly strike partnership with Dwight Yorke, he went on to win a host of honours with United. Then, following the signing of Ruud van Nistelrooy, he joined Blackburn Rovers for £7.5 million, having scored 121 goals in 275 games. Teaming up with Yorke again, he helped his new club triumph in the 2002 Football League Cup Final at the Millennium Stadium, netting the winner against Tottenham Hotspur. A regular in Rovers' first-team line-up, he ended the 2002/03 season as the club's joint-leading scorer.

Andy Cole in action during a friendly with France at the Stade de France in September 2000. The match was drawn 1–1.
(Clive Brunskill/Getty Images)

Stan COLLYMORE

Position	Forward
Born	Stanley Victor Collymore, Cannock, 22 January 1971
Height	6ft 3in
Weight	13st 10lb
Clubs	Wolverhampton Wanderers, Crystal Palace, Southend United, Nottingham Forest, Liverpool, Aston Villa, Fulham, Leicester City, Bradford City
England Caps	3
	1995 v Japan (won 2–1), v Brazil (lost 1–3)
	1998 v Moldova (won 4–0)

A TRAINEE at both Walsall and Wolverhampton Wanderers, Stan Collymore, who went on to win three caps for England, started out at Molineux as a non-contract player while manager Graham Turner pondered over offering him a full contract. Finally released, he joined neighbouring Stafford Rangers, and in 1990/91 he scored eight goals in ten consecutive games, prompting Crystal Palace to pay £100,000 for his services. He made his League debut as a substitute against Queen's Park Rangers in February 1991, but it was another 13 months before he made his full debut. He then moved to Southend United and scored 15 goals in 30 games before joining Nottingham Forest. In his first season at the City Ground, 1993/94, he was the club's top scorer with 19 goals, as he was again in 1994/95 when he scored 22 goals in 37 games. He had scored 45 goals in 78 games for Forest when, in July 1995, he moved to Liverpool for a club transfer record of £8.5 million.

Despite being in and out of the Liverpool side, he was a great favourite with the Anfield crowd, scoring 35 goals in 81 first-team outings before a £7 million transfer took him to Aston Villa in the summer of 1997. Following his well-documented problems at Villa Park, he joined Fulham on loan before Leicester City manager Martin O'Neill offered him another chance to prove himself. However, following O'Neill's departure and the appointment of Peter Taylor, Collymore found his face didn't fit at Filbert Street and he moved to Bradford City. After just a handful of games, he went on the transfer list and was eventually allowed to join Spanish club Real Oviedo. That too failed to work out and he announced his retirement. Collymore was a powerful striker whose great talent was never fully exploited.

Gary NEVILLE

Position	Right-back
Born	Gary Alexander Neville, Bury, 18 February 1975
Height	5ft 11in
Weight	12st 8lb
Clubs	Manchester United
England Caps	61
	1995 v Japan (won 2–1), v Brazil (lost 1–3)
	1996 v Colombia (0–0), v Norway (0–0), v Switzerland (won 3–1), v Portugal (1–1),

Gary Neville during the during the World Cup Group 9 qualifier against Greece in October 2001. England qualified after the match ended 2–2. (Gary M. Prior/Getty Images)

v Bulgaria (won 1–0), v Croatia (0–0), v Hungary (won 3–0), v China (won 3–0),
v Switzerland (1–1), v Scotland (won 2–0), v Holland (won 4–1), v Spain (0–0 aet, England won 4–3 on penalties)

1997 v Moldova (won 3–0), v Poland (won 2–1), v Italy (lost 0–1), v Georgia (won 2–0),
v Poland (won 2–0), v Italy (won 2–0), v France (won 1–0), v Brazil (lost 0–1)

1998 v Moldova (won 4–0), v Chile (lost 0–2), v Portugal (won 3–0), v Saudi Arabia (0–0),
v Belgium (0–0), v Romania (lost 1–2), v Colombia (won 2–0), v Argentina (2–2 aet, Argentina won 4–3 on penalties)

1999 v Bulgaria (0–0), v Poland (won 2–1)

2000 v Luxembourg (won 6–0), v Poland (0–0), v Brazil (1–1), v Malta (won 2–1), v Portugal
(lost 2–3), v Germany (won 1–0), v Romania (lost 2–3)

2001 v Germany (lost 0–1), v Italy (lost 0–1), v Spain (won 3–0), v Finland (won 2–1),
v Albania (won 3–1)

2002 v Holland (lost 0–2), v Germany (won 5–1), v Albania (won 2–0), v Greece (2–2),
v Sweden (1–1), v Holland (1–1), v Italy (lost 1–2), v Paraguay (won 4–0), v Slovakia
(won 2–1), v Macedonia (2–2)

2003 v Australia (lost 1–3), v Liechtenstein (won 2–0), v Turkey (won 2–0)

2004 v Macedonia (won 2–4), v Liechtenstein (won 2–0), v Turkey (0–0), v Denmark
(lost 2–3)

MANCHESTER UNITED FULL-BACK Gary Neville's rise to fame and international honours was nothing short of meteoric. Furthermore, his adaptability in filling two positions has ensured his place in the national side. When his younger brother Phil joined him in the England side, they were the first brothers from the same club to represent England since Nottingham Forest's Frank and Fred Foreman in 1899!

Gary Neville first came to prominence as captain of Manchester United's successful Class of '92, which captured the FA Youth Cup. He made his League debut for the Reds in the final home game of the 1993/94 season against Coventry City but had already made a brief appearance as a substitute in European competition. An injury to Paul Parker allowed him to establish himself in the United side, and by the end of the 1994/95 campaign Terry Venables had included him in the international squad. A most versatile defender, able to play on either flank or at the heart of the defence, he has won a host of honours with United, including five Premier League titles and the European Cup. He continues to be a consistent and vital cog in the United side, while at international level he earned his 50th cap against Holland in February 2002. Sadly, he missed out on a place in the squad for the World Cup Finals after breaking a metatarsal in his left foot. On his return to action, Neville's goal as stand-in United skipper against Basle in the Champions League came on his 77th outing in European football – more than any other player in the competition's history.

John SCALES

Position	Defender
Born	John Robert Scales, Harrogate, 4 July 1966
Height	6ft 2in
Weight	13st 5lb
Clubs	Bristol Rovers, Wimbledon, Liverpool, Tottenham Hotspur, Ipswich Town
England Caps	3
	1995 v Japan (won 2–1), v Sweden (3–3), v Brazil (lost 1–3)

AFTER SIGNING FOR Leeds United on a YTS scheme in the summer of 1984, John Scales was freed the following summer and joined Bristol Rovers. He spent two years with the Pirates, but when Bobby Gould was made manager of Wimbledon Scales was among his former manager's first signings. At the end of his first season with the Dons, Scales won an FA Cup winners' medal after coming on as a substitute for Terry Gibson during the 1–0 victory over Liverpool. He later switched from full-back to a more central role, replacing Eric Young, and was the rock upon which Joe Kinnear built his defence. His consistent displays at the heart of the Wimbledon back line led to him being voted the club's Player of the Year in seasons 1992/93 and 1993/94.

Scales had appeared in 288 games for Wimbledon when, in September 1994, he was transferred to Liverpool for £3.5 million. Full international honours came his way soon after, the first of his three caps coming against Japan. Despite being Liverpool's best player in the 1996 FA Cup Final defeat by Manchester United, he was allowed in December of that year to join Tottenham Hotspur for £2.6 million.

He soon demonstrated his great aerial ability with Spurs, but during his three-and-a-half seasons at White Hart Lane he was ravaged by injuries and only made 37 appearances. Given a free transfer, he joined Ipswich Town but, again constantly dogged by injuries, he decided to retire to concentrate on his business interests.

David UNSWORTH

Position	Defender
Born	David Gerald Unsworth, Chorley, 16 October 1973
Height	6ft 1in
Weight	14st 2lb
Clubs	Everton, West Ham United, Aston Villa, Everton
England Caps	1
	1995 v Japan (won 2–1)

DAVID UNSWORTH made his Football League debut for Everton against Tottenham Hotspur in April 1992 while still a trainee. Although he was substituting at left-back for the injured Andy Hinchcliffe, he scored a stunning equalizing goal for the Blues with a first-touch volley from a corner in a 3–3 thriller. In his early days with the club, Everton fans thought he would prove the natural long-term successor to Welsh international Kevin Ratcliffe for, like the former skipper, Unsworth proved to be a quick, powerful and efficient left-sided central defender. During the 1994/95 season he developed a fine central defensive partnership alongside Dave Watson, helping Everton lift the FA Cup at the end of that campaign.

England manager Terry Venables called him up to the full international squad and he played against Japan, but has since failed to add to his collection.

Much to the consternation of many Everton supporters, Unsworth left Goodison in the summer of 1997, joining West Ham United for a fee of £1 million, with the Hammers' Danny Williamson moving in the opposite direction. Despite having an excellent season at Upton Park, a year later he was involved in one of the most bizarre transfers in Premiership history. After joining Aston Villa, he realized that his former club Everton also coveted his signature. Following pleas to the Villa board, and without kicking a ball for his new club, he was allowed to rejoin the Blues for the £3 million fee Villa had paid the Hammers. Back at Everton, he was appointed club captain and he developed into one of the Premiership's most solid and reliable defenders, having appeared in more than 300 games for the Blues and equalled the club record of 23 successful spot-kicks in a game against Liverpool.

Colin COOPER

Position	Defender
Born	Colin Terence Cooper, Sedgefield, 28 February 1967
Height	5ft 10in
Weight	11st 9lb
Clubs	Middlesbrough, Millwall, Nottingham Forest
England Caps	2
	1995 v Sweden (3–3), v Brazil (lost 1–3)

AFTER JOINING MIDDLESBROUGH on a YTS scheme, Colin Cooper progressed through the ranks to make his League debut against Crystal Palace in March 1986. By the start of the following term, he had won a regular place at left-back and was ever-present in the Boro side that won promotion from the Third Division in 1986/87. The following season he missed just one game as the club won another promotion, this time to the top flight. Predominantly right-footed, he was switched to right-back following the signing of Jimmy Phillips, but then Lennie Lawrence was appointed manager and Cooper found his days at Ayresome Park numbered.

Cooper joined Millwall, where Mick McCarthy converted him into a centre-back. After a number of impressive performances at the heart of the Millwall defence, Nottingham Forest manager Frank Clark paid £1.5 million to take him to the City Ground. In 1995, he won two full international caps to go with the eight he had earned at Under-21 level Then, following Stuart Pearce's departure, he was made Forest club captain. Though Forest later accepted a £2.5 million bid from West Ham, Cooper refused to move, going on to play in 213 games before rejoining Middlesbrough in the summer of 1998.

Strong and fearless in the tackle, Colin Cooper has now taken his total number of appearances for Middlesbrough in his two spells with the club to more than 370, though it is 18 years since he made his debut.

Jamie REDKNAPP

Position	Midfielder
Born	Jamie Frank Redknapp, Barton-on-Sea, 25 June 1973
Height	6ft 0in
Weight	12st 10lb
Clubs	Bournemouth, Liverpool, Tottenham Hotspur
England Caps	17 Goals 1

1996 v Colombia (0–0), v Norway (0–0), v Switzerland (won 3–1), v China (won 3–0),
  v Scotland (won 2–0)
1997 v Mexico (won 2–0), v Georgia (won 2–0), v South Africa (won 2–1)
1999 v Sweden (lost 1–2), v Bulgaria (0–0), v France (lost 0–2), v Poland (won 3–1),
  v Hungary (1–1), v Bulgaria (1–1)
2000 v Belgium (won 2–1) 1 goal, v Scotland (won 2–0), v Scotland (lost 0–1)

JAMIE REDKNAPP seemed certain to establish himself in the England side for a good number of years but then suffered a serious injury in the early stages of an international against Switzerland. He came back for England in Euro '96 and continued to feature in successive England managers' plans until another injury robbed them and his club, Liverpool, of his services.

The son of Portsmouth manager Harry Redknapp, Jamie was courted by Tottenham Hotspur as an associated schoolboy, but on leaving school he joined his father, who was then managing Bournemouth. He was just 16 years 202 days old when he made his Football League debut for the Cherries against Hull City. Clearly a player of great potential, he was signed by Liverpool in January 1991 as an investment for the future, for at the time Redknapp wasn't even sure of a first-team spot at Dean Court. Replacing Paul Stewart, he was to prove Liverpool's major discovery of the 1992/93 season, a campaign that saw him make his debut for the England Under-21 side. He won his first honour with Liverpool in 1995 when the Reds defeated Bolton in the League Cup Final. He married pop star Louise in the summer of 1998, and the following season was to be his best in a Liverpool shirt. He was sidelined the next season following an operation, and as Liverpool enjoyed success in FA, League and UEFA cups, he found his opportunities at Anfield limited. In 2002 he moved to Tottenham Hotspur, where, in his own words, he is 'simply happy to be playing again'. Sadly, injury problems continued to blight this talented midfielder's progress back to international status.

Steve STONE

Position	Winger
Born	Steven Brian Stone, Gateshead, 20 August 1971
Height	5ft 8ins
Weight	12st 7lb
Clubs	Nottingham Forest, Aston Villa, Portsmouth
England Caps	9 Goals 2

1996 v Norway (0–0), v Switzerland (won 3–1) 1 goal, v Portugal (1–1) 1 goal, v Bulgaria (won 1–0), v Croatia (0–0), v China (won 3–0), v Switzerland (1–1), v Scotland (won 2–0), v Spain (0–0 aet, England won 4–3 on penalties)

NICKNAMED 'BULLDOG', Steve Stone suffered three broken legs during his time at Nottingham Forest but recovered to become a player willing to run himself into the ground for the good of his team. Originally a central midfielder, he never looked back after being converted to a wide position, and by the end of the 1995/96 season he had established himself as a near-automatic choice in the England team. A hard-working player with great skill and confidence on the ball, he scored for England in the 3–1 win over Switzerland, and to prove this was no fluke he also scored in his next international, against Portugal. A serious knee injury forced him to miss virtually the whole of the 1996/97 season, but when he finally returned to action in 1997/98 he proved to be an important member of Forest's First Division Championship-winning side. He went on to score 27 goals in 229 games for Forest before joining Aston Villa in March 1999 for a fee of £5.5 million.

A loss of form and a series of niggling injuries limited his first-team appearances at Villa Park, but following the appointment of John Gregory he was rarely absent from first-team duties. However, after Gregory's departure he struggled to secure a regular place in the Villa side, and subsequently moved to Portsmouth where he helped the Fratton Park club win promotion to the Premiership.

Gareth SOUTHGATE

Position	Defender
Born	Gareth Southgate, Watford, 3 September 1970
Height	6ft 0in
Weight	12st 8lb
Clubs	Crystal Palace, Aston Villa, Middlesbrough
England Caps	55 Goals 2

1996 v Portugal (1–1), v Bulgaria (won 1–0), v Hungary (won 3–0), v China (won 3–0), v Switzerland (1–1), v Scotland (won 2–0), v Holland (won 4–1), v Spain (0–0 aet, England won 4–3 on penalties), v Germany (1–1 aet, Germany won 6–5 on penalties)

1997 v Moldova (won 3–0), v Poland (won 2–1), v Georgia (won 2–0), v Mexico (won 2–0), v Georgia (won 2–1), v South Africa (won 2–1), v Poland (won 2–0), v Italy (won 2–0), v France (won 1–0), v Brazil (lost 0–1)

1998 v Moldova (won 4–0), v Italy (0–0), v Cameroon (won 2–0), v Switzerland (1–1), v Saudi Arabia (0–0), v Morocco (won 1–0), v Tunisia (won 2–0), v Argentina (2–2 aet, Argentina won 4–3 on penalties)

1999 v Sweden (lost 1–2), v Bulgaria (0–0), v Luxembourg (won 3–0) 1 goal, v Bulgaria (1–1)

2000 v Belgium (won 2–1), v Scotland (won 2–0), v Argentina (0–0), v Ukraine (won 2–0), v Malta (won 2–1), v Romania (lost 2–3)

2001 v France (1–1), v Germany (lost 0–1), v Finland (0–0), v Italy (lost 0–1), v Mexico (won 4–0)

Gareth Southgate in a friendly against Portugal at Villa Park in September 2002. The match ended as a 1–1 draw. (Phil Cole/Getty Images)

2002 v Holland (lost 0–2), v Sweden (1–1), v Holland (1–1), v Italy (lost 1–2), v Paraguay (won 4–0), v S. Korea (1–1), v Cameroon (2–2), v Portugal (1–1), v Slovakia (won 2–1)

2003 v Liechtenstein (won 2–0), v S. Africa (won 2–1) 1 goal, v Serbia (won 2–1), v Slovakia (won 2–1)

AFTER MAKING his international debut as a substitute in the match against Portugal, Gareth Southgate forced his way into England's Euro '96 squad. Despite his penalty shoot-out miss, he was one of the stars of an England team that reached the semi-finals of the competition. A member of England's World Cup party for France '98, he was injured in the opening game, but returned for the last 50 minutes of the Argentinian match following David Beckham's dismissal, only to have another nightmare experience of the penalty shoot-out system.

Southgate started his career with Crystal Palace and was the only ever-present when the Eagles dropped out of the Premiership in 1993/94. As Palace captain, he had led by example right up to the final whistle of the last match of that campaign, but in the summer he left Selhurst Park to join Aston Villa in a £2.5 million deal. Though he arrived at Villa Park as a midfield player, he joined Ugo Ehiogu and Paul McGrath in a three-man defensive system. A hard-working player with two good feet, he was able to bring the ball out of defence and distribute it effectively. Following the departure of Andy Townsend, he took over the Villa captaincy and led the club to the FA Cup Final in 2000, going on to play in 243 games for Villa before a £6.5 million transfer to Middlesbrough in the summer of 2001.

Voted Boro's Player of the Year at the end of his first season in the north-east, Southgate was a member of Sven-Goran Eriksson's 2002 World Cup squad, but the Middlesbrough captain's international career now appears to be over.

Robbie FOWLER

Position	Forward
Born	Robert Bernard Fowler, Liverpool, 9 April 1975
Height	5ft 11in
Weight	11st 10lb
Clubs	Liverpool, Leeds United, Manchester City
England Caps	26 Goals 7

1996 v Bulgaria (won 1–0), v Croatia (0–0), v China (won 3–0), v Holland (won 4–1), v Spain (0–0 aet, England won 4–3 on penalties)

1997 v Mexico (won 2–0) 1 goal

1998 v Cameroon (won 2–0) 1 goal

1999 v Czech Republic (won 2–0), v Bulgaria (1–1)

2000 v Luxembourg (won 6–0), v Poland (0–0), v Brazil (1–1), v Ukraine (won 2–0) 1 goal, v Malta (won 2–1)

2001 v Italy (lost 0–1), v Finland (won 2–1), v Mexico (won 4–0) 1 goal, v Greece (won 2–0)

2002 v Holland (lost 0–2), v Albania (won 2–0) 1 goal, v Greece (2–2), v Sweden (1–1), v Italy (lost 1–2) 1 goal, v Paraguay (won 4–0), v Cameroon (2–2) 1 goal, v Denmark (won 3–0)

Robbie Fowler on the ball in a friendly against Mexico at Pride Park, Derby, 24 May 2001. (Clive Brunskill/Getty Images)

ROBBIE FOWLER grew up an Everton fan but made the transition from the Goodison terraces to the Anfield playing staff because the Reds were the quickest to recognize his obvious talent for scoring goals. Frustratingly, he hasn't found the target as prolifically when on international duty, scoring just seven times in 26 appearances.

He scored on his Liverpool debut in the League Cup at Fulham and followed this up in the Anfield return by becoming the first Liverpool player to score five times in a game since Ian Rush achieved the feat a decade earlier. Netting a hat-trick in a 4–2 win over Southampton in what was only his fifth League game, he began his first full season by scoring the fastest hat-trick in Premiership history as Arsenal were beaten 3–0. He ended tthe 1993/94 season by breaking the 30-goal barrier and picking up a League Cup winners' medal. In 1995/96 he scored four goals in a 5–2 defeat of Bolton Wanderers, on his way to another best-ever total of 35 goals. Another four against Middlesbrough in December 1996 saw him reach the milestone of 100 goals for Liverpool in 165 matches – one match fewer than Ian Rush had taken. Though he continued to find the net on a regular basis, he proceeded to shoot himself in the foot with some well-documented examples of extraordinary behaviour, which swiftly overshadowed his footballing talent. He had to sit on the bench for two of the three finals that the Reds won in 2000/01, but capped a great season by scoring Liverpool's goals in the League Cup Final victory over Birmingham City. Though Fowler, who had scored 171 goals in 330 games for Liverpool, pledged his future to the Merseyside club, he left to join Leeds United for a fee of £11 million in November 2001. Beset by injuries during his time at Elland Road, he left the Yorkshire club to join Manchester City in January 2003, but struggled to hit his best form for much of the 2002/03 season.

Phil NEVILLE

Position	Defender/Midfielder
Born	Philip John Neville, Bury, 21 January 1977
Height	5ft 11in
Weight	12st 0lb
Clubs	Manchester United
England Caps	44
	1996 v China (won 3–0)
	1997 v S. Africa (won 2–1), v Poland (won 2–0), v Italy (won 2–0), v France (won 1–0), v Brazil (lost 0–1)
	1998 v Moldova (won 4–0), v Cameroon (won 2–0), v Chile (lost 0–2), v Portugal (won 3–0), v Saudi Arabia (0–0), v Belgium (0–0)
	1999 v Luxembourg (won 3–0), v Finland (won 3–1), v Hungary (1–1), v Sweden (0–0), v Bulgaria (1–1)
	2000 v Luxembourg (won 6–0), v Poland (0–0), v Belgium (won 2–1), v Scotland (won 2–0), v Scotland (lost 0–1), v Argentina (0–0), v Brazil (1–1), v Ukraine (won 2–0), v Malta (won 2–1), v Portugal (lost 2–3), v Germany (won 1–0), v Romania (lost 2–3)
	2001 v Finland (0–0), v Spain (won 3–0), v Mexico (won 4–0), v Greece (won 2–0)

Phil Neville in a friendly against Mexico at Pride Park, Derby, in May 2001. (Phil Cole/Getty Images)

2002 v Sweden (1–1), v Holland (lost 0–2), v Italy (lost 1–2), v Paraguay (won 4–0)
2003 v S. Africa (won 2–1), v Serbia (won 2–1), v Slovakia (won 2–1)
2004 v Croatia (won 3–0), v Macedonia (won 2–1), v Liechtenstein (won 2–0), v Denmark (lost 2–3)

AFTER APPEARING FOR ENGLAND at Under-21 level, Phil Neville won his first full cap against China in May 1996, when he and Gary became the first pair of brothers to play for England since the Charltons 26 years previously.

A talented all-round sportsman, Phil represented England schoolboys at both cricket and football. In fact, he was offered a contract at the other Old Trafford to play county cricket for Lancashire, but he opted for a career in football, which has proved to be the right decision.

In 1994/95 he captained United's youth team to the FA Youth Cup and made his first-team debut against Wrexham in the League Cup, before going on to make his League debut in the Manchester derby at Maine Road. During the 1996/97 season he went down with glandular fever – losing a stone and a half in four days – which could so easily have ended his career. His adaptability has often kept him in the United team, enabling him to slot into a different role when more senior players have returned to take up their normal positions. Rumours abounded early on about his long-term future at Old Trafford, but Alex Ferguson gave him a massive vote of confidence and he went on to end the 1998/99 season with European Cup, FA Cup and Premier League winners' medals. During the 1999/2000 season he appeared in all 12 England matches but had the great misfortune to concede a last-minute penalty in the Euro 2000 match against Romania, which saw England eliminated from the competition. Although his achievements have often been overshadowed by the exploits of brother Gary, every manager in the country would dearly love to have a player of Phil Neville's talent in their squad.

Ugo EHIOGU

Position	Defender
Born	Ugochuku Ehiogu, Hackney, 3 November 1972
Height	6ft 2in
Weight	14st 10lb
Clubs	West Bromwich Albion, Aston Villa, Middlesbrough
England Caps	4 Goals 1
	1996 v China (won 3–0)
	2001 v Spain (won 3–0) 1 goal
	2002 v Holland (1–1), v Italy (lost 1–2)

UGO EHIOGU made his international debut against China in 1996, but then in February 2001 won a deserved recall for England's game against Spain, when he scored in a 3–0 win.

Unable as a youngster to force his way into the West Bromwich Albion side on a permanent basis, Ehiogu joined Aston Villa for a fee of £40,000 in the summer of

1991. Though he struggled to make much of an impact, he worked hard at his game to become one of the most improved defenders in the Premier League. Possessing good pace and strong in the air, he showed himself to be dangerous at set pieces, scoring a number of vital goals for Villa. He formed a defensive triumvirate with Gareth Southgate and Paul McGrath, and his displays were rewarded with his first England cap. A member of the Villa side that beat Leeds United in the League Cup Final, he later suffered a fractured left eye-socket following a collision with Alan Shearer. It was thought that the injury would keep him out of the game for a long time, but after three months and three operations he returned to first-team action. Possibly Villa's best player in their 2000 FA Cup Final defeat against Chelsea, Ehiogu went on to appear in 303 games for the club before, following a much-publicized transfer request, he moved to Middlesbrough for £8 million – a new club-record fee. Well received by the Riverside faithful, he readily joined in the club's fight against relegation to become an important member of the Middlesbrough side

Sol CAMPBELL

Position	Defender
Born	Sulzeer Jeremiah Campbell, Newham, 16 September 1974
Height	6ft 2in
Weight	14st 1lb
Clubs	Tottenham Hotspur, Arsenal
England Caps	56 Goals 1

1996 v Hungary (won 3–0), v Scotland (won 2–0)
1997 v Georgia (won 2–0), v Italy (lost 0–1), v Georgia (won 2–0), v S. Africa (won 2–1), v Poland (won 2–0), v France (won 1–0), v Brazil (lost 0–1)
1998 v Moldova (won 4–0), v Italy (0–0), v Cameroon (won 2–0), v Chile (lost 0–2), v Portugal (won 3–0), v Morocco (won 1–0), v Belgium (0–0), v Tunisia (won 2–0), v Romania (lost 1–2), v Colombia (won 2–0), v Argentina (2–2 aet, Argentina won 4–3 on penalties)
1999 v Sweden (lost 1–2), v Bulgaria (0–0), v Luxembourg (won 3–0), v Czech Republic (won 2–0), v Poland (won 3–1), v Sweden (0–0), v Bulgaria (1–1)
2000 v Scotland (won 2–0), v Scotland (lost 0–1), v Argentina (0–0), v Brazil (1–1), v Ukraine (won 2–0), v Malta (won 2–1), v Portugal (lost 2–3), v Germany (won 1–0), v Romania (lost 2–3)
2001 v France (1–1), v Spain (won 3–0), v Finland (won 2–1), v Albania (won 3–1)
2002 v Germany (won 5–1), v Albania (won 2–0), v Holland (1–1), v Italy (lost 1–2), v S. Korea (1–1), v Cameroon (2–2), v Sweden (1–1) 1 goal, v Argentina (won 1–0), v Nigeria (0–0), v Denmark (won 3–0), v Brazil (lost 1–2), v Macedonia (2–2)
2003 v Australia (lost 1–3), v Turkey (won 2–0)
2004 v Macedonia (won 2–1), v Turkey (0–0)

A VERSATILE PLAYER who can play right-back or in midfield, Sol Campbell swiftly established himself at the centre of Tottenham's defence. He is comfortable on the ball and happy to come out of defence to set up an attack. His early displays for the White Hart Lane club led to his selection for England's Euro '96 squad, Campbell coming on

Sol Campbell runs with the ball during the England v Argentina World Cup Finals match at Sapporo, 2002. England won 1–0. (Laurence Griffiths/Getty Images)

as a substitute in the 2–0 defeat of Scotland (though he had also come on as a substitute a month earlier in a friendly against Hungary). After that he matured into a reliable and intelligent defender for both club and country. He took on the captain's armband, his understanding of the game grew with every match, and in 1997 he was named as the England Player of the Year. He had a good World Cup in 1998, where his back-to-the-wall defending against Argentina was outstanding. Four years later, in the 2002 World Cup, he netted his and England's first goal of the competition.

Facing some of the best attackers at both Premiership and world level, he emerged as one of the most complete central defenders to be found. Not surprisingly, with interest in the highly rated defender growing both at home and abroad, speculation mounted as to whether he would be moving on to pastures new. Though assurances came from both Alan Sugar and Director of Football David Pleat that the club were ready to break the bank to keep their captain, he eventually left White Hart Lane in the summer of 2001, joining North London rivals Arsenal.

Campbell, who had appeared in 315 games for Spurs, soon settled in at the heart of the Gunners' defence and was one of the cornerstones of the club's double triumph in 2001/02.

Ian WALKER

Position	Goalkeeper
Born	Ian Michael Walker, Watford, 31 October 1971
Height	6ft 2in
Weight	13st 1lb
Clubs	Tottenham Hotspur, Oxford United, Leicester City
England Caps	3
	1996 v Hungary (won 3–0), v China (won 3–0)
	1997 v Italy (lost 0–1)

SON OF the former Norwich City and Everton manager Mike Walker, Ian was instrumental in Spurs winning the FA Youth Cup in 1990 with a series of outstanding displays. However, due to the consistency of Erik Thorstvedt, he was unable to get a game in the first team and was loaned out to Oxford United, where he made his League debut in a 1–1 draw against Wolverhampton Wanderers. Such was his talent that he made his debut for the England Under-21 team against Wales in December 1990. His Spurs debut came in an end-of-season game at Norwich in April 1991. With the advantage of first-hand coaching by former England keeper Ray Clemence, Walker developed into a fine keeper and was soon a regular member of the England squad. However, his self-confidence took a massive knock in a 7–1 Spurs defeat at Newcastle and a 6–2 League Cup exit at Bolton, not to mention the media-wide criticism of his part in Gianfranco Zola's goal in England's 1–0 defeat by Italy in the World Cup qualifier at Wembley.

Despite conceding some soft goals over the next couple of campaigns, Walker gradually regained his confidence and there were calls for him to be reinstated into the England squad. However, following the signing of Neil Sullivan to Spurs, he found himself his club's second choice and, after making 313 appearances for Spurs, he joined Leicester City for £2.5 million. His performances there earned him selection for a number of Sven-Goran Eriksson's squads. He ended the 2002/03 season with a healthy tally of clean sheets that was just short of the all-time record and he was the club's only ever-present as they won promotion to the Premiership.

Jason WILCOX

Position	Winger
Born	Jason Malcolm Wilcox, Farnworth, 15 July 1971
Height	5ft 11in
Weight	11st 10lb
Clubs	Blackburn Rovers, Leeds United
England Caps	3
	1996 v Hungary (won 3–0)
	1999 v France (lost 0–2)
	2000 v Argentina (0–0)

LEFT-WINGER JASON WILCOX worked his way through the ranks at Blackburn Rovers to make his League debut against Swindon Town in April 1990. However, it wasn't until 1991/92 that he established himself as a first-team regular. Many of his games were on the right-hand side of midfield owing to the fine form of Scott Sellars. Sadly, injury prevented him from playing any part in the play-off matches that saw Rovers promoted to the Premier League. Following Sellars' departure to Leeds in the summer of 1992, Wilcox claimed the left-wing position as his own and went on to have an impressive first season in the top flight. His career was thrown into doubt in the summer of 1993 after he contracted legionnaires' disease, which put him out of action for a good number of weeks. He returned towards the end of the year and his form was such that he won selection to the England squad, eventually making his full debut against Hungary in 1996.

Wilcox's subsequent progress with Rovers was hampered by a series of operations. When he returned to action, new manager Brian Kidd made him the onfield captain, but in December 1999, having taken his tally of goals to 34 in 286 games, he left Ewood Park to join Leeds United for a fee of £3 million. His time at Elland Road has been fraught with injuries but he remains an important member of the Yorkshire club's squad.

David BECKHAM

Position	Midfielder		
Born	David Robert Joseph Beckham, Leytonstone, 2 May 1975		
Height	6ft 0in		
Weight	11st 12lb		
Clubs	Manchester United, Preston North End, Real Madrid		
England Caps	65	Goals	13
	1997 v Moldova (won 3–0), v Poland (won 2–1), v Georgia (won 2–0), v Italy (lost 0–1),		
	v Georgia (won 2–0), v S. Africa (won 2–1), v Poland (won 2–0), v Italy (won 2–0),		
	v France (won 1–0)		
	1998 v Moldova (won 4–0), v Italy (0–0), v Cameroon (won 2–0), v Portugal (won 3–0),		

David Beckham celebrates scoring England's goal in their World Cup victory over Argentina, 2002. (Alex Livesey/Getty Images)

v Saudi Arabia (0–0), v Belgium (0–0), v Romania (lost 1–2), v Colombia (won 2–0) 1 goal, v Argentina (2–2 aet, Argentina won 4–3 on penalties)

1999 v Luxembourg (won 3–0), v Czech Republic (won 2–0), v France (lost 0–2), v Poland (won 3–1), v Sweden (0–0)

2000 v Luxembourg (won 6–0), v Poland (0–0), v Scotland (won 2–0), v Scotland (lost 0–1), v Argentina (0–0), v Brazil (1–1), v Ukraine (won 2–0), v Malta (won 2–1), v Portugal (lost 2–3), v Germany (won 1–0), v Romania (lost 2–3)

2001 v France (1–1), v Germany (lost 0–1), v Italy (lost 0–1), v Spain (won 3–0), v Finland (won 2–1) 1 goal, v Albania (won 3–1), v Mexico (won 4–0) 1 goal, v Greece (won 2–0) 1 goal

2002 v Holland (lost 0–2), v Germany (won 5–1), v Albania (won 2–0), v Greece (2–2) 1 goal, v Sweden (1–1) 1 goal, v Argentina (won 1–0) 1 goal, v Nigeria (0–0), v Denmark (won 3–0), v Brazil (lost 1–2), v Slovakia (won 2–1) 1 goal, v Macedonia (2–2) 1 goal

2003 v Australia (lost 1–3), v Liechtenstein (won 2–0) 1 goal, v Turkey (won 2–0) 1 goal, v S. Africa (won 2–1)

2004 v Croatia (won 3–1) 1 goal, v Macedonia (won 2–1) 1 goal, v Liechtenstein (won 2–0), v Turkey (0–0), v Denmark (lost 2–3)

MADE CAPTAIN OF ENGLAND by new coach Sven-Goran Eriksson, who saw qualities in him that the media had missed, David Beckham was instrumental in the nation reaching the World Cup Finals in 2002. He scored some stunning goals, though it was feared that a broken metatarsal would prevent him from playing in the Finals themselves.

Beckham is another of the famed Manchester United Class of '92 to make the breakthrough to the big time. He made his first-team bow in a League Cup tie at Brighton in September 1992 but had to wait another two years before his next taste of action. Following a loan spell at Preston North End, he replaced the departed Kanchelskis on the right-hand side of United's midfield, though manager Alex Ferguson reckoned the player's best position at that time was in a more central role. He possesses excellent vision and is able to turn defence into attack with a superb range of passes. His first full season in the United side brought him both Championship and FA Cup winners' medals – a tremendous achievement for a 21-year-old. The following season he scored the goal of the campaign in the match against Wimbledon, when he chipped the keeper from the halfway line. Promoted to the full England side, he went from strength to strength, especially as a regular scorer of outstanding goals, and ended the season as the PFA's Young Player of the Year.

Though every aspect of his life began to dominate the headlines – notably his engagement to Posh Spice – his form continued to earn rave notices. Thought by many to be a player who would grace the World Cup stage in France '98, he was sent off against Argentina, effectively limiting England's chances of victory. He returned to England a marked man, and it was feared that he might have to move abroad to escape the fierce hostility shown towards him. However, demonstrating that he had the necessary character to rise above adversity, he was ever-present as United lifted the Premier League title, FA Cup and European Cup.

However, after his marriage to Victoria Adams, the back pages of the newspapers continued to portray him as either hero or villain. Taking the runner-up spot behind Rivaldo in the 2000 European Footballer of the Year, Beckham continued to juggle his showbiz lifestyle with his career as a professional footballer with great dexterity. His performances as England skipper are high class and he was instrumental in the country qualifying for the Euro 2004 finals.

Awarded an OBE in the 2003 Queen's Birthday Honours List, he became the latest superstar to join the exodus to Spain when he signed for Real Madrid that summer.

David Beckham is, quite simply, the most outstanding English footballer of his generation.

Andy HINCHCLIFFE

Position	Left-back
Born	Andrew George Hinchcliffe, Manchester, 5 February 1969
Height	5ft 10in
Weight	13st 7lb
Clubs	Manchester City, Everton, Sheffield Wednesday
England Caps	7
	1997 v Moldova (won 3–0), v Poland (won 2–1), v Georgia (won 2–0)
	1998 v Cameroon (won 2–0), v Switzerland (1–1), v Saudi Arabia (0–0)
	1999 v Bulgaria (1–1)

BEGINNING HIS CAREER with Manchester City, Andy Hinchcliffe played a prominent part in the Maine Road club's promotion to the First Division in 1988/89, scoring five times from the left-back position. In the summer of 1990 he was transferred to Everton in exchange for Neil Pointon and a large cash adjustment in City's favour. Once regarded as one of the most promising left-backs in the country, he was only an occasional performer in his early days at Goodison, but when Joe Royle arrived in 1994 he was switched to a midfield role wide on the left. His game was transformed and his brilliant crossing and dead-ball play were key to the Blues' FA Cup success in 1995. His form won him international recognition, with the first of his seven caps coming against Moldova in 1997.

Injuries subsequently hampered Hinchcliffe's Everton career and in January 1998 he was transferred to Sheffield Wednesday for £2.85 million. His wholehearted and enthusiastic approach was greatly appreciated by the Hillsborough faithful, but sadly this polished performer's career was ended by an Achilles heel injury that forced his retirement after 462 games for his three clubs.

David JAMES

Position	Goalkeeper
Born	David Benjamin James, Welwyn Garden City, 1 August 1970
Height	6ft 5in
Weight	14st 5lb
Clubs	Watford, Liverpool, Aston Villa, West Ham United, Manchester City
England Caps	11

1997 v Moldova (won 3–0)
2001 v Italy (lost 0–1), v Spain (won 3–0), v Mexico (won 4–0)
2002 v Holland (lost 0–2), v Holland (1–1), v Italy (lost 1–2), v S. Korea (1–1), v Cameroon (2–2), v Portugal (1–1)
2003 v Australia (lost 1–3), v Liechtenstein (won 2–0), v Turkey (won 2–0), v S. Africa (won 2–1), v Serbia (won 2–1), v Slovakia (won 2–1)
2004 v Croatia (won 3–1), Macedonia (won 2–1), v Liechtenstein (won 2–0), v Turkey (0–0), v Denmark (lost 2–3)

DAVID JAMES began his career with Watford, where he spent two years in the shadow of Tony Coton, but when the latter moved to Manchester City he got the break he'd been looking for. Playing a large part in Watford's recovery from a relegation position to mid-table security, he showed outstanding form that he was soon called up into the England Under-21 squad. His name became repeatedly linked with Liverpool and his eventual departure to Anfield in the summer of 1992 was hardly unexpected.

During his first season with the Reds he lost his place three times and showed a great deal of uncertainty in dealing with crosses and corners. A goalkeeper in the mould of Bruce Grobbelaar, he eventually, however, made the No. 1 jersey his own, displaying the ability to produce world-class saves with his spectacular athleticism. His good form for Liverpool following two ever-present seasons eventually earned him full international honours, beginning with a clean sheet in a 3–0 win over Moldova.

After losing his place to Brad Friedel, James left Anfield to play for Aston Villa, who paid £1.7 million for his services. His performances helped Villa reach the 2000 FA Cup Final, where they were beaten by Chelsea. In the summer of 2001 he left Villa to join West Ham United for £3.5 million. Shortly after signing, he suffered a bad knee injury playing for England against Holland, but after his long-awaited Hammers debut in November 2001 he soon showed why he is rated one of the best keepers in the country. However, despite a number of commanding goalkeeping displays, he couldn't prevent West Ham's relegation, and midway through the following season he left to join Manchester City.

Nicky BUTT

Position	Midfielder
Born	Nicholas Butt, Manchester, 21 January 1975
Height	5ft 10in
Weight	11st 3lb
Clubs	Manchester United
England Caps	31

1997 v Mexico (won 2–0), v S. Africa (won 2–1)
1998 v Moldova (won 4–0), v Italy (0–0), v Chile (lost 0–2), v Belgium (0–0), v Czech Republic (won 2–0)
1999 v Hungary (1–1)

2001 v Italy (lost 0–1), v Spain (won 3–0), v Finland (won 2–1), v Albania (won 3–1),
v Mexico (won 4–0), v Greece (won 2–0)

2002 v Sweden (1–1), v Holland (1–1), v Italy (lost 1–2), v Paraguay (won 4–0), v Argentina
(won 1–0), v Nigeria (0–0), v Denmark (won 3–0), v Brazil (lost 1–2), v Portugal (1–1),
v Slovakia (won 2–1), v Macedonia (2–2)

2003 v Liechtenstein (won 2–0), v Turkey (won 2–0)

2004 v Croatia (won 3–1), v Macedonia (won 2–1), v Turkey (0–0), v Denmark (lost 2–3)

A MEMBER OF the England side that reached the 2002 World Cup quarter-finals, Nicky Butt first came to prominence with the Manchester United team that won the FA Youth Cup in 1992. During his early days in the game, Butt was often in trouble and his disciplinary record for one so young was open to improvement.

Further youth honours came his way when he played alongside team-mates Gary Neville and Paul Scholes in the England Under-18 side that participated in the European Under-18 Tournament in 1992/93. After helping England reach the final, Butt was injured and had to watch from the stands as they beat Turkey 1–0. Following the departure of Paul Ince, he established himself in United's midfield, and in 1995/96 was an important member of the side that completed a League and Cup double. By then he was captain of the England Under-21 side, and in 1997 he was elevated to full international status when he played against Mexico.

A gritty midfielder with neat skills and a hardened edge, he won Premier League and European Cup winners' medals in 1998/99 but was missing from the United side that lifted the FA Cup. He has gone on to win six Premier League Championship medals, and though he may not be one of United's most high-profile players, Sir Alex Ferguson knows he is one of the most dependable.

Paul SCHOLES

Position	Midfielder
Born	Paul Scholes, Salford, 16 November 1974
Height	5ft 7in
Weight	11st 10lb
Clubs	Manchester United
England Caps	59 Goals 13

1997 v South Africa (won 2–1), v Italy (won 2–0) 1 goal, v Brazil (lost 0–1)

1998 v Moldova (won 4–0) 1 goal, v Cameroon (won 2–0) 1 goal, v Portugal (won 3–0),
v Saudi Arabia (0–0), v Tunisia (won 2–0) 1 goal, v Romania (lost 1–2), v Colombia (won
2–0), v Argentina (2–2 aet, Argentina won 4–3 on penalties)

1999 v Sweden (lost 1–2), v Bulgaria (0–0), v Luxembourg (won 3–0), v France (lost 0–2),
v Poland (won 3–1) 3 goals, v Sweden (0–0)

2000 v Poland (0–0), v Scotland (won 2–0) 2 goals, v Scotland (lost 0–1), v Argentina (0–0),
v Brazil (1–1), v Ukraine (won 2–0), v Malta (won 2–1), v Portugal (lost 2–3) 1 goal,
v Germany (won 1–0), v Romania (lost 2–3)

2001 v France (1–1), v Germany (lost 0–1), v Finland (0–0), v Spain (won 3–0), v Finland
(won 2–1), v Albania (won 3–1) 1 goal, v Mexico (won 4–0) 1 goal, v Greece (won 2–0)
1 goal

Paul Scholes in the 2002 World Cup quarter-final against Brazil. (David Cannon/Getty Images)

2002 v Holland (lost 0–2), v Germany (won 5–1), v Albania (won 2–0), v Greece (2–2), v Sweden (1–1), v Holland (1–1), v Paraguay (won 4–0), v S. Korea (1–1), v Cameroon (2–2), v Sweden (1–1), v Argentina (won 1–0), v Nigeria (0–0), v Denmark (won 3–0), v Brazil (lost 1–2), v Slovakia (won 2–1), v Macedonia (2–2)
2003 v Australia (lost 1–3), v Liechtenstein (won 2–0), v Turkey (won 2–0), v S. Africa (won 2–1), v Serbia (won 2–1), v Slovakia (won 2–1)
2004 v Croatia (won 3–1), v Turkey (0–0)

PAUL SCHOLES was man-of-the-match in England's opening World Cup game in France '98 – a 2–0 win over Tunisia in which he scored. Scholes appeared in all four England games before the side went out of the competition on penalties. He then netted a hat-trick playing for England against Poland in a European Championships qualifier at Wembley the year after.

He is equally at home playing up front or in central midfield, and his meteoric rise delighted Alex Ferguson so much that he likened the young Manchester United player to a young Kenny Dalglish. During the course of the 1995/96 season, Scholes scored 11 goals in his first 23 outings – an amazing feat when one considers that he only completed five of those games. He went on to win League and FA Cup winners' medals. Despite the arrival of several big-money stars, he continued to hold down a place in the United side and won the first of his England caps when he played against South Africa in 1997. In 1999, his yellow-card offence in the European Cup semi-final against Juventus ruled him out of the final. Despite his immense disappointment, he remained one of United's key players and played an inspiring role in the FA Cup Final that year, scoring the club's deciding goal which completed the second leg of an historic treble.

England's Player of the Year for 1999/2000, Scholes has remained an influential presence for both club and country. The 2002/03 season was one of his best in terms of goals scored. He netted a hat-trick in an 8-goal thriller at Newcastle to take his healthy quota of goals for Manchester United to 101 in 375 games.

Rio FERDINAND

Position	Defender
Born	Rio Gavin Ferdinand, Peckham, 8 November 1978
Height	6ft 2in
Weight	12st 1lb
Clubs	West Ham United, Bournemouth, Leeds United, Manchester United
England Caps	33 Goals 1

1998 v Cameroon (won 2–0), v Switzerland (1–1), v Belgium (0–0)
1999 v Luxembourg (won 3–0), v Czech Republic (won 2–0), v France (lost 0–2), v Hungary (1–1), v Sweden (0–0)
2000 v Argentina (0–0)

2001 v Italy (lost 0–1), v Spain (won 3–0), v Finland (won 2–1), v Albania (won 3–1),
   v Mexico (won 4–0), v Greece (won 2–0)
2002 v Germany (won 5–1), v Albania (won 2–0), v Greece (2–2), v Sweden (1–1),
   v Holland (1–1), v S. Korea (1–1), v Cameroon (2–2), v Sweden (1–1), v Argentina (won
   1–0), v Nigeria (0–0), v Denmark (won 3–0) 1 goal, v Brazil (lost 1–2), v Portugal (1–1)
2003 v Australia (lost 1–3), v Liechtenstein (won 2–0), v Turkey (won 2–0), v S. Africa (won
   2–1)
2004 v Croatia (won 3–1)

....

THE COUSIN OF Tottenham Hotspur's Les Ferdinand, Rio made his League debut for West Ham United against Sheffield Wednesday in the final game of the 1995/96 season. Following a loan spell at Bournemouth he consistently impressed over the next couple of seasons, being calm under pressure and strong in the air. He was selected for England's squad for the World Cup qualifier against Moldova in September 1997, only for Glenn Hoddle to send him home following a drink-driving charge. However, he soon became a regular in the England squad, quite unfairly being compared to Bobby Moore at both club and international level.

A thoughtful and stylish player, comfortable on the ball, displaying excellent distribution and showing maturity beyond his years, he remained a steady figure in the West Ham back four before he was eventually sold to Leeds United in November 2000 for a new club-record fee of £18 million. It made him the world's most costliest defender.

Ferdinand soon settled into the Elland Road club's side, his partnership with Lucas Radebe at the heart of the Leeds defence coinciding with an upturn in fortunes for the Yorkshire club. His leadership qualities impressed David O'Leary so much that he appointed him club captain, but, following a good World Cup and the appointment of Terry Venables as Leeds' new manager, Ferdinand was sold to Manchester United for £30 million. After missing a number of games through injury he began to show the kind of form that had persuaded Sir Alex Ferguson to part with that huge cheque. In December 2003 he was banned by the FA for eight months for failing to attend a drugs test.

Chris SUTTON

Position	Forward
Born	Christopher Roy Sutton, Nottingham, 10 March 1973
Height	6ft 3in
Weight	13st 5lb
Clubs	Norwich City, Blackburn Rovers, Chelsea, Celtic
England Caps	1
	1998 v Cameroon (won 2–0)

....

CHRIS SUTTON was capped against Cameroon in 1998, but after failing to win a regular spot in the national side he told Glenn Hoddle he didn't want to be considered for any future internationals.

The son of former Norwich City player Mike Sutton, Chris joined the Canaries on his father's recommendation. It was 1992/93 before he became a fixture in the Norwich side, netting a hat-trick in a 4–2 home win over Leeds United, despite missing a penalty. The following season he emerged as a goalscorer of real quality, netting 28 League and Cup goals and prompting Blackburn Rovers to splash out £5 million for his services. He was an instant success for Rovers, netting another treble in only his third game for the club as Blackburn won 4–0 at Coventry City, and collecting a Premier League Championship medal at the end of the campaign. The following season he injured tendons and ligaments and missed most games. Injuries hampered his progress in 1998/99 and at the end of the season, having scored 59 goals in 161 games for Blackburn, he commanded the third-highest transfer between British clubs when he left to play for Chelsea for £10 million. He had a disappointing season at Stamford Bridge and in the summer of 2000 joined Scottish giants Celtic for £6 million. A huge favourite at Parkhead, he helped the Bhoys win the Scottish Premier League, Cup and League Cup in his first season there.

Dion DUBLIN

Position	Forward
Born	Dion Dublin, Leicester, 22 April 1969
Height	6ft 1in
Weight	12st 4lb
Clubs	Norwich City, Cambridge United, Manchester United, Coventry City, Aston Villa, Millwall
England Caps	4
	1998 v Chile (lost 0–2), v Morocco (won 1–0), v Belgium (0–0)
	1999 v Czech Republic (won 2–0)

DESPITE SIGNING professional forms for Norwich City in March 1988, Dion Dublin was released during the summer and joined Fourth Division Cambridge United on a non-contract basis. In only his second appearance for the club he scored a hat-trick in a 5–1 victory at Peterborough United, and then in 1989/90 he topped the club's scoring charts and helped United to both reach the sixth round of the FA Cup and qualify for the play-offs. Cambridge eventually won promotion after beating Chesterfield 1–0 at Wembley, with Dublin the scorer. In 1990/91 Cambridge won the Third Division Championship and again reached the sixth round of the FA Cup.

Dublin had scored 74 goals in 202 games for Cambridge when Manchester United manager Alex Ferguson paid £1 million to take him to Old Trafford, but, in only his sixth game, he broke his leg. On regaining full fitness he found it difficult to win a regular place, and consequently joined Coventry City for a fee of £2 million. He was the Highfield Road club's leading scorer for four consecutive seasons, and his form led to international recognition, with four full caps for England.

He had scored 68 goals in 159 games for the Sky Blues when Aston Villa paid £5.75 million for his services in the summer of 1998. After a sensational start to his Villa career, injury brought his first season at Villa Park to a premature end, though he did return to help the club to the 2000 FA Cup Final. Injuries have since blighted his career but he did have a loan spell at Millwall, where he became an influential figure for the Lions during the closing stages of the 2001/02 season. He was then transformed from the forgotten man to linchpin of the Villa side, scoring his 100th Premiership goal in November 2003.

Michael OWEN

Position	Forward
Born	Michael James Owen, Chester, 14 December 1979
Height	5ft 9in
Weight	11st 2lb
Clubs	Liverpool
England Caps	53 Goals 24

1998 v Chile (lost 0–2), v Switzerland (1–1), v Portugal (won 3–0), v Morocco (won 1–0) 1 goal, v Belgium (0–0), v Tunisia (won 2–0), v Romania (lost 1–2) 1 goal, v Colombia (won 2–0), v Argentina (2–2 aet, Argentina won 4–3 on penalties) 1 goal

1999 v Sweden (lost 1–2), v Bulgaria (0–0), v Luxembourg (won 3-0) 1 goal, v France (lost 0–2)

2000 v Luxembourg (won 6–0) 1 goal, v Poland (0–0), v Belgium (won 2–1), v Scotland (won 2–0), v Scotland (lost 0–1), v Brazil (1–1) 1 goal, v Portugal (lost 2–3), v Germany (won 1–0), v Romania (lost 2–3) 1 goal

2001 v France (1–1) 1 goal, v Germany (lost 0–1), v Spain (won 3–0), v Finland (won 2–1) 1 goal, v Albania (won 3–1) 1 goal, v Mexico (won 4–0), v Greece (won 2–0)

2002 v Holland (lost 0–2), v Germany (won 5–1) 3 goals, v Albania (won 2–0) 1 goal, v Italy (lost 1–2), v Paraguay (won 4–0) 1 goal, v S. Korea (1–1) 1 goal, v Cameroon (2–2), v Sweden (1–1), v Argentina (won 1–0), v Nigeria (0–0), v Denmark (won 3–0) 1 goal, v Brazil (lost 1–2) 1 goal, v Portugal (1–1), v Slovakia (won 2–1) 1 goal, v Macedonia (2–2)

2003 v Australia (lost 1–3), v Liechtenstein (won 2–0) 1 goal, v Turkey (won 2–0), v S. Africa (won 2–1), v Serbia (won 2-1), v Slovakia (won 2-1) 2 goals

2004 v Croatia (won 3–1) 1 goal, v Macedonia (won 2–1), v Liechtenstein (won 2–0) 1 goal

MICHAEL OWEN, who notched up a hat-trick for England in a memorable 5–1 win in Germany, played a major role in his country reaching the 2002 World Cup Finals, where his goals against Denmark and Brazil further enhanced his reputation as a finisher of the highest class.

Having got his Liverpool career underway in 1996/97, Owen began his international career in February 1998 against Chile at Wembley when, at the age of 18 years 59 days, he became the youngest player of the 20th century to play for England. It was a magnificent season for the goalscoring wizard – he scored 23 goals and was named as the PFA Young Player of the year.

Held back during England's opening game of the 1998 World Cup Finals against Romania, he was introduced in the 73rd minute and scored an equalizer, before the Romanians snatched a last-minute winner – even then 'Boy Wonder' nearly equalized in the dying moments when he struck a post. Owen then showed his true worth against Argentina when he raced past two defenders to shoot across the keeper for one of the goals of the competition.

Michael Owen celebrates after scoring a goal against Germany in the World Cup qualifier at Munich, 1 September 2001. England won 5–1. (Ben Radford/Getty Images)

The 1998/99 season was another spectacular one for Michael Owen and, after netting a hat-trick in a 4–1 win at Newcastle United, his relentless running in the Liverpool cause destroyed the myth that he had expended too much energy during England's World Cup campaign. A hamstring injury hampered his progress the following season, but in 2000/01 he rewrote Liverpool's FA Cup history when he grabbed two goals in the last seven minutes to turn the final around and steal the trophy from an Arsenal side that had dominated the game. Since then he has continued to be an automatic first choice for Liverpool.

Lee HENDRIE

Position	Midfielder
Born	Lee Andrew Hendrie, Birmingham, 18 May 1977
Height	5ft 10in
Weight	10st 3lb
Clubs	Aston Villa
England Caps	1
	1999 v Czech Republic (won 2–0)

THE ASTON VILLA MIDFIELDER Lee Hendrie was unfortunate to be sent off in his Premier League debut at Queen's Park Rangers in December 1995, when, after coming on as a substitute, he was dismissed by a referee who made no allowances for youthful exuberance. He hails from a football family – he is the son of Paul, a former Birmingham star, and the cousin of John, who starred for Middlesbrough and Bradford City among others. His early displays led to England Under-21 honours. He finally became a regular in the Villa side in 1997/98, when he also represented England against Russia at international 'B' level. The following season he was capped at full international level when he came off the bench to make his debut against the Czech Republic.

Hendrie proved to be a key member of John Gregory's title-chasing side, his attacking strength, all-round hard work and commitment to the Villa cause always being in evidence. Possessing the skills to unlock the tightest of opposition defences, he was hampered by a series of injuries, being restricted in 1999/2000 to appearances from the substitute's bench, which included replacing Alan Wright for the final few minutes in the FA Cup Final. Over the next few seasons, he began to feature much more, though after suffering a hamstring injury during the 2001/02 season, he lost his place to Thomas Hitzlsperger. In 2002/03 he was rarely absent and, encouraged to shoot on sight, netted a Premiership double against Everton.

Ray PARLOUR

Position	Midfielder
Born	Raymond Parlour, Romford, 7 March 1973
Height	5ft 10in
Weight	11st 12lb
Clubs	Arsenal
England Caps	10
	1999 v Poland (won 3–1), v Sweden (0–0), v Bulgaria (1–1)
	2000 v Luxembourg (won 6–0), v Scotland (lost 0–1), v Argentina (0–0), v Brazil (1–1)
	2001 v Germany (lost 0–1), v Finland (0–0), v Italy (lost 0–1)

RAY PARLOUR was named in the 30-strong England squad – later whittled down to 22 – for World Cup '98 in France. His increased strength, fitness and pace enabled him to score some quality goals, and though ultimately he missed out on that World

Cup he received a belated call-up to the England squad in 1999 for a match against Poland, making his international debut when he came on as a substitute.

After making his League debut for Arsenal against Liverpool at Anfield in January 1992, where he conceded a penalty in a 2–0 defeat, Ray Parlour came on in leaps and bounds over the next couple of seasons, impressing as an integral part of the club's engine room. A former Essex schoolboy star, he had an outstanding season when helping Arsenal win both the FA and League cups in 1992/93, and the following season, although he didn't appear in any of the European fixtures, he won a winners' medal as one of the non-playing reserves. Always recognizable by his shock of blond hair, he won Premier League Championship and FA Cup winners' medals in 1997/98 as the Gunners stormed to the 'double'. He scored the first hat-trick of his career in the away leg of the UEFA Cup quarter-final at Werder Bremen as the Gunners won 4–2. His impressive form earned him a start in England's line-up for the first time against Luxembourg. This often underrated midfielder was also an influential member of Arsenal's double-winning side in 2001/02, scoring a cracking effort to help the Gunners on their way to victory over Chelsea in the FA Cup Final. In the 2002/3 season a series of niggling injuries and a loss of form kept him out of the side for long periods, yet despite this he remains a valuable member of the Arsenal squad.

Tim SHERWOOD

Position	Midfielder
Born	Timothy Alan Sherwood, St Albans, 6 February 1969
Height	6ft 0in
Weight	12st 9lb
Clubs	Watford, Norwich City, Blackburn Rovers, Tottenham Hotspur, Portsmouth
England Caps	3
	1999 v Poland (won 3–1), v Hungary (1–1), v Sweden (0–0)

AFTER BEGINNING HIS CAREER with Watford, Tim Sherwood joined Norwich City in the summer of 1989 when the Canaries paid £175,000 for his services. Playing in a variety of positions, he soon won selection for the England Under-21 squad. Following Andy Townsend's departure from Norwich, he settled into a midfield role, but just when it seemed his career would take off he was fined and suspended for a breach of club discipline.

In February 1992 Sherwood left Carrow Road and joined Blackburn Rovers for a fee of £500,000. Appointed club captain, he led Rovers to the Premier League title in 1994/95 and was on the short-list for the PFA Player of the Year award. He went on to score 31 goals in 288 League and Cup games before joining Tottenham Hotspur in February 1999 for £3.8 million. Finding White Hart Lane the ideal platform on which to rebuild his reputation as one of the best midfielders in England, he won three full caps for England, but after suffering a spate of niggling injuries, he dropped out of Glenn Hoddle's long-term plans and was allowed to join Portsmouth. Adding strength, guile and balance to the south coast club's side, he helped them win promotion to the Premiership.

Wes BROWN

Position	Defender
Born	Wesley Michael Brown, Manchester, 13 October 1979
Height	6ft 1in
Weight	12st 4lb
Clubs	Manchester United
England Caps	7
	1999 v Hungary (1–1)
	2001 v Finland (won 2–1), v Albania (won 3–1)
	2002 v Holland (1–1), v S. Korea (1–1), v Cameroon (2–2)
	2003 v Australia (lost 1–3)

HAVING EARNED RAVE REVIEWS in the reserves, Manchester United's Wes Brown made his Football League debut as a substitute against Leeds United during the 1997/98 season. Early in the following campaign he won international recognition when he was capped for England at Under-21 level, and towards the end of that season Kevin Keegan rewarded him with a full England cap in the friendly against Hungary.

After picking up Premier League and European Cup winners' medals, Brown was forced to miss the next 15 months after suffering a ruptured cruciate ligament that nearly wrecked his career. He eventually returned to form a solid central defensive partnership at United with Jaap Stam, but following the Dutchman's departure to Lazio, a huge weight of expectation fell on his shoulders.

Able to play at full-back or in the centre of defence, Brown is good in the air and has pace and confidence to match. He has the potential to be an England regular for many years to come.

Michael GRAY

Position	Left-back
Born	Michael Gray, Sunderland, 3 August 1974
Height	5ft 7in
Weight	10st 10lb
Clubs	Sunderland
England Caps	3
	1999 v Hungary (1–1), v Sweden (0–0), v Bulgaria (1–1)

SUNDERLAND-BORN MICHAEL GRAY worked his way through the ranks before making a goalscoring debut for his home-town club against Barnsley in December 1992. After three seasons as a fringe player, he was ever-present in 1995/96 as the club won the First Division Championship. During that campaign he also represented a Football League Under-21 XI against an Italian Serie 'B' side and was chosen by his fellow professionals as a member of the PFA First Division Select XI.

Gray continued to impress in the Premier League even though he had switched from his usual position on the left side of midfield to left-back to accommodate Chris

Waddle. A player of undoubted class, he showed great strength of character in 1998/99 to overcome his penalty miss against Charlton Athletic in the play-off final, helping the Wearsiders to win the First Division title. His form during that Championship-winning season led to full international honours for England. Since then he has been one of Sunderland's most consistent players and, following the retirement of Steve Bould, he was appointed team captain. Though the north-east club were relegated at the end of the 2002/03 season, Gray made his 400th appearance in a red and white shirt at Fulham in March 2003.

Kevin PHILLIPS

Position	Forward
Born	Kevin Mark Phillips, Hitchin, 25 July 1973
Height	5ft 7in
Weight	11st 0lb
Clubs	Watford, Sunderland, Southampton
England Caps	8
	1999 v Hungary (1–1)
	2000 v Belgium (won 2–1), v Argentina (0–0), v Brazil (1–1), v Malta (won 2–1)
	2001 v Italy (lost 0–1)
	2002 v Sweden (1–1), v Holland (1–1)

ONE OF THE GAME'S most prolific goalscorers, Kevin Phillips has yet to hit the target in his eight appearances for England.

Signed from non-League Baldock for £10,000, he began his Football League career with Watford, but early in his first full season with the Vicarage Road club he suffered a broken foot. He was still troubled by the injury in 1996/97, but on his return netted his first hat-trick of his League career in a 3–0 win over Bristol City. His goalscoring feats for the Hornets attracted the attention of a number of top clubs, and in the summer of 1997 Sunderland paid £300,000 for his services. He scored on his debut for the Black Cats in a 3–1 win over Manchester City in what was the club's first League game at the Stadium of Light. Possessing tremendous pace, he formed a deadly strike partnership with Niall Quinn and earned a call-up to the England 'B' squad. During the course of that 1997/98 season he scored in nine consecutive home League games and netted four goals in a 5–1 FA Cup win at Rotherham United. He ended a remarkable campaign with 35 goals, his 29 in the League making him the First Division's leading marksman. His form the following season led to full international honours as a member of Kevin Keegan's England team.

Having made the step-up into the Premiership, Phillips continued to find the net with great regularity and in 1999/2000 scored on 30 occasions, becoming only the third forward to reach this target since the Premiership's inception. He rounded off a great season by finishing runner-up to Roy Keane in both the PFA and Football Writers' Association Player of the Year awards. The following season he broke Gary Rowell's post-war scoring record for Sunderland and despite suffering from a spate of niggling injuries, this striker, who can certainly live with the very best, scored 121 goals in 199 games for the north-east club.

In the summer of 2003, following Sunderland's relegation, Phillips signed for Southampton and immediately struck up a potent partnership with Saints striker James Beattie.

Emile HESKEY

Position	Forward
Born	Emile William Ivanhoe Heskey, Leicester, 11 January 1978
Height	6ft 2in
Weight	13st 12lb
Clubs	Leicester City, Liverpool
England Caps	38 Goals 5

1999 v Hungary (1–1), v Bulgaria (1–1)
2000 v Belgium (won 2–1), v Scotland (lost 0–1), v Argentina (0–0), v Ukraine (won 2–0), v Malta (won 2–1) 1 goal, v Portugal (lost 2–3), v Romania (lost 2–3)
2001 v Finland (0–0), v Italy (lost 0–1), v Spain (won 3–0) 1 goal, v Finland (won 2–1), v Albania (won 3–1), v Mexico (won 4–0), v Greece (won 2–0)
2002 v Germany (won 5–1) 1 goal, v Albania (won 2–0), v Greece (2–2), v Sweden (1–1), v Holland (1–1), v Italy (lost 1–2), v S. Korea (1–1), v Cameroon (2–2), v Sweden (1–1), v Argentina (won 1–0), v Nigeria (0–0), v Denmark (won 3–0) 1 goal, v Brazil (lost 1–2), v Portugal (1–1), v Slovakia (won 2–1)
2003 v Liechtenstein (won 2–0), v S. Africa (won 2-1) 1 goal, v Serbia (won 2-1)
2004 v Croatia (won 3–1), v Macedonia (won 2–1), v Turkey (0–0), v Denmark (lost 2–3)

EMILE HESKEY, who has won 38 caps for England, was chosen for a number of England squads but had to drop out because of injury until the trip to Hungary in 1999, when he came on as a substitute for Kevin Phillips.

Beginning his career with his home-town club, Leicester City, Heskey was a promising first-year YTS striker when he was thrown in at the deep end against Queen's Park Rangers, the Foxes having been ravaged by a flu epidemic. He won a regular spot under manager Martin O'Neill, continuing to impress

Emile Heskey during the first-round match of the 2002 World Cup against Sweden. The match was drawn 1–1. (Ross Kinnaird/Getty Images)

with his strength and speed. Affectionately nicknamed 'Bruno' by the Leicester fans, he scored some stunning goals during 1996/97, his first Premiership season. Promoted to the England Under-21 team, he scored the vital last-ditch equalizer at Wembley in the League Cup Final against Middlesbrough after previously hitting the bar twice. He again struck the woodwork in the replay, on his way to a Cup winners' medal.

After helping Leicester beat Tranmere in the 2000 League Cup Final, Heskey left Filbert Street to join Liverpool; City received a club-record £11 million fee. Although some observers questioned Gerard Houllier's decision to sign him, their doubts were soon laid to rest when he netted a hat-trick in a 4–0 win at Derby County. A run of 12 goals in 12 games confirmed his status as one of the top strikers in the country and he ended the 2000/01 season with FA Cup, League Cup and UEFA Cup winners' medals. Although not as prolific a scorer, he established himself as the strike partner of Michael Owen for both club and country, though he now faces stiff competition at international level from Wayne Rooney.

Jamie CARRAGHER

Position	Defender
Born	James Lee Duncan Carragher, Bootle, 28 January 1978
Height	6ft 1in
Weight	13st 0lb
Clubs	Liverpool
England Caps	9
	1999 v Hungary (1–1)
	2001 v Italy (lost 0–1), v Mexico (won 4–0)
	2002 v Holland (lost 0–2), v Germany (won 5–1), v Albania (won 2–0), v Sweden (1–1),
	v Paraguay (won 4–0)
	2003 v Serbia (won 2–1)

JAMIE CARRAGHER would most certainly have been a member of England's 2002 World Cup squad but for impending knee surgery.

Showing the potential to become a powerful midfield dynamo, he marked his first full appearance for Liverpool against Aston Villa at Anfield with a firm header into the Kop End net to open the scoring in a 3–0 win. He made his mark, however, as a central defender, and during the course of the 1997/98 season was selected for both of the England 'B' matches as well as playing in seven of the eight England Under-21 matches.

Under Gerard Houllier, Carragher proved to be a very versatile player, one day doing a marking job, the next occupying a holding midfield role before returning to the centre of defence a few days later. A fierce tackler, he sometimes allowed his youthful exuberance to get the better of him on and off the pitch, but eventually Houllier's strict regime and sense of discipline brought the young defender into line. He played in all but four of Liverpool's 63 matches in 2000/01, when the Reds won the FA Cup, League Cup and UEFA Cup.

Jonathan WOODGATE

Position	Defender
Born	Jonathan Simon Woodgate, Middlesbrough, 22 January 1980
Height	6ft 2in
Weight	13st 0lb
Clubs	Leeds United, Newcastle United
England Caps	4
	1999 v Bulgaria (1–1)
	2002 v Portugal (1–1), v Slovakia (won 2–1), v Macedonia (2–2)

OF ALL THE TALENTED YOUNGSTERS breaking through the ranks at Elland Road, none benefited more from the appointment of David O'Leary as manager than Jonathan Woodgate, a centre-back of great skill and composure. Able to combine his defensive skills with the ability to break forward, he is most dangerous at set pieces. At the end of his first season, 1998/99, he made his full international debut for England in a 1–1 draw with Bulgaria.

Woodgate quickly learned from playing alongside Lucas Radebe at Leeds and began the 2000/01 season in fine form before picking up a number of injuries that restricted his first-team appearances. He returned to give his best performance of the season in the 1–0 victory at Lazio but then stepped back to focus on a well-documented off-the-field matter. On his return this cultured defender looked as though he had never been away, but midway through the 2002/03 season he left Leeds for Newcastle United in a £9 million deal. He has become the cornerstone of the Magpies' defence and was called up by England for the Euro 2004 qualifiers against Slovakia and Macedonia.

2000
and Beyond

The New Millennium

Despite some poor showings, England gained a place, thanks to Sweden's defeat of Norway, in the 2000 European Championship play-offs against Scotland. They beat the Scots 2–1 on aggregate. After a 3–2 defeat by Portugal, an Alan Shearer goal helped England beat Germany, but an 89th-minute penalty, rashly conceded by Phil Neville, gave Romania victory when Keegan's side only needed a draw to reach the Euro 2000 quarter-finals.

In October of the same year, Keegan stunned England by quitting his 19-month reign as coach minutes after his side lost 1–0 to Germany in a World Cup qualifier at Wembley. Howard Wilkinson assumed the caretaker's mantle again, until the FA appointed Sven-Goran Eriksson as England's new manager.

England made a bright start under Eriksson, beating Spain 3–0 at Villa Park and then securing World Cup qualifying victories over Finland (home 2–1), Albania (away 3–1) and Greece (away 2–0). On 1 September 2001 an historic Michael Owen hat-trick helped England devastate Germany with a stunning 5–1 victory in Munich, sparking a carnival atmosphere at home. The victory was the first in a World Cup qualifier on German soil and England's first success there since 1965. Thousands of dejected German fans headed for the exits after Heskey netted the fifth goal in the 74th minute and, later, Eriksson was even greeted by a round of applause in the press room. The following month, with England trailing 2–1 in Greece and in the final seconds of the game, the inspirational David Beckham sent a trademark 25-yard free kick whistling into the net, dramatically securing England's World Cup Finals spot.

England started the 2002 tournament with an unconvincing draw against Sweden, but five days later skipper Beckham wiped out four years of misery with a penalty winner against Argentina. This was followed by a goalless draw against Nigeria and a place in the last 16. After a number of defensive errors England beat Denmark 3–0, only to be beaten 2–1 by Brazil in the quarter-finals. The dream was over for another four years.

England's Euro 2004 campaign saw the emergence of Wayne Rooney. However, disgraceful crowd scenes marred England's Rooney-inspired feisty win over Turkey at the Stadium of Light, almost resulting in England having to play their next qualifier behind closed doors. Results continued to go England's way, leaving them needing a point in Turkey to qualify for the finals. David Beckham missed a penalty, had a headed goal disallowed and there was a tunnel bust-up at half-term before England survived a searching examination of their character. But a courageous performance deservedly brought Sven-Goran Eriksson's side to the point they needed to put a smile back on the face of English football.

Kieron DYER

Position	Midfielder
Born	Kieron Courtney Dyer, Ipswich, 29 December 1978
Height	5ft 7in
Weight	9st 7lb
Clubs	Ipswich Town, Newcastle United
England Caps	19

2000 v Luxembourg (won 6–0), v Poland (0–0), v Belgium (won 2–1), v Argentina (0–0),
v Ukraine (won 2–0)
2001 v France (1–1), v Germany (lost 0–1), v Italy (lost 0–1)
2002 v Paraguay (won 4–0), v Sweden (1–1), v Denmark (won 3–0), v Brazil (lost 1–2),
v Slovakia (won 2–1)
2003 v Australia (lost 1–3), v Liechtenstein (won 2–0), v Turkey (won 2–0)
2004 v Croatia (won 3–1), v Macedonia (won 2–1), v Turkey (0–0)

ONE OF A NEW BREED of players, the product of Ipswich Town's revitalized youth policy, Kieron Dyer is a versatile performer, able to play in a number of positions, including midfield and wing-back. Able also to run at players and set up chances for others, he represented England at Under-21 level in only his second season in the game, before being promoted to the England 'B' team and eventually making his full debut against Luxembourg in 2000.

Newcastle United manager Ruud Gullit paid out £6 million in the summer of 1999 to bring Dyer to St James' Park, and the latter's performances in his first season in the Premiership confirmed him as a footballer of exciting potential. Since then, however, he has suffered more than his fair share of injuries – a stress fracture of the shin, a bone-graft operation in which he had a pin inserted in his leg, and a stress fracture in his left foot. Back to full fitness, he captained the Magpies in the absence of Alan Shearer and Gary Speed.

Kieron Dyer during the Euro 2004 qualifier against Turkey at the Stadium of Light, 2 April 2003.
(Ben Radford/Getty Images)

Steve GUPPY

Position	Winger
Born	Stephen Andrew Guppy, Winchester, 29 March 1969
Height	5ft 11in
Weight	11st 12lb
Clubs	Wycombe Wanderers, Newcastle United, Port Vale, Leicester City, Celtic
England Caps	1
	2000 v Belgium (won 2–1)

LEFT-WINGER STEVE GUPPY began his career with Wycombe Wanderers, where he made an immediate impact, helping the club win two FA Trophies and the GM Vauxhall Conference title. During the summer of 1994 a £150,000 transfer took him to Newcastle United, but he was unable to hold down a first-team place and after only three months on Tyneside he joined Port Vale. Soon his dazzling wing play began to receive rave notices and top-flight club scouts flocked to watch him. On one occasion, due to heavy traffic, he had to run two miles to the ground to make the kick-off for the FA Cup tie against Everton – going on to star in a 2–2 draw! After helping Vale challenge for the play-offs in 1996/97, he joined Premier League Leicester City for a fee of £950,000. Soon adapting to the wing-back position, he won a call-up to the England 'B' team and, as an over-age player, to the Under-21 line-up. One of the best crossers of a ball in the Premiership, he also added the odd spectacular strike. His consistent level of performance regularly saw him touted as a possible England contender, particularly in light of the national side's paucity of naturally left-footed players, but he had to wait until October 1999 to make his full debut against Belgium.

Despite a season hampered by injuries, Guppy's trademark corners helped Matt Elliott head vital goals at Wembley as the Foxes won the League Cup. A regular under Martin O'Neill, he was, however, unable to hold down a place under Peter Taylor, and in August 2001 he moved north of the border to play for Glasgow Celtic, helping the Parkhead club win the Scottish League Championship.

Frank LAMPARD junior

Position	Midfielder
Born	Frank Lampard, Romford, 20 June 1978
Height	6ft 0in
Weight	12st 6lb
Clubs	West Ham United, Swansea City, Chelsea
England Caps	16 Goals 1
	2000 v Belgium (won 2–1)
	2001 v Spain (won 3–0)
	2002 v Holland (lost 0–2), v Sweden (1–1), v Holland (1–1), v Italy (lost 1–2), v Paraguay (won 4–0)
	2003 v Australia (lost 1–3), v S. Africa (won 2–1), v Serbia (won 2–1), v Slovakia (won 2–1)
	2004 v Croatia (won 3–1) 1 goal, v Macedonia (won 2–1), v Liechtenstein (won 2–0), v Turkey (0–0), v Denmark (lost 2–3)

THE SON OF the former West Ham United legend, Frank junior also began his career with the Hammers but made his Football League debut while on loan with Swansea City. He impressed the Vetch Field crowd as a strong attacking midfielder with a high work-rate and plenty of skill. Back at Upton Park, he led the young Hammers to the Championship and to the FA Youth Cup Final. During the course of the 1996/97 season he had the misfortune to break his leg against Aston Villa, but he recovered to establish himself in the Hammers' first team, going on to make his debut for both the England 'B' and Under-21 teams, and eventually his full debut against Belgium in October 1999.

Very talented and with an eye for goal, Lampard has vision, allied to great passing skills, and he became the Under-21 side's captain, leading the side in the European Championship Finals in Slovakia in 2000.

He was placed in a difficult situation at Upton Park after his father and uncle were replaced as the Hammers' management team, and in the summer of 2001 he joined Chelsea for a fee of £11 million. During his first season at Stamford Bridge, he switched to the right flank, away from the more favoured central midfield position in which he had established a reputation as a consistent goalscorer, but a switch back to the centre brought a return to his best form. Though disappointed to be omitted from England's 2002 World Cup squad, his inspired displays made him an automatic choice for the Blues, this despite an influx of big-money signings at Stamford Bridge.

Steven GERRARD

Position	Midfielder
Born	Steven George Gerrard, Huyton, 30 May 1980
Height	6ft 2in
Weight	12st 4lb
Clubs	Liverpool
England Caps	21 Goals 3
	2000 v Ukraine (won 2–0), v Germany (lost 0–1)
	2001 v Finland (won 2–1), v Mexico (won 4–0), v Greece (won 2–0)
	2002 v Germany (won 5–1) 1 goal, v Albania (won 2–0), v Greece (2–2), v Holland (1–1),
	v Paraguay (won 4–0), v Portugal (1–1), v Slovakia (won 2–1), v Macedonia (2–2) 1 goal
	2003 v Liechtenstein (won 2–0), v Turkey (won 2–0), v S. Africa (won 2–1), v Serbia (won
	2–1) 1 goal, v Slovakia (won 2–1)
	2004 v Croatia (won 3–1), v Liechtenstein (won 2–0), v Turkey (0–0)

THE LIVERPOOL MIDFIELDER Steven Gerrard was invited to train with Kevin Keegan's England team during his first season in the Reds' side before being diagnosed with a stress fracture at the base of his back. Thankfully, he was given the all-clear after several tests. Tigerish in the tackle, he can also deliver a penetrating through-ball to his forwards, and it was these qualities that helped him win his first full cap for England against the Ukraine in May 2000, aged 19. The following season, having coped admirably with all the pressures of being a star at such a young age, he scored ten goals, all impressive strikes but none better than his 35-yard bullet in the

2–0 win over Manchester United. He also scored the second goal in the unforgettable UEFA Cup Final against Deportivo Alaves and was voted PFA Young Player of the Year.

Gerrard started the 2001/02 season in outstanding form, with a majestic display for England in the historic 5–1 win over Germany in Munich. However, on his own admission, his form throughout the campaign was inconsistent, especially during the Reds' mid-season slump. Despite a relatively injury-free season, he was declared unavailable for his country in the 2002 World Cup Finals, due to a recurrence of a groin strain requiring an operation. He returned to action in the 2002/03 season but his form was patchy in the first half of the campaign. He achieved more consistency in the 2003/04 season, for which he was named captain.

Gareth BARRY

Position	Defender
Born	Gareth Barry, Hastings, 23 February 1981
Height	6ft 0in
Weight	12st 6lb
Clubs	Aston Villa
England Caps	8
	2000 v Ukraine (won 2–0), v Malta (won 2–1)
	2001 v France (1–1), v Germany (lost 0–1), v Finland (0–0), v Italy (lost 0–1)
	2003 v S. Africa (won 2–1), v Serbia (won 2–1)

ASTON VILLA DEFENDER Gareth Barry graduated from the YTS ranks to turn professional in February 1998 after starting out at the club as a midfielder. In 1998/99, his first full season in the Villa side, he went from strength to strength, replacing Steve Staunton as the left-hand side of defence. The club were so impressed with his progress that, on his 18th birthday, they offered him a five-year contract, confirming him to be a youngster with a bright future. Featuring regularly in the England Under-21 side, he was a member of the Villa side that lost to Chelsea in the 2000 FA Cup Final. That season also saw him win full international honours when he came on as a substitute against both the Ukraine and Malta in the run-up to Euro 2000. By then an established figure in Villa's defence, he impressed with his composure and a maturity beyond his years.

Barry has developed into a versatile defender who can slot into any position in the back line. Though he lost his place following the arrival of Alpay and Mellberg, the return of Graham Taylor as manager saw him back in favour. Under new manager David O'Leary, the 23-year-old has taken his total of games for Villa to over 200.

Richard WRIGHT

Position	Goalkeeper
Born	Richard Ian Wright, Ipswich, 5 November 1977
Height	6ft 2in
Weight	13st 0lb
Clubs	Ipswich Town, Arsenal, Everton
England Caps	2
	2000 v Malta (won 2–1)
	2002 v Holland (lost 0–2)

RICHARD WRIGHT won his first full cap against Malta, saving a late penalty to spare England's blushes in a 2–1 win. He began his Football League career with his home-town club Ipswich Town, replacing the injured Craig Forrest. Unflappable and with a physique that belied his age during his early days at Portman Road, it wasn't long before he won Under-21 honours, keeping a clean sheet on his debut. As well as being a regular in the Under-21 side, he won selection for England at 'B' level and was also asked to train with the England first-team squad for the game against Chile in February 1998.

In 1998/99, Wright equalled the Ipswich record for clean sheets in a season with 26 and, not surprisingly, was recognized by his fellow professionals with selection to the PFA award-winning First Division side. When Ipswich won promotion to the Premier League in 1999/2000 via the play-offs, he was outstanding in the Wembley final, saving a Darren Barnard penalty. His performances during the campaign earned him a place in the PFA award-winning First Division side for the second season in succession.

Following the appointment of Sven-Goran Eriksson as England manager, Wright was named in Eriksson's first three squads. He had played in 291 games for Ipswich when, in the summer of 2001, he joined Arsenal for £6 million. Though he always performed competently for the Gunners when called upon, he was essentially the back-up to David Seaman, and in the close season, having helped the club win the 'double', he left Highbury to join Everton. Following a nervous and uneasy start, he found his feet and his improved performances led to a recall into the England squad. If he can reduce his lapses of concentration, he will be one of the leading candidates to replace David Seaman as his country's No. 1.

Seth JOHNSON

Position	Midfielder
Born	Seth Art Maurice Johnson, Birmingham, 12 March 1979
Height	5ft 10in
Weight	11st 0lb
Clubs	Crewe Alexandra, Derby County, Leeds United
England Caps	1
	2001 v Italy (lost 0–1)

JUST 18 YEARS OF AGE and a first-year Crewe professional, Seth Johnson made his Football League debut in March 1997 as a left-back against Preston North End. Not only did he keep his place, but he also made an appearance as a substitute at Wembley as Crewe went into the First Division via the play-offs. Through the quality of his play he continued to emphasize how far he had progressed in such a short time and was delighted to score for the England Under-18 team at Gresty Road prior to the European Championships in Cyprus in the summer of 1998.

Playing mainly in midfield, though he did fill in at full-back occasionally, Johnson was chased by a posse of scouts before eventually signing for Derby County in the summer of 1999 for a fee of £3 million.

In his first season in the top flight his aggressive style meant that he was yellow-carded more than any other player in the Premier League. Despite this, he appeared regularly for the England Under-21 side, and it was clearly only a matter of time before he made his full international debut. This duly arrived in November 2000 when he came on as a second-half substitute in a friendly against Italy – the first Derby player to be capped for England for nine years.

In October 2001, Leeds United paid £7 million for his services but he was to suffer soon afterwards from the Elland Road 'injury jinx', a blood clot on the knee keeping him out of action for almost half of his first season. He was again frustrated by injuries in the 2002/03 season when he was restricted to just a handful of appearances.

Chris POWELL

Position	Left-back
Born	Christopher George Robin Powell, Lambeth, 8 September 1969
Height	5ft 10in
Weight	11st 7lb
Clubs	Crystal Palace, Aldershot, Southend United, Derby County, Charlton Athletic
England Caps	5
	2001 v Spain (won 3–0), v Finland (won 2–1), v Mexico (won 4–0)
	2002 v Holland (lost 0–2), v Holland (1–1)

UNABLE TO HOLD DOWN a regular place with Crystal Palace, left-back Chris Powell had a loan spell with Aldershot before joining Southend United on a free transfer. Made the Shrimpers' club captain, his cultured performances led to many enquiries from top clubs. He had appeared in 290 games for the Roots Hall club when Derby manager Jim Smith paid £750,000 to take him to the Baseball Ground. Very calm under pressure, Powell is skilled at developing counter-attacking play down the left flank and this made him one of the best players in his position in the Premier League.

In June 1998, Charlton Athletic broke their transfer record by paying Derby £825,000 for Powell's services, and the following season he was ever-present. In 1999/2000 he helped the Addicks win the First Division Championship, and was selected by his fellow professionals for the PFA award-winning First Division side. The following season was memorable for Powell as he became only the third Addicks player since 1946 to play for the full England side. He also scored his long-awaited first goal for the club in the London derby against Spurs. Adding two more international caps to his collection in 2001/02, he became Charlton's most-capped England player.

Michael BALL

Position	Defender
Born	Michael John Ball, Liverpool, 2 October 1979
Height	5ft 10in
Weight	11st 2lb
Clubs	Everton, Glasgow Rangers
England Caps	1
	2001 v Spain (won 3–0)

HANDED A TESTING Football League debut in a crucial Everton relegation battle against Spurs, Michael Ball showed maturity and composure well beyond his 17 years. Such was the quality of his performances that the Blues' caretaker boss Dave Watson had no qualms about introducing him after just 23 minutes into a fierce Merseyside derby. A sharp-tackling, overlapping left-back, he is equally at home in central defence and also possesses an enormously long throw. It was these qualities that allowed Howard Kendall to sell Andy Hinchcliffe to Sheffield Wednesday, the former England defender tipping Ball for a full international call-up if he maintained his progress. Sure enough, in his first full season in the Premier League, Ball was called up to the England squad for the friendly international against Hungary and represented the Under-21 side.

Ball subsequently suffered a loss of form and had trouble in convincing Everton manager Walter Smith that he was worth a starting place in a full-strength Blues side. Despite being a regular for the Under-21 side, he was left out of the 2000 European Championships in Slovakia. In 2000/01, he was forced by an injury crisis to play in central defence. His development as a player, however, was acknowledged by Sven-Goran Eriksson with a first full cap, against Spain in February 2001.

In the 2001 close season, Ball joined Glasgow Rangers but was then hampered by a spate of injuries.

Gavin McCANN

Position	Midfielder
Born	Gavin Peter McCann, Blackpool, 10 January 1978
Height	5ft 11in
Weight	11st 0lb
Clubs	Everton, Sunderland, Aston Villa
England Caps	1
	2001 v Spain (won 3–0)

A SHARP, SNAPPY central-midfielder, with a good range of passing skills and a fine shot, Gavin McCann began his career with Everton but a series of injuries, including a hairline fracture of his leg, hampered his progress. Unable to break into the Everton side on a regular basis, he joined Sunderland for £500,000 to provide extra cover and competition for midfield places in the squad. A box-to-box player, he is a tremendous competitor who always gives his best, but in his early days in the north-east he suffered a cruciate knee-ligament injury. When he returned to action in 2000/01, he went on to enjoy a season of significant achievement, his displays immediately catching the eye of England coach Sven-Goran Eriksson. Selected for the squad for the friendly against Spain, he received his first full cap as a second-half substitute.

The industrious midfielder had a disappointing season in 2001/02, failing to win the ball and distribute it accurately with his usual consistency. He also picked up his share of bookings, causing him to miss a number of games through suspension. Following the Black Cats' relegation in 2003, McCann joined Aston Villa.

Ashley COLE

Position	Left-back
Born	Ashley Cole, Stepney, 20 December 1980
Height	5ft 8in
Weight	10st 8lb
Clubs	Arsenal, Crystal Palace
England Caps	23

2001 v Albania (won 3–1), v Mexico (won 4–0), v Greece (won 2–0)
2002 v Holland (lost 0–2), v Germany (won 5–1), v Albania (won 2–0), v Greece (2–2), v S. Korea (1–1), v Sweden (1–1), v Argentina (won 1–0), v Nigeria (0–0), v Denmark (won 3–0), v Brazil (lost 1–2), v Portugal (1–1), v Slovakia (won 2–1), v Macedonia (2–2)
2003 v Australia (lost 1–3), v Serbia (won 2–1), v Slovakia (won 2–1)
2004 v Croatia (won 3–1), v Macedonia (won 2–1), v Turkey (0–0), v Denmark (lost 2–3)

ASHLEY COLE IS AN adventurous left-back, who, given his age, could go on to surpass former Gunner Kenny Sansom's international appearance record in that position.

A product of the Arsenal youth scheme, he was loaned to Crystal Palace to gain first-team experience. He impressed with his displays at left wing-back, showing excellent timing in the tackle. He then returned to Highbury to make his full Arsenal debut in the Premiership at Newcastle United. He had an outstanding first full season for Arsenal in 2000/01, his surging runs, timely tackles and accurate crosses winning him a regular place in the England Under-21 side before England's new coach Sven-Goran Eriksson gave him his first full cap in the World Cup qualifier against Albania.

At club level, Cole has showed a maturity beyond his years, putting in accomplished performances against the cream of Europe in the Champions League. His 2001/02 season was disrupted by a knee-ligament injury, but once fully recovered he went on to feature for England in the 2002 World Cup Finals in the Far East, having earlier helped the Gunners complete the 'double'. He continued to develop both at club and international level and he was one of five Arsenal players voted into the PFA Premiership team of the season.

Ashley Cole during the World Cup quarter-final with Brazil on 21 June 2002.
(David Cannon/Getty Images)

Michael CARRICK

Position	Midfielder
Born	Michael Carrick, Wallsend, 28 July 1981
Height	6ft 0in
Weight	11st 10lb
Clubs	West Ham United, Swindon Town, Birmingham City
England Caps	2
	2001 v Mexico (won 4–0)
	2002 v Holland (lost 0–2)

AFTER MAKING his West Ham debut in the Inter Toto Cup game against FC Jokerit in the summer of 1999, Michael Carrick was loaned to Swindon Town, where he scored a wonder goal in the home game against Charlton Athletic, finishing off a move he had begun from inside his own half. Another loan period followed with Birmingham City before he returned to Upton Park. Displaying an elegant style with great passing and vision, Carrick was initially used sparingly by the Hammers' boss Harry Redknapp, but in 2000/01, after being thrust into action because of an injury crisis, he rarely missed a match. He featured regularly for England at Under-21 level and made his full international debut when he came on as a half-time substitute in the friendly game against Mexico in May 2001.

At West Ham, Carrick formed a good understanding with Joe Cole in the Hammers' midfield, the two complementing each other's talents. Though he missed some games midway through the 2001/02 season after undergoing surgery to resolve a groin problem, the young left-sided midfielder gained many more admirers after some brilliant displays. He enjoyed an excellent season in 2002/03 despite the disappointment of his club's relegation and took his tally of Under-21 caps to 13.

Joe COLE

Position	Midfielder		
Born	Joseph John Cole, Islington, 8 November 1981		
Height	5ft 9in		
Weight	11st 0lb		
Clubs	West Ham United, Chelsea		
England Caps	13	Goals	2
	2001 v Mexico (won 4–0)		
	2002 v Holland (lost 0–2), v Italy (lost 1–2), v Paraguay (won 4–0), v S. Korea (1–1), v Cameroon (2–2), v Sweden (1–1), v Portugal (1–1)		
	2003 v S. Africa (won 2-1), v Serbia (won 2–1) 1 goal		
	2004 v Croatia (won 3-1), v Liechtenstein (won 2–0), v Denmark (lost 2–3) 1 goal		

THIS EXTREMELY TALENTED MIDFIELDER established himself as a regular in the England Under-21 side before making his long-awaited full international debut when he replaced Steven Gerrard for the second half of the friendly against Mexico in 2001.

After much media hype, Cole, who had represented England in the European Youth Championships and helped the Hammers win the FA Youth Cup, made his League debut after only a matter of days as a professional. Taking it all in his stride, he showed enough skill to suggest that he would be a future star. He established himself as a first-team regular in 1999/2000, coping well with the pressures of intense media attention, before a broken leg brought his season to a premature close.

During the course of the 1999/2000 campaign he made his bow for the England Under-21s against Argentina but was ruled out of the European Championships in Slovakia. At the start of the 2001/02 season, he again appeared for the England Under-21s, but his stunning displays soon elevated him to the senior team and he travelled to the World Cup Finals as a member of England's 23-man squad. He matured considerably as a player during the Hammers' relegation season of 2002/03 but then left Upton Park to join Chelsea.

Danny MILLS

Position	Right-back
Born	Daniel John Mills, Norwich, 18 May 1977
Height	5ft 11in
Weight	11st 9lb
Clubs	Norwich City, Charlton Athletic, Leeds United, Middlesbrough
England Caps	18
	2001 v Mexico (won 4–0)
	2002 v Holland (lost 0–2), v Sweden (1–1), v Italy (lost 1–2), v Paraguay (won 4–0),
	v S. Korea (1–1), v Cameroon (2–2), v Sweden (1–1), v Argentina (won 1–0),
	v Nigeria (0–0), v Denmark (won 3–0), v Brazil (lost 1–2), v Portugal (1–1)
	2003 v Australia (lost 1–3), v S. Africa (won 2–1), v Serbia (won 2–1), v Slovakia (won 2–1)
	2004 v Croatia (won 3–1)

DANNY MILLS' DISPLAYS at right-back for Leeds United were rewarded with his first full cap in the friendly against Mexico. In 2001/02, he became a regular squad member for England and featured in the World Cup Finals in the Far East.

A calm and authoritative defender, Danny Mills began his career with his home-town club, Norwich City, being one of eight players to wear the No. 2 shirt in his debut season of 1995/96. The following season he spent much of the campaign on the opposite flank, but still won England Under-21 honours and selection for the Football League Under-21 side that played their Italian Serie 'B' equivalent. His impressive display that night caught the eye of the Charlton Athletic manager Alan Curbishley, who was in charge of the side, and he secured Mills' services for a fee of £350,000.

Mills, who loves to get down the flank and put in crosses, left the Valley in the summer of 1999, joining Leeds United for £4 million. He began the new season as the club's first-choice right-back, but lost his place to Gary Kelly. In 2000/01 he more than made his mark in an injury-ravaged season for the Yorkshire club, playing in all four positions in the back four before making the right-back spot his own. After playing a major role for England in the World Cup Finals, he became one of Leeds United's most consistent players. He then moved to Middlesbrough.

Danny Mills runs with the ball during the World Cup match with Nigeria on 12 June 2002. The match ended in a 0–0 draw. (Stu Forster/Getty Images)

Alan SMITH

Position	Forward
Born	Alan Smith, Rothwell, 28 October 1980
Height	5ft 9in
Weight	11st 10lb
Clubs	Leeds United
England Caps	6 Goals 1
	2001 v Mexico (won 4–0), v Greece (won 2–0)
	2002 v Holland (lost 0–2), v Portugal (1–1) 1 goal, v Slovakia (won 2–1), v Macedonia (2–2)

IF HE CAN IMPROVE his disciplinary record, Leeds United's Alan Smith has a great future ahead of him at international level, having won the first of his six caps in the friendly against Mexico in 2001 and retained his place in the squad for the World Cup qualifier in Greece.

Just three weeks after his 18th birthday, Alan Smith came on as a substitute for Leeds and with his first touch in senior football scored in front of the Anfield Kop in a 3–1 win for the Yorkshire club. Keeping his place in the side, he went on to average a goal every other game in that 1998/99 season, demonstrating that he was a real prospect for the future. A real team player, he is full of unselfish running and works hard to close down defenders. He also has a deadly eye for goals and can score with both feet, displaying both aggression and desire. Though he had to undertake a different role in the Leeds side following the departure of Jimmy Floyd Hasselbaink, he continued to give as good as he got and was capped by England at Under-21 level.

In 2000/01 he forged a formidable strike partnership with Australian international Mark Viduka, scoring 18 goals in all competitions. Sadly, his 2001/02 season was curtailed by injury and suspensions, the latter after picking up two red cards, but in 2002/03 the fiery striker, who appeared in a variety of roles for Leeds, developed into a much more complete player.

Wayne BRIDGE

Position	Left-back
Born	Wayne Michael Bridge, Southampton, 5 August 1980
Height	5ft 10in
Weight	11st 11lb
Clubs	Southampton, Chelsea
England Caps	15
	2002 v Holland (1–1), v Italy (lost 1–2), v Paraguay (won 4–0), v S. Korea (1–1), v Cameroon (2–2), v Argentina (won 1–0), v Nigeria (0–0), v Portugal (1–1), v Macedonia (2–2)
	2003 v Liechtenstein (won 2–0), v Turkey (won 2–0), v Serbia (won 2–1)
	2004 v Croatia (won 3–1), v Liechtenstein (won 2–0), v Denmark (lost 2–3)

WAYNE BRIDGE began his career as a midfielder, playing wide on the left. In 1998/99, his first season at senior level, he made rapid progress and was capped by England at Under-21 level. However, the following season, with so many midfielders on the club's books, he adapted to a more defensive role in Southampton's reserve side. In 2000/01 he was ever-present for the club's Premier League matches and was on the bench for England in the Under-21 game in Italy. That game fell victim to fog but he added a further cap when he appeared in the friendly against Spain.

His continued improvement at club level for the Saints reaped rewards when Bridge was deservedly called up into the England side on a regular basis. His outstanding displays for the south coast club, with his impressive forward running and pinpoint crosses, led to his being selected for the PFA's Premiership team for 2001/02. Again ever-present that season, he had featured in every minute of the club's Premiership football since March 1999. An injury against Liverpool in January 2003 brought an end to the run and in the close season after appearing in 174 games for the Saints, he joined Chelsea.

Trevor SINCLAIR

Position	Midfielder
Born	Trevor Lloyd Sinclair, Dulwich, 2 March 1973
Height	5ft 10in
Weight	12st 10lb
Clubs	Blackpool, Queen's Park Rangers, West Ham United, Manchester City
England Caps	12
	2002 v Sweden (1–1), v Italy (lost 1–2), v Paraguay (won 4–0), v S. Korea (1–1), v Cameroon (2–2), v Argentina (won 1–0), v Nigeria (0–0), v Denmark (won 3–0), v Brazil (lost 1–2), v Portugal (1–1)
	2003 v S. Africa (won 2–1)
	2004 v Croatia (won 3–1)

A MEMBER OF the England side that reached the quarter-finals of the 2002 World Cup, Trevor Sinclair began his career with Blackpool but spent his first couple of seasons at Bloomfield Road in and out of the side, before winning a regular place in 1991/92. The scorer of a number of spectacular goals, he left the Seasiders in August 1993 when a £600,000 transfer took him to Queen's Park Rangers.

Sinclair turned in a series of performances that soon led to Under-21 honours for England. A fast, skilful, wide player, he is difficult to dispossess when in full flow, and it was no surprise when a number of clubs made enquiries regarding a possible big-money transfer.

In January 1997 he pulled off a memorable bicycle kick, volleying a cross that was drifting behind him into the top corner of the Barnsley net as Rangers beat the Yorkshire club 3–2 in the fourth round of the FA Cup. He went on to score 21 goals in 190 games for Rangers, before West Ham United manager Harry Redknapp paid £2.3 million for his services in January 1998.

A regular in the Hammers side for his first few seasons, Sinclair later suffered a knee cartilage injury that forced him to miss several matches, but he returned in 2001/02 to win the first of ten caps and become one of the stars of the England team in the World Cup Finals. On his return to Upton Park he found it difficult to achieve his best form and, following the Hammers' relegation, he joined Manchester City.

Danny MURPHY

Position	Midfielder
Born	Daniel Benjamin Murphy, Chester, 18 March 1977
Height	5ft 9in
Weight	10st 8lb
Clubs	Crewe Alexandra, Liverpool
England Caps	9 Goals 1

2002 v Sweden (1–1), v Italy (lost 1–2), v Paraguay (won 4–0) 1 goal, v S. Korea (1–1),
   v Portugal (1–1)
2003 v Australia (lost 1–3), v Liechtenstein (won 2–0)
2004 v Croatia (won 3–1), v Denmark (lost 2–3)

ALTHOUGH OMITTED FROM the 23-man squad for the 2002 World Cup Finals, Danny Murphy was put on standby and called up almost immediately as a replacement for Steven Gerrard, only to miss out in turn after chipping a bone in training.

One of Crewe's youngest-ever players, Murphy captained the club's 1994/95 youth side while also playing, on occasions, for the Gresty Road club's first team. A talented midfield player, he began to score regularly over the next couple of seasons and was a key player in the Wembley play-off final that saw Alexandra promoted to the First Division at the expense of Brentford.

In July 1997, Murphy joined Liverpool for a fee of £1.5 million. Fast, fierce and highly competitive for a small player, he soon won England Under-21 honours. Competition for places restricted him to just a few appearances and he returned to his former club on an extended loan.

On his return to Anfield, he rarely had a long enough run in the side to prove himself in the first team, although he continued to shine in the reserves. In 2000/01 he enjoyed some of the best form of his career, helping the Reds win the FA Cup, League Cup and UEFA Cup. The following season he was called up to the England squad and made his international debut against Sweden.

Owen HARGREAVES

Position	Midfielder
Born	Owen Hargreaves, Calgary, Canada, 20 January 1981
Height	5ft 10in
Weight	11st 10lb
Clubs	Bayern Munich
England Caps	15

2002 v Holland (lost 0–2), v Germany (won 5–1), v Italy (lost 1–2), v Paraguay (won 4–0),
   v S. Korea (1–1), v Cameroon (2–2), v Sweden (1–1), v Argentina (won 1–0),
   v Portugal (1–1), v Slovakia (won 2–1)
2003 v Australia (lost 1–3), v Serbia (won 2–1), v Slovakia (won 2–1)
2004 v Macedonia (won 2–1), v Liechtenstein (won 2–0)

Owen Hargreaves in action against Sweden in the 2002 World Cup. The game was drawn 1–1. (David Cannon/Getty Images)

CALGARY-BORN OWEN HARGREAVES was just 20 and playing for German club Bayern Munich when he was called up to the full England squad to face Holland at White Hart Lane in a friendly in August 2001. He had shot to prominence the previous season, helping Bayern to win both the European Cup and the German League Championship. In the final of the Champions League, his non-stop running and tigerish tackling were prominent throughout, helping his side draw 1–1 with Spanish side Valencia before triumphing 5–4 on penalties.

A 78th-minute substitute for Steven Gerrard in the 5–1 demolition of Germany in Munich, Hargreaves has impressed every time he has donned the white shirt of England. He played in most of the international friendlies leading up to the 2002 World Cup Finals and, unsurprisingly, was selected in the 23-man squad. He played in the opening match against Sweden and started the all-important game against Argentina but was forced by injury to leave the field after just 19 minutes. Replaced by Trevor Sinclair, he took no further part in the competition.

Michael RICKETTS

Position	Forward
Born	Michael Barrington Ricketts, Birmingham, 4 December 1978
Height	6ft 2in
Weight	11st 12lb
Clubs	Walsall, Bolton Wanderers, Middlesbrough
England Caps	1
	2002 v Holland (1–1)

MICHAEL RICKETTS made a sensational entrance onto the Football League stage when, in Walsall's final game of the 1995/96 season, he calmly chipped the Brighton keeper within three minutes of coming on as a substitute. Possessing an excellent football brain and good feet, coupled with aerial ability, Ricketts soon made the grade with the Saddlers and, though injuries then hampered his progress, he was Walsall's leading scorer in 1999/2000. Unsettled at the Bescot Stadium, he left to join Bolton Wanderers in July 2000, the Trotters paying £500,000 for his services.

Ricketts scored on his Wanderers debut against Preston North End and continued to find the net regularly for the remainder of the campaign, finishing as the club's top scorer with 24 goals in all competitions. After the Wanderers won promotion to the top flight via the play-offs, he made an immediate impression on the Premiership stage, scoring some fantastic goals. His form led to his first England cap against Holland in February 2002, but after that the goals dried up and he went almost a year before scoring again in open play. Hoping to resurrect his goalscoring touch, he left the Reebok in January 2003 to join Middlesbrough for a fee of £3.5 million. His only goal of the campaign came in the final game of the season, a 3–1 defeat at his old club Bolton, a win that kept the Trotters in the Premiership.

Darius VASSELL

Position	Forward
Born	Darius Vassell, Birmingham, 13 June 1980
Height	5ft 7in
Weight	12st 0lb
Clubs	Aston Villa
England Caps	15 Goals 4

2002 v Holland (1–1) 1 goal, v Italy (lost 1–2), v Paraguay (won 4–0) 1 goal, v S. Korea (1–1), v Cameroon (1–1) 1 goal, v Sweden (1–1), v Nigeria (0–0), v Brazil (lost 1–2), v Macedonia (2–2)

2003 v Australia (lost 1–3), v Turkey (won 2–0) 1 goal, v S. Africa (won 2–1), v Serbia (won 2–1), v Slovakia (won 2–1)

2004 v Turkey (0–0)

DARIUS VASSELL scored a spectacular goal on his international debut against Holland in February 2002 and was later selected in England's 23-man squad for the World Cup Finals in the Far East.

Progressing through the Aston Villa youth academy to reach the first team in 1998/99, the young Vassell featured on the substitute's bench in over half of the games during that season. Then, in the UEFA Cup game against Stromgodset, he scored two of Villa's goals after replacing Darren Byfield. By the end of the campaign he had been capped by England at Under-21 level. The 1999/2000 season saw him hit by a string of injuries, and he failed to establish himself in the Villa side. The following season he featured mostly from the substitute's bench again but was still a regular for the England Under-21s, for whom he won five more caps. Finally earning himself a regular place in the Villa line-up in 2001/02, he formed a successful strike partnership with Juan Pablo Angel. Without doubt, he was one of the revelations of the Premiership campaign, scoring regularly and being voted the *Sunday Mercury* Midlands Football Young Player of the Year.

Fast and skilful on the ball, with plenty of trickery, he likes to run at defenders and get in shots on goal. He featured on a number of occasions for England in the 2002/03 season and scored a vital goal in the Euro 2004 qualifiers against Turkey.

Ledley KING

Position	Defender
Born	Ledley Brenton King, Stepney, 12 October 1980
Height	6ft 2in
Weight	13st 6lb
Clubs	Tottenham Hotspur
England Caps	2

2002 v Italy (lost 1–2)

2003 v Australia (lost 1–3)

A TALENTED YOUNG DEFENDER, Ledley King made his Tottenham Hotspur debut as a substitute in the match against Liverpool in May 1999, before going on to represent England Under-21s against Luxembourg. He then appeared in all three games in the European Championship Finals in Slovakia.

Terrific aerial ability coupled with a no-nonsense commitment in the challenge has made King hugely popular with Spurs' fans – a ready-made replacement for Sol Campbell who moved to Arsenal in the summer of 2001. During the course of the 2000/01 season, King scored after just 10 seconds of the match at Bradford City, thus setting a new official record for the Premiership's fastest goal. His height makes him a threat at set pieces and his confidence means that he is quick to seize opportunities to help out his forwards. He settled well into the Spurs back four and made his international debut as a substitute against Italy.

Lee BOWYER

Position	Midfielder
Born	Lee David Bowyer, London, 3 January 1977
Height	5ft 9in
Weight	10st 6lb
Clubs	Charlton Athletic, Leeds United, West Ham United, Newcastle United
England Caps	1
	2002 v Portugal (1–1)

LEE BOWYER began his career with Charlton Athletic, joining the professional ranks a year earlier than usual from the Addicks' youth team. During the course of 1995/96, his first full season in the side, he won England Under-21 honours and became Charlton's most valuable asset. Then, in July 1996, he became the country's most expensive teenager when he joined Leeds United for £2.6 million. After scoring on his debut, he sustained an horrific eye injury in the game against Manchester United, which temporarily caused the loss of sight in his right eye. Sidelined for two months, he soon settled in at Elland Road and was the club's most consistent outfield player in the 1996/97 and 1997/98 seasons.

A player with endless stamina, Bowyer blossomed in 1998/99 into an all-action midfielder and was one of the final nominations for the PFA Young Player of the Year. His consistent dynamic performances in the Leeds' midfield increased speculation that he would soon play for England. Despite his well-documented and long-drawn-out court appearance, he continued to produce the goods on the pitch, and his displays finally received recognition when he was selected for the friendly against Portugal.

Bowyer left Elland Road in January 2003 and joined West Ham United in their battle for Premiership survival. He subsequently moved on in the close season to Newcastle United.

David DUNN

Position	Midfielder
Born	David John Ian Dunn, Blackburn, 27 December 1979
Height	5ft 10in
Weight	12st 3lb
Clubs	Blackburn Rovers, Birmingham City
England Caps	1
	2002 v Portugal (1–1)

A MEMBER OF the Blackburn side that reached the final of the FA Youth Cup in 1998, David Dunn was not expected to feature in the first team during 1998/99 but injuries necessitated his promotion. A tough tackler and a hard worker, he was selected for the England Under-21 side to face the Czech Republic towards the end of his first season in League football. However, he endured a frustrating time at Blackburn in 1999/2000, failing to hold down a regular first-team place. He requested a transfer, but this was turned down. Under new manager Graeme Souness he gained fresh momentum, finishing the campaign on a high after being selected for the England Under-21 squad for the European Championships in Slovakia.

In 2000/01 Dunn established himself as a first-team regular, netting a hat-trick of penalties in a 6–1 Worthington Cup win over Rochdale. He continued to be a regular for England at Under-21 level, often captaining the side, and was honoured by his fellow professionals in the PFA's First Division team. Injuries hampered his progress in 2001/02, but on his return he began to use his natural body strength to tackle and cover in midfield. After helping Rovers win the League Cup, he won full international recognition when he was selected for the friendly against Portugal in September 2002. At the end of the 2002/03 season he was signed by Steve Bruce for Birmingham City.

James BEATTIE

Position	Forward
Born	James Scott Beattie, Lancaster, 27 February 1978
Height	6ft 1in
Weight	12st 0lb
Clubs	Blackburn Rovers, Southampton
England Caps	5
	2003 v Australia (lost 1–3), v Serbia (won 2–1)
	2004 v Croatia (won 3–1), v Liechtenstein (won 2–0), v Denmark (lost 2–3)

JAMES BEATTIE began his Football League career with Blackburn Rovers, when he was thrust into the side during the 1996/97 season due to an injury crisis. Until then, the public schoolboy had been considering a career in medicine.

Unable to take his considerable scoring exploits into the Rovers first team – he averaged a goal a game for the club's reserve side – he joined Southampton for a fee of £1 million in July 1998, as Kevin Davies moved in the opposite direction for £7.5 million.

Capped by England at Under-21 level, Beattie ended his first season at the Dell as the club's Player of the Year, in recognition of his non-stop effort and passion. He is very strong in the air and has great physical presence in and around the opponents' box, but injuries marred his 1999/2000 season and when he finally recovered he found that competition for places had intensified. He bounced back in 2000/01, however, hitting a rich vein of form that included ten goals in ten games to win the Carling Player of the Month award for December. His exploits included a stunning free kick in the 3–2 win over Chelsea and a 40-yard effort at Sunderland. Despite further injuries in 2001/02, he proved to be the perfect foil for Marian Pahars, netting 12 goals in 24 Premiership starts. The following season he was a revelation and fully deserved his call-up to the England side for the friendly against Australia. In 2002/03 he netted 23 Premiership goals, staying in contention for the Golden Boot until the closing day of the season.

Francis JEFFERS

Position	Forward
Born	Francis Jeffers, Liverpool, 25 January 1981
Height	5ft 10in
Weight	10st 7lb
Clubs	Everton, Arsenal
England Caps	1 Goals 1
	2003 v Australia (lost 1–3) 1 goal

FRANCIS JEFFERS became only the second 16-year-old in Everton's history to figure in a first-team game when he was introduced a minute after half-time in the 1997 Boxing Day game against Manchester United. A clever, pacey striker, he had to sit out two months of that season after suffering a mysterious heart virus, but he returned to score a crucial goal in Everton's FA Youth Cup Final defeat of Blackburn Rovers. In 1998/99 he was given an extended run in the side, scoring on his home debut and ending the campaign as the club's second-top scorer with seven goals.

Called up into the England squad for the trip to Hungary, he then made his Under-21 debut in September 1999 against Luxembourg, going on to play in all three games in the European Championship Finals in Slovakia. He was increasingly reproducing the form that had marked him down as a star of the future, though it was obvious he still had disciplinary problems to attend to.

The start of the 2000/01 season saw a devastating scoring burst – five goals in five Premier League games – but then an ankle ligament injury sidelined him for five months. Though he returned towards the end of the season, Jeffers, who had scored 20 goals in 60 games, turned down the offers of a new contract and signed for Arsenal for a fee of £8 million. He spent much of his first season at Highbury struggling with an ankle injury that eventually required surgery, but he figured more prominently in the Gunners' side in the 2002/03 season and scored on his international debut as England lost 1–3 to Australia.

He did well for England Under-21s, scoring twice against Slovakia and securing a hat-trick against Macedonia a few days later. In the close season he rejoined Everton on loan.

Jermaine JENAS

Position	Midfielder
Born	Jermaine Anthony Jenas, Nottingham, 18 February 1983
Height	5ft 11in
Weight	11st 2lb
Clubs	Nottingham Forest, Newcastle United
England Caps	4
	2003 v Australia (lost 1–3), v S. Africa (won 2–1), v Serbia (won 2–1)
	2004 v Denmark (lost 2–3)
Honours	PFA Young Player of the Year 2003

A HARD-TACKLING midfield player able to distribute the ball accurately, Jermaine Jenas made his Football League debut for his home-town team Nottingham Forest against Crystal Palace during the course of the 2000/01 season. He had already appeared in the FA Cup third-round tie with Wolves. During the course of that season he also won representative honours with the England Under-17 and Under-18 teams.

Playing in either central midfield or out wide on the left, Jenas moved from Nottingham Forest in January 2002 when Newcastle United manager Bobby Robson paid £5 million to take him to St James' Park. He made his debut for the Magpies in the heat of the north-east derby at Sunderland, which the Magpies won 1–0. He then settled down to win a regular place in the side, looking very much at home in the higher grade of football.

Tall and willowy, Jenas is an elegant footballer with a fine turn of pace. Seemingly mature beyond his years, he won his first cap against Australia in February 2003 when he was one of the few success stories in England's 1–3 defeat. His talent was recognised by his selection as the PFA Young Player of the Year.

Paul ROBINSON

Position	Goalkeeper
Born	Paul William Robinson, Beverley, 15 October 1979
Height	6ft 2in
Weight	13st 4lb
Clubs	Leeds United
England Caps	4
	2003 v Australia (lost 1–3), v S. Africa (won 2–1)
	2004 v Croatia (won 3–1), v Denmark (lost 2–3)

A MEMBER OF Leeds United's successful youth sides, Paul Robinson made the breakthrough during the course of the 1998/99 season, following Nigel Martyn's rib injury in Roma. He kept a clean sheet in a goalless draw with Chelsea.

Big and agile, he is a very good shot-stopper, and while on England Under-21 duty he was called into the full squad for training. Though he failed to make a Leeds first-team appearance in 1999/2000, he took over in goal from the injured Martyn in

October 2000 and retained his place until the end of January. During that time he provided many inspirational performances, none more so than in the Champions League encounter with Barcelona when at times the match seemed to be 'Robbo' versus Rivaldo.

Though Nigel Martyn was ever-present in 2001/02, Paul Robinson began the 2002/03 season in pole position and, despite Leeds United's disastrous start to the season under Terry Venables, his consistent displays between the posts led to his first full cap against Australia as a half-time substitute for West Ham's David James.

Wayne ROONEY

Position	Forward
Born	Wayne Rooney, Croxteth, 24 October 1985
Height	5ft 9in
Weight	11st 5lb
Clubs	Everton
England Caps	9 Goals 3
	2003 v Australia (lost 1–3), v Liechtenstein (won 2–0), v Turkey (won 2–0), v Serbia (won 2–1), v Slovakia (won 2–1)
	2004 v Macedonia (won 2–1) 1 goal, v Liechtenstein (won 2–0) 1 goal, v Turkey (0–0), v Denmark (lost 2–3) 1 goal

WAYNE ROONEY became England's youngest-ever player, aged 17 years and 111 days, when he made his international debut against Australia on 12 February 2003. This was followed by an appearance as substitute against Liechtenstein. Controversy preceded his selection for the national side's Euro qualifier against Turkey, with many claiming that Rooney was too inexperienced to face a team that finished fourth in the 2002 World Cup. Eriksson's brave decision to play the youngster ahead of Emile Heskey was fully justified with a glorious display that raised England's game to new heights. In 2004 Rooney later became England's youngest-ever goalscorer when, aged just 17 years and 317 days, he broke Michael Owen's record, netting in the 2–1 defeat of Macedonia.

The teenage sensation burst onto the national stage in October 2002 following a ten-minute cameo appearance against unbeaten Premiership Champions Arsenal. The then 16-year-old came on as a substitute for Tomasz Radzinski in the 81st minute with a game deadlocked at 1–1. Within mintues he had beaten David Seaman with a wicked, dipping, swerving drive from 25 yards.

Just six months previously, Wayne had played an important role in Everton's run to the 2002 FA Youth Cup Final, scoring eight goals in eight games. He was still an unknown when he scored a wonder goal in an FA Youth Cup tie at Tottenham that had Glenn Hoddle and David Pleat turning to Everton officials and asking, 'Who is this kid?'

Still painfully shy, he was grateful to Everton boss David Moyes for maintaining a ban on media interviews – it was lifted only to launch his first professional contract and his discomfort then was clear to see. So what now for Rooney? Arsenal manager

Wayne Rooney during the Euro 2004 qualifier against Turkey.
(Ben Radford/Getty Images)

Arsene Wenger has hailed him as the greatest young talent he has ever seen, while Newcastle boss Sir Bobby Robson says, 'He takes my breath away. He is sensational. He can do things that are way out of the reach of any other player. He is precocious, cheeky and confident, with a great football brain.'

Perhaps the last word should come from Everton owner Bill Kenwright who called on everyone in the game – from club to country – to 'cherish' his talent.

Paul KONCHESKY

Position	Defender
Born	Paul Martyn Konchesky, Barking, 15 May 1981
Height	5ft 10in
Weight	10st 12lb
Clubs	Charlton Athletic
England Caps	1
	2003 v Australia (lost 1–3)

LEFT-SIDED DEFENDER PAUL KONCHESKY was just 16 years 93 days old when he made his Football League debut for Charlton Athletic against Oxford United in the second game of the 1997/98 season. He was the youngest player in the club's history. Very self-assured and composed, he uses the ball well when coming out of defence. He found himself playing out of position for his club, either in midfield or occasionally in the centre of defence, due to the consistency of Chris Powell at left-back. However, he was still called into the England Under-21 squad, and scored his first senior goal in the match against Everton at Goodison Park on 29 December 2001. Konchesky has the potential to be a top-class player. He is both quick and a strong tackler, and his solid displays for Charlton Athletic during the 2002/03 season led to his first international cap in the friendly against Australia at Upton Park.

Matthew UPSON

Position	Defender
Born	Matthew James Upson, Stowmarket, 18 April 1979
Height	6ft 1in
Weight	11st 4lb
Clubs	Luton Town, Arsenal, Nottingham Forest, Crystal Palace, Reading, Birmingham City
England Caps	6
	2003 v South Africa (won 2–1), v Serbia (won 2_1), v Slovakia (won 2–1)
	2004 v Croatia (won 3–1), v Liechenstein (won 2–0), v Denmark (lost 2–3)

UNABLE TO BREAK into Arsenal's first team on a regular basis, Matthew Upson joined Birmingham City during the January 2003 transfer window. He soon settled in alongside Kenny Cunningham and his decisive form earned the club's first England call-up for 25 years when he made his international debut against Australia the following month.

After beginning his career with Luton, Upson joined the Gunners for a fee of £1 million, basically as cover for the likes of Tony Adams, Martin Keown and Steve Bould. He certainly benefited from training alongside those players and became a regular in the England Under-21 side. A good tackler and strong in the air, he ruptured a cruciate ligament and was out of action for much of the 2000/01 season. Once fit, he had loan spells with Nottingham Forest and Crystal Palace before returning to Highbury to fight for a first-team place. He had just begun to win more first-team action when he suffered a broken fibula.

After recovering he had a very successful loan spell with Reading, where his arrival coincided with a run of six consecutive wins without conceding a goal. However, he was then sold to Birmingham for the bargain fee of £1 million.

John TERRY

Position	Central defender
Born	John George Terry, Barking, 7 December 1980
Height	6ft 0in
Weight	12st 4lb
Clubs	Chelsea, Nottingham Forest
England Caps	6
	2003 v Serbia (won 2–1)
	2004 v Croatia (won 3–1), v Macedonia (won 2–1), v Liechtenstein (won 2–0), v Turkey (0–0), Denmark (lost 2–3)

JOHN TERRY'S 2002/03 campaign certainly ended on a high – Champions League qualification was bolstered by call-up to the full England squad.

Terry found himself playing in the Chelsea first team before his 18th birthday when he came on as a substitute in his accustomed central defensive position against Aston Villa in the 1998/99 Worthington Cup competition. To underline his versatility, his next two appearances were in central midfield and at right-back. He made enormous strides the following season after a loan spell to gain experience at Nottingham Forest. On his return to Stamford Bridge he was selected as one of Chelsea's substitutes for the FA Cup Final at Wembley, where he collected a winners' medal. In October 2000 he won his first England Under-21 cap, later being made captain. That season he claimed a regular place in the Chelsea side alongside Marcel Desailly and Frank Leboeuf as new manager Claudio Ranieri tried a new three-man central defensive system.

His meteoric rise continued despite some adverse publicity following two off-field incidents and in 2001/2 he was named as the club's 'Player of the Season'. Despite a bizarre pre-season injury that resulted in keyhole surgery to a knee, Terry won his place back in the side.

Glen JOHNSON

Position	Defender
Born	Glen McLeod Johnson, London, 23 August 1984
Height	6ft 0in
Weight	12st 0lb
Clubs	West Ham United, Millwall, Chelsea
England Caps	1
	2004 v Denmark (lost 2–3)

THOUGH HE SIGNED FOR West Ham United in the summer of 2001, Glen Johnson joined Millwall on loan in October 2002 and spent six weeks as cover for injured Lions defenders. He made an immediate impact at the New Den, producing some excellent displays and looking comfortable at both full-back and in the centre of defence.

He was recalled to Upton Park and came into the West Ham United side at right-back. During the Hammers' fight against relegation, Johnson showed a level of maturity beyond his years. After playing for the England Under-20 side in December 2002, he stepped up to the Under-21s the following April. Though the season ended in disappointment as the Hammers lost their Premiership status, Johnson deservedly won the 'Young Hammer of the Year' award.

He later left Upton Park to join Chelsea and shortly after his arrival at Stamford Bridge, he made his full international debut in the defeat against Denmark when he replaced Gary Neville after just 17 minutes.

Scott PARKER

Position	Midfielder
Born	Scott Matthew Parker, Lambeth, 13 October 1980
Height	5ft 7in
Weight	10st 7lb
Clubs	Charlton Athletic, Norwich City, Chelsea
England Caps	1
	2004 v Denmark (lost 2–3)

AN INFLUENTIAL AND skilful footballer, Scott Parker was named the Addicks' Player of the Year for 2002/03. He won his first full cap for England when he came on as a substitute for Wayne Rooney in the 3–2 defeat by Denmark in 2003.

Despite his obvious talent, Parker was unable to break into the Charlton side on a regular basis in his early years with the club but looked impressive when he did play and made sufficient appearances to earn a First Division championship medal in 1999/2000. Very self-assured, he likes to take players on and is not afraid to hit long crossfield passes or shoot from distance when the opportunity arises.

He had a brief loan spell with Norwich City before returning to the Valley following an injury to Mark Kinsella. In February 2004 he moved to Chelsea.

Statistics

MOST-CAPPED PLAYERS since 1946

1.	Peter Shilton	125	12.	Tom Finney	76
2.	Bobby Moore	108	13.	David Seaman	75
3.	Bobby Charlton	106	14.	Gordon Banks	73
4.	Billy Wright	105	15.	Alan Ball	72
5.	Bryan Robson	90	16.	Martin Peters	67
6.	Kenny Sansom	86	17.	Tony Adams	66
7.	Ray Wilkins	84	18.	Dave Watson	65
8.	Gary Lineker	80		David Beckham	65
9.	John Barnes	79	19.	Kevin Keegan	63
10.	Stuart Pearce	78		Alan Shearer	63
11.	Terry Butcher	77		Ray Wilson	63

TOP GOALSCORERS since 1946

1.	Bobby Charlton	49	12.	Mick Channon	21
2.	Gary Lineker	48		Kevin Keegan	21
3.	Jimmy Greaves	44	13.	Martin Peters	20
4.	Tom Finney	30	14.	Johnny Haynes	18
	Nat Lofthouse	30		Roger Hunt	18
	Alan Shearer	30	15.	Tommy Taylor	16
7.	David Platt	27		Tony Woodcock	16
8.	Bryan Robson	26	16.	Martin Chivers	13
9.	Michael Owen	25		Paul Mariner	13
	Geoff Hurst	24		Paul Scholes	13
10.	Stan Mortensen	23		Bobby Smith	13
11.	Tommy Lawton	22		David Beckham	13

Index of Player Entries

Ferdinand, Les 414
Ferdinand, Rio 457
Finney, Tom 15
Flowers, Ron 91
Flowers, Tim 410
Foster, Steve 311
Foulkes, Bill 81
Fowler, Robbie 442
Francis, Gerry 252
Francis, Trevor 276
Franklin, Neil 13
Froggatt, Jack 43
Froggatt, Redfern 68

Garrett, Tommy 65
Gascoigne, Paul 365
Gates, Eric 305
George, Charlie 276
Gerrard, Steven 473
Gidman, John 278
Gillard, Ian 254
Goddard, Paul 313
Grainger, Colin 100
Gray, Andy 400
Gray, Michael 464
Greaves, Jimmy 122
Greenhoff, Brian 269
Gregory, John 325
Guppy, Steve 472

Hagan, Jimmy 26
Haines, Jack 32
Hall, Jeff 94
Hancocks, Johnny 33
Hardwick, George 9
Harford, Mick 361
Hargreaves, Owen
    486
Harris, Gordon 185
Harris, Peter 40
Harvey, Colin 222
Hassall, Harold 56
Hateley, Mark 335
Haynes, Johnny 84
Hector, Kevin 243
Hellawell, Mike 150
Hendrie, Lee 462
Henry, Ron 157

Heskey, Emile 466
Hill, Freddie 155
Hill, Gordon 274
Hill, Ricky 313
Hinchcliffe, Andy 453
Hinton, Alan 152
Hirst, David 393
Hitchens, Gerry 140
Hoddle, Glenn 293
Hodge, Steve 354
Hodgkinson, Alan
    102
Holden, Doug 119
Holliday, Edwin 129
Hollins, John 194
Hopkinson, Eddie 104
Howe, Don 105
Howe, Jack 25
Howey, Steve 426
Hudson, Alan 255
Hughes, Emlyn 206
Hughes, Laurie 47
Hunt, Roger 145
Hunt, Steve 335
Hunter, Norman 183
Hurst, Geoff 187

Ince, Paul 411

James, David 453
Jeffers, Francis 492
Jenas, Jermaine 493
Jezzard, Bedford 79
Johnson, David 258
Johnson, Glen 497
Johnson, Seth 476
Johnston, Harry 19
Jones, Bill 47
Jones, Mick 182
Jones, Rob 401

Kay, Tony 165
Keegan, Kevin 240
Kennedy, Alan 329
Kennedy, Ray 266
Keown, Martin 402
Kevan, Derek 102
Kidd, Brian 213

King, Ledley 489
Knowles, Cyril 195
Konchesky, Paul 496

Labone, Brian 153
Lampard, Frank, jnr
    472
Lampard, Frank, snr
    234
Langley, Jim 109
Langton, Bobby 18
Latchford, Bob 284
Lawler, Chris 223
Lawton, Tommy 6
Le Saux, Graham 420
Le Tissier, Matt 422
Lee, Francis 203
Lee, Jack 51
Lee, Rob 425
Lee, Sammy 316
Lindsay, Alec 252
Lineker, Gary 332
Little, Brian 259
Lloyd, Larry 227
Lofthouse, Nat 54
Lowe, Eddie 21

Mabbutt, Gary 316
McCann, Gavin 478
McDermott, Terry
    281
Macdonald, Malcolm
    229
McDonald, Colin 113
McFarland, Roy 218
McGarry, Bill 80
McGuinness, Wilf 117
McMahon, Steve 362
McManaman, Steve
    427
McNab, Bob 200
McNeil, Mick 138
Madeley, Paul 224
Mannion, Wilf 17
Mariner, Paul 279
Marsh, Rodney 228
Martin, Alvin 307
Martyn, Nigel 407

Marwood, Brian 369
Matthews, Reg 99
Matthews, Stanley 5
Meadows, Jimmy 88
Medley, Les 53
Melia, Jimmy 160
Merrick, Gil 61
Merson, Paul 369
Metcalfe, Vic 57
Milburn, Jackie 28
Miller, Brian 141
Mills, Danny 482
Mills, Mick 232
Milne, Gordon 161
Milton, Arthur 63
Moore, Bobby 146
Morley, Tony 310
Morris, Johnny 36
Mortensen, Stan 21
Mozley, Bert 40
Mullen, Jimmy 20
Mullery, Alan 175
Murphy, Danny 486

Neal, Phil 261
Neville, Gary 434
Neville, Phil 444
Newton, Keith 186
Nicholls, Johnny 78
Nicholson, Bill 58
Nish, David 242
Norman, Maurice 149

O'Grady, Mike 155
Osgood, Peter 211
Osman, Russell 300
Owen, Michael 460
Owen, Sid 78

Paine, Terry 163
Pallister, Gary 363
Palmer, Carlton 409
Parker, Paul 374
Parker, Scott 498
Parkes, Phil 244
Parlour, Ray 462
Parry, Ray 132
Peacock, Alan 150

Pearce, Stuart 358
Pearson, Stan 24
Pearson, Stuart 270
Pegg, David 103
Pejic, Mike 244
Perry, Bill 98
Perryman, Steve 312
Peters, Martin 189
Phelan, Mike 379
Phillips, Kevin 465
Phillips, Len 63
Pickering, Fred 172
Pickering, Nick 326
Pilkington, Brian 86
Platt, David 380
Pointer, Ray 143
Powell, Chris 477
Pye, Jesse 41

Quixall, Albert 70

Radford, John 202
Ramsey, Alf 30
Reaney, Paul 201
Redknapp, Jamie 439
Reeves, Kevin 292
Regis, Cyrille 311
Reid, Peter 348
Revie, Don 83
Richards, John 242
Richardson, Kevin 423
Rickaby, Stan 72
Ricketts, Michael 488
Rimmer, Jimmy 270
Ripley, Stuart 417
Rix, Graham 307
Robb, George 74
Roberts, Graham 320
Robinson, Paul 493
Robson, Bobby 107
Robson, Bryan 297
Rocastle, David 367
Rooney, Wayne 494

Rowley, Jack 31
Royle, Joe 221
Ruddock, Neil 426

Sadler, David 194
Salako, John 394
Sansom, Kenny 289
Scales, John 437
Scholes, Paul 455
Scott, Laurie 8
Seaman, David 369
Sewell, Jackie 62
Shackleton, Len 27
Sharpe, Lee 388
Shaw, Graham 117
Shearer, Alan 404
Shellito, Ken 163
Sheringham, Teddy 415
Sherwood, Tim 463
Shilton, Peter 215
Shimwell, Eddie 33
Sillett, Peter 91
Sinclair, Trevor 485
Sinton, Andy 400
Slater, Bill 86
Smith, Alan 373
Smith, Alan 484
Smith, Bobby 138
Smith, Lionel 52
Smith, Tommy 226
Smith, Trevor 125
Southgate, Gareth 440
Spink, Nigel 327
Springett, Ron 129
Staniforth, Ron 74
Statham, Derek 319
Stein, Brian 328
Stepney, Alex 196
Sterland, Mel 372
Steven, Trevor 341
Stevens, Gary 341
Stevens, Gary 346
Stewart, Paul 398

Stiles, Nobby 177
Stone, Steve 439
Storey, Peter 223
Storey-Moore, Ian 211
Streten, Bernard 42
Summerbee, Mike 196
Sunderland, Alan 303
Sutton, Chris 458
Swan, Peter 136
Swift, Frank 7

Talbot, Brian 280
Tambling, Bobby 156
Taylor, Ernie 73
Taylor, Jim 57
Taylor, Peter 267
Taylor, Phil 24
Taylor, Tommy 68
Temple, Derek 183
Terry, John 497
Thomas, Danny 323
Thomas, Dave 253
Thomas, Geoff 388
Thomas, Michael 372
Thompson, Peter 169
Thompson, Phil 264
Thompson, Tommy 60
Thomson, Bobby 168
Todd, Colin 231
Towers, Tony 268
Tueart, Dennis 256

Ufton, Derek 72
Unsworth, David 437
Upson, Matthew 496

Vassell, Darius 489
Venables, Terry 173
Venison, Barry 424
Viljoen, Colin 257
Viollet, Dennis 137

Waddle, Chris 344
Waiters, Tony 171
Walker, Des 368
Walker, Ian 449
Wallace, Danny 351
Walsh, Paul 326
Ward, Peter 304
Ward, Tim 23
Watson, Dave 245
Watson, Dave 337
Watson, Willie 43
Webb, Neil 360
Weller, Keith 250
West, Gordon 200
Wheeler, Johnny 82
White, David 413
Whitworth, Steve 254
Whymark, Trevor 283
Wignall, Frank 174
Wilcox, Jason 450
Wilkins, Ray 272
Williams, Bert 38
Williams, Steve 323
Willis, Arthur 59
Wilshaw, Dennis 71
Wilson, Ray 135
Winterburn, Nigel 382
Wise, Dennis 389
Withe, Peter 308
Wood, Ray 80
Woodcock, Tony 286
Woodgate, Jonathan 468
Woods, Chris 350
Worthington, Frank 251
Wright, Billy 9
Wright, Ian 387
Wright, Mark 330
Wright, Richard 476
Wright, Tommy 199

Young, Gerry 174